EVIDENTIAL LEGAL REASONING

This book offers a transnational perspective of evidentiary problems, drawing on insights from different systems and legal traditions. It avoids the isolated manner of analyzing evidence and proof within each Common Law and Civil Law tradition. Instead, it features contributions from leading authors in the evidentiary field from a variety of jurisdictions and offers an overview of essential topics that are of both theoretical and practical interest. The collection examines evidence not only as a transnational field, but in a cross-disciplinary context. Each chapter engages with the interdisciplinary themes cutting through the issues discussed, benefiting from the expertise and experience of their diverse authors.

Jordi Ferrer-Beltrán is full professor of Legal Philosophy and director of the Chair of Legal Culture at the University of Girona. He is co-editor of Quaestio Facti, International Journal on Evidential Legal Reasoning and member of the International Association of Procedural Law and of the Council of the International Association of Evidence Science.

Carmen Vázquez is Associate Professor of Legal Philosophy at the University of Girona. She is _academic coordinator of the Master's Degree on Evidentiary Reasoning at the University of Girona and the Università degli Studi di Genova. She is a member of the editing committee of Quaestio Facti, International Journal on Evidential Legal Reasoning. Member of the Council of the International Association of Evidence Science.

Evidential Legal Reasoning

CROSSING CIVIL LAW AND COMMON LAW TRADITIONS

Edited by

JORDI FERRER BELTRÁN
University of Girona

CARMEN VÁZQUEZ
University of Girona

CAMBRIDGE UNIVERSITY PRESS

CAMBRIDGE
UNIVERSITY PRESS

University Printing House, Cambridge CB2 8BS, United Kingdom

One Liberty Plaza, 20th Floor, New York, NY 10006, USA

477 Williamstown Road, Port Melbourne, VIC 3207, Australia

314–321, 3rd Floor, Plot 3, Splendor Forum, Jasola District Centre, New Delhi – 110025, India

103 Penang Road, #05–06/07, Visioncrest Commercial, Singapore 238467

Cambridge University Press is part of the University of Cambridge.

It furthers the University's mission by disseminating knowledge in the pursuit of education, learning, and research at the highest international levels of excellence.

www.cambridge.org
Information on this title: www.cambridge.org/9781316516997
DOI: 10.1017/9781009032049

First published 2022

A catalogue record for this publication is available from the British Library.

Library of Congress Cataloging-in-Publication Data
NAMES: World Congress on Evidential Legal Reasoning (1st : 2018 : Universitat de Girona) | Ferrer Beltrań, Jordi, editor. | Vázquez Rojas, Carmen, editor.
TITLE: Evidential legal reasoning : crossing civil law and common law traditions / edited by Jordi Ferrer Beltrán, Universitat de Girona; Carmen Vázquez, Universitat de Girona.
DESCRIPTION: Cambridge, United Kingdom ; New York, NY : Cambridge University Press, 2020. | Includes bibliographical references and index.
IDENTIFIERS: LCCN 2021041366 (print) | LCCN 2021041367 (ebook) | ISBN 9781316516997 (hardback) | ISBN 9781009032049 (ebook)
SUBJECTS: LCSH: Evidence (Law) – Congresses. | LCGFT: Conference papers and proceedings.
CLASSIFICATION: LCC K2261.A6 W67 2018 (print) | LCC K2261.A6 (ebook) | DDC 347/.06–dc23/eng/20220208
LC record available at https://lccn.loc.gov/2021041366
LC ebook record available at https://lccn.loc.gov/2021041367

ISBN 978-1-316-51699-7 Hardback

Contents

Figures

Tables

Contributors

RONALD J. ALLEN, Northwestern University

AMALIA AMAYA, National Autonomous University of Mexico and University of Edinburgh

MAURICIO DUCE, Diego Portales University

GARY EDMOND, University of New South Wales

JORDI FERRER BELTRÁN, University of Girona

MARINA GASCÓN ABELLÁN, University of Castilla La Mancha

DANIEL GONZÁLEZ LAGIER, University of Alicante

HOCK LAI HO, National University of Singapore

JOHN JACKSON, University of Nottingham

DALE NANCE, Case Western Reserve University

FREDERICK SCHAUER, University of Virginia

SARAH SUMMERS, University of Zurich

MICHELE TARUFFO, University of Girona

GIOVANNNI TUZET, Bocconi University

WILLIAM TWINING, University College London

CARMEN VÁZQUEZ, University of Girona

PING YANG, China Academy of Discipline Inspection and Supervision

BAOSHENG ZHANG, China University of Political Science and Law

ADRIAN A. S. ZUCKERMAN, University of Oxford

Introduction

Jordi Ferrer Beltrán and Carmen Vázquez

The First World Congress on Evidential Legal Reasoning, organised by the Legal Culture Chair of the University of Girona, was held between 6 and 8 June 2018. The Congress was attended by 350 participants and featured 18 speakers from 4 continents. The three days of formal and informal presentations and discussions yielded excellent results, strengthening the interrelation between the legal communities and specialists of different traditions. The eighteen papers from the Congress, reviewed by their authors based on the discussions and the suggestions made at the Congress, have been compiled in this book.

The leitmotif of the Congress and of the book is coloured by the subject matter, namely evidence and proof in judicial proceedings, addressed by different judicial traditions and with the emphasis placed on different specific problems. This book does therefore not constitute a mixed debate or discussion of a specific evidential area. The value of this book lies in the variety of topics, approaches, bibliographies used, case law analysed and even the concepts taken as its point of departure.

Twining, whose chapter opens the volume, proposes that a multidisciplinary approach be taken to evidence:

> Evidence as a multidisciplinary subject is a 'field concept', that is a label for a broad, varied, ever-changing field with no stable boundaries or agendas. Viewed thus it would be a mistake to start with trying to construct a precise definition of the field or a Grand Theory of Evidence just as it would be a mistake to try to explicate 'Law' in the phrase 'the Harvard Law School'.

Without taking up the discussion as to whether a general theory of evidence is or is not possible, in the way that Kelsen conceived the general theory of law, we believe that there is a clear common leitmotif in the studies in this field that operates on different levels. The first one is conceptual: it is indeed possible to debate the key notions of the field of evidence (inside and outside law), such as

1

'evidence', 'proof', 'burden of proof', 'expert testimony', and 'standard of proof'. The second level pertains to evidential reasoning and is comprised of studies about the argumentation of facts and epistemology. The third level is clearly institutional, characterised by the legal regulation of evidence in judicial proceedings. Finally, there is a fourth – normative – level which includes debates in the field of political and moral philosophy about, for example, what scope we should afford to the right to silence or what the most suitable distribution of risk of error should be in certain types of proceedings.

The first two levels pave the way for discussions that do not depend upon each country's legal specificities or on the different families of legal systems and in this regard are clearly common to all of them. The third level depends on specific national regulations, although there are clear lines of convergence, and comparative studies are highly useful. Once again, the fourth level is general in scope and does not depend directly on the regulation of specific legal systems. Of course, all four levels are related and are not watertight compartments, although a distinction can be made between them, which is useful in order to individualise the analysis perspectives and to see how in most of them it makes sense to begin the discussion beyond the confines of the actual legal tradition.

Sometimes there are specific institutions of a judicial system or family of systems which in other systems use different technical terminology that has to be clarified in order to avert purely verbal disagreements. Thus, in the English-speaking literature it is common practice to use a gradual concept of burden of proof, which affords meaning to the question of how much burden of proof one of the parties to the process has. This is because the notion of burden of proof already includes the standard of proof applicable, meaning that one may say that the party has the burden of proof beyond reasonable doubt, for example. On the other hand, in Roman-Germanic tradition countries, the burden of proof responds strictly to the question as to which party will lose the case if there is insufficient proof, leaving aside the concept of determination of the threshold of sufficiency of evidence (perhaps because normally less attention has been dedicated to it as well). Only when these conceptual differences have been understood is it possible to have a proper understanding of the institutions and avoid purely verbal discussions. However, once these 'translation' problems have been dispelled, it transpires that there is also a common leitmotif, shared theoretical options and very similar problems and discussions. This is why it is so important to make the effort to go beyond parochial debate and broaden the focus of our studies.

This was one of the core objectives of the First World Congress on Evidential Legal Reasoning: to offer a meeting point between different legal traditions to debate evidential problems. We believe that this book clearly mirrors the highly encouraging outcomes of this debate.

Nevertheless, the reader will realise that the presence of the different families of legal systems is unequal: English- and Spanish-speaking countries obviously enjoyed the greatest representation, which is why the book places particular emphasis on a dialogue between the way the doctrine is being developed in the field of evidence in English- and Spanish-speaking traditions. This is also a novel aspect of the Congress and of the book, because the comparison between common law and continental traditions has usually been addressed taking the French or German models as points of reference for the continental tradition. However, we believe that the vitality of the procedural reforms and doctrinal debates ongoing in the last twenty-five years in Spanish-speaking countries also provides a very interesting point of view on or for the subject matter studied in this book.

The book is organised into five thematic blocks: Part I: Evidence As an Area of Knowledge, Part II: Convergences Between Systems, Part III: On Evidential Inferences, Part IV: Expert Evidence and Part V: Standards of Evidence As Decision-Making rules.

The first part, 'Evidence As an Area of Knowledge', is comprised of two works that stress highly important aspects of this enterprise, namely its multi-disciplinary nature, as well as the complexity of a legal system of which evidence is a part. In 'Evidence as a Multi-Disciplinary Field: What Do the Law and the Discipline of Law Have to Offer?', William Twining shows how inferential evidential reasoning for validating hypotheses and for justifying conclusions is an axis that renders it possible to generate a 'multidisciplinary focus' that transcends law, even although legal evidence is a semi-autonomous area. He wonders how we jurists can contribute to an exchange, co-operation and a search for a core of evidence as an area of multidisciplinary knowledge, and in answer he gives us two major challenges: to reach a solid consensus about a point of departure and to identify whether there is something charac-teristic in evidence in the law. Moreover, Ronald J. Allen, in 'New Directions for Evidence Science, Complex Adaptive Systems, and a Possibly Unprovable Hypothesis about Human Flourishing', departs from the consideration that trials, legal systems, governments and market economies are all complex adaptive systems. Viewing them in that light opens up new avenues for research and leads to a possibly unprovable supposition that human flourish-ing will be enhanced at the intersection of societies with a commitment to the rule of law that embraces free elections, market economies and responsive legal systems of which the common law is the paradigmatic example. These complex adaptive systems have the advantage of feedback mechanisms that may facilitate the intelligent exploitation of the vast amount of information contained in each of the systems.

The second part, 'Some Convergences Between Legal Systems', is comprised of four chapters that address different ways in which legal systems have gradually changed and are curiously shifting towards points of convergence, very commonly on account of their relationships with other countries, and in many other cases even as an unexpected result of a specific procedural reform that actually pursued other goals. In order to plot the differences between the legal systems, essentially between the common law and civil law families, a distinction has traditionally been made between 'inquisitive systems' and 'adversarial systems'; although the label does not necessarily have a specific content and its uses vary, it can sometimes prove useful to emphasise certain aspects that are regarded as key. Thus, for example, in 'Truth-Finding and the Mirage of Inquisitorial Process', Adrian Zuckerman takes, as his central axis, a reform in the English civil law system regarding free legal aid, and with this a new demand upon judges to guarantee procedural equality for citizens who eventually represent themselves. A demand which, in his opinion, by translating into a more active role on the part of judges in the presentation of evidence, may involve inquisitive elements inconsistent with the obligation of judicial impartiality, including the prevention of cognitive biases. The fact that it is only the parties who determine the object of litigation and the presentation of evidence, which Zuckerman identifies as an 'adversarial system', would prevent the judge from being involved in activities which could make him or her more vulnerable to corrosive factors.

On the other hand, in 'Common Law Evidence and the Common Law of Human Rights: Towards a Harmonic Convergence?', John Jackson explores the role played by the European Court of Human Rights in diluting certain rules of exclusion in a common law system such as the English model, particularly the impact of certain criteria on the right to legal aid during police questioning or the right to question witnesses. In particular it has developed certain rules that have had the effect of encouraging common law judges to engage more holistically with the effect of certain kinds of evidence on the weight of the evidence as a whole and on the fairness of the proceedings as a whole. The effect has been to reinforce a shift in the nature of both their epistemic and non-epistemic reasoning during the trial. In doing so, the ECHR takes on a more supervisory position of 'director of operations' to ensure that the right to a fair trial and the rights of the defence are made sufficiently 'practical and effective' within the member states.

Sarah Summers is another theoretician who in recent years has extensively questioned the 'inquisitive' and 'adversarial' distinction. In her chapter,

'Evidential Remedies for Procedural Rights Violations: Comparative Criminal Evidence Law and Empirical Research', she provides an example to demonstrate how this classification is not only over-reductionist, but also that it does not properly reflect what criminal proceedings are like in the real world. Moreover, her work reveals how the implementation of idealised procedural models has influenced national and even supranational courts, promoting a certain reluctance to establish absolute evidential rules instead of allowing for discretion of the court, which would obviously involve a discussion on the cases in which this is legitimate. The specific example provided by Summers is the right to be represented by a lawyer in Switzerland, more specifically the right to be informed about the right to legal aid, demonstrating, with empirical data, violations of this right, not because the accused was not informed but rather because they were informed in an incomplete or biased way, being told insistently that lawyers are unnecessary and costly.

In 'The Transformation of Chinese Evidence Theories and System: From Objectivity to Relevancy', Baosheng Zhang and Ping Yang show the impact of not only the dissemination of Common Law evidence in China but also on the concept of evidence. The 'objective fact theory', which has been playing a dominating role in Chinese legal scholarship and judicial practice over a long period of time, confuses empirical fact with objective existence. As a result, the theory of 'objective evidence' was established, and judicial notions such as 'seeking truth from fact', 'the perpetrator of every murder case must be captured', 'zero tolerance to wrongful convictions or acquittals', are derived from this theory. They not only accounted for the deficiencies in Chinese evidence theories and system, but also led to judicial injustices. In recent years, however, Chinese evidence theories and system have shown a trend of transformation from adhering to the 'objective evidence theory' to evidence relevancy. Nevertheless, such a transformation is still unfinished, with the coexistence of both new and conventional notions and systems. To establish relevance as the foundational principle of the modern evidence system is of great significance to advancing the Chinese evidence system and evidence law scholarship.

The third part, 'On Evidential Inferences', compiles chapters dealing explicitly with different questions about inferential reasoning in evidential matters: the basic premises, the role of ostension versus inference, the influence of ethical and political questions and even the process of deliberation that may take place in collegiate bodies.

Michele Taruffo, in 'Inferences in Judicial Decisions about Facts', presents a map of types of evidential inference and inferential schemes based on the work of Toulmin. To this end, Taruffo's point of departure is the non-mathematical probabilistic nature of evidential reasoning, geared towards the objective of ascertaining the truth, understood as correspondence.

Giovanni Tuzet, in 'On Probatory Ostension and Inference', discusses two theses on juridical evidence: the *ostension thesis* and the *inference thesis.* According to the first, the process of juridical proof typically requires some ostensive act. In this sense the evidence consists in some element susceptible of being shown, or exhibited, or indicated to someone in a given context. According to the second thesis, the process of juridical proof requires necessarily some inference. In this process juridical evidence becomes the content of one or more inferences performed by the parties or by the fact-finders (judges or jurors). It can be the content of a premise which, together with other premises, leads to a conclusion about the disputed facts; or the content of a conclusion the premises lead to. Tuzet will rather concentrate on the first thesis, whose subject is somewhat neglected by the literature. He will address the probatory role of ostension, the logical structure of the ostensive act, and some points that pertain to the pragmatics of evidence discourse, namely the role of indexicals and demonstratives in this kind of discourse. Tuzet emphasises that in the fact-finding process ostension comes first: parties present fact-finders with pieces of evidence and then elaborate probatory arguments out of them. No probatory inference can be performed without an ostensive input.

In 'Silence as Evidence', Hock Lai Ho tells us that the right to remain silent and not to incriminate oneself in the criminal process is recognised in some quarters as a human or fundamental right, but the right is not given this exalted status everywhere; indeed, it has its fair share of ardent critics. The existence of the right, constitutionalised or not, varies across jurisdictions. There is much debate on its significance and desirability. His work looks at the position taken (i.e. what the law is and how it got there) and discourse (i.e. how officials talk when they go about defending legislative amendments or praising the current law) on the right of silence in Singapore. Does the experience in Singapore reveal a distinctly Asian perspective to the right of silence? The study of Singapore will be used as a springboard for theoretical reflections on the right in general. Beyond the example of Singapore, the work illustrates a basic general question related to evidential reasoning: while it is primarily theoretical, it is legally regulated by rules that are often shaped by practical – including political and ethical – considerations.

Finally, in 'Group-Deliberative Virtues and Legal Epistemology', Amalia Amaya highlights the social dimensions of argumentation about factual questions in law and, more specifically, analyses the character traits that are conducive to good group deliberation. Considering the effectiveness of deliberative groups and the process of exchange of reasons allows us to broaden the scope of the analysis on the quality of the argumentative process that leads to the acquisition of true beliefs.

The next part, 'Expert Evidence', comprises a further four chapters around a kind of evidence that is acquiring increasingly greater importance in judicial proceedings, namely the expert witness. As in the previous blocks, very different topics are covered, from a general model of expert evidence, taking in an analysis by court-appointed experts, through to the obstinate judicial practice of insisting upon the continued use of unfounded practices despite the scientific information available and the legal errors resulting from such practices.

In 'From Institutional to Epistemic Authority: Rethinking Court Appointed Experts', Carmen Vázquez deals with court-appointed experts in the Spanish system. On the one hand, she demonstrates that court-appointed experts is an institution that can be implemented in highly diverse ways, although in systems that systematically (not exceptionally) avail themselves of such experts, the most common form consists of generating lists to make it easier to identify experts. On the other hand, she also sets out to expose the irrationality of the courts' reliance on these experts, given how they are selected, since their selection and appointment processes are fraught with certain aspects that render it totally unjustifiable. The court's assessment of expert evidence cannot be reduced to who the expert is or how he or she was selected, since attention must be paid to what they actually say, and if this duty is to be observed then this selection process is not the right way.

Gary Edmond, in 'Unreliable Law: Legal Responses to Latent Fingerprint Evidence', focuses on reported decisions in four common law jurisdictions, namely England and Wales, the United States, Canada and Australia, examining the overwhelmingly accommodating response to forensic scientific evidence from its inception to the present day. Through examples the chapter demonstrates sustained legal insensitivity to scientific knowledge and the actual reliability of fingerprint evidence.

Marina Gascón Abellán, in 'Prevention and Education: The Path towards Better Forensic Science Evidence', provides an up-to-date discussion on the traditional debate between expert evidence models that defer to experts and decision-maker educational models, taking forensic science as her basis. As we shall see, she advocates a preventivist and educational system.

Finally, in 'Evidentiary Practices and Risks of Wrongful Conviction: An Empirical Perspective', Mauricio Duce offers an empirical study performed in the Chilean context about how poor- or zero-quality expert evidence, eye witnesses and identification parades generate evidential errors that lead to wrongful convictions.

The final part, 'Standards of Evidence As Decision-Making Rules', includes three chapters that address the problem of the applicability of standards of proof to transnational cases, and the debate about the possibility of formulating general rules that objectively determine the threshold of sufficiency of evidence and its distinction with evidence assessment criteria.

In 'Burdens of Proof and Choice of Law', Dale Nance focuses on private international law and its traditional view that all aspects of the burden of proof are procedural. It is typically inferred that a forum court properly uses the law of the forum on such matters even when comity dictates the recognition and application of the substantive law of another jurisdiction to the matter in dispute. However, this characterisation has never been entirely accurate, at least in American law. Moreover, there has been discernible movement towards the opposite conclusion over the last century, at least as to certain aspects of the burden of proof. In order to make sense of this, it is necessary to recognise that the two components of the burden of proof, the burden of persuasion and the burden of production, have quite different functions in an adversary system. Once these functions are identified, it becomes clear that only the burden of production, in both its allocation and the severity of the burden that it imposes, should be governed by forum law, while the burden of persuasion, in both its allocation and the severity of the burden that it imposes, should be treated as part of the substantive law that the forum court chooses to apply. Thinking through the reasons for these conclusions provides an interesting lens through which to view the nature of evidential legal reasoning and the rules that provide.

Daniel González Lagier, in his work 'Is It Possible to Formulate a Precise and Objective Standard of Proof? Some Questions Based on an Argumentative Approach to Evidence', asserts that the relationships and differences between the standard of proof and the evidence assessment criteria remain unclear in civil law systems. This lack of precision can make it difficult to discuss which evaluation criteria and which particular standards are appropriate, or even to discuss the possibility of formulating a precise, objective standard of proof. For this reason, he seeks to offer a set of conceptual suggestions that could be used to make progress in the search for a shared terminological and conceptual basis on this point. To do so, he focuses on the structure of evidentiary inference, the reasons that count as good reasons for establishing the degree of corroboration of a hypothesis and the possibility of formulating a precise, objective standard of proof.

In 'Prolegomena to a Theory of Standards of Proof: The Test Case for State Liability for Undue Pre-trial Detention', Jordi Ferrer Beltrán presents the methodological requirements that must be fulfilled by a standard of proof in order to fulfil the function of determining the threshold of sufficiency of evidence. To this end, his point of departure is, on the one hand, that the institutional aim of evidential reasoning in any type of judicial proceedings can only be ascertaining the truth surrounding the facts, and on the other that probative reasoning is of a non-mathematical probabilistic nature (probably Baconian). On this basis, the chapter also presents certain factors to be taken into consideration in order to take the political decision as to the degree of evidentiary requirement according to which the standard will be defined, distributing the risk of error among the parties. Finally, the case law of Spain and the European Court of Human Rights are analysed with regard to indemnity for undue pre-trial detention, serving as a test case for a proper understanding of the role of standards of evidence.

As the reader will have noticed, these works address different topics, written by authors from highly diverse judicial cultures and in which oftentimes parallel and somewhat impermeable debates have taken place. Nevertheless, reading all of them leads to a very interesting conclusion: the evidential problems and the fundamental aspects under discussion are, to a great extent, shared. Sometimes, there are specific institutions of a legal system or family of systems, in others there are different technical terminologies that have to be clarified in order to avoid purely verbal disagreements, although there is also a common leitmotif, shared theoretical options and highly similar problems and discussions. This is why it is so important to make the effort to go beyond parochial debate and broaden the focus of our studies. By doing so, we can also learn from the successes and failures of the experiences of other systems and thus be able to avoid both a shallow understanding of them and even hasty transplantations.

PART I

EVIDENCE AS AN AREA OF KNOWLEDGE

1

Evidence as a Multidisciplinary Field

What Do the Law and the Discipline of Law Have to Offer?

William Twining

The field of evidence is no other than the field of knowledge.

Jeremy Bentham, 1843

The law has no mandamus on the logical faculty.

James B. Thayer, 1898

So let us forget about psychology, sociology, technology and mathematics, ignore the echoes of structural engineering and collage in the words 'grounds' and 'backing', and take as our model the discipline of jurisprudence. Logic (we may say) is generalised jurisprudence.

Stephen Toulmin, 1964: 7

1.1 THE CONTEXT

Anyone who reads this chapter will have drawn inferences from evidence in the past twenty-four hours. I state this confidently because almost all human beings draw inferences from evidence in their daily lives; scholars, investigators and journalists do so; so do workers, decision-makers and other actors in more or less specialised contexts; anyone who has not done so, perhaps some newborn, brain-damaged or insensible individuals, are not part of my audience. This kind of inferential reasoning is a basic human activity, often mixed in with other activities and practised at many different levels of competence.[1]

---

[1] An empirical enquiry could usefully identify and analyse in general terms a demography of common activities and decisions involving inferential reasoning from evidence in different contexts, using some rough standard taxonomy such as Santos' map of structural-agency contexts which includes 'the Householdplace, workplace, marketplace, community place, citizen place, workplace' (Santos, 1995: 416 ff.) or more sophisticated or elaborate ones in the sociological literature.

All established and emerging disciplines, sub-disciplines and fields of enquiry involving empirical questions are more or less concerned about inferential reasoning from evidence. But we do not yet have an established, let alone institutionalised, multidisciplinary field of Evidence within which relevant disciplines and activities regularly converse, stimulate and cross-fertilise each other.

In recent years major public events, the media, popular culture, evidence-based medicine and evidence-based policy-making have given greater salience to evidentiary issues in public consciousness.[2] Theorising about evidence has a long tradition in Western culture, dating back before Greek philosophy and historiography through classical and medieval rhetoric, debates about the existence of God, probability theory, the STEM sciences, various forms of scepticism, postmodernism and relativism, to artificial intelligence, neuroscience and many other enclaves of our contemporary intellectual life. Yet, so far as I know, evidence and inference as such have not been a sustained focus of sharp cross-disciplinary attention until quite recently. Nearly all of the theorising, technology and scholarly research has been rooted in quite limited spheres. Evidence is not an established field in intellectual history or the history of ideas.[3]

Law is probably the main discipline in which the study of Evidence has been institutionalised, especially in the common law tradition, as a recognised sub-discipline with courses, journals, specialists and satellite professions, such as forensic science. A few other fields, such as epistemology, historiography, statistics, informal logic and the philosophy of science might make similar, but more modest, claims.

My standpoint today is that of an anglophone jurist who has taken a theoretical interest in Evidence in legal contexts for many years.[4] This has

[2] Many streams have fed into this phenomenon, including DNA, the War in Iraq, dope testing of athletes; detective fiction expanded its horizons to include forensic science (Patricia Cornwell), Forensic Anthropology (Kathy Reichs), scenes-of-crime officers (especially on television) and various forms of intelligence analysis. Evidence-based medicine and evidence-based policy became fashionable. Now in the Trump era Fake News, viral rumours, the Mueller (Russia) Enquiry and disparaging of experts have continued the trend. See Twining, 2003; Twining, 2006 for further and more detailed examples.

[3] Hacking, 1975, Haack, 1993 and Haack, 2014 are significant partial exceptions, but my thesis is broader than these.

[4] A note on terminology. I use Evidence, the Law of Evidence and Evidence in Legal Contexts (capitalised) as field concepts, that is as broad labels to designate an area of study or a discipline or sub-discipline. Field concepts tend to vary over time and space and to have no fixed boundaries nor much analytical purchase. I use lower case terms such as evidence, materiality, probative value and admissibility as analytical concepts. Wigmore divided the study of Evidence in Legal Contexts into two parts: The Principles of Proof and the Trial Rules (Wigmore, 1913; Wigmore, 1937). This distinction is broadly reflected in such contemporary labels as 'Evidence and Proof', which signal a willingness to treat the Law of Evidence as the only part of the study of Evidence in Law. In my early writings I used 'Evidence, Proof and Fact-finding' (EPF) as an organising

made me acutely aware of the extent of my ignorance of aspects of the field in other languages, other legal traditions and even quite adjacent disciplines and sub-disciplines. In this chapter I shall focus almost exclusively on the Anglo-American tradition, in the hope that colleagues from other legal traditions can extend the analysis.

My concern here is with articulating what Law as a discipline or the subject-matters that it studies may have to offer to a distinct and semi-autonomous multidisciplinary field.[5] However, it is worth emphasising that throughout history, and especially in the twentieth century, our discipline has been quite open to outside influences in respect of evidence. Wigmore categorised his 'Principles of Proof' as being grounded in 'Logic, Psychology and General Experience'. 'General Experience' ranges from beliefs in the most rigorous repeated random clinical trials to expert practical knowledge to common sense to myths, fairy tales, prejudices and fallacies – in short, a society's or community's stock of beliefs. At a fairly general level there have been sustained academic interdisciplinary movements in relation to Psychology,[6] Forensic Science, Probabilities and Proof and so on. 'Scientific Evidence' has been a major interface between Law and the hard and not-so-hard 'sciences',[7] including quite specialised areas such as Forensic Anthropology and Narratology. Although bits of the Law of Evidence have sometimes seemed to be 'high among the unrealities', on the whole Evidence in Legal Contexts has been quite responsive to outside influences. Moreover, as the scope of the common law rules of admissibility has steadily narrowed over the last two centuries, the field has become closer to Wigmore's idea of 'General Experience'. Accordingly, we have a lot to build on when we reflect on how best we might contribute to the broader cause.

category signalling that I was also concerned with empirical as well as logical dimensions. I also tried stimulate the idea of 'information in litigation' (Twining, 2006: 248–62) but, understand-ably, this did not catch on. Interestingly, Jeremy Bentham used 'Adjective Law' as his main organising category and his manuscripts reveal that he had considerable difficulty in maintaining a distinction between Evidence and Procedure. For the purposes of this chapter the choice of an appropriate label or organising concept for the relevant field of study is not important, so long as it is clear that in this context the Law of Evidence is only one part of the broad field of Evidence in Legal Contexts.

[5]   The breadth and complexity of the discipline of Law is a central theme of (Twining, 2019).

[6]   In the 1970s and 1980s I was a consultant to the Centre of Socio-Legal Studies in Oxford, mainly helping a Social Psychologist, Dr Sally Lloyd-Bostock, who organised an exemplary series of workshops involving a wide range of academics and practitioners. These resulted in several edited books. See, for example, Lloyd-Bostock, 1980.

[7]   See the recent excellent American overview in Diamond and Lempert, 2018.

Stimulated by the work of David Schum,[8] for almost twenty-five years I have taken an intermittent interest in the idea of Evidence as a broad multidisciplinary field. It is worth summarising the narrative of my involvement under his influence, although I am well aware that there have been other places and centres which have had similar concerns.

In the 1960s Schum, a social psychologist and statistician at Rice University, encountered Wigmore's *Science of Judicial Proof* (1937) almost by chance. He was intrigued theoretically, but also used Wigmore's 'chart method' in training intelligence analysts for the CIA. This led to a brilliant two-volume work, *Evidence and Inference for Intelligence Analysts* (1987), which was probably considered too daunting by the intelligence community and failed to attract attention beyond it.[9] However, Schum persisted and produced some important papers, culminating in another major work, *Evidential Foundations of Probabilistic Reasoning* (1994/2001). This synthesised basic ideas about evidence and inference from several more disciplines, including Logic, Philosophy, Semiotics, Artificial Intelligence and Psychology, as the basis of a multidisciplinary 'substance-blind' approach not confined to theoretical enquiries. Schum pointed out that accountants, actuaries, air traffic controllers and other practitioners on through the alphabet all have to make decisions on the basis of drawing inferences from evidence.

I shall not try to do justice to Schum's work here, but it is worth making three points: first, he has been the leading pioneer in emphasising shared concerns and continuities across disciplines, which justifies talking of a 'substance-blind' approach to inferential reasoning from evidence.[10] Second, he was most interested in practical decision-making and how cross-fertilisation between different kinds of decisions could make a difference in the worlds of practice. However, his main approach was analytical, focussing

---

[8] Sadly, David Schum died on 29 March 2018 after a long illness. This chapter is dedicated to his memory.

[9] See now Tecuci et al., 2016. Although presented as a practical training manual for intelligence analysts, this contains a wealth of interesting ideas of wider interest, including some that will be contested from various points of view.

[10] Schum's 'substance-blind' approach was controversial during the UCL programme (discussed later in this chapter). Underlying the scepticism were various strands: those who believed in the autonomy of disciplines; those who emphasised context and the importance of specialised knowledge; epistemological sceptics and postmodernists, who raised doubts about rationality and even the very idea of evidence; and at the opposite end of the spectrum, those who questioned the originality of the idea of 'substance-blind' by pointing out that logic, mathematics and other abstract forms of enquiry also fit that category. In my view Schum emerged almost unscathed from these critiques, although they raise issues that need to be addressed within a multidisciplinary field of Evidence. For his defence of the idea, see Dawid et al., 2011: 18–26.

on concepts and properties of evidence. Third, David Schum, having discovered Wigmore, paid a great deal of attention to law in a broad sense, analysing concepts involved in reasoning about questions of fact both in trials and in police investigations, as well as in the secondary legal literature. He went as far as to say that legal scholarship on Evidence 'forms the major source of inspiration for anyone interested in a study of the general properties and uses of evidence' (Schum, 1994/2001: 6). I find that encouraging, but a bit overstated. Later I shall point to some of the limitations of the subject of Evidence in Law, especially in regard to the kinds of enquiry most commonly involved in litigation, viz. particular past events.

Schum's *magnum opus* came out just before Terry Anderson and I were Research Fellows at the Netherlands Institute for Advanced Study (NIAS) in Wassenaar in 1994–5. Our group project related to the Netherlands Criminal Justice System, but we set up an extra multidisciplinary group from the other Fellows to explore methodological problems relating to evidence, inference and interpretation based on Schum's approach. Towards the end of the year we invited him to come over to Wassenaar to lead the final session and, in due course, an edited volume of papers from the project was published, with an overview and commentary by Schum.[11]

At NIAS I formulated the following hypothesis as a starting point:

> Notwithstanding differences in (i) the objectives of our particular enquiries; (ii) the nature and extent of available source material; (iii) the culture of our respective disciplines (including their histories, conventions, states of development etc.); (iv) national backgrounds; and (v) other contextual factors, all of our projects involve, as part of their enterprise, drawing inferences from evidence to test hypotheses and justify conclusions, and the logic of this kind of enquiry is governed by the same principles.[12]

As mentioned above, since the 1990s evidence became particularly newsworthy (Twining, 2003). It may have been such developments that stimulated the Leverhulme Foundation in 2002 to invite bids for a £1 million grant for a project on Evidence in the UK. At University College London (UCL) Philip

---

[11] Twining and Hampsher-Monk, 2003. The title *Evidence and Inference in History and Law* reflects the fact that nearly every contributor adopted the standpoint of 'the historian', but their papers exemplify the varieties of historiography, including ones on Theatre Iconography, Musicology, the History of Ideas, Labour History and Assyriology, as well as Law.

[12] The formulation was deliberately provocative, but I do not remember anyone at NIAS seriously challenging it; this contrasts with the UCL project in which there was no consensus about its working assumptions and Schum's approach was challenged. That remains unfinished business, because I suspect that evidence as a multidisciplinary field needs a broader and richer agenda of questions.

Dawid, a distinguished statistician, led the initiative to invite expressions of interest within UCL. Academics from over twenty departments responded and a multidisciplinary proposal, along with one from the London School of Economics, secured the grant (enhanced by the Economic and Social Research Council), which seemed enormous to those in the Humanities and some Social Sciences who were not accustomed to such expansive funding.[13] Ably led by Philip Dawid, with participants from nearly twenty disciplines, the project struggled valiantly with the intransigent problems of multidisciplinary work (see Davies, 2011: ch. 3). It culminated in a major conference held at the British Academy in 2007 and a substantial volume in 2011 which describes and evaluates the project (Dawid et al., 2011).

I was a bit disappointed at the outcome of this project. The main reason, in my view, was that four years was too short a period for establishing an essentially new field. Moreover, there was not a consensus on the aims and working assumptions. The initial focus was based on Schum's 'substance-blind' approach, but this was challenged early on by some different post-modernist and discipline-relative approaches (Dawid et al., 2011: chs. 2–4). After 2007 several of us tried to revive the project, but except for a multidisciplinary seminar in the Graduate School at UCL, it eventually fizzled out.[14]

The UCL project involved a relatively large grant, over fifty participants and a multidisciplinary management committee from several different academic cultures. There were bureaucratic constraints, problems of coordination and the normal, and some unexpected, problems of cross-disciplinary work. Nevertheless, a lively 'evidence community' was maintained and most of us learned a lot. However, what might be more appropriate at the next stage could be more like a decentralised movement involving informal networking at a variety of levels directed to establishing better cross-disciplinary communication and cooperation about evidence.

I am personally interested in finding practical ways forward, but this chapter addresses a more intellectual question: what might we as jurists, and our heritage of both theory and practical decision-making, contribute to an enterprise devoted to stimulating cross-fertilisation, cooperation and the search for a reasonably common core or family of cross-disciplinary relations for

---

[13]   The LSE project was led by Mary Morgan, an economic historian, and culminated in Howlett and Morgan, 2010.
[14]   This was largely because we could find no one to lead a second stage. In my view there is a lot to build on from these initial projects and the experience, but if something like this programme were to revive, it would have to be more sharply focussed and based on a clear consensus about the nature of the enterprise.

Evidence as a recognised multidisciplinary field? Here are some preliminary suggestions for one way to approach this question.

First, Evidence as a multidisciplinary subject is a 'field concept', that is a label for a broad, varied, ever-changing field with no stable boundaries or agendas. Viewed thus it would be a mistake to start with trying to construct a precise definition of the field or a Grand Theory of Evidence – just as it would be a mistake to try to explicate 'Law' in the phrase 'the Harvard Law School'.

Second, however, there needs to be an agreed starting point. I think that there could be quite a strong consensus among jurists that our central *focus* of attention should (at least to begin with) be *inferential reasoning from evidence in the context of argumentation* about both theoretical and practical issues and those in between.[15] This does not preclude a much wider agenda but makes the subject manageable at the start.

Third, is there something special about Evidence in legal contexts? Let me list some candidates from the anglophone world.

1.2 SPECIAL FEATURES OF EVIDENCE IN LEGAL CONTEXTS

1.2.1 *Well-Developed Concepts and Ones Recognised as Problematic*

Law is particularly rich in this regard.[16] For example, here is a sample of concepts that have been subjected to sustained analysis in the Anglophone literature: Admissibility, ancillary evidence, authenticity, credibility of witnesses (verity, veracity, bias (Schum)), catenate inferences, cognitive competence, cognitive consensus (contested), evidence, issues of fact/rule (law), fiction, free proof, general experience (common sense generalisations), induction, inference, materiality, persuasive effect, pre-appointed evidence (Bentham), presumption, probative force or weight or probative value, real evidence, relevance (including minimum relevance), reliability, standards of proof and standards for decision.[17]

---

[15] This formulation is close to but wider than Wigmore's 'Logic of Proof' (see Wigmore,1913; Wigmore, 1937). I am presenting this as a useful working assumption for this enterprise rather than a profound truth. The idea is derived from James Bradley Thayer who many common law evidencers acknowledge as having triumphed in respect of both the Law of Evidence and whatever might be subsumed under Wigmore's Principles of Proof. (See Swift, 2000.) There is, of course, plenty of room for debate about this. Wigmore's term 'the logic of proof' is criticised by Haack, 2014.

[16] Most of these are discussed in Anderson et al., 2005 and Schum, 1994.

[17] For further examples see the indexes of Schum, Wigmore and Twining works cited in the bibliography. Other specific examples include Gaskins, 1992. Jonathan Cohen's *The Probable and the Provable* (Cohen, 1977) and his articles in several fields (Philosophy, Law, Medical Diagnosis, Psychology, are notable for his controversial critique of Kahneman and Tversky

They have been subjected to intense scrutiny in response to a wide variety of theoretical and practical problems. It is worth asking of each: how well does this travel across what disciplinary borders? A few may be peculiar to Law, but many have considerable potential. In order to concretise the discussion, by way of illustration the next section of this chapter briefly examines four concepts that are widely treated as of central importance to Evidence in the common law: materiality, relevance, weight (or probative force) and admissibility.

1.2.2 *Four Concepts*

Like David Schum I think the value of this enterprise will be mainly at middle order and quite concrete levels. I also agree that analysing some key concepts may be a good place to start. By way of illustration let me look briefly at four basic concepts which belong to both the Law of Evidence and the Logic of Proof: materiality, relevance, weight and admissibility.[18] Two points are worth emphasising at the start. First, although closely linked under common law, they are governed by different bodies or norms as is expressed in the following mantra:

(a) The test of materiality is substantive law;
(b) The test of admissibility is the Law of Evidence;
(c) The test of relevance is 'Logic and General Experience'
(d) The test of weight or probative force is 'Logic and General Experience' (Twining, 2006: ch. 6).

What is striking about this scheme is that not only is the operation of each concept governed by different norms, but two of them are explicitly not governed by law, but rather by the rules of informal logic and 'common sense'.

A second point is that these concepts transcend differences between Criminal Evidence and Civil Evidence and between the Law of Evidence and what Wigmore called 'The Principles of Proof'. (Twining, 2006: ch. 6).

1.2.2.1 Materiality and Hypotheses

The concept of materiality is unfamiliar to most lay people. In orthodox evidence discourse it refers to the ultimate and penultimate probanda –

(Cohen, 1981). There are, of course, many other examples. Some of the literature on cross-disciplinary cooperation would help in the evaluation of these (see Davies, 2011).

[18] Other promising concepts include coherence, standards for decision, burdens and standards of proof, cogency and presumptions.

what has to be established at trial to a certain standard of proof (or of other decision)[19] for the charge or claim to be proved. For example, in English law where X is accused of murdering Y the prosecution has to prove beyond reasonable doubt that (a) Y is dead; (b) the cause of Y's death was an unlawful act; (c) that the act was intentional; (d) that it was X who committed the act; and (e) that the act was committed without lawful justification or excuse.[20]

Outside the law this kind of ultimate or penultimate *probandum* is generally known as a hypothesis. At first sight the law's approach to hypothesis formation, formulation, refinement, testing and elimination may appear to be distinctive.[21] But it is worth pausing to consider two different perspectives on 'materiality'.

Much evidence discourse in Law is based on an 'adjudication model', in which decisions on questions of fact and law are made by authoritative third-party adjudicators – judges, juries, lay magistrates, tribunal members and other authoritative fact-finders. The ideal type of 'materiality' under that model includes some such working assumptions as:

(a) the choice of ultimate probandum (the charge, the claim) are determined in advance by someone other than the adjudicator (e.g. by the prosecutor or the claimant);

(b) the penultimate probanda (the material facts) are specified in advance by law (e.g. the elements of a specific crime);

(c) they are generally, but not invariably, articulated with some precision;

(d) the hypothetical outcome of each particular case (e.g. the verdict) is typically binary (guilty/not guilty; liable/not liable);

(e) the final decision should be based on and justifiable by ordinary inferential reasoning, with deduction and abduction playing limited roles ('soft logic'); and

(f) the evidence supports the verdict according to a specified standard of proof.[22]

---

[19] On the distinction between standards of proof and other standards of decision see Anderson et al., 2005: 230–45.

[20] 'X murdered Y' is the ultimate probandum; (a) to (e) constitute the penultimate probanda (the material facts) each of which has to be established beyond reasonable doubt. I do not enter here into possible complications about (e).

[21] On abduction, imaginative reasoning and hypothesis formation see Anderson et al., 2005: 46–62, (based largely on Schum, 1994: ch. 9, but including an example from post-mortems on the Twin Towers attack, 9/11). See also Tecuci et al., 2016, index under hypothesis.

[22] This is a simplified normative ideal type for the adjudicative model frequently underlying Evidence discourse. It is, of course, subject to various exceptions and deviations in both theory and practice.

At first sight these factors make adjudicative decisions and evidential reasoning on questions of fact appear to be exceptional. For example, an ordinary citizen deciding whether to accept a job or where to go on holiday, or a historian reaching a conclusion about the causes of a particular war or who killed President Kennedy, or a scientist trying to assess the potential environmental impact of a proposal for a brewery may all deviate from this model in several respects. Evidence in Law looks very different from other kinds of deciding or concluding from this perspective.

However, litigation involves much more than adjudication and Law involves much more than litigation. A different ideal type of the role of evidence in decisions made in the course of litigation may suggest that Evidence in Law is not so distinctive or peculiar as the adjudication model suggests. For example, even a simple linear total process model of evidence in litigation in 'modern' Western societies depicts a much more complex, flexible and, in many respects, less distinctive, picture in respect of hypotheses.[23] To take two simple examples: first, in the early stages of a typical criminal process, investigators and others are involved in abduction and imaginative reasoning in constructing, refining and eliminating hypotheses (the Sherlock Holmes model) in ways which may be quite similar to orthodox historians (if such historians exist). Indeed, police are regularly warned against being tempted by 'suspect driven enquiries', in short premature settling on single hypotheses. At a later stage prosecutors very often have discretion to choose between specific charges (i.e. hypotheses); and in plea bargaining and some kinds of civil proceeding the selection of hypotheses to be adjudicated on may be the subject of negotiation. In short, from the point of view of a total process model of litigation, the formation, adjustment, testing and choice of hypotheses may be quite similar to some kinds of 'non-legal' processes of decision or enquiry. Conversely, the lawyers' conception of 'materiality' may help to illuminate some puzzles about evidence outside legal contexts. For example, is it true to say: materiality is of no concern to historians?

1.2.2.2 Relevance

Unlike materiality the concept of relevance has been the subject of considerable attention in several disciplines, from Gricean pragmatics and

---

[23] The literature on dispute processing, including litigation, suggests that linear models tend to be too simple (Twining, 2006: 175–80, 249–52).

conversation analysis to informatics and cross-cultural studies[24] The most extensive literature is probably to be found in law libraries. In ordinary usage 'relevance' is a vague word of relation normally meaning '[closely] connected or appropriate' to something ('A is relevant to B'). Talk of relevance in the abstract has been widely condemned but, even if B is specified, the term on its own is still vague unless more or less clear criteria of relevance are specified. A first question is: connected/relevant to what? The answer may be a goal or goals, a standard, a rule, a conversation, a decision, a story or a hypothesis to mention some obvious ones. A second question is what kinds of criteria of relevance might there be in each context? For example, in respect of a goal, does this advance or undermine the goal? In conversation, does it advance the conversation? Or the criterion may be looser: for example, does it have any connection with the conversation? In law the connection is to a probandum, ultimate, penultimate or intermediate. The criteria of relevance are: does it tend to support or to negate this probandum?

The concept of relevance is central to the subject of Evidence in Law. In broad terms, under the adjudication model at common law the predominant Thayerite view is that the reference point is the material facts in a given case and relevance means 'tends to support or tends to negate' one or more penultimate probanda directly or indirectly in the circumstances of the particular case.[25] Significantly, the main criteria of relevance are not formal rules or even general guidelines but 'logic and general experience'. Hence Thayer's famous dictum: 'The law has no mandamus on the logical faculty' (Thayer, 1898).

Under the total process model the picture is only a bit more complex, with a good deal of space needed for 'potentially relevant evidence' and different standards for decision such as those governing arrest, decisions to prosecute and release on parole. Throughout the process relevance is a key concept and the

---

[24] The search engine in *The Stanford Encyclopaedia of Philosophy* lists nearly 1,000 documents under 'relevance' with numerous further links, including two on the Law of Evidence. One of these by Ho, 2015 is an excellent overview of theoretical aspects of Evidence and Proof and in nearly all respects is close to the interpretations in this paper: https://plato.stanford.edu/entries/evidence-legal.

[25] The best known formulation is in the Federal Rules of Evidence 401 (re-styled in 2011): 'Relevant evidence means evidence having any tendency to make the existence of any fact that is of consequence to the determination of the action more probable or less probable than it would be without the evidence'.

   (The classic theoretical account is Tillers, 1983). I skip over here the supposed distinction between 'logical' and 'legal' relevance for which Wigmore is often blamed (see Ho, 2015 and Twining, 1985: 152–5). I find it useful to distinguish the question 'Is there any connection?' (relevance) from the question: 'How strong is the connection?' (weight or probative force), but in practice the *de minimis* principle blurs the distinction. See Michael and Adler, 1931.

context is argumentation and justification. There are, of course, problems, for example in relation to narrative and styles of argumentation and story-telling across different cultures. In short there is plenty of scope for cross-disciplinary enquiry about conceptions and applications of the idea of relevance. Clearly the closest are those related to argumentation.

1.2.2.3 Weight, Probative Force or 'Strength' of Evidence

Similar considerations apply to the concept of 'weight' or 'probative force' or 'value' of evidence across disciplines. For instance, one of the most important tests of admissibility at common law is whether the prejudicial effect outweighs the probative value of an item of evidence *in the circumstances of the case*.[26] How well might this intriguing concept travel to 'non-legal' contexts? Might it for instance suggest a way of mitigating the drive to develop hierarchies of the strength of classes of evidence in evidence-based medicine and evidence-based policy? From Bentham onwards the common law has resisted the very idea of having rules of weight.[27] In an era of bureaucratisation and IT algorithms, the experience of Law may be highly suggestive for anyone worried by such developments (Twining, 2006: 436–9, 452).[28]

1.2.2.4 Admissibility

The fourth core concept of Evidence in Legal Contexts is *admissibility*. At first sight this looks peculiarly legal. The concept itself and its proper scope and form constitute a large part of the bread-and-butter of common law evidence

---

[26] FRE 403: 'The court may exclude relevant evidence if its probative value is substantially outweighed by a danger of one or more of the following: unfair prejudice, confusing the issues, misleading the jury, undue delay, wasting time, or needlessly presenting cumulative evidence'.

 For English Law see, for example, Roberts and Zuckerman, 2010 (index under 'prejudicial effect', 'prejudicial evidence' and 'probative value').

[27] In the nineteenth century Jeremy Bentham attacked, and effectively destroyed, Chief Baron Gilbert's 'False Theory of Evidence' (Gilbert, 1754; Twining, 2006: 38–41) which was based on priority rules of the weight of classes of evidence with official documents under seal trumping official documents not under seal and so on down to oral witness testimony. Bentham's main critique is still worth reading (*An Introductory View of the Rationale of Judicial Evidence for use of Non-lawyers as well as Lawyers* (Bowring (ed.)) *Works* vi. Appendix C). This covers ground not included in Bentham's *Rational of Judicial Evidence*.

[28] I do not here discuss 'the probabilities' debates that have persisted in Anglo-American circles since the late 1960s. I am personally sceptical about the broad applicability of Bayesianism in legal contexts on grounds that have been trenchantly set out in Haack, 1993; Haack, 2014. For a useful summary of the issues see Roberts and Zuckerman, 2010: 116–39.

scholarship. For the sake of argument, let me accept Thayer's view that to treat a class of evidence in a particular legal system as inadmissible is to say that it cannot be used for a given purpose as part of a valid argument based on evidence. Thus to take a standard example: under the adjudication model the classical doctrine of hearsay evidence (now much eroded) states that (subject to exceptions) hearsay evidence may not be *admitted* to support the truth of the statement, but it may be *used* as evidence that the statement was in fact made (Roberts and Zuckerman, 2010: 364–7). This is probably counterintuitive to a lay person, but makes sense within the framework of the logic of proof: in Wigmorean terms the two propositions ('W said Y'/ 'Y is true') belong in different parts of the same chart.[29]

Not being allowed to take certain factors into account is common in practical life: for example, under equality law in recruitment or promotions most employers may not take into account protected characteristics (such as age, disability, gender reassignment, race, gender or sexual orientation) in making appointments or promotion; other considerations may be inadmissible by convention or general conceptions of respect and fairness. Not all of these can be subsumed under 'irrelevance'. One area in which legal experience may be particularly illuminating concerns to what extent admissibility in adjudication and other legal contexts has been treated, normatively and in practice, as matters to be treated by strong or weak discretion, directives, mandatory rules, guidelines, balancing tests, standards, conventions and so on.[30]

Thus, the significance of the four basic evidentiary concepts is not confined to legal contexts. Making comparisons between the use of these concepts or their equivalents or analogues in other contexts is one quite promising line of enquiry. Some topics for consideration in this way may be fairly obvious; a few may have been considered already; and there may be quite a few surprises. The possibilities are endless, especially if one adopts a total process model rather than an adjudication model of Evidence in Legal Contexts.

Schum may be partly right about the richness of legal experience and theorising. However, there are some clear limitations of our heritage in the context of this enterprise. For example, (a) the main focus of attention (with some notable exceptions) has been on *particular past events*: it is less strong on evidence of empirical *generalisations*; prediction of *future* events; and evidence of other objects of enquiry, such as the existence of imaginary, metaphysical or fictional entities and phenomena from ghosts and fairies to the soul

---

[29] Within Jurisprudence, Ronald Dworkin's ban on policy and consequentialist arguments by judges (Dworkin, 1977: chs. 2 and 4) can be read as a thesis about *admissibility*.

[30] On nuanced differences between types of norms see Twining, 2019: ch. 11.

and God and abstract concepts such as injustice;[31] (b) the main emphasis in the legal literature has been on practical decision-making rather than fundamental philosophical and other theoretical enquiries relating to rationality, epistemology, logic and metaphysics; (c) on a spectrum of hard and soft disciplines, on the whole legal concerns and approaches tend towards the soft, qualitative, local, particularistic, humanist pole rather than the hard, quantitative, general, even universalist scientific one.

1.2.3 A Theoretical Literature

Apart from being intertwined with Logic, Rhetoric and Probability theory, much theorising about Evidence in Law in the Anglo-American tradition was specifically about Evidence doctrine (the Law of Evidence); there are some important exceptions to this within the common law tradition. For example, Bentham (who said there should be no rules of evidence or procedure – 'the anti-nomian thesis') (Twining, 1985: 66–75) and Wigmore; and the debate between Pascalians and Baconians (including Jonathan Cohen's thesis that non-Pascalian reasoning is particularly well-exemplified by Law).[32] The civil law tradition has a rather different ancestry which can illuminatingly be compared from various perspectives.[33] Of course, other legal traditions have also dealt with evidentiary issues and there is a rather fragmented literature in Comparative Law.

1.2.4 Reasoning

Because of the dominance of the mainstream doctrinal traditions, the term 'legal reasoning' has usually been confined to reasoning about doctrine and 'questions of law' (see Twining, 2019: chs. 10, 19). 'Evidential reasoning' in the

---

[31]   A conference at UCL on Bentham on Evidence organised by the Bentham project in 2018 may develop into a symposium or other publication. On Bentham's account of real and fictitious entities see Schofield, 2006: ch.1; on its significance for the study of Evidence see Postema, 1983; Twining, 1985: 60–3.

[32]   Cohen, 1977. In Cohen's usage a distinction is drawn between Baconian (inductivist, non-mathematical) and Pascalian (mathematical) probabilities. These concepts are contested.

[33]   I have found Verges et al., 2015 particularly helpful as an introduction to the French tradition, which has a transnational aspect and it filled some major gaps in my awareness of the literature. Hazard and Taruffo, 1993 is still a useful introduction to comparative civil procedure. I am informed that the most important books on evidence in Spanish from a theoretical perspective include Ferrer Beltrán, 2007 and Gascón, 2010. A comparative intellectual history of theories of evidence in different Western traditions would be particularly useful for the present enterprise.

title of this conference breaks with this practice. There is now, as is well known, a leaner, but quite sophisticated literature on reasoning about questions of fact. Although the distinction between law and fact (and between interpretation, application of rules and fact-determination in relation to rules) is recognised as problematic, in the Anglo-American tradition we have the all too common phenomenon of two bodies of literature talking past each other. There are many kinds of reasonings in legal contexts and questions about their nature, their relationship to each other, whether any are really distinctive or unique and whether all can be subsumed under a single concept of 'practical reasoning' are issues that remain relatively unexplored.[34] Such questions are central to theorising about evidence in general.

1.2.5 A Social Science Literature[35]

This literature is particularly interesting in Psychology, Discourse Analysis and Decision Theory. Rather than generalise about the vast expanse of relations between Law and the Social Sciences, I shall focus on 'Psychology and Law' as an example because this is one area where evidentiary topics have been perceived to be important. Consider the following statement:

> Law and psychology are two separate disciplines, but have much in common. While psychology's goal is to understand behaviour and law's goal to regulate it, both fields make assumptions about what causes people to act the way they do (Kazdin, 2000: 4118).

This bold formulation, although simplistic, brings out the breadth of the two disciplines; each is concerned with (almost) all human behaviour. Each has numerous sub-disciplines, specialisms and schools of thought. Accordingly, it is reasonable to assert that there are many interfaces in many different contexts and at many levels of abstraction. It is dangerous to generalise about the relationship. There are, nevertheless, many general manuals, encyclopaedias and handbooks on 'Law and Psychology' which illustrate this variety and the unevenness of scholarship in the general area (e.g. Memon et al., 2003). This category, and even the more sharply focussed 'Forensic Psychology', are just not coherent fields.

---

[34] The relationship between questions of fact and questions of law in adjudication is the subject of a forthcoming paper. Still a very useful discussion is Zuckerman, 1986.

[35] For reasons of space I omit here discussion of the massive literature on expert evidence, expertise, and distrust of experts which transcends, among others, Forensic Science, Psychology and the developing cross-disciplinary interest in 'trust', 'trustworthiness'. See, for example, Diamond and Lempert, 2018 and Haack, 2014: chapters 3–8.

In respect of Evidence there has been considerable interest in such topics as the role of narrative in jury decision-making, the psychology of witnesses in relation to identification evidence[36] and confessions and interrogation. A general weakness in the area in the Anglo-American tradition is that it has tended to be court-centric and even jury-centric. This is partly because classical theorists, such as Bentham and Wigmore, focussed on 'judicial evidence', but also because psychologists have tended to adopt an adjudicative model rather than a total process model of legal processes. Thus, in respect of confessions the focus has been on confessions that have not been retracted, whereas in practice most confessions in Anglo-American criminal processes are retracted (vide for example the guilty plea). This can distort perceptions of the significance of coercion and 'robust' interrogation techniques in bringing about guilty pleas and plea bargains. Similarly, it is easy to assume that the role of identification parades ('line ups') is solely to generate fresh evidence, whereas it has other uses such as to eliminate suspects, persuade a suspect that the game is up or to lead to a decision not to prosecute (Twining, 2006: ch. 5). There is a general lesson to be drawn from this about interdisciplinary communication. It is wise for lawyers to check that their interlocutors have appropriate or shared perceptions and working assumptions about the legal phenomena under consideration.[37]

1.2.6 *Disputes*

Disputes bring to the surface differences about values, facts and concepts, as Karl Llewellyn regularly emphasised.[38] Similarly, central to Schum's claim that the discipline of Law has something special to offer is the idea that evidentiary issues are argued about in 'the crucible of litigation' and that 'the disciplines of law, and perhaps history, are the only ones known to me in

---

[36]   Anderson et al., 2005: 65–71, based on the classic account in Schum, 1994: ch. 7.3.

[37]   In teaching a course on Law for non-lawyers, which was very popular with accountancy students who wanted to study the Law of Contract, I used to insist that they start with a general overview of law and legal processes so that they did not assume that what they needed to know about contracts in accounting was just a semi-codified bunch of rules. On the assumption that the training of detectives should focus on the Law of Evidence rather than the Logic of Proof see Twining, 2019.

[38]   For example, 'The case of trouble, again, is the case of doubt, or is that in which discipline has failed, or is that in which an unruly personality is breaking through into new paths of action or leadership, or is that in which an ancient institution is being tried against emergent forces. It is the case of trouble which makes, breaks twists or flatly establishes a rule, an institution, an authority . . . not only the making of new law and the effect of old, but the hold and thrust of all other vital aspects of the culture, shine clear in the crucible of conflict' (Llewellyn and Hoebel, 1941: 29).

which evidence of every substantive variety imaginable must be evaluated' (Schum, 1994/2001: 58).[39]

1.2.7 *Archives*

Legal documents, documents of the most technical kind, are the best, often the only evidence that we have for social and economic history, for the history of morality, for the history of practical religion.

(Maitland, 1911)

This dictum by F. W. Maitland, perhaps England's greatest legal historian, has been echoed many times by archivists, historians and others in many languages. Statements of this kind are sometimes exaggerated, but they are often justified for good reason (Twining and Quick, 1994: ch. 2). Recently in England the concept of 'legal records' has been extended beyond court records and formal documents to the much broader and more diverse category of 'records of institutions specialised to law'.[40] This signals a rich heritage, but unfortunately public records have been restricted by financial concerns, private sector legal records have received little attention and the digital revolution has created new challenges that have yet to be confronted adequately. Academic lawyers not only are skilled in interpreting and handling these kinds of material; they also have a special responsibility in raising awareness of the importance of preserving a proportionate selection of our heritage of such records for practical reasons as well as for posterity.[41]

1.3 CONCLUSION: THE LIMITATIONS OF THE DISCIPLINE OF LAW IN RELATION TO EVIDENCE AS A MULTIDISCIPLINARY FIELD

This enterprise of developing a general field of Evidence involves recognised disciplines ranging from agronomy, algebra, archaeology, architecture and

---

[39] I have argued elsewhere that focusing on the contested trial tends to distract attention from other stages in litigation and other kinds of dispute processes in which evidence is important. That broadens Schum's point, rather than undermining it (Twining, 2006: chs. 5 and 6).

[40] In the UK the preservation of private sector legal records has generally been perceived narrowly and largely neglected. For example, only recently have archivists recognised that 'solicitors' records' extend beyond wills and deeds to include all the records of legal firms, including their business records, correspondence and so on. See https://ials.sas.ac.uk/researc h/areas-research/legal-records-risk-lrar-project.

[41] See https://ials.sas.ac.uk/research/areas-research/legal-records-risk-lrar-project.

astronomy (which may be especially interesting) through probability theory and proof of the existence of God right up to Zoology and Zymurgy. Why should lawyers of all people claim to be potentially significant contributors, even pioneers, in this enterprise? I have already given my tentative answer. 'Evidence is no other than the field of knowledge', wrote Bentham (1838–43) who focused mainly on judicial evidence and who wrote more on this subject, broadly conceived, than any other. Of course this is a huge enterprise, especially if one adopts a largely bottom-up approach and emphasises middle order theorising.[42] This chapter has concentrated on what we as jurists can offer to such an enterprise.

There is a vast amount of evidence-related work, including cross-disciplinary and multidisciplinary projects, going on at various levels, for example in relation to health, evidence-based policy and evidence-based policing; in addition to the UCL and LSE programmes there have been some events which treated Evidence in general as a focus of attention;[43] but these have tended to be mainly subject-specialists explaining to a general audience how evidence is viewed or treated in their own particular field. There are also large-scale developments, for instance in health, evidence-based policy and evidence-based policing.[44] If the purpose is to stimulate interdisciplinary communication, co-operation and cross-fertilisation, it may be wise not to attempt to start with a Grand Theory or a multi-million dollar programme or institution – the potential field is so vast and the possibilities so extensive.[45] One has to start somewhere and, like Schum, I think that exploring the similarities and differences between evidence-related concepts and their uses in different disciplines is one promising way to start, especially for a lawyer.

---

[42]   On middle-order theorising, see Twining, 2019: ch. 1.
[43]   For example, the President's seminar at Wolfson College Oxford in 2017–18 on 'What counts as evidence?' organised by Professor Philomen Probert, a specialist in historical linguistics.
[44]   One of the most impressive is the transnational Cochrane Collaboration ('Trusted evidence, informed decisions, better health') (https://community.cochrane.org): 'A non-profit, non-governmental organization formed to organize medical research findings so as to facilitate evidence-based choices about health interventions faced by health professionals, patients, and policy makers'. Cf. the Campbell Collaboration (info@campbellcollaboration.org).
[45]   At the World Congress on Evidential Legal Reasoning I was surprised to hear Professor Ron Allen suggest that I favoured a top-down, rather than a bottom-up approach in this area. (Allen, 2021: Ch. 2 in this book). I see the relationship between generality and particularity, between the abstract and the concrete, as being one largely of reciprocal interaction. In my work in Jurisprudence and Evidence my bias has if anything been towards middle-order theorising and emphasising complexity. I deplore the widespread tendency to skip up and down ladders of abstraction missing out the middle rungs. In the tension between Italo Calvino's Kublai Kahn who wishes to reduce his Empire to order and the elusive anti-reductionism of Marco Polo (Calvino, 1994), I tend to the anti-reductionist tendencies of the latter (see Twining, 2019: Preface and ch. 20.

REFERENCES

Allen, R. (2021). New Directions of Evidence Science, in C. Vázquez and J. Ferrer Beltrán, eds., *Evidential Legal Reasoning*, Cambridge: Cambridge University Press.

Anderson, T., Schum, D. and Twining, W. (2005). *Analysis of Evidence*, 2nd ed., Cambridge, New York: Cambridge University Press.

Bentham, J. (1837–43). *An Introductory View of the Rationale of the Law of Evidence for Use by Non-lawyers as well as Lawyers* (ed. James Mill, circa 1810). VI Works 1–187. Bowring edition, 1837–43. Edinburgh: William Tait.

Calvino, I. (1974). *Invisible Cities*. Weaver, W. translator, New York: Harcourt Brace and Company.

Cohen, J. (1977). *The Probable and the Provable*, Oxford: Oxford University Press.

Cohen, J. (1981). Can Human Irrationality be Experimentally Demonstrated?, *Behavioral and Brain Sciences*, 4 (3), 317–31.

Damaška, M. (1986). *The Faces of Justice and State Authority*, New Haven, CT: Yale University Press.

Dawid, P., Twining, W. and Vasilaki, M. (2011). *Evidence, Inference and Enquiry*, Oxford: Oxford University Press.

Diamond, S. and Lempert, R. (2018). When Law Calls, Does Science Answer? A Survey of Distinguished Scientists and Engineers, *Daedalus*, 147 (4), 41–60.

Dworkin, R. (1977). *Taking Rights Seriously*, London: Gerald Duckworth and Co. Ltd.

Ferrer Beltrán, J. (2007). *La valoración racional de la prueba*, Madrid: Marcial Pons.

Gascón, M. (2010). *Los hechos en el derecho. Bases argumentales de la prueba*. 3rd ed., Madrid: Marcial Pons.

Gaskins, R. (1992). *Burdens of Proof in Modern Discourse*, New York: Yale University Press.

Gilbert, J. (1754). *The Law of Evidence*. Dublin: P. Byrne.

Haack, S. (1993). *Evidence and Inquiry: Towards Reconstruction in Epistemology*. Cambridge, MA: Blackwell.

Haack, S. (2014). *Evidence Matters*, Cambridge: Cambridge University Press.

Hacking, I. (1975). *The Emergence of Probability*, Cambridge: Cambridge University Press.

Hazard, G. and Taruffo, M. (1993). *American Civil Procedure: An Introduction*, New Haven, CT: Yale University Press.

Ho, J. L. (2015). The Legal Concept of Evidence, *Stanford Encyclopaedia of Philosophy*. https://plato.stanford.edu/archives/win2015/entries/evidence-legal/.

Howlett, P. and Morgan, M. (2010). *How Well Do Facts Travel? The Dissemination of Reliable Knowledge*, Cambridge: Cambridge University Press.

Jackson, J. and Summers, S. (2012). *The Internationalisation of Criminal Evidence: Beyond the Common Law and Civil Law Traditions*, Cambridge: Cambridge University Press.

Kazdin, A. E. ed. (2000). *Encyclopedia of Psychology*, New York: Oxford University Press.

Llewellyn, K. and Hoebel, E. (1941). *The Cheyenne Way. Conflict and Case Law in Primitive Jurisprudence*, Norman: University of Oklahoma Press.

Lloyd-Bostock, S. M. (1980). *Psychology in Legal Contexts: Applications and Limitations*, Chichester: John Wiley and Sons Ltd.

Maitland, F. (2011). *The Collected Papers of Frederic William Maitland*, H. A. L. Fisher ed., Cambridge: Cambridge University Press.

Memon, A., Vrij, A. and Bull, R. (2003). Psychology and Law: Truthfulness, Accuracy and Credibility, Chichester: Wiley.

Michael, J. and Adler, M. (1931). *The Nature of Judicial Proof: An Inquiry into the Logical, Legal and Empirical Aspects of the Law of Evidence* (private printing).

Postema, G. (1983). Facts, Fictions and Law: Bentham on the Foundations of Evidence, in W. Twining ed., *Facts in Law*, Wiesbaden: Franz Steiner Verlag.

Roberts, P. and Zuckerman, A. (2010). *Criminal Evidence, 3rd edition*. Oxford: Oxford University Press.

Santos, B. (1995). *Toward a New Common Sense: Law, Science and Politics in the Paradigmatic Transition*. London, New York: Routledge.

Schofield, P. (2006). *Utility and Democracy: The Political Thought of Jeremy Bentham*. Oxford: Oxford University Press.

Schum, D. (1994/2001). *Evidential Foundations of Probabilistic Reasoning*. Evanston, IL: Northwestern University Press.

Swift, E. (2000). One Hundred Years of Evidence Law Reform: Thayer's Triumph. *California Law Review*, 88 (6), 2437–76.

Taruffo, M. (1992). *La prova dei fatti giuridici*. Milan: Giuffre.

Tecuci, G., Schum, D., Marcu, D., and Boicu, M., (2016). *Intelligence Analysis As Discovery of Evidence, Hypotheses, and Arguments: Connecting the Dots*, New York: Cambridge University Press.

Thayer, J. (1898). *A Preliminary Treatise on Evidence at Common Law*. Boston, MA: Little Brown and Company.

Tillers, P. (1983). Modern Theories of Relevancy, *Wigmore on Evidence*, 1-1A, Boston, MA: Little Brown and Company.

Toulmin, S. (1964). *The Uses of Argument*, Cambridge: Cambridge University Press.

Twining, W. (1985). *Theories of Evidence: Bentham and Wigmore*, London: Weidenfeld and Nicolson.

Twining, W. (2006). *Rethinking Evidence*, Cambridge: Cambridge University Press.

Twining, W. (2019). *Jurist in Context. A Memoir,* Cambridge: Cambridge University Press.

Twining, W. and Monk, I., eds. (2003). *Evidence and Inference in History and Law,* Evanston, IL: Northwestern University Press.

Twining, W. and Quick, E. (1994). *Legal Records in the Commonwealth,* Aldershot: Dartmouth Publishing Co. Ltd.

Vergès E., Vial, G. and Leclerc, O. (2015). Droit de la preuve. París: Presses Universitaires de France.

Wigmore, J. H. (1913). *The Principles of Judicial Proof as Given by Logic, Psychology and General Experience,* Boston, MA: Little Brown and Company. 3rd ed., 1937. *Sub Nom the Science of Judicial Proof.*

Zuckerman, A. (1986). Law, Fact or Justice? *Boston University Law Review,* 66, 487–508.

2

New Directions for Evidence Science, Complex Adaptive Systems, and a Possibly Unprovable Hypothesis About Human Flourishing

Ronald J. Allen

The title to this chapter will be heard by scholars from different parts of the world differently. It will not sound strange at all to the burgeoning field of evidence scholars in China, who conceive of the study of evidence precisely in these terms, and who have created the International Association of Evidence Science that holds quite successful biennial conferences that blend together what the Anglo-American world would call evidence scholarship and forensic science. It may sound a bit odd to European scholars who tend to approach questions of evidence from more of a philosophical than empirical perspective. And I suspect it will sound oddest to the Anglo-American scholars for two reasons. The first is the lingering effects of the attack by the Legal Realists in the first half of twentieth century on the alleged pretensions to science by their doctrinal predecessors that led to the term "legal science" becoming something that no self-respecting legal scholar would admit to pursuing.[1] Quite remarkably, even the rise of Law and Economics – by far the most important development within legal scholarship in the second half of the twentieth century – did not scrub this term of the disdain heaped upon it by the Realists. The second reason may be the more recent disappointing results of a multidisciplinary effort at identifying the components of an "integrated science of evidence,"[2] notwithstanding the optimistic tone set at the beginning of the project by David Schum.[3] The scope of that effort was not limited to law and legal systems and was motivated by the thought that perhaps there are commonalities in the concept and implications of evidence across many

[1] See, e.g., Robert Gordon, The Case for and against Harvard, 93 *Mich. L. Rev.* 1231 (1995).
[2] Philip Dawid, William Twining & Mimi Vasilaki, *Evidence, Inference and Enquiry* (2011).
[3] David A. Schum, A Science of Evidence: Contributions from Law and Probability Law, 8 *Probability and Risk* 197 (2009).

disciplines that could be synthesized. In the words of one of our participants here, William Twining, "the idea of a shared enterprise that also focused on some shared general questions was lost sight of. My personal hopes were not realized. The development of a new subject matter is a major undertaking."[4]

I suspect that there is a common reason for the lack of success in both enterprises, to-wit that one does not make sciences top-down; one becomes aware of them as they grow up around you.[5] Moreover, "sciences" are unruly and so far as I am aware (I don't claim to have an encyclopedic knowledge of "the sciences") none of them can be easily characterized by monolithic descriptions of either subject matter or method except at the most banal level. Take the King of Science – physics (mathematics seems to be the queen) – as an example. Such references almost always are actually to a small subset of physics – particle physics, which has had stunning success in large measure driven by its mathematic underpinnings. But there are other branches of physics that lack this conceptual purity, such as fluid dynamics and those involving nonlinear physical electromagnetic phenomena that exhibit chaotic effects beyond the competence of the mathematicians to tame.[6] No physicist would try to predict where a molecule of water in a mountain stream is going to end up. And of course there are many other "sciences" that have achieved remarkable successes without being tied at the hip to mathematics in the way that particle physics has been. Biology, for example, and the neurosciences. The more telling point for my purposes, though, is that no one set out to create particle physics or biology or the neurosciences in their present form; rather, they grew up around their practitioners pursuing more or less common aims.[7]

The burden of this chapter is that in my opinion a "science of evidence" is evolving as it applies to legal institutions. What I mean by "legal institutions" are the methods and modes of governance in a representative democracy (the only form of governance within my competence) with at least a modest commitment to the rule of law, of which legal systems and dispute resolutions are an important part. I realize that these are simple definitions, but I believe that they will prove adequate to the task. What I mean by "science" is equally

---

[4] William Twining, Moving Beyond Law: Interdisciplinarity and the Study of Evidence, in Philip Dawid, William Twining & Mimi Vasilaki, *Evidence, Inference and Enquiry* (2011) 111.

[5] Professor Twining is sensitive to the point. See id. at 113, but the efforts described in the Dawid book are most easily understood as the failure of the "development of a new subject." Id. at 111.

[6] For a brief introduction, see https://en.wikipedia.org/wiki/Electromagnetism.

[7] And a perhaps even more telling point may be the argument of Sabine Hossenfelder in Lost in Math: How Beauty Leads Physics Astray (2018) that physicists' preoccupation with elegant mathematics may account in part for the lack of significant progress in particle physics over the last half-century.

naïve, but like naïve realism, it may be better than its more sophisticated cousins. What I mean by it is the systematic study of some more or less common phenomena from a more or less common perspective using compatible methodologies.

An evidence science has grown up around these legal institutions that tends to focus on various forms of dispute resolution but that has much wider implications than that. Although virtually no one to my knowledge presently engaging in this science thinks explicitly in the following terms, in fact we are collectively engaging in a subset of the study of complex adaptive systems. I will briefly describe complex adaptive systems, demonstrate that collectively this captures in an important way what we are studying, and then conclude with some thoughts as to whether or not, even if I am right, the recognition of what we are doing has any consequences, like for example for human flourishing.

A critical difference exists between something that is complicated and something that is a complex adaptive system, something that is static as compared to something that is dynamic, a good metaphor being the distinction between a tree farm and a rain forest. It is sensible to ask what the point of a tree farm is, but not a rain forest. The distribution of the grains of sand on a beach is complicated, as is the progression of a hurricane, but neither are complex adaptive systems. Chess is complicated, but static. It is closed deductively and the rules are complete. Complex adaptive systems by contrast involve massive discrete interactions, emergent properties, and often involve feedback mechanisms. Examples are the immune system, traffic on roads, the progression of infectious diseases and as I shall return to later, elections, markets, and adaptable legal systems, of which the common law is probably the paradigm. They are dynamic, not static. Unpredictable consequences emerge. These are examples and generalizations. There is no universally accepted specification of the meaning of "complex adaptive system"; the study of complexity is a science that is emerging in precisely the manner of its objects of inquiry. Indeed, even the meaning of "complex" is complex.[8] A useful description that captures the central concept of complex adaptive systems across many different definitions, in the words of Melanie Mitchell, is "a system in which large networks of components with no central control and simple rules of operation give rise to complex collective behavior, sophisticated information processing, and adaptation via learning or evolution."[9] Similarly, Neil Johnson identifies

---

[8]   See Melanie Mitchell, *Complexity: A Guided Tour*, Chapter 7, *Defining and Measuring Complexity* (2009).

[9]   Melanie Mitchell, Complexity: A Guided Tour, at p. 13. For a general discussion of the pertinent ideas, see Matt Ridley, *The Evolution of Everything: How New Ideas Emerge* (2015).

"Complexity Science ... as the *study of Phenomena which emerge from a collection of interacting objects* ...[10] that ... can arise in the absence of any controller or coordinator."[11] Precursors to these ideas include both the Hayekian distinction between made and grown systems[12] and the concept of autopoiesis first penned by Humberto Maturana and Francisco Varela to refer to the self-sustaining nature of cells[13] and extended to social systems most famously by Niklas Luhmann.[14]

In an important sense, a complex adaptive system is more a frame of reference than a natural kind. Conceptualizing the immune system as a complex adaptive process is completely uncontroversial, but this is also true of the human body of which the immune system is a part, and so too with the surrounding ecology of which the human body is a part. The most spectacular adaptive system may be the universe as a whole (from a singular quantum event we get stars, galaxies, giraffes, and immune systems) with the human mind perhaps a close second. The idea of complex adaptive systems is thus in part an analytical tool whose payoff is in the work that it can do to advance understanding.

Nothing guarantees that a complex system will adapt in a direction that a participant in that system might view as beneficial. Dinosaurs, had they thought about the matter, were probably not too pleased with the aftermath of large meteors striking the earth or stupendous volcanoes erupting that made life decidedly unpleasant for them. However, those same processes laid the

---

[10] Neil Johnson, *Simply Complexity: A Clear Guide to Complexity Theory* (2009) at Kindle location 139.

[11] Id. at Kindle location 211. A more complicated set of conditions include:

- The System contains a collection of many interacting objects or agents:
- These objects' behavior is affected by memory or feedback
- The objects can adapt their strategies according to their history
- The system is typically "open" — influenced by its environment
- The system appears to be "alive." ... evolves in a highly non-trivial and often complicated way, driven by an ecology of agents who interact and adapt under the influence of feedback
- The system exhibits emergent phenomena which are generally surprising, and may be extreme.
- The emergent phenomena typically arise in the absence of any sort of "invisible hand" or central controller
- The system shows a complicated mix of ordered and disordered behavior.

Id. at Kindle Location 343–93.

[12] See, e.g., F. A. Hayek, *Rules and Order*, vol. 1 of *Law, Legislation, and Liberty* (Chicago: University of Chicago Press, 1973).

[13] *Autopoiesis and Cognition: the Realization of the Living* at p. 78 (2nd ed. 1980).

[14] *Essays on Self-Reference* (1990).

groundwork for the age of mammals. The human immune system keeps the average person alive notwithstanding a constant assault from trillions of pathogens, some of which are quite threatening, yet at other times the pathogens prevail (which they might think is a good thing).

Because of the evolution of the human brain that has allowed the species to control to a considerable extent its environment, humans are not entirely at the mercy of nature, obviously. One of the consequences of this capacity to control the environment is the possibility of exploiting the benefits of complex systems, and there is one potential benefit that looms large. That is the capacity of complex adaptive systems to process vast amounts of information without a top-down central controller. Evolution is an example. The human species (or any other) is the product of close to an infinite number of local interactions that led to the emergent property of life and then speciation. The immune system is another, quite stunning example. With no central command system, it does a remarkable job of keeping us alive in the face of the onslaught noted above.

A remarkable example of this is the centrifugal governor invented by Thomas Watt to regulate the rate of a flywheel attached to a steam engine that was critical to the success of the textile industry in Britain, which in turn fueled the industrial revolution. A close to infinite amount of information is transmitted between the regulator, the flywheel, and the valve, all without any central command system or computation.[15]

Humans can exploit these phenomena by the creation of cognizant feedback mechanisms to attempt to guide emergence, and there are at least three that in my opinion help explain (along with many other variables, I'm sure) the success of the western world, and they are the three I mentioned above: elections, markets, and the common law. These three permit the intelligent exploitation of vast amounts of information, much too much information for any central command and control center to process and act upon. This, of course, was Hayek's central insight about price theory, but it applies to markets generally. It is not just information about price that markets are accommodating, but also consumer desires and needs. Elections do something similar because of the feedback mechanism of removing and replacing office holders.

Responsive legal systems do the same thing. The paradigmatic example is the common law. In fact, the common law is both an example of an adaptive

---

[15] Tim Van Gelder, What Might Cognition Be, If Not Computation, 92 *J. of Philosophy* 348 (1995). He was inspired by an invention by Christian Huygens to regulate the distance and pressure between millstones in windmills. Richard E. Bellman, *Adaptive Control Processes: A Guided Tour* (2015).

system that can accommodate large amounts of information and an example of how "intelligent" systems can evolve in the absence of a central control mechanism. No one thought up the "law" in the common law. As Matt Ridley says, it "is a code of ethics that was written by nobody and everybody ... It is a beautiful example of spontaneous order." He continues:

> Judges change the common law incrementally, adjusting legal doctrine case by case to fit the facts on the ground. When a new puzzle arises, different judges come to different conclusions about how to deal with it, and the result is a sort of genteel competition, as successive courts gradually choose which line they prefer. In this sense, the common law is built by natural selection.[16]

Ridley is not a lawyer, and he leaves out three important parts of the story, all involving feedback mechanisms that assist the system to process information in an intelligent way: appellate judges, legislatures, and citizens. Appellate judges act to facilitate the competition by providing competing perspectives on whatever is the question at hand, and legislatures can intervene whenever there is the political will to do so. The critical variables of the common law are information processing and responsiveness, which can exist in other systems as well, in particular in democracies with a strong commitment to the rule of law.

What about other citizens? In my opinion this is the most important but least noted attribute that makes a responsive legal system like the common law work as well as it does.[17] When a decision is reached, it ripples out across a complex neural network structure formed by the citizens of the pertinent jurisdiction and anyone with any interest can become aware of it. A decision may be helpful to some and such people can work towards its adoption or exploitation; the same decision may be harmful to others, and they can work towards its constraint or elimination. Both activities can be through further litigation, agitation for statutory change, social protest, or whatever. All of these messages likewise traverse the network, which facilitates the examination

---

[16] Ridley, supra n. 9, at loc. 761.
[17] There is a large literature about the common law, see e.g. John H. Langbein, Renee L. Lerner, & Bruce P. Smith, *History of the Common Law: The Development of Anglo-American Legal Systems* (2009) but to my knowledge none of it analyzes the role that citizens and their knowledge play in its success. The informational benefits of the common law as a complex adaptive system is completely absent from the analysis even in work that focuses on the contingency of life and analogizes to evolution. Allan C. Hutchinson, *Evolution and the Common Law* (2005). Other work focuses on the perennial question of common law reasoning. See, e.g., Melvin A. Eisenberg, *The Nature of the Common Law* (1988). For a good sampling of this literature, none of which touches on complex adaptive processes, see Douglas E. Edlin (ed.), *Common Law Theory* (2007).

and probing of the issue in question by vast numbers of individuals with varying perspectives, knowledge, and backgrounds. Whatever happens, happens, and once again messages go out across the network in iterated fashion until some form of stability (not an equilibrium) is achieved. All of this is facilitated by the principle of the common law that the judges only decide the facts and arguments presented to them. If a first decision is reached that did not consider what a third party to the litigation thought to be important and determinative, the next judge can. It should also be immediately obvious that appellate opinions and legislation have these same network effects. All three ripple through the system, engaging the cognition of others in the system and allowing responses.

All of this is a bit stylized in today's world that is the culmination of more than a century of increasing statutory and regulatory intrusions into private lives,[18] but core elements remain true. Legal systems can be more or less top-down versus bottom-up; they can be more or less responsive to nuance; they can be more or less tolerant of discretion. And, admittedly, there are pitfalls everywhere. Rules have strengths as well, in particular in view of the demand to treat like cases alike. Discretion can be wisely administered or arbitrarily. But analogously it can be the rules themselves that become arbitrary, where there is a distance between the letter of the law and its spirit. Rules become oppressive in part because of their inability to respond to dynamic contexts. Another advantage of viewing legal processes through the lens of complexity is to highlight the significance of the distinction between static systems where rules often work fine, and dynamic ones where they don't.

What does all of this have to do with the law of evidence? In my opinion, quite a lot, as I will now try to demonstrate. I will attempt to show that understanding of the pertinent object of inquiry of both the philosophers examining juridical proof and the evidence scholars is enhanced by looking at that object through the lens of complexity theory.

Many scholars, I believe, view the law of evidence as involved primarily with advancing accurate outcomes subject to certain policy constraints, and thus the field of evidence is associated primarily with epistemology, echoing the statement from Bentham almost two hundred years ago that the study of evidence is the study of knowledge.[19] This is true to a considerable extent in both his world and ours, and for a very good reason. Efficiently and effectively

---

[18] See, e.g., Guido Calabresi, A Common Law for the Age of Statutes (1982).
[19] "[T]he field of evidence is no other than the field of knowledge." Jeremy Bentham, An Introductory View of the Rationale of Judicial Evidence, Works, Vol. VI(5) (1843) (Bowring ed. 2002).

establishing the facts at trial is critically dependent upon the field and the law of evidence, and without accurate decision-making rights are meaningless. Moreover, without orderly decision-making errors cannot be allocated consistently with political preferences.

But there are two complexifying factors that the facile equation of the field of evidence with epistemology neglects. First, the law of evidence does much more than structure an epistemological episode, and second theories of evidence are contingent political constructs.

First, consider the complex objectives of the law of evidence in the Anglo-American world, which the field of evidence must accommodate in some way. In addition to epistemology, the law of evidence accommodates at least four other variables.

The Organizational Problem: In addition to structuring the context of fact-finding, the law of evidence regulates the interactions of the various participants in the legal system: trial judge, jurors and other lay assessors, attorneys, parties, and witnesses (both lay and expert) and constructs the framework for a trial. It allocates both power and discretion to each of the actors. For example, by determining how much discretion the trial judge has, the law of evidence affects how much control the parties have over the trial process. Similarly, the law of evidence structures the relationship between trial judges and appellate judges. Should there be trial de novo in the appellate court, or is appellate review limited to the resolution of legal errors, which essentially insulates from appellate review factual decision in the trial court? Are small civil cases different from large commercial cases in ways that justify different treatment? What is unique about criminal cases? The law of evidence also regulates the relationships among branches of government, in particular but not limited to the judiciary and legislature: whoever writes the rules at least partially determines the outcome. An interesting example for this audience is the European Court of Human Rights mandating confrontation rights in criminal cases. These rulings take power from courts and local legislatures and locate it in parties.

The Governance Problem: Notwithstanding the importance of accurate fact-finding, there are other social goals in addition to sensible trials that accurate fact-finding competes with, often through the creation of incentives of various kinds. The list of social policies that conflict with accurate adjudication is long and culturally contingent. For example, the law of privileges may foster and protect numerous relationships, including spousal, legal, medical, spiritual, and governmental. Perhaps settlement of disputes is preferred to litigation, which leads to the exclusion of statements made during settlement talks. In the United States and more and more in the world at large, a body of exclusionary rules is premised on the perceived need to regulate police investigative activities. The important point here is that the legal analyst cannot limit attention to the epistemological question, for epistemology competes with social policy. One important social policy is the satisficing of the four possible outcomes at trial, which itself adds a complexifying variable that I will return to below.

The Social Problem: In some societies, trials serve additional functions to dispute resolution, such as symbolic and political purposes. Both institutions and individuals can make statements through the means of trials, and impart lessons of various kinds. Trials also can be the means of vindicating reputations and obstructing governmental overreaching. Obviously, the law of evidence can impact all such issues. Principles of fairness and equity may also influence the law of evidence, although the precise effect of this variable is often hard to sort out from more overtly utilitarian motivations. Some think that the limit on unfairly prejudicial evidence reflects not only the concern about accuracy but also the concern about humiliation, as is also the case with character evidence rules. The limits on prior behavior and propensity evidence reflect in part a belief that an individual should not be trapped in the past. The hearsay rule reflects the values of the right to confront witnesses against oneself.

The Enforcement Problem: There is a critical distinction between the law on the books and the law in action. It is one thing to write laws and rules; it is another to enforce them in the way anticipated by the drafter of those provisions. The drafter of an evidence code may think that a rule has a precise meaning or that allocating discretion to someone, whether trial judge or attorney, makes sense, but the drafter may have in mind an approach to interpreting the rule or exercising that discretion that might not be shared by those implementing the rule. More generally, it is hard to enforce complex codes in social events such as trials. The event itself, the trial, is often fluid and unpredictable, and it would be impossible to have every decision made at trial second-guessed by some other authority. The field of evidence must consider how to respond to such matters and incorporate those conclusions into the law of evidence.

This catalogue of complexifying variables of the field of evidence is not complete. It omits, for example, the complex interaction of substantive law on the one hand, and procedural and evidentiary law on the other, and there are surely other variables that have escaped my notice. In addition to being incomplete, it is decidedly parochial and associates "the field of evidence" with contemporary thought in western democracies. Unfortunately, life is again more complicated than that. To be sure, the law of evidence emerges from the field of evidence, but it does so by at least implicitly adopting or furthering a theory or set of objectives of litigation. Theories of litigation themselves are derived from more fundamental understandings of the nature or objectives of legal systems, but legal systems are derived from even more fundamental theories or objectives of government. These are all interconnected and the field of evidence cannot neglect this point. "Evidential reasoning" occurs in a context. It has universal attributes like cognition and the nature of rationality, but it also has highly idiosyncratic components fashioned from the community in which it resides.

So one sees a bubbling cauldron of complexity that the evidentiary scientist has to deal with. The more abstract one's lens, moving from mundane questions of admissibility to governments and legal systems for example, the more obvious it is that the object of inquiry is a complex adaptive system. Consider just one example of this that I mentioned above – the focus on mistakes at trial that often seems to preoccupy students of burdens of persuasion. No sensible social planner would look just at mistakes at trial, but instead would expand the horizon to include both correct decisions and the associated mistakes in cognate procedures such as settlement, as well as the adaptive effects on primary behavior.

The objective of the legal system is the overall optimization of social welfare, not just the optimization of litigation behavior. Thus, the interactive effect of the legal regime with primary behavior must be accommodated. For example, there is surely an optimal level of litigation. The promise of fair and accurate findings of fact at trial give citizens and the government incentives to follow the law as do the transaction costs of litigation. It is often a pointless waste of resources to dispute ownership of property, for example, if the outcome is predetermined by fair and accurate resolution of disputes. This creates strong incentives to talk among ourselves about disputes, determine where we disagree, and work out an equitable resolution, rather than waste resources on litigation. Cost of litigation thus is probably socially useful in giving people incentives to structure their affairs to avoid it and thus to reduce overall transactions costs, as well as foster social relations. The field of evidence cannot limit its horizon to just the legal system, in other words, but instead must take into account the more general social contributions that the legal system makes to society. The law of evidence is an important tool to implement these social objectives. But this is surely an adaptive process. As the law changes, both litigation and primary behavior change in response.[20] Conceptualizing the law of evidence as involving a static rather than

---

[20] The inability to accommodate the dynamic nature of this phenomenon largely explains the failure of Louis Kaplow's ambitious effort to explain burdens of proof from an economic perspective. For a discussion, see Ronald J. Allen & Alex Stein, Evidence, Probability, and the Burden of Proof, 55 *Arizona L. Rev.* 557 (2013).

a dynamic process obscures these important components of a sensible field of evidence.

At a more discrete level, even trials are adaptive. Trial judges make rulings both out of fidelity to the law as well as a desire to avoid reversal, and for other reasons, desires that can be in a complicated relationship. An even clearer complication results from the desire to follow the law and the desire to effect an outcome. The parties have a wide range of options to respond to trial judges' behavior, and to each other, which can then reverberate across this set of relationships prompting further moves in one direction or another. Even the basic concept of relevance has to be seen through the lens of complexity rather than the rather sterile lens of doctrinal analysis. The standard doctrine taught at least in American law schools that relevancy is determined by whether a reasonable person would conclude that an offer of evidence increases or decreases the probability of a fact of consequence (a material proposition at common law) is at a minimum quite unhelpful, and in fact probably just false.[21] Any offer of evidence at trial can be conditioned upon any other offer of evidence that has or will be made. At the time of the offering of evidence, one simply has no clear idea what its role will be once all the rest of the evidence is admitted. Evidence that a person was observed near the scene of a murder increases the probability of guilt, until evidence is admitted that he was visiting his dying mother in the locale as he always does at exactly that time, until evidence is admitted that the times of the two observations were different, until evidence is admitted that at least one of the "timekeepers" was malfunctioning, until . . . . Perhaps the best example of this analytical problem is a criminal case with an alibi, for which the standard understanding of relevancy makes no sense. The prosecution's case is completely irrelevant and should not be admitted if the alibi is true, and vice versa.

This leads to another correction of conventional views of the law of evidence when viewed through the lens of complexity. Often the only thing that can be determined at the time of admission is whether or not evidence furthers a party's explanation of events, as exemplified by an alibi. But both parties get to give their explanations in their own terms, and thus in the typical case the evidence at trial is massively overlapping. Most witnesses after the first on a particular topic largely repeat what has already been said. If the conventional understanding of meaning of relevancy is true, all that evidence is irrelevant

---

[21] FRE 401 and 402 adopt this perspective, but these rules obviously do not control what actually occurs at trial. The evidence of this is in real trials and their transcripts. One example is the transcript that begins my evidence book, Ronald J. Allen, Eleanor Swift, David S. Schwartz, Michael S. Pardo, & Alex Stein, *An Analytical Approach to Evidence: Text Problems, and Cases* (2016). Other examples abound.

because, in the words of FRE 401, it does NOT have "any tendency to make a fact [of consequence] more or less probable than it would be without the evidence," and thus should be inadmissible by reference to FRE 402's exclusion of "irrelevant evidence."[22] But of course it isn't. The conventional understanding articulates a sufficient but not a necessary condition of admissibility – as does the furthering of a party's explanation.

Returning to whether or not approaching these phenomena from the perspective of complexity theory is of any use, as we have already seen it is at least true that viewing the evidentiary process as a complex adaptive system helps clarify a number of important issues concerning the nature of juridical proof. Its significance goes much further. It also explains a paradigm shift that is presently occurring concerning the understanding of juridical proof from the probabilistic paradigm that has dominated western thought to an explanationist paradigm that involves the analysis of the explanatory alternatives offered at trial.

The probability paradigm was first undercut by a recognition that trials were too complicated to be handled appropriately. This, of course, is the well-known problem of computational complexity. Additionally, no satisfactory interpretation of conventional probability could be given in the absence of plentiful, and reliable, relative frequencies. While true, these were not the deepest problems. The deepest problem is that the probabilistic paradigm accurately explains virtually nothing that occurs at trial, from the initial admission of evidence, to its processing, to the ultimate conclusions that are reached. Explanationism, by contrast, does. Evidence is admitted if it forms a part of a party's explanation. Evidence is "processed" not in an updating way but in an educational process in which the fact-finder is educated about the parties' explanations, and in which all the cognitive tools in the cognitive tool chest are available, including probability. The alibi problem noted above goes away, because each side gets to provide its explanation. Subject to a few nuances,[23] the conclusion is reached in civil cases by deciding which explanation is more plausible, and in criminal cases by deciding if there is a plausible story of guilt, and if so whether there is a plausible story of innocence.

A length exegesis of relative plausibility, as this theory has come to be known, was recently published.[24] As is typical with paradigm shifts, there are

---

[22] The references are to federal law, but every state, and to my knowledge every Anglo-American jurisdiction, has similar structures.

[23] Fact-finders can obviously construct their own explanation in light of the trial evidence and their experiences in life.

[24] Ronald J. Allen & Michael Pardo, Relative Plausibility and Its Critics, 23 *Int. J. Evidence and Proof* 5 (2019).

objectors and resistors, and answers to these objections are given. Along with the main article, twenty responses and criticisms were also published, and so these issues have been thoroughly aired. I will thus not belabor any of the details here today, but I do want to emphasize one matter. The evolution of relative plausibility has been associated with the psychological story model, and indeed thirty years ago the consanguinity of the two seemed to yield support to both. However, relative plausibility has no necessary analytical relationship to the story model, and the failure to recognize that has been misleading. The early psychological research, like the early analytical legal work, focused on criminal cases and torts, in which there are indeed usually stories in classic chronological narrative form, but the trial of disputes ranges far beyond these simple examples. There are not "stories" in the typical anti-trust case, nor in many contract cases, nor in no-fault divorce cases, nor in disparate impact cases, and so on. There are, by contrast, explanations in all of them.

Viewing the litigation process through the lens of complexity also points to the direction of the future of evidence science in my opinion, and that is to empirical work done with complex adaptive systems in mind. Interestingly, there is an important example of this work being done today, and it is by the artificial intelligence branch of evidence science – the people interested in argument structure, scenarios, and the like. I have no idea whether people like Floris Bex, Douglas Walton, Bart Verheij, Henry Prakken, and many others that could be named think in these terms or not, but they are exploring the way in which people reason in adaptive situations.[25] Their disparate results are also indicative of the underlying dynamic they are studying, which resists reduction to simple propositions and simple deductions.

Another important scholar who in my opinion has at least implicitly recognized the complex adaptive structure of litigation and the limits of the probability paradigm, and is examining these matters head-on, is Dale Nance. In discussing what actually occurs at trial, he says:

> Such argument forms serve important functions relative to both the assessment of discriminatory power and the choice of Keynesian weight... [P]lausible reasoning serves as a tool for the analysis of evidence in commonsense terms. Even as litigation comes with ready-made contending hypotheses (C and not-C), those general claims typically will be refined at trial to specific theories of the case, one or more for the claimant instantiating C and one or more for the

---

[25]   Among the many examples, see Floris J. Bex, *Arguments, Stories and Criminal Evidence: A Hybrid Theory* (2010); Douglas Walton, Chris Reed & Fabrizio Macagno, *Argumentation Schemes* (2008).

defendant instantiating not-C. In deliberation, though, the fact-finder will often find it necessary to consider other alternatives. And as Peirce noted, abduction (or inference to the most plausible explanation) becomes a critical tool by which commonsense reasoning develops such additional hypotheses. An assessment of Keynesian weight must be made relative to the contending hypotheses, and as these hypotheses change, some modification of the practical optimization of Keynesian weight may become necessary.[26]

Remove the reference to Keynesian weight, and I and my coauthors could have written that paragraph. Moreover, although Professor Nance may disagree, the extent to which Keynesian weight actually plays a role in the best explanation of juridical proof is orthogonal to the question of probabilism as compared to explanationism. It could play a role in a system best characterized by either. And his other major argument about somewhat free-floating utility judgments is, I believe, more aspirational (in his words interpretive) than positive, and thus equally orthogonal to the positive effort to provide the best explanation of juridical proof as it is today. So, we count him as a part of this paradigm shift.

Perhaps another person who may disagree with much of my presentation should also be counted as further evidence of the paradigm shift, and that is William Twining. In a telling passage in his interesting book on evidence, he quotes, approvingly I believe, Bentham's comment: "To find infallible rules for evidence, rules which insure a just decision is, from the nature of things, absolutely impossible; but the human mind is too apt to establish rules which only increase the probabilities of a bad decision."[27] That is exactly right, precisely because rules are often ineffective tools in dynamic environments, as for example in the legal context, whether they are designed to control the admission of evidence, its processing, or the inferential process.

What does this have to say about the future of evidence science? It is at least somewhat explanatory of both doctrinal points and the significant paradigm shift discussed above. It also explains other attributes of evidence law, such as the interesting shift away from epistemic rules of exclusion, and provides justification for furthering that development.[28] Viewing things through the complexity lens in addition points to the kind of work that may be most fruitful. That work will attempt to accommodate the dynamic nature of the systems under inquiry, such as evidence law, the field of evidence, litigation theories, theories of government, rationality, and so on.

---

[26] Dale A. Nance, *The Burdens of Proof: Discriminatory Power, Weight of Evidence, and Tenacity of Belief* 140–1 (2016).

[27] William Twining, *Rethinking Evidence: Exploratory Essays* 40 (1990).

[28] See, e.g., Ronald J. Allen, The Hearsay Rule as a Rule of Admission Revisited, 84 *Fordham L. Rev.* 1395 (2016).

Such a mode of thinking may lead to the extension of the work we do into other areas as well. For example, I hypothesize that human flourishing will be found to be enhanced at the intersection of well-functioning markets,[29] governments based on relative free elections with at least a modest commitment to the rule of law,[30] and responsive legal systems, of which the common law is probably the exemplar.[31] Each of these involves a complex adaptive system that permits extremely complicated information about human preferences to affect the structure of social systems in a way that leads to human flourishing.[32] At this point I am not sure that I can prove or disprove this hypothesis for precisely the reasons at the heart of this chapter: the concept of human flourishing is complicated and contested,[33] the three variables identified have complex interactive effects,[34] and there are countless other pertinent variables as

[29] On markets as complex adaptive systems and how that contributes to wealth creation, see Eric D. Beinhocker, *The Origin of Wealth: Evolution, Complexity, and the Radical Remaking of Economics* (2006); Sheri M. Markose, Computability and Evolutionary Complexity: Markets as Complex Adaptive Systems (CAS), 115 *The Economic Journal* F159 (2005).

[30] On complexity theory and governance, see Robert Jervis, Complexity and the Analysis of Political and Social Life, 112 *Pol S. Q.* 569 (1997); Andreas Duit & Victor Galaz, Governance and Complexity—Emerging Issues for Governance Theory, 21 *Governance: An International Journal of Policy, Administration, and Institutions* 311 (2008); Laurence Whitehead, Enlivening the Concept of Democratization: The Biological Metaphor, 9 *Perspectives on Politics* 291 (2011).

[31] See, e.g., Daniel Martin Katz, Joshua R. Gubler, Jon Zelner, Michael J. Bommarito II, Eric Provins, & Eitan Ingall, Reproduction of Hierarchy? A Social Network Analysis of the American Law Professoriate, 61 *J. Legal Educ.* 76 (2011): "As many have observed, the common law is a complex adaptive system in which an array of agents, institutions, and social contexts together act to produce its substantive jurisprudence." Many have observed it, but there hasn't much analysis of the observation or its implications. In a seminal paper, Prof Ruhl analyzed legal systems more generally as complex adaptive systems without focusing on the common law. J. B. Ruhl, The Fitness of Law: Using Complexity Theory to Describe the Evolution of Law and Society and its Practical Meaning for Democracy, 49 *Vanderbilt Law Review*, 1406 (1996).

[32] For an interesting discussion that traces the gradually increasing effect of complexity theory on economics and public policy, see David Colander & Roland Kupers, *Complexity and the Art of Public Police: Solving Society's Problems from the Bottom Up* (2014).

[33] I have identified over forty measures of some aspect of human flourishing, and not surprisingly there is not much consistency in the rankings. Still, western Europe and the United States dominate many of the rankings probably because of their economic success, which created the space for both welfare programs and liberationist politics. But then there are rankings such as the Global Peace Index of the Institute for Economics and Peace, which ranks the United States 149 in terms of its "level of peacefulness." Available at http://visionofhumanity.org/app/uploads/2018/06/Global-Peace-Index-2018-2.pdf.

[34] As an example of the complexities of the hypothesis about flourishing, on whether the common law is efficient and thus relatively effective at wealth creation, compare Todd J. Zywicki & Edward Peter Stringham, Common Law and Economic Efficiency, Encyclopedia of Law and Economics (2d ed., Francesco Parisi & Richard Posner, eds.) to Adam J. Hirsch, Evolutionary Theories of Common Law Efficiency: Reasons for (Cognitive) Skepticism, 32 *Fl. St. L. Rev.* (2005). See generally Paul H. Rubin (ed.), *The Evolution of Efficient Common Law* (2007).

well (although my hunch is that they are less significant).[35] And at the end of the day there may lie in wait the accusation of the creation of a just-so story. These are to be sure daunting obstacles but also exhilarating challenges, and one might think that enterprises with a low risk of failure may not be worth the effort.

In conclusion, I hope that I have answered the question I posed at the beginning of this chapter concerning the relationship of complex adaptive systems to the field of evidence. As in many areas of science (by which I mean the systematic study of phenomena), the implications of trials, legal systems, and the governments they constitute in part will be informed by aspects of complexity theory because all of these are in fact complex adaptive processes. I may be unable to establish the hypothesis concerning human flourishing, but there will be an endless number of other hypotheses emanating from the recognition that trials, legal systems, and governments are dynamic and not static.[36]

---

[35] The legal origins literature has claimed that certain aspects of the legal origins of states explain economic success. See, e.g., R. La Porta, F. Lopez-de-Silanes, & A. Shleifer, The Economic Consequences of Legal Origins, *Journal of Economic Literature* 285–332 (2008). These claims have been met with withering criticism that basically points out the complexity of the matter. See, e.g. Eric Helland & Jonathan Klick, Legal Origins and Empirical Credibility, in *Does Law Matter? On Law and Economic Growth* 99 (Michael Faure & Jan Smits eds., 2011).

[36] In the mid-1990s, J. B. Ruhl began to introduce complexity theory into legal scholarship in quite far-sighted articles. See, e.g., J. B. Ruhl, Complexity Theory as a Paradigm for the Dynamical Law and Society System: A Wake Up Call for Legal Reductionism and the Modern Administrative State, 45 *Duke L. J.* 849 (1996); J. B. Ruhl, The Fitness of Law: Using Complexity Theory to Describe the Evolution of Law and Society and Its Practical Meaning for Democracy, 49 *Vand. L. Rev.* 1407 (1996). Another early contribution to the legal literature was Eric Kades, The Laws of Complexity and the Complexity of Laws: The Implications of Computational Complexity Theory for the Law, 49 *Rutgers L. Rev.* 403 (1997). See also Hope M. Babcock, Democracy's Discontent in a Complex World: Can Avalanches, Sandpiles, and Finches Optimize Michael Sandel's Civic Republican Community?, 85 *Georgetown L. J.* 2085 (1997). Regrettably, in my opinion, the implications of these seminal articles were not, and have not been, grasped by mainstream legal scholarship, so that twenty years later Professor Ruhl was writing of Law's Complexity: A Primer, 24 *Georgia State U. L. Rev.* 885 (2008). Nonetheless, interest in the relationship between law and complexity seems to be growing. For a recent article reprising many of the lessons of this early work, see Steven Lierman, Law as a Complex Adaptive System: The Importance of Convergence in a Multi-Layered Legal Order, 21 *Maastricht J. Eur. & Comp. L.* 611 (2014).

PART II

CONVERGENCES BETWEEN SYSTEMS

3

The Transformation of Chinese Evidence Theories and System

From Objectivity to Relevancy

Baosheng Zhang and Ping Yang

3.1 INTRODUCTION

The principle of adjudication by evidence has been basically established after almost forty years of reforms in China's modern justice system. This principle is aimed at preventing arbitrariness in adjudication and pursuing a correlative relationship between the factual premise and the judgment. However, the operation of such a principle still encounters both theoretical and institutional barriers. Specifically, as the concept of empirical fact and that of objective existence were mixed up, objectivity instead of relevancy has been regarded as the basic principle of evidence. As a result, although there are many evidence rules scattered among the three procedural laws of China (namely: Criminal Procedure Law, Civil Procedure Law and Administrative Procedure Law), as well as judicial interpretations promulgated by the Supreme People's Court (SPC), such rules are sporadic, like a pile of pearls without a thread, constituting an operational barrier to adjudication by evidence (Zhang and Yang, 2018: 7). Moreover, such notions as 'seeking truth from fact', 'the perpetrator of every murder case must be captured', 'zero tolerance to wrongful convictions or acquittals', 'correcting every wrong whenever discovered', 'a lifelong accountability system for the judiciary personnel' have been held as foundational principles of the Chinese judiciary. These conventional ideas distort Chinese evidence system, constitute a major cause for wrongful convictions, and bring about risks to judges' occupation security. For the above concerns, this chapter endeavours to systematically expose the fallacies of the 'objective evidence theory' while elaborating the relationship between empirical fact and objective existence, the uncertainty of fact-finding and the probability of proof standards. Subsequently, it discusses a trend of transformation from objectivity to relevancy in Chinese evidence theories and system, and finally proposes a brief plan to advance such a transformation.

3.2 EMPIRICAL FACT AND OBJECTIVE EXISTENCE

Fact is the logical starting point of evidence law. In terms of features of fact, an unavoidable issue is the debate between 'objective fact' and 'legal fact' (Yongsheng, 2003). 'Chinese criminal judicial philosophy has always equated fact of a case with objective fact, asserting that every case has an "objective fact" accessible to human cognition' (Ruihua, 2013: 168). The theoretical origin of such a judicial notion of 'objective fact', as opposed to a substitute for 'formal truth theory', was first put forward as an important principle by the Former Soviet Union scholars. The target of their criticisms was 'formal truth theory' applied in civil proceedings of some capitalist countries (Hao, 2004: 32).

The 'objective fact theory' holds that 'objectivity' is the foundational attribute of fact, and thus confuses fact with existence, for both are two different concepts. Existence is purely objective, referring to the objective world independent from human consciousness. Existence and consciousness are a pair of philosophical ontology concepts. Whereas, fact is something that actually exists (Garner, 2004: 1775), that is, the real existence perceptible by human mind and senses. In short, fact, as a concept of epistemology, is truthful, empirical and describable.

The truthfulness of fact can be illustrated from two aspects. Firstly, a fact takes place at a certain time–space dimension. In the space dimension, a fact takes place at a certain location. In the time dimension, a fact has its past or present tense. Henry Wigmore said: 'a fact is any act or condition of things, assumed (for the moment) as happening or existing' (Wigmore, 1935, from Garner, 2004: 1775). Things that would happen in the future mean possibilities rather than facts. Secondly, a fact is something that has occurred. Professor Jin Yue Lin illustrated that 'fact is not subject to any changes' (Yue Lin, 2011: 817). Once a fact occurs, whether you like it or not, it is unchangeable in history. As an old saying goes 'it is no way to cry over the spilled milk', neither the fact of committing a crime nor that of a wrongful conviction could be changed, for people cannot transcend time and space to correct an error that has already been made.

The difference between objective existence and empirical fact is the very one between the knowable and the known. The knowledge about objective existence can be acquired by human thinking, for instance, that 'the cosmos has no limit' is a kind of abstract knowledge not directly relying upon human senses. By contrast, fact is real knowledge. Judgments about facts require people's perceptions and experience. In this regard, Wittgenstein Ludwig stated that 'the world is the totality of facts, not of things' (Wittgenstein, 1974: 11). The difference between empirical fact and objective existence can be illustrated by the international ratio of the explicit number of drug abusers to the implicit one: in 2014 approximately three million people were registered as drug abusers in China, which was an explicit number and an empirical fact. According to such a ratio of 1:5, about fifteen million people in China were estimated to be implicit drug abusers in the same year. That was an objective existence.[1] However, we have no knowledge about this implicit group of drug abusers, including their identities, types of drugs they took, as well as the time and place they did so. Therefore, that there were about fifteen million drug abusers in 2014 in China is not a fact truly known by us, but a knowable objective existence. Jürgen Habermas made a similar point that 'veridical being or being-the-case must not be confused with the existence of an object'.[2] 'Generally speaking, what are called facts (being the case) are exactly empirical facts' (Yilian, 2015: 6).

Empirical fact is expressible. This proposition can be illustrated by knowledge presentation and knowledge acquisition, upon which three arguments are made.

The first argument is that what is known can always be expressed. From the perspective of knowledge presentation or the speaker, we must turn to the medium of language if we want to share with others or process in mind the perceptual knowledge acquired by observation. That is why Wittgenstein Ludwig argued that 'the limits of my language mean the limits of my world . . . We cannot say what we cannot think' (Wittgenstein, 1974: 86). For instance, suppose there is a case that '15 minutes ago, a traffic accident took place in the street outside this building' and you are asked to describe the accident. If you cannot do so, it is safe to conclude that you do not have knowledge of such an accident. In this sense, 'a fact is precisely a person's statement of the actuality of something (i.e. something has certain features or relationship with the other) based on his or her direct perceptions' (Yilian, 2015: 75).

The second argument is that the listener is supposed to know a fact described by the speaker's statement. From the perspective of knowledge acquisition or the listener, knowledge can be acquired simply because

---

[1] See 2014 *China Drug Situation Report*, published by the Office of China National Narcotics Control Commission, http://news.xinhuanet.com/legal/2015-06/25/c_127949443.htm (visited 17 May 2018).

[2] Habermas, 1996: 12. Cited from Tugendhat, 1982: 21–34.

a proposition and a fact are isomorphic. A proposition or a statement is a linguistic representation of a judgment. Wittgenstein Ludwig illustrated that 'the proposition is a picture of reality, for I know the state of affairs presented by it, if I understand the proposition' (Wittgenstein, 1974: 34). Therefore, in the above case, although we do not have a perceptual knowledge of the accident, yet we can still acquire the knowledge of it from the statement made by a passer-by (identified as Witness No. 1) that 'a grey car hit a red one'.

However, why cannot the fact-finder at a trial simply take the statement of the Witness No. 1 as a fact without evidential reasoning? The reason can be found in the third argument that a proposition or a statement could be true or false. A proposition represents a judgment. Two scenarios are involved when a judgment expresses a thought or belief: 'if such a thought is true, then the sentence that expresses it reports a fact' (Habermas, 1996: 11); otherwise, what it reports is not a fact. Suppose in the above case there is another passer-by (identified as Witness No. 2), who testified that 'it was a red car that hit a grey one'. As a result, there appears a scenario where 'a single fact has two opposite stories'. The truthfulness or falseness of a proposition depends on whether the speaker's statement is consistent with the fact concerned.

As the 'objective fact theory' fails to recognise the empirical and describable nature of fact, it inevitably misperceives objectivity as the basic attribute of evidence.[3] Such theory would find itself caught in the following three dilemmas:

(a) There is no test standard for the so-called objectivity of evidence. Suppose there is a cup, how can the judge decide whether it is objective to factum probandum? It is obviously impossible to make such a decision. Under Federal Rule of Evidence 401, however, there is a 'test for relevant evidence',that is, whether the cup has any tendency to make facts of consequence more or less probable than it would be without the cup. As there is no standard for testing whether evidence is objective or not, it is neither impossible to examine the objectivity of evidence presented, nor does the theory have any epistemic significance.

(b) In order to resolve dilemma (a), the 'objective evidence theory' often turns to the aid of its opposite side, that is, subjectivity, claiming that evidence has both features, namely, objectivity and subjectivity.[4] This actually produces another logic error of 'taking a part as the whole'. In fact, everything in epistemology involves the interaction between the subject and the object.

---

[3] See Jianwei, 2014; Jianlin and Shigui, 2014; Jiahong and Weiping, 2011.
[4] See Jianwei, 2014: 124; Jianlin and Shigui, 2014: 144–53.

(c) Since evidence can be true or false, the 'objective evidence theory' finds it impossible to answer such a question as 'which kind of evidence, true or false, is objective'.

3.3 FACT-FINDING AND THE 'MIRROR OF EVIDENCE'

The relationship between fact and evidence should not be examined only in a static way, for only when an epistemic subject is involved could such a relationship acquire epistemic significance. Three models can be generalised with regards to the involvement of an epistemic subject in the relationship.

The first model is an epistemic subject's direct interaction with the factual object in the present tense. The epistemic subject can actively know facts by repeated observations and practices in his or her daily life.

The second model refers to the relationship between the witness and the fact in the present tense too. However, it does not necessarily indicate that the witness's observation is neutral. 'Seeing is a "theory-laden" undertaking. Observation of x is shaped by prior knowledge of x.'[5] It is safe to conclude that the accuracy of an observation or a statement could be affected by the witness' identity, perception, memory, sincerity, and narrative ability, as well the location of his or her seeing.

The third model involves the fact-finder's ascertaining past facts only by evidential reasoning. At trial, the fact-finder has no personal knowledge about what happened in the past. Therefore, evidence serves as the only 'bridge' that connects the object and the subject, or a 'mirror' reflecting past facts to the present. On one hand, without the 'mirror' of evidence, it is impossible to find the truth of a case. On the other hand, the doctrine of 'Mirror of Evidence' also reveals the limits of evidential reasoning, that is, the fact of a case, to some extent, is like 'flowers in the mirror'. According to the 'correspondence theory of truth', we could take 'truth' as synonyms for 'correspondence of fact'.[6]Professor

---

[5] Hanson, 1965: 19. Hanson developed this theory by first citing an example that 'the physicist and the layman see the same thing, but they do not make the same thing of it. The layman must learn physics before he can see what the physicist sees'. He continued to argue that 'it is important to realize that sorting out differences about data, evidence, observation, may require more than simply gesturing at observable objects. It may require a comprehensive reappraisal of one's subject matter'. Hanson then concluded that 'the observer may not know what he is seeing: he aims only to get his observations to cohere against a background of established knowledge. This seeing is the goal of observation. It is in these terms, and not in terms of "phenomenal" seeing, that new inquiry proceeds'. (Hanson, 1965: 16–20).

[6] To Popper, Tarski 'vindicated the free use of the intuitive idea of truth as correspondence to the facts', based on which, Tarski made his greatest achievement in the philosophy of the empirical sciences. See Popper, 2002: 303–9.

Shu Weiguang held that 'if the subjective knowledge is consistent with the objective world by over fifty percent in the interaction between the subject and the object, this knowledge can be regarded as truth' (Weiguang, 1993: 206). This notion of truth is well demonstrated by the preponderance of evidence as a proof standard in civil proceedings.

The conventional Chinese judicial notion of 'seeking truth from fact' regrettably misapplies the relationship between the subject and the object in the present tense described by the second model for that in the past tense implied by the third model, thereby failing to perceive a conclusion inferred from evidence as truth in the 'mirror of evidence'. In the trial, as the fact-finder has no personal knowledge about past events, neither the judicial notion of 'seeking truth from fact', nor the 'correspondence theory of truth' is applicable. Instead, the target of the fact-finder is evidence rather than fact. Therefore, a right judicial philosophy should be 'seeking truth from evidence'.

The doctrine of 'Mirror of Evidence' reveals the limits of evidential reasoning, that is, truth, as the conclusion of evidential reasoning, is an epistemic 'brainchild'. In short, 'the fact-finding in adjudication reconstructs past events not susceptible to direct observation' (Stein, 2005: 34). Hence, the function of evidence law is to eliminate the uncertainty of fact-finding. In this regard, relevance rules could perfectly demonstrate the accuracy value of evidence law, which 'are designed to present to the trier of fact all of the information which will assist in making the decision. The exclusion of irrelevant evidence also serves the truth value because it keeps the fact-finder's attention focused on the proper information and only the proper information' (Bergland, 1973: 166).

In contrast with the trial by ordeal in ancient times and the statutory proof doctrine in the modern times, the contemporary evidence system is established on the foundation of relevant evidence, which serves as a rational basis for modern judicial civilisation and confidence. The reason is that 'a method of fact-finding is "rational" if, and only if, judgments about the probable truth of the allegations of the facts in issue are based on inferences from relevant evidence presented to the decision-maker' (Twining, 1985: 14).

Evidence is the information relevant to facts of consequence, used to prove whether a proposition of fact is more or less probable. 'The central issue of relevancy is whether an evidentiary fact relates the fact-finder's prior knowledge and experience in order to permit the fact-finder to rationally process and understand the evidence' (Allen, 2010a: 371). In the chain of evidential inferences, the fact-finder tries to connect evidence with facts of consequence through inferences, so as to prove whether the evidence is relevant to facts of consequence, and evaluate the degree of such a relevance, that is, the probative force. There is no established rule preset by lawmakers for judging whether evidence is relevant in proving facts of consequence and the relevancy degree. This job, instead, must be done by the trier primarily based on his or her 'logic and general experience', which determines that the logical form of fact-finding is inductive reasoning; in other words, fact-finding is a process of empirical inferences. That is why Sidgwick emphasised that 'since, then, our inferences from fact to fact depend upon our belief in general rules of connection between fact and fact, generalizations of the way things happen in nature, so the work of criticizing inferences resolves itself into that of criticizing generalizations' (Anderson et al., 2005: 262).

Professor William Twining, along with others in chapter ten of their coauthored book *Analysis of Evidence* (Anderson et al., 2005: 262–8) harshly criticised generalisations as 'necessary but dangerous'. Generalisations are necessary because each step in inferential reasoning from evidence must rely on the stone piers of generations (labelled G_1, G_2, G_3, G_4 ... G_n (Anderson et al., 2005: 261) to reach 'the other side' of factum probandum. Generalisations can also be labelled dangerous simply because society's stock of knowledge upon which generalisations are made usually consists of stereotypes, impressions, speculations and prejudices, which determine differentiated degrees of certainty of generalisations. If the 'stone pier' stepped upon by the fact-finder is dangerous itself, then there would involve risks of the fact-finder's slipping into the river (i.e. erroneous fact-finding). To some extent, every step in the chain of inferential reasoning could probably be sources of uncertainty.

In the case of Nian Bin prosecuted for poisoning,[7] the judgment made by the court of first instance read that:

> This court finds that . . . on the night of July 26th in 2006, the defendant Nian Bin found that some customers who seemed to walk towards his grocery store finally turned away for Ding Yunxia's, and thus borne a grudge against Ding. At 1:00 a.m. in the next day, the defendant put a half bag of rat poison taken from his home into a mineral water bottle, dissolved the poison with water, and then dumped it into the aluminium kettle Ding Yunxia shared with others in the kitchen.

The above judgment was concluded based on the following generalisations as shown in Figure 3.1.

---

[7] *Written Judgment of First Instance on the Case of Nian Bin Guilty for Throwing Dangerous Substance*（No. 84(2007) 榕刑初字）, see the website: www.fjcourt.gov.cn/Page/Court/N ews/ArticleTradition.aspx?nrid=1e77d372-0ce6-4144-a7ca-92b3d40ee753 (visited 17 May 2018).

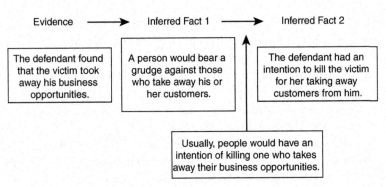

FIGURE 3.1 Generalisation used in the judgment made by the Court of First Instance in the case of Nian Bin

The above generalisation with the implicit relevance or common connection constitutes the major premise of a syllogism that 'one would harbour an intention of killing someone who takes away his or her business opportunities'; the minor premise is that 'the defendant saw customers, who initially walked towards his grocery store, finally walked into Ding Yunxia's one, and thus bore a grudge against Ding'. The conclusion is drawn that 'the victim took away the defendant's business opportunities, so the defendant had the intention to kill the victim'.

If the judge holds, based on common knowledge, that 'one would produce an intention of killing someone who takes away his or her business opportunities' is truly a reasonable generalisation, then he or she would admit it as relevant evidence. Alternatively, if the judge has doubts over the rationality of the generalisation, he or she would raise such a question as whether a person would certainly resort to killing someone who takes away his or her business opportunities and might thus request additional evidence to further prove the rationality of the generalisation. Regrettably, in the case of Nian Bin, the judge failed to raise any doubts over the soundness of the generalisation, and thus found that the defendant was guilty. Obviously, if empirical inferences are built on dangerous generalisations, an erroneous conclusion would be unavoidable.

3.4 PROBABILITY OF TRUTH AND STANDARDS OF PROOF

There are basically five reasons why, in any context including law, conclusions based on evidence are necessarily probabilistic in nature, that is, the incomplete, inconclusive, ambiguous, dissonant, and imperfect credibility of evidence (Anderson et al., 2005: 246). These reasons account for error risks of evidential reasoning.

The probability of truth finds expression in standards of proof. In civil proceedings, the fact-finder must ascertain on the ground of a preponderance of evidence that the plaintiff's claims are true. In criminal proceedings, the burden of persuasion is guilty 'beyond reasonable doubt'. According to Article 53 of the Criminal Procedure Law of China, the proof standard must reach such a level that 'evidence shall be deemed to be sufficient and concrete', and 'based on the comprehensive assessment of all evidence for the case, the ascertained facts have been proved beyond reasonable doubt'.'Reasonable doubt' refers to a kind of 'moral certainty' rather than an absolute certainty in mathematics. It allows for a certain error rate. For instance, in the United States, statistics show that the error rate of felony trials is somewhere between 3.5 per cent and 5.0 per cent in convictions of capital rape-murders at trial (Allen, 2010b: 756).

The probability of the proof standard raises challenges to the traditional judicial notion of 'zero tolerance to wrongful convictions or acquittals', which holds that impartial justice must meet the requirement of 'neither convicting an innocent person nor acquitting a guilty one' (Xiaoqin, 2013). In response to this idea, Justice Shen Deyong of the SPC argued that 'pursuing absolute certainty in judicial proceedings appears to be impartial, but in practice it is most likely to lead to the tendency that wrongful convictions are better rather than wrongful acquittals'. By contrast, he upheld a new judicial notion that 'a wrongful acquittal is better than a wrongful conviction' (Deyong, 2013b: 8). The above debate indicates that, influenced by such conventional judicial notions as 'objective evidence theory' and 'objective truth theory', there are two problems with China's accountability system for misjudged cases. One is that some legal professionals are still not ready to recognise the possibility of committing errors in justice, insisting instead that impartial justice should involve neither wrongful conviction nor wrongful acquittal. The second problem is that the accountability system fails to distinguish between 'wrongful conviction' and 'wrongful acquittal'. Such two problems are mainly reflected in the judicial slogan of 'correcting every wrong whenever discovered', which indicates two ideas. The first is that every misjudged case must be rectified. The second is that judges must be held accountable for judicial errors. The slogan, theoretically rooted in the ignorance of the probabilistic judicial proof, is harmful in at least three aspects. At first, it is at odds with the principle of presumption of innocence. If an erroneous acquittal, due to the insufficiency of evidence and the failure to meet the statutory proof standard, is also regarded as an error supposed to be corrected, with judges held accountable for such an error, foundations of the rule of law would be severely undermined. Secondly, it conflicts with the principle of efficiency. From the experience of the retrial procedure across the globe, the principal aim of this procedure is to correct 'errors in the fact-finding part in the judgment with res judicata' (Yinghui, 2003: 164) as well as erroneous convictions, otherwise, the emphasis of legal remedies on misjudged cases would be distracted. Thirdly, this slogan keeps the defendant far away from the protection of 'the principle of non bis in idem' and 'the principle against dangers of double jeopardy'. Therefore, in respect for judicial nature, the slogan of 'correcting every wrong whenever discovered' should be replaced by that of 'correcting every wrongful conviction'.

Due to a lack of understanding of the probability of truth and the proof standard, in the reform of Chinese judicial accountability system, a lifelong accountability system for judges has been put in place, which upholds the notion of 'correcting every wrong whenever discovered' and that judges should be permanently held accountable for misjudged cases. This system requires a 100 per cent accuracy for adjudicative fact-finding, a standard far beyond a judge's capability that nobody but the God could meet. According to *China Justice Index in 2015*, the average score for the secondary-class index on 'occupation guarantee for legal professionals' was 67.6 points with 100 in total, a figure calculated based on 6,200 questionnaires conducted in 31 provinces in China. When asked about views on the 'protection mechanism for judges' performance of statutory duties', only 19.2 per cent of judges surveyed expressed their satisfactions with it. (Zhang et al., 2017: 98) In judicial practice, a judge named Wang Guirong at the Chuanhui District court of Zhoukou, Henan Province, China, was sentenced to one year and nine months in 2011 for being guilty of dereliction of duty,[8] which put at risk the profession of judges. To solve the above problems, admittedly, it is important to establish a judicial immunity system so that the judge would not be held accountable for performing proper official duties, yet it is far more important, also a long-term mission, to be committed to exposing fallacies of 'objective evidence theory' and 'objective truth theory' to eliminate theoretical foundations of the unrealistic assessment criteria for judges.

3.5 A TREND OF TRANSFORMATION IN CHINESE EVIDENCE THEORIES AND SYSTEM: FROM OBJECTIVITY TO RELEVANCY

A society undergoing transformation is typically characterised with the coexistence or alteration of new and old things. In a period of social transformation,

---

[8] *Written Criminal Judgment of First Instance on Defendant Wang Guirong Guilty of Dereliction of Duty*, made by the People's Court in Wuyang County, Henan Province, China (No. 167 （2011） 舞刑初字).

Chinese scholars' views on the basic attributes of evidence are also undergoing changes. In recent years, the theory that upholds objectivity as the basic principle of evidence has received more scepticism and criticism; while evidence relevance rules have played an increasingly important role in legislation and judicial practice and received much more attention in textbooks and academic research on the law of evidence.

Firstly, legislators of Chinese evidence rules are altering previous obstinate adherence to 'objective evidence theory' and introducing the concept of evidence relevancy. Both the 1979 Criminal Procedure Law and 1996 Criminal Procedure Law defined evidence in such a way that 'any fact that can prove the truth of a case is evidence',[9] and thus adhered to the 'fact of evidence theory'. Moreover, evidence rules in the above two Criminal Procedure Laws even did not contain a single word of 'relevancy' (with the Chinese characters being '相关性'), except the provision that the presiding judge has the authority to stop the prosecution and the defence from raising irrelevant questions.[10]

Nevertheless, this phenomenon gradually changed subsequently. The Judicial Interpretations of SPC on the Application of the Criminal Procedure Law promulgated in 1998 allowed both the prosecution and the defence to raise objections to the presiding judge over questions irrelevant to the case asked by the other party, and requested each party to explain to the presiding judge facts they intend to prove when applying to summon a witness to testify or presenting evidence in a trial.[11] Such provisions demonstrate that relevance rules began to be applied in procedures of presentation and cross-examination. Subsequently, the Provisions on Evidence in Civil Procedure by SPC (hereinafter Provisions on Evidence

---

[9]   See Article 31 of 1979 Criminal Procedure Law of PRC and Article 42 of 1996 Criminal Procedure Law of PRC.

[10]   See Article 115 of the 1979 Criminal Procedure Law of PRC and Article 156 of 1996 Criminal Procedure Law of PRC.

[11]   See Article 136 of Judicial Interpretations of the SPC on the Application of the Criminal Procedural Law, which stipulates that: 'where the ways in which the prosecution or the defence of a case conducts interrogation or questioning to the defendant, the victim, the plaintiff of the supplementary civil action, or the defendant in the action are inappropriate or where the contents of the interrogation or questioning are irrelevant to the case, the presiding judge shall stop the interrogation or questioning. Where one party of a case believes that the other party's contents of interrogation or questioning are inappropriate or ways of the interrogation or questioning is irrelevant to the case, and raises objections, the presiding judge shall correctly judge the situation before upholding or dismissing the application.' Similarly, Article 139 of the Interpretation regulates that: 'When applying for a witness to testify in court or producing real evidence, documents, or audio-visual materials, the prosecution or the defence of a case shall state the facts they intend to prove. The presiding judge shall grant permission where he or she deems the application necessary; the presiding judge may also decide not to grant permission if he or she deems the evidence to be produced is irrelevant to the case, repetitive, or unnecessary.'

in Civil Procedure) and Provisions on Evidence in Administrative
Procedure by SPC (hereinafter Provisions on Evidence in Administrative
Procedure) first introduced the concept of 'relevance', with both regulating
that the judge shall review the relevance of evidence in the process of
evaluation and deliberation of evidence.[12] In addition, a complete description of evidence relevance was found afterwards in Article 48 of the 2012
Criminal Procedure Law, which reads that 'any material that can prove
facts of a case is regarded evidence'. This Article can be deemed as
a Chinese definition of evidence relevance. Also, there are all together
four Articles in The Judicial Interpretations of SPC on the Application of
the 2012 Criminal Procedure Law that request deliberation of 'relevance' for
different types of evidence. Another example for a raised status of relevance
rules in Chinese evidence legislations lies in Article 27 of Opinions on
Comprehensively Advancing the Trial-Centered Criminal Procedure
System enacted by SPC, which stipulates that 'evidence including real
evidence and documents collected by such investigation measures as
inspection, examination and search cannot be held as basis for resolving
a case without proving its relevance to the fact of a case by way of identification and forensic examination'.

Secondly, relevance rules have been increasingly applied in China's judicial practice since 1996. According to the data in the database of Chinese
adjudication documents, presented in the following chart, (1) of the 389
criminal judgments in total made during the period from 1 January 1979 to
31 December 1995, there was no criminal judgment that contains the word
'relevance'; (2) of the 3,388,689 criminal judgments made between
1 January 1996 and 31 December 2017, there were 67,928 criminal judgments
that include the word 'relevance', accounting for about 2 per cent of the total.

The contrast of figures in the Table 3.1 demonstrates that it was after 1996
that the word 'relevance' appeared frequently in criminal judgments, which is
approximately consistent with the phenomenon that relevance rules have

[12] For example, Article 54 of Provisions on Evidence in Administrative Procedure stipulates that:
      'the relevant people's court shall examine each piece of evidence confronted at the court or the
      evidence unnecessary to be confronted, and make an overall examination of all evidence, . . .
      ensure the evidence presented has any tendency to prove the fact of a case and eliminate those
      irrelevant evidence, in order to accurately ascertain the fact of a case'. Article 50 of Provisions
      on Evidence in Civil Procedure states that: 'when conducting confrontation at the court, the
      parties shall focus on the truthfulness, relevance, or lawfulness of evidence presented, ques-
      tion, explain or contest over issues as the likelihood or the weight of the probative force of the
      evidence concerned'. Article 66 similarly stipulates that: 'the judges shall comprehensively
      review and examine all evidence of a case regarding the relevancy of each evidence to the fact
      of a case, the connection among each evidence'.

TABLE 3.1 *The Number of Criminal Judgments Containing the Word 'Relevance' during the Period from 1979 to 2017.*[13]

Year	the word 'relevance'/criminal judgments	
	1979–1995	1996–2017
The ratio of the number of criminal judgments containing the word 'relevance' to that of criminal judgments	0/389	67928/3388689

gained an increasing significance in the legislation of evidence law since 1996. Even though the percentage of the application of relevance rules by judges in judgments is still low, progress has been made if this figure is compared with that prior to 1996. A deeper analysis of the content of criminal judgments that contain the word 'relevance' made between 1996 and 2017 shows that the concept of 'relevance' was understood or applied in the following three aspects: (a) relevance was regarded as one of attributes of evidence, with the principle of evidence-based adjudication applied in considering the relevance of evidence;[14] (b) the investigation department was requested to demonstrate sources of real evidence and documents in order to establish their connection with the fact of a case;[15] (c) irrelevant evidence was found to have no probative force and should be excluded as a result.[16] The judge's experience and logic were applied for considering whether evidence is relevant or not.[17] Therefore, Chinese judges' perception of relevance in their work is almost in line with the standard definition of relevance.

[13] See the website of Chinese judgment documents, http://wenshu.court.gov.cn (visited 13 February 2018).

[14] 'Regarding the drugs collected in the vehicles controlled by the drug traffickers, efforts should be made to review whether there is evidence that can demonstrate relevance of the drug traffickers to the drugs and vehicles.' See CAI Lukai, CAI Shiqiang, *Examination of Evidence in Cases of the Uncertainty of Source of Drugs*, 17 People's Justice, 4–6 (2017).

[15] See *Written Judgment of Second Instance* (No. (2015) 浙刑三终字), which read: 'when collecting real evidence and documentary evidence, the investigation department shall make a record of evidence collection and lists of evidence collected, in order to show sources of the real evidence, and establish 'the connection between the real evidence and facts of a case'.

[16] For example, the people's court in the case (No. (2016) 黔27刑终157) found that the appellant Chen Minghua was guilty of misappropriation of public funds, embezzlement, and dereliction of duty on the ground that the request for leniency offered by the People's government of Zhangbu Town in Guizhou, China were irrelevant evidence.

[17] See *Written Judgment of First Instance* (No. 0439 (2009)昆刑初字); *Written Judgment of the Retrial Procedure* (No. 0219 (2009)苏中刑终字).

What is more, in recent years, some Chinese scholars have discarded the 'objective evidence theory' and stressed that relevance is the basic attribute of evidence. Their understanding of evidence relevance is close to its definition in the Common Law evidence. For instance, a textbook on evidence defined relevance in such a way that evidence is relevant if it has any tendency to prove facts of consequence and is useful for the judge to evaluate the probability of the occurrence of a fact at issue' (Zhang, 2018: 29).

In short, the acceptance of the concept and rules of relevance by Chinese evidence legislations, judicial practice and the academia has undergone a progressive change: from the absence of relevance in Chinese evidence rules at the beginning, the initial application of it in procedures of evidence investigation, cross-examination, evaluation and deliberation of evidence, to the subsequent establishment of its definition in Criminal Procedure Law. This is also a process where the 'objective evidence theory' and 'objective truth theory' were dismissed, as well as one where people's awareness of relevance rules gradually deepened. Additionally, the establishment of the evidence-based adjudication principle in China, thanks to the exposure of a few wrongful convictions, the advancement of the trial-centred criminal procedural reform, and the increasing influence of the Common Law evidence in China all served as interrelated driving forces for the transformation of evidence theories and system in China.

Nevertheless, the transformation from objectivity to relevancy in evidence theories or system has not concluded in China, as the notion that relevance serves as the fundamental attribute of evidence has yet to be established. In evidence law scholarship, conventional evidence theories that argue for evidence objectivity are still influential in the academia.[18] In judicial practice, 'some courts are still accustomed to the principle of presumption of guilt in hearing big criminal cases, worrying that the presumption of innocence principle might lead to wrongful acquittals'.[19] In evidence legislations, relevance rules have yet to be established as a fundamental principle for the evidence system. For example, relevance rules are placed at a lower position

---

[18]   For instance, representative works on 'three-attribute theory of evidence' (i.e., objectivity, relevance and lawfulness) include: Gaoqing, 2010: 75–81; Yiyun, 2010: 61–7; Jiahong and Weiping, 2011: 23–7; Chongyi, 2012; Jingui, 2013, holding that the ' three-attribute theory of evidence' has increasingly become the mainstream proposition; Qing, 2013: 51, arguing that the conventional 'three-attribute theory of evidence' is more scientific than other evidence theories. Representative textbooks on 'two-attribute theory of evidence' (i.e., objectivity and relevance) include: Jianwei, 2014; Jianlin and Shigui, 2014.

[19]   See Understanding and Application of the Supreme People's Court of PRC on Provisions on Several Issues Concerning the Examination and Judgment of Evidence in Death Penalty Cases.

between the fourth and the eighth section along the hierarchy ladder of evidence rules in the Interpretations of SPC on the Application of the 2012 Criminal Procedure Law, namely, Article 69, Article 84, Article 92 and Article 93, which, as is mentioned above, put in place regulations on considering 'relevance' for different types of evidence.

To achieve the success of the transformation from objectivity to relevancy, the key is to draw up a logical evidence law system and evidence theory with relevance as the logical thread. As one of the commitments to this goal, *A Research Project on the Provisions of Procedural Evidence* was approved in 2011 supported by the National Social Science Foundation of China, with Justice Shen Deyong, Executive Vice-President of SPC as the Chief Expert. Members of the project included fifteen judges from different levels of courts in China, fifteen faculty members and PhD candidates at the Institute of Evidence Law and Forensic Science, China University of Political Science and Law, with Professor Ronald J. Allen from the Northwestern University of the USA as the project's sole foreign advisor. The major task of the project is to construct a legal system of Chinese evidence, and draft Provisions on Procedural Evidence of the People's Courts, which is expected to be used as parts of future judicial interpretations by SPC and be also applicable for courts at all levels in China, thereby integrating evidence provisions in China's three procedural laws. The structure of the Provisions on Procedural Evidence of the People's Courts can be summarised into four points: (a) one logical thread, namely, relevance; (b) two proof requirements, that is, the burden of proof and standards of proof; (c) three statutory stages including presentation, cross-examination and confrontation, evaluation and deliberation of evidence; (d) four 'value pillars' consisting of accuracy, fairness, harmony and efficiency (Zhang and Yang, 2018: 17–18).

3.6 CONCLUSION

Firstly, in contrast with objective existence, the fundamental feature of fact is empirical. It is the empirical feature of fact that shapes the basic attribute of evidence, that is, relevance, and determines that fact-finding is a process of empirical inferences. Both the truth ascertained by empirical inferences and standards of proof are probabilistic. Thanks to an increasing exposure of fallacies of the 'objective evidence theory' or 'objective fact theory', judicial notions in China are transforming from 'seeking truth from fact' to 'seeking truth from evidence', from 'zero tolerance to wrongful convictions or wrongful acquittals' to 'preferring wrongful acquittals over wrongful convictions', from 'correcting every wrong whenever discovered' to 'correcting every wrongful conviction whenever discovered', and from the 'lifelong accountability system' to the 'professional security system for judges' performing statutory duties'.

Secondly, over a long period of time, the 'objective evidence theory' has served as the philosophical foundation for Chinese evidence theories and system. However, in recent years, a trend of transformation from objectivity to relevancy is witnessed in evidence legislations, judicial practice and academic research, while traditional judicial notions were dismissed during this period. A major dynamic for this transformation is the criticism and rethinking in the academia of the 'objective fact theory', 'objective evidence theory', paving a theoretical foundation for understanding the relationships among fact, evidence and fact-finding. Also, the exposure of wrongful convictions in China advanced the establishment of the principle of adjudication by evidence and the principle of presumption of innocence. More importantly, the trial-centred criminal procedural reform laid institutional foundations for the establishment of relevance principle.

Thirdly, the transformation from objectivity to relevancy in Chinese evidence system is still underway, with the notion of evidence objectivity still exerting influences in both evidence law scholarship and judicial practice. To achieve the complete success of such a transformation, it is suggested that a definition of relevance should be clearly expounded in the legislation of evidence law, and a modern evidence system with relevance as the logical thread be built up. More importantly, great efforts should be made to conduct in-depth research on the law of evidence, develop the education of modern evidence law notions and cultivate a new generation of legal scholars, judges, prosecutors and lawyers to master modern evidence science theories.

REFERENCES

Allen, R. (2010a). Relevancy and Admissibility, *Evidence Science*, 18, 375–82.
Allen, R. (2010b). The Relationships among Evidence Law, Procedural Law and Substantive Law, *Evidence Science*, 18, 750–60.
Anderson, T., Schum D. and Twining W. (2005). *Analysis of Evidence*, 2nd ed., Cambridge, New York, etc.: Cambridge University Press.
Baosheng, Z. (2014). *Evidence Law*, 2nd ed., China University of Political Science and Law of Beijing.
Baosheng, Z. (2018). *Evidence Law*, 3rd ed., China University of Political Science and Law of Beijing.
Baosheng, Z. and Yang Ping (2018). *Rethinking Chinese Evidence Theories and Reconstructing System of Evidence: A Thread for the Pearls of Chinese Evidence*, Frontiers of Law in China, 1, vol. 13.

Baosheng, Z., Zhang Zhong and Wu Hongqi (2016). *China Justice Index Report*, China University of Political Science and Law of Beijing.

Bergland, D. (1973). Value Analysis in the Law of Evidence, *Western State University Law Review*, 1, 162 ff.

Bian, J. and Tan Shigui (2014). *Law of Evidence*, 3rd ed., Beijing: China University of Political Science and Law.

Chen, R. (2013). *Visible Justice*, Beijing: Peking University Press.

Chen, Y. (2003). Convergence and Departure of Legal Facts and Objective Facts: A New Perspective on History of Evidence System, 8 *Journal of the National Procurators College*.

Chen, Y. (2010). *The Law of Evidence*, Beijing: Renmin University of China Press.

Fan, C. (2012). *The Law of Evidence*, 5th ed., Beijing: Law Press China.

Garner, B. ed. (2004). *Black's Law Dictionary*, 8th ed., St. Paul, Minneapolis: Thomson Reuters.

Habermas, J., (1996). *Between Facts and Norms: Contributions to a Discourse Theory of Law and Democracy*. William Rehg translator, 2nd ed., Cambridge, MA: MIT Press.

Hao, Li (2004). On Finding Legal Truth Exemplified by Civil Procedures, *Law and Social Development*, 3.

Jiahong, H. and Zhang Weiping (2011). *Concise Evidence Law*, Beijing: Renmin University of China Press.

Jianwei, Z. (2014). *Essence of Evidence Law*, Beijing: Peking University Press.

Jingui, P. (2012). *The Law of Evidence*, Beijing: Law Press China.

Lukai, C. and Cai Shiqiang (2017). Examination of Evidence in Cases of the Uncertainty of Source of Drugs, *People's Justice*, 17.

Norwood Russell , Hanson (1965). *Patterns of Discovery: An Inquiry into the Conceptual Foundations of Science*, The Syndics of Cambridge University Press.

Peng, Y. (2015). *On Fact*, Guangxi: Guangxi Normal University Press.

Popper, K. (2002). *Conjectures and Refutations: The Growth of Scientific Knowledge*, London: Routledge and Kegan Paul.

Qing, Y. (2013). *Procedural Evidence Law*, Beijing: Peking University Press.

Shen, D. (2013a). How Should We Prevent Miscarriages of Justice, *People's Court*.

Shen, D. (2013b). On In Dubio Pro Reo, *China Legal Science*, 5.

Song, Y. (2003) *Principles of Criminal Procedure*, Beijing: Law Press China.

Stein, A. (2005). *Foundations of Evidence Law*, London: Oxford University Press.

Tugendhat, E. (1982). *Traditional and Analytical Philosophy*. Corner, P. A. translator, Cambridge: Cambridge University Press.

Twining, W. (1985). *Theories of Evidence: Bentham and Wigmore*, California: Stanford University Press.

Wang, J. (2013). *New Trends of Criminal Evidence Law in China*, Beijing: Law
    Press China.
Weiguang, S. (1993). *The Comprehensive Design of Scientific Knowledge*,
    Beijing: Jinlin Renmin Press.
Wigmore, J. (1935). A Student Textbook of the Law of Evidence. In *Black's
    Law Dictionary*, 8th ed., St Paul: Thomson Reuters.
Wittgenstein, L. (1974). *Tractatus Logico Philosophicus*, 2nd ed., Pears, D. and
    B. F. McGuinnes trans., London: Routledge and Kegan Paul.
Wu, G. (2010). *The Law of Evidence*, Beijing: Tsinghua University Press.
Yue Lin, J. (2011). *On Knowledge*, Beijing: The Commercial Press.

4

Truth Finding and the Mirage of Inquisitorial Process

Adrian A. S. Zuckerman

4.1 INTRODUCTION

(1) The court represents a quintessential element of a society governed by law. The rule of law principle dictates that disputes between individuals or between citizens and the Government be decided according to the law. This means that a court deciding a contested issue, whether criminal or civil, has to determine the true facts and correctly apply the law to the situation.

(2) When it comes to deciding which contested version of the facts is correct, the adjudicator's final conclusion is necessarily a matter of probability, never certainty. This means that there is always an inevitable risk of error. The question therefore arises as to how we can have confidence that the court decision on factual issues is correct; that is, conforms with the fact as they actually happened.

(3) This problem of verification, of ascertaining whether a factual inference from evidence is correct, is common to all empirical enterprises. In some fields of research procedures have developed for testing the validity of factual inference, or of factual generalisations drawn from evidence. Accordingly, in science a theory derived from experiments will be tested by replication. That is to say, a theory will not be accepted unless the experiments on which it is based are capable of replication and the results can be shown to be explicable only by the theory offered.

(4) The replication method is unavailable where past facts are in question. Consequently, alternative testing strategies are used in some areas of scholarship concerned with the past. For instance, in historical research when a historian proposes an account of the past, other historians will subject it to critical analysis that may involve examining the sources and testing the hypotheses offered. When a historian advances an account of

some particular event there are bound to be others who would contest it. Historical accounts, we may conclude, are invariably tested in the market of ideas.

(5) However, neither the strategy of replication nor public debate can be employed in testing judicial judgments, for obvious reasons. Since there is no way of testing the factual correctness of individual judgments, we must therefore adopt procedures which are calculated to promote accurate determination. Furthermore, such procedure must command public confidence in the rectitude of judgments, for in the absence of widespread confidence in the judicial authority there is no reason to behave according to the law.

(6) The one universal and timeless strategy that has been pursued in court dispute resolution has been the adversarial process, about which I will have more to say later. For now, it suffices to note its central features: each party to the dispute is entitled to a fair hearing, also known as the principle of *audi alteram partem*. This means that each party is entitled to present its arguments and evidence and to an opportunity to respond to the adversary's arguments and evidence.

(7) However, the adversarial process is being eroded in England in significant ways. To explain how this has come about, I need to say something about recent developments in litigation funding. In 2013 legal aid was withdrawn in England and Wales from all but a small number of civil cases.[1] This resulted in a dramatic rise in civil cases where one or both parties appear without legal representation. Self-represented litigants are referred to in England as litigants in person; LIPs for short.

(8) Since lay persons are not familiar with the substantive law and court procedure, they are frequently poorly prepared for litigation. They tend to make procedural mistakes, such as failing to comply with rules and court orders or missing deadlines. All too frequently LIPs are ill equipped to argue the appropriate law, deploy documentary evidence or effectively challenge the opponent's case.

(9) These shortcomings lead to inefficiency and injustice. Inefficiency, because the court is forced to devote disproportionate time and effort to cases involving LIPs. Injustice because LIPs are more exposed to the risk of an erroneous judgment; that is, to the risk of an adverse

---

[1]   According to Government figures, 623,000 of the 1,000,000 people who benefited from Legal Aid annually were denied access to this aid from 1 April 2013, when the Legal Aid, Sentencing and Punishment of Offenders Act 2012 became effective.

judgment resulting from inadequate preparation or presentation rather than lack of merit.

(10) To cope with the flood of LIPs a committee recommended the insertion into the Civil Procedure Rules of 'a specific power ... that would allow the court to direct that, where at least one party is a litigant in person, the proceedings should be conducted by way of a more inquisitorial form of process'.[2] CPR 3.1A now states that in any proceedings where at least one party is unrepresented the court must adopt such procedure at any hearing as it considers appropriate to further the overriding objective (of enabling the court to deal with cases justly and at proportionate cost), including '(a) ascertaining from an unrepresented party the matters about which the witness may be able to give evidence or on which the witness ought to be cross-examined; and (b) putting, or causing to be put, to the witness such questions as may appear to the court to be proper'.

(11) A report in 2013 recommended the creation of an online procedure for claims up to £25,000 (Euro 28,550) which will include an inquisitorial element.[3] This procedure would require litigants to present their cases at the outset in some detail, using online software that would lead both the claimant and the defendant through a set of questions, the answers to which would then be collated and organised online as detailed statements of case, uniformly structured (Stage 1). Next, some case management and conciliation would be attempted by a Case Officer (Stage 2). In the final stage (Stage 3), a judge would decide whether to conduct a trial or to determine the case on the documents. If a trial were deemed necessary, the judge would still have to consider how to conduct the hearings. Phone calls and video conferences are the preferred methods. Oral face-to-face hearings would not only cease to be the default form of adjudication but would become a last resort. The judge would have to take a leading role and act more inquisitorially than is currently acceptable.

(12) The English court now accepts that it would be wrong for the court to treat all parties as if they all had the same strength of advice and representation. In order to equalise access, the court should vary the level of assistance it gives according to whether a litigant is represented

---

[2] Judicial Working Group on Litigants in Person Report, headed by Hickingbotton J., July 2013, paras. 2.10, 5.11.

[3] Lord Justice Briggs, *Chancery Modernisation Review: Final Report* (2013), available at: www .judiciary.gov.uk/wp-content/uploads/JCO/Documents/CMR/cmr-final-report-dec2013.pdf.

or unrepresented, and according to the litigant's level of competence and understanding. The court has, however, acknowledged that achieving the appropriate level of assistance is constrained by the requirement that the court must at all times be, and be seen to be, impartial as between the parties, and that injustice to either side must be avoided.

(13) My argument is that it is impossible for a judge to both provide unrepresented and poorly qualified litigants with meaningful legal assistance while at the same time avoiding impartiality.

4.2 ADVERSARIAL PROCESS

As already noted, a common and timeless feature of all conflict resolution procedures is the adversarial principle, or a*udi alteram partem*, whereby each party is entitled to be heard. That is, to present his argument and evidence and respond to his opponent's case. An additional and essential feature of the legal dispute resolution process is that the adjudicator is bound to consider impartially the evidence and arguments presented by each party.

Central to the legal adversarial process is the separation of roles between the parties and the adjudicator. The parties define the controversy, present evidence in support of their allegations, and test each other's evidence and arguments. The judge's role is limited to supervising the process to ensure it is conducted in an appropriate manner and deciding the controversy according to the evidence presented by the parties.

The separation of functions in the litigation process is designed to place a distance between the judge, on the one hand, and on the other hand the investigation of the issues, the probing of evidence and the development of the legal argumentation that take place in front of the court. It is for the parties, normally represented by advocates, to clarify the issues, to deploy evidence, to test it, to debate the inferences to be drawn from the evidence and to argue about the strengths and weaknesses of the competing accounts.

In modern Anglo-American civil procedure, the judge has a managerial role, intended to ensure that the litigation process is effectively concluded within a reasonable time and by the use of proportionate means and resources. However, it must be stressed that the court's managerial role is distinct from the investigation of the issues. Today's judge is no more permitted to take part in the choice of issues to be decided, in directing the parties what evidence to adduce, or in cross-examining witnesses, to any greater extent than it was permissible in the past.

It will have become clear that the court's function is distinguishable from the role that the parties and their lawyer play in litigation. Theirs is an inherently mercenary or adversarial role: to advance a particular position in opposition to another. Advancing a party case inevitably involves an intellectual or emotional commitment to the correctness and justness of the case advanced. Detachment, even-handedness and an open mind, are attributes that cannot be expected from the parties or their advocates.

4.3 COGNITIVE REASONS FOR SEPARATION BETWEEN INVESTIGATION AND ADJUDICATION

The insistence by both the common law and the civilian traditions on an adversarial system is based on the long-standing belief that judicial involvement in the investigation of the issues would undermine the integrity of the decision-making process. Studies in cognitive psychology show how well founded is this belief due to the confirmation bias. Confirmation bias is the tendency to search for, interpret, favour and recall information in a way that confirms one's pre-existing beliefs or hypotheses (Plous, 1993). It is a type of cognitive bias and a systematic error of inductive reasoning. People display this bias when they gather or remember information selectively, or when they interpret it. The effect is stronger for emotionally charged issues and for deeply entrenched beliefs. In the judicial decision-making context, confirmation bias represents a tendency to seek evidential support for the hypothesis that the decision-maker has already formed and to ignore evidence or explanations that undermine this hypothesis.

A series of experiments in the 1960s showed that people tend to be biased in favour of their existing beliefs. More recent experiments have found that people tend to test hypotheses in a one-sided way, by searching particularly for evidence consistent with the hypothesis that they have formed, rather than looking at all the relevant evidence and considering different hypotheses. In oral questioning, for instance, investigators tend to phrase questions to receive an affirmative answer that supports their hypothesis. They look for the consequences that they would expect if their hypothesis were true, rather than what would happen if it were false.

Confirmation bias is unintentional and unconscious. It takes the form of unselfconsciously adopting a biased strategy. Confirmation bias affects researchers and decision-makers who honestly and conscientiously seek to reach a correct conclusion by employing the most appropriate and reliable method available to them. Notwithstanding best intentions, bias tends to creep in and infect the investigative process in a variety of ways.

Where the investigator defines the question to be examined, the very framing of the issue may point the search in a particular direction, leaving out other possible lines of investigation. Investigations may consist of numerous decisions about what to look for, where to look and how to interpret what has been found. An inclination, albeit unintended, towards a particular position may, therefore, affect the investigation process at many different points and in a variety of ways.

While the confirmation bias has been known for a long time, and its effects have been empirically confirmed in numerous experiments, what is less known is the self-consciousness of the possibility of bias can itself lead to distortion through over compensation or correction for a biased inclination.[4]

4.4 THE INFLUENCE OF BACKGROUND ASSUMPTIONS

The impact of the confirmation bias is magnified by the role that prior generalisations play in factual reasoning. The process of drawing inferences from data necessarily involves the use of generalisations which enable us to move from evidence to conclusion. Some generalisations used in the inferential process are scientifically proven and universally accepted. For instance, we are able to reason from the presence of a particular DNA to the identification of a decomposing body because it is accepted that every person's DNA is unique. But many generalisations are informed by assumptions that may be held only in a particular society, or are shared only by persons of similar background, or are formed as a result of particular experience. Consequently, many assumptions used in common sense reasoning are relative to time, to place and to the investigator's experience and background.

Personal experience, and the beliefs which go with it, are moulded by class, gender, age, ethnicity, nationality and religion. There is consequently much variation between the background assumptions used in reasoning from data to conclusions by differently situated groups and individuals. In this sense, there is a subjectivity factor in factual reasoning.

A particular type of bias which is the product of social background is known as in-group bias. People tend to be familiar with others belonging to their own social group and have less knowledge or understanding of people from other social groups. This tends to lead to unconscious preference and sympathy for member of the familiar group. Experiments have identified a pattern of favouring members of one's in-group over out-group members, which may

---

[4] Early US female judges over-corrected in rape cases by imposing more lenient judgments than their male counterparts: Guttel, 2004: 241; Schul, and Goren, 1997: 133–55.

be expressed in evaluation of others, in allocation of resources, and in many other ways.[5]

4.5 STRATEGIES FOR OVERCOMING DISTORTION IN FACT-FINDING: REPLICATION AND DEBATE

Two strategies, as already noted, are employed to overcome the distorting effects of bias and subjectivity: validation and debate. Validation is the common method used in science. To be validated an experiment supporting a theory must be capable of being independently replicated with the same results. Further, it must be shown that there is no other plausible explanation for the result obtained other than that claimed.

The methodology of validation through replications is unavailable for the investigation of unique past events. We can know the past by means of drawing inferences from evidential data, such as witness accounts, documents and circumstantial evidence. To form a conclusion about the occurrence of a particular past event we need to piece together the relevant evidence in support of a particular hypothesis and eliminate other possible hypotheses.

Persons who research the past, whether professional or amateurs, whether inside or outside an institutional framework, are vulnerable to cognitive bias and subjective relativism no matter how hard they try to overcome them. The reconstruction of the past is therefore bound to be influenced by the intellectual and cultural baggage brought to the task, whether by historians, journalists or professional judges. Moreover, we are bound to remain unconscious of the effects that these cognitive factors have on our thought processes.

In most contexts these latent cognitive limitations pose no special difficulty because accounts of the past are usually offered as explanations to be tested by open debate before they are accepted or before they are relied upon in a decision-making process. For every historian, scientist, journalist, political pundit or economic analyst, pronouncing a view about events there are many others looking into the same question or phenomenon who would be only too ready to expose the flaws in the view offered. To gain widespread public confidence a factual account of any consequence must first be tested by open debate. Robust knowledge of the past is therefore reached only through the exposure of competing explanations to the rigours of the market of ideas.

---

[5] Moses, and Zussman, 2011: 1447–84; Charness et al., 2007: 1340–52; Bornhorst et al., 2004; Turner et al., 1987.

4.6 ADVERSARIAL PROCESS: THE ONLY GUARANTEE OF INTEGRITY OF JUDICIAL PROCESS

Since judgments are meant to be determinative of the parties' rights and final, court decisions are not amenable to testing in the market of ideas. Court findings cannot be further assessed once the appeal process has been exhausted. There is no mega-test by which to gauge the factual accuracy of final judgments. Given that court judgments cannot be tested outside the legal process, the only guarantee of rectitude of decision has to be found within the process itself.

The time-honoured solution adopted in the judicial context consists of the adversarial system. The adversarial process does not seek to immunise judicial reasoning against confirmation bias and subjective relativism, which is of course impossible. Instead, it distances the judge from the activity which is most prone to these corrosive factors: the investigation of the issues. For this reason, the subject-matter of the investigation is determined by the parties and it is they who take turns in offering competing accounts, adducing evidence and challenging each other's explanations and theories. In other words, the adversarial process mirrors the open market of ideas that operates outside the law for testing factual accounts outside the court.

If a judge were to take part in defining the issues in controversy, if the judge were to direct which evidence is to be sought and presented, if the judge were to direct the questioning of witnesses and experts and develop the legal dispute, the entire process would be liable to be distorted by confirmation bias, by over-correction bias or by in-group bias. Personal involvement by the decision-maker always carries a risk that the decision-maker would form sympathy or dislike for one of the other parties and would unconsciously be influenced by such feelings (Lind et al., 1976: 271–83).

A person who conducts an investigation will necessarily form a hypothesis at some stage in the investigation, commonly early on. Once a hypothesis has been formed, the investigator would tend to focus attention on that hypothesis and be less inclined to devote adequate attention to other possibilities.

It is for this reason that the common law insists on keeping the judge out of the investigation of the issues until the parties or their advocates have concluded their presentations. This position in founded on the belief, going back a long way, that once a judge starts to take a hand in the investigation (such as by pressing witnesses about the cogency of their accounts), the judge is likely to form a view about the merits of the parties' respective positions. And once such a view has been formed, the judge becomes less receptive to counter-indicators. Put differently, a judge who attempts to present both parties' cases, tends to press harder for the case of one party long before he retires to decide the outcome. The perception of partiality that arises when a judge takes an active role in the investigation reflects the widely understood cognitive limitations that affect all of us.

Equally important, the effects of the confirmation bias could well remain hidden because it subtly and unselfconsciously affects the entire process so that it would not be easy to discover it on appeal. True, even in an adversarial process the judge's decision-making process may be affected by subjective assumptions and choices. But in an adversarial process the parties will have presented in open court the opposing accounts so that nothing relevant remains hidden from appellate, or for that matter public, review.

To their credit, English judges have demonstrated reluctance to assume an inquisitorial role. This is illustrated by the case of Q v. Q which was decided in the Family Division of the High Court, a civil court.[6] As a background I should mention that in criminal proceedings legislation forbids a person accused of a sex offence to cross-examine in person child witnesses or alleged victims of sex offences.[7] But the case under consideration was not a criminal case. It consisted of several appeals involving a common issue. Each concerned a father who was seeking access to his child. The fathers were unable to afford legal representation and could not obtain legal aid. The mothers were represented with public funding. In each case the mother objected to access alleging that the father had committed a sexual offence against her or one of her other children. The fathers denied the allegations and wished to cross-examine the mothers.

The Matrimonial and Family Proceedings Act 1984 section 31G(6) states:

> Where in any proceedings in the family court it appears to the court that any party to the proceedings who is not legally represented is unable to examine or cross-examine a witness effectively, the court is to
> (a) ascertain from that party the matters about which the witness may be able to depose or on which the witness ought to be cross-examined, and
> (b) put, or cause to be put, to the witness such questions in the interests of that party as may appear to the court to be proper.

The trial judge found it inappropriate to permit the father to conduct the cross-examination. However, the judge also considered that the court was ill-placed to conduct a satisfactory cross-examination on behalf of the father. First, because the judge could not take instructions from the father. And,

---

[6] Q [2014] EWFC 31.
[7] Criminal Justice Act 1988 s. 34A; Youth Justice and Criminal Evidence Act 2005 s. 35.

secondly, the preparation for such cross-examination required legal advice that would explain to the father the consequences of various options that could be pursued; something that the court was in no position to offer.

On appeal, Sir James Munby P., stated the problem bluntly:

> The absence of public funding for those too impoverished to pay for their own representation potentially creates at least three major problems: first, the denial of legal advice and of assistance in drafting documents; second, and most obvious, the denial of professional advocacy in the court room; third, the denial of the ability to bring to court a professional witness whose fees for attending are beyond the ability of the litigant to pay.[8]

None of these deficiencies could be cured by the court itself, the Court of Appeal held:

> These are not matters which the judge conducting the fact-finding hearing can determine without the benefit of legal argument on both sides. If the judge is deprived of adversarial argument, and if the father is denied access to legal advice both before and during the hearing, there must, in my judgment, be a very real risk of the father's rights under Articles 6 and 8 being breached.[9]

Having concluded that the court could not do justice in the absence of legal representation for the fathers the appropriate course was for the court to appoint counsel for the purpose of cross-examination paid out of the court's budget.

4.7 ADVERSARIAL PROCESS SHIELDS THE COURT FROM RESPONSIBILITY FOR ERROR

By distancing the judge from the investigation of the disputed issues the adversarial process shields the court from responsibility for erroneous decisions. Where the court's role is limited to deciding according to the evidence adduced by the parties and tested by them, the court's responsibility for the correctness of the outcome is commensurably limited to drawing the appropriate inferences from what it has seen and heard during the trial. The judge has no higher responsibility for the correctness of judgments. However, were the court to undertake the role of settling the issues, of articulating each party's positions and of deciding which witnesses to call and how to examine them, the court would in effect undertake responsibility for the factual rectitude of its decisions. If miscarriage of justice occurred,

---

[8] Q [2014] EWFC 31 at [43].
[9] Ibid. at [85].

it could be laid squarely at the court's door and the court could become the target of public criticism which in the long term could undermine confidence in the judicial process.

There would also be questions of redress. Litigants who have been let down by their legal representatives could hold them accountable for negligence. A self-represented litigant who mismanaged her own case can blame only herself. But if the court undertook to advance her cause, the litigant could justly feel aggrieved when the judge mishandled the task. Judicial responsibility for outcomes in cases where the judge conducted the parties' cases would be greater. Were inquisitorial proceedings to take root, public pressure could build up over time to recognise rights to compensation for judicial mistakes, similar to rights of compensation from other public authorities. There are therefore good policy reasons for distancing the court from the investigation process, quite apart from the cognitive factors discussed earlier.

4.8 THE MYTH OF AN INQUISITORIAL SYSTEM

Behind the legislative introduction in England of inquisitorial elements to assist litigants in persons lies the assumption that an inquisitorial system (in the sense of judicial investigation of the issues by the judge of merits) is employed in civilian legal systems. This is a misconception. The court in civilian systems may have a greater role in managing the hearings and in eliciting witness testimony, but the process remains strictly adversarial. As in England, the parties define the issues. The continental civil court has no greater power than the English court to decide what matters to investigate or what evidence should be presented.

The litigation process in civilian systems is largely conducted in written form. In France, for example, oral evidence is rarely taken. The rules of procedure in these systems lay down fairly detailed requirements concerning documentary evidence. The formalistic aspects of the continental legal process assume a high degree of learning which untrained persons cannot hope to muster, even if they were permitted to represent themselves. Accordingly, the major Continental European systems impose mandatory legal representation in civil proceedings, except in very low value claims. This is true of Germany, France, Italy and other European systems, where the advocates are expected to define the issues and present evidence and argument.[10]

---

[10] Legal representation is mandatory in Austria, Belgium France, Germany, Greece, Italy, Luxembourg, the Netherlands, Portugal and Spain; see e.g., Layton and Mercer, 2004: Vol. 2.

In civilian systems, the litigation process is conducted by lawyers. The advocates present their parties' allegations and indicate to the court the evidence they wish to adduce and witnesses they wish to call. The court summons only witnesses indicated by the parties; it does not seek witnesses of its own motion. While it is true that witnesses in civilian systems are questioned by the court and not the parties' advocates, the court tends to pursue the line of questioning suggested by the advocates. This is only to be expected since it is the advocates who define the issues and therefore determine the matters that require examination. The mandatory requirement of legal representation in such systems is more a reflection of the reality that litigation is practically impossible without lawyers than of an ideological commitment to high procedural standards.

4.9 CONCLUSION

The English system of civil justice offers poor access to litigants of limited means. This has been the case for a long time, but the situation has greatly deteriorated since the abolition of legal aid in civil cases and there it is now urgent to address it. The strategy that seems to appeal to the legislator favours procedures that can be conducted without the involvement of professional advocates, of inquisitorial proceedings. This strategy is misconceived. While there is much to be said for simplifying the litigation system through use of technology, online resources and other labour-saving measures, there is no substitute for adversarial process. Shortcutting the adversarial principle may well save cost, but it has the potential of creating injustice and undermining the legitimacy of court resolution of civil disputes.

REFERENCES

Briggs, Lord Justice (2013), *Chancery Modernisation Review: Final Report*, available in: www.judiciary.gov.uk/wp-content/uploads/JCO/Documents/CMR/cmr-final-report-dec2013.pdf.

Bornhorst, F., Ichino, A., Schlag, K. and Winter, E. (2004). *Trust and Trustworthiness Among Europeans: South-North Comparison*, available at www.researchgate.net/publication/5009344_Trust_and_Trustworthiness_Among_Europeans_South-North_Comparison.

Charness, G., Rigotti, L. and Rustichini, A. (2007). Individual Behavior and Group Membership. *American Economic Review* 97(4), 1340–52.

Ehud, G. (2004). Overcorrection, *Geo. LJ*, 93, 241.

Jackson, J. and Summers, S. (2012). *The Internationalisation of Criminal Evidence: Beyond the Common Law and Civil Law Traditions*, Cambridge: Cambridge University Press.

Layton, A. and Mercer, H., eds. (2004). *European Civil Practice*, 2nd ed., London: Sweet and Maxwell.

Lind, A., Thibaut, J. and Walker, L. (1976). A Cross-Cultural Comparison of the Effect of Adversary and Inquisitorial Processes on Bias in Legal Decision Making. *Virginia Law Review*, 64(2), 271–83.

Plous, S. (1993). *The Psychology of Judgment and Decision Making*, New York: McgrawHill Book Company.

Schul, Y. and Goren, H. (1997). When Strong Evidence Has Less Impact than Weak Evidence: Bias, Adjustment, and Instructions to Ignore. *Social Cognition* 15(2), 133–55.

Shayo, M. and Zussman, A. (2011). Judicial Ingroup Bias in the Shadow of Terrorism, *The Quarterly Journal of Economics*, 126(3), 1447–84.

Turner, J. C., Hogg, M. A., Oakes, P. J., Reicher, S. D., and Wetherell, M. S. (1987). *Rediscovering the Social Group: A Self-Categorization Theory*, Oxford: Basil Blackwell.

5

Evidential Remedies for Procedural Rights Violations

Comparative Criminal Evidence Law and Empirical Research

Sarah Summers

5.1 INTRODUCTION

The comparative criminal evidence scholarship continues to be influenced by 'the old debate as to whether adversarial or inquisitorial systems are better at finding the truth' (Jackson and Summers, 2012: 10). 'Adversarial' or 'accusatorial' systems are criticised on the grounds that the parties are afforded too much responsibility for gathering and presenting the evidence leading to a clear risk of bias. The triers of fact, meanwhile, are required to maintain a position of neutrality and prohibited from undertaking any sort of active judicial inquiry. These concerns are compounded by a vision of the law of evidence as a highly-regulated system of rules for the admission of evidence at trial (Jackson and Summers, 2012: 10). The 'inquisitorial systems', a term often used loosely to describe the procedural systems of 'continental Europe', are also subject to criticism. In such systems, fact-finders are able to conduct their own inquiries, but here the risk is said to be the probability that fact-finders form hypotheses too early (Damaška, 1997: 92). Such systems, which rely heavily on the judge to reach accurate conclusions and espouse notions of 'free proof', are sometimes said not to have a law of evidence at all.[1]

This characterization of the two main procedural traditions is unduly narrow and 'obscures two important truths about any system of adjudication which subscribes to the importance of evidence and proof. Firstly, any system which gives triers of fact the task of evaluating evidence must subscribe to some extent to a doctrine of free proof; and, secondly, any adjudicative system must have *some* rules of evidence and proof' (Jackson and Summers, 2012: 11). The comparative criminal evidence debate has tended to degenerate into

---

[1] For example, South African Law Commission, Discussion Paper 102 (Project 107) Sexual Offences, at 12.11.3.1.4.

highly partisan views as to the merits of one mode of proof over the other, rather than more considered analysis of evidential remedies as such.

Adherence to the idea of idealised procedural models might be understood as having contributed to the reluctance on the part of the supranational bodies responsible for defining procedural standards to consider the importance of evidential rules in determining the extent of procedural rights. This is well-illustrated by the case law of the European Court of Human Rights (ECtHR). It is common to find statements in the judgments of the ECtHR to the effect that it does not regulate the law of evidence and that criminal evidence is essentially a matter for the contracting states.[2] This, though, is quite obviously not entirely true: Strasbourg has been busy dictating the use of evidence in all sorts of situations from confrontation[3] to torture.[4] Such statements are problematic, not least because they seem to reinforce an understanding of a separation of the law of criminal evidence on the one hand and criminal procedure on the other which is quite obviously conceptually flawed.

In addition, the focus on idealised procedural models serves as a distraction from important issues which lie outside this debate. There has been little examination of whether these two theoretical models which are used for the purposes of comparison actually reflect real-life criminal processes. This is, however, of essential importance to the comparative criminal evidence law debate. It is important to stress at the outset that this is not to suggest that there are not differences between the various legal systems; rather, it is to argue that these differences are not necessarily accurately reflected in the accusatorial – inquisitorial typology. By engaging more with the realities of criminal process it should be possible to overcome the traditional adherence to the exclusionary rules versus free proof dogma and to provide new insights into comparative criminal evidence.

In this chapter, these arguments will be illustrated with reference to the evidential consequences of a violation of the right to counsel in Switzerland. This chapter will draw on data collected in the course of a large empirical

---

[2] See e.g. *Schenk* v. *Switzerland*, 12 July 1988, Series A No. 140, § 40: 'While Article 6 of the Convention guarantees the right to a fair trial, it does not lay down any rules on the admissibility of evidence as such, which is therefore primarily a matter for regulation under national law'; *Khan* v. *United Kingdom*, No. 35394/97, ECHR 2000-V, § 34: 'it is not the role of the ECtHR to determine, as a matter of principle, whether particular types of evidence – for example, unlawfully obtained evidence – may be admissible'.

[3] Famously the subject of considerable disagreement between the UKS Supreme Court and the ECtHR in *Al-Khawaja and Tahery* v. *United Kingdom*, No. 26766/05 and 22228/06, 20 January 2009. See further Jackson and Summers, 2013.

[4] *Jalloh* v. *Germany* [GC], No. 54810/00, ECHR 2002-VII, § 99; *Harutyunyan* v. *Armenia*, No. 36549/03, 28 June 2007, § 66.

study of criminal trials, the *Trial Observation Project*, funded by the Swiss National Science Foundation.[5] In the course of the study, the project team spent two years observing a total of 439 criminal trials in the courts of four Swiss cities.[6] The study aimed to document the nature of the implementation of trial rights in practice in order to challenge some of the principal assumptions underlying the normative theorising on trial rights.

The chapter will begin by challenging the assumption that the Swiss criminal procedure system, which clearly falls within the 'continental European' tradition, allows the fact-finder total freedom of proof in considering the evidence. The Swiss criminal procedure code provides, if not for exclusion, then certainly for the prohibition on the use of evidence. In this regard, reference will be made, by way of example, to the strong evidential remedies which exist to protect the right to counsel. The chapter will then consider the ways in which this strong right is undermined in practice and for attention to be drawn to the relationship between de facto restrictions on the right and evidential remedies. This will provide the basis for a number of concluding thoughts. The aim of this chapter is to move the focus of the discussion away from abstract notions of truth-finding to consider the relevance of evidential remedies for rights violations in practice and then to come back to consider the theoretical and comparative implications.

5.2 PROHIBITIONS ON THE USE OF UNLAWFULLY OBTAINED EVIDENCE

The use of evidence in Swiss criminal proceedings is regulated by Article 141 of the Federal Code of Criminal Procedure (CCP). Article 141 CCP sets out two distinct types of prohibition on the use of evidence obtained in violation of the provisions of the CCP: a mandatory prohibition on the use of the evidence and a discretionary prohibition, which allows the judge to rely on the evidence provided that various criteria are fulfilled. All other evidence obtained in violation of provisions which are deemed technical in nature (*Ordnungsvorschriften*) can be relied on by the judge in convicting the accused.[7]

The mandatory prohibition on the use of evidence covers both evidence obtained by compulsion or by recourse to force, threats, promises or deception and evidence obtained in violation of one of the provisions of the CCP,

---

[5] Summers and Studer, 2016: 45–72; Summers, 2014: 217–32.
[6] Strafgericht Basel Stadt, Regionalgericht Bern-Mitteland, Bezirksgericht Zürich and the Tribunal Pénal de Genève.
[7] Art. 141 para. 3 CCP.

providing that the provision expressly states that in such circumstances the evidence is not to be used.

The discretionary prohibition on the use of evidence stipulates that evidence obtained in violation of rules 'protecting the validity of the evidence' (*Gültigkeitsvorschriften*) is not to be used, unless the use of the evidence is essential for the purposes of solving a serious criminal case. The test allows substantial room for interpretation.[8] There is considerable disagreement in the literature as to the determination of terms such as 'serious offence',[9] 'essential' (Wohlers, 2014) and even with regard to the identification of those provisions of the code which are to be understood as 'protecting the validity of the evidence'.[10] The judge then has considerable discretion in individual cases for determining whether these tests are met.

It is important to think very briefly about the nature of these evidential provisions. Article 141 CCP cannot strictly speaking be characterised as an exclusionary rule, if exclusionary rules are to be understood as operating only within a system of admissibility as is the case in common law systems. In the common law context, the bifurcation of the proceedings means that the judge will determine the admissibility of the evidence and ultimately, if necessary, exclude the evidence; this means that the fact-finder – the jury – will not hear the evidence. This is without doubt an important difference from systems, such as the Swiss system, which do not separate the tasks of fact-finding and judging. It is questionable whether a person who has heard evidence is really able to exclude it from the decision-making process (Schünemann, 2000: 159–65). This is without doubt an important issue. Nevertheless, it is important, in the comparative context, not to over-estimate its relevance. Many common law trials are heard without a jury: studies suggest that jury trials constitute less than 1 per cent of all criminal cases in England and Wales.[11] In cases heard without a jury, the English judge – just like his or her Swiss counterpart – will both make decisions on 'admissibility' and act as the fact-finder.

With this brief overview of the evidential framework for the use of the evidence in mind, it is now possible to turn to examine the manner in which these remedies are applied in practice in the context of the right to counsel and the relevance of the extent of the evidential remedy for the scope of the protection afforded by the procedural right.

---

[8]   See further W. Wohlers, Art. 141 n.19ff., in Donatsch et al., 2014.
[9]   Donatsch and Cavegn, 2008: 158–66; Häring, 2009: 225–48; Gless, 2014.
[10] Wohlers, 2014: n.19; see also the judgment of the Federal Supreme Court BGE 130 I 126, 133.
[11] See e.g. Thomas, 2010. Ministry of Justice Research Series 1/10, 1, available from the Ministry of Justice Website: www.justice.gov.uk/publications/research.htm.

5.3 RIGHT TO COUNSEL

The right to counsel is acknowledged across Europe to be a crucial aspect of the right to be heard and the right to a fair trial as set out in provisions such as Article 6 of the ECHR. Following ground-breaking judgments of the ECtHR in cases such as *Salduz*[12] and *Pischalnikov*,[13] it has been firmly established that the accused has the right to counsel not just at trial but also during pre-trial hearings. These principles are reflected in the CPP, according to which the accused is entitled to the assistance of counsel at any time and at every stage of the proceedings.[14] This strong level of protection afforded in law is reflected in the high levels of legal representation in practice.

The data from the *Trial Observation Project* shows that in almost 90 per cent of cases which made it to trial in Switzerland,[15] the accused was assisted by counsel at trial (Figure 5.1).

In addition, legal aid is readily available. The CPP stipulates that legal aid shall be granted, inter alia, if the accused does not have sufficient funds to appoint a lawyer and defence counsel is necessary to safeguard his or her interests.[16] The strong right to legal aid is mirrored in practice by high levels of legal aid representation. According to the *Trial Observation Project* data, accused persons received legal aid in around 60 per cent of cases (Figure 5.2).

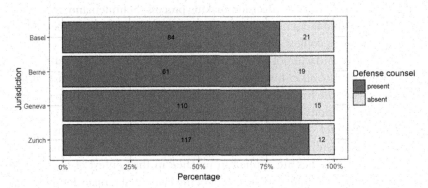

FIGURE 5.1 Presence of counsel at trial

---

[12] *Salduz* v. *Turkey* [GC] No. 36391/02, 27 November 2008.
[13] *Pischalnikov* v. *Russia*, No. 7025/04, 24 September 2009.
[14] Art. 129 CCP.
[15] In line with most European criminal justice systems only about 5 per cent of cases make it to trial.
[16] Art. 132b CPP.

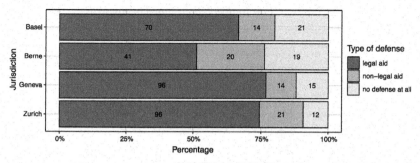

FIGURE 5.2 Extent of legal aid provision by the court

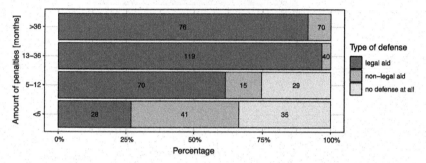

FIGURE 5.3 Extent of legal aid provision according to the charge

When the cases were sorted by severity, according to the sentence requested by the prosecutor, the legal aid provision was similarly impressive. Those facing a sentence of more than a year received legal aid in more than 95 per cent of cases (Figure 5.3).[17]

Finally, consideration of the number of cases in which the defence complained of a violation of the right to counsel or in which the right was discussed by the judge ('raised' at trial), demonstrates that this occurred just 14 times out of 436 cases (Table 5.1).

This suggests that the right to counsel is enforced in exemplary fashion in Switzerland. On the basis of this data one might assume that there are few impediments to the right to counsel. The accused, aware of his or her rights, will make use of these and those involved in the proceedings will make sure that the accused is able to do so. In fact, during the study

[17] This is unsurprising when one takes into account the fact that if the accused is facing a sentence of more than one-year imprisonment, the authorities are obliged to appoint legal aid counsel, see Art. 131 CCP.

TABLE 5.1 *Fair trial violations raised or observed*

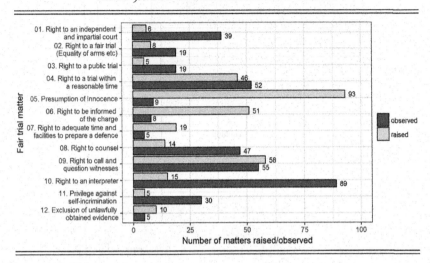

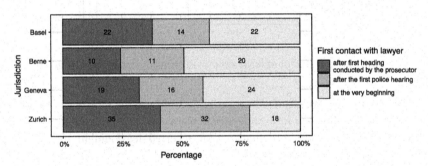

FIGURE 5.4 First contact with the accused (according to counsel)

problems with the enforcement of the right of the accused to counsel were identified, albeit not at the trial stage. The most important of these concerned delay.

On conclusion of the proceedings, the accused and counsel were asked at what point in the proceedings counsel had been appointed. Although 90 per cent of accused persons in our study were represented by counsel at trial, in 65–68 per cent of these cases there was delay in access to counsel, in the sense that counsel was not present at the first hearings with the police or prosecution (Figure 5.4).

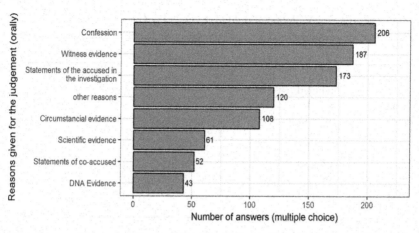

FIGURE 5.5 Type of evidence referred to in the oral verdict in convicting the accused

This is not an insignificant issue but represents a considerable interference with the right to counsel in practice. The significance of statements made at an early stage in the proceedings should not be underestimated. In more than 40 per cent of the cases observed, statements made by the accused during the investigation were relied upon by the court in convicting the accused and mentioned in the course of the oral reasoning of the verdict (Figure 5.5).

This suggests that despite strong procedural rules, the courts routinely rely on statements made by the accused before he or she has received the assistance of counsel. In spite of this, as noted above, the right to counsel is rarely complained about at trial. Taking a closer look at the matters raised at trial, we see that the defence complained about restrictions on the right to counsel issue on just 11 occasions out of a total of 439 trials observed (Table 5.2). Ten of these eleven cases concerned delay in counsel becoming involved in the case.[18] Similarly, of the twelve violations observed by the project team (and not mentioned during the proceedings) which were deemed to constitute a 'likely' violation of the right to counsel, ten concerned delay in access to counsel.

Why this disconnect between the extent of the exercise of the right and complaints about interferences with the right at trial? One of the principal reasons is that even if the accused or the defence complains about the delay, it is highly unlikely that this will result in an effective remedy in the sense of restriction on the use of the evidence.

---

[18] These cases are discussed in detail in Summers et al., 2016: 133–70.

TABLE 5.2 *Violation of right to counsel raised or observed at trial*

		Accused	Defence	Judge	Prosecutor	Observer
Matters raised		1	11	2	o	47
Reaction	ignored	o	4	o	o	-
	rejected	o	3	o	o	-
	accepted	1	4	2	o	-
Success?	likely	o	4	1	o	12
	possible	1	7	1	o	35
	unlikely	o	o	o	o	o
Acquittal/	yes	o	1	o	o	-
Sentence Reduction	no	1	10	2	o	-

5.4 DE FACTO RESTRICTIONS ON THE RIGHT TO COUNSEL AND THE ROLE OF EVIDENTIAL REMEDIES

JUDGE: Have you read the indictment? Do you understand the case brought by the prosecutor?

ACCUSED: No, I couldn't afford a lawyer.

JUDGE: There is the opportunity to obtain a legal aid lawyer; in your case it is very likely that you would fulfil the criteria to be entitled to legal aid.

ACCUSED: Yes, I did ask, but they told me that I would have to pay for the first meeting with the lawyer myself and Fr. 280.00 was simply too much. Would a lawyer have been useful?

JUDGE: Well it wouldn't have done any harm! But I will consider both the facts that speak against you and those which speak for you . . .[19]

One of the principal factors which will influence the decision of the accused to seek the assistance of counsel is the cost of the lawyer. In the case mentioned above, the accused's decision not to request legal counsel appears to have been influenced by the fact that he may have had to pay for the first hour of any legal assistance. During the study, accused persons were asked on completion of the trial, why they had not insisted on having counsel appointed at an earlier stage. Common replies included that the accused was concerned about not being able to afford counsel or that they were unaware of the right to legal aid at the beginning of the proceedings (Summers et al., 2016, 133–70).

[19] Dialogue between judge and accused recorded by the trial observer in Case ID 47 City of Basel (Theft).

The right to be informed of the right to counsel is set out in Article 158 CPP. According to Article 158(1) CCP, the accused is to be informed by the police or the prosecution at the beginning of the first examination hearing 'that he or she is entitled to appoint defence counsel or where appropriate to request a legal aid defence counsel'. Failure to inform the accused of his or her right to counsel will result in a mandatory prohibition on the use of any statements made to the investigating authorities: 'Examination hearings which were conducted despite the fact that this information was not provided shall not be used in evidence.'[20]

It will seldom be the case, however, that the police or prosecution fail entirely to inform the accused of the right to counsel, especially in light of the introduction of standardised protocols. In fact, it would not be unreasonable to suggest that this type of scenario does not actually exist in practice. The data from the study suggests that other less dramatic scenarios are of relevance. The problem was not that the accused had not been informed of the right to counsel but rather that the information was incomplete. Either the accused was not informed about the legal aid entitlement or he or she was informed of the right to legal aid but also informed that the costs might have to be repaid on conclusion of the proceedings and that lawyers were expensive and unnecessary. Such statements clearly have the potential to have a chilling effect on the extent of the right to counsel. In view of this, it is useful to consider the evidential consequences of the provisions of incomplete or potentially misleading information on the legal aid entitlement.

The first issue to consider in this regard is the matter of waiver. An accused in such a situation will be assumed to have waived the right. He or she will have to prove that the waiver was invalid, and it will be difficult to establish that the information provided by the authorities was insufficient or that the police or prosecution sought to dissuade the accused from taking counsel. Assuming that the accused can cross the waiver hurdle, it is instructive to consider the evidential consequences of an incomplete or misleading 'caution'.

According to the CPP, a failure to inform the accused of his or her right to counsel will result in an absolute prohibition on the use of the evidence. What about the right to be informed about the legal aid entitlement? If the right to be informed about legal aid is considered an independent aspect of the provision, the failure to mention this entitlement would result in an absolute prohibition on the use of any subsequent statements made during the hearing in evidence.[21] If, however, it is assumed that the mandatory prohibition on the

---

[20]   Art. 158(2) CPP in conjunction with Art. 141(1) CPP.
[21]   In the sense of Art. 158(2) in conjunction with Art. 141(1).

use of the evidence refers to cases in which the accused was not informed at all about right to counsel, then it will not apply to cases in which the accused was informed of the right to counsel but not about the legal aid entitlement. This situation would give rise at most to a discretionary prohibition on the use of the evidence.[22]

The situation looks similar if we consider a scenario in which the police or prosecution informed the accused of the right to legal aid counsel but immediately qualified this information in order to dissuade the accused from taking counsel, by stressing the cost of counsel, the possibility that costs would have to be repaid or by suggesting that lawyers were unnecessary and would only complicate things. In this scenario, the mandatory prohibition would certainly not apply. Once again the only available remedy would be the discretionary prohibition on the use of the evidence, providing that the necessary conditions were fulfilled.[23] In such cases the court would be required to consider whether the evidence was obtained in violation of a provision protecting the validity of the evidence (*Gültigkeitsvorschrift*), but even in such cases, if the matter at issue concerned a 'serious offence', then it is likely that the evidence would be used.

In summary, despite the fact that the right to counsel is protected by a strong evidential remedy, the police and prosecution can caution the accused in such a way as to dissuade him or her from immediately insisting on the assistance of counsel without seriously having to fear that this is going to impact on use of the evidence at trial. In essence, weak discretionary evidential remedies protecting the right to information about the legal aid entitlement have the potential to contribute to substantial de facto restrictions on the right to counsel. There are, of course, a number of ways in which this situation could be ameliorated. One possibility would be to introduce a blanket right to three hours of free legal assistance at the beginning of proceedings (Summers et al., 2016: 133, 169). This would ensure that the accused was properly informed of his or her procedural rights and that any decision to refuse legal assistance was in fact made unequivocally, freely and perhaps most importantly, in full understanding of the procedural consequences of the waiver.[24]

5.5 CONCLUSIONS

This examination of the right to counsel in practice leads to a number of conclusions as regards normative theorising about comparative criminal

---

[22] Art. 158(1)/Art. 143 in conjunction with Art. 141(2).
[23] Art. 141(2) in conjunction with Art. 143 CPP.
[24] *Sejdovic* v. *Italy* [GC], No. 56581/00, §§ 96–104.

evidence law. First, systems can compensate for strong procedural rights by restricting the extent of evidential remedies. There is considerable potential for criminal procedure systems to compensate for strong procedural rights by restricting the availability of strong evidential remedies, such as a total prohibition on the use of the evidence. Here, the provision of an absolute right to counsel protected by red-line evidential remedies is mitigated in practice by the fact that interferences with this right, such as incomplete cautions, are subject to discretionary judicial balancing exercises weighted in favour of the use of the evidence.

It is perhaps not entirely disingenuous to suggest that concerns that the right of the accused to take counsel early on in the proceedings might hinder the investigating potential of the prosecution and police have been alleviated by allowing some leeway in informing the accused of their rights and thus preventing broad early access to legal counsel. It is also important to note that this situation might be aggravated further by steps taken ostensibly to strengthen procedural rights, such as by way of the introduction of a written letter of rights.[25] Such developments may in fact prove counterproductive if there is no regulation of ways in which the right to counsel can be undermined in practice. The introduction of a letter of rights which the accused must sign, essentially results in a cast iron waiver. The fact that the accused was informed of the right does not however necessarily mean that he or she has *understood* the right. Here it is essential that serious consideration be paid to the argument that a waiver of counsel should only be valid, if made after the accused has had legal advice on the procedural consequences of the waiver.[26]

This all gives rise to issues of legitimacy and forces consideration of whether strong procedural rights are in fact dependent on de facto restrictions on the exercise of these rights for their existence and acceptance.

Second, the nature of the implementation of the right to counsel in practice demonstrates the importance of evidential remedies for the uniform application of procedural rights. If it is accepted that the nature of evidential remedies impacts on the extent of the protection afforded to the procedural rights, then this seems to call into question the suggestion that procedural rights can be applied uniformly in different procedural, institutional or evidential environments. In other words, if the aim is to ensure uniform application of procedural rights, then it will also be necessary to regulate evidential remedies.

---

[25] Directive 2012/13/EU of the European Parliament and of the Council of 22 May 2012 on the right to information in criminal proceedings, Art. 4.
[26] *McGowan (Procurator Fiscal, Edinburgh) (Appellant)* v. *B (Respondent) (Scotland)* [2011] UKSC 54, paras. 103 and 108 (per Lord Kerr, dissenting).

Third, the debate on exclusionary versus free proof principles within the context of the adversarial–inquisitorial typology is of little relevance. Switzerland clearly has 'exclusionary type' rules. The interesting issue is rather to what extent procedural rights should be protected by red-line rules and in which cases is it legitimate to allow judicial discretion to play a role in determining whether the evidence can be used and according to which criteria (harm doctrine, seriousness of the offence, proportionality etc.). The Swiss criminal justice system, as a system falling within the continental tradition, might be understood as being governed by the free evaluation of evidence, but the reality is much more complex. The judge is bound by rules of evidence and the interesting question is rather the extent of discretion in the determination of whether the evidence can be used or not and the factors impacting on this decision.

It seems likely that the issues discussed here are common to many jurisdictions, or at least to those jurisdictions in which there is underlying agreement on the procedural rights in question or regarding the definition of improperly or unlawfully obtained evidence. In fact, it may well be the case that other lines are being drawn. As the Strasbourg court propagates a vision of the judge as the 'ultimate guardian of fairness',[27] and as European jurisdictions enact provisions which afford the judge considerable control in determining whether it is fair to use the evidence in convicting an accused,[28] we can see room for considerable difference of approach between the USA and Europe.

Finally, these findings highlight the importance of paying attention to real-life practices in the context of comparative criminal evidence. It is essential that normative theorising is based on accurate descriptive accounts of criminal proceedings. We need a new approach in which the realities of criminal proceedings – and data about the manner in which rules of evidence and procedure operate in practice – are placed at the centre of the discussion.

REFERENCES

Damaška M. (1997). *Evidence Law Adrift*, New Haven: Yale University Press.
Donatsch A. and Cavegn C. (2008). Ausgewählte Fragen zum Beweisrecht nach der schweizerischen Strafprozessordnung, ZStrR, 126, 158–66.
Gless S. (2014). Art 141 N 72, in M. A. Niggli, M. Heer and H. Wiprächtiger (eds.), *Basler Kommentar, Schweizerische Strafprozessordnung/Jugendprozessordnung*, 2nd ed., Basel, Helbling and Lichtenhahn, 2014.

---

[27] *Cuscani v. United Kingdom*, no. 32771/96, § 39.
[28] See too Police and Criminal Evidence Act 1984, s. 78.

Häring, D. (2009). Verwertbarkeit rechtswidrig erlangter Beweise gemäss schweizerische Strafprozessordnung – alter Zopf oder substanzielle Neuerungen?, *ZStrR* 127, 225–48.

Jackson, J. and Summers, S. (2012). *The Internationalisation of Criminal Evidence: Beyond the Common Law and Civil Law Traditions*, Cambridge: Cambridge University Press.

Jackson, J. and Summers, S. (2013). Confrontation with Strasbourg: UK and Swiss Approaches to Criminal Evidence, *Criminal Law Review*, 60 (2), 115–31.

Schünemann, B. (2000). Der Richter im Strafverfahren als manipulierter Dritter? Zur empirischen Bestätigung von Perseveranz- und Schulterschlusseffekt. 3 *Strafverteidiger* 159–65.

Summers, S. (2014). Observing Criminal Trials, in R. Anderson, J. Chalmers and J. MacLeod (eds.), *Glasgow Tercentenary Essays: 300 Years of the School of Law*, Edinburgh: Avizandum Publishing, 217–32.

Summers, S. and Studer, D. (2016). Fairness im Strafverfahren? Eine empirische Untersuchung, *Schweizerische Zeitschrift für Strafrecht*, 134 (1), 45–72.

Summers, S., Garland, L. and Studer, D. (2016). Das Recht auf Verteidigung – Anspruch und Wirklichkeit, *Schweizerische Zeitschrift für Strafrecht*, 134(2), 133–70.

Thomas, C. (2010). *Are Juries Fair?*, Ministry of Justice Research Series 1/10 www.justice.gov.uk/publications/research.htm.

Wohlers, W. (2014). Art 141 N 19ff, in A. Donatsch, T. Hansjakob and V. Lieber (eds.), *Kommentar zur Schweizerischen Strafprozessordnung*, 2nd ed., Zurich: Schulthess.

6

Common Law Evidence and the Common Law of Human Rights

Towards a Harmonic Convergence?

John Jackson

6.1 INTRODUCTION

This chapter considers what impact human rights law has made on the common law of evidence which has been developed in common law jurisdictions as a discrete body of law and practice with a particular focus on exclusionary rules of evidence. Particular emphasis will be given to the jurisprudence of the European Court of Human Rights (ECtHR) which it will be argued has tried to steer an uneasy path between two positions. The first position is one of minimal interference towards the way in which evidence is regulated in member states on the basis that as an international court it must respect the traditions of member states and that member states should be the driving force in the matter of applying the Convention. This has meant the Court taking a back seat, arbitrating on how the fair trial principles have been applied in individual cases and intervening only where in a given case the result has led overall to an unfair outcome. The second position is to take a more supervisory position of 'director of operations' to ensure that the right to a fair trial and the rights of the defence are made sufficiently 'practical and effective' within the member states.[1] It will be suggested that in its early days the Court gravitated in favour of the first approach. But in more recent times it has come closer to the second approach. In particular it has developed certain rules that have had the effect of encouraging common law judges to engage more holistically with the effect of certain kinds of evidence on the weight of

---

[1] The phrases 'arbitrator of principles' and 'director of operations' derive from R. Spano, 'Terrorism and Article 6 of the European Convention on Human Rights', 6th Annual Lecture of the Human Rights Law Centre's International Humanitarian Unit, University of Nottingham, 10 March 2017.

the evidence as a whole and on the fairness of the proceedings as a whole. The effect has been to reinforce a shift in the nature of both their epistemic and non-epistemic reasoning during the trial.

Two particular rules developed by the ECtHR will be considered: the so-called *Salduz* doctrine and the so-called sole or decisive rule applied to un-examined statements. The '*Salduz*' doctrine is a kind of European '*Miranda*' rule whereby access to a lawyer should be provided from the first interrogation of a suspect by the police and any use of incriminating statements at trial which have been made during police interrogation without such access will in principle irretrievably prejudice the rights of the defence.[2] The 'sole or decisive' rule provides that defence rights are unduly restricted if the convic-tion of a defendant is solely or mainly based on evidence provided by witnesses whom the accused is unable to question at any stage of the proceedings.[3] In its most recent decisions, however, it will be argued that the Court would seem to have drawn back from its more activist stance of setting standards of fairness in evidentiary matters and become more fixated on the traditional common law concern with reliability. This has somewhat pushed back the potential that the ECtHR has to shift the common law towards achieving a more harmonic convergence between achieving truth and fairness in criminal proceedings. Before we come to the approach of the ECtHR towards issues of evidence, however, we need to set out what the common law approach has been.

6.2 THE COMMON LAW MODEL OF EVIDENCE LAW

For many centuries evidence has been regulated in common law countries by a law of evidence which is often contrasted with a 'free' system of proof that operates in civil law countries. The core of the contrast is sometimes wrongly attributed to the fact that common law systems have rules of evidence while civil law systems do not. In fact contemporary continental systems place a variety of constraints on the use of certain types of evidence similar in many respects to evidentiary devices and doctrines familiar to common law-yers. The common law system is, however, distinctive in two important respects.[4] First of all, it is unitary in nature applying across all types of litigation freed from the procedural regulations that govern particular types of proceed-ings. Secondly, it is exclusionary in nature. Thayer, one of the giants of Anglo-American common law scholarship, viewed the common law system as

---

[2] See *Salduz* v. *Turkey* (2009) 49 EHRR 421.
[3] See *Al-Khawaja and Tahery* v. *UK* (2009) 49 EHRR 1; (2012) 54 EHRR 23.
[4] For further detail, see Jackson and Roberts, 2019.

radically peculiar because a great mass of evidentiary matter, logically important and probative, is shut out from the view of the judicial tribunal by a rule
while the same matter is not excluded anywhere else. He predicated common
law evidence on two strikingly simple, complementary principles: (1) that
nothing is to be received which is not logically probative of some matter
requiring proof; and (2) that everything which is probative should be received
unless excluded by some rule or principle of law (Thayer, 1898: 265, 530). The
effect is to disaggregate the law of evidence from the logic of proof by excluding from the fact-finding arena certain kinds of evidence even though such
evidence is *ex hypothesi* relevant. As Thayer put it, the law has 'no mandamus
to the logical faculty' (Thayer, 1898: 314). This approach is made particularly
effective by a binary trial structure with a judge ruling on questions of
admissibility and able to exclude evidence from the jury. The structure of
continental proceedings by contrast makes it difficult to enforce a system
of exclusionary rules in a context where all of the evidence is heard by the fact-
finding tribunal.

It would be wrong to conclude from this that the common law system of
evidence is not concerned with truth-finding. Wigmore, another giant of
common law evidence scholarship, divided the rules into two types: 'rules
of auxiliary probative policy' and 'rules of extrinsic policy' (Wigmore, 1904:
§37–§38). Many of the former such as hearsay and the rules on bad character
are designed to promote rectitude of outcome by excluding evidence on the
ground that it is potentially unreliable or might otherwise (so it is thought)
unduly prejudice or confuse a jury. In this respect, accuracy is a core institutional value in the common law system. But it is achieved, at least in the
traditional scheme, by means of excluding whole classes of evidence rather
than by rules specifying how particular evidence should be evaluated. It is true
that judges have increasingly come to exercise greater judicial discretion over
the admissibility of evidence and commentators have discerned a 'powerful
trend' towards expanding judicial discretion (Swift, 2000: 2437, 2441). One sees
this in the most recent legislative attempts in the UK to regulate hearsay
evidence by an innovation that gives judges an overriding discretion to
admit probative hearsay in the interests of justice.[5] However, one must not
overstate this trend. Some modern legislation, at least in the UK context, has
come to narrow judicial discretion – for example, in relation to the cross-
examination of complainants on previous sexual history. Another trend that
one can see in more recent times has been the use of what Roberts and
Zuckerman have called 'forensic reasoning rules' where judicial directions

---

[5]   Criminal Justice Act 2003, s. 114(1).

must directly engage with how evidence should be evaluated – for example, in areas such as directions on drawing inferences against silence and how to approach probative hearsay or bad character evidence that has been admitted by virtue of increasingly relaxed admissibility rules or increasing judicial inclusionary discretion (Roberts and Zuckerman, 2010). Again, one should not overstate the case. Once the evidence is filtered through to the jury, it is still remarkably free to engage in its own common sense reasoning with little appellate supervision of its reasoning processes.

Another sign of change has been a shift away from the traditional common law approach whereby the rules of admissibility are applied in an undifferentiated manner to both civil and criminal proceedings. Increasingly, individual procedural rights have supplied enduring rationales for many characteristically common law rules of evidence as evidentiary devices such as compulsory process, legal professional privilege, the exclusion of unlawfully obtained evidence and the right of silence (largely confined to criminal adjudication) have come to be given constitutional status in many common law (as well as civilian) jurisdictions.[6] This trend has been reinforced by a global human rights law which at least in its European embodiment, through the jurisprudence of the ECtHR, has been developing fair trial standards for criminal proceedings such as the presumption of innocence, the protection of the accused against abusive coercion, the right to examine witnesses and the need for 'equality of arms' and an 'adversarial procedure' between the investigating or prosecuting authorities and the accused.[7] The question that we now turn to is whether in its development of these fair trial standards the ECtHR has had a tangible impact on the development of common law evidence law or whether it has merely had a rhetorical effect with no real bite in individual cases.

6.3 FROM MINIMAL INTERFERENCE TO A GREATER SUPERVISORY ROLE

Although from the beginning the European Commission (ECommHR) and Court (ECtHR) emphasised that the right to a fair trial embodied in Article 6 of the European Convention on Human Rights (ECHR) holds a prominent place in a democratic society with the result that it must be given a broad construction, they seemed particularly reluctant to be prescriptive when it came to evidentiary matters. A number of limiting principles have been adopted. First of all, from its early days the Commission established that the

---

[6] See Jackson and Roberts, 2019. For greater detail, see Hunter and Roberts, 2012.
[7] See generally, Jackson and Summers, 2012.

Strasbourg authorities do not constitute a further court of appeal from the national courts.[8] This fourth instance doctrine together with the doctrine of the margin of appreciation has meant that the national courts are given considerable discretion concerning the evaluation of evidence. The Strasbourg authorities will only intervene if the judgment of the national court is found to be wholly arbitrary.[9] This is not a surprising stance for a human rights body to take and has been emulated by the UN Human Rights Committee (UNHRC) which has held that it is generally the task of the national courts to review facts and evidence and the application of domestic law in a particular case, 'unless it can be shown that such an evaluation or application was clearly arbitrary or amounted to a manifest error or denial of justice'.[10] As we shall see, however, the ECtHR would seem to be increasingly considering the reliability of the evidence in determining whether in individual instances the applicant received a fair trial.

Second, in line with the general principle that the member states enjoy considerable freedom in the choice of the appropriate means of ensuring that their judicial systems comply with the requirements of Article 6,[11] the ECtHR does not require states to adopt any particular rules governing the admissibility of evidence, although we shall see that it has embraced certain evidentiary principles that have had to be translated into national systems. Instead, it has considered that it is for the competent authorities to determine the relevance of proposed evidence and that rules on the admissibility of evidence are 'primarily a matter for regulation under national law'.[12] The ECtHR's unwillingness to prescribe rules of evidence or concepts such as admissibility was a clear signal that it had no wish to impose a common law system of evidence on member states. But it equally sent a clear signal that it would not interfere with the admissibility rules of the common law system. The UNHRC has likewise held that it is 'primarily for the domestic legislatures of the States parties to determine the admissibility of evidence and how their courts assess it'.[13]

---

[8]   X v. FRG (dec), 16 December 1957. See further *Kemmache v. France (No. 3)*, 24 November 1994, [44]. Other trans-national courts have taken a similar approach: see, e.g., Inter-American Commission on Human Rights in *Juan Santaella Telleria et al v. Venezuela*, 12 October 2005 at 40.

[9]   See, e.g., *Khamidov v. Russia*, 15 November 2007 at 174; *Berhani v. Albania*, 27 May 2010 at 50.

[10] See, inter alia, *Cuartero Casado v. Spain*, 15 July 2005 [4.3]; *Riedl-Riedenstein et al. v. Germany*, 2 November 2004 [7.3]; *Errol Simms v. Jamaica*, 3 April 1995 [6.2].

[11] *Hadjianastassiou v. Greece*, 16 December 1992 [33].

[12] *Engel and others v. Netherlands*, 8 June 1976 [46]; *Schenk v. Switzerland*, 12 July 1988 [40]; *Delta v. France*, 19 December 1990 [35].

[13] Human Rights Committee, General Comment No. 32 [90]: *Article 14: Right to equality before the courts and tribunals and to a fair trial*, adopted on 27 July 2007, [39].

Third, the ECommHR and ECtHR both stated at an early stage that their task is to determine whether they can be satisfied that the proceedings taken 'as a whole' were fair.[14] On the one hand, this has enabled the ECtHR to give an expansive interpretation to Article 6, and to hold that the rights accorded to defendants in Article 6(2) and 6(3) are 'specific aspects of the general principle stated in paragraph 1 and are to be regarded as a non-exhaustive list of 'minimum rights' which form constituent elements amongst others, of the notion of a fair trial in criminal proceedings'.[15] This expansionist principle has enabled the ECtHR to read other important protective rights into Article 6 such as the privilege against self-incrimination.[16] On the other hand, however, contrary to what would seem to be required in the English text which refers to the specific rights in Article 6(3) as 'minimum rights',[17] in a number of cases the ECtHR has considered that it is not essential for the specific rights to be respected in every case if the trial, when examined as a whole, has been fair. Thus in *Asch* v. *Austria*[18] where the applicant was not given the opportunity to cross-examine the main witness in an apparent breach of the right to examine witnesses under Article 6(3)(d), the Court decided that taken as a whole, the trial could not be characterised as having been unfair. Sometimes the Court has adopted a stricter proportionality analysis by considering if measures restricting the rights of the defence are 'strictly necessary' and there are adequate compensating measures taken to protect the accused at trial.[19] But the clear signal sent to domestic jurisdictions is that they may make inroads into the specific rights in Article 3(d) provided that the trial as a whole may be considered fair.[20]

While these limiting principles have enabled the Court to adopt a cautionary approach towards the regulation of evidence in national courts, they have not prevented the Court from developing principles that it has considered to be at the heart of a fair trial, such as the privilege against self-incrimination, as already mentioned, and the principles of equality of arms and adversarial procedure (Jackson and Summers, 2012). Inevitably, this meant that there would come a point when the development of such principles was going to come into conflict with taking a 'hands off' approach

---

[14]   *Nielsen* v. *Denmark* (report), 15 March 1961, 518; *Barberà, Messegué and Jabardo* v. *Spain*,
     6 December 1988; *Delta* v. *France*, 19 December 1990 [35]. For criticism of the 'fairness as
     a whole' doctrine, see Trechsel, 2005: 87.
[15]   *Deweer* v. *Belgium*, 27 February 1980 [56].
[16]   See, e.g., *Funke* v. *France*, 25 February 1993.
[17]   See Trechsel, 2018: 19. See also Goss, 2017: 1137.
[18]   (1993) 15 EHRR 597.
[19]   See, e.g., *Van Mechelen* v. *Netherlands* (1988) 25 EHRR 647 [58].
[20]   See, e.g., *Brown* v. *Stott* [2001] 2 All ER 97.

towards the way national courts regulated evidence. Admittedly, when one looks across both common law and civil law systems, there is a great deal of agreement on how certain types of evidence which have been obtained by coercion should be treated. Despite its 'mantra' that it is not the role of the ECtHR to determine as a matter of principle whether particular types of evidence may be admissible or not, the Court has over time come to accept that the use in criminal proceedings of evidence obtained by way of torture will automatically violate the right to a fair trial,[21] as will the use of incriminating statements obtained in defiance of the will of the accused.[22] Such rules are quite in keeping with the common law approach. The common law has long considered that statements obtained by torture of by threats or inducements will automatically be inadmissible.[23]

Things became more controversial, however, when the ECtHR used the concepts of equality of arms and adversarial procedure to develop a vision of defence rights as not only protecting defendants from abuse and coercion but also enabling defendants to participate fully in the trial process.[24] Attention has focused on two of the minimum rights specified under Article 6(3): the right to counsel under Article 6(3)(c) and the right to examine witnesses under Article 6(3)(d). In November 2008 the ECtHR issued its famous judgment in *Salduz* v. *Turkey*[25] stating that suspects had a right of access to a lawyer when first questioned by the police. Although there has been much debate about what the nature of such access should mean,[26] the prescription that *some* access was required when suspects were first questioned by the police had major repercussions across the member states of the Council of Europe (see Giannoulopoulos, 2016: 103). This included common law systems such as Scotland, though less so England and Wales where statutory legislation had already provided for a right of access to a lawyer in the police station.[27] The evidential impact of the judgment had an effect on both these jurisdictions, however, by in effect imposing what seemed like an almost blanket

---

[21] *Harutyunyan* v. *Armenia* ECtHR 28 June 2007, *Levinta* v. *Moldova* ECtHR 16 December 2008; *Husayn* v. *Poland* ECtHR 24 July 2014.

[22] *Saunders* v. *UK* (1996) 23 EHRR 313.

[23] See in relation to torture, *A and others* v. *Secretary of State for the Home Department* [2005] UKHL 71; [2005] 3 WLR 1249. The common law requirement that confessions must be voluntary dates back to the eighteenth century: see *R* v. *Warickshall* (1783) 1 Leach 263.

[24] Jackson, 2005: 737; Jackson and Summers, 2012.

[25] (2009) 49 EHRR 421.

[26] Jackson, 2016: 987; Pivaty, 2018: 62.

[27] See s. 58 of the Police and Criminal Evidence Act 1984. The *Salduz* principle was endorsed and applied to Scotland in the UK Supreme Court decision of *Cadder* v. *HM Advocate* [2010] 1 WLR 2601.

exclusionary rule on the use made of any incriminating statements when access to a lawyer was denied, no matter how reliable such statements were and how voluntarily they were made, thereby fettering the discretion that judges had hitherto exercised to decide for themselves whether voluntary or reliable statements obtained unfairly should be excluded.[28]

The 'sole or decisive' rule that was applied to unexamined witness evidence proved even more controversial. Whereas as we have seen in cases like *Asch v. Austria* the Court at first adopted a flexible approach towards the right to examine witnesses by looking for compensatory safeguards when defendants were not able to examine witnesses against them, in later years it developed a stricter approach towards the right. In a number of cases culminating in *Al-Khawaja and Tahery v. UK*[29] in 2009 the ECtHR considered that the right to examine witnesses in Article 6(1)(d) was an aspect of the right to a fair trial guaranteed by Article 6 which in principle requires that all evidence must be produced in the presence of the accused in a public hearing with a view to adversarial argument. A pretty much absolute rule came to be developed to the effect that where a conviction is based solely or to a decisive degree on depositions that have been made by a person whom the accused has had no opportunity to examine or have examined, whether during the investigation or at trial, the rights of the defence are restricted to an extent that is incompatible with the guarantees provided by Article 6.[30]

At first sight, it is hard to see why these particular Strasbourg rules should rub up against the common law system evidence. After all, exclusionary rules are very much its hallmark. The common law has long had a rule excluding the use of involuntary confessions and the *Salduz* rule excluding the use of incriminating statements made in the absence of legal advice might seem little more than an extension of the privilege against self-incrimination long recognised in English law. Similarly, rules such as the hearsay rule have long been designed to encourage witnesses to give oral evidence at trial by effectively excluding out-of-court witness statements adduced to prove the truth of the facts asserted. In fact, however, both these rules, particularly the sole or decisive rule propounded by the ECtHR, have provided a challenge both to the common law method of excluding evidence and to the increasingly flexible approach that the English courts have been taking towards

---

[28]   For an analysis of the impact of *Salduz* on the English law of evidence, see Dennis, 2020: 242–6.
[29]   *Al-Khawaja and Tahery v. UK* (2009) 49 EHRR 1.
[30]   *Luca v. Italy* (2003) 36 EHRR 46 [40]; *Solakov v. Former Yugoslavia Republic of Macedonia*, 31 October 2001 [58], *Al-Khawaja and Tahery v. UK* (2009) 49 EHRR 1 [36].

exclusionary rules such as the hearsay rule. We will examine the methodological challenge first before considering the content of the new Strasbourg rules.

6.4 THE METHODOLOGICAL CHALLENGE

The common law system of evidence requires judges to rule on the admissibility of evidence in a piecemeal, 'atomistic' manner as the evidence is adduced rather than to make sweeping assessments about the impact of the evidence on the case as a whole. By contrast, the ECtHR has considered that a much more 'holistic' approach is called for by considering how decisive or substantial any 'suspect' evidence is in relation to the case as a whole. This requires that judges are in a position to make some assessment of the strength of the other evidence against the accused, something that judges are not used to doing in criminal trials involving juries. It is true that at the end of the prosecution case judges have been traditionally asked to rule on whether there is a case to answer, which has required them to consider whether on one possible view of the facts there is evidence on which a jury could conclude the defendant is guilty.[31] But the new rules would seem to call for a much more searching analysis of the strength of the evidence as a whole. In its own terms, the sole or decisive rule governing the use made of unexamined statements requires a judgment to be made as to whether such evidence is the sole or decisive evidence in the case as a whole. The *Salduz* principle as enunciated by the ECtHR in *Salduz* did not seem to call for such a judgment to be made. The court appeared to suggest that if incriminating statements were made after there has been a denial of access to a lawyer, then the rights of the accused are irretrievably prejudiced.[32] However as we shall see in its later application of the rule, the ECtHR would seem to have changed tack and in considering whether the lack of access affected the fairness of the proceedings as a whole, the court has put particular emphasis on the quality and significance of the incriminating statements that were obtained in the context of the evidence as a whole.[33]

The UK judges were quick to voice their concerns about the sole or decisive rule. Soon after the ECtHR applied the 'sole or decisive' rule to the UK in *Al-Khawaja and Tahery v. UK*, the UK Supreme Court delivered a seven judge ruling in *R v. Horncastle*[34] raising concerns about the practicability of the test

---

[31] See, e.g., *R v. Galbraith* [1981] 1 WLR 1039.
[32] *Salduz v. Turkey* (2009) 49 EHRR 421 [55].
[33] See *Ibrahim and others v. UK* (2015) 61 EHRR 9.
[34] *R v. Horncastle and others* [2009] EWCA Crim 964 (CA); [2009] UKSC 14, [2010] 1 Cr App R 17.

under the common law system. In the jury system, the judge will not know whether a piece of evidence is decisive or not in the jury's eyes, so it was suggested that the judge would have to rule inadmissible any witness statement capable of proving decisive. If 'decisive' means capable of making a difference between a finding of guilt and innocence, then this seemed to point to all hearsay evidence being excluded.

When the fourth section decision in *Al-Khawaja and Tahery* was referred to the Grand Chamber, the ECtHR clarified that the word 'decisive' should not be construed broadly to mean that almost all evidence would qualify as 'decisive' but should be narrowly understood as indicating evidence of such significance or importance as is likely to be determinative of the outcome of the case.[35] But the broader methodological challenge that the sole or decisive rule poses to the common law model is that it re-engages the law of evidence in the logical analysis of evidence. The judge is no longer required to apply a technical rule (hearsay) and its exceptions in a binary fashion, determining whether the evidence is accordingly admissible or inadmissible, but is instead required to make a wholesale rounded assessment of the importance of the evidence to the case as a whole and the jury under judicial direction must then likewise make its own assessment of the evidence in this manner. This is a shift towards 'forensic reasoning rules', as Roberts and Zuckerman have called them, as opposed to the conventional exclusionary rules of evidence at common law. In contrast to the common law's atomistic admissibility determinations (deferring holistic evaluation of evidence to the jury), the ECtHR is requiring judges to engage in holistic evaluation before the evidence gets to the jury.

Interestingly, however, the Grand Chamber defended its rule against the charge that the rule could not be practically applied in the common law system on the ground that the common law courts had *themselves* resorted to the very same sole or decisive rule when it had considered whether anonymous witness evidence should be admissible in criminal trials. Rather than formulating a binary approach towards anonymous witness evidence whereby it was either admissible or not, the House of Lords in *R v. Davis*[36] had fashioned a rule (drawing it would seem from the language of the ECtHR) that a conviction which was based solely or to a decisive extent on statements or testimony of anonymous witnesses could not be regarded as 'fair', adding that 'this was the view traditionally taken by the common law of England'.[37]

---

[35] *Al-Khawaja and Tahery v. UK* (2012) 54 EHRR 23 [131].
[36] *R v. Davis (Iain)* [2008] UKHL 36.
[37] Ibid. [25] per Lord Bingham.

This case prompted the UK to reverse the binding effect of such a bright line rule by replacing it with legislation that allowed judges to make witness anonymity orders, but interestingly the effect of such a rule was not wholly extinguished, as one of factors to which judges were to have regard in deciding to make such an order was whether the witness's evidence might be the 'sole or decisive' evidence against the accused.[38] The ECtHR also drew attention to another context in which a 'sole or decisive' rule had been incorporated into English law relating to the drawing of adverse inferences from an accused's silence. In *Murray* v. *UK*[39] the Court had approved the drawing of inferences from accused persons in certain circumstances when the evidence against the accused called for an explanation, but it hedged this with various safeguards, one of which was that it would be incompatible with the right of silence to base a conviction 'solely or mainly' on the accused's failure to give evidence or on a refusal to answer questions put to him. The Court did not add but it seemed to imply, rightly, that such a rule had been successfully integrated into English law without much protest.[40] Moreover in the latest legislative attempt to codify hearsay law in the Criminal Justice Act 2003, the UK Parliament had itself begun to shift the moorings of hearsay law away from a purely exclusionary or inclusionary approach by empowering the trial judge at the end of the prosecution case to direct an acquittal where he or she is satisfied that the case against the defendant is based 'wholly or partly' on a statement not made in oral evidence in the proceedings and the evidence provided by the statement is so unconvincing that, considering its importance to the case against the defendant, his conviction of the offence would be unsafe.[41]

Rather than pointing to the impracticality of applying the sole or decisive rule in the common law context, these shifts away from a purely exclusionary approach towards the need to adopt a more holistic approach towards 'suspect' evidence point to the fact that such a rule could be successfully integrated into English law. This has produced a far more harmonic convergence than was suggested possible in the *Horncastle* decision between the common law as it has been developing in more recent years and the human rights approach. The challenge that the 'sole or decisive' rule posed to the more flexible approach towards the admissibility of hearsay that had been developed in the Criminal Justice Act 2003 was more serious.

---

[38]   Coroners and Justice Act 2009, s. 89(2)(c).
[39]   [1996] 22 EHRR 29.
[40]   The 'solely or mainly' phraseology has been incorporated into judicial directions to the jury. See *R* v. *Petkar* [2003] EWCA Crim 2668.
[41]   Criminal Justice Act 2003, s. 125(1).

6.5 THE FAIR PARTICIPATION CHALLENGE

The more substantive challenge that the new Strasbourg rules mounted to the common law approach lay in the way in which these appeared to elevate considerations of fair participation in the proceedings above the traditional considerations of truth-finding that had long provided a motivating factor for rules governing confessions and hearsay. The common law as we have seen had always accepted that involuntary confessions were inadmissible but the new *Salduz* doctrine now prescribed that *any* use of incriminating statements for a conviction when made during police interrogation without access to a lawyer would in principle prejudice the rights of the defence, even when presumably it is considered that they are reliable and voluntary. Furthermore, the Court suggested that this would be the case even where, as the Court conceded there could be, compelling reasons for not granting access to a lawyer. This suggested that the right of access to a lawyer is grounded in more than simply the privilege against self-incrimination, long embedded as a principle within the common law. In justification of its rule, the ECtHR stated that access to a lawyer would help ensure the right of an accused not to incriminate himself. Such a right presupposed that the prosecution in a criminal case must seek to prove their case against the accused without resort to evidence obtained through methods of coercion or oppression in defiance of the will of the accused. But the Court also seemed to extend its justification for access to a lawyer on the broader, more participative principle of equality of arms between the investigating or prosecuting authorities and the accused.[42] In later judgments the ECtHR expressly linked the *Salduz* doctrine to the need to secure 'the fundamental aspects' of . . . (the) defence' such as the 'discussion of the case, organisation of the defence, collection of evidence favourable to the accused, preparation for questioning, support of an accused in distress and checking of the conditions of detention'.[43]

This participative strand to the fair trial standards is also very evident in the 'sole or decisive' rule relating to unexamined statements which in *Al-Khawaja* was applied even where there was a good reason for the non-attendance of the witness. The common law has long recognised the importance of the defendant being able to confront his accusers and cross-examine them. Indeed the 'sole or decisive' rule relating to anonymous statements articulated by the House of Lords in *Davis* gave particular expression to the content of these principles. However, there has also been a strong reliability strain built into the common law, reinforced by the statutory provisions relating to hearsay in the

---

[42] (2009) 49 EHRR 421 [53].
[43] *Dayanan v. Turkey* ECtHR, 13 October 2009 [32].

Criminal Justice Act 2003, which has admitted hearsay where it is reliable or is the best evidence available. Before Al-Khawaja's case came to be determined in Strasbourg, the Court of Appeal had stressed that where a witness who is the sole witness of a crime has made a statement to the police and that witness has since died (as happened in *Al-Khawaja*), there may be a strong public interest in the admission of the statement as evidence so that the prosecution may proceed.[44] This did not mean that such a statement would automatically be admissible. There was a provision under the legislation for the judge to exclude the statement if he or she considered it had insufficient value and as we have seen there is also provision to direct an acquittal where reliance on such a statement would make a conviction unsafe.[45] When the case came to Strasbourg, however, the Court in its fourth section decision ruled that the use of such a statement constituted a violation of Article 6(1) and Article 6(3)(d) of the Convention. The Court could envisage no counterbalancing factors that would be sufficient to justify the introduction in evidence of an untested statement which was the sole or decisive basis for the conviction of an applicant other than in an exceptional case where the witness had been kept from giving evidence through fear induced by the defendant.[46]

For the justices of the Supreme Court in *Horncastle* this went too far. According to Lord Phillips, who gave the sole unanimous judgment of the Court, *Al-Khawaja* was the first case where the sole or decisive test had been applied in a case so as to produce a finding of a violation of Article 6 where there had been justification for not calling the witness (since the witness had died) and where the evidence was demonstrably reliable.[47] This was also the first case where the rule was applied in a case from England and Wales and no consideration had been given as to whether it was necessary or appropriate to apply the rule having regard to the safeguards contained in the Criminal Justice Act. His lordship considered that the justification for the sole or decisive test appeared to be that the risk of an unsafe conviction based solely or decisively on anonymous or hearsay evidence was so great that such a conviction can never be permitted.[48] But by building in safeguards the Criminal Justice Act had shown that there were less draconian ways of protecting against that risk. His lordship's preoccupation was very much about ensuring the reliability of the evidence. Earlier his lordship indicated that there are two principal objectives of a fair criminal trial – that

---

[44] *R* v. *Al-Khawaja* [2005] EWCA Crim 2697.
[45] Criminal Justice Act 2003, s. 125 (1), s. 126(1).
[46] *Al-Khawaja and Tahery* v. *UK* (2009) 49 EHRR 1 [37].
[47] [2009] UKSC 14, [94].
[48] Ibid. [86].

a defendant who is innocent should be acquitted and that a defendant who is guilty should be convicted.[49] He stated that the first objective carries more weight than the second, but the emphasis placed on these objectives emphasises that a clear priority should be given to epistemic concerns in the criminal trial. On this view, the right to cross-examination is not sacrosanct; instead, everything turns on the presumptive reliability of the statements made by witnesses.

What this view fails to encapsulate, however, is that a fair verdict is more than simply a reliable verdict (Hoyano, 2014). The sole or decisive rule may be justified on a participatory, rather than on a pure epistemic basis, which holds that witnesses put forward by either party must be able to be effectively tested by the other. The more a case rests upon witness statements in respect of whom there is an absence of supporting evidence, the more it can be said that fairness requires that there should be an opportunity to examine these witnesses. The point is not that the witness needs to be examined to determine whether his or her evidence is reliable. The question is rather whether, as a matter of fairness, the defence ought to be given an opportunity to put a version of events directly to an important witness which is different from that advanced by the prosecution. If the prosecution has been able to question a witness and rely on a statement which is clearly incriminatory, why should the defence not be able to probe the witness who made it? Institutional equality between the parties in order that the tribunal of fact can reach an impartial evaluation of the evidence would seem to demand this.

Unfortunately, however, the strong claims that the Strasbourg rules in *Salduz* and *Al-Khawaja* seemed to make for meaningful defence participation in both the investigatory and trial processes have since been rolled back by the ECtHR in favour of what would seem to be the classic common law concern for the reliability of the verdict, with fairness relegated as a mere side-constraint to ensuring that defendants are treated fairly in the criminal justice process and not coerced into making involuntary statements. It did not take long for this rolling back to start to happen. When the UK government asked for the fourth section decision in *Al-Khawaja and Tahery* to be referred to the Grand Chamber, the Grand Chamber issued a decision which turned the 'sole or decisive' rule into more of a flexible standard, restoring a strong reliability rationale into the Court's decision making and reaffirming the dominance of the common law approach.[50]

---

[49] Ibid. [18].
[50] *Al-Khawaja and Tahery* v. *UK* (2009) 49 EHRR 1.

6.6 STRASBOURG ROLLS BACK ITS OWN RULES

Much of the language in the Grand Chamber in *Al-Khawaja* express a strong determination to uphold the sole or decisive rule. The UK based its challenge to the rule on the Supreme Court judgment in *Horncastle*. It was argued that the rule seemed to have been particularly directed at civil law jurisdictions which had not accommodated the right to examination as comprehensively as common law jurisdictions. Common law countries had by contrast long developed a hearsay rule which addressed that aspect of fair trial that Article 6(3)(d) of the ECHR was designed to ensure. The Grand Chamber accepted that much of the impact of Article 6(3)(d) was on continental procedures which previously allowed an accused person to be convicted on the basis of evidence from witnesses whom he or she had not had an opportunity to challenge. However, the cases of *Al-Khawaja and Tahery* where the accused had been convicted on hearsay evidence would not have arisen if the strict common law rule against hearsay had been applied and the Criminal Justice Act had not provided for exceptions which allowed for the admission of witness statements in these cases. While it was important for the Court to have regard to substantial differences in legal systems and procedures, it had to apply the same standard of review under Article 6(1) and (3)(d) irrespective of the legal system from which a case emanates. As we have seen, the Court similarly rejected the argument that the rule could not be applied within the common law system.

When it came to consider the substance of the rule, however, we see the Court coming to a gradual acceptance of the 'reliability' grounds that were used to attack the rule and finally coming almost to a full-scale endorsement of a reliability approach which has arguably fatally undermined the right to examine witnesses. The Court rejected the UK submission based on *Horncastle* that the rule was predicated on the false assumption that all hearsay evidence which is crucial to a case is either unreliable or incapable of proper assessment. Instead, the Court said it is predicated on the principle that the greater the importance of the evidence, the greater the potential unfairness to the defendant in allowing a witness to remain anonymous or to be absent from the trial. So far, so good. But it then conceded that the rule is based largely on a reliability rationale by saying that where there was such potential unfairness, there was a greater need for 'safeguards to ensure that the evidence is demonstrably reliable or that its reliability can properly be tested and assessed'.[51] It then went on to undercut the significance of the right to examine witnesses under Article 6(3)(d) by saying that it has always 'traditionally' interpreted Article 6(3) in the context of an overall

---

[51] Ibid. [139].

examination of the fairness of the proceedings. Directing itself specifically to the sole or decisive rule, it stated that it should not be applied in an inflexible manner. Seemingly reining back from its earlier statement about the need to apply objective standards across all the member states, it considered that it would not be correct to ignore entirely the specificities of the particular legal system concerned and in particular its rules of evidence. To do so would transform the rule into a blunt instrument and indiscriminate instrument that runs counter to the traditional way in which the Court approaches the issues of overall fairness of the proceedings, namely to weigh in the balance the competing interests of the defence, the victim, and witnesses and the public interest in the effective administration of justice.[52] Far from introducing a more flexible element into the rule, however, it seemed then to take the bite out of the rule altogether when it said that where a conviction is based solely or decisively on the evidence of absent witnesses, this was now only one important factor to be balanced in the scales and the question in each case was whether there were 'sufficient counterbalancing factors' in place including strong procedural safeguards to permit a 'fair and proper assessment of the reliability of the evidence to take place' so that a conviction based on such evidence would only be permitted where it was sufficiently reliable given its importance to the case.[53]

When the Court came to apply these principles, it ironically seemed to come close to appropriating for itself a fourth instance role, something it has always said it would not do, by looking not only for strong procedural safeguards but also by making an overall assessment of the reliability of the evidence. The Court first looked at the safeguards in the English legislation that enabled judges to prevent juries considering sole or decisive witness statements, even though convictions may be based on such statements, and considered that they were in principle strong safeguards to ensure fairness. It then looked at the facts of the particular cases before it and considered whether there was corroborative evidence to establish the reliability of the hearsay, ruling that in the *Al-Khawaja* case, involving the statement of a dead witness, there was but that in the *Tahery* case, involving the statement of a witness in fear, there was not. The counterbalancing factors that were considered, in other words, were not only whether there were procedural safeguards assisting the defence to overcome the disadvantage they were under in not being able to examine the witnesses but also evidential considerations such as the strength of any corroborating evidence. In subsequent cases the ECtHR has taken a similar approach, determining the question whether the proceedings were

---

[52] Ibid. [146].
[53] Ibid. [147].

fair overall according to whether there was or was not 'strong corroborative evidence' or in some cases determining whether the witness evidence was sole or decisive evidence in the first place.[54]

The most recent Grand Chamber decision in *Schatschaschwili* v. *Germany*[55] on the non-attendance of important witnesses seems to accentuate this trend towards examining the reliability of the evidence and diminishing the importance of defence participation, in terms of being able to examine witnesses. In this case the ECtHR considered that the lack of a good reason for the non-attendance of a witness did not in itself violate the accused's right to a fair trial. In *Al-Khawaja and Tahery* the Court had said that the requirement that there be a good reason for admitting the evidence of an absent witness was a preliminary question to be examined before any consideration is given as to whether that evidence was sole or decisive.[56] In a number of decisions before *Al-Khawaja and Tahery*, the Court had found that even where the evidence of an absent witness had not been sole or decisive, there was a violation of Articles 6(1) and 3(d) when no good reasons had been shown for failing to have the witness examined.[57] In *Schatschaschwili*, however, the Grand Chamber considered that even though there were good reasons why in the instant case two decisive witnesses who had been robbed in their apartment could not attend (as the trial court had taken all reasonable steps to try to secure their attendance after they had fled to Latvia), the absence of a good reason for the non-attendance of a witness was not in itself conclusive of the unfairness of a trial. Following the approach adopted in *Al-Khawaja and Tahery* where the Grand Chamber departed from the indiscriminate sole or decisive rule and had regard in the 'traditional' way to the fairness of the proceedings as a whole, the Grand Chamber said that it would amount to a new indiscriminate rule if a trial were considered to be unfair for lack of a good reason for a witness's non-attendance alone, even if the untested evidence was neither sole nor decisive and was possibly even irrelevant to the outcome of the case.

Although the Court went on to say that the lack of a good reason for a prosecution witness's absence was a very important factor to be weighed in the balance when assessing the overall fairness of the proceedings, the extent to which the Court is prepared to tolerate the non-attendance of an important (if not decisive) witness for no good reason, thereby depriving the defence of an opportunity to cross-examine the witness, can be illustrated in *Seton*

---

[54] Jackson and Summers, 2013.
[55] *Schatschaschwili* v. *Germany*, 15 December 2015.
[56] Ibid. [120].
[57] See e.g., *Ludi* v. *Switzerland*, 15 June 1992; *Mild* v. *Finland*, 26 July 2005; *Bonev* v. *Bulgaria*, 8 June 2006; *Pello* v. *Estonia*, 12 April 2007.

v. *UK*.[58] In this case the English Court of Appeal had upheld the judge's decision to admit under the Criminal Justice Act the hearsay evidence of a phone call by a serving prisoner in which the prisoner denied responsibility for a murder which the defendant alleged that he had committed.[59] The prisoner had refused to give a statement to the police or to testify. In its decision the fourth section of the ECtHR considered that there was no good reason for the non-attendance of the witness (he could have been compelled to attend), but nevertheless found there had been no violation of Article 6 as there was other 'overwhelming' evidence against the defendant. The case serves as a classic illustration of how the apparent reliability of the rest of the evidence was deemed to make the proceedings as a whole fair, thereby aligning reliability of the evidence very closely with fairness.

The reiteration of the traditional approach of looking at the overall fairness of the proceedings has also come into play in the Court's more recent interpretation of the *Salduz* rule. In *Ibrahim and others* v. *UK*[60] the ECtHR introduced a two-tier test into considering whether restricting the *Salduz* right of access to a lawyer violated a fair trial. The first question was whether there were compelling reasons for the restriction of access and the second question was whether the restriction had an impact on the overall fairness of the proceedings. The rigour of the *Salduz* doctrine rule seemed to be diluted here in two respects. First of all, it will be recalled that in *Salduz* the Court had accepted that there could be compelling reasons for the restriction of access but considered that where there were not Article 6 required that 'as a rule' access be provided. The question left unanswered was what meaning to give to 'as a rule'. Was it to be interpreted to mean that where there were not compelling reasons for the restriction, there would be an automatic breach of Article 6 as, on one view, the Court intended? Or did it mean only that where there were no compelling reasons there would be merely a presumption of unfairness and that the Court could go on in the traditional manner to consider whether the proceedings as a whole were fair? In *Ibrahim*, the Court was satisfied that there were compelling reasons for restricting access to three of the applicants given the urgent need in the circumstances to question them about the whereabouts of bombs which it was feared they had planted in the London underground. But then paralleling its stance in *Schatschaschwili* where the Court said that the absence of good reasons for the non-attendance of a witness would not necessarily violate a fair trial, the Court

---

[58] *Seton* v. *UK*, 31 March 2016.
[59] *R* v. *Seton* [2010] EWCA Crim 450.
[60] *Ibrahim and others* v. *UK* (2015) 61 EHRR 9.

took the view that the absence of compelling reasons similarly does not necessarily violate a fair trial. Instead, there was a presumption of unfairness in such a case which it was for the government to rebut.

A good illustration of how this can dilute the rigour of the *Salduz* rule can be seen in the Grand Chamber case on the interpretation of the *Salduz* rule, *Simeonovi* v. *Bulgaria* where the Court found by twelve votes to five that despite the absence of compelling reasons for restricting the applicant's access to legal assistance while he had been in custody, the government had rebutted unfairness by showing that he had not been prejudiced by this restriction.[61] The applicant's right to legal assistance had been restricted for the first three days of his police custody. He had then made a voluntary confession two weeks later in the presence of a lawyer. The Court said that no causal link was ever posited between the absence of a lawyer for the first three days of custody and the confession that was used, amongst other evidence, to convict him. The Court found that although there had not been compelling reasons for restricting his right of access to a lawyer, the fairness of the proceedings, taken as a whole, had not been irretrievably prejudiced by the absence of a legal assistance while he had been in police custody.

The second respect in which the *Salduz* rule seemed to be diluted in *Ibrahim* relates to what is meant by the fairness of the proceedings. In *Salduz* as we have seen fairness seemed to be equated with not unduly prejudicing the rights of the accused under Article 6 even where there were compelling reasons for restricting the right of access. Such rights were considered to be irretrievably prejudiced when incriminating statements were made in the absence of a lawyer. In *Ibrahim*, a somewhat different approach was taken to fairness. The decision was made in the context of a case where the applicants had been convicted of conspiracy to murder for detonating bombs which failed to explode on three underground trains and a bus in central London two weeks after four suicide bombs exploded on three underground trains and a bus, killing fifty-two people and injuring hundreds more. The Court considered that there could be no question of watering down fair trial rights for the sole reason that the individuals in question were suspected of involvement in terrorism.[62] But then, in the very next sentence it appeared to contradict itself, by stating that when determining whether the proceedings as a whole have been fair the weight of the public interest in the investigation and punishment of the particular offence in issue may be taken into consideration,

---

[61] *Simeonovi* v. *Bulgaria*, ECtHR, 12 May 2017. See also *Beuze* v. *Belgium*, ECtHR, 9 September 2018.

[62] *Ibrahim and others* v. *UK* (2015) 61 EHRR 9, [252].

while not extinguishing the very essence of the applicants' defence rights.[63] This balancing of the individual defence rights against the public interest seemed then to lead the Court, as it had done previously in *Al-Khawaja and Tahery*, towards putting a high premium on the weight or reliability of the evidence against the defendant when considering the fairness of the proceedings as a whole. In setting out a number of relevant factors to be considered the Court put considerable emphasis on the quality and significance of the evidence that was obtained in the context of the evidence as a whole.[64] The Court appeared to be suggesting that the more important the evidence in the context of the prosecution case, the more vulnerable the suspect and the greater the risk of unreliability, the greater the impact will be on the fairness of the proceedings. On the facts of the case, the Court considered that the three applicants who had lied to the police when questioned in the absence of a lawyer had had these lies admitted as evidence against them as merely one element of a substantial prosecution case and in their cases it was satisfied that the proceedings as a whole were fair. By contrast, the admissions which the fourth applicant had made when questioned without being cautioned by the police in the absence of a lawyer had formed an integral and significant part of the evidence on which his conviction was based and the Court considered that in his case the proceedings were unfair.

In both respects in which it can be argued that the *Salduz* rule was diluted in *Ibrahim* – in regard to the need to assess the fairness of the proceedings as a whole even where there are not compelling reasons for restricting access to a lawyer and in regard to how the fairness of the proceedings as a whole is assessed– it is troubling that just as we saw in respect of the watering down of the 'sole or decisive' rule as applied to unexamined statements, the ECtHR has shifted the emphasis away from defence rights and put greater reliance on balancing these against the public interest in ensuring that the guilty are punished. It is true that in *Ibrahim* the Court emphasised that public interest concerns cannot extinguish 'the very essence' of an applicant's rights. But if these rights can be overridden in the interests of an overall fairness test that puts a heavy weight on the reliability of the evidence as a whole, it is hard to see how their essence is not taken away (see also Goss, 2017). As the minority judgment makes clear, there was no logically compelling ground to claim that only an 'overall fairness' evaluation (based on the outcome of the trial) can

---

[63]   Ibid. See Goss, 2017: 1148–9, arguing that the ECtHR attempts to have it both ways: Article 6 rights cannot be watered down when a particularly serious offence has been committed but the rights can be 'balanced away' when terrorism is concerned.
[64]   Ibid. [274].

result in a finding of a violation of Article 6.[65] When one looked at the history of the court's case law, there was nothing unique in the *Salduz* approach of considering a specific factor to be so decisive to fairness of the proceedings as to enable the fairness of the trial to be assessed simply on the basis of this factor. In other words, violations of certain bright line rules are so prejudicial per se to the overall fairness of the proceedings that there is no need to make any further assessment. Instead the ECtHR would seem to have adopted the common law approach of giving weight to the reliability of evidence and the outcome of the trial over defence rights, without realising that a harmonic convergence between truth-finding and fairness requires that these two considerations are not put in opposition, with one necessarily dominating the other, but that in the interests of the overall integrity of the proceedings truth-finding is only achieved through fairness.

6.7 CONCLUSION: THE COMMON LAW VINDICATED OR RE-IMAGINED?

In earlier sections we have reviewed how in recent jurisprudence of the ECtHR through the development of strong principles like the *Salduz* rule and the 'sole or decisive' rule, common law judges have been encouraged to shift away from atomistic towards more holistic approaches to factual reasoning and to shift away from the common law emphasis on truth-finding where fairness is considered to be a mere side-constraint on the overall search for rectitude. It is true that there were signs of these shifts occurring anyway, as judges have come to grapple more with 'forensic reasoning rules' and with the importance of procedural rights. But the emphasis of the ECtHR on defence participation as a vital element of a fair trial at both investigatory and trial processes has been a distinctive contribution that has encouraged a shift away from purely protective rights towards more participatory rights. More recently, however, the ECtHR has taken some of the bite out of its participatory rules by equating fairness of the proceedings as a whole with whether there has been a fair (reliable) outcome. This might seem to be a vindication of the traditional common law approach and has led to a more harmonic convergence between common law evidence and human rights law. But in another sense, it can be said to set back the potential for a harmonic convergence between truth and fairness where each goal is achieved through procedures that allow for meaningful participation between the parties.

---

[65] Joint partly dissenting, partly concurring opinion of Judges Sajo and Laffranque.

It would be wrong to end on too negative a note. The ECtHR continues to play a useful role in giving an independent voice to important principles which have the potential to influence the development of the common law of evidence and push it in the direction of a more harmonic convergence of principles. This can be illustrated by looking at two more positive features of the Grand Chamber decisions in *Schatschaschwili* and *Ibrahim*. Although we have seen that the *Schatschaschwili* decision gave priority to the 'fairness as a whole' principle when there has been no good reason for the non-attendance of witnesses, it went on to give a majority decision that has potentially wide-ranging significance for common law evidence. The Court concluded that on the facts of the case the evidence of the two witnesses was decisive in terms of being determinative of the applicant's conviction. The trial court had scrutinised the reliability of their statements in a careful manner but hardly any procedural measures had been taken to compensate for the defence's lack of opportunity to directly cross-examine the witnesses at trial. In particular, the Court pointed to the failure at the investigation stage when the investigating judge had heard the witnesses to provide for any defence examination of the witnesses. Overall, the ECtHR concluded that given the importance of the statements, the counterbalancing measures had been insufficient to permit a fair and proper assessment of the reliability of the untested evidence.

This re-assertion of the importance of procedural measures to compensate for the absence of examination at trial is a welcome expression of the continuing importance of finding a way to provide for some measure of defence participation other than giving the defendant an opportunity simply to give his own version of the facts. *Salduz* heralded an important change in terms of the participation of defence counsel at the investigative stage of police questioning of suspects and now it would seem that *Schatschaschwili* is exhorting member states to build in mechanisms for the participation of the defence at the investigatory stage of questioning witnesses. It has repercussions, however, for the common law model of evidence which has traditionally focused on the principle of defence participation at trial. Although it would seem that common law systems have adjusted to the *Salduz* principle, the notion that counsel should have a role in questioning witnesses who are likely to be absent at trial is a new challenge.

The other example of the ECtHR's role in encouraging states to comply with principle is to be seen in the *Ibrahim* decision itself. We have seen that the Court considered that there were compelling reasons to restrict access to legal advice to three of the four applicants based on the urgency of the situation. This was another respect in which the majority judgment referred to the need to balance rights against the public interest. When it came to the fourth applicant, however, it considered there were not compelling reasons to restrict access here because the police had chosen to act completely outside the framework of domestic law. In particular, they failed to caution him at the point when it became clear he was no longer only a witness but was about to incriminate himself which was a deliberate flouting of the code of practice governing the detention and questioning of suspects. A significant minority of judges considered that it is hard to understand why if the urgent factual circumstances were enough to constitute compelling reasons to restrict access to the first three applicants, these were not enough to constitute compelling reasons in respect of the fourth applicant.[66] The minority, correctly it is submitted, considered that breaches of the code should have been more properly considered at the second stage of the test when considering the fairness of the proceedings as a whole, for one of the factors mentioned by the Court here was whether the framework governing pretrial proceedings and the admission of evidence had been complied with. The minority considered that the fact that the trial judge had discretion at trial to exclude the evidence when there had been breaches of the code meant there had been sufficient compliance with the rule of law. But this overlooks the need for a human rights court to be seen to be affirming the rule of law. Here there was no mere technical breach of the code; there was a deliberate flouting of the whole basis underlying the questioning of suspects which the trial judge had failed to consider when exercising his discretion to admit the statement.

The common law has long subscribed to principles such as a right to a fair trial and the rule of law. As we have seen, however, the common law model of evidence tended to give priority to the weight or probative value of the evidence in any particular case, although it has upheld protective principles such as the need to protect defendants against abuse and compelled incrimination. The ECtHR's wider agenda of introducing participatory principles into the forensic process has challenged this approach and although it has rolled back somewhat from imposing these principles on member states by making it clear that it will always look at the fairness of the proceedings as a whole, recent decisions show that this does not mean that the Court will always give overwhelming weight to the fairness or reliability of the outcome but will wish to ensure that counterbalancing procedures have been taken to try to accommodate participatory principles and that

---

[66] Partly dissenting opinion of Judges Hajuyev, Yudkivska, Lemmens, Mahoney, Silvis and O'Leary.

ultimately there has been respect for the rule of law in the procedures that have been followed.

REFERENCES

Dennis, I. (2020). *The Law of Evidence*, 6th ed., London: Sweet and Maxwell.

Giannoulopoulos, D. (2016). Strasbourg Jurisprudence, Law Reform and Comparative Law: A Tale of the Right to Custodial Legal Assistance in Five Countries. *Human Rights Law Review*, 16(1), 103–12.

Goss, R. (2017). Out of Many, One? Strasbourg's *Ibrahim* Decision on Article 6, *Modern Law Review*, 80(6), 1137–50.

Hoyano, L. (2014). What Is Balanced on the Scales of Justice? In Search of the Essence of the Right to a Fair Trial. *Criminal Law Review*, 1, 4–29.

Hunter, J. and Roberts, P. (2012). *Criminal Evidence and Human Rights: Reimagining Procedural Traditions*, London: Hart Publishing.

Jackson, J. (2005). The Effect of Human Rights on Criminal Evidentiary Processes: Towards Convergence, Divergence or Realignment. *Modern Law Review*, 68(5), 737–64.

Jackson, J. (2016). Responses to *Salduz*: Procedural Tradition, Change and the Need for Effective Defence. *Modern Law Review*, 79(6), 987–1018.

Jackson, J. and Roberts, P. (2018). Beyond Common Law Evidence: Reimagining, and Reinvigorating, Evidence Law as Forensic Science, in D. Brown and J. Turner, eds., *Oxford Handbook of Criminal Process*, New York: Oxford University Press.

Jackson, J. and Summers, S. (2012). *The Internationalisation of Criminal Evidence*. Cambridge: Cambridge University Press.

Jackson, J. and Summers, S. (2013). Confrontation with Strasbourg: UK and Swiss Approaches to Criminal Evidence. *Criminal Law Review*, 60(2), 115–31.

Pivarty, A. (2018). The Right to Custodial Legal Assistance in Europe: In Search for the Rationales. *European Journal of Crime, Criminal Law and Criminal Justice*, 26(1), 62–98.

Roberts, P. and Zuckerman, A. (2010) *Criminal Evidence*, 2nd ed., Oxford: Oxford University Press.

Spano, R. (2017). Terrorism and Article 6 of the European Convention on Human Rights, *6th Annual Lecture of the Human Rights Law Centre's International Humanitarian Unit*, University of Nottingham, 10 March 2017.

Swift, E. (2000). One Hundred Years of Evidence Law Reform: Thayer's Triumph. *California Law Review*, 88, 2439–76.

Thayer, J. B. (1898). *A Preliminary Treatise on Evidence at Common Law*, Boston: Little-Brown.

Trechsel, S. (2005). *Human Rights in Criminal Proceedings*, Oxford: Oxford University Press.

Trechsel, S. (2018). The Character of the Right to a Fair Trial, in J. Jackson and S. Summers, eds., *Obstacles to Fairness in Criminal Proceedings: Individual Rights and Institutional Forms*, London: Hart Publishing.

Wigmore, J. H. (1904). *A Treatise on the System of Evidence in Trial at Common Law*, 1st ed., Boston: Little-Brown.

PART III

ON EVIDENTIAL INFERENCES

7

Group Deliberative Virtues and Legal Epistemology

Amalia Amaya

7.1 INTRODUCTION

Collective agents play a critical role in the legal determination of facts. The jury remains the primary fact-finding institution in many legal cultures and multi-member courts are also entrusted, in some legal systems, with the task of determining the facts at trial. Notwithstanding the relevance of group decision-making in evidential reasoning in law, legal epistemology, for the most part, embraces a highly individualistic perspective. A focus on the individual processes of legal decision-making is also a characteristic of attempts to address problems of legal epistemology by using the framework of virtue theory. In this chapter, my aim is to contribute to the study of the social dimensions of deliberation about factual issues in law. More specifically, I will examine the relevance of group deliberative virtues, that is, the traits of character that enable sound group deliberation, to the epistemology of legal proof.

Group deliberation is a highly neglected topic in the burgeoning field of virtue theory. While interesting work has been done on the possibility of attributing virtues to collective decision-making bodies, such as whether the jury was fair, impartial or courageous, the (distinct) issue of which traits of character may foster a genuine and productive group deliberation have been largely obliterated in current virtue-oriented approaches to social epistemology.[1] However, deliberative virtues have been studied in different (and apparently unrelated) bodies of literature, most importantly, virtue politics, communicative theory and argumentation theory. In this chapter, I will draw on work on the deliberative virtues in these domains in order to provide an account of the relevance of group deliberative virtues to legal epistemology.

---

[1] See Fricker, 2010a; Lahroodi, 2007; Cordell, 2017.

The structure of this essay is as follows. In Section 7.2, I shall propose a typology of the main kinds of traits of character that are virtues in the context of group deliberation about factual issues in law. In Section 7.3, I will defend the value of these virtues by explicating the ways in which they contribute to sound legal decision-making about the facts being litigated on the part of juries and composite courts. Section 7.4 argues that group deliberative virtues help us correct critical deliberative distortions that threaten to undermine group decision-making on disputed questions of fact. I shall conclude by exploring some implications of the argument developed in this chapter for legal education as well as the design of legal fact-finding institutions.

7.2 DELIBERATIVE VIRTUES

Group deliberative virtues are those traits of character that foster a productive group deliberation. The criteria for determining whether a trait of character is a deliberative virtue is tied up with the goals of deliberation (see Cohen, 2017: 183). The ultimate end of group deliberation about factual issues in law is the acquisition of true beliefs about the facts being litigated.[2] As in any other deliberative setting, group deliberation about factual issues in law aims at finding the truth in a certain way, namely, through a process of reason exchange. Effective deliberating groups have a positive 'synergy,' where such synergy is not only a function of the output – the acquisition of true beliefs – but also of the quality of the argumentative process that results in such an output (see Aikin and Clanton, 2010: 414). Group deliberative virtues are traits of character that enhance group synergy insofar as they promote a kind of deliberative engagement that produces optimal epistemic outcomes.

Now, which traits of character best foster positive group synergy when deliberating about the facts at trial? First of all, members of the jury or composite courts should possess and exercise a number of *epistemic virtues*, such as open-mindedness, intellectual courage, perseverance, intellectual autonomy and thoroughness.[3] Secondly, there are a number of *moral virtues* that are critical to creating a deliberative environment that results in good epistemic outcomes. Friendliness, civility, humility, kindness, cooperativeness, temperance and respectfulness are some of the traits of character that promote the background conditions needed to enable a productive deliberation.[4] Thirdly,

---

[2] Subject to constraints, of course, deriving from other values that trials seek to protect.
[3] On epistemic virtues, see, among other, Zagzebski, 1996; Montmarquet, 1993; Roberts and Wood, 2007.
[4] On the importance of some of these moral virtues to deliberation see Aikin and Clanton, 2010: 415–20, and Harden Fritz, 2018.

deliberation is first and foremost a process of argumentation and this makes *argumentative virtues* pivotal for securing that group deliberation strikes a positive synergy (Cohen, 2005 and Aberdein, 2010). Willingness to engage in communication, to listen to others, to modify one's position and to question the obvious are some of the dispositions that contribute to enhancing the quality of group deliberation (Cohen, 2017: 183). Finally, group deliberation is a kind of communicative practice. Thus, those engaged in group deliberation should also exhibit a number of *communicative virtues*, such as sincerity, receptivity, and clarity (Cooper, 1994: 465–6).

　　These kinds of traits of character contribute in various ways to fostering a productive deliberation within the jury or the court. While distinct, there are interesting connections between the different categories of virtues that should not go unnoticed. Epistemic virtues have, of course, an epistemic rationale but they are also morally relevant. For example, there are epistemic reasons to be open-minded, but also moral reasons in that the open-minded person gives minority and marginalized voices a hearing (Aikin and Casey, 2016: 438). Not only there is a moral undercurrent to epistemic virtues, but there is also an epistemic undercurrent in moral virtues. Kindness towards other members of the deliberating group or temperance in the face of the heated emotions that might arise in the midst of the discussion are helpful in getting at the truth, for where there is a cooperative and friendly deliberative climate, people are more willing to share information, more open to criticism and more sincere about their views, all of which positively contribute to better epistemic outcomes. There are also important connections between epistemic and argumentative virtues in that the possession of some intellectual virtues manifests itself in a number of valuable dispositions in the context of argumentation.[5] For instance, the intellectually humble person will be willing to listen to others, question her own views, and revise them accordingly. Finally, communicative virtues are also importantly connected with both argumentative and epistemic virtues. For example, clarity in stating one's views is a critical virtue for a successful proponent and receptivity is central to genuinely exhibiting open-mindedness.

　　It is also important to notice that deliberative virtues contribute to group synergy both synchronically and diachronically. Group synergy depends not only on how a group deliberates at a time but also on whether it performs well over time (see Aikin and Clanton, 2010: 414). This distinction is critical in the

[5]　There is some controversy on how to distinguish argumentative virtues from epistemic virtues, see Aberdein, 2010: 173; Aikin and Clanton, 2010: 421; Aberdein, 2014: 88–9; and Cohen, 2007: 4–5.

context of legal fact-finding for jury deliberation may extend over the course of
several sessions and court members are likely to sit often in the same court
within a given jurisdiction. Deliberative virtues create a deliberative environment that facilitates a truth-conducive deliberation both at a specific instance
of group deliberation about the facts being litigated and over the course of
a trial or several trials. For example, civility 'keeps the avenues of communication open and it promotes continued dialogue' (see Cohen, 2017: 182),
which is arguably essential to secure not only a productive deliberation at
a given time but also the well-functioning of a jury or a multi-member court in
the longer run.

7.3 THE VALUE OF DELIBERATIVE VIRTUES

Deliberative virtues facilitate, as argued, group synergy, which is a function
not only of the goodness of the outcome but also of the quality of the
deliberative process in both a synchronic and a diachronic dimension.
Insofar as group deliberative virtues enable a productive group deliberation,
they are valuable, I would argue, from an epistemic, practical and moral-
political point of view.

7.3.1 Epistemic Value

Group deliberation often outperforms individuals in producing good epistemic outcomes. There is, as it were, a 'wisdom of the crowds' (Suroweicki,
2004) that the law may benefit from by entrusting fact-finding to composite
bodies. Group deliberation may lead to epistemic results which are not only
superior to those reached by solitary deliberation, but also better than the
statistical averaging of individual views within a group. There are also, however, as will be discussed below, important risks in group deliberation – which
may lead group deliberation seriously astray. Thus, it is critical to determine
the conditions under which group deliberation is likely to strike a positive,
rather than a negative, group synergy. There are several conditions concerning
the composition of the group – in terms of gender, social status, expertise, race
or cognitive diversity – that have been shown to have a significant impact on
the quality of group deliberation (see, among others, Karpowitz and
Mendelberg, 2007). The norms that structure deliberation (e.g. unanimity
rule versus majority rule) are also an important factor that determines whether
group deliberation is likely to be effective (Karpowitz and Mendelberg, 2007:
649). The character of individual deliberators and, more specifically, the
extent to which they possess and exercise the deliberative virtues has

a momentous influence in the truthconduciveness of group deliberation as well. Thus, group deliberative virtues – in conjunction with other criteria – are crucial for increasing the epistemic credentials of collective determinations of facts in law.

7.3.2 *Practical Value*

Accurate determinations of fact in law are to be reached in a specific way, namely, through the dialectical exchange of reasons with a view to solving disagreement and reaching consensus (or a qualified majority, in some legal systems). Thus, even if deliberation about factual matters in law is oriented towards the search for truth, it also has practical goals (i.e. the resolution of conflict) that are to be reached by argumentative means (rather than by flipping a coin or striking a bargain, for example). Group deliberative virtues are instrumental to the goal of resolving conflict by the force of argument. Argumentative and epistemic virtues are pivotal for promoting an effective group deliberation about the contested evidence and the beliefs about the facts under dispute and have thus an important dialectical value. Moral and communicative virtues help generate a deliberative environment that enables the group to successfully deal with disagreement and reach consensus (or at least a qualified majority). Critically, they are essential in bringing about the cooperative background that is needed for an argumentative practice to rationally solve conflict.[6] Thus, there is a practical rationale (in addition to an epistemic one) for promoting the possession and exercise of group deliberative virtues within legal fact-finding bodies.

7.3.3 *Moral-Political Value*

Legal fact-finding collegiate bodies (whether the jury or the court) are sites for public deliberation. As such, they are expected to conduct deliberation in a way that realizes the moral and political values enshrined in the legal and political culture. Group deliberative virtues, I would argue, contribute to bringing group deliberation about factual issues in law closer to the exemplary deliberative practice that is characteristic of a well working democracy. To begin with, the epistemic and practical reasons that have been given in support of group deliberative virtues have a moral and political import. To be sure, that factual determinations be accurate and reached through a rational process is a pivotal element of a democratic system of justice. Thus, to the extent that deliberative virtues help groups achieve epistemically justified outcomes and

---

[6]   On argumentation as a cooperative practice, see Gensollen, 2017.

rationally solve disagreement, they contribute to the realization of important democratic values. However, the relevance of group deliberative virtues for the affirmation of democratic values goes beyond their role in facilitating group deliberations that aim at the truth by way of argument. Group deliberation about factual determinations in law is also a critical public venue for social interaction and deliberative engagement among citizens and judges. In virtuous group deliberation, participants relate to each other with civility, kindness and respect; there reigns an egalitarian ethos that yields an inclusive deliberative environment in which different views are given a hearing and taken seriously; and argument exchange is done against a background of cooperation in pursuit of common ends. Given that all these features are a landmark of the kind of social relationships and deliberative endeavours that a democracy aspires to establish and promote, group deliberative virtues may be also justified on moral and political grounds.

7.4 GROUP-DELIBERATIVE VIRTUES AND DELIBERATIVE DISTORTIONS

Thus far I have argued that group-deliberative virtues (1) help groups reach epistemically justified outcomes; (2) contribute to successfully deal with disagreement and reach consensus; (3) generate a deliberative climate where (1) and (2) occur. Furthermore, I have argued that group-deliberative virtues not only help juries and courts effectively reach a decision about the facts being litigated that is based on epistemically sound factual determinations, but also enhance the moral quality of the deliberative process whereby such decisions are made. Now, I would like to argue that group-deliberative virtues, in addition to having a positive role in enabling productive group deliberation, also play a negative, remedial, role in that they may prevent certain distortions that threaten to taint group deliberation from arising.

There are four kinds of phenomena that distort group deliberation, with the result that groups often do not improve on and sometimes even do worse than their average median member.[7] These phenomena may result in the group converging on falsehood rather than truth. The four kinds of deliberative failure are as follows:

(1) *Amplification.* As is well known, individuals use heuristics that lead them to predictable errors and they are also subject to a number of identifiable bias (see Kahneman, 2011). There is significant evidence

---

[7]   See Sunstein and Hastie, 2015, ch. 1. See also Luskin et al., 2017.

that shows that individual cognitive errors are usually amplified as a result of group deliberation.

(2) *Homogenization.* Deliberation usually reduces variance as shared information crowds out information that is held by one or few members (common-knowledge effect) and people follow the statements of their predecessors, ignoring their private knowledge (cascade effects).

(3) *Polarization.* Members of deliberating groups end up adopting a more extreme version of their pre-deliberative tendencies.[8]

(4) *Domination.* The attitudes of members of deliberating groups shift towards the attitude of their socially advantage members.

There are two main reasons that help explain these deliberative failures. The first source for these failures is informational influences, that is, if group members share a particular belief, isolated or minority members might not speak out on the grounds that their own judgement must be wrong. A second reason for self-silencing involves social, rather than informational, influences in that people in a minority position might silence themselves out of fear for social sanctions, such as the risk of suffering reputational injury, being ridiculed, disliked or disapproved.[9]

Several strategies have been proposed to overcome the foregoing problems and increase the likelihood that group deliberation will outsmart individual deliberation (see Sustein and Hastie, 2015: ch. 6). My suggestion is that group deliberation is more likely to avoid deliberative distortions when group members embody the deliberative virtues. The claim is thus that deliberative virtues play a corrective role in that they prevent group deliberation from falling victim to amplification, polarisation, homogenisation and domination. In so doing, they crucially aid to achieve the aims of deliberation, as these phenomena make it less likely that the truth will emerge as a result of group deliberation and yield deliberative processes where consensus is impaired (polarisation) or badly reached (homogenisation and domination). As both psychologists and philosophers have argued, the virtues of character provide a way to correct a number of heuristics and biases that lead to systematic errors in individual reasoning.[10] Similarly, virtuous character traits may arguably help correct the epistemic functioning of groups.[11]

8   The phenomenon of group polarisation is well documented and there is also considerable support for the claim that group polarisation might also take place in multi-member courts. See Sunstein, 2000: 102–4.
9   See Sunstein and Hastie, 2015. See also Sunstein, 2008: 65–9.
10 See Kahneman, 2011: 46; Stanovich, 2009: 69; Roberts and West, 2015; Samuelson and Church, 2015; Bruin, 2013; and Correia, 2012.
11 This point is also argued by Talisse, 2007: 51.

A first way in which deliberative virtues may mitigate deliberative distortions is, precisely, by way of attenuating individual cognitive biases. As explained, the amplification of individual's cognitive errors is one of the reasons for deliberative failure. Thus, and pretty straightforwardly, the epistemic performance of a group will improve if there are fewer individual errors that may be augmented as a result of group deliberation. In addition, some biases have been shown to aggravate deliberative failures, such as group polarisation, so the correction of individual biases indirectly ameliorates group deliberation by mitigating the import of these failures (see Correia, 2012: 227).

Deliberative virtues also directly address the two main forces driving deliberative distortions, to recall, informational and social self-silencing. Self-silencing on the grounds that one's beliefs are likely to be incorrect given that they are contradicted by the majority position would arguably be less likely if individual deliberators are intellectually autonomous. Social self-silencing may also be attenuated if those in a minority position exhibit courage, which would be greatly facilitated if there is a cooperative and friendly deliberative environment, and those in a majority position are willing to listen to other viewpoints and show proper respect.

Deliberative virtues may effectively reduce the specific failings involved in group polarisation, homogenisation and domination as well. Group polarisation may be attenuated if individual deliberators have some key epistemic virtues, such as open-mindedness and intellectual humility, argumentative virtues, critically, willingness to listen to others and to modify one's position and moral virtues, like prudence or temperance. These virtues, among others, will help group deliberators to deal with disagreement and reach consensus, thereby avoiding problems of hang juries and difficulties associated to the court's reaching a joint judgment – which might compromise the group synergy of the court in future cases. Homogenisation –through both the cascade and the common knowledge effects – is less likely to take place if members of the jury and collegiate courts are tenacious, inquisitive and intellectually energetic – rather than simply following the lead of those who first happen to express their views, have a willingness to question the obvious – even when deeply held beliefs shared by the group are at stake, have intellectual autonomy, and thus are able to come up with their own independent views about the case instead of falling back on previously stated positions or uncritically accepting shared views within the group. These traits of character, among others, will enable group deliberation to reach a verdict that is fully responsive to the different perspectives hold by the group members and that is properly informed by the range of information and reasons available within the group. Domination is also mitigated when individual deliberators are humble – and thereby committed to an egalitarian stance,[12] civil and respectful, all of which generate a climate in which group members cooperate on an equal footing and social disadvantage does not translate into loss of credibility or lack of participation.

The claim that deliberative virtues may correct deliberative distortions may be questioned on the grounds that these distortions operate automatically and unconsciously, and thus are difficult to control even by the most well-intentioned member of the jury or the trial court.[13] However, there are several reasons why the seemingly unconscious and automatic nature of these failures does not detract from the remedial value of deliberative virtues. First, the virtues, once inculcated, become a kind of 'second nature', so that the virtuous response is in many cases automatic and does not require a conscious effort on the part of the individual deliberator (see Correia, 2012: 234 and Fricker, 2010b). In this sense, it may often counteract the unconscious process that leads to deliberative failures without taxing our cognitive resources and with the rapidity and efficacy required in contexts of legal decision-making about facts that are limited by severe time constraints.

Second, virtue, even if habitual, does involve in difficult cases a proper amount of reflection. Reflective abilities, alongside intuition, form the core of virtuous deliberation. For example, one may need to engage one's reflective abilities in order to determine when one needs to be open to other's peers arguments and when, to the contrary, one should ignore indefensible views or irrelevant objections.[14] Thus, hitting the right mean in a particular deliberative context may require a conscious effort on the part of the deliberator. Reflection may also be called for to deliberate in situations in which the virtues impose conflicting demands upon one's behaviour, for instance, to address conflicts between intellectual autonomy and intellectual humility or between willingness to modify one's position and intellectual integrity. In addition, virtue acquisition is the result, at least partially, of a conscious effort on the part of the individual. Just as self-reflective regulation has been shown to be an effective safeguard against a number of cognitive bias, which are also automatic and unconscious, virtuous deliberation – insofar as it involves conscious

---

[12] On the connection between humility and egalitarianism in the context of legal decision-making, see Amaya, 2018.
[13] This is an objection analogous to the objection according to which virtue cannot correct for non-volitional prejudices. On this objection, see Anderson, 2012; Alcoff, 2010. For a reply, see Fricker, 2010b.
[14] On failing to be open-minded by the vice of excess, see Aikin and Casey, 2016: 439 and Cohen, 2009.

reflection – may also be capable of mitigating deliberative distortions, even if these distortions, are, like individual cognitive biases, non-volitional (see Fricker, 2010b).

Third, structural remedies may nudge virtue remedies. Different structural mechanisms may be put in place to foster virtuous deliberation (see Anderson, 2012: 168). If deliberative virtue has not been practised enough to become habitual and if the reflective capacities involved in virtue have not been developed to a degree sufficient to enable virtuous responses in difficult situations, we can still facilitate the exercise of deliberative virtue in those that are less than virtuous through institutional design. Fact-finding institutions may structure jury and court deliberations in ways that enable the exercise of virtuous dispositions: for instance, one may indirectly promote impartiality by instructing jurors to seriously consider alternative views[15] and foster open-mindedness by asking them to overshoot on the side of charity in interpreting arguments, since we are naturally disposed towards dogmatism.[16] Norms of deliberation and even the framing of the deliberative setting may prove instrumental to nudging group deliberation in accordance to virtue.[17]

Thus, deliberative virtue may be effective in correcting deliberative distortions even if these operate at an unconscious level. This is not to say, of course, that virtue is the only way to avoid deliberative failures. There is an array of strategies, which are not virtue based, for structuring group deliberation that may prove useful for reducing deliberative failures, for example, the Delphi method – which involves the anonymous statement of private opinions prior to deliberation – or rewarding success (see Sunstein and Hastie, 2015: ch. 6). In addition, addressing deliberative failures seems to require structural remedies that go well beyond the design of fact-finding deliberative environments. Indeed, as seen, social segregation is a major factor leading to group dynamics that result in distortions in deliberation. Thus, large-scale social changes seem necessary to promote the kind of social of integration that is conducive to the well-epistemic functioning of group deliberation.[18] While important, the deliberative virtues –whether individually inculcated or structurally triggered – provide only part of the solution to the problem of deliberative distortions.

[15] This is the 'consider the opposite' instruction. See Simon, 2004.
[16] As demanded by the Aristotelian doctrine of compensation, see Aikin and Casey, 2016: 439.
[17] Even if, admittedly, they may not suffice to elicit genuinely virtuous behaviour. For a discussion of this objection, see Horowitz, 2009: 65–70.
[18] On group integration as a structural remedy for the lack of epistemic justice as an individual virtue, see Anderson, 2012: 171.

7.5 CONCLUSIONS

Legal determinations of fact are oftentimes the result of collective deliberation and this makes it imperative that the epistemology of legal proof pay attention to the social aspects of evidential reasoning in law. In this chapter, I have suggested that virtue epistemology may prove to be a useful framework for addressing the social dimensions of legal arguments about evidence and proof. More specifically, I have argued that deliberative virtues are critical for ensuring sound group deliberation. Communicative, epistemic, moral and argumentative virtues importantly contribute to realizing a number of values – epistemic, practical as well as moral and political values – which lie at the core of legal fact-finding institutions. In addition, they also have a momentous remedial value in that they provide a corrective to a number of deliberative distortions that undermine the epistemic well-functioning of group deliberation.

The claim that group deliberative virtues have an important place in the social epistemology of legal proof is not hopelessly idealistic, but it has important implications for both public policy and legal reform. In order to ensure virtuous group deliberation, it is necessary to shape citizens education and legal education so that there are opportunities for discursive engagement and training in the practice of argumentation. The design of fact-finding institutions is also pivotal to create the conditions under which virtuous dispositions are triggered. Larger structural reforms –as argued – are ultimately needed to bring about the kind of group integration which results in good epistemic outcomes. At the end of the day, virtuous group deliberation requires nothing less than the inculcation of civic virtues and an egalitarian ethos, both of which are necessary for a properly functioning democracy. Thus, the epistemological concerns driving inquiry into the inner workings of group determinations of legal facts end up overlapping with distinctively political concerns. In short, a virtue approach to the epistemology of legal proof turns out to be inextricably linked with a virtue politics.

REFERENCES

Aberdein, A. (2010). Virtue in Argument. *Argumentation*, 24, 165–79.
Aberdein, A. (2014). In Defense of Virtue: The Legitimacy of Agent-Based Argument Appraisal. *Informal Logic*, 34(1), 77–93.
Aikin, S. F. and Casey, J. P. (2016). Straw Men, Iron Men and Argumentative Virtue. *Topoi*, 35(2), 431–40.
Aikin, S. F. and Clanton, J. C. (2010). Developing Group Deliberative Virtues. *Journal of Applied Philosophy*, 27(4), 409–24.

Alcoff, L. M. (2010). Epistemic Identities. *Episteme*, 7(2), 128–37.

Amaya, A. (2018). The Virtue of Judicial Humility. *Jurisprudence*, 9(1), 97–107.

Anderson, E. (2012). Epistemic Justice as a Virtue of Social Institutions. *Social Epistemology*, 26(2), 163–73.

Cohen, D. H., (2005). Arguments that Backfire, in D. Hitchcock and D. Far (eds.), *The Uses of Argument*, OSSA, Hamilton, 58–65.

Cohen, D. H. (2007). Virtue Epistemology and Argumentation Theory, in H. V. Hanse et al. (eds.), *Dissensus and the Search for Common Ground*, OSSA, Windsor, 1–9.

Cohen, D. H. (2009). Keeping an Open Mind and Having a Sense of Proportion as Virtues in Argumentation. *Cogency*, 1(2), 49–64.

Cohen, D. H. (2017). The Virtuous Troll: Argumentative Virtues in the Age of Technologically Enhanced Argumentative Pluralism. *Philosophy and Technology*, 30(2), 179–89.

Cooper, N. (1994). The Intellectual Virtues. *Philosophy*, 69(270), 459–69.

Cordell, S. (2017). Group Virtues: No Great Leap Forward with Collectivism. *Res Publica*, 23(1), 43–59.

Correia, V. (2012). The Ethics of Argumentation. *Informal Logic*, 32(2), 222–41.

De Bruin, B. (2013). Epistemic Virtues in Business. *Journal of Business Ethics*, 113(4), 583–95.

Fricker, M. (2010a). Can There Be Institutional Virtues?, in T. Szabo and J. Hawthorne (eds.), *Oxford Studies in Epistemology*, Oxford: Oxford University Press, 235–52.

Fricker, M., (2010b). Replies to Alcoff, Goldberb, and Hookway on Epistemic Injustice. *Episteme*, 7(2), 164–78.

Gensollen, M. (2017). El lugar de la teoría de la virtud argumentativa en la teoría de la argumentación contemporánea, *Revista Iberoamericana de Argumentación*, 15, 41–59.

Harden Fritz, J. M. (2018). Communication Ethics and Virtue, in N. Snow (ed.), *The Oxford Handbook of Virtue*, Oxford: Oxford University Press.

Horowitz, P. (2009). Judicial Character and does It Matter. *Constitutional Commentary*, 26, 96–167.

Kahneman, D. (2011). *Thinking Fast and Slow*, New York: Farrar, Straus and Giroux.

Karpowitz C. F. and Mendelberg, T. (2007). Groups and Deliberation. *Swiss Political Science Review*, 13(4), 645–62.

Lahroodi, R. (2007). Collective Epistemic Virtues. *Social Epistemology*, 21(3), 281–97.

Luskin, R. C., Sood, G., Fishkin, J. S., and Hahn, K. S. (2017). Deliberative distortions? Homogenization, polarization, and domination in small group deliberations. Unpublished manuscript from the Center for Deliberative

Democracy, available at: https://cdd.stanford.edu/mm/2017/07/luskin-deliberative-distortions.pdf.

Montmarquet, A. J. (1993). *Epistemic Virtue and Doxastic Responsibility*, Lanham, MD: Rowman and Littlefield.

Roberts, R. C. and West, R. (2015). Natural Epistemic Defects and Corrective Virtues. *Synthese*, 192(8), 2557–76.

Roberts, R. C. and Wood, W. J. (2007). *Intellectual Virtues*, Oxford: Clarendon Press.

Samuelson, P. L. and Church, I. M. (2015). When Cognition Turns Vicious: Heuristics and Biases in Light of Virtue Epistemology, *Philosophical Psychology*, 28(8), 1095–113.

Simon, D. (2004). A Third View of the Black Box: Cognitive Coherence in Legal Decision-Making, *The University of Chicago Law Review*, 71, 511–86.

Stanovich, K. E. (2009). *What Intelligence Tests Miss: The Psychology of Rational Thought*, New Haven: Yale University Press.

Sunstein, C. (2000). Deliberative Trouble? Why Groups Go to Extremes, *The Yale Law Journal*, 110(1), 71–119.

Sunstein, C. (2008). *Infotopia: How Many Minds Produce Knowledge*, Oxford: Oxford University Press.

Sunstein, C. and Hastie, R. (2015). *Wiser: Getting Beyond Groupthink to Make Group Smarter*, Cambridge: Harvard Business Review Press.

Suroweicki, J. (2004). *The Wisdom of Crowds: Why Many Are Smarter than the Few and How Collective Wisdom Shapes Business, Economics, Societies and Nations*, New York: Doubleday.

Talisse, R. B. (2007). Why Democrats Need the Virtues, in L. E. Goodman and R. B. Talisse (eds.), *Aristotle's Politics Today*, Albany: State University of New York Press, 45–52.

Zagzebski, L. (1996). *Virtues of the Mind*, Cambridge: Cambridge University Press.

8

On Probatory Ostension and Inference

Giovanni Tuzet

8.1 INTRODUCTION: TWO THESES ON EVIDENCE

This chapter discusses two theses on juridical evidence: the *ostension thesis* and the *inference thesis*. According to the first, the process of juridical proof typically requires some ostensive act. In this sense the evidence consists in some element susceptible of being shown, or exhibited, or indicated to someone in a given context. According to the second thesis, the process of juridical proof requires necessarily some inference. In this process juridical evidence becomes the content of one or more inferences performed by the parties or by the fact-finders (judges or jurors). It can be the content of a premise which, together with other premises, leads to a conclusion about the disputed facts; or the content of a conclusion the premises lead to.

The two theses concern the *process* of juridical proof, but also the *evidence* involved in the process. For some characters of the process affect its content. Evidence is ostensively shown and inferentially processed.

I think that the second thesis is already well-established and well-received in the literature. For it is hard to deny that evidence per se does not prove anything: for probatory purposes, we need inferences and arguments constructed out of the evidentiary items that fit the admissibility requirements of the relevant context. So, I will rather concentrate on the first thesis, whose subject is somewhat neglected by the literature. I will address the probatory role of ostension, the logical structure of the ostensive act, and some points that pertain to the pragmatics of evidence discourse, namely the role of indexicals and demonstratives in this kind of discourse.

Let me stress that in the fact-finding process ostension comes first: parties present fact-finders with pieces of evidence and then elaborate probatory arguments out of them. No probatory inference can be performed without an ostensive input.

The structure of the chapter is as follows: I will outline the ostension thesis in Section 8.2, discussing in particular the indexical dimension of evidence discourse, the logical structure of the ostensive act, and what I call the 'Principle of Maximal Proximity'; then I will briefly address the inference thesis in Section 8.3; I will finally claim in Section 8.4 that both theses are necessary to an account of juridical evidence and proof, even if it can be argued that the ostension thesis is only synthetically true (true of many but not of all things we call 'evidence') while the inference thesis is analytically true (true of everything we call 'evidence', or true in virtue of the meaning of 'evidence').

8.2 THE OSTENSION THESIS

In order to move from evidence to verdict five requirements at least must be satisfied: *first*, evidence must be admissible according to the rules of the relevant legal system; *second*, it must be presented to fact-finders; *third*, it must be 'inferentialised' by parties and fact-finders, since evidence doesn't speak for itself and the participants to a dispute have to construct evidentiary arguments based on the items presented; *fourth*, evidence must be assessed to determine its probative value (or, better, the evidentiary inferences and arguments at stake must be assessed to determine the evidential support, or warrant, or justification provided by the premises to the conclusions); *fifth*, fact-finders need to consider whether the evidence (as assessed) meets the relevant standard of proof, or whether the relevant burden of proof has been satisfied.[1]

This section of the present chapter is on the second requirement of the above list; the next section will be on the third.

However, before addressing the ostension thesis, we must distinguish the relevant idea from that of an 'ostensive definition'. As the name makes clear, the act of ostensive definition consists in showing some item that indicates the meaning of a word or expression. Nicholas Rescher, for instance, takes ostensive definition to be the 'procedure of defining by *giving examples*' in that 'it frequently takes the form of actually pointing to instances, rather than simply listing them' (Rescher, 1964: 37–8).

This is not the place to recall and discuss the merits and limits of ostensive definitions. Suffice it to say that, on the one hand, they were cherished by (some of) the logical positivists of the Vienna Circle, who tried to use them to explain how our words and concepts connect to the world of empirically

---

[1] On this last point, see Allen, 2014.

detectable things.[2] On the other hand, they were deeply criticised by Wittgenstein (1953: § 28ff.), since he claimed that no ostensive act can convey any meaning unless it is part of an already established language game.[3]

Suppose I point my finger in the direction of Ludwig: am I pointing at Ludwig as a person? Am I pointing at him as a philosopher? Am I pointing at his face? At his nose? Etc. The ambiguity of pointing is remarkable.

That kind of ambivalence toward ostensive definitions can be found in Quine's work.[4] On the one hand, his writings frequently go back to the idea of learning a language through ostension; on the other, he insists on the inscrutability of reference and the indeterminacy of translation. The following passage exemplifies the first attitude:

> Many expressions, including most of our earliest, are learned *ostensively*; they are learned in the situation that they describe, or in the presence of the things that they describe. They are conditioned, in short, to observations; and to publicly shared observations, since both teacher and learner have to see the appropriateness of the occasion. (Quine, 1970/1986: 6)

But in many other passages, as well known, Quine claims that our theory of nature is underdetermined by all possible observations.[5]

An interesting thing that he points out, in any event, is the dependence of ostension success on identity criteria. This is an example he makes in *Identity, Ostension, and Hypostasis* (a paper originally published in 1950):

> if we were to point to *a*, and then wait the required two days and point to *b*, and affirm identity of the objects pointed to, we should thereby show that our pointing was intended not as a pointing to two kindred river stages but as a pointing to a single river which included them both. The imputation of identity is essential, here, to fixing the reference of the ostension. (Quine, 1953: 66)

I am going to assume that criteria of this sort exist in the legal domain too. (Of course, they exist in law. Every claim and every dispute about goods

---

2   Notice that also the logical positivists' *protocol sentences*, like 'Blue patch now' or 'Here now blue', had an ostensive aspect (if they are read in a non-solipsistic way, they point to public data). See Coffa, 1991: 176–7, 242, 249 ff. and 354 ff. See also Misak, 1995: 89–96.
3   'So one might say: the ostensive definition explains the use – the meaning – of the word when the overall role of the word in language is clear. Thus, if I know that someone means to explain a colour-word to me the ostensive definition 'That is called 'sepia' will help me to understand the word … One has already to know (or be able to do) something in order to be capable of asking a thing's name. But what does one have to know?' (Wittgenstein, 1953: § 30). Many references to showing, pointing to, etc. are also in Wittgenstein, 1968, where the limits of the ostensive act are pointed out along with the necessity of it for certain purposes.
4   See e.g., Quine, 1953: 66–7, Quine, 1960: 100–18 and Quine, 1969: 30–47, 121–5.
5   See e.g., Quine, 1969: 35, 45–7 and Quine, 1976: 254.

require identity conditions of such goods.) Now, that makes possible the use of ostension *for probatory purposes*. Identity imputation criteria are background conditions of ostensive proof. A successful pointing to some object for probatory purposes requires an understanding of the pointing intention based on the ontological criteria we share.

So, do not confuse (a) giving a sample to indicate how double bass sounds like, and (b) using a sample to show what instrument I play. The former can be taken as an ostensive definition of the double bass sound; the latter is a probatory ostension when someone disputes what musical instrument I play.

The ostension thesis does not concern the use of ostensive acts for definition or clarification purposes. It concerns the use of ostension for proof purposes. It concerns the use of ostension to support a factual claim, pointing at the evidence that justifies some such claim.

To restate it, consider that the process of juridical proof typically requires some ostensive act. In this sense the evidence consists in elements which are *not only perceptible but also susceptible of being shown, or exhibited, or indicated to fact-finders in the relevant context.*

The value of probatory ostension can be stressed going back to the classical distinction between knowledge by acquaintance and knowledge by description.[6] When I say 'I know Ludwig', I claim to have a kind of knowledge which is different from the one I claim when I say 'I know that Constantinople was taken by Mehmet the Conqueror in 1453'. The latter is knowledge by description (of the relevant fact or event put into propositional terms). The former is knowledge by acquaintance (of the relevant thing, person or situation, in virtue of perceptual connection with it). The description form is crucial for the transmission and preservation of knowledge. Typically, books contain knowledge by description. But description alone is unable to tell you where truth is.

Consider these descriptions and assume that one of them is true and the other false:

(1) On 2 January 1934 Ludwig had for breakfast a croissant, a cup of tea and some orange juice.
(2) On 2 January 1934 Ludwig had for breakfast some sausages, black coffee and a herring.

---

[6] See Russell, 1912/1998: 25–32, but also James, 1890/1981: 216–18. In fact, Russell conceived of the two as knowledge of things, while I think that knowledge by acquaintance is properly knowledge of things and knowledge by description is knowledge of facts. So, I use Russell's distinction with some liberty.

Which is the true one? 'The real world cannot be distinguished from
a fictitious world by any description', said Peirce (CP 2.337, c. 1895). Were
you there, you could have acquired by acquaintance some knowledge of
Ludwig's breakfast; in that very moment you could have shown to someone
else what Ludwig was having; later in time you could have shown a picture of it
in case you took one; and you could give a testimony about it if needed for
some purpose. Acquaintance conditions are a crucial part of ostension
conditions.

In the following of this section I will address more closely the probatory
value of ostension, together with its indexical dimension (Section 8.2.1); then
I will point out what the logical structure of ostension is (Section 8.2.2), and
I will present the Principle of Maximal Proximity (Section 8.2.3).

8.2.1 *Evidence, Ostension and Indexicality*

When we talk about ostension, the first thing that likely comes to mind is
pointing with one's finger. This is the kind of ostension which is most natural
when there is a material thing that we want to draw someone else's attention
to. This is pretty natural for babies. But also, adult life takes advantage from it.
In many situations pointing to something is easier, faster, and cheaper than
giving a description of it. If you ask me 'Where's Ludwig?', it's easier for me to
point at him and say 'There!', instead of saying 'He is on the third seat of
the second row of the Concert Hall'. Pointing is not the only modality of
ostension, though. As the pragmatist philosopher and social theorist George
Herbert Mead observed, we can accomplish an ostensive act in many different
ways:

> Whether one points with his finger, or points with the glance of the eye, or
> motion of the head, or the attitude of the body, or by means of a vocal gesture
> in one language or another, is indifferent, provided it does call out the
> response that belongs to that thing which is indicated. (Mead, 1934/1967: 97)

Provided the context and the background conditions make salient what
we are interested in, the glance of an eye may suffice. This calls for
a *functional conception of ostension*, where ostensive intention and response
are connected by several ostensive modalities such as pointing with one's
finger, pointing with the glance of the eye, or motion of the head, or vocal
gesture.

In legal proceedings rarely a gesture suffices. True, in a line-up identification procedure a pointed finger may suffice. But that is a kind of peculiar
situation. In the central case of ostension in legal proceedings the act is

accompanied by words or statements uttered by the relevant party to the relevant hearer in the relevant context. A material object is shown to the jury and the prosecutor explains it was found in the defendant's apartment; a picture is shown to the jury and the defendant explains that it was taken just before the crime; etc.

Notice that showing the thing without saying a word would be interlocutory to say the least. Fact-finders would wonder why the party behaves like that. (In exceptional circumstances a gesture might suffice, though.) On the other hand, a statement describing something which is not shown to the audience has far less probatory impact than a statement accompanying the thing shown. In the central case of ostension fact-finders perceive the thing, listen to what the party has to say about it and make up their minds as to its probative value.

I do not have data that support this intuition, but I believe that probatory discourse is characterised by the use of indexicals and demonstratives much more than normative discourse is. This is a point about the *pragmatics of legal discourse*, in one of its areas.

Contemporary pragmatics calls *indexicals* such words as 'I', 'you', 'here', 'now', words that refer to something without naming it, nor giving a description of it. And it calls *demonstratives* the words that perform a similar function pointing to something, like 'this' and 'that'.[7] It is not essential to discuss their properties and distinction here. We can simply talk of 'indexicality' in a broad sense encompassing the use of demonstratives and of indexicals properly understood.

The interesting feature of indexicality from a philosophical viewpoint is the connection it establishes with real world things. The use of indexicals is a linguistic way to perform the ostensive function outlined above. Charles Sanders Peirce pointed out that feature and discussed the 'existential connection' that indexicals have with their reference.[8] Hilary Putnam, among others, has elaborated on this and has claimed that ignoring the indexicality of most words is ignoring the contribution of the environment to our language and cognition (Putnam, 1975: 271).[9]

Now, evidence discourse as performed by the parties in a dispute is likely to be significantly characterised by the use of demonstratives and indexicals.

---

[7] The (disputed) difference between the two categories is that only indexicals enjoy semantic rules which determine their reference (for instance, 'I' refers to the speaker). See Levinson, 1983: 54 ff. As to the legal domain, see Capone and Poggi, 2016 and 2017.

[8] For an illuminating comment see Burks, 1949. See also Short, 2007.

[9] Cf. Putnam, 1975: 229–35 on indexicality, ostension and rigidity. See also Kripke, 1980. Consider in addition the indexicality of proper names (of parties, places, etc.) in the trial oral exchange and in the written documents including judicial opinions (case-specific information with proper names is necessary, for an indexicality-free description of the case is impossible); but note that this form of indexicality does not necessarily require ostension.

'Here is the object that was found'; 'That is the picture which was taken'; 'Listen to this declaration'; 'Look at that letter': these are some simple examples of what we are considering, that is, indexical evidentiary statements made with the ostension of the relevant item. Similarly, for the linguistic interaction with witnesses: 'Did you see him?'; 'That is the person I saw run away from the house'; 'Do you recognise this voice?'; 'This is John's voice, Paul's is that', etc.

At this point of the present discussion someone might critically observe that the ostension thesis fits the presentation of material or tangible evidence, of documents, pictures and the like, but not the use of testimony and of expert testimony in particular. Witnesses do not show anything, they do not point at ostensible things – in fact, so the argument would go, such things would be directly pointed at by the relevant party were they available. Witnesses tell stories; or, better, they report what they (think they) know about the litigated facts.

No doubt there is a difference between being show a picture of the event and listening to what a witness has to say about it. But notice the following things: (1) witnesses must be present in the relevant context, they are brought in, on the witness stand, and in a sense, as sources of information, they are exhibited to the fact-finders; (2) witnesses make statements and fact-finders listen to them in order to draw some probatory conclusion from their testimony. These are ostensive and perceptual aspects of fact-finding. They explain, and justify to a certain extent, Jerome Frank's notorious worries about testimony: errors can affect not only the witnesses' own perception of the facts, their memory and the ways of reporting it, but also the fact-finders' perception of what witnesses report, let alone its interpretation and assessment (Frank, 1949/1973: 14 ff. and 316 ff.).

In addition, of course, the witness's demeanour is a part of the story. Because fact-finders make up their minds considering also how the witness behaves while being on the stand.

As to expert testimony, one might insist that the great bulk of what it relies upon is out-of-court expert knowledge. Technical or scientific expertise grows out of a mass of data, experiments and tests that are run in laboratories, not before fact-finders, and that are possibly published in scientific journals or the like.[10] This is obviously true. But we should not disregard the fact that experts are supposed to present fact-finders with their results. They must do it in the relevant context and in the appropriate way (they cannot simply email them,

---

[10]   Misak, 2017: 68: 'in science, we rely on the reports of those in the lab – we do not have to have the experiences ourselves'; this is not completely true of juridical fact-finding.

as it were). And they must be ready to answer critical questions about the matter. So the fact-finder '*listens* to the screened experts and decides to what extent to credit their testimony and what impact that testimony should have on the case as a whole' (Brewer, 1998: 1544, my emphasis).

However, when only statistical evidence is provided (be it by expert or counsel) the ostensive and perceptual aspects of the process seem to be negligible. The proponent just needs to provide a number. Of course, not a number coming from nowhere: a statistical number coming from reliable research and carving the right reference class. Still, we know that it is awkward to decide cases based only on 'naked statistical evidence'.[11] Why is this? Because our preferences go to ostensible evidence relating to the case in hand, or case-specific evidence. The information that patients of a certain age range, in certain conditions, survive a given disease in a certain percentage of cases, if treated promptly, is not enough to decide a medical malpractice case: we want to learn more *about the case in hand*, about that patient's age and conditions, about the severity of the disease, about what was feasible in those very circumstances, etc. All this information does not come from statistics. It comes from ostensible evidence about the particular case.

Even in some hypotheticals as in the gatecrasher case (Cohen, 1977: 74–6) there should be one significant ostension at least: the plaintiff, claiming that only 499 spectators out of 1000 paid for a rodeo admission, sues spectator A arguing that there is a .501 probability that A did not pay and concluding that this meets the balance of probabilities civil standard; however, in a possible world not too far from the actual one, the rodeo organisers should provide evidence of the 499 paid admissions (presumably, some documents should be shown to the fact-finders).[12]

A more sophisticated way to address such reservations about the ostension thesis would consist in using Quine's distinction between *direct* and *deferred* ostension. What characterises the former is that 'the term which is being ostensively explained is true of something that contains the ostended point', whereas the latter occurs 'when we point at the gauge, and not the gasoline, to show that there is gasoline' (Quine, 1969: 39–40). One thing is pointing to the gauge to indicate the reference of 'gauge'. Another thing is pointing to the gauge to indicate the gasoline level. Note also that the first is a kind of ostensive definition, the second of probatory ostension. In semiotic terms, with

---

[11] See Schauer, 2003: 79–107 in particular.

[12] Cohen, 1977: 75 avoids this by assuming that 'it is common ground that 499 people paid for admission' and adding that, however, 'no tickets were issued and there can be no testimony as to whether A paid for admission or climbed over the fence'.

probatory ostension the thing pointed at is the sign of what is proven (in Peirce's terminology, the gauge is an index of the gasoline; see Short 2007: 207 ff.). Similarly, there is deferred ostension when we point at a recorded utterance from which a probatory conclusion can be drawn; and there is deferred ostension when we point at witnesses and their statements as sources of information.

A wonderful quote from a joint work on evidence sums up the whole question in this way:

> All evidential data presented at trial must be presented in a form that the triers of fact can perceive with their senses. This evidence consists of only two types: testimonial assertions made by a witness from the witness stand, that is, oral statements the triers of fact actually hear, and physical objects displayed to the triers of fact or, rarely, other forms of evidential data that can be perceived by one or more of the senses. (Anderson et al., 2005: 91)

Be it heard, seen, smelled or otherwise sensed; evidence is perceived by fact-finders in virtue of ostensive acts.

Written judicial opinions do not perform ostensive acts, of course. But insofar as they rely on what happened at trial, they are parasitic on trial ostension, as appeal decisions are when the check is only on the legal appropriateness of the trial decision.

Before addressing the logical structure of such ostensive acts, let me clarify a point about *direct and circumstantial evidence*. This distinction does not separate what is ostensible from what is not. Both kinds of evidence are ostensible. The difference lies, to my understanding, in the strength of the inference they license, since the conclusions we are supposed to draw from direct evidence are certainly stronger than those of the circumstantial kind.[13]

8.2.2 *The Logical Structure of Ostension*

What is the logical structure of the ostensive act in a trial or a like context? We must distinguish the components it has, at least the most important ones.

---

[13] 'Evidence is often said to be direct if it goes in one reasoning step to a matter revealed in the evidence. If you believe the evidence to be perfectly credible, that settles the matter. Evidence is said to be *circumstantial* if, even though perfectly credible, it provides only some but not complete grounds for belief in some probandum or proposition. In other words, circumstantial evidence, even though perfectly credible, is always just *inconclusive* on some probandum' (Anderson et al., 2005: 76). Consider also the difficulties that affect the notion of direct evidence, given that (1) such evidence depends on how we structure the argument based on it, and (2) 'every argument can be further decomposed to reveal new sources of doubt or uncertainty' (Anderson et al., 2005: 77).

Once we distinguish its components, it is not hard to see the logical structure of the act.

Basically, the ostensive act has this structure: *A* shows *B* to *C* in context *D* to draw inference *E*. *A* is the party that exhibits the evidence. *B* is the evidentiary item. *C* is the fact-finder to whom the evidence is shown. *D* are the spatiotemporal coordinates defined by law, namely the relevant context. And *E* is the inference that the fact-finder is expected to draw given the evidence.

Some comment is needed on *D*. The relevant context, for instance a trial or a hearing, is defined by the law. Legal rules – procedural and evidentiary ones – establish the relevant spatiotemporal coordinates. Where, when, how, by whom and to whom the evidence can be shown. This is a peculiar aspect of law. It makes juridical fact-finding significantly different from ordinary cognition and from scientific inquiry, which is in general conducted without normative delimitations and constraints. Scientists, as well as historians, can choose the subject-matter of their inquiry, the ways to perform it, the amount of time they devote to it, the kind of evidence they look for, or even the conclusions they are more inclined to. Parties and fact-finders, instead, play their roles in a context which is highly regulated by the law (notwithstanding Bentham's call for a 'free proof' system; see Haack, 2004b: 56–9). Players are bound by the rules in several respects, including spatiotemporal limitations, bans on certain kinds of evidence, legal criteria of evidence assessment, and mandatory standards of proof.[14]

Imagine, *per absurdum*, a lawyer showing a piece of evidence to the jury in an extralegal context like a Friday night party at the judge's place. Imagine also that jurors draw the correct inference from it. Epistemically speaking, nothing would be wrong with this party scenario. *A*, *B*, *C* and *E* would be in order. What would be missing is *D*, namely the proper context. Even though fact-finders would form the right mental states based on the evidence, there would be something wrong – obviously wrong – from a practical and institutional point of view. That hypothetical state of things would not be what is supposed to happen according to the law, regardless of the substantial correctness of the epistemic outcome.

In any case, notice that the above structure better fits certain kinds of proceedings than others. Ostensive acts take place when different actors collect the evidence and make decisions on it. Were the procedure inquisitorial, the same actor would play both roles and the need of ostension would evaporate. Public ostensive acts take place before independent (and supposedly impartial) fact-finders. The purely adversarial model of adjudication is the one that maximises the importance of probatory ostension.

---

[14] See, e.g., Haack, 2004a; Goldman, 2005; Bulygin, 2015: 219, 257–61.

This calls for a clarification on the logical structure of the ostensive act. Does it reflect the role of the opposing party? Where is it in the structure we adopted? Adversary proceedings have a dialectical dimension and I see two ways of making it apparent. The first is to include the opposing party in D (namely, to say that D stands for the context including, in adversary sets, the opposing party). The second is to include it in C (namely, to say that when a party shows B to the triers of fact it also shows it to the other party). I prefer the first option because, from the strategic point of view of the party that performs the ostensive act, the audience is basically the fact-finder: the point of the act is to persuade the fact-finder, not the other party. Therefore, I prefer to locate the other party in the ostension context.

This rather technical point signals a more important aspect, though. Remember one thing that William Twining pointed out, namely that evidence is 'the means of proving or disproving facts' (1984: 267); remember also that evidence can be used for the purpose of hypothesis falsification: now, we should not forget that ostensive acts, especially in adversarial contexts, can either have the purpose of supporting a factual claim or the purpose of attacking it (showing it is inconsistent, inadequate, inaccurate, etc.). Do not commit the error of thinking that evidence is collected and exhibited only for verification or confirmation purposes. Do not let our interest in the epistemic and logical aspects of probation distract you from the dialectical dimension of trials and of adversary trials in particular. Ostensive acts are part of this dialectical dimension.

8.2.3 *The Principle of Maximal Proximity*

Consider what you prefer between: (1) attending an interesting event yourself, (2) seeing a picture of it and (3) listening to some testimony about it. Of course, you prefer the first, unless you have some weird attachment to pictures or to narratives. And if you have some such attachment, you are expected to give it as a reason for preferring the second or the third option. Otherwise, the default preference is for the first and you need not justify your choice.

Similarly, if fact-finders can choose between a direct perception of the thing at stake and a picture of it, it is reasonable for them to select the first option. If they can choose between a picture and a testimony, it is reasonable to select the picture (unless it is a very bad one). And of course, by the transitivity property of rational preferences, it is rational to prefer first-hand knowledge to testimony.[15]

---

[15]   They should prefer what Wigmore, 1913: § 3 called 'autoptic proference'.

The general reason for those attitudes is obvious enough: first-hand knowledge is generally better. In other words, knowledge by acquaintance is better than knowledge by description if the description source is a picture, or a document or a testimony. True, there are some exceptions to this general point: if the thing at stake requires some technical understanding, acquaintance is not enough. Think of attending a surgical operation as a lay person: you cannot perceptually grasp many relevant details unless otherwise informed. Put these exceptions aside, first-hand information is better.

The reason why first-hand information is generally better is its being less error-exposed than information derived from other sources. Of course, perception is not immune from error. And memory of perception is not immune from error either. 'Since both memory and perception are capable of playing us false, we run a twofold risk when we appeal to the memory of a perception' (Chisholm 1977: 79). But the risk is threefold with testimony. And it is greater with hearsay.

In a passage of *An Essay Concerning Humane Understanding* (1690, Book IV, Ch. XVI, § 10), Locke says that 'any Testimony, the farther off it is from the original Truth, the less force and proof it has'. Locke's 'original Truth' is the correct account of the original relevant facts (who committed the robbery, for instance). A witness who perceived them can give an accurate testimony of what happened. But perception can be wrong; memory of it can be wrong; suggestion can distort it; reporting conditions can generate misleading declarations; interpretation of these can be wrong; etc. And it is even worse with the testimony of a testimony: at any and every passage of the perceptual-memorial-cum-testimonial chain, error can creep in and alter the outcome. So, as Locke said, the probative value of a testimony decreases 'the farther off it is from the original Truth'.

In the same part of Locke's *Essay* we find what we may call the 'copy issue': Locke says that, according to the law of England, the attested copy of a record is admitted as proof, while the copy of a copy cannot be so. More in general, the copy of a copy has lower epistemic value than the copy, as the testimony of a testimony has lower epistemic value than the testimony.

That explains the traditional distrust toward hearsay and the traditional ban on hearsay in English law.[16] However, I am not going to revive the 'the British fetishism' (Allen, 2016: 1398) with first-hand knowledge, for we all know that in many circumstances of our life it is necessary and extremely important to rely on the testimony of others and even on hearsay.[17] We also know that many

---

[16] Notice that the general rationales of the exclusion are in fact two: (1) low epistemic value; (2) very limited possibility of cross-examination.

[17] See, as an excellent work, Lackey, 2008.

contemporary legal systems, notwithstanding the common law traditional ban on hearsay, are rather liberal toward it.[18]

The thought I want to convey is this: we can explain the foregoing (including the preference for first-hand knowledge and certain ostensible evidence) with a general principle that I suggest to call *Principle of Maximal Proximity*. It is the idea that we should go as close as we can to the 'original Truth'. For this minimises the error risk.[19] Everything else being equal, we are supposed to prefer first-hand knowledge to pictures, and pictures to testimonies. Because first-hand knowledge is the closest to the 'original Truth', and pictures are closer to it than testimonies.

This principle has some affinity with Stein's 'Principle of Maximal Individualization' (Stein, 2005: 91 ff.). But the latter has a number of features that include moral and political dimensions, while the former is simpler. Perhaps the proximity principle is a version of the 'Best Evidence Principle'.[20] It makes the 'best' idea straightforward by focusing on the proximity condition (for there are various ways of reading that 'best').

For our purposes here, the Principle of Maximal Proximity also explains why we care about ostension in juridical fact-finding. Ostension is the act that gives direct knowledge of the thing shown. We want fact-finders to perceive the thing directly, if possible, or at least perceive a representation of it, such as a picture, or a document or a testimony. We care about the knowledge fact-finders can get by acquaintance. Then the relevant information will be put into propositional form and inferentially processed. Hopefully the final outcome, namely the verdict, will reflect the knowledge by description generated in this way. And hopefully it will be faithful to the 'original Truth' of the case.

8.3 THE INFERENCE THESIS

Let me quote some well-known scholars who have written on evidence and the purpose of fact-finding. In a paper of 1984 (still a quite interesting one) William Twining defines evidence as:

> the means of proving or disproving facts, or of testing the truth of allegations of fact, in situations in which the triers of fact have no first-hand knowledge of the events or situations about which they have to decide what happened (Twining, 1984: 267).[21]

[18] Cf. Allen, 1992 and 2016; Damaška, 1997: 15–16, 64–5, 130; Ho, 1999; Roberts and Zuckerman, 2010: 364 ff.; Combs, 2010: 215–16; Jackson and Summers, 2012: 328–9.
[19] I leave aside the issue of error *distribution*. See, among others, Laudan, 2006.
[20] See Nance, 1988 and Twining, 2006: 38–41, 60–6.
[21] Note that this raises an interesting conceptual point: with first-hand knowledge, no evidence is needed according to Twining. A similar assumption was also in Austin's work on perception:

More broadly speaking, he contends, evidence is 'information from which further information is derived or inferred in a variety of contexts for a variety of purposes' (Twining 1984: 267–8). Notice the connection between evidence as information and the inferential processing of it. In the relevant context, for the relevant purpose, further information is *inferentially* obtained from the evidence at disposal.

As to the purpose of it, Twining claims that fact-finding is instrumental to adjudication. We are not interested in the knowledge of the litigated facts per se. Fact-finding is performed in the sake of rectitude of decision, or of substantive justice. And a true or correct account of the facts is a necessary component of it.

> There is undoubtedly a dominant underlying theory of evidence in adjudication, in which the central notions are truth, reason and justice under the law. It can be re-stated simply in some such terms as these: the primary end of adjudication is rectitude of decision, that is the correct application of rules of substantive law to facts that have been proved to an agreed standard of truth or probability. (Twining 1984: 272)

Alvin Goldman, similarly, claims that the primary aim of adjudication is substantive justice, that a truthful account of the facts is instrumental to it, and that, as to the process of fact-finding, this has the paramount aim of truth.

> The overarching aim (of adjudication) is securing *substantively just* treatment of individuals ... Thus, truthful determination of facts becomes a derivative aim of the legal system, but the paramount aim in matters of evidence handling. (Goldman, 2005: 164)

Evidence handling, or the process of fact-finding, is truth-oriented. Were it not generally so, it would badly serve the purpose of justice.[22]

Now, the only way we have to achieve or approximate those results (truth and justice) is through inference. We start from evidentiary items, we process them inferentially and we draw conclusions as to the case in hand. Why is that? Why do we need inference? Because no evidence is sufficient by itself. By itself, evidence proves nothing. Nor does it yield verdicts. It must be 'inferentialised'.

'The situation in which I would properly be said to have *evidence* for the statement that some animal is a pig is that, for example, in which the beast itself is not actually on view, but I can see plenty of pig-like marks on the ground outside its retreat'; 'if I actually see one man shoot another, I may *give* evidence, as an eye-witness, to those less favourably placed; but I don't *have* evidence for my own statement that the shooting took place, I actually *saw* it' (Austin, 1962: 115–16). See also Wigmore, 1913: § 3.

[22] See also Summers, 1999; Haack, 2004a; and Ferrer, 2005.

Ron Allen rightly puts it, when he says that 'evidence does not announce its own implications' (1994: 613). Scott Brewer puts it even more strongly, when he offers a conception of evidence as argument (2017).

The inference thesis has it that the process of juridical proof requires necessarily some kind of inference. Juridical evidence presented to fact-finders is 'translated' into probatory inferences or arguments. It becomes the content of one or more inferences performed by the parties or by the fact-finders. It can be the content of a premise which, together with other premises, leads to a conclusion about the litigated facts; or the content of a conclusion the relevant premises lead to.[23]

What inferences? Any kind of them, but especially *abductive* inferences and inferences to the best explanation. This is the case because, usually, the information at disposal is not complete. We just know a part of what we would like to. We just happen to have some evidence that points to certain inferential directions, often incompatible. The evidence we usually have is the effect of certain unknown causes. Then it is processed as the content of one or more premises contributing to some conclusion about the causes that would explain it. This is abduction, which is the inference formulating an explana-tory hypothesis, or the inference we usually perform in conditions of incom-plete information. And when incompatible hypotheses are so formulated, we face 'factual ambiguity' (Allen, 1994) and must select the 'best explanation' of the evidence we have (Pardo and Allen, 2008).

Still, there is room for other inferences. Inductive generalisations are neces-sary to establish the major premises of probatory arguments. Twining, in particular, has discussed the topic of 'background generalisations' used in fact-finding. He claims that generalisations are *necessary* because every inferential step from particular evidence to particular conclusion 'requires justification by reference to at least one background generalization' (Twining, 2006: 334).[24] Every abductive inference, I would say, requires a major premise stating some generalisation. Without it, it would be impossible to move from a minor premise reporting some evidence to a conclusion providing an explanatory hypothesis. Twining also claims, famously, that generalisations are *dangerous*:

> Generalizations are dangerous in argumentation about doubtful or disputed questions of fact because they tend to provide invalid, illegitimate, or false

---

[23]   With cascaded inference, in addition, the conclusion of an inference is also a premise of another inference. See Taruffo, 1992: 248–52.

[24]   Generalisations are a continuum that goes from scientific laws and well-founded scientific opinions, through commonly held, but unproven or unprovable, beliefs, to biases and prejudices (Anderson et al., 2005: 102; cf. Dahlman, 2017).

reasons for accepting conclusions based on inference. They are especially dangerous when they are implicit or unexpressed. (Twining, 2006: 335)

Of course, abductive inferences are invalid from a deductive point of view. They instantiate the 'affirming the consequent' fallacy. Their conclusions can be false even if their premises are true. But we cannot dispense with them if we want to explain puzzling facts. In any case I agree with Twining on the importance of making them explicit.

Indeed, there is reasoning *from* evidence and reasoning *to* evidence. Testing is moving to further evidence. (There is also, of course, reasoning *about* evidence, namely evidence assessment.) Confirming evidence is processed in this way: once an explanatory hypothesis is formulated, the additional evidence that is found contributes to the best explanation of the case via some generalisation supporting the conclusion.[25] Here the evidence figures as the expected conclusion given the hypothesis and the relevant generalisation. Inference makes it expected and ostension presents it to fact-finders.

And there is room for deduction also. The explanation of evidence can hardly be deductive. But the finding of a conclusive alibi can be cast into deductive terms (in the *modus tollens* form). Consider for instance the following situation: imagine that we assume as minor premise, given a testimony, that the defendant is materially guilty of a robbery that took place in Milan on some day at a given time, and we also assume as true major premise that no human being can be at the same time in different places; then we would not expect to find the defendant in Rome on the same day at the same time. If, to the contrary, conclusive evidence is found that the defendant was in Rome on that day at that time, that evidence falsifies the starting hypothesis. As Popper has extensively shown in the context of philosophy of science,[26] falsification has the logical character of deductive *modus tollens*: it is impossible that the starting hypothesis be correct if the falsifying evidence is correct.[27]

Then two comments are in order, to make the inference thesis clearer from an analytical point of view. First, arguments are not identical to inferences. They can be conceived as *public inferences*, in that they are performed before a certain audience and certainly have other dimensions than the logical one (in particular, they have a rhetorical dimension and a specific point:

---

[25] The point can be rephrased in probabilistic terms, using Bayes' theorem. But the use of mathematical tools such as Bayes' theorem is highly disputed in this context. See, among others, Taruffo, 1992: 166 ff., Allen and Pardo 2007, Ferrer, 2007: 93 ff. and Gascón, 2010: 140 ff.

[26] See Popper, 1934/1959 in particular.

[27] Analogy can play a role too, but I do not discuss it here. Just consider that, for some logicians, it is a complex inferential pattern made of basic inferences such as abduction, induction and deduction. See Brewer, 1996 and McJohn 1993; cf. Canale and Tuzet 2009.

persuading the audience). On arguments as public inferences, consider this aspect of our everyday experience: we need not make arguments in front of ourselves, properly speaking. If you are alone in your room and make an argument in a loud tone of voice, with dramatic gestures and facial expressions, either you are preparing an argument you will perform before others, or you have some mental troubles.[28]

Second comment – trivial but analytically true – arguments are about disputed points. We need not argue about what we agree upon. No one is supposed to argue about a fact that everyone agrees upon. So, there is no need to collect, present and discuss evidence about a fact that is already established.

8.4 CONCLUSION: ANALYSIS AND SYNTHESIS

Both theses presented here are necessary to an account of juridical evidence and proof. But there is a significant difference as to their status. I take the inference thesis to be correct regardless of the kind of evidence at stake. For every kind of evidence, it is true that it must be inferentialised. This is true, by my lights, of any kind of juridical evidence and, more in general, of evidence of any kind (be it in law, history, empirical science, etc.). In this sense the inference thesis is analytically true of 'evidence'.

The ostension thesis, instead, is true of many kinds of evidence but not universally true of juridical evidence, nor of evidence in general. As I said at the beginning of the chapter, the process of juridical proof *typically* requires some ostensive act. The ostension thesis is synthetically true of some typical subcategories of what we mean by 'evidence', and it is arguably false of some of them. It is true of material evidence and even of testimony, but it is arguably false of statistical evidence (or at least it is not true of it in the same sense). In addition, the ostension thesis better fits the adversary model of fact-finding and adjudication: where independent fact-finders make the relevant decision, parties are supposed to present them with evidence and to argue about it. Remember that ostension is a source of knowledge for those who do not have it. Investigators go around looking for evidence; fact-finders do not do this in adversary proceedings. Both investigators and fact-finders get knowledge by acquaintance, but fact-finders get it because they are shown evidentiary items. Inquisitorial proceedings, instead, seem to be far less concerned with public

---

[28]   However, the order of explanation might be reversed: one could claim that inference is argument internalised, that is, that our capacity to perform inferences comes from the practice of making arguments before others.

ostensive acts and arguments.[29] When fact-finders are involved in the investigation they get some knowledge by acquaintance, but they need not perform an ostensive act before others: they will simply use that knowledge for decision purposes.

That difference in theoretical status does not make one of the theses less important than the other. If describing and explaining the world is important as much as analysing our language and conceptual apparatus, both theses are equally important and necessary to an account of fact-finding. They make sense of our usual ways of processing evidence and of deciding cases on their factual merits.

REFERENCES

Allen, R. J. and Pardo, M. (2007). The Problematic Value of Mathematical Models of Evidence, *The Journal of Legal Studies*, 36 (1), 107–40.

Allen, R. J. (1992). The Evolution of Hersay Rule to a Rule of Admission, *Minnesota Law Review*, 76, 797–812.

Allen, R. J. (1994). Factual Ambiguity and Theory of Evidence, *Northwestern Law Review*, 88, 604–34.

Allen, R. J. (2014). Burdens of Proof, *Law, Probability and Risk*, 13(3–4), 195–219.

Allen, R. J. (2016). The Hearsay Rule as a Rule of Admission Revisited, *Fordham Law Review*, 84, 1395–405.

Anderson, T., Twining, W. and Schum, D. A. (2005). *Analysis of Evidence*. Cambridge: Cambridge University Press.

Austin, J. L. (1962). *Sense and Sensibilia*. Oxford: Clarendon Press.

Brewer, S. (1996). Exemplary Reasoning: Semantics, Pragmatics, and the Rational Force of Legal Argument by Analogy, *Harvard Law Review*, 109 (5): 923–1028.

Brewer, S. (1998). Scientific Expert Testimony and Intellectual Due Process, *Yale Law Journal*, 107: 1535–681.

Brewer, S. (2017). *The Logocratic Conception of Evidence as Argument*. Manuscript.

Bulygin, E. (2015). *Essays in Legal Philosophy*. C. Bernal Pulido, C. Huerta Ochoa, T. Mazzarese, J. J. Moreso, P. E. Navarro and S. L. Paulson, eds. Oxford: Oxford University Press.

Burks, A. W. (1949). Icon, Index, and Symbol, *Philosophy and Phenomenological Research*, 9 (4), 673–89.

---

[29] Still, they are concerned with evidentiary inferences: even the most stubborn and biased inquisitors must make up their minds about their cases.

Canale, D. and Tuzet, G. (2009). The A Simili Argument: An Inferentialist Setting, *Ratio Juris*, 22 (4), 499–509.

Capone, A. and Poggi, F. (2016). *Pragmatics and Law. Philosophical Perspectives*. Cham, Switzerland: Springer.

Capone, A. and Poggi, F. (2017). *Pragmatics and Law. Practical and Theoretical Perspectives*. Cham, Switzerland: Springer.

Chisholm, R. M. (1977). *Theory of Knowledge*, 2nd ed. Englewood Cliffs: Prentice-Hall.

Coffa, J. A. (1991). *The Semantic Tradition from Kant to Carnap. To the Vienna Station*. Cambridge: Cambridge University Press.

Cohen, L. J. (1977). *The Probable and the Provable*. Oxford: Clarendon Press.

Combs, N. A. (2010). *Fact-Finding without Facts: The Uncertain Evidentiary Foundations of International Criminal Convictions*. Cambridge: Cambridge University Press.

CP, *Collected Papers of C.S. Peirce* C. Hartshorne, P. Weiss (vols. 1–6) and A. Burks (vols. 7–8), Cambridge, MA: Harvard University Press, 1931–58. (References by volume and paragraph number).

Dahlman, C. (2017). Unacceptable Generalizations in Arguments on Legal Evidence, *Argumentation*, 31 (1), 83–99.

Damaška, M. (1997). *Evidence Law Adrift*. New Haven and London: Yale University Press.

Ferrer, J. (2005). *Prueba y verdad en el derecho*, 2nd ed. Madrid: Marcial Pons.

Ferrer, J. (2007). *La valoración racional de la prueba*. Madrid: Marcial Pons.

Frank, J. (1949). *Courts on Trial. Myth and Reality in American Justice*. Princeton: Princeton University Press, 1973.

Gascón, M. (2010). *Los hechos en el derecho. Bases argumentales de la prueba*, 3rd ed. Madrid: Marcial Pons.

Goldman, A. (2005). Evidence. In M. P. Golding and W. A. Edmundson (eds.), *The Blackwell Guide to the Philosophy of Law and Legal Theory*. Oxford: Blackwell, 163–75.

Haack, S. (2004a). Truth and Justice, Inquiry and Advocacy, Science and Law, *Ratio Juris*, 17, 15–26.

Haack, S. (2004b). Epistemology Legalized: Or, Truth, Justice, and the American Way, *The American Journal of Jurisprudence*, 49, 43–61.

Ho, H. L. (1999). A Theory of Hearsay, *Oxford Journal of Legal Studies*, 19, 403–19.

Jackson, J. D. and Summers, S. J. (2012). *The Internationalisation of Criminal Evidence. Beyond the Common Law and Civil Law Traditions*. Cambridge: Cambridge University Press.

James, W. (1890). *The Principles of Psychology*, vol. 1. Cambridge, MA: Harvard University Press, 1981.

Kripke, S. A. (1980). *Naming and Necessity*, 2nd ed. Oxford: Blackwell.

Lackey, J. (2008). *Learning from Words. Testimony as a Source of Knowledge*. Oxford: Oxford University Press.

Laudan, L. (2006). *Truth, Error, and Criminal Law. An Essay in Legal Epistemology.* Cambridge: Cambridge University Press.

Levinson, S. C. (1983). *Pragmatics.* Cambridge: Cambridge University Press.

McJohn, S. M. (1993). On Uberty: Legal Reasoning by Analogy and Peirce's Theory of Abduction, *Willamette Law Review*, 29, 191–235.

Mead, G. H. (1934). *Mind, Self, and Society.* Chicago: University of Chicago Press, 1967.

Misak, C. J. (1995). *Verificationism. Its History and Prospects.* London and New York: Routledge.

Misak, C. J. (2017). James on Religious Experience, *Philosophical Inquiries*, 5, 63–74.

Nance, D. A. (1988). The Best Evidence Principle, *Iowa Law Review*, 73, 227–97.

Pardo, M. S. and Allen, R. J. (2008). Juridical Proof and the Best Explanation, *Law and Philosophy*, 27, 223–68.

Putnam, H. (1975). *Mind, Language and Reality. Philosophical Papers*, vol. 2. Cambridge: Cambridge University Press.

Quine, W. V. O. (1953). *From a Logical Point of View.* Cambridge and London: Harvard University Press.

Quine, W. V. O. (1960). *Word and Object.* Cambridge: The MIT Press.

Quine, W. V. O. (1969). *Ontological Relativity and Other Essays.* New York: Columbia University Press.

Quine, W. V. O. (1970). *Philosophy of Logic*, 2nd ed. Cambridge and London: Harvard University Press, 1986.

Quine, W. V. O. (1976). *The Ways of Paradox and Other Essays*, 2nd ed. Cambridge and London: Harvard University Press.

Popper, K. R. (1934). *The Logic of Scientific Discovery.* London: Routledge, 1959.

Rescher, N. (1964). *Introduction to Logic.* New York: St. Martin's Press.

Roberts, P. and Zuckerman, A. (2010). *Criminal Evidence*, 2nd ed. Oxford: Oxford University Press.

Russell, B. (1912). *The Problems of Philosophy.* Oxford: Oxford University Press, 1998.

Schauer, F. (2003). *Profiles, Probabilities, and Stereotypes.* Cambridge. MA: Harvard University Press.

Short, T. L. (2007). *Peirce's Theory of Signs.* Cambridge: Cambridge University Press.

Stein, A. (2005). *Foundations of Evidence Law.* Oxford: Oxford University Press.

Summers, R. S. (1999). Formal Legal Truth and Substantive Truth in Judicial Fact-Finding – Their Justified Divergence in Some Particular Cases, *Law and Philosophy*, 18, 497–511.

Taruffo, M. (1992). *La prova dei fatti giuridici.* Milano: Giuffrè.

Tuzet, G. (2016). La prova ragionata, *Analisi e diritto*, vol. 2016, 127–61.

Twining, W. (1984). Evidence and Legal Theory, *Modern Law Review*, 47, 261–83.

Twining, W. (2006). *Rethinking Evidence. Exploratory Essays*, 2nd ed. Cambridge: Cambridge University Press.

Wigmore, J. H. (1913). *The Principles of Judicial Proof* Boston MA: Little, Brown and Company.

Wittgenstein, L. (1953). *Philosophical Investigations* G. E. M. Anscombe and R. Rhees, eds. Oxford: Blackwell.

Wittgenstein, L. (1968). Notes for Lectures on 'Private Experience' and 'Sense Data', *The Philosophical Review*, 77, 275–320.

9

Inferences in Judicial Decisions About Facts

Michele Taruffo

9.1 SOME PREMISES

The arguments that will be shortly developed in this chapter move from some premises concerning the goals and the main features of the decision that the trier of fact has to make on the facts in issue in any procedural context.

(1) The basic premise is that such a decision deals with statements (usually a set of statements) describing events that are relevant for the application of a legal rule in the specific case. In a sense, it is the rule that is taken as the legal standard determining the decision that is applied to as the criterion to determine the legal relevance of the facts in issue.

(2) The second basic premise is that among the goals of any judicial decision on facts there is the judgment about the truth or falsehood of such statements. In a sense, the judicial process may be interpreted as a complex proceeding oriented to the search of truth about the facts in issue. It means that the decision about such facts has to be *accurate*: all the statements concerning facts should be taken as true or false, and the truth or falsehood of such statements should be justified in a detailed and analytical way.

(3) The third basic premise is that such a final decision about all the factual statements should be based upon: (1) all the available evidence concerning the facts in issue; (2) a rational reasoning based upon such evidence. This second point is especially important in order to reject various theories according to which the decision about the facts in issue could or should be no more than the outcome of an irrational *intime conviction*.

(4) A further fundamental premise is that in the judicial context any talk about the search of truth is properly referred (setting aside the other several theories of truth) to the concept of truth as correspondence of factual

statements to the events that are described in such statements. So to say, the decision about the facts in issue should be based upon an accurate and complete *reconstruction* of what happened in the reality of such facts. However, it seems obviously clear that for many reasons in a judicial proceeding no *absolute truth* can ever be achieved; judicial truth is obviously a *human truth*, and therefore it cannot but being *relative*, that is, depending on the amount and the quality of the information provided by the evidence, and on the rational validity of the reasoning that is used to process such information and to reach the decision about the facts.

(5) Evidence is the only means by which the trier of fact may reconstruct what happened in the reality. Private knowledge of such facts is not admissible as a basis of the decision. In a very general sense, *evidence* is any kind of information that is relevant (i.e., useful) for the knowledge of any fact in issue.

(6) Usually in any judicial proceeding several items of evidence are presented and collected with the aim of gathering all the possible information about the facts in issue. As abovesaid, all this information should be considered and used *rationally*, that is, with the aim of deriving from them a rationally justified decision about the truth or falsehood of the facts in issue. Some theories, proposed mainly with the purpose of describing how *jurors* deal with the evidence, say that jurors make a *holistic* evaluation of all the items of evidence, and of all the facts in issue, ending up with a complete *narration* of the facts that is supposed to be the final outcome of such a 'global' judgment. Not discussing here whether or not this is a reliable description of how jurors reach their verdict, a criticism is that in such a way it is impossible to determine whether their judgment is rational and accurate (also because a verdict of a jury never is justified).

On the contrary, saying that the decision of the trier of fact has to be accurate and rational, being oriented to finding out the truth about the facts in issue, requires the adoption of a different perspective about the evaluation of evidence, that is: an analytical perspective, according to which *any* item of evidence concerning *any* fact should be taken in specific consideration in order to determine which information it provides, and whether or not such an information is relevant for the final decision about the truth of the factual statements.

9.2 SOME THEORIES OF FACTUAL DECISION

Leaving aside the theories that consider the decision about the facts in issue as a merely irrational activity, and those that deal only with the psychology of judicial decisions, it is worth stressing that there are several tentative explanations of how a decision about the facts in issue may or should be achieved. All these explanations cannot be discussed here in detail, but some of them deserve to be mentioned.

According to one of these theories that is rather widely accepted in legal theory, the decision on the facts should be derived from an *inference to the best explanation*. The basic idea is that in a judicial context there are two (or more) descriptions of the facts connected with the evidence, and that such a connection provides an *explanation* of such facts. Between the explanation offered by the plaintiff and the explanation offered by the defendant, the trier of fact should choose the *best* one. At first glance this seems reasonable, but there are at least four problems here: (1) there are no clear criteria by which such a choice should be made. Sometimes it is said that the best explanation has to be coherent with the common sense, reasonable, able to connect in one narration the facts and the evidence, but all these criteria seem to be too vague and uncertain. (2) Such a theory is clearly based upon an *holistic perspective*, since each explanation has to be taken as a *whole*, but this is in conflict with what has been said above in favour of an analytical consideration of each fact and of each item of evidence. (3) Moreover, if the best explanation has to be narratively coherent, this means that it has nothing to do with the truth or falsehood of the statements concerning the facts in issue, while – as it has been told above – this is just the problem that the decision must solve. (4) The relatively best explanation may even have a very low degree of evidentiary confirmation, and it may be 'relatively' best while the other explanations are worse, but once again this has nothing to do with the truth or falsehood of the factual statements.

Among the theories that try to offer a rational analysis of the factual decision based upon the evidence, perhaps the more popular – since its beginning in the Seventies in some areas of the American legal theory – is based on the application of the calculus of quantitative ('pascalian') probability, and in particular on the use of the so-called *Bayes theorem*. About such a theory there is a number of books and essays: then it cannot be discussed in all its aspects, but the basic idea may be expressed in synthetic terms. Such an idea is roughly the following: we start with the *prior probability* of a factual statement and then, applying the Bayes theorem, we can establish how much a new information or evidence about that fact determines a variation in its probability. The outcome is an *a posteriori probability*, that is a number between 0 and 1 (or between 0 and 100) that is the resulting probability of that statements on the basis of the new evidence.

Here the problem is neither the calculus of mathematical probability nor about the Bayes theorem, the validity of which is not discussed. The problem is whether or not this type of calculus is applicable – as several scholars say – in a judicial context. The solution of this problem is negative, for various reasons. The main negative reason is that in a judicial context we almost never have a prior probability numerically determined of anything, and we cannot *create from nothing* such a probability just in order to start the calculus: clearly any number we can produce as an outcome would be arbitrary and nonsense. Another relevant reason is that, according to the most recent versions of this theory, it could explain only how to calculate the effect of just *one* item of evidence, but so far it cannot be applied to the most common judicial situation, in which there are several or even many items of evidence. Moreover, the calculus that such a theory suggests is so complex and sophisticated that no juror or judge would be able to perform it in a correct way.

However, since the judicial truth is never absolute and is always *relative*, it seems that we may analyse the structure of the factual decision in terms of *probability*. Of course, not in terms of bayesian probability, but in terms of *logical (Baconian) probability*. Logical probability is – speaking in very simplified terms – the logic of the connections among statements, that is, the logic of the inferences that are constructed in order to justify reasonings about statements and to reach a conclusion about one statement according with the information provided by other statements. This kind of logic derives from the classical tradition (the Aristotelian syllogism was an inference connecting two premises with a conclusion) and is applied in a variety of areas in which there are no numbers or statistics but there are rational and logically valid arguments. For these reasons it may be taken as a useful tool for the analysis of the reasoning about evidence, aimed to achieve the confirmation of statements concerning the facts in issue.

9.3 MODELS OF INFERENTIAL REASONING

The inferential structure of the reasoning that the trier of fact has to develop in order to evaluate the evidence and to draw conclusions from the information provided by the evidence may be described in various ways. However, a useful way is to apply the inferential model that was proposed in 1958 by Stephen Toulmin and is currently used by several authors.

Such a model basically combines three factors and allows us to determine whether a hypothesis H, the liability of which has to be established, is confirmed by the available information E. The outcome may be positive if a reference may be made to a *warrant* W that connects E and H in such a way that, given E, H is logically confirmed. Then the structure of the inference is

$$E \rightarrow H \qquad (1)$$
$$\uparrow$$
$$W$$

That is: H is logically confirmed by E on the basis of W.

Such a model is very useful because it is very simple and may be applied in order to analyse very different inferences. If, for instance, I have to establish in H if Socrates is mortal, and I know in E that Socrates is a man, I can say that Socrates is mortal because I refer to a warrant that says that all humans are mortal.

Of course, then, it is easy to see that the real basis of the inference is W: then the degree of logical confirmation of H on the basis of E is determined by W. When W is a general law, as in the example of Socrates, the inference is *deductive*, but in many cases W is a statistical regularity or even a common sense generalisation: in such cases the confirmation of H may be only *probabilistic*. However, in such cases the problem is to determine the real cognitive content of such generalisations. If such a content is uncertain, then the conclusion concerning H cannot be validly drawn.

9.3.1 *Complex Inferences*

The model of inference just described explains the *simplest* and *atomic* logical structure of evidential inferences, but the situation in which it corresponds to the *whole* inference is rather infrequent.

What often happens, actually, is that the evidentiary inference is much more complex, consisting in a combination of *basic* inferences as the one just described. There is a wide variety of such combinations, that cannot be analysed here. However, the basic structure of some of such combinations may be analysed.

(1) One possibility exists when there is an *inferential linear chain*, in which the final inference about H is the outcome of another previous inference, such as

$$E' \rightarrow H' \quad \text{where } H'=E \rightarrow H \qquad (2)$$
$$\uparrow \qquad\qquad \uparrow$$
$$W' \qquad\qquad\qquad W$$

However, also E' may be in its turn a hypothesis confirmed by another inference, and so on. Therefore, we may have a complex linear chain of this type

$$E^n \rightarrow H^n \rightarrow ....E' \rightarrow H' = E \rightarrow H \qquad (3)$$
$$\uparrow \qquad\qquad \uparrow \qquad \uparrow$$
$$W^n \qquad\qquad W' \qquad W$$

In such a situation, the confirmation of the final H is given by W, and the confirmation of all the Hs is given by the respective Ws. The basic principle is that the *force* of the whole chain is equivalent to the force of its *weakest* ring: if one ring breaks down, the whole chain breaks down.

(2) A situation that is rather frequent in judicial context but has a complex inferential structure, is that in which for the same H there are various evidentiary items E', E'' and E'''. If we admit that E' $\rightarrow$ H; E'' $\rightarrow$ H, and that E''' $\rightarrow$ H, and also that these inferences (each one with its own W) are reciprocally compatible and independent, we have a situation like

$$E' \qquad\qquad (4)$$
$$\searrow$$
$$E'' \rightarrow H$$
$$\uparrow$$
$$E'''$$

in which each of the three converging inferences provides a positive confirmation of H. Correspondingly, such a confirmation is given by the combination (we could say the *sum*) of the outcomes of the three inferences. We should consider, however, that each of the Es may be in its turn the outcome of a linear chain of inference of the type described above in A).

(3) A special but frequent situation of converging inferences may happen when none of the Es is by itself sufficient to give H a real confirmation (although each E gives H *some* confirmation, although insufficient). This is the case in which there are several items of circumstantial evidence, but none of them is able by itself to support H. However, usually it is admitted that in such a situation a set of insufficient circumstantial evidence may lead to a final positive confirmation of H. The solution is not of summing up the outcome of different (but each insufficient) inferences, but to build up a different inference corresponding to:

$$E' \qquad\qquad (5)$$
$$E'' \ \} \rightarrow H$$
$$E''' \ \uparrow$$
$$W$$

In this type of inference, the three Es are not different premises of different inference but are – taken *together* – a *unique* E, that is the premise of a *unique* inference that may justify H according to W. Obviously such a W should connect the set of E', E" and E"' with H.

(4) Moreover, we may then imagine a group of situations in which the common feature is that the items of evidence that are available as Es are not converging in the same direction, that is: are not univocally supporting the final H. It means that there are *diverging inferences* that may be based upon the existing evidence.

The simplest of such situation may be that of the *ambiguous* E, which means that E does not support only H, but also 'not H', in such a way:

$$E \rightarrow H \qquad (6)$$
$$\searrow \text{not H}$$

In such a case the problem is about the Ws justifying different conclusions, and a choice is possible only when one of the two inferences is supported by a W. If none is supported, no conclusion is possible about H.

A different form of ambiguity of E may be the following:

$$\begin{array}{c} H \\ \uparrow \\ E \rightarrow H' \\ \downarrow \\ H'' \end{array} \qquad (7)$$

That is a situation in which from the same E different inferences (on the basis of different Ws) may be drawn about different Hs. It may happen that the various Hs are compatible (for instance when they refer to different facts). In such a case we might say that E is *plural*.

We may also have a different and more complex situation, that is unfortunately very frequent, when at the same time there are different items of evidence, but each of them supports different Hs according to different Ws, in this way:

$$\begin{array}{c} E \rightarrow H \\ \uparrow \\ W \\ E' \rightarrow H' \\ \uparrow \\ W' \\ E'' \rightarrow H'' \\ \uparrow \\ W'' \end{array} \qquad (8)$$

Here the problem arises when the several Hs are about the same fact, and that each H has its own confirmation supported by a specific E and by a specific W. Then the choice that the trier has to make should be in favour of the H that has a strongest degree of confirmation. There is no problem, however, when the various Hs refer to different facts.

(5) Last, but not least, we have to consider the very frequent situation in which there are items of evidence leading to opposite conclusions about the same H, in this way:

$$E \rightarrow H \qquad (9)$$
$$\uparrow$$
$$W$$
$$E' \rightarrow not\ H$$
$$\uparrow$$
$$W'$$

In this case we have an inference confirming that H is true and an inference, based upon a different E, confirming that H is false. Once again, in such a situation the choice of the trier of fact should be guided by the comparison between the degrees in which the two inferences support their respective conclusion.

Of course this list of situations is far from complete, since the reality of many judicial decisions about the facts in issue requires an extremely complex and sophisticated logical analysis. However, we may think that a thorough use of these inferential models, and of their combinations, may help the trier of fact to reach a logically justified decision and to give rational reasons for such a decision.

9.4 A SPECIAL PROBLEM: STATISTICAL EVIDENCE

The problem of the inferences connecting rationally the evidence at hand with a conclusion concerning the facts in issue may be interpreted – and actually it is interpreted – on the basis of various conceptual models. A complete analysis of all these models cannot be made here, then a specific attention will be paid only to situations in which statistics may be or are actually used.

However, one of these models may be set aside immediately, that is the theory according to which the so-called *naked statistical evidence* may support a conclusion about the facts in issue even when there is no other evidence. It is a well-known and disputed theory but a full discussion of it is not relevant here, because of at least two reasons. One is that in the administration of justice there is no interest in paradoxes as those of the blue bus or the public of a rodeo. The judge does not play with paradoxes: he has to deal with specific and concrete empirical facts that occurred in the past. Another reason is that – as it is commonly said – statistics have nothing to say about specific past facts, since they deal with populations or sets of events and – moreover – are oriented towards the future rather than towards the past. This does not prevent, of course, the reference to statistics in the analysis of the evidence, but it shows that *naked* statistics cannot be taken as an autonomous and sufficient item of evidence.

A more positive and fruitful approach to the problem of the judicial use of statistics requires a due consideration of the inferences by which evidence is connected to a conclusion concerning the facts in issue. The set of such inferences is sometimes very complex and may be analysed by means of different logical models.

One of these models is the Hempel's model of a *nomological-deductive* inference. This kind of inference is so called because it connects a premise with a conclusion on the basis of a *general covering law*, and therefore the conclusion is certain in a *deductive* way. So far, however, we are simply dealing with a modern version of the Aristotelian syllogism, and there is no problem of statistics. The problem arises when the reference is made to a *quasi* nomological-deductive model, that is to a *probabilistic* version of the original model. It happens when there is not a covering general law, but there is a *statistical frequency* of the connection between premise and conclusion, and such a frequency has a specially high value (of 90 per cent or even more). In such a case it is said that the conclusion may be considered as *practically certain*, since its truth is highly probable. There are, however, some criticisms that can be addressed to this theory. On the one hand, it may be said that it does not represent what normally happens in judicial contexts, where the reference to general laws, but also to very high probabilities, is not impossible but is not frequent. Then this model cannot be taken as a general model of judicial inferences.

On the other hand, the role of statistics in such a model deserves to be properly defined. It seems clear that if there are statistics suggesting that A provokes B in 95 per cent of the cases, it provides a good reasonable justification for believing that most probably A provoked B also in the specific case. But it would be incorrect to say that in such a case the occurrence of B has a 95 per cent probability, since statistics provide frequencies but do not say anything about a specific instance. Rather, it could be said that in such a case the statistical frequency offers a nice justification for a *practical decision*. In other words, a judge would be reasonably justified in taking the conclusion of the inference *as if* such a statement were true, and to behave as if it were true.

It seems, therefore, that the reference to statistics may have a relevant role in providing a rational justification for judicial decisions, bur here a further problem arises. Actually, such a justification may be rational when the probability at stake is very high (that is when the statistical information is *quasi general*) mainly because in such cases the rate of error is very low, and then the probability of a wrong decision is also very low, or at any rate tolerable. But what about the much more frequent case in which the statistical frequency is lower (for instance, of 80 per cent or 70 per cent), and then taking the conclusion of the inference 'as if it were true' has a much higher probability to be wrong? Moreover: what about the case in which the statistical frequency is low or very low (for instance 30 per cent or 20 per cent), with the corresponding high probability of error concerning the conclusion? In a sense, it could be roughly said that the *degree of confidence* (or of *belief*) in the truthfulness of the conclusion depends on the degree of probability of the statistics that are used as the basis of the inference.

This does not mean that only statistics with high probabilities should be used, since also low probabilities may be useful. However, an important aspect of the problem is whether and when statistics may or may not be sufficient to achieve the standard of proof that is required in each specific case although it may be admitted that even 'low' statistics may be relevant in reaching a conclusion about the facts in issue.

9.4.1 A Doubtful Case: Toxic Torts

Toxic torts are the domain in which the reference to statistics, mainly provided by epidemiology, is most frequent. However, it is also the domain in which the use of statistical evidence raises several problems.

First of all, it is commonly said that in the cases concerning toxic torts the general causation about the toxic effects of the use of dangerous medicaments or of the exposure to dangerous materials needs to be properly demonstrated, and then that also the specific causation of such effects in individual cases needs to be proven. As to the proof of general causation there are no special problems since statistics may provide such a proof. The problem arises concerning the proof of specific causation: it is usually said that statistical probabilities have nothing to say about specific causation, but sometimes it is also said that statistics *may* prove such a causation, since they could provide a proof that achieves the civil standard of the preponderance of evidence, that is a probability of at least 51 per cent. This theory has been accepted by several American courts. The main argument is –in extreme synthesis, the following: if the *relative risk* of disease of those who used a medicament or were exposed to a dangerous material is two times the risk of the non-users or unexposed, *therefore* in such cases there would be a proof of the specific causation in the individual cases, because the standard of the more probable than not has been achieved. Moreover, sometimes it is said that the statistics showing the *double risk* are a *sufficient* proof of the specific causation, and sometimes it is even said that such statistics are *necessary* to prove such a causation.

There is no need to develop here a thorough analysis of this argument, but some critical remarks are necessary. First of all, one may be inclined to believe that if – for instance – the non-users of the medicament or the nonexposed suffer the disease in the proportion of 5 per cent, and the users or the exposed suffer the same disease two times more (that is with a risk of 2), the outcome would be that for the users or the exposed the risk of such a disease is of 10 per cent, but this would not say anything about the specific causation concerning particular individuals. It would just be an information about the general causation in the population of the users or of the exposed, but nothing more. After all, a probability of 10 per cent of risk for users and exposed may be relevant within the general assessment of evidence, but it is in no way equivalent to a probability of 50 per cent in any case of specific causation.

On the other hand, even admitting that the double risk produces a probability of 50 per cent in specific cases, this does not mean that the standard of the preponderance of evidence (or of the more probable than not) is achieved: 50 per cent is not preponderant upon another 50 per cent, then with 50 per cent of probability the proof is not achieved.

SELECTED BIBLIOGRAPHY

Ferrer Beltrán, J. (2007). *La valoración racional de la prueba*, Madrid; Barcelona; Buenos Aires: Marcial Pons.

Frosini, B. V. (2002). *La prove statistiche nel processo civile e nel processo penale*, Milán: Giuffrè.

Garbolino, P. (2014). *Probabilità e logica della prova*, Milan: Giuffrè.

González Lagier, D. (2005). *Quaestio Facti, Ensayos sobre prueba, causalidad y acción*, Lima; Bogotá: Palestra.

Green, M. D., Freedman, D. M. and Gordis L. (2011). Reference Guide on Epidemiology, *Reference Manual on Scientific Evidence*, 3rd ed., Washington, DC: Federal Judicial Center.

Haack, S. (2014). *Evidence Matters. Science, Proof and Truth in the Law*, Cambridge: Cambridge University Press.

Kaye, D. H. and Freedman D. (2011). Reference Guide on Statistics, in *Reference Manual on Scientific Evidence*, 3rd ed., Washington, DC: Federal Judicial Center.

MacCrimmon, M. and Tillers, P. eds. (2002). *The Dynamics of Judicial Proof. Computation, Logic, and Common Sense*, Heidelberg; New York: Physica Verlag.

Nieva Fenoll, J. (2010). *La valoración de la prueba*, Madrid; Barcelona; Buenos Aires: Marcial Pons.

Taruffo, M. (2009). *La semplice verità. Il giudice e la costruzione dei fatti*, Bari: Laterza.

Taruffo, M. (2012). *La prova nel processo civile*, Milan: Giuffre.

Toulmin, S. (1958). *The Uses of Argument*, Cambridge: Cambridge University Press, 2008.

Tuzet, G. (2013). *Filosofia della prova giuridica*, Torino: G. Giappichelli Editore.

Twining, W. (2006). *Rethinking Evidence. Exploratory Essays*, 2nd ed., Cambridge: Cambridge University Press.

10

Silence as Evidence

Hock Lai Ho

10.1 INTRODUCTION

The right to remain silent and not to incriminate oneself in the criminal process is recognised in some quarters as a human or fundamental right. Examples of such recognition can be found in international instruments,[1] regional human rights texts[2] and national Constitutions or Bills of Rights.[3] But the right is not given this exalted status everywhere; indeed, it has its fair share of ardent critics. The right is not mentioned in the ASEAN Human Rights Declaration[4] and is not among the fundamental rules of natural justice protected under the Singapore Constitution.[5] Obviously, there may exist (aspects of) a legal right of silence even if it is not constitutionalised. The existence of the right, constitutionalised or not, varies across jurisdictions. There is much debate on its significance and desirability.

This chapter looks at the position taken and discourse on the right of silence in Singapore. By position, I mean what the law is and how it got there. By discourse, I mean how officials talk when they go about defending legislative

---

[1] E.g., UN General Assembly, International Covenant on Civil and Political Rights, United Nations (New York), 16 December 1966, in force 23 March 1976, Treaty Series, vol. 999, p. 171. International Covenant on Civil and Political Rights, Art. 14(3)(g).

[2] E.g., Organization of American States, American Convention on Human Rights, 'Pact of San Jose', Costa Rica, 22 November 1969. Arts. 8(2)(g) and 8(3). The privilege against self-incrimination, though not explicitly mentioned, is recognised as an implicit component of the right to a fair trial in Art. 6 of the European Convention on Human Rights.

[3] E.g., United States Constitution, Fifth Amendment; Canadian Charter of Rights and Freedoms, s. 11(c); South African Constitution, s. 35(1)(a), (b) and (c), and s. 35(3).

[4] It is not mentioned in the 'fair trial' provision in Art. 20(1) of the Declaration. It is also not explicitly mentioned in the African Charter on Human and Peoples' Rights (missing from Art. 7) and the Arab Charter on Human Rights (missing from Arts. 6 and 7).

[5] PP v. Mazlan bin Maidun [1992] 3 SLR(R) 968.

amendments or praising the current law. Does the experience in Singapore reveal a distinctly Asian perspective to the right of silence? The study of Singapore will be used as a springboard for theoretical reflections on the right in general. I hope to illustrate or instantiate this general point: while evidential reasoning is primarily theoretical, it is legally regulated by rules that are often shaped by practical – including political and ethical – considerations.

To begin with, we need some clarity on the meaning of the right of silence.

10.2 ASPECTS OF THE RIGHT OF SILENCE

The term 'right of silence' does not have a clearly settled meaning and tends to be used loosely. At its broadest, it encompasses that which is known as the privilege against self-incrimination.[6] The right has many aspects. Adopting a Hohfeldian scheme, I set out below the major aspects that are especially relevant in Singapore (Hohfeld, 1913: 16; Hohfeld, 1917: 710). The first set is about silence in the context of police questioning. The second arises at the trial. These two sets contain four equivalent components. The third aspect cuts across both contexts.

Pre-trial: context of police questioning

(1a) The *privilege* (or *liberty*) of a person under police investigation to remain silent or to refuse to answer questions that are potentially self-incriminating; there is an absence of a duty of disclosure on his or her part and no rights of others are violated in remaining silent.

(1b) The *immunity* from legal sanction ('non-liability') should he or she exercise the privilege in (1a).

(1c) The *duty* of the police to forbear from interfering with or denying the choice to exercise the privilege in (1a) and the person's claim-right to such police forbearance.

(1d) The *duty* of the police to take positive measures to protect this freedom of choice and the person's claim-right to such positive measures.

Trial

(2a) The *privilege* (or *liberty*) of an accused person not to testify at his or her trial; there is an absence of a duty to testify and no rights of others are violated in remaining silent.

(2b) The *immunity* from legal sanction ('non-liability') where he or she elects to exercise the privilege in (2a).

---

[6]   See *R* v. *Director of Serious Fraud Office, ex parte Smith* [1993] 1 AC 1 at 30.

(2c) The *duty* of the judge to forbear from interfering with or denying the choice to exercise the privilege in (2a) and the person's claim-right to such forbearance.

(2d) The *duty* of the judge to take positive measures to protect this freedom of choice and the person's claim-right to such positive measures.

Adverse Inference

(3) The *immunity* from adverse *evidential* consequences (whether of the nature of an adverse comment by the prosecutor or judge to the jury or an adverse inference drawn by the fact-finder) where a person exercises the privilege in (1a) or (2a).

10.3 RIGHT OF SILENCE IN SINGAPORE

Some of these aspects of the right exist in Singapore and some do not (see Ho, 2013: 826). Let me summarise the position following the same sequence as above.

The person who is being questioned by the police has a privilege against self-incrimination (1(a)). He 'need not say anything that might expose him to a criminal charge'.[7] In general, no criminal sanction attaches to the exercise of this privilege (1(b)).[8] There is some duty on the police to forbear from interfering with or denying the person the choice whether or not to speak (1(c)). This duty is enforced by criminal sanctions. For instance, it is an offence under the Penal Code for a police officer to cause hurt in order to extort a confession.[9] The breach of this duty of forbearance may also invite sanctions of an evidential nature. If a statement was made by a person as a result of police interference with or denial of the privilege – specifically, if the police had obtained the statement by an inducement, threat or promise[10] or by oppression[11] or torture[12] – it would be inadmissible as evidence. However, this duty of forbearance is not accompanied by a positive obligation to inform the person that he or she has the privilege against self-incrimination (1(d)).[13]

---

[7] Criminal Procedure Code (CPC), s. 22(2).

[8] An exception is where a person is asked to provide information under the Prevention of Corruption Act (PCA). See *Taw Cheng Kong v. PP* [1998] SGCA 37, [1998] 2 S.L.R.(R.) 489; PCA, s. 27 (creating legal duty to give information) and s. 26(d) (prescribing punishment for refusing to give information).

[9] Penal Code, ss. 330 and 331; these provisions apply also to private persons (*PP v. GBZ* [2017] SGDC 271).

[10] CPC, s. 258(3) (provided other conditions are satisfied).

[11] CPC, Explanation 1 to s. 258(3).

[12] See *Yong Vui Kong v. PP* [2015] 2 SLR 1129 at 64.

[13] *PP v. Mazlan bin Maidun* [1992] 3 SLR(R) 968.

Should the case proceed to trial, the accused may elect not to enter the witness box and to remain silent (2(a)). Unlike ordinary witnesses, the accused is not subject to any substantive legal sanctions, such as being held in contempt of court, should he or she decline to testify (2(b)).[14] Not only does the judge have a duty to forebear from interfering with or denying the person the choice to testify or remain silent (2(c)), the judge has a positive duty to inform the person of this choice (2(d)).[15]

I now come to the last aspect. The evidential immunity (3) was removed in 1977. Where a person chooses to withhold information from the police in the course of criminal investigation or chooses to remain silent at his or her trial, the fact-finder has the power to draw such inferences from the non-disclosure or silence as appear proper in determining his or her guilt.[16]

10.4 POWER TO DRAW ADVERSE INFERENCES

This power to draw adverse inferences is not punitive. To treat it as punitive would be inconsistent with the immunity from legal sanctions in (1b) and (2b) that exists under Singapore law. In principle, the drawing of adverse inferences must be based on epistemic considerations. It is improper to draw an adverse inference against the accused simply to punish him or her for failing to co-operate or be candid with the authorities (see, e.g. Leng, 2001: 240). An adverse inference that p is permissible only to the extent that it is justifiable epistemically in the sense that silence under the circumstances is capable of supporting the belief or the proposition that p. The non-disclosure or silence must be such that it provides a good enough basis – and there are different interpretations of what counts as good enough – for drawing a factual inference against the accused that go some way to support the overall finding that he or she is guilty as charged.

10.5 PROBATIVE VALUE OF SILENCE

How is the accused's silence or non-disclosure of information probative? Analysis of its probative value will have to rest on some general theory of evidential reasoning. Some contend that evidential reasoning is mainly atomistic and probabilistic; others believe that it is primarily holistic and

---

[14] CPC, s. 291(4).
[15] CPC, s. 230(1)(m).
[16] In both contexts, the court has the power to draw such inferences as appear proper: CPC, s. 261(1) and s. 291(3), respectively.

explanatory.[17] Without wading into the controversies, let me show how the probative value of silence fits nicely with a theory that has been advanced by Allen together with Pardo and other collaborators.[18] They contend that, in legal disputes, fact-finders do not reason in the fashion portrayed by the Bayesian model. Instead, fact-finders engage in generating explanations for, or hypotheses from, the evidence adduced at the trial by a process of abductive reasoning or drawing 'inferences to the best explanation', and these competing explanations or hypotheses are compared in the light of the evidence.[19] The comparison is not of a hypothesis with the negation of that hypothesis, where the probability of a hypothesis is compared with the probability of its negation. Instead, the comparison is of one hypothesis with one or more specific alternative hypotheses as advocated by a party or as independently constructed by the fact-finder. On this approach, the plausibility of X, the factual account of the case that establishes the accused's guilt, is compared with the plausibility of a hypothesis Y, an alternative account that points to the accused's innocence, and there may be more than one such alternative account. To establish the standard of proof beyond reasonable doubt, there must be a plausible explanation of the evidence that includes all of the elements of the crime and, in addition, there must be no plausible explanation that is consistent with – or, more accurately, that points to – innocence.

There is some support for this theory of proof in cases decided in Singapore although the term 'possibility' is more commonly used than 'plausibility'. Singapore has an adversarial system. There is no jury system. Fact-finding is conducted by the trial judge. As in other common law jurisdictions, the burden is on the prosecution to prove its case beyond reasonable doubt. This standard of proof has been held to mean that the court 'cannot be satisfied beyond reasonable doubt on circumstantial evidence unless no other explanation than guilt is reasonably compatible with the circumstance'.[20] The key question is 'whether the cumulative effect of all the evidence leads ... to the irresistible conclusion that it was the accused who committed this crime. Or is there some reasonably possible explanation ..., for example – "Was it an accident?"'[21]

---

[17] See generally Ho, *Stanford Encyclopaedia of Philosophy*, https://plato.stanford.edu/entries/evidence-legal/.
[18] The latest addition to their writings on the subject is Allen and Pardo, 2019.
[19] For another sophisticated model of legal fact-finding based on inference to the best explanation and coherence, see Amaya, 2009: 135–59; Amaya, 2015: especially ch. 2.
[20] *PP v. Chee Cheong Hin Constance* [2006] 2 SLR(R) 24 at 84.
[21] *Sunny Ang v. PP* [1965–7] SLR(R) 123 at 13.

At the trial, the prosecution will advance a factual hypothesis that establishes the accused's guilt. This 'theory of guilt', as it is sometimes called, must sufficiently explain and be supported by the evidence adduced before the court.[22] The prosecution's theory lacks sufficient explanatory power where the evidence is also consistent with a different theory that points to the reasonable plausibility of the absence of one or more elements of the crime. Since the accused has an interest in preventing the prosecution from succeeding in discharging its burden for proof, he or she has an interest in raising the reasonable plausibility of some such alternative theory. While the defence does not have to prove this alternative theory, it is insufficient to simply suggest some 'fanciful or speculative possibilities'.[23] The Court of Appeal has distinguished between a mere doubt and a reasonable doubt. A 'mere doubt' that is not 'concretely ... articulated in relation to the evidence in the case ... remains an untested hypothesis and may be rejected'.[24]

Here is where the accused's silence may be probative. It is probative where it undermines the plausibility of the alternative hypothesis of innocence raised by the defence. In *Oh Laye Koh* v. *PP*,[25] the accused was prosecuted on a charge of murder. He was the driver of a school bus and the victim was one of the students who regularly took his bus. At the trial, circumstantial evidence was adduced by the prosecution to prove facts that included the following: the victim was last seen alive boarding a bus that looked like the accused's bus. There was no one else in it apart from the two of them. The accused had previously teased and made other upsetting remarks to the victim, including remarks about her body. The accused lied about his bus undergoing repair in the afternoon on the day the girl went missing and had asked a mechanic to support his lie. He had eventually led the police to the spot where the victim's decomposed body was found and to another spot where her schoolbooks were discovered. There was expert evidence that certain injuries on the victim were caused by a blow delivered with great force. In the face of these and other incriminating evidence, the accused elected to remain silent at the trial.

The trial judge in applying the standard of proof beyond reasonable doubt proceeded by considering 'whether on a review of the whole case, the facts proved are not only consistent with [the accused's] guilt but also such that they are inconsistent with any other reasonable conclusion'. The fact that the

---

[22]   See, e.g. *XP* v. *PP* [2008] 4 SLR(R) 686 at 94.

[23]   *PP* v. *Chee Cheong Hin Constance* [2006] 2 SLR(R) 24 at 85.

[24]   *Took Leng How* v. *PP* [2006] 2 SLR(R) 70 at 29, quoting from Tan Yock Lin, *Criminal Procedure* (Singapore: LexisNexis, 2005) vol. 2, ch. XVII at [2952].

[25]   [1994] SGCA 102 (Court of Appeal).

accused chose to remain silent and the absence of an explanation from him 'greatly strengthened the Prosecution case'. The judge was 'satisfied that the various circumstances [were] not capable of any explanation consistent with [his] innocence' and convicted the accused.[26]

There was an appeal against the conviction. The defence counsel argued that the trial judge had misapplied the standard of proof in failing to consider the possibility that the victim might have died as a result of being hit by the bus in an accident and that the lies told by the accused could have been told to dissociate himself from the incident.

The Court of Appeal accepted that 'if it were a reasonable hypothesis that the deceased could possibly have died in an accident, the appellant's guilt would not have been proved beyond reasonable doubt'.[27] However, the hypothesis was not a reasonable one. 'It is not the duty of the courts to devise and conjecture possible defences for an accused, particularly ... when the accused could so easily have explained what actually happened to the deceased.'[28]

In the present case, silence of the accused (E) is probative and supports the prosecution's theory (X = that it was the accused who had intentionally caused the death of the victim) insofar as it undermined the plausibility of the competing – and guilt-defeating – hypothesis (Y) raised by the defence (that the accused had accidently hit the victim with his bus). To flesh this out in explanatory terms, we may draw on the notion of 'normic support' developed by Martin Smith (2018):

> E (the silence of accused at the trial) normically supports not-Y (where Y is the proposition that the accused had accidently hit the victim with his bus) insofar as the circumstance in which E and Y are both true requires more explanation than the circumstance in which E is true and Y is false.

For Smith, normalcy is not just a matter of statistical generalisations where 'normal circumstances are circumstances that frequently obtain while abnormal circumstances are circumstances that infrequently obtain'. It is highly improbable that I will win a fair lottery where I hold just one out of a million tickets. But it is not 'abnormal' for me to win in the sense that if I do win, I will not go look for some special explanation for winning – it just so happened that my ticket was the winning ticket, and it could equally have been any of the tickets.

Silence is evidence that calls for explanation. Given our general beliefs about the world, including human psychology, we may think that in the circumstance,

---

[26]   *PP* v. *Oh Laye Koh* [1994] SGHC 129 (High Court).
[27]   *Oh Laye Koh* v. *PP* [1994] SGCA 102 at 19.
[28]   *Ibid.* at 20.

it is normal for an innocent person to speak and not remain silent, and that silence where the accused is factually innocent calls for more explanation than silence where he or she is factually guilty. It is abnormal for an accused person who is in fact innocent to remain silent – special explanation is called for, and especially so, as in the case under discussion, where the accused's guilt has emerged as a highly plausible explanation of the evidence adduced at the trial, and where the accused alone is in a position to and can easily give evidence in support of the hypothesis that is being relied upon to counteract the prosecution's theory.[29] In the absence of some special explanation for the accused's silence, it normically supports the falsity of the defence hypothesis.

A similar reasoning is applicable to pre-trial silence. Silence during police questioning may undermine the plausibility of the competing hypothesis that the defence raises only later at the trial. Where facts supporting the hypothesis was not disclosed by the accused during police interrogation, the law in Singapore allows an adverse inference to be drawn from the non-disclosure. Judges tend to treat pre-trial silence as a phenomenon that begs for some special explanation. If the facts that the accused now allege in his or her defence are true, why did he or she not mention them earlier on? The circumstance of non-disclosure to the police where the defence hypothesis is true requires more explanation than the circumstance of non-disclosure to the police where the defence hypothesis is false. As compared to silence at the trial, the normic support of pre-trial silence for the falsity of the defence hypothesis is easier to rebut. This is because many explanations are potentially available in the circumstance of non-disclosure. The non-disclosure could be the result of stress or mental disorientation caused by an oppressive interrogative environment or the lack of knowledge (especially likely if the person had no access to counsel) at that point in time about the legal significance of the undisclosed facts.

10.6 RELATIONSHIP BETWEEN POWER TO DRAW ADVERSE INFERENCES AND THE PRIVILEGE OF SILENCE

It has been argued before the Privy Council (which was then Singapore's highest appellate court) that the power to draw an adverse inference from silence (that is, the lack of the evidential immunity in (3)) violates the

---

[29] This reasoning will have to rely on generalisations. As L. Jonathan Cohen wrote in *The Probable and the Provable* (Cohen, 1977: 247), generalisations in judicial fact-finding 'are not statable as exact and fully determinate correlations . . . They function instead as common-sense presumptions, which state what is normally to be expected but are rebuttable in their applications to a particular situation if it can be shown to be abnormal in some relevant respect.'

accused's privilege against self-incrimination at the pre-trial stage (1a) and the liberty to remain silent at the trial (2a) because it has the effect of compelling speech in both situations.[30] In rejecting this argument, the Privy Council reasoned that the power to draw an adverse inference does not *compel* but merely *induces* the accused to speak.[31] This stands at odd with a recent Court of Appeal decision concerning legal professional privilege. It was held that, in principle, no adverse inference may be drawn from the exercise of this privilege because 'to draw an adverse inference ... in such a situation would be to render [the] privilege otiose'.[32] If this be so for legal professional privilege, why cannot something similar be said of the privilege of silence? I think it can be.

The privilege to remain silent during police questioning (1a) and at the trial (2a) may be understood as the liberty to exclude oneself from being utilised as a source of evidence in the legal determination of one's guilt. Allowing the trial court to draw an adverse inference from the exercise of this privilege will significantly undermine the value of the privilege. One is no longer at full liberty to exclude oneself from being a source of incriminating evidence – by remaining silent at the trial or refusing to answer potentially self-incriminating questions put by the police – if silence itself can be treated as a form of self-incriminating evidence. Where silence will result in an adverse inference, there is self-incrimination even in silence. The absence of the immunity in (3) undermines the value of the privilege in (1a) and (2a).

10.7 LEGAL REGULATION OF EVIDENTIAL REASONING

Unlike the position in Singapore, some legal systems afford immunity in the form of a prohibition against adverse comments being made on, or adverse inferences being drawn from, the accused's silence during police questioning or at the trial.[33]

---

[30] Assuming the accused is aware of the judicial power to draw adverse inferences from silence.

[31] *Jaykumal v. PP* [1981–2] SLR(R) 147; *Haw Tua Tau v. PP* [1981–2] SLR(R) 13.

[32] *Mykytowych v. VIP Hotel* [2016] SGCA 44 at 55.

[33] Examples may be found in the law of the United States (*Griffin v. California*, 380 US 609 (1965)); Canada (*R. v. Chambers*, 1990 CanLII 47 (SCC), [1990] 2 SCR 1293); India (s. 315(1) (b) of the Code of Criminal Procedure 1973 provides that accused's 'failure to give evidence shall not be made the subject of any comment by any of the parties or the Court or give rise to any presumption against himself'); Scotland (in a 2011 review of the criminal justice system commissioned by the Scottish government, it was recommended that 'no change be made to the current law ... that prevents inferences being drawn at trial from an accused's failure to answer questions during the police investigation': *The Carloway Review – Report and Recommendations* (17 November 2011) at 328, available at: www.gov.scot/Resource/Doc/925/0122808.pdf (last accessed on 4 July 2018) and the Rome Statute of the International Criminal Court (Article 67(1)(g) states that the accused's silence shall not be 'a consideration in the determination of guilt or innocence').

A rule that prevents the accused's silence from being used as evidence in the legal determination of guilt requires justification insofar as it runs against the truth-seeking objective of the trial. Epistemic justification for this is possible. It may be that fact-finders, for various reasons, tend to be overly dismissive of innocent explanations for the accused's silence. If so, it may promote fact-finding accuracy in the long run by barring the use of silence as incriminating evidence as a rule (Schauer, 2008a: 165; Schauer, 2008b: 295). I do not know whether this is empirically true in Singapore or elsewhere. Let me set it aside.

The justification for prohibiting the use of the accused's silence as incriminating evidence may also draw on practical – political or ethical – considerations. I claimed earlier that allowing adverse inferences to be drawn from silence would impair the privilege or liberty to remain silent. If this is right, a possible practical justification for the evidential immunity (aspect (3)) is that it serves to uphold the privilege of silence (aspects (1a) and (2a)). The strength of this practical justification would depend on whether upholding the privilege (1a and 2a) through the immunity (3) is worth the sacrifice of silence as a form of probative evidence.

In Singapore, the view is taken that it is not. As I mentioned, the evidential immunity was abolished in 1977. The removal of the immunity has been officially defended on two fronts: first by emphasising that recognition of the immunity will result in a loss of probative incriminating evidence, thus harming the effectiveness of crime control and secondly by de-valuing the privilege of silence as a due process right. Political legitimacy is claimed for striking the balance in favour of removing the immunity on the ground that it reflects Asian or national values and that Singaporeans mostly value crime control more than they do the rights of individuals suspected or accused of having committed an offence.

10.8 LEGISLATIVE HISTORY

In Singapore, the power to draw adverse inferences from silence was introduced by the Criminal Procedure Code (Amendment) Act. This Act was passed in 1976 and came into force in 1977. The relevant amendments were based substantially on the recommendations made in 1972 by the Criminal Law Revision Committee of England and Wales (the CLRC) in its 11th Report on Evidence. During the second reading of the amendment bill in 1975, the Minister for Law explained in Parliament the need for reforming the law:

> Experience has shown that determined criminals are not sufficiently deterred by merely enhancing the punishments for various offences. A greater

deterrent would be to increase the chances of their conviction when they are apprehended and, with this in mind, it has been decided through this Amendment Bill to adopt certain of the recommendations of the Criminal Law Revision Committee of the United Kingdom.[34]

According to the Minister, the amendment bill 'proposes to restrict greatly the so-called right of silence enjoyed by suspects when interrogated by the police or by anyone charged with the duty of investigating offences'. In moving the passage of the bill, the Minister stated that '[i]t is as much in the public interest that a guilty person should be convicted as it is that an innocent person should be acquitted', and he drew support from the following passage in the CLRC Report:

> In our opinion it is wrong that it should not be permissible for the jury or magistrates' court to draw whatever inferences are reasonable from the failure of the accused, when interrogated, to mention a defence which he puts forward at his trial. To forbid it seems to us to be contrary to common sense and, without helping the innocent, to give an unnecessary advantage to the guilty. Hardened criminals often take advantage of the present rule to refuse to answer any questions at all, and this may greatly hamper the police and even bring their investigations to a halt. Therefore the abolition of the restriction would help justice.[35]

In England, the CLRC's proposal to abolish the right of silence met with vociferous opposition, both in and outside of parliament (e.g., Gerstein, 1979a: 81). The proposal was not implemented. While acknowledging the 'severe criticisms' faced by the CLRC proposal in England, the Minister noted that local conditions were different:

> we have no jury in Singapore and we have to assume that our magistrates and judges can empathise. It is relevant to note here that whereas a very high proportion of the criminal cases heard in the magistrates' courts in England and Wales are tried by lay justices, all the magistrates in Singapore are today legally trained.

What we can see from these passages is that the power to draw adverse inferences from non-disclosure or silence is defended mainly on two grounds. The first is the interest in crime-control and rests on the belief that introducing a power to draw adverse inferences from non-disclosure or silence would remove an obstacle that 'greatly hampers' police investigation and make it easier to secure criminal convictions. The Blackstonian ratio,

---

[34] *Parliamentary Debates Singapore, Official Report*, 19 August 1975, vol. 34, columns 1217–18.
[35] *Ibid.* at column 1218.

which prioritises the avoidance of one kind of false positive over another (better to acquit ten guilty persons than to convict one innocent man or woman), is reframed in terms of true positives and given equal weight: it is 'as much in the public interest' to convict the guilty as to acquit the innocent. The second point is about a structural difference between the criminal justice system in Singapore and that in England and Wales; the fact that fact-finders in Singapore, unlike in England and Wales, are legally trained judges provides some assurance that the proposed power will not be misapplied or abused. Judges are less likely than laypersons to read too much into silence.

Neither of these two grounds are based on any assertion of Asian-ness or Asian values, however, we define Asia and Asian values. This is obvious in relation to the second ground; the lack of a jury system is neither characteristic of nor unique to legal systems in Asia. As for the first ground, it is not only in Asia that the criminal legal system has been shaped by the felt pressure to be tough on crime. For instance, a study by two American scholars shows that the willingness of Anglo-American law to uphold the right of silence has swung four times over the course of history from one extreme to the other. The shifts in the degree of interrogative pressure that was used and legally tolerated corresponded to the social perception of the level of internal and external threats (Thomas III and Leo, 2012).

It would have been somewhat ludicrous for the Minister to have pressed for reform of Singapore law in 1975 by arguing that it promoted distinctly Asian values – which he did not do. After all, the reform was based on the recommendations in a report written by fourteen British jurists presented to the Parliament in the United Kingdom by command of Her Majesty. What prompted these fourteen jurists to recommend the diminution of the right of silence had nothing to do with values characteristic of Asians nor conditions unique to Asia. In taking a negative view of the right of silence, the CLRC was adopting the position articulated by their fellow Englishman, Bentham, in the early nineteenth century.[36] It is true that the CLRC's proposal to erode the right of silence met with fierce opposition and had to be abandoned. But it is equally true that decades later, the right of silence came to eroded in England

---

[36] A *Treatise on Judicial Evidence* (London: J. W. Paget, 1825) at 241 (anonymous English translation of Etienne Dumont (ed.), *Traité des Preuves Judiciares* (Paris, 1823)): 'If all criminals of every class had assembled, and framed a system after their own wishes, is not this rule the very first which they would have established for their security? Innocence never takes advantage of it. Innocence claims the right of speaking, as guilt invokes the privilege of silence.' This passage is commonly attributed to Bentham but was in fact written by his French translator, Dumont: Lewis, 1990: 139; Lewis, 1988: 40–1.

and Wales.[37] I have not heard anyone say that this was the result of a Western turn to Asian values.

10.9 ASIAN VALUES

It was only much later that talk about Asian values came into the picture. In a speech given in 1990 by the then prime minister, he gave his take on the 'philosophical approach to the development of the law and the legal system in Singapore'.

> The basic difference in our approach springs from our traditional Asian value system which places the interests of the community over and above that of the individual.
>
> In English doctrine, the rights of the individual must be the paramount consideration. We shook ourselves free from the confines of English norms which did not accord with customs and values of Singapore society.
>
> In criminal law legislation, our priority is the security and well-being of law-abiding citizens rather than the rights of the criminal to be protected from incriminating evidence.[38]

Much has been written on the political use or misuse of the discourse on Asian values.[39] As I just noted, as a matter of history, the language of Asian values post-dated the legislative reform that undermined the right of silence. Be that as it may, my interest is in considering the argument on its own terms. Can anything be drawn from the Asian values discourse that might support the dilution of the right of silence? But there is more of the story to tell: the discourse has been elided with or morphed into something that is not quite identical.

10.10 NATIONAL VALUES AND SOVEREIGNTY

'We are Asians' is no longer a popular idiom in the defence of Singapore criminal law (cf. Chan, 2000a). Taking its place in the last decade or so is an assertion of national sovereignty. The emphasis is no longer explicitly on Asian values but on the right of a sovereign nation to set her own priorities in the crafting of her laws. A balance has to be struck between competing interests that is acceptable to and reflects the will of the majority of the populace. An

---

[37] On the history of the legislative erosion of the right of silence in England, see Quirk, 2017: ch. 2.
[38] 'Address by the Prime Minister, Mr Lee Kuan Yew' (1990) 2 *Singapore Academy L. J.* 155 at 155.
[39] For a balanced critique, see Chan, 1997: 35.

oft-repeated message is that the people of Singapore generally places greater value on 'crime control' than on 'due process'. Speaking extra-judicially, and employing the well-known lexicon of an American scholar writing on the law in the United States, the then chief justice observed that 'Singapore ceased to give maximum due process to accused persons from 1976 and has progressively favoured the crime control model' (Chan, 2000b: 42). The idea that value choices underpin the design of criminal justice systems was borrowed explicitly from Western scholarship.[40]

The crime control ideology takes the suppression of crime as the dominant aim and is premised on an assumption about the negative impact of individual rights on the containment of criminal activities. It is assumed that to be strong on rights is to be soft on crime, and, conversely, those rights, including the right of silence, needs to be weakened in order to be effective in crime control. The fact that Singapore has a low crime rate is said to vindicate encroachments on individual rights (see, e.g. Shanmugan, 2012: 360–1). This has been the consistent line taken by the government and the judiciary in the last decade or two. The remainder of this section recounts many instances where this stand was officially articulated.

In a speech given at a New York State Bar Association Rule of Law Plenary Session in 2009, the Singapore Minister in charge of Law and Home Affairs reminded his foreign audience of the following:[41] 'Every society seeks to strike a balance between the rights of the individual and the rights of society, in enacting its criminal legislation. How that balance is struck depends on the philosophy of the society . . .. We do tend to weight the balance more towards the society compared with you.'

In response to a question about the diminution of the right of silence in Singapore, the minister defended the approach as one that 'works for us and enjoys broad public support'.[42] He stressed that it has been very effective in keeping crime down and maintaining order and security.[43]

---

[40] Packer, 1964; later developed into Part II of Packer, 1968.
[41] Shanmugan, 2012: 78–9 of the speech which is available at www.nas.gov.sg/archivesonline/speeches/view-html?filename=20091104002.htm (last accessed 4 July 2018).
[42] *Ibid.* at [99].
[43] *Ibid.* at [96]–[97]:
What is the result of our approach?:

1) If you asked any Singaporean lady in this room: she will have not too much concern about taking the metro or taxi or bus at any time, to any location.
2) You can walk downtown, to any area, at any time, without fear or concern.
3) Many parents will let their children under 10 take public transport, on their own. Children move about freely – as children should.

This is not just the personal view of one minister. It is the official position taken by the state. Singapore has participated twice in the Universal Periodic Review (UPR). The UPR is conducted under the auspices of the United Nations' Human Rights Council for the purpose of reviewing the human rights records of member states. The first UPR of Singapore was conducted in 2011 and the second in 2016.

In the National Report submitted for the 2011 UPR, the government drew attention to the fact that the Singapore Constitution 'guarantees due process and fair trial'.[44] However, there is a need to subject 'individual rights ... to legal limits in order to protect the rights of others, as well as to maintain public order and general welfare'.[45] The section of the Report on criminal justice stresses that 'it is a fundamental human right of all citizens to live in a safe environment, free from drugs, guns, random street violence and terrorism'.[46] The laws in Singapore 'are designed to protect the public against crimes, while ensuring that persons accused of alleged crimes have due process and fair trials. Singapore's crime rate is one of the lowest – 684 per 100,000 population in 2008, with 111 violent crimes per 100,000 population – despite a relatively small police force.'[47]

In the 2015 National Report for the second UPR,[48] the government reiterated that it considers 'the safety and security of the person to be a fundamental human right, without which other rights cannot genuinely be enjoyed'.[49] It is pointed out that the island state is the 'world's second safest city, after Tokyo (Economist Safe Cities Index 2015). All residents, including women and minorities, can go where they please freely and without fear, in any part of Singapore, at any time of day or night'.[50] The priority and 'cardinal objective' of Singapore's criminal justice system is to 'deter crime and protect society against criminals'.[51]

---

4) There are no slums, no 'no go' areas, no deprived inner city areas. More than 90 per cent of the population own their homes.

Our crime rate is low. Last year, we had a crime rate of 684 per 100,000 population. New York, which has made significant steps to becoming one of the safest large cities in the USA, had 2,400 per 100,000. If you look at violent crimes, we have 111 per 100,000 population. New York has 580 per 100,000 population.

[44] National report submitted in accordance with paragraph 15 (a) of the annex to Human Rights Council resolution 5/1 (2 February 2011) at [23].
[45] *Ibid.* at [110].
[46] *Ibid.* at [119].
[47] *Ibid.* at [119].
[48] National report submitted in accordance with paragraph 5 of the annex to Human Rights Council resolution 16/21 (28 October 2015).
[49] *Ibid.* at [100].
[50] *Ibid.*
[51] *Ibid.* at [101].

The views of the government have been echoed by judges.[52] In a speech given in India, the then chief justice of Singapore gave this positive portrayal of Singapore law.

> Singapore has a relatively safe and secure environment that is free from crime because our leaders had the political will to enact an appropriate legal framework to achieve it. . . . Amongst other things, a suspect is encouraged to be candid during interrogation . . .
>
> In the realm of procedural justice, many of the provisions in the CPC and the Evidence Act have been modified to give greater effect to crime control. . . . [T]he original provisions of these two Acts reflected an adherence to *due process*, rather than crime control, values. This approach was best illustrated by the rules regarding an accused person's testimony. Upon his arrest, an accused did not have to answer *any* incriminating questions. His silence during interrogation could *not* be raised as a relevant consideration at trial . . . . During the trial itself, an accused could continue to maintain his silence *with* impunity . . . .
>
> In 1976, the CPC was amended to incorporate the recommendations of the 11th Report of the UK Criminal Law Committee by modifying the right to silence . . . . This amendment has greatly assisted our law enforcement agencies in investigating offences, leading to many more factually guilty persons being convicted through guilty pleas or convictions at trial.
>
> . . . A suspect still has a right *not* to answer a question that may incriminate him, but any omission by the police to inform him of this right will not affect the admissibility of any admission he makes. When he is charged and asked to state his defence, he remains silent at the risk of an adverse inference being drawn against him if he subsequently offers an explanation as part of his defence at trial . . . . During the trial, . . . if he fails to testify, an adverse inference may be drawn against him.[53]

The same speaker had aired similar views on at least two other occasions before his appointment as the chief justice. The first occasion was in a speech given in his capacity as the attorney-general at the opening of the Legal Year in 1995. He stated:

> The common law and rules of equity reflect ideas and principles of right and justice in English society at various periods of history. We cannot change our legal history but we can continue to adapt and modify our legal inheritance to promote the social and cultural values appropriate to our society, as for

---

52   See generally Jayasuriya, 1999; cf. Palmer, 2017: 505.
53   Chan Sek Keong CJ, 'From Justice Model to Crime Control Model', address before the International Conference on Criminal Justice Under Stress: Transnational Perspectives, New Delhi, India (24 November 2006) at [13]–[16].

example, giving primacy to community rights over individual rights and promoting the virtue of social obligations over the demand of individual rights.[54]

After noting that the right to silence is one of the 'principles which in the past have erected an iron curtain to protect an accused in a criminal trial', the Attorney-General went on to ask:[55] 'whether the right to silence is so fundamental to the fairness of our criminal justice system that any diminution of this right will render a fair trial difficult or impossible. What value should we give to the right of silence in a criminal justice system that is fair to society as well as the accused?'

In defending the 1976 amendments that diminish the right of silence in Singapore, the Attorney-General cited Bentham's view that 'innocence claims the right of speaking as guilt invokes the privilege of silence', and added that while it 'is in the public interest that an accused should have due process', 'at the same time the public is entitled to a criminal justice system which does not make it easy for the guilty to go free'.[56]

The second occasion was in a lecture given at the National University of Singapore in 1996. In defending the 'Singapore model' of the criminal process, the attorney-general stressed the following:

> Each country must have a criminal justice system which meets its own needs.... Most Singaporeans, I believe, appreciate the safe environment they live in and support a criminal justice system that is responsible for it .... (Chan, 1996: 434)

> What that balance should be, between community needs and individual rights in the criminal process, is determined by the ideological and social goals of the government of the day. If anything has been made clear in Singapore, it is that crime control has always been and is a high priority on the Government's action agenda. (Chan, 1996: 438)

The airing of these views is not confined to speeches and lectures. These views have found their way into legal judgments. For example, in the 2008 case of *Law Society of Singapore* v. *Tan Guat Neo Phyllis*,[57] the High Court (sitting as a bench of three judges) stated:

> Whilst we pay great respect to the decisions of the appellate courts in Australia, Canada and England ..., we must also bear in mind that the

---

[54] (1995) *Singapore Academy of Law Newsletter* 2 at 2.
[55] *Ibid.* at 2–3.
[56] *Ibid.* at 3.
[57] [2008] 2 SLR(R) 239.

legal and social environments in these jurisdictions are not the same, and that the courts in each jurisdiction must take into account the values and objectives of the criminal justice system which they wish to promote. The common law is infused with common or universal values which are applicable in all common law jurisdictions, but, in the field of criminal law, national values on law and order may differ not only in type, but also in intensity of adherence.

A year earlier, the High Court had similarly remarked:[58]

... the judicial philosophy and approach to crime control in each jurisdiction is a policy decision based on the balancing of communitarian values and concerns against individual interests. It is pointless to attempt to distil from the various strands of foreign criminal legal jurisprudence a universal consensus that could or should be applied in Singapore. The present crime control model premised on a judicious and focussed application of deterrence coupled with the effective apprehension of offenders has worked well for Singapore.[59]

These extracts serve to illustrate the common line that the state and its officials, including judges, have taken in shaping and defending the criminal justice system in Singapore.[60] As a sovereign nation, she has the right to strike a balance between the social interest in combating crime and respect for individual rights.

10.11 TAKING STOCK OF THE OFFICIAL DISCOURSE

The argument advanced by the state and its functionaries, at its simplest, is that the vast majority of Singaporeans value security against crime much more than they do individual rights of criminal justice, and, on the assumption that they are negatively correlated, this legitimises the sacrifice (to some extent) of the latter for the sake of achieving the former. This ordering of priorities reflects values shared by most Singaporeans, in particular, the value of placing 'society above self'.[61]

---

[58] *PP* v. *Law Aik Meng* [2007] 2 SLR(R) 814 at 19 (remarks made in the context of sentencing). See also *Yuan Suan Piau Steven* v. *PP* [2013] 1 SLR 809 at 31.

[59] This was an entrapment case. For a critique, see Ho, 2012: 232.

[60] See also the Practice Statement (Judicial Precedent) issued by the judiciary on 11 July 1994 and published in [1994] 2 SLR 689: 'We recognize the vital role that the doctrine of stare decisis plays in giving certainty to the law and predictability on its application to similar cases. However, we also recognize that the political, social and economic circumstances of Singapore have changed enormously since Singapore became an independent and sovereign republic. The development of our law should reflect these changes and the fundamental values of Singapore society.'

[61] This is one of the five values proposed for promotion among Singaporeans in the White Paper presented to Parliament on 2 January 1991 ('Shared Values', Paper Cmd. No. 1 of 1991) and adopted by Parliament on 15 January 1991.

The argument as framed raises – or conceals – all sorts of difficult questions. Some are empirical (and largely unanswered): to what extent can an increase in efficiency in law enforcement or a decrease in the number of crimes be causally attributed to the dilution of any individual right of criminal justice? There is also a variety of theoretical questions. What exactly do we mean by Asian or national values (definitional)? Are there such things (ontological)? If there are such things, how do we know what they are (epistemic)? Then there is the socio-political question: is law shaped by the character of a society that is defined by the values held by the majority or most (powerful) of its members or is it determined (decisively or to a greater extent) by the circumstances in which a particular society (be it in the East or in the West) happen to find itself at a particular moment in history? (Could it be true as a general proposition that the greater the criminal threat that is perceived by *any* society, the stronger the call for 'crime control' measures?) How should we see the differences? Are societies subscribing to different values or do they differ only in the manner in which they express or rank or weight or operationalise the values that they have in common? And so on. These general and important questions cannot be addressed on this occasion. My concern is more specific: in what sort of (supposedly non-liberal or communitarian) perspective is the discourse on the right of silence in Singapore grounded?

Serving as a good launch pad for discussion is the English case of *Rice v. Connolly*.[62] A police constable questioned a man whom he had spotted behaving suspiciously. The issue was whether the man had committed the offence of 'wilfully' obstructing the constable in the execution of his duty by refusing to answer his questions. The court held that the accused had a legal right to silence and therefore his refusal to answer was not 'wilful'. In a telling passage, Lord Parker CJ explained:

> though every citizen has a moral duty or, if you like, a social duty to assist the police, there is no legal duty to that effect, and indeed . . . the whole basis of the common law is the right of the individual to refuse to answer questions put to him by persons in authority.[63]

Is silence, then, immoral or anti-social? And if so, how is the legal privilege of silence defensible?[64]

---

[62] [1966] 2 QB 414.

[63] *Ibid.* at 419.

[64] Academic literature exploring the rationale is vast. For critical overviews, see Dolinko, 1986; 1063; Roberts and Zuckerman, 2010: 547–63.

10.12 JUSTIFICATIONS FOUNDED ON LIBERAL INDIVIDUALISM

The privilege to remain silent would seem to run against ordinary practices of morality. After all, we are taught from young that the right thing to do when we have done wrong is to own up.[65] Confession is good for our moral health. And, according to some religions, it frees us from our sins.[66]

But this criticism needs to be handled with care. Even if confessing to a crime is the morally right thing to do, it does not follow that the law should force suspects to confess their guilt. It is a mistake to read a law that permits a type of action as necessarily encouraging it. A legislation that allows euthanasia under certain circumstances is not affirming the principle that the morally right thing for a person to do in those circumstances is to end his or her life (Waldron, 1981: 23). Similarly, in giving the suspect the right not to confess, the law is not thereby promoting silence as the right course of action – or, rather, inaction. The right of silence gives the suspect the liberty, and protects the liberty, not to self-incriminate or confess; the right itself provides no reason for the suspect either to remain silent or to disclose his or her guilt. The decision is left to the individual to make.

From a liberal perspective, the right of silence upholds individual freedom. The liberty in question has been interpreted in moral and political terms. Let me give an example of each of these interpretations.

A possible moral interpretation proceeds as follows.[67] The right of silence recognises and protects individual freedom in a specific respect – a person's freedom to make an autonomous moral decision on a matter that is of significance to his or her life and identity. In the moral realm, to self-incriminate or confess is not merely to divulge or let slip incriminating facts; it is also about recognising one's error and accepting responsibility for one's

---

[65] As noted by, among others, Friendly, 1968: 680 '[T]he lesson parents preach is that a misdeed, even a serious one, will generally be forgiven, a failure to make a clean breast of it will not be. Every hour of the day people are being asked to explain their conduct to parents, employers and teachers. Those who are questioned consider themselves to be morally bound to respond, and the questioners believe it proper to take action if they do not.'

[66] Examples may be found in Christianity (e.g. 1 John 1.9: 'If we confess our sins, he is faithful and just to forgive us our sins and to cleanse us from all unrighteousness') and Hinduism (see Pandurang Vaman Kane, *History of Dharmaśāstra (Ancient and Mediæval Religious and Civil Law in India)* (Poona: Bhandarkar Oriental Research Institute, 1977) at 40, quoting an Ancient Hindu text on the belief that 'by confession, by repentance, by austerity, by reciting Vedic texts . . . a sinner is freed from guilt').

[67] The argument is that the legal right to silence has a moral foundation and not that there is a moral right to remain silent. On the distinction, see Donagan, 1984; 147. On the issue of whether the accused has a moral right to remain silent, see Bronaugh, 1998: 86; Greenawalt, 1981: 15.

action. It is these qualities in or associated with a confession that pave the way for personal reform. A confession that has this moral value must ultimately be voluntary; it cannot be extracted by command and compulsion. The right of silence ensures that the suspect or accused person has, according to Gerstein, 'the opportunity to come to terms in his own conscience with the accusation against him' (Gerstein, 1979b: 343–4). To coerce a person into self-condemnation is, he claims, 'to stultify his ability sincerely to take responsibility for his actions' and to weaken 'the very capacities for self-evaluation and regeneration that we rely upon for rehabilitation in punishment' (Gerstein, 1971: 84–8. See also Gerstein, 1970; 87).

From a different liberal perspective, the right of silence is an expression of the political right of individuals to offer resistance against the state. Hobbes, for instance, argued that no man is bound to confess to a crime, thereby exposing himself to punishment, when interrogated by the sovereign or by his authority (Hobbes, 1962 [1651]: at 164). He deduced the right not to confess from the broader principle that 'no man can transfer, or lay down his right to save himself from death, wounds, and imprisonment, the avoiding whereof is the only end of laying down any right' (Hobbes, 1962 [1651]: 110. See, further Hobbes, 1962 [1651]: chs. 14 and 21). Ristroph has offered this reading of Hobbes. In entering into civil society, one exchanges most of one's natural rights – on the condition that other individuals will do likewise – for the security that only the all-powerful sovereign can provide. If the grant of authority to the sovereign is for the sake of my self-preservation, to protect myself from harm, it must come with the implicit reservation of my right to resist should the sovereign attempt to harm me (Ristroph, 2009: 615–16). The individual's right to resist punishment by the sovereign is not a legally enforceable claim but merely a 'blameless liberty'.[68] It 'simply means that we should not be surprised if the condemned man fights back, nor can we say that he is wrong to do so' (Ristroph, 2009: 619 footnote 89). Since there can be no punishment without a conviction, the right not to confess is a derivative of the right to resist punishment. Unlike the right to resist punishment, the right not to confess, as with other due process rights, is legally enforceable. In refusing to confess, a person is resisting a criminal conviction. Legal recognition of this right to resist – whether the person is factually innocent or guilty, or even especially if he or she is guilty – is, on this view, a form of respect for the

---

[68] Hobbes, 1889 [1640]: 71 as quoted by Ristroph, 2009: 617: '[T]hat which is not against reason, men call RIGHT, or *jus*, or blameless liberty of using our own natural power and ability. It is therefore a *right of nature*, that every man may preserve his own life and limbs, with all the power he hath.'

individual. 'Hobbesian respect for criminals refuses to blame humans for acting on the fundamental and rational drive for self-preservation.'[69]

This political justification for the privilege of silence views the criminal process as, in the words of Griffiths, 'a struggle – a stylized war – between two contending forces' (Griffiths, 1970; 367) where there is 'profound and irreconcilable disharmony of interest' between the state and the person suspected or accused of a crime. The former is interested in putting the 'suspected criminal in jail' for preventive or retributive reasons whereas the latter is interested in getting acquitted.

10.13 A COMMUNITARIAN PERSPECTIVE

Suppose we take a non-liberal, communitarian, perspective. Let us consider Confucianism which was the principal source of the Singapore school of Asian Values. At first blush, it is absurd to think that classical Confucianism can have anything to say about a legal right that, in its time, had yet to emerge from Western legal history.

This is true. But it is a little too hasty. Confucianism has been interpreted as a variety of virtue-ethics (e.g. Sim, 2015) and as a form of role-ethics (e.g. Rosemont Jr. and Ames, 2016). Moral virtues or social roles take centre-stage in the ethical analysis. Suppose we take the standpoint of a virtuous person or social role-bearer who is accused of or questioned about a crime. What will he or she do?

Ethical theories of the deontological variety put primary emphasis on rules and duties. Consequentialist ethical theories focus on the evaluation of consequences. In contrast, virtue ethics places primary analytical importance on the virtues of the agent and role-ethics focuses on reciprocal interactions of persons that are defined by their social roles. Human or social flourishing is the way of life of the virtuous. This may well call for a remorseful confession when one is accused of or questioned about a crime. A confession, followed by repentance and atonement, is likely to contribute to repairing the social relationship that has been disrupted by an antisocial criminal act. This is a perspective that lends itself to what John Griffith has described as the family model of the criminal justice system (see generally Rosemont Jr., 2015: 167–71 and 63). A criminal process that is modelled on family relations would be based on an 'assumption of reconcilable – even mutually supportive – interests' between state and individual (Griffiths, 1970; 371). Reconciliation is emphasised. Members of

---

[69] Ristroph, 2009: 628. For a related discussion drawing on Lockean contractarianism, see Green, 1999: 627.

society are perceived as bearing roles that come with responsibilities; they are not free but necessarily and desirably encumbered in an interrelated co-existence that aspire to human and social flourishing (see generally Rosemont Jr., 2015). Conversely, if society is but an aggregate of agents who bear rights that protect their inherent and separate claims to freedom and autonomy, individuals should be protected against the state under a battle model of criminal justice system. (It is ironic that Singapore officials adopt this individualistic portrayal of the criminal justice system when they purport to rely on communitarian values.)

All that I am suggesting is that Confucianism offers a perspective that differs from the liberal one. I do not suggest that this perspective is available only from Confucianism. Other communitarian theories originating from the West or within Asia may well cast the same light on the right of silence.

A different perspective does not necessarily lead to a different conclusion. I am not suggesting that Confucianism is necessarily in favour of using the law to compel self-incrimination. In the first place, it is well known that classical Confucianism favours the use of rites and moral exemplars over the law as primary sources of guiding social behaviour. 'Confucius himself was ... skeptical about the ability of laws and punishments to create and/or maintain a decent human society' (Rosemont Jr., 2015: 165). In this connection, the following passage from the Analects is frequently cited (Ames, 2011: 189):

> The Master said: 'Lead the people with policies and keep them orderly with penal law, and they will avoid punishments but will not develop a sense of shame. Lead them with excellence and promote social order through attainment of propriety in their roles and relations and they will develop a sense of shame, and moreover, will order themselves'.

Secondly, Confucianism – whether we see it is as a version of virtue ethics or a form of role-ethics – is particularistic. There is no categorical imperative to tell the truth though heavens may fall. Nor is the agent guided by a decision procedure that involves calculation of what would maximise happiness or utility in some way. What virtue or a social role calls for depends on the specific context. It is possible that silence is what a virtuous social-being would do when questioned by an officer investigating a crime. Relatedly, in a famous passage in the Analects, Confucius purportedly thought well of a son who covered for his father's crime by lying to the authority.[70]

---

[70] Ames and Rosemont Jr, 1998: 167 [13.18]: 'The Governor of She in conversation with Confucius said, 'In our village there is someone called "True Person". When his father took a sheep on the sly, he reported him to the authorities'.' Confucius replied, 'Those who are true in my village conduct themselves differently. A father covers for his son, and a son covers for

Thirdly, virtue has an emotional component. An unrepentant person can be forced to disclose incriminating facts by threats. The sort of confession that is associated with remorse and repentance is a voluntary one. In this respect, there is an affinity with the emphasis on freedom in the liberal justification that is founded on the value of moral autonomy.[71] As I said, legal recognition of the right of silence does not imply – and the liberal account does not claim – that the morally right thing to do is to remain silent. What it does say is that the individual should be left free to choose whether to confess or admit to the crime. Even if liberty is not in itself a basic good, it may be a feature of an environment that is conducive to, or needed for, human and social flourishing.

The first point about scepticism on the appropriateness of law as a tool for regulating human behaviour suggests that legal compulsion to self-incriminate would be disfavoured. It follows from the second point about particularism that silence, as an ethical choice, cannot be governed by an across the board rule. The third point about voluntariness suggests the desirability of according individuals the freedom to act as the context calls for. In these three senses, the Confucianist perspective would seem consistent with the right of silence. Legal compulsion to speak cannot be grounded in an ethical theory that does not regard self-incrimination as necessarily virtuous across all contexts and that prefers to have human behaviour motivated by an internalised sense of shame than to be dictated by external compulsion of law.

10.14 CONCLUSION

Silence is probative. Its probative value can be explained in explanatory and comparative terms. If silence is probative and the trial aims at the truth, why would we want to exclude or restrict the use of silence as evidence? A practical justification for the immunity against having adverse evidential consequences attached to one's silence (aspect (3) of the right of silence) is that it upholds one's privilege of non-disclosure or silence (aspects (1a) and (2a)). This pushes the search for justification for the immunity to a search for the value and significance of the privilege. Different accounts of the privilege, corresponding to different ways of understanding the purpose and nature of the criminal process, emerge from liberal and communitarian perspectives. But I do not think they necessarily lead us to different conclusions on the privilege. While

---

his father. And being true lies in this.' For insightful discussion of this passage, see Rosemont Jr and Ames, 2008: 163–8.
[71] On Confucius's belief in moral choice and autonomy, see Brindley, 2011: 257.

my discussion has been cautiously tentative, I hope to have illustrated how legal regulation of evidential reasoning might invite engagement with multiple fields – not only with epistemology but also with political and ethical theories.

REFERENCES

Allen, R. J. and Pardo, M. S. (2019). Relative Plausibility and Its Critics, *International Journal of Evidence and Proof*, 23 (1–2), 5–59.

Amaya, A. (2015). *The Tapestry of Reason*, Oxford: Hart Publishing.

Amaya, A. (2009). Inference to the Best Explanation, in H. Kaptein, H. Prakken and B. Verheij (eds.), *Legal Evidence and Proof: Statistics, Stories and Logic*, Burlington: Ashgate, 135–59.

Ames, R. T. (2011) *Confucian Role Ethics. A Vocabulary*, Hong Kong: Chinese University Press.

Ames, R. T. and Rosemont Jr., H. (1998). *The Analects of Confucius: A Philosophical Translation*, New York: Ballantine.

Bentham, J. (1825). *A Treatise on Judicial Evidence*, Dumont E. ed., London: J. W. Paget.

Brindley, E. (2011). Moral Autonomy and Individual Sources of Authority in the Analects, *Journal of Chinese Philosophy*, 38 (2), 257–73.

Bronaugh, R. (1998). Is There a Duty to Confess?, *American Philosophical Association Newsletter*, 98, 86–7.

Chan, J. (1997). Hong Kong, Singapore, and 'Asian Values': An Alternative View, *Journal of Democracy*, 8 (2), 35–48.

Chan, S. K. (2000a). Cultural Issues and Crime, *Singapore Academy of Law Journal*, 12: 1–25.

Chan, S. K. (2000b). Rethinking the Criminal Justice System of the Singapore for the 21th Century, in Singapore Academy of Law, *The Singapore Conference: Leading the Law and Lawyers into the New Millennium @2020*, Singapore: Butterworths.

Chan, S. K. (1996). The Criminal Process – The Singapore Model, *Singapore Law Review*, 17: 433–503.

Cohen, L. J. (1977). *The Probable and the Provable*, Oxford: Oxford University Press.

Dolinko, D. (1986). Is There a Rationale for the Privilege Against Self-Incrimination?, *UCLA Law Review*, 33, 1063–148.

Donagan, A. (1984). The Right Not to Incriminate Oneself, *Social Philosophy and Policy*, 1 (2): 137–48.

Friendly, H. J. (1968). The Fifth Amendment Tomorrow: The Case for Constitutional Change, *University of Cincinnati Law Review*, 37 (4): 671–726.

Gerstein, R. S. (1979a). The Self-Incrimination Debate in Great Britain, *The American Journal of Comparative Law*, 27 (1), 81–114.

Gerstein, R. S. (1979b). The Demise of *Boyd*: Self-Incrimination and Private Papers in the Burger Court, *UCLA Law Review*, 27 (2), 343–97.

Gerstein, R. S. (1971). Punishment and Self-Incrimination, *American Journal of Jurisprudence*, 16, 84–94.

Gerstein, R. S. (1970). Privacy and Self-Incrimination, *Ethics*, 80 (2), 87–101.

Green, M. S. (1999). The Privilege's Last Stand: The Privilege Against Self-Incrimination and the Right to Rebel Against the State, *Brooklyn Law Review*, 65 (3), 627–716.

Greenawalt, R. K. (1981). Silence as a Moral and Constitutional Right, *William and Mary Law Review*, 23 (1), 15–71.

Griffiths, J. (1970). Ideology in Criminal Procedure or a Third 'Model' of the Criminal Process, *The Yale Law Journal*, 79 (3), 359–417.

Ho, H. L. (2015). The Legal Concept of Evidence, *Stanford Encyclopaedia of Philosophy*, in https://plato.stanford.edu/entries/evidence-legal/.

Ho, H. L. (2013). The Privilege Against Self-Incrimination and Right of Access to a Lawyer. A Comparative Assessment, *Singapore Academy Law Journal*, 25, 826–46.

Ho, H. L. (2012). 'National Values on Law and Order' and the Discretion to Exclude Wrongfully Obtained Evidence, *Journal of Commonwealth Criminal Law*, 2012, 232–56.

Hobbes, T. (1640). *Elements of Law, Natural and Politic*, Tonnies F., ed., 1889, London: Simpkin, Marshall.

Hobbes, T. (1651). *Leviathan*, Oakeshott M. ed., New York: Touchstone, 1962.

Hohfeld, W. N. (1913). Some Fundamental Conceptions as Applied in Judicial Reasoning, *The Yale Law Journal*, 23 (1), 16–59.

Hohfeld, W. N. (1917). Fundamental Legal Conceptions as Applied in Judicial Reasoning, *The Yale Law Journal*, 26 (8), 710–70.

Jayasuriya, K. (1999). Corporatism and Judicial Independence Within Statist Legal Institutions in East Asia, in K. Jayasuriya (ed.), *Law, Capitalism and Power in Asia: The Rule of Law and Legal Institutions*, London-New York: Routledge, 173–204.

Kane, P. V. (1977). *History of Darmaśāstra (Ancient and Mediœval Religious and Civil Law in India)*, Poona: Bhandarkar Oriental Research Institute.

Lee, K. Y. (1990). Address by the Honourable the Prime Minister, Mr. Lee Kuan Yew, *Singapore Academy of Law Journal*, 2, 155–60.

Leng, R. (2001). Silence Pre-trial, Reasonable Expectations and the Normative Distortion of Fact-Finding, *International Journal of Evidence and Proof*, 5 (4), 240–56.

Lewis, A. D. E. (1988). Bentham and the Right of Silence, *The Bentham Newsletter*, 12, 37–42.

Lewis, A. D. E. (1990). Bentham's View of the Right of Silence, *Current Legal Problems*, 43 (1), 135–57.

Packer, H. (1964). Two Models of the Criminal Process, *University of Pennsylvania Law Review*, 113 (1), 1–68.

Packer, H. (1968). *The Limits of the Criminal Sanction*, Stanford: Stanford University Press.

Palmer, M. (2017). Constitutional Dialogue and the Rule of Law, *Hong Kong Law Journal*, 47, 505–24.

Quirk, H. (2017). *The Rise and Fall of the Right of Silence*, Oxford: Routledge.

Ristroph, A. (2009). Respect and Resistance in Punishment Theory, *California Law Review*, 97 (2), 601–32.

Roberts, P. and Zuckerman, A. (2010). *Criminal Evidence*, 2nd ed., Oxford: Oxford University Press.

Rosemont, Jr., H. (2015). *Against Individualism. A Confucian Rethinking of the Foundations of Morality, Politics, Family and Religion*, London: Lexington Books.

Rosemont, Jr., H. and Ames, R. T. (2016). *Confucian Role Ethics. A Moral Vision for the 21st Century*, Taipei: National Taiwan University Press.

Rosemont, Jr., H. and Ames, R. T. (2008). Family Reverence as the Source of Consummatory Conduct, *Dao: A Journal of Comparative Philosophy*, 7 (1), 9–19.

Schauer, F. (2008a). On the Supposed Jury-Dependence of Evidence Law, *University of Pennsylvania Law Review*, 155 (1), 165–202.

Schauer, F. (2008b). In Defense of Rule-Based Evidence Law: And Epistemology Too, *Episteme*, 5 (3), 295–305.

Shanmugam, K. (2012). The Rule of Law in Singapore, *Singapore Journal of Legal Studies*, Dec. 2012, 357–65.

Sim, M. (2015). Why Confucius' Ethics Is a Virtue Ethics, in L. Besser-Jones and M. Slote (eds.), *The Routledge Companion to Virtue Ethics*, New York-London: Routledge: 63–76.

Smith, M. (2018). When Does Evidence Suffice for Conviction?, *Mind*, 127 (508), 1193–218.

Tan, Y. L. (2005). *Criminal Procedure*, Vol. 2, Singapore: LexisNexis.

Thomas III, G. C. and Leo, R. A. (2012). *Confessions of Guilt*, Oxford: Oxford University Press.

Waldron, J. (1981). A Right to Do Wrong, *Ethics*, 92 (1), 21–39.

11

Sanctions for Acts or Sanctions for Actors?

Frederick Schauer[*]

11.1 A TIMELY EXAMPLE

I begin with a not-so-hypothetical example. Suppose someone, whom we can call Harvey, has been accused by four different women of sexual assault or other acts of serious sexual misconduct. As is common in such instances, there were no witnesses to any of the alleged acts, nor is there any physical evidence. But each of the women presents a largely believable account, and for each it is an account that contains occasional inconsistencies but is otherwise highly persuasive. In response to each of these accusations, Harvey offers a forceful denial, each denial being somewhat believable and persuasive, but, again, containing some inconsistencies.

Assume, but only for the sake of the example, that each of the accusations, taken in light of the denials and in light of the other available evidence,[1] is .80–80 per cent likely to be true. Accordingly, if the individual

[*] This chapter was prepared for the World Congress on Evidential Reasoning held at the University of Girona on 6–8 June 2018. An earlier version was presented at the Centre for Law and Philosophy of the University of Surrey on 15 May 2018, and a much, much earlier version of the central claims in this chapter was discussed in 1978 (!) at the University of Cambridge at a seminar on statistical evidence organised by Dr Ian White of the Cambridge University Faculty of Philosophy. I am grateful to the participants at Girona and Surrey for their questions and comments, for discussions with Larry Alexander, Kim Ferzan, Alon Harel, Dale Nance, Barbara Spellman and Peter Westen, and for references and sources provided by all of them.

[1] Examples of other possible supporting evidence might be that the accuser and the person accused were in the same city on the same date, or that the accuser had almost immediately after the alleged events recounted her story to an acquaintance. Such evidence, especially the former, would not be even close to sufficient for criminal conviction or civil liability, but would nevertheless increase the likelihood of the truth of the accusation above what the likelihood would have been without the evidence, making the evidence, at least in the United States, presumptively admissible. See *Federal Rules of Evidence*, Rule 401. In some circumstances, the absence of the evidence that would typically be offered or available for events of some type evidence might constitute evidence of the

accusations, assessed individually, were each to be the foundation for a criminal prosecution based solely on the single act alleged by a single accuser, and if the standard for conviction were proof beyond a reasonable doubt – often understood to be in the vicinity of .95[2] – then Harvey will be acquitted in each of these four prosecutions, and as a consequence will not be subject to criminal sanctions.

But now suppose we ask a different question, and ask whether Harvey has committed at least one act of serious sexual misconduct. If this is the question, the statistics now look very different. Assuming, crucially, that there is genuine independence among the multiple accusations,[3] the likelihood that Harvey has committed at least one of these acts is $1 - ((1 - .80) \times (1 - .80) \times (1 - .80) \times (1 - .80)$, which is .99984, a likelihood that is, for all (or at least most) practical purposes, equivalent to absolute certainty.[4]

---

act's non-occurrence, as James Brook (1985: 301) argues with respect to the absence of evidence of the bus company's identity in the widely discussed *Smith* v. *Rapid Transit Inc.*, 58 N.E.2d 754 (1945). But this kind of inference from the lack of evidence of occurrence to evidence of non-occurrence is rarely warranted in sexual misconduct cases.

[2] See, e.g., Fisher, 2012: 833; Newman, 2006: 267; Schauer and Zeckhauser, 1996: 27; Wansley, 2013: 309. For a highly sophisticated and balanced discussion of whether reducing degrees of confidence to numerical probabilities is even possible, see Nance, 2016: 21–62.

[3] As there might not be, for example, if the accusers had discussed their experiences with each other before making their accusations, or even if an accuser were aware of other accusations before making her own.

[4] As I write these words, the comedian and actor Bill Cosby has recently been convicted (subsequently overturned on other and unrelated ground) in a Pennsylvania state court of felony sexual assault. See *Commonwealth* v. *Cosby*, CP-46-CR-0003932–2016 (Pa. Ct. Comm. Pl.). In a previous trial in the same jurisdiction for the same offence, there was testimony by the complaining witness, and also by one other witness, this other witness testifying that the defendant had sexually assaulted her in a manner similar to that alleged by the complaining witness. After the jury was unable to reach a verdict, the judge declared a mistrial, and some months later Cosby was tried again for the same alleged sexual assault. In this second trial, five women, in addition to the complainant, testified to similar assaults by Cosby against them, and now the defendant was convicted. The parallels between this case and my hypothetical are obvious, but my hypothetical was constructed without detailed knowledge of the Cosby scenario. The admission of the testimony from other victims in the second trial is on the surface inconsistent with American positive law, which typically treats prior similar acts as generally inadmissible. See Federal Rules of Evidence, Rule 404(b)(1). But there are many exceptions or ways of avoiding the prohibition on the use of prior similar acts, see Rule 404(b) (2), and the trial judge allowed the testimony largely because the 'striking' similarity of methods among the six alleged events suggested a 'common plan or scheme', a generally accepted exception to the prohibition on 'prior bad acts' evidence. And although the Cosby trial and most other sexual assault criminal prosecutions in the United States take place in state and not federal courts, it is noteworthy that the Federal Rules of Evidence, which are not applicable to state prosecutions, do specifically (Federal Rules of Evidence, Rule 413) allow prior acts of sexual misconduct, even if not similar in method, to be introduced against a defendant in criminal trials for sexual assault.

Thus, under circumstances in which it is virtually certain that Harvey has committee at least one act of sexual assault – that he is a sexual assaulter – he will be acquitted in four serial criminal prosecutions, and will accordingly not be punished. Whether this outcome is problematic or troubling, in criminal trials or in other contexts, is the principal theme of this chapter.

11.2 A RELATED EXAMPLE

In his 1977 book, *The Probable and the Provable* (Cohen, 1977), the philosopher L. Jonathan Cohen presented what he described as The Paradox of the Gatecrasher. Cohen asks his readers to imagine an event – a rodeo – in which there is a charge for admission. The organisers 'count the house,' with the result that there appear to have been 1000 spectators in attendance. But it turns out that only 499 tickets were sold and presented.[5] Accordingly, we are led to conclude that 501 spectators entered without tickets – there were 501 gatecrashers, 501 spectators who entered fraudulently.

Cohen then hypothesises a civil lawsuit for damages by the rodeo organisers against any one of the 1000 spectators. The organisers present evidence of the number of seated spectators and the number of tickets bought and presented, but there is no other evidence against the defendant. And then the question – Cohen's question – is why the organisers, in a civil action in which the standard of proof for imposing liability is proof by a preponderance of the evidence,[6] should not be able to recover solely on the basis of the statistical evidence, given that they appear to have proved their case to a probability of .501, which indeed represents a preponderance of the evidence?[7]

---

[5] In Cohen's example (Cohen, 1977: 75), no tickets were issued, but changing the example makes the point clearer without any material modification of the problem.

[6] In most of the British Commonwealth, the standard is described as proof by a 'balance of probabilities' (Tapper, 2010: 154–7). An important and thorough historical and analytical treatment of the preponderance standard is John Leubsdorf (Leubsdorf, 2016: 1569). Also, especially valuable is Edward K. Cheng (Cheng, 2013: 1254).

[7] This sketch of Cohen's position, and Cohen's position itself, ignores an important qualification, one whose neglect can be misleading, even if orthogonal to the concerns of this chapter. The typical legal cause of action contains multiple elements, each of which must be proved if the plaintiff (or prosecutor) is to prevail. If each of those elements must be proved according to the applicable standard of proof, the composite standard of proof turns out to be higher than the 'official' or canonical standard of proof. And if the official standard of proof is in fact a composite standard, then the standard of proof for any of the elements may fall below the official standard as long as the composite standard is met. See Nance, 2016: 74–8; Allen, 1991a: 373; Allen, 1986: 401.

Cohen takes the question to be rhetorical – 'There is something wrong somewhere. But where?' – and for him it is self-evident that the organisers should not be permitted to recover on the basis of what the literature refers to as 'naked statistical evidence' (see Kaye, 1979a: 601; Wright, et al., 1996: 677). And he uses what he takes to be the patent impermissibility of such an outcome to ground an inquiry into just why it is impermissible.[8]

But perhaps basing a judgment, especially a judgment in a civil action for damages, on statistics alone is not impermissible at all, as some number of commentators have argued over the years.[9] If we accept that all evidence is probabilistic,[10] and if we assume that we are within a broadly probability/ statistical paradigm,[11] there may be no defensible distinction between the evidence that comes from a not-very-reliable (.501 likely to be true, for example) eyewitness and the evidence that comes from naked statistics having exactly the same probabilistic likelihood of truth (see Schauer, 2003: 101–7).

More importantly, however, it may be that Cohen's engaging example has led us down a false path. And the example has done so by seductively hypothesising 501 identical wrongs – 501 gatecrashers and thus 501 identical fraudulent entries. But the fact that the 501 wrongs are identical turns out to be no more than a quirk of this particular example. So, let us consider a different example. Suppose that in the month of December 2017, there were 100 murders committed in the city of New York. And suppose that a person, Smith, has been heard to say, prior to December 2017, that he intended to commit a murder in New York in December 2017, and has also been heard to say, at a later date, that he committed one of the 100 murders. Smith is then prosecuted, and there is no other evidence. Can Smith be convicted?

Our initial reaction is that under the prevailing practices of most common law legal systems, Smith cannot be convicted. Smith would not be prosecuted simply for committing a murder, or even an unspecified one of 100 murders. He would have to be prosecuted for having committed a particular murder,

---

[8] The literature that Cohen's example has spawned is extensive. See, e.g., Allen, 1991b: 1093; Kaye, 1979b: 101; Thomson, 1986: 225–40; Williams, 1979: 297.

[9] See, for example, Shaviro, 1989: 530; See also Schauer, 2003: 79–107; Finkelstein and Fairley, 1970: 489.

[10] See *Milan* v. *State Farm Mutual Insurance Co.*, 972 F.2d 166, 170 (7th Cir. 1992) (Posner, J.).

[11] A paradigm that not all commentators accept. See, for a broad-based challenge to the paradigm, Allen, 2016: 133. See also Tribe, 1971: 1340. And for an important recent defence of a probabilistic account of knowledge in general, an account including legal proof, see Moss, 2018.

and could not be convicted unless there was sufficient evidence that he committed the particular murder he was charged with having committed. Or so we (or most legal systems) believe.[12]

We can imagine similar examples of even greater specificity, and thus with numbers smaller than 100 but still greater than 1. But we would still say that we do not convict a person for having committed some robbery, some burglary, some arson or some murder. A particular crime must be charged, and a particular crime must be proved. Without identifying a particular crime or, generally in civil contexts,[13] a particular wrong, the prosecution or other legal action is a non-starter. Whether it be the murder example or Cohen's rodeo example, we typically require specification of *which* of the 100 murders, or *which* of the 501 fraudulent entries, provides the basis for the legal claim, whether that claim be by way of criminal prosecution or civil action for damages.

As a descriptive matter, if Cohen's example is to be representative of most actual legal systems, it would be necessary to prove to the relevant standard of proof that the defendant in any one lawsuit committed a particular fraudulent entry. The fact that there were 500 other fraudulent entries in the same general location and on the same day and even at approximately the same time is no more relevant than it would be in the prosecution for murder that there were 99 other murders in New York in the same month. Therefore, if we were initially to identify a particular fraudulent entry, the probability, without additional evidence, that a particular person among the spectators committed that particular fraudulent entry is no longer .501. It is 1/1000, or .001. That 500 other and very similar entries occurred on the same day and in the same place does not in any way increase the probability of this defendant having committed this particular wrong above .001. The other acts are logically and ordinarily legally irrelevant, and would not be admitted as evidence in a trial.

The central point is worth emphasising. It is tempting to reason along the following lines: we have identified a fraudulent entry; 501 out of 1001 entries were fraudulent; therefore, there is a .501 probability that this was a fraudulent entry. But the fallacy lies in the fact that the legal system as currently constituted in most common law jurisdictions requires that we identify the wrong – the particular fraudulent entry – prior to commencing

---

[12]	Representative of the prevailing view is. Capra and Richter, 2018: 432.
[13]	But see *Sindell* v. *Abbott Laboratories*, 607 P.2d 924 (Cal. 1980), on so-called market share liability. A recent, important and comprehensive treatment of the issue is Fennell, 2018: 2371.

a criminal prosecution or any other legal action. We do not identify a person first; we identify a particular wrong first. Cohen's mistake is thus in supposing that the legal system starts with the person and then goes to the wrong, when in reality it is just the opposite. And if it is necessary to identify a particular wrong at the outset, then the number of other wrongs that have occurred in locational and temporal proximity is of no legal relevance. Indeed, things become clearer once we realise that each fraudulent entry took place at a different moment, and each took place at a different (if only by centimetres) place. The difference between Cohen's alleged paradox and the 100 murders in New York is only a matter of degree, and Cohen's paradox disappears if we exclude as legally irrelevant the other 500 fraudulent entries for the same reason that we exclude the other 99 murders in New York in December.

11.3 BUT SHOULD IT BE?

My discussion of Cohen's gatecrasher paradox was intended to be descriptive of the prevailing practice and underlying assumptions in most common law (and, I suspect, civil law) jurisdictions. The argument just offered was not intended to be normative. But we can now ask the normative question, and inquire into why the legal system operates in this way, and whether it *should* do so. Indeed, if we switch Cohen's example from the context of civil liability to that of criminal prosecution, and if we adjust the numbers so that there are 800 fraudulent entries out of 1000 identified spectators in attendance, and consequently a .80 probability of guilt, then we can then again address the case of Harvey: can or should the legal system convict Harvey of having committed at least one sexual assault, even if the probability of him having committed a particular sexual assault against a particular accuser is less than the presumed .95 necessary to support a legitimate criminal conviction?

For many people, the idea of sanctioning Harvey (or anyone else) for having committed an unspecified sexual assault (or any other crime) appears initially unjust or otherwise misguided. But it is possible that some or even much of the resistance to the idea of sanctioning for non-specified wrongs is premised upon a series of worries that in the final analysis may not be dispositive, or may not even be very much on point. So, let us examine some of the possible objections to sanctioning actors for having committed at least one wrongful act, under circumstances in which we cannot specify the wrongful act.

One potential objection stems from a set of evidentiary worries constructed around the paradigm case of the criminal defendant. And given the Blackstonian 'better that ten guilty persons escape ...' maxim,[14] it is not surprising, and in most contexts not troubling,[15] that the principles of proof are heavily skewed to minimise false convictions, even at the cost of increasing the number of false acquittals. But if the objection to criminal sanctions for having committed unspecified acts is based simply on a generalised and almost intuitive fear of increasing in any way the state's power to prosecute, it is worth considering that multiple protections against state overreaching are already incorporated into some number of other procedural devices, including, in many jurisdictions, the presumption of innocence, the privilege against self-incrimination, the prohibition on double jeopardy, and additional restraints on police and prosecutorial practices. As Laudan (2006: 63) argues, adding additional prosecutorial hurdles may in some contexts be a form of double-counting. The example of Harvey suggests, therefore, that it might be possible to create a system of sanctions for having committed an unspecified act without relaxing either the burden of proof or any of the other just-mentioned protections for defendants in criminal prosecutions. More generally, it cannot be the case that anything that facilitates prosecution is for that reason impermissible, at least without specifying which features of which prosecutions are in need of anti-prosecutorial revision.

Even if we assume, contrary to the argument in the previous paragraph, that the appropriately skewed nature of criminal procedure is an argument against the aggregation of evidence in the form now under discussion, that concern goes away when we are not talking about the criminal law. Thus, if we shift our attention from the criminal context to civil awards or (sometimes) administrative remedies, we are, in theory, as troubled by a non-award (or non-recompense of any form) to a wronged victim/plaintiff as we are about an award against a non-culpable defendant.[16] If we therefore remove the distracting spectre of wrongful imprisonment and consequently the presence of

---

[14] 'It is better than ten guilty persons escape, than that one innocent suffers' (Blackstone, 1769). The philosopher Larry Laudan has provided a list of commentators throughout history who have offered similar ideas but with different ratios, those ratios ranging from Moses Maimonides (1000:1) down to Voltaire (2:1), and including Matthew Hale (5:1), John Fortescue (20:1) and Benjamin Franklin (100:1). See Laudan, 2006: 63. See also Volokh, 1997: 173.

[15] But Laudan, 2006: 63, has offered an important and comprehensive challenge to the basic idea.

[16] And even in administrative context, we may be as troubled (or, commonly, more troubled) by a non-remedy against a socially detrimental situation than we are by a mistaken remedy against a situation that is not in fact socially detrimental.

pervasive defendant preferences, it becomes easier, as it was for Jonathan Cohen, to examine the issue more closely. Indeed, removing the diversion of the actual, potential or simply feared totalitarian state makes open-mindedly examining the statistical and decision-theoretic issue at hand far more straightforward.

Even in a civil context, however, there remains a looming series of worries and potential objections that it is necessary to address. One of these objections is that common law legal systems are, in general, averse to sanctioning people, whether civilly or criminally, for their *character*, as opposed to sanctioning them for the acts that that character may have caused (in a probabilistic sense of causation)[17] them to commit. And one reason for the traditional aversion to the use of character evidence is that people with characters that might make them more likely than others to commit certain acts might still not commit those acts. And once the fear of sanctioning people for their character is articulated in terms of the possibility that people with certain characters may nevertheless not commit the acts that the characters might cause or non-causally indicate, there emerge the familiar worries and objections couched in the language of thought control, mind control, 1984 and much else.

But although mind control might (or might not)[18] be scary, the argument for aggregating wrongs is less an argument from thoughts than it is an argument from acts. Harvey, in my opening example, is not being sanctioned for what he was thinking, but for the aggregated probabilities of multiple *acts*. Moreover, the argument against imposing liability because someone with certain thoughts, motives, intentions, or proclivities might not actually commit the acts they have thought about is in some tension with the various crimes that are sometimes labelled as preparatory offences.[19] Possession of burglar tools and possession of drug paraphernalia are, after all, compatible with the possessor never committing the act for which the devices are preparatory, but such possession is often in many jurisdictions treated an independent criminal offence whose proof does not require that the act for which the preparatory offence was preparatory was ever committed.[20] But even if there *are* sound arguments against punishing people for their intentions or for the commission

---

[17] Among the important philosophical analyses of the basic idea of probabilistic (as opposed to deterministic) causation are Suppes, 1970; Cartwright, 1979: 319; Eels, 1991: 52; Good, 1961: 305; Papineau, 1985: 57; Rosen, 1978: 604; Salmon, 1980: 50.

[18] Perhaps it depends on whose mind is being controlled and who is doing the controlling. But that is for another day. A valuable recent contribution to the question is Mendlow, 2018: 2342.

[19] See Schauer, 2003: 224–50. See also Schauer, 2015: 427; Schauer, 2011: 363.

[20] On such preparatory offences, see Bein, 1993: 185; Kessler Ferzan, 2011: 1273. For the view that such crimes are liberty-denying, see Byrne Hessick, 2011: 853.

of preparatory acts, those arguments miss the mark in the context of the form of
evidentiary aggregation now under discussion. The basic point, which is not
undercut by the concerns about punishment for character or punishment for
thoughts, is that some form of liability for a non-specified but already committed act is unlike liability for an act likely to lead to some further act, and unlike
liability for merely intending or even planning to commit an act. Here an act
has already taken place, even if we do not know exactly which act, and as
a result the worry about punishment for character or for unacted-on thoughts
or preparatory acts appears to be very much of a misplaced objection.

In addition to potentially resembling the problematic category of evidence
of character, the aggregation of evidence of wrongs in order to show that at
least one wrong has been committed appears to resemble even more the
equally problematic category of evidence of past acts to prove current conduct.
As discussed above (Cohen, 1977), most developed legal systems, especially in
common law jurisdictions, are reluctant to admit into evidence the past acts
that someone charged with a wrong has committed in order to show they have
committed the similar act for which they are charged.[21] But the argument from
the impermissibility of past-act evidence is strained. At least part of the
concern with the use of past acts is the worry that such use might be the
equivalent of multiple or increased punishment for the same act.[22] If committing crime C_1 justifies punishment P_1, then perhaps using the evidence that
a person has committed C_1 in order to prove the commission of crime C_2 is
equivalent to increasing the punishment for C_2 beyond P_1. But apart from the
concern with an implicit increase in the sanction, there is also the concern
that jurors (or judges) will over-value such evidence of past acts. Even if an
agent's past acts are relevant in determining whether he or she committed this
act, the worry is that jurors (or judges) will take the past act as conclusive and

---

[21]   Thus, it is impermissible to admit a driver's past speeding citations to show that he was
       speeding at the time of an accident now being litigated, *Sparks* v. *Gilley Trucking Co., Inc.*,
       992 F.2d 50 (4th Cir. 1993), and it is impermissible to admit a defendant's criminal history in
       order to prove that he committed a crime on a particular occasion. See *United States*
       v. *Mothershed*, 859 F.2d 585 (8th Cir. 1988). When the prior acts are almost identical to the
       presently charged act, when those acts are in some way unusual, and when there are multiple
       past acts, courts have tended to find a way to admit the previous acts into evidence. The most
       famous example is *R.* v. *Smith*, 11 Cr. App. R. 229, 84 L.J.K.B. 2153 (1915), in which a defendant
       was convicted of drowning his wife in a bathtub, his two previous wives also having died in
       bathtub 'accidents'. An American analogy is *United States* v. *Woods*, 484 F.2d 127 (4th Cir.
       1973), allowing against a foster mother accused of suffocating her foster child evidence of seven
       previous cyanosis-caused deaths of children in her foster care. But *Smith* and *Woods* are
       exceptional, see Redmayne, 1999: 659, and the general rule remains that a past crime or other
       past act cannot normally be used to show commission of a crime or act on this occasion.
[22]   See the discussion in Lempert et al., 2014: 355–6.

not just as probative evidence of commission of the current act. And thus mandatory under-valuing is taken as the appropriate precaution against the expected over-valuing.[23] But however valid these concerns about the use of past acts are in general, they are inapplicable to the case of aggregation of evidence of multiple wrongs or multiple crimes. First, a finding that some defendant has committed one or more prohibited (or liability-incurring) acts does not entail any increase in the sanction or liability beyond what would have been the case for higher-probability proof of a particular act, and thus the fear of inappropriate increases in sanctions is no longer relevant. Moreover, although it is true that the use of evidence of multiple acts to prove the commission of at least one act may increase the likelihood of guilt or its equivalence beyond what that likelihood would have been without the aggregate evidence, there is still no suggestion that the probative value of the aggregated evidence would be higher than would otherwise be necessary to impose sanctions. If we accept that there is some baseline burden of proof for the imposition of sanctions of some kind for engaging in conduct of some kind, nothing about the use of aggregate evidence to prove the existence of at least one unspecified wrong or crime need not, and normally would not, involve lowering the standard of proof below the otherwise applicable baseline.

The worry about using past acts to prove current conduct may thus not be particularly relevant when the question is whether a single unspecified wrong or act has occurred, and the same holds for the traditional worry about the use of evidence of character to prove conduct. But perhaps the objection to aggregation is different, and is in fact based on an alleged similarity between liability for an unspecified act and liability for having some kind of status – the so-called status crimes. It is true that status crimes – being a vagrant, being a drug addict, being a 'habitual drunkard', or having 'no visible means of support' – do have a long and mostly ugly history, and the aversion to status crimes is often based on the possibility of official abuse, as with the crime of vagrancy (see Goluboff, 2016), or with challenges to the criminalisation of a status that may be beyond the power of the alleged perpetrator to change, as with some number of drug-related status crimes and with the crime of being without visible means of support.

The objection to aggregation liability because of its seeming similarity to status crimes issue is important because it raises the question whether there is any difference between the idea of a status crime and the conclusion in the aggregation case that Harvey is putatively being sanctioned for having the status of a sexual assaulter. Similarly, the putative defendant in Cohen's

---

[23] *United States v. Daniels*, 770 F.2d 1111 (D.C. Cir. 1985).

example is being held liable not for having committed an act, but for having the status of being a fraudulent enterer.

But now we must examine the idea of a status crime more closely. Under the law of Virginia, for example, it is a crime to be a habitual drunkard, and it is not surprising that there is scepticism about the moral and social legitimacy of using the criminal law in this way. But would the common scepticism about such crimes be the same if the crime was that of being a habitual murderer, or a habitual rapist?[24] It may be that the argument against aggregation liability from its similarity to long-scorned status crimes is more to the status that undergirds such crimes than it is to the idea of a status crime more generally.

We may now have reached the heart of the matter. At bottom, the question is about the difference, if any, between sanctioning people because they have committed particular murders or sanctioning them because they are murderers. Is there a difference between holding someone liable for an act of negligent operation of a motor vehicle on a particular occasion or for being a negligent driver? Do we – or should we – distinguish between punishing a person because he committed this burglary and punishing him for being a burglar?

For many people, the difference between the two is enormous. But we have just seen the typical objections cannot stand up to close scrutiny. On closer inspection it appears that the immediate negative reaction to prosecuting or otherwise sanctioning people for what they are, in this precise sense, rather than for what they have done on a particular occasion is sometimes a product of an aversion to sanctioning people in part for their past acts. But we have just seen that this is a false equivalence, for here the sanction is not for a past act, in this technical sense of a past act, but for a present one, even if we do not know exactly which present act is involved. Sometimes the negative reactions to this form of aggregation stem from a related but different aversion, the aversion to sanctioning people for their character, or for their dispositions. But again the equivalence is a false one, because the sanctions under discussion are not sanctions for having a certain character or disposition without evidence of having acted on that character or disposition, as might be the case with

---

[24] And certainly, most jurisdictions have little reluctance to take such multiplicity of offences into account at the sentencing stage of the criminal process, although sometimes the practice remains controversial. The controversy, however, is about whether, for example, a thrice-convicted shoplifters should be sentenced more harshly than they would have been for three individual shopliftings, but that is not the issue here. Whatever may be the arguments for or against so-called Three Strikes laws, see Sutton, 2013: 37, what is being discussed in this chapter is sanctioning someone for having committed one act, and imposing the sanction appropriate for one act, even if we cannot specify to the requisite standard of proof precisely which act that was. Enhanced sanctions for multiple acts are a different issue.

sanctioning a person for having a short temper without evidence that the temper has led to a violent act, or sanctioning people for their sexual proclivities, again without evidence that they have acted on them.[25] But when we are talking about aggregation evidence, the putative sanctions are sanctions for having committed an act, and not just for having the character or disposition to commit one, even if, again, we are not sure which precise act was committed.

At the very least, therefore, it appears that some of the typical reactions to the form of aggregation under discussion are based on false equivalencies or misleading analogies, and that, as has occasionally been argued earlier, there might be a plausible argument in favour of even criminal prosecution under the circumstances just described.[26] But it is also likely that some of the typical negative reactions are based on the what we can think of as the looming overhang of the criminal process. If we set aside fears of excess prosecution,[27]

---

[25] This is a source of major contemporary controversy with respect to child pornography. Putting aside the possibility that prohibiting the sale, use or possession of child pornography is grounded on views about the inherent immorality of the act, for some the prohibition is premised on the belief that users are potential or actual sexual predators, and thus that the potential dangers to children are sufficient to justify sanctioning on the basis of the inference, for which there is some evidence, of a probabilistic connection between possession and disposition, and of a probabilistic connection between disposition and acts, while others have argued, in opposition, that such probabilistic connections are insufficient to justify sanctions without evidence of actual acts, in which case it is the acts and not the probabilistically causal indicators that should be subject to punishment. On all of this, see the various contributions in Byrne Hessick, 2016.

[26] See especially Harel and Porat, 2009: 261. Harel and Porat's important article reaches conclusions similar to those offered here, and does so in a way that is less qualified than those offered earlier in Schauer and Zeckhauser, 1996. Moreover, the idea of aggregation across cases – for liability even without specification of the act that grounds the sanction – as argued for here, by Schauer and Zeckhauser, and by Harel and Porat, is closely related to the question whether there can be or should be liability for a specified liability-incurring act, even if the exact grounds of liability are unspecified. As Larry Alexander has put it in correspondence to me, what if we know that it is certain beyond a reasonable doubt that Miss Scarlett killed Professor Plum, but we cannot be certain beyond a reasonable doubt whether she used the lead pipe in the dining room or the candlestick in the conservatory. The different methods describe two different crimes that may even carry the same sentence, producing a quandary about what to do. And see also Westen and Ow, 2007: 153. Similar aggregation problems are explored in Levmore, 2001: 723, and in Porat and Posner, 2012: 2. And an important response to all of these claims is Clermont, 2012: 165. The reader is thus cautioned to read the present chapter with awareness that the arguments offered here, although perhaps especially timely in light of examples like the one that opened this chapter, arise against the background of an existing literature, albeit a small and unfortunately under-appreciated one.

[27] Arguably some of these fears are already incorporated into the proof beyond a reasonable doubt standard, the presumption of innocence, and the typical special protections of defendants in criminal proceedings, such as the privilege against self-incrimination. And thus, it is possible that additional fears beyond those already accounted for in the foregoing protections are an example of double-counting. See Laudan, 2006, discussed above.

we might consider the same questions in the context of civil liability rather than criminal punishment. Assuming a preponderance of the evidence standard, the numbers are now different, but the basic analytics, with one important qualification, are similar. The qualification is that in the civil context the typical remedy is an award of damages against a particular victim, thus requiring, to continue with the example of Harvey and the four accusers, a particular victim who establishes that she was the one assaulted, rather than just that an assault has occurred, that requirement being a function of the nature of the underlying cause of action – tort, in this example – rather than the nature of the legal system. But without this qualification, we might still observe that, under a preponderance of the evidence standard, and supposing that each complaint is only 40 per cent persuasive, and thus unable to prove her case,[28] the probability that Harvey has committed at least one sexual assault is now $1 - ((1-.40) \times (1-.40) \times (1-.40) \times (1-.40))$, which is .944. This does not even reach the standard for proof beyond a reasonable doubt, but is still far above the civil standard of proof by a preponderance of the evidence, and thus it is still considerably more than probably the case that Harvey has committed at least one act of sexual assault.

11.4 GETTING REALISTIC

There may be many reasons to doubt the likelihood of the kind of aggregation discussed here ever becoming part of common law legal systems, whether in the context of criminal law or even civil liability. The necessity of commencing with a particular act before focusing on a potential perpetrator is simply too entrenched for that and raises issues going to the very operation of the sanctioning dimension of law. But the point of this exercise, even apart from academic (in the best sense, and not as a pejorative) interest, is that the issue has important implications in many non-formal or non-judicial administrative contexts. Where the question is not criminal or civil sanctions, but instead whether this or that person or entity should receive a licence to engage in an activity or lose the licence that he, she or it already has, the question may have special salience. How should an attorney licensing board deal with an attorney who has been accused by four former clients of financial improprieties? Should a company, three of whose former employees have accused the company of unlawful disposal of pollutants, be subject to sanctions for environmental violations? Should a student who has thrice been weakly suspected of cheating be suspended or dismissed? And so on.

---

[28] I put aside the important issue discussed above in note 7.

As the opening example illustrated, the issue is especially relevant in the context of charges of sexual misconduct. Because of the typical lack of witnesses or physical evidence, and because of the sad but still present practice of disbelieving women who make allegations of sexual misconduct, it will often be the case that multiple allegations will individually be treated as inconclusive.[29] But can such individually inconclusive (and perhaps even individually unlikely, albeit not conclusively so) allegations be aggregated for purposes of concluding that the likelihood of truth of one or more becomes conclusive, as is more than arguably the case with two recent American presidents, large number of other political figures, and even larger numbers of prominent business people, athletes, entertainers and other celebrities? As a mathematical matter, such aggregation seems the right course when the sanctions are the sanctions of public opinion, but again the overhang of the criminal law – the mistaken belief that negative judgments in public and private life should mirror the protections of the criminal process – is often a distraction. This is not to deny as well that statistical independence may be less present in public matters and public life than it is in the statistics books. And this is especially problematic when there are personal and political motives, when charges may beget other charges, and when individual charges may lack independence in other ways. When that is the case, unwarranted aggregation may be as much of a problem as underused but statistically warranted aggregation.

In an even more pervasive way, the mechanisms that we often describe as rumour or gossip may operate in the same way, sometimes for good and sometimes for ill. And it is even more often the case that multiple allegations in the domain of social relations (and especially in the new world of social media) no longer share the characteristic of statistical independence, without which all of the calculations and all of the analysis above become invalid. But on the rare occasions when unsubstantiated rumours come from multiple genuinely independent sources, even the sanctions that ensue from rumour and gossip may as a descriptive matter be based on the aggregation principle discussed are, and may, as a normative matter, in some contexts be better for it.

REFERENCES

Allen, R. J. (1986). A Reconceptualization of Civil Trials, *Boston University Law Review*, 66, 401–37.
Allen, R. J., (1991a). The Nature of Juridical Proof, Cardozo *Law Review*, 373, 413–20.

---

[29] Depending, of course, on the standard for conclusiveness.

Allen, R. J. (1991b). On the Significance of Batting Averages and Strikeout
  Totals: A Clarification of the 'Naked Statistical Evidence' Debate, the
  Meaning of 'Evidence,' and the Requirement of Proof Beyond
  Reasonable Doubt, *Tulane Law Review*, 65, 1093–110.
Allen, R. J. (2016). The Nature of Juridical Proof: Probability as a Tool in
  Plausible Reasoning, *The International Journal of Evidence and Proof*, 21(1–
  2), 133–42.
Bein, D. (1993). Preparatory Offences, *Israel Law Review*, 27(1–2), 185–212.
Blackstone, W. (1769). Commentaries on the Laws of England, London, 352
Brook, J. (1985). The Use of Statistical Evidence of Identification in Civil
  Litigation: Well-Worn Hypotheticals, Real Cases, and Controversy,
  St. Louis University Law Journal, 29, 293–352.
Capra, D. and Richter, L. (2018). Character Assassination: Amending Federal
  Rule of Evidence 404(B) to Protect Criminal Defendants, *Columbia Law
  Review*, 118(3), 769–832.
Cartwright, N. (1979). Causal Laws and Effective Strategies, *Noûs*, 13(4),
  419–37.
Cheng, E. K. (2013). Reconceptualizing the Burden of Proof, *Yale Law
  Journal*, 122, 1254–79.
Clermont, K. M. (2012). Aggregation of Probabilities and Illogic, *Georgia Law
  Review*, 47, 165–80.
Cohen, L. J. (1977) *The Probable and the Provable*, Oxford: Clarendon Press.
Eels, E. (1991). *Probabilistic Causality*, Cambridge: Cambridge University
  Press.
Fennell, L. A. (2018). Accidents and Aggregates, *William and Mary Law
  Review*, 59, 2371–445.
Ferzan, K. K. (2011). Inchoate Crimes at the Prevention/Punishment Divide,
  San Diego Law Review, 48(4), 1273–98.
Finkelstein, M. O. and Fairley W. B. (1970). A Bayesian Approach to
  Identification Evidence, *Harvard Law Review*, 83(3), 489–517.
Fisher, T. (2012). Conviction Without Conviction, *Minnesota Law Review*, 96,
  833–85.
Goluboff, R. L. (2016). *Vagrant Nation: Police Power, Constitutional Change,
  and the Making of the 1960s*, New York: Oxford University Press.
Good, I. J. (1961). A Causal Calculus I-II, *British Journal for the Philosophy of
  Science*, 11(44), 305–18.
Harel, A. and Porat A. (2009). Aggregating Probabilities Across Cases:
  Criminal Responsibility for Unspecified Offenses, *Minnesota Law Review*,
  94, 261–310.
Hessick, C. B. (2011). Disentangling Child Pornography from Child Sex
  Abuse, *Washington University Law Review*, 88(4), 853–902.
Hessick, C. B., ed. (2016). *Refining Child Pornography Law Crime, Language,
  and Social Consequences*, Ann Arbor, MI: University of Michigan Press.

Kaye, D. H. (1979a). Naked Statistical Evidence, *Yale Law Journal*, 89(3), 601–11.

Kaye, D. H. (1979b). The Paradox of the Gatecrasher and Other Stories, *Arizona State Law Journal*, 1979 (1), 101–10.

Laudan, L. (2006). *Truth, Error, and Criminal Law: An Essay in Legal Epistemology*, Cambridge: Cambridge University Press.

Lempert, R. O. and Saltzburg, S. A., et al. (2014). *A Modern Approach to Evidence*, St. Paul, MN: West Academic Publishing.

Leubsdorf, J. (2016). The Surprising History of the Preponderance Standard of Civil Proof, *Florida Law Review*, 67(5), 1569–618.

Levmore, S. (2001). Conjunction and Aggregation, *Michigan Law Review*, 99 (4), 723–56.

Mendlow, G. S. (2018). Why Is It Wrong to Punish Thoughts?, *Yale Law Journal*, 127(8), 2342–86.

Moss, S. (2018). *Probabilistic Knowledge*, Oxford: Oxford University Press.

Nance, D. A. (2016). *The Burdens of Proof – Discriminatory Power, Weight of Evidence, and Tenacity of Belief*, Cambridge: Cambridge University Press.

Newman, J. O. (2006). Quantifying the Standard of Proof Beyond a Reasonable Doubt: A Comment on Three Comments, *Law, Probability and Risk*, 5(3–4), 267–9.

Papineau, D. (1985). Probabilities and Causes, *Journal of Philosophy*, 82(2), 57–74.

Porat, A. and Posner, E. A. (2012). Aggregation and Law, *Yale Law Journal*, 122 (2), 1–69.

Redmayne, M. (1999). A Likely Story!, *Oxford Journal of Legal Studies*, 19(4), 659–72.

Rosen, D. (1978). In Defence of a Probabilistic Theory of Causality, *Philosophy of Science*, 45(4), 604–13.

Salmon, W. (1980). Probabilistic Causality, *Pacific Philosophical Quarterly*, 1980(2), 25–37.

Schauer, F. (2003). *Profiles, Probabilities, and Stereotypes*, Cambridge MA: Harvard University Press.

Schauer, F. (2011). Bentham on Presumed Offenses, *Utilitas*, 23(4), 363–79.

Schauer, F. (2015). On the Distinction Between Speech and Action, *Emory Law Journal*, 65(2), 427–54.

Schauer, F. and Zeckhauser R. (1996). On the Degree of Confidence for Adverse Decisions, *The Journal of Legal Studies*, 25(1), 27–52.

Shaviro, D, (1989). Statistical-Probability Evidence and the Appearance of Justice, *Harvard Law Review*, 103(2), 530–54.

Suppes, P. (1970). *A Probabilistic Theory of Causality*, Amsterdam: North-Holland Pub. Co.

Sutton, J. R. (2013). Symbol and Substance: Effects of California's Three Strikes Law on Felony Sentencing, *Law and Society Review*, 47(1), 37–71.

Tapper, C. and Cross R. (2010). *Cross and Tapper on Evidence*, Oxford: Oxford University Press.

Thomson, J. J. (1986). *Rights, Restitution, and Risk: Essays, in Moral Theory*, W. Parente ed., Cambridge, MA: Harvard University Press.

Tribe, L. H. (1971). Trial by Mathematics: Precision and Ritual in the Legal Process, *Harvard Law Review*, 84(6), 1329–93.

Volokh, A. (1997). N Guilty Men, *University of Pennsylvania Law Review*, 146 (1), 173–216.

Wansley, M. (2013). Scaled Punishments, *New Criminal Law Review: An International and Interdisciplinary Journal*, 16(3), 309–63.

Westen, P. and Ow, E. (2007). Reaching Agreement on When Jurors Must Agree, *New Criminal Law Review: An International and Interdisciplinary Journal*, 10(2), 153–209.

Williams, G. (1979). The Mathematics of Proof, *Criminal Law Review*, 1979 (2), 340–54.

Wright, E. F., Maceachern, L., Stoffer E. and Macdonald N. (1996). Factors Affecting the Use of Naked Statistical Evidence of Liability, *The Journal of Social Psychology*, 136(6), 677–88.

PART IV

EXPERT EVIDENCE

12

From Institutional to Epistemic Authority: Rethinking Court-Appointed Experts

Carmen Vázquez

12.1 INTRODUCTION

Traditionally, there are two types of expert opinion, depending on whether the expert is appointed by one of the parties (*expert witness*) or is appointed by the judge (*court-appointed expert*). Expert witnesses have tended to be more a characteristic of common law systems, whereas opinions by court-appointed experts have enjoyed greater presence in civil law.

In fact, in some civil law systems, the term 'expert' or 'expert opinion' has been applied exclusively to the court-appointed expert, whereas the parties would only have the possibility of appointing a kind of assessor whose function would be to challenge the court-appointed expert, albeit without being allowed to engage in their own expert analysis. Or in other words, the assessor would only be able to analyse what is done and said by the court-appointed expert, having no direct access to the object of the analysis that would enable her to suitably reach her own conclusions about the case. For years, this situation has led both case law and scholars to discuss whether experts provide genuine evidence or whether, on the other hand, they are assistants to the administration of justice. Indeed, it has been held that 'in many continental jurisdictions, an expert is considered an extension of the court itself, with corresponding consequences for the reliability of his/her findings' (Appazov, 2016: 149).

In common law systems, it has often been said that 'to solve the problems of expert evidence . . . a central feature [is]: the use of expertise obtained outside the usual adversarial channels. The most frequently suggested reform, how-ever, is the use of court appointed expert witnesses' (Gross, 1991: 1188). The supposedly negative aspects of expert witnesses are: (1) the selection of the expert is partial; (2) the expert can be prepped by the parties' lawyers; and (3) the financial compensation received by the expert from the parties. In civil law systems, on the other hand, more or less the same arguments have been adduced to defend the assertion that court-appointed experts would therefore enjoy the presumption of greater credibility.

However, and beyond any theoretical suppositions or assumptions regarding the greater reliability of court-appointed experts as opposed to expert witnesses, very few analyses have been conducted to test the hypothesis in current legal systems. And this is precisely the objective of this work: taking the current Spanish procedural system as my example, I will set out to question not only the necessary epistemic superiority of court-appointed expert opinions, but also the fact that the mere origin of the expert opinion is a relevant factor that should be considered. As we shall see, the selection, prepping and remuneration of the expert could be regulated in such a way that they do not even guarantee the impartiality of the court-appointed expert; however, in order to assess the reliability of an expert opinion we would have to evaluate what the expert did and asserted in the specific case, and this is independent of their origin.

In Spain, the expert model historically used is that of the court-appointed expert. However, the Spanish Civil Procedure Act of 2000 (hereinafter, the LEC) spawned a new situation, not only opening up the possibility for parties to present their own expert witnesses, but also highlighting a preference for the latter over the court-appointed expert. Through this reform, the legislature explicitly and clearly stated that the expert provides genuine evidence and is not an extension of the court. Thus, according to a certain part of the Spanish procedural scholars, the case law that made a very subjective interpretation of the Article in the LEC as a criterion for the admissibility of expert opinions was rendered outmoded, since the admissibility of an expert opinion could no longer depend on any knowledge that the judge could personally have and or depend on a restricted judgment as to the relevance or the usefulness thereof.

Nevertheless, not all the regulatory panorama favours the presentation of opinions by expert witnesses; there are some points in proceedings when the only expert opinion that can be requested is that of a court-appointed expert. This obviously assumes that an expert opinion may be admitted at different moments before and after the filing of the claim and the answer, which are generally the points at which such expert opinions are required in civil actions.[1] One of these procedural moments could be decisive in a court proceeding, the so-called *diligencia final*: in cases in which, once all the

---

[1] The scholars have branded the regulation governing the different points when an expert opinion may be used as 'procedural gibberish' (Muñoz Sabaté, 2001: 335). Joan Picó i Junoy (2001: 83 et seq.) identified at least twelve different moments, in six of which the expert must be court-appointed. One example is when handwriting whose authenticity has been discussed in a pre-trial hearing has to be examined prior to the proceedings or the hearing.

evidence that has been admitted has been heard in the oral proceedings, the judge considers that the evidence is neither sufficiently clear nor suitable to reach a finding in the case and may request an expert opinion, which should be furnished by a court-appointed expert. One of the most common cases of the use of this competence seems to occur when two expert witnesses disagree with each other. In fact, in a recent empirical study dealing with expert opinions in financial cases in the Spanish procedural setting, in which judges were asked in which situation they tended to resort most to court-appointed experts, 35 per cent of them responded that they did so when the findings of the parties' expert witnesses differed significantly.[2]

Another curious aspect of the regulation of the court-appointed experts in the LEC is that it provides for the possibility of the parties requesting that the judge appoint an expert. This involves, by necessity, cases where the State meets the cost of such expert opinions in view of the precarious financial situation of the party requesting the opinion. If the petitioner is not in this predicament, then it will be obliged to pay for the expert opinion given by the court-appointed expert. This situation has led some judges to consider that, 'while these opinions are usually identified as court-appointed expert evidence, they are actually expert witness opinions, since the fees are ultimately paid for by one of the parties' (Laguna and Palomo, 2008: 19). Not only must the parties pay for such an expert opinion, they must also contend with a series of inconveniences, such as, by way of example, being limited to the list of experts compiled every year by the competent authority, or running the

Scholars are virtually agreed about the need to define a single point in proceedings when the inclusion of this type of information may be allowed. And while this generally makes sense, we have to consider certain characteristics of legal systems which, like Spain's, eventually require that at least some types of evidence are allowed to be presented continuously in order to guarantee equality of arms, the parties' right to their defence or even a finding issued on the strength of a rich or sufficient body of proof. In my opinion, these characteristics are: 1) the lack of clear obligations upon the parties to disclose the information held by each other before the legal machinery is engaged; 2) the immense variety of appeals that provide an incentive to the parties to appeal most findings not only in the first instance, but also to the last possible instance, rendering it highly difficult to finish court proceedings earlier; and, 3) the still latent possibility through which judges can change the evidential panorama by requesting evidence on their own.

[2] See Laguna and Palomo, 2008: 20. Besides the differences between parties' expert witnesses, the other reasons for judges to appoint an expert are: 'to settle specific aspects of particular relevance', which enjoys the highest percentage, 37 per cent; 'when the parties have not provided expert opinions', 18 per cent; and in 'cases in which an expert witness is lacking in professional competence', 4 per cent. It should be mentioned that all of these eventualities fit within the scope of *diligencia final* (proceedings to examine further evidence), although not necessarily. For example, a court-appointed expert could be called in at the beginning of the procedure if the parties have not produced expert opinions and the rules so permit.

risk of the chosen expert rejecting the appointment and having to resolve whether such a refusal is warranted according to the eventualities established for it, etc. Despite this, the aforementioned empirical study shows that judges appoint an expert witness on request by the parties in 9 per cent of the cases of court-appointed expert opinions considered (Laguna and Palomo, 2008: 20). This may be explained by the fact that, at least for some parties, there is a major perverse incentive in requesting a court-appointed expert: namely that the courts prefer the court-appointed expert over the expert witness.

Judges' preference for court-appointed experts is mirrored in the fact that they attach greater probative value to their expertise, to the detriment of the expertise provided by the expert witness. For example, in the mentioned empirical study about expert opinions in financial cases, 73 per cent of the judges stated that they attach great relevance to the expert opinion when reaching a finding, particularly when the evidence is furnished by court-appointed experts. The rationale for this greater probative value would lie in the fact that the expert is impartial because of the way in which they were selected; it is therefore the selection that is regarded as relevant for this purpose rather than the general impartiality obligation established in the actual LEC upon all experts.[3] This is why it would be worthwhile to analyse the selection process of court-appointed experts in Spain in greater detail in order to ascertain whether the court's preference enjoys any degree of justification, and what it would actually justify. I am of the opinion that these considerations may be useful to us in order to rethink the system of court-appointed experts in general, that is, beyond the purely Spanish setting.

To conclude this introduction, we have to distinguish between two types of court-appointed experts: those from public institutions, who in formal terms are the genuine 'court's experts', and the private experts who circumstantially participate as such experts in a legal action. The former are public officials reporting permanently to the organs of the Administration of Justice, or to the latter's dependent organisations; for example, forensic examiners, regional and provincial forensic medicine institutes, and the Institute of Toxicology.[4] Not only is there abundant case law of the Supreme Court that confers great value on the reports

---

[3] The LEC stipulates that all experts must take all available information into account, i.e., that which favours and jeopardises the parties (art. 335.2). Beyond that, however, there are no further legal controls in place for this purpose.

[4] The workload of these institutions focuses on criminal affairs. For example, the *Instituto de Medicina Legal* [Institute of Forensic Medicine] in Catalonia recorded, in the course of 2013, the last year for which official statistics are available, 75,694 actions in criminal proceedings (bodily injury, psychiatric evaluations, sex offences, domestic violence, autopsies, etc.); whereas it attended to 16,836 civil affairs (legal guardianship, psychiatric internments, the civil registry, etc.). These data are available at: www.poderjudicial.es/cgpj/es/Temas/Estadisti

issued by such experts from public organisations, since 'experts provided by the Administration are presumed to be impartial',[5] but furthermore, this type of expert opinion tends to be included in the proceedings as documentary evidence, whereby their reports can be read in court without the testimony of the experts that performed them or the people who headed an analysis conducted by a team.[6]

It should also be emphasised that the public nature of an institution or an expert does not presuppose that they are reliable, and neither does it necessarily follow that the performing individuals are experts in the matter. For this reason, empirical information should be available about how the methods or the instruments used by experts actually work, distinguishing between those who hold technical positions following a recruitment process that guarantees their relevant expertise and those who do not, and in any event, always being on the look-out for the so-called institutional biases.[7] In any event, hereinafter I will not be alluding to these institutions, which merit an independent

ca-Judicial/Plan-Nacional-de-Estadistica-Judicial/Actividad-Judicial/Actividad-de-los-Instituto s-de-Medicina-Legal.

[5] The historic criterion in this regard holds that: 'Jurisprudence has asserted that the expert evaluations performed by administrative bodies, removed from any interests at stake, when conducted with all the legal formalities and procedural guarantees, must, by dint of their competence, impartiality and objectivity, enjoy the utmost credence, close to the value of *praesumptio iuris tantum* (rebuttable presumption) provided that other expert opinions or evidence do not prove that they may have made a mistake.' Cf. SSC (Sentence of the Supreme Court) of 23 December 1993. Therefore, the accumulation of mere formalities that are taken into consideration to attribute a presumptive nature to it is rather striking.

[6] The same situation occurs in Germany where, unlike Spain, the law provides for replacing the expert in person with the reading of the report in the oral hearing. Article 256 of the German Code of Criminal Procedure (StPO) refers to public organisations, forensic examiners, traffic radars, blood analyses to determine blood group or degree of alcohol (cf. Bachmaier 2009: 134).

This situation was also addressed in the United States in the case *Melendez-Díaz v. Massachusetts* 557 U.S. 305 (2009), resolved by the Supreme Court. The finding established that the DA presenting an analysis of the nature of the drug seized without the presence of the expert who had done it, i.e., it was presented as a kind of documentary evidence, was a violation of the constitutional right to the '*confrontation clause*' provided for in the Sixth Amendment to the United States Constitution. Nevertheless, it also found that: 'A state would not violate the Constitution through a "notice-and-demand" statute by both putting the defendant on notice that the prosecution would submit a chemical drug test report without the testimony of the scientist and also giving the defendant sufficient time to raise an objection.'

[7] In the United States, the *National Research Council of the National Academies* conducted an analysis of the current state-of-the-art of forensic sciences in the country, uncovering some major issues: economic problems caused by the precarious situation of many laboratories and an excessive workload; political problems because they depend broadly on the legal framework and operate fundamentally as an extension of the district attorneys' offices; and legal problems, because they fail to meet the system's demands for the admission of *expert evidence*. This is compounded by serious shortcomings in their own practices. For example, the enormous divergence between types of training, certification, controls of the methodologies and the protocols used by forensic examiners seems to cast serious doubts on their validity and

analysis, and will dwell solely on private experts who act occasionally as court-appointed experts.[8]

I will proceed as follows: first of all, I will analyse the task of providing Spanish courts with a broad group of experts who would be willing to act as such if appointed by the courts, and which would result in the generation of the so-called lists of experts. Secondly, I will be addressing how courts select the experts available on the list to act as the expert that will examine the case in question, attaching a certain emphasis to incentives to experts, judges and the parties in this Spanish scenario. Finally, I will analyse the circumstances that would make it possible to improve the system of court-appointed experts and the possible scope of this model, and then compare it to a system in which the expert is selected by one of the parties with a view to regulating the preparation of and payments to experts.

12.2 MAKING LISTS, THE CONTROL OF EXPERT GROUPS AND THE COURT-APPOINTED EXPERT MARKET

Following the precedent enshrined by the Spanish Supreme Court, two activities should be distinguished in the appointment of experts by the court: one is governmental and the other is judicial. The former would consist of all the activities needed to provide judges with a list of experts willing to act as such in court proceedings, which is regarded as a clearly instrumental activity. The second, on the other hand, would consist of selecting, from among this list, the individual to act as the expert in a specific case and to whom 'an undoubted transcendence' would be attached 'because the core value of impartiality is implied'.[9] This section will deal with governmental activity, that is, the formation of the group of experts available for acting occasionally as experts, leaving the judicial activity for the following section.

---

reliability. For a very interesting analysis of this study and how it is related to the evidence theory, see Pardo (2010).

[8] The public resources invested in these institutions, and through them their capacity to provide expert opinions, are amply surpassed by the number of expert opinions rendered by court-appointed experts who act occasionally in legal proceedings. For example, in 2017, the Ministry of Justice of Catalonia stated that it had provided 24,297 expert opinions by both in-house and external personnel. Payment was requested for 15,768 of the opinions, which would infer that this is the number of expert opinions given by external professionals, for a total amount of €972,566.69. The highest annual expenditure was recorded in 2008: €1,423,866.29 in Catalonia alone.

[9] STS of 3 March 2010, *Sala de lo Contencioso-Administrativo* (the part of the court that hears appeals against administrative decisions).

In the Romano-Germanic legal tradition, producing lists of experts willing to act as court-appointed experts seems to be constant,[10] and at least two ways of making such lists are known: through open calls by the competent authorities inviting any professional interested to come forward, or by asking certain expert groups to send, with a certain frequency, lists of their members who are available for such work. In Spain, Article 341 of the LEC establishes that:

1. In January each year, the different professional colleges, or as applicable the relevant corresponding organisations, as well as the cultural and scientific academies and institutions, will be asked to submit a list of members or associates who would be willing to act as experts. ...
2. When a person without an official title but who is practiced in or conversant with the subject has to be appointed as an expert, the parties will be convened and the appointment will be made according to the procedure described in the preceding paragraph, for which purpose a list of individuals that will be requested every year from unions, associations and appropriate organisations will be used, and which must be comprised of at least five of these persons. If on account of the unique nature of the matter in question only the name of one person practised in or conversant with the topic were available, the consent of the parties will be secured and this person will only be appointed as an expert if they all agree.

A priori, there appears to be a difference between the making of a list of experts produced by lay persons and another list made by the actual experts. When lay persons make up the list of experts, at most they are asked to guarantee the formal fulfilment of certain requirements by the candidate: titles/qualifications, years of experience, no criminal record in certain offences, etc.[11] On the other hand, when the list is produced by the experts themselves, they are in a position to exercise greater supervision over the requirements to be expected of their colleagues who may be included in it. Of course, there are different types

[10] This, as far as I know, is not the case of common law. For example, in the United States, different procedures have been used to select court-appointed experts who will testify in a specific case. In a civil liability case regarding defective breast implants, a committee was named to appoint a panel of independent experts (see Hooper, Cecil and Willging, 2001).
   On the other hand, the *European Guide for Legal Expertise* (EGLE), produced in 2015 by the *European Expertise and Expert Institute* with financial support from the *Civil Justice Programme of the European Union*, envisages the compilation of expert lists in all the Member States as the ideal form of appointment. In view of the importance of this guide, I will be referring to it again, citing it as the EGLE.
[11] For example, in France it is the Court of Cassation that draws up lists of experts, although if need be, judges may appoint an expert who is not on the list in question (CPP. 159).

of direct and indirect controls that the experts may avail themselves of, but in any event the question will be whether and how they do it.

In Spain, the first control imposed upon official qualifications was through the professional colleges. Based on the premise that it falls to the professional colleges to regulate the exercise of professions, the Spanish legislature, or at least this is how it was interpreted, established that only the colleges could send lists of experts in all the official qualifications who are willing to act as such; and other groups of experts would only be resorted to if such qualifications were not available. Hence, the General Council of the Judiciary established the following.

For cases in which the expert opinion sought calls for a mandatory collegiate qualification, the presidents of the Higher Courts of Justice and Senior Judges will obtain lists from all the professional colleges or associations in the jurisdiction linked to a profession whose qualification could be directly related to and be suitable for the provision of a court-required expert opinion. For cases in which being a member of the college is not an indispensable requirement for exercising the profession, or if there are different qualifications and/ or professions that could suitably provide the expert evidence requested, the presidents of the Higher Courts of Justice and the Senior Judges will secure lists of experts from all the non-official professional associations, corporations and colleges in the jurisdiction.[12]

In this context of preference for colleges over other associations, in 2008, the Asociación Nacional de Grafólogos, Peritos Calígrafos y Documentólogos (GRAPECA) (National Association of Graphologists, Handwriting Experts and Documentologists) filed a contentious-administrative appeal before the Supreme Court against an agreement by the General Council of the Judiciary which confirmed, in turn, a resolution by the President of the Higher Court of Justice of the Balearic Islands rejecting the inclusion of its members on the list of experts as possible court-appointed experts. The argument was that the respective association was not analogous to a college because there was no record that its rules of operation could be equated to those of an official college. Basically, it was said that the association: (1) did not require any qualification for membership; and (2) that it had not been authorised by or was not overseen by the Administration. However, in 2010, the Supreme Court found in favour of GRAPECA, arguing that the list that it submitted was

[12]   Cf. Directive 5/2001 of 19 December, of the Plenary of the General Council of the Judiciary, pertaining to the annual submission to the courts of lists of professionals for court appointment as expert witnesses. Published in the Official Gazette of the Government of Spain (BOE) no. 312, 29 December 2001.

comprised of experts without an official qualification and that in this case the LEC provided for the possibility of private associations submitting list of experts.[13]

At the same time as the previous case, as of 2009, and in the wake of a set of Spanish and European regulations that deregulated the real estate industry and the exercise of the profession, a series of administrative actions were filed by professional associations of real estate property agents (generally known as Realtors) before the Supreme Court, who had submitted their own list of members who were willing to act as court-appointed experts and had been denied the possibility of being part of the group of court-appointed experts because there was an official college that was already submitting lists.[14]

In this case, the Plenary of the General Council of the Judiciary issued an agreement that distinguished between the obligatory membership and voluntary membership in official colleges.[15] In other words, in principle, official colleges would only enjoy preference when being a member thereof was mandatory in the profession. The Supreme Court confirmed this by finding in favour of the state lawyer in the sense that 'the requirement of an official college which voluntarily brings together qualified professionals who may engage in an activity in a non-excluding way cannot be a barrier that excludes other legally-qualified professionals from engaging in this same activity'.[16]

The situation went beyond what a reading of the previous paragraph would suggest, since not only was the preference for colleges in professions in which college membership is voluntary eliminated, but it was also applied to other cases in which membership is mandatory. While section 8 of the aforementioned Agreement seems to underline this preference for colleges, it subsequently established that when there are *different qualifications and/or professions that may suitably provide the expert opinion requested*, the lists of experts from all professional associations and corporations will be used (section 9). In practice, this means that in most cases, all the aforementioned lists must be used, since there are very few cases involving expert evidence

---

[13] See the SSC of 3 March, 2010, Sala de lo Contencioso-Administrativo (court that hears appeals against administrative decisions).

[14] See the sentences of the SSC of 6 June 2011; SSC of 6 July 2011; SSC of 21 September 2011 and SSC of 26 July 2012, all of which were issued by the Sala de lo Contencioso-Administrativo (court that hears appeals against administrative decisions).

[15] 28 October 2010. Thereby amending the General Council's Directive 5/2001 of 19 December on the annual submission to the courts of lists of professionals for court appointment as expert witnesses, and the Protocol for action on common procedural services for the appointment of expert judicial witnesses, of 9 February 2005.

[16] See STS 5737/2012.

that fall solely to the competence of a single qualification for which membership of a college is compulsory and in which, moreover, other qualifications or professions are not concurrently involved. Thus, the Agreement and the subsequent finding formally opened up the market for court experts in Spain.

All of these court decisions on the 'governmental sphere' of the production of expert lists has meant that: (1) to be a court-appointed expert, one need only be in possession of a qualification that is regarded as suitable for the expertise in question, regardless of professional experience; and (2) any association of experts may submit a list of the members who are willing to act as such. The courts were therefore suddenly obliged to manage more or less twice the number of lists,[17] each one with different contents that they had to harmonise, and for which purpose they have gradually implemented different mechanisms in each autonomous region and/or each judicial district in order to cope with the ensuing deluge. Some districts did a better job of managing all this by creating a common expert appointment service, whereas in others the function was transferred directly to the government of the autonomous region in question (Madrid, Valencia and Catalonia are examples of this).

Hence, the ministries of justice of certain autonomous regions began to engage in the governmental task of producing the lists that are sent every year to the different Spanish courts.[18] To do this, they performed two tasks geared towards harmonising and guaranteeing the service's efficacy: (1) produce a list of specialities and sub-specialities into which the different experts on the list must be classified[19] and (2) establish a system of communication (basically

---

[17] For example, in 2017, forty-eight associations and eighty-four colleges were registered in Catalonia. In Girona, there were eighty-four colleges and fifty-two associations in 2018. The names of twenty-five of these fifty-two associations include the words 'legal experts' or 'forensic examiners'. It is important to note that, in Spain, an association can be incorporated by as few as three individuals, although the lists of any association must contain five specialists.

[18] In Germany, the Registry of accredited experts, öffentlich bestellte Sachverständigen, is produced by the Kammern, a public agency of the state. And, as in France, the judge may choose not to use this list if needs so dictate (StPo 73). In Russia, the government is also in charge of evaluating who produces the list of experts. A committee evaluates qualifications for this purpose (Appazov, 2016: 169).

[19] The lists are all very different. For example, if we compare the lists produced in Valencia and Catalonia, to begin with, the former makes a distinction between 'categories' and 'specialities' and the latter between 'speciality' and 'sub-specialities'. In Valencia, a number of specialities have been included in the 'alternative medicine' category, such as acupressure, homeopathy, traditional Chinese medicine, naturopathy, reflexology or sexology. This is not the case in Catalonia, where this category does not exist. There are also differences when we compare the contents of the sub-specialities. For example, in 'Realtors' in Valencia we have 'commercial agent', 'urban leasings', 'real estate in general, evaluation and appraisal'; whereas in Catalonia there are fifteen sub-specialities, for example, 'tourist properties', 'urban properties', 'industrial

technological) between the agency of the corresponding autonomous region and the expert groups for the latter to directly provide the information that will be sent to the courts.

Set aside any possible criticism that may be levelled at the different lists of specialities and sub-specialities that have gradually been devised by the different ministries in the different autonomous regions, and the difficulty encountered by judges to work outside them, it would be worthwhile to dwell on the only substantive datum contained in the expert lists: the qualification declared by the person who wishes to be included in the list,[20] where fundamentally university degrees, as well as any courses that accredit them as a specialist in any of the administrative classifications for which the subject in question applies, are specified. In these lists, there is a notable difference between official and certain non-official qualifications, there being experts who are clearly suited for a single speciality or sub-speciality, and 'all-terrain experts', in other words, experts who are accredited to furnish very different types of expertise.[21]

In this context, the salient point is that there is an absolute dependence on what each expert group, be it a college or organisation, does, both in terms of accrediting the *expertise* of members as well as in preparing the list of experts sent to the corresponding ministries. The first situation is much more complicated in professions that do not require official qualifications, since some expert associations have become akin to machines churning out qualifications which first of all accredit an individual as an expert and subsequently add that individual to their own list of experts who may be court-appointed in a given case.[22] Here it should be stressed that these associations are private, having

premises', 'lots of land', and rustic and urban 'leasings'. In general, the lists are more detailed in Catalonia than they are in Valencia.

[20] The remaining information pertains solely to the identification of the expert and their contact particulars. When the LEC was debated in Congress, the Spanish Socialist Workers' Party proposed that the lists contain all the information a judge needs to be able to select the expert in a specific case. In the same line, and according to some of the judges polled in the aforementioned empirical study on expert evidence in financial cases in the Spanish procedural setting, 'one of the measures that should be taken so that court-appointed experts will furnish a higher-quality service would be the production of more-detailed lists of experts, or with certain filters, such as proven prior experience in similar matters, speciality, available resources, etc.; they suggest that these lists should be drawn up with the help of exhaustive controls by independent organisations or agencies, such as the Professional Colleges' (Laguna and Palomo, 2008: 19).

[21] See, for example, www.aspejure.com/microsite/formulario-adscripcion-2018-2019.pdf which says that the association 'will accredit up to 8 different specialities'. Last visited on 25 May 2018.

[22] However, neither can it be forgotten that official qualifications are by no means free of certain problems. As Nieva Fenoll rightly asserts (2017: 99), '... something that has been hit by a major crisis that occurred a long time ago and which no one seems willing to remedy [are] university

their own objectives and interests, and in many cases are profit-making entities with no limitation on their participation in the courts of law.

The associations have not only taken charge of issuing certain qualifications, they are also responsible for acknowledging an individual as an expert on account of their *years of experience as an expert* in legal proceedings.[23] Indeed, not only do they attest to the expertise of an individual as attained by means of courses, but also that the period of time in which someone is engaged in an activity would make it possible to assume that this person is an expert, irrespective of their more formal credentials.[24] All the foregoing is compounded by the constant practice of including, in the actual name of the association, a reference to 'court experts' or 'forensic examiners', which is clearly misleading, because they are neither.[25]

Moreover, and with regard to how the lists are drawn up by the colleges, the procedure – if one actually exists – is somewhat shrouded in darkness: members are included in the lists sent by their institution to the ministries of Justice or the corresponding departments.[26] One of the exceptional cases, for example, is the Official College of Physicians of Madrid, which has implemented a specific procedure for producing the list of experts it submits to the courts every year in the Autonomous Region of Madrid, evaluating substantive (beyond purely formal credentials) and ethical aspects of the physician (no conflicts of interest, no negative reports issued by code of conduct committees, no criminal or administrative penalties as a practising physician).[27]

---

qualifications. There was a time, quite a long one, when a university degree conferred the condition of expert upon its holder, a qualification that nobody doubted.'

[23] See, for example, www.asociacion-anpc.es/anpc/admision/.

[24] For example, membership in the Catalan Association of Legal and Forensic Experts, which works with the Administration of Justice, requires proof of two years of experience as an expert witness in the courts, although the governing board may waive this requirement for applicants who can validate having attended courses that provide the necessary training to exercise as an expert witness. Evidently, these courses are organised by the very same expert associations.

[25] The latest statistics provided by the Spanish General Council of the Judiciary (2015) show that the most sought-after expert opinions are those involved in the appraisal of property, vehicles, jewellery and valuable objects. Experts of this type would appear to be the most sought after in the court-appointed expert system referred to in the aforementioned report. In Catalonia at least, this information is confirmed by the actual statistics of the Ministry of Justice where property appraisal and evaluation has been the most requested expertise since 2005, and more specifically in 2017 it accounted for 45.98 per cent of court-appointed expert opinions. Cf. www .poderjudicial.es/cgpj/es/Temas/Estadistica-Judicial/Plan-Nacional-de-Estadistica-Judicial/Activi dad-Judicial/Actividad-Pericial-Judicial.

[26] The EGLE asserts that the public nature of the lists 'does away with the obstacle posed by discretionary appointments [by judges] based on hidden lists produced in accordance with unknown criteria the existence of which has been proven in numerous Member States'. In Spain, this situation is prompted not by the judges, but rather by the experts themselves.

[27] See the relevant information at: www.icomem.es/comunicacion/noticias/2947/Abierto-el-plazo-para-formar-parte-del-listado-de-peritos-para-el-ano-2018. Last visited on 25 May 2018.

On the other hand, many colleges do not seem to exercise, at least publicly, any specific control over the drawing-up of expert lists,[28] and the willingness or the availability of each member to act as an expert witness if necessary will suffice for this to occur. Evidently, one might argue that college affiliation helps to control at least certain substantive aspects, but to corroborate this, the conditions established in associations' by-laws for admission to the corresponding professional college would need to be known. And this is where things start to get complicated, because not only is there one college per profession, but rather these colleges have demerged into very different cells, which are known as 'organizaciones colegiadas' [collegiate organisations], all over Spain.[29]

Regarding this situation, the same thing occurs with associations, whose regulations would need to be examined in order to ascertain whether in each case they implement any type of control to substantiate eligibility for membership or even to be included in the corresponding list of experts. Thus, and by way of example, la Asociación de Peritos Colaboradores con la Administración de Justicia of the Valencian Community requires a

> prior report by the Deontological Commission, in which fulfilment of the demands envisaged by the professional college for each expert appraisal must be addressed. In cases in which the activity does not enjoy the support of a college, a report should be provided about the candidate's competence by the person responsible for the activity in which the candidate seeks to engage. This report will deal exclusively with technical and ethical and professional questions.[30]

If our aim is the quality control of the experts on the list, maybe the best way of producing the list of expert witnesses available to the courts would be through expert groups, and in this regard perhaps the matter should be taken much more seriously. Indeed, the vast experience accumulated in the United States in matters of expert opinions has demonstrated that if we are to

---

[28] Another option would be to exclude experts from the lists, in certain circumstances, as does the Agrupación de Arquitectos Peritos y Forenses del Colegio Oficial de Arquitectos de Madrid, whose regulations provide for such course of action in the following eventualities: falsehood in the merits alleged for inclusion in the list, accepting an appointment when the candidate is incompatible with the job, the technical insufficiency of a finding or opinion, manifest incompetence or partiality, issuing opinions on questions that were not part of the mandate, etc. This organisation's code of conduct also includes responsibility for damages for incompetence, negligence, mistakes, lack of foresight or dedication or deficient performance.

[29] The Collegiate Medical Organization is comprised of the Official Provincial Colleges of Physicians and of the General Council. The General Council of Official Colleges of Physicians is the organ that brings together, coordinates and represents all the Official Colleges of Physicians in Spain.

[30] See www.asociaperitos.com/upload/Reglamento.pdf.

ascertain and even improve the quality of the expert evidence that is submitted in legal proceedings, then we must make the leap towards the expert community and not focus solely on specific expert witnesses who participated in a given case.[31] It is evident that asking an experts group to send a yearly list of its members who are willing to act as court-appointed experts solely on the strength of their qualifications is hardly the most useful or enriching type of approach. More rational methods must be devised that allow us to leverage the work either already done or which could be done by these groups, to which end we would need to think about which groups to approach as well as the type of information we request of them.

When approaching groups of experts, care should be taken to identify genuine expert communities. For example, if an area of expertise is dubious, its community of experts cannot be very capable and should not be treated with blind deference. It would be misguided to relinquish to them areas of great relevance with regard to how the law is applied. For example, currently in the Valencian Community lists of experts are produced in areas whose non-reliability has been demonstrated by a spate of empirical tests, such as so-called 'alternative medicine'. Applying the Frye criterion, the general acceptance of the expert community, if we went to groups of homeopaths to find out whether their methods are reliable, they would definitely tell us that they are. Therefore, it would not only be a question of knocking on the doors of communities simply to ask about the reliability of what they do, but rather of calling for controlled empirical studies that actually demonstrate that what they do is reliable. It is not a question of launching 'missiles' to label a given area as pseudoscience or junk science, but rather of demonstrating why the use thereof in the legal setting would be justified.[32]

In this line, for example, referring to the European Guide for Legal Expertise (EGLE) is interesting, as it establishes that organisations commissioned with managing the transparency, admission, training and quality of legal experts would have the following functions: promoting the quality of expert evidence; establishing basic quality standards applicable to all expert

---

[31] I am referring to the famous Frye criterion (1923), 'the general acceptance of the scientific community', repeated in the finding of the Supreme Court in the Daubert case (1993), along with its other criteria, and the judicial findings and legislative changes of the subsequent years. The available bibliography about experiences in the United States is very broad. See Vázquez (2015 and 2016) for an analysis of the case and multiple references to the different aspects debated.

[32] It should be emphasised, although this may seem self-evident, that the quality of evidence and our *knowledge* of the quality of evidence are two entirely different matters (Pardo, 2010: 367).

witnesses; establishing basic standards for the certification of expert witnesses; establishing basic standards for the accreditation of expert witness service providers; establishing quality standards for the different specific areas of expertise; besides the general CEN/ISO6 standards, and to the extent possible, establishing quality standards that include the best practices and specific competencies that should be demanded of each one of the different areas of expertise; implementing evaluation and re-evaluation procedures of expert witnesses and of expert witness service providers; etc.[33]

However, it must be clearly understood that all the work done to corroborate and oversee the reliability of the methods or techniques used by the experts and the professionalism with which they carry out their work will not solve all the problems of using expert opinion in legal proceedings. It will still be necessary to assess what experts *actually do* in specific cases. In other words, in the best of cases, this information will tell us something about the general reliability of at least certain methods or techniques, irrespective of how they were used in the specific case. Nevertheless, however reliable a method may be, mistakes may be made in its application in a specific case, whereby it will always be necessary to evaluate what the expert said or did in the specific context.

Returning to the Spanish case, we find that so-called 'government activity' in the court appointment of the experts has created a market for experts willing to provide expertise. This is a situation in which not only have the advantages of having the experts themselves generate lists of expert witnesses clearly *not* been exploited, but where these groups regulate their own interactions with the courts and where greater attention has not been paid to the overall reliability of the methods, techniques, theories, etc. they use. Next we will analyse 'judicial activity', that is, the selection of experts who will act as expert witnesses in specific cases.

12.3 SELECTING AN EXPERT FOR A SPECIFIC CASE: A JURISDICTIONAL FUNCTION?

In Spain, once the names and the information about all the individuals who will make up the annual list of experts are available, the list is usually classified in alphabetical order and in accordance with the speciality and sub-speciality

---

[33] In an empirical study, to which I have already referred (Laguna and Palomo, 2008: 42), judges were asked which measure they would take to improve the degree of specialization in the expert witness profession. The vast majority chose required accreditation of ongoing training of these professionals (44 per cent) and oversight by professional colleges (41 per cent), while a much smaller percentage chose the entrance examination to the profession (15 per cent).

that the administration in question has drawn up. Once this has been done, at the beginning of every year a date is set for holding a draw with the letters of the alphabet for the purpose of generating the letter that will be used for the correlative appointments of experts in each judicial district.[34] For example, if the letter C comes up in the draw, then the first expert appraisal of the respective sub-speciality will be conducted by the first person on the list in this letter, and so on in strict order down the list throughout the year. To put it another way, randomness decides which expert will be assigned to a specific case; the only thing 'judicial' about an appointment of this type are the purely formal aspects of the call.

In recent years, at least in some autonomous communities, software tools have had an impact on the selection of experts. For example, in Catalonia, virtually the entire court appointment process is computerised: the turn of the expert who should be appointed according to the order of the list is parametrised in the application, the petition issued by the judge, and even part of the notification sent to the expert about the appointment. And a step beyond the Catalan system is a recent Valencian one: BOPERIT ('buen perito' in Valencian). It is a computing system that directly assigns the expert who will take part in the case in hand once the judge has issued the petition through the system, indicating the speciality or sub-speciality required. What is more, the system will even inform the judge, for example, which specialities can produce certain types of expert opinions; hence, an expert opinion about the 'environment', according to the system, can be rendered by a philosopher, different types of engineers or even by a graduate in environmental sciences.

Some (albeit few) representatives of the judges have expressed an opinion about these expert selection procedures, asserting that they deliver advantages such as clarity, simplicity and objectivity.[35] At the same time, it has also been said that such automation does not allow the judge to introduce any nuances about the expert's suitability.[36] However, in my opinion, there is an even more controversial issue: the jurisdictional aspect involved in the appointment of

---

[34] Article 341 of the LEC establishes that 'the first appointment from each list will be made by a draw in the presence of the Clerk to the Court. The following appointments shall be made in sequential order.'

[35] The same opinion was voiced by the National Spokesperson of the Senior Judges of Spain, Pedro Luis Viguer Soler, http://lawyerpress.com/2017/02/22/la-asociacion-de-peritos-colaboradores-con-la-administracion-de-justicia-de-la-comunidad-valenciana-celebra-su-200-aniversario/.

[36] It is not merely a question of assessing whether the expert has a greater degree of academic specialisation, since sometimes it will be better to choose someone with fewer formal, but more practical, credentials. For example, let us imagine an expert opinion that appraises building work finishes, where it might be more advisable to consult a construction coordinator

the expert is obviated in its entirety, and the actors involved in the process are randomness and the regional administration[37] (which, let it be said in passing, is also a party to certain legal actions). In such a system, one must wonder about what the incentives and the responsibilities of the participants (i.e., the parties, the judge, and the expert) are.

Why would one of the parties request a court-appointed expert with this procedure? In other words, if the parties have a greater interest in having evidence that benefits them included in the court proceedings, and, to the extent possible, that it be quality evidence, is there anything that would provide one of them with an incentive to relinquish control over the expertise in the probative reasoning? Perhaps these cases could be explained by the Spanish courts' case law, which establishes that a court-appointed expert, simply on account of being selected in an impartial way, merits greater probative value than a party expert.[38] And beyond such case law, the preference for court-appointed experts is clearly mirrored in a survey conducted by the General Council of the Judiciary, in which 77 per cent of the judges, at least in the criminal jurisdiction, opined that the creation of a corps of experts exclusively at the service of the courts was highly necessary, whereas 22 per cent stated that it was quite necessary.[39] Scholars also reassert the idea

---

or a company that specialises in renovations rather than a professor of structural engineering or an academic with a master's degree in insulation.

[37] BOPERIT is managed in its entirety by the Ministry of Finance and Economic Model of the Autonomous Government of the Valencian Community.

[38] The sentence of 15 December 2015 by the Civil Chamber of the Supreme Court 'does not categorically and absolutely reject expert opinions provided by one of the parties with their statements of pleas, but rather, taking as the maxim that they always tend to be favourable to the party that provides them, which is not absurd either, because if they were unfavourable then there would be no sense in having them, it concludes that they must be assessed with caution, and that as this prevention does not generally exist in opinions provided by court-appointed experts, which is why the courts usually attach greater value to them. . . . By this, the Court does not mean that expert witnesses should be disqualified, but rather that, and assuming that the opinion given is an honest one, if it is unfavourable to the party then it is hardly likely to include it in the action against its own best interests.' Or, more recently, in the SSC of 3 March 2016, the review of the same Civil Chamber of the finding of the lower court reads thus: 'The challenged decision reasons that both experts use valid and commonly-accepted criteria as their principal criteria, reaching, with regard to most of the premises, substantively identical results, to the extent that the expert witness for the accused acknowledged that practically the relevant discrepancy was related to premises (venue) number 1. With such background, the Court continues to reason that it is logical and not arbitrary that the court should give priority to the report that evinced greater impartiality and objectivity, because the expert had been appointed by ballot by the court in the prior action finding on the legal division of an inheritance.'

[39] The survey was answered by 1205 practising judges and magistrates of the 5390 practising in Spain in 2015, thus amounting to 23.8 per cent of the total. Although the question about experts is limited to financial or accounting experts in criminal matters (p. 77), an earlier question was put to them

that it will always be preferable to opt for the court-appointed expert in view of the greater advantages, such as 'the greater credibility of the court-appointed expert, who is appointed impartially and is not chosen by only one of the parties' (Serra Domínguez, 2000: 310).

The seemingly most solid argument put forward in the Spanish context for attaching greater probative value to evidence provided by a court-appointed expert is the impartial *selection* of the expert who acts as such. And I italicise the word *selection*, because this is the only thing that the configuration of the current system guarantees. It does not in fact guarantee that an impartial expert will be appointed, it does not guarantee that the expert selected is the best one out of the available experts or even that he is a genuine expert in the specific issue in dispute. Naturally, there are procedural mechanisms in place for the parties to intervene and avert potential disasters,[40] but this will depend almost exclusively on their interests. Nevertheless, an impartial system is not the same as an impartial expert. Obviously, leaving the designation to chance is impartial; leaving it to an unfamiliar computer system is not necessarily.

Another possible argument for one of the parties to request a court-appointed expert is the cost of the services or, in other words, to control costs. In fact, the General Council of the Judiciary had provided for 'professional colleges, when sending the official lists of their members to the jurisdictional organs, attaching an addendum with a scale of approximate fees of each one'.[41]

However, the National Commission on Markets and Competition (CNMC in Spanish) considers that these scales of fees constituted unfair competition and prohibited the colleges from implementing them. Thus, colleges, associations and the like are only asked for an opinion when the fees established by an expert are challenged (article 246 LEC). In this case, the National

---

about the creation of expert units or court assistance units attached to the specialised first-instance provincial courts and under their functional dependence (p. 71). Agreement with the legislative amendment that this would require stood at 86 per cent. Cf. www.poderjudicial.es/cgpj/es/Tem as/Estadistica-Judicial/Estadistica-por-temas/Opinion-y-quejas-sobre-el-funcionamiento-de-la-jus ticia/Opinion-de-los-profesionales-y-usuarios-de-la-Administracion-de-Justicia-/Encuestas-a-la-Ca rrera-Judicial/.

[40] For example, recusal or disqualification. The former conceived as a closed list of reasons that the parties can bring into play to oppose the appointment of a court-appointed expert (see Picó i Junoy, 2001: 70 ff).

[41] Protocolo de Actuación del Servicio Común Procesal [Action Protocol of the Procedural Common Service] for the appointment of judicial expert witnesses, approved by Agreement of the Plenary on 9 February 2005. This resolution was consistent with Article 5.5 of the Royal Decree-Law 5/1996 on deregulation measures in land matters and professional colleges in which the main function attributed to the colleges was that of 'establishing scales of fees, which will be purely approximate'.

Commission on Markets and Competition recommended that colleges take the following points into consideration: the degree of complexity of the issues addressed, the degree of specialisation or experience required, the breadth or difficulty involved in collecting data and the diversity of sources consulted, travelling required to do the job, the financial amount of the claim and the weighting of all the aspects depending on the extent of their significance to the finding.

Moreover, some judges have asserted that the goal was precisely to 'make the (expert) selection process more objective, disassociating it form the decisions of the actual organ'.[42] The main argument is the protection of judges' impartiality, since they do not participate directly (and very often not even indirectly) in the appointment; of course, following this line of argument, tossing a coin to decide the expert would also be an objective process disassociated from the organ's decisions. The *risk* of judicial partiality is always present in every legal decision, and this is obviously no impediment for judges to continue to exercise their decision-making function or to prevent them from tossing a coin whenever they have to decide or whenever they fear they may lapse into partiality.

The concern about judicial impartiality should lead us to bolster the tools available to the parties to participate not only in the selection of the expert witness but also during the latter's performance as such, or even in determining what will be addressed by the appraisal, and not to deprive judges of their decision-making capacity.[43] All of these tools constitute a kind of ongoing dialectic exercise between the parties and the judge, in which the latter must be receptive to the parties' arguments, imposing nothing, and in which the parties should support their requests or petitions with suitable arguments. This, in my opinion, is the way to guarantee legal impartiality in a decision that should be the responsibility of Spanish judges, that is, selecting the court expert, as occurs in other European countries.[44]

If the Spanish judge is not responsible for appointing the expert, then who is? The answer is nobody, if it all depends on luck, then there is no responsibility: not

---

[42] At the beginning of last year, the secretary of the Government Chamber of the Higher Court of Justice of Andalusia, Ceuta and Melilla, in a proposal to follow in the footsteps of other autonomous regions. See the resolution of the complaint number 00000216/2016.

[43] The French system seems to have fully comprehended the importance of the *contradictorio* (adversarial proceedings) in court-appointed evidence. For example, the French legislation establishes that if, during their operations, the expert needs any document or clarification, then they must convene all the parties; if the expert has been authorised to request information from a third party, then they must first submit this material to the consideration of the parties before using it, etc. Cf. Orellana de Castro, 2017: 120

[44] For example, France or Germany.

even of the colleges or associations that send the list or of the systems used to select the expert for the case or the court staff. Thus, if, when all is said and done, after the court-appointed expert has been heard in court and it transpires that the expert was not suitable for the case or that they proved to be partial in their declarations, despite their impartial appointment, etc., the courts are unlikely to regard them as legally responsible.[45] In this scenario, once again, there is a kind of delegation in the expert groups, since the consequences that may arise, for example, from accepting a commission that is beyond the expert's competence, fall to the latter's College or association if thus provided for in its statutes; the same applies if the expert has acted wrongly as such, and the option of not renewing their presence in the corresponding lists is considered, etc.

The Criminal Code, for example, envisages the offence of false witness against the Administration of Justice, and this could be used as a limitation on experts by way of a penalty for certain conduct. However, it would appear to be very difficult to prove the facts provided for by the legislator for its enforcement, since not only must the falsehood in itself be accredited (obviously requiring, in turn, expert opinions), but it should also be proved to have been malicious (article 459 CP). Hence, the Supreme Court has warned that it is necessary: (1) from an objective standpoint, that what is expressed in the report or in the ratification must be contrary to reality, be insufficiently justified or change facts already verified; and (2) in subjective terms, the conscious and voluntary knowledge that a lie has been told.[46] Hence, 'since the untenable opinion must be issued maliciously, any issue involving negligence or insufficient capacity or lack of expertise precludes the enforcement of such charges, which are reserved solely for deliberately false opinions'.[47]

This situation is even worse in the case law of the Spanish Supreme Court regarding the responsibility of experts when acting as such. For example, in one case in which one of the parties sued their opponent's expert witness for 'damage to honour' on the grounds of the report's contents regarding their personality, the Supreme Court ultimately exonerate the psychologist by saying that 'the report basically involves the exercise of freedom of expression,

---

45 Civil, criminal and disciplinary liability is provided for. For example, in civil issues, recourse could be had to the expert's extra-contractual liability, obviously with the difficulty of proving the resulting damage and the relationship of causality between the expert opinion and the damage caused. In disciplinary matters, the reasons are more informal in nature, for example, if in the court proceedings the expert shows a lack of due consideration of, respect for and obedience to the Court. In this regard, see Picó i Junoy (2001: 63 et seq.) and Abel Lluch (2009: 81 et seq.).
46 SSC of 18 February 2009.
47 Sentence of the Provincial Court of the Balearic Islands of 3 November 2006.

whereby its legal consequences must be calibrated mainly around this concept'.[48] Regardless of whether or not the exoneration of the defendant is correct, the argument used by the Spanish highest court is worrying: it does not take the expert's professional performance in a proceedings into account, but rather regards the psychologist as if she were just another citizen who had voiced an opinion elsewhere, failing to consider her as a participant in the workings of the administration of justice.

While there may be no legal-institutional incentives, there still remain personal incentives for each expert to act diligently, leaving this up to the subjectivity of each one of them. One of the incentives that court-appointed experts could have is to do a good job so that the court would procure their services on another occasion, although now it is virtually impossible for an expert to participate more than once a year if their speciality has many candidates. In any event, this does not depend on good performance alone. On the other hand, if the speciality or sub-speciality has few experts, then naturally the person will be called back as an expert witness, albeit virtually without any external or institutional incentives, since the system is not sensitive to the quality of the expert or of the expert appraisals.

Moreover, if besides the foregoing we recall that court-appointed experts may also be engaged as expert witnesses in other cases, the scenario is somewhat disturbing, as it is one in which at least the differences between both types of expert opinion seem to be increasingly blurred: there is a very large market of experts available to act as such, there are no judicial controls as to who the expert that will act as court expert will be, sometimes the court-appointed expert is paid by one of the parties, etc. In summary: it is a context in which judges must control the quality of such expert opinions exactly in the same way in which they control the opinion of an expert witness chosen by a party.

12.4 THE RELATIVE IMPORTANCE OF WHETHER AN EXPERT IS APPOINTED BY THE COURT OR CHOSEN BY ONE OF THE PARTIES

Assuming that one of the only ways to eliminate partiality and improve expert evidence is to prevent experts from being appointed by the parties,[49] then by

---

[48] SSC of 3 March 2011, Civil Chamber.
[49] Like when it is said that 'in a system in which each party provides their own expert, the doubts regarding the experts' objectivity must increase, particularly when they do not come from public organizations' (Bachmaier, 2009: 136).

definition an expert witness chosen by one of the parties would be partial, and a court-appointed one would be impartial. Expressed in this way, however, the argument becomes purely conceptual and in no way speaks to the reliability of the chosen expert, and even less about their expertise. Thus, the basic issue for establishing *qualitative* differences between expert witnesses chosen by a party and court-appointed experts lies in considering the criteria used to select a good and appropriate expert for the specific case – not the impartial selection system – and how they developed their expertise.

In any case, it is noteworthy that when the term 'court-appointed expert' is used, no reference is usually made to how the expert is appointed, as if it were not important or there were a single system that made it possible to refer to this figure regardless of the specific type of designation. Perhaps the strategy of having a list of experts available as witnesses would be appropriate in a judicial system that appoints experts in a consistent way, but more work certainly needs to be done on the criteria and guarantees for the preparation of the list. What kind of information, other than their qualifications (if they have completed degree), should be taken into account when compiling expert lists?

The EGLE, for example, recommends a European-wide organisation to manage lists. In particular, it would be empowered to verify the experts' technical competence according to their qualifications, professional record and other expertise (pp. 9 and 10). Section 3.13 of the EGLE refers to university qualifications, professional experience included in their CV, membership in professional associations, references, professional titles and initial and ongoing expert training, relevant publications, awards or prizes obtained, courses taught and teaching experience.

Naturally, the difficulties of setting up an organisation such as the one proposed by the EGLE are not few, and are even more numerous when a Europe-wide strategy is proposed, not merely a national one. The proposal, however, has some undeniably positive points: the size of the group and the distance between its various members could help to reduce certain risks of camaraderie that occur in small groups, where particular interests of individuals are often very influential. Obviously, communities of experts should not only be asked to merely verify compliance with requirements, they should also be required to control the names of the experts on the lists, revealing those who might be there for their expertise, and those who should not be there for their lack thereof or for their poor performance as experts in previous cases.[50] But,

---

[50] These expert communities also exist in England and seek to control the quality of experts that will act as such, although in a different way, not through lists. See www.academyofexperts.org/training-courses.

prior to that, the expert communities should provide empirical information to demonstrate the reliability of the methods, techniques, theories, etc. that their individual members use. Without that kind of data, it is difficult to justify giving them the power to make up the lists.

Another type of empirical information to be sought might be that which is provided by the users of the expertise, that is, judges, lawyers, prosecutors, etc. As is apparently done by the Chilean Public Defender's Office, which has a list of registered experts, the organisation would only ensure formal completion of qualifications when the counsels who contacted it are asked to evaluate the report submitted by the court-appointed expert and to defend the expert's opinion in the oral hearing. They would be asked about issues such as whether or not the objectives of the expert opinion or witness were met; the methodology, quantity and quality of the instruments applied and the relevance of the outcome of the expert opinion to the objective addressed.[51] This kind of information might complement the work done by the expert communities, joining efforts with legal actors to substantially improve the system used to compile lists of experts. Nevertheless, even with the best experts on the list, the selection made for any specific case would not be left to chance. Rather, in each case, the most suitable expert available would be chosen by the judge, whose choice would be facilitated by an established list of accredited experts.

Nevertheless, consideration should be given to the costs involved in a large-scale or comprehensive system of properly controlled court-appointed experts. First of all, if we want to assemble a list of available experts, consideration must be given to the cost of setting it up and the factors that might encourage qualified experts to participate in the process. Secondly, if we want to bring in the best expert available for a particular case, the selection process will obviously represent additional work for the courts, and especially for the judges. A feasibility study would reveal if the costs are much higher than the advantages, and if that were the case, then it might be best to forgo a list of experts. Deciding about the model would require knowing the cost of each method of selecting experts and the quality of the expert opinions produced with each selection method. Moreover, empirical information on how the methods and techniques used by experts actually work is needed to know where it is worthwhile to invest public resources.

---

[51] See www.dpp.cl/pag/7/63/introduccion.
  The aforementioned assessment criteria are more substantive in nature, although they are also asked about purely formal questions such as clarity, simplicity or confidence in the exposition of the contents of the opinion; the expert's capacity to convince and their credentials.

Whatever the model of expert selection, one fundamental issue must not be overlooked: defining the purpose of the expertise and the information provided to the expert for this purpose is essential for the success of the expert evidence. Whatever the expert is asked to do is always crucial. This should be taken into consideration, especially when there are procedural limits that restrict experts' tasks to what they were asked to do when they were appointed, as in the Spanish case, where experts cannot overreach, suggest changes or request extensions. It is curious, however, that while a close relationship between the judge and the court-appointed expert is precluded in order to properly establish the ends or purpose of the expertise, the Spanish Civil Procedure Act (LEC) does not prohibit experts, after their appointment, from contacting the party that has requested the expert opinion, nor does it provide for control of experts and the tasks to be carried out.

Orellana de Castro highlights the preceding concern and advises in favour of contact between court-appointed experts and the parties who requested their appointment. Experts might need further details about the scope of the evidence required and it may also happen that 'once the agreed formulation of the expert evidence is known, the expert may consider that it has been poorly formulated, and may therefore suggest to the lawyer the possibility of amending it'. An expert appointed by a judge at the request of one of the parties who has a connection with that party would be an obvious contradiction of the thesis defended by a good part of the procedural doctrine. According to that thesis, the most important difference between the American and the Romano-Germanic systems of law with regard to expert evidence is that in the American system the parties choose the expert opinion they consider relevant to a decision in their favour by offering an expert also selected by them (see, e.g. Taruffo, 1996: 241). In the Spanish case, parties can request a court-appointed expert who would be chosen by chance. But what is even more problematic is that the parties can define the ends or purposes of the expertise and even control the information provided for it.[52]

The point of contention clearly lies in the *absence of judicial control* over both the boundaries of the expert opinion and the information provided to the expert witness to carry out the task commissioned to them. However, if this is consistently considered so relevant to attributing evidentiary value to an expert

[52] Although the doctrine acknowledges the legal loophole, it suggests that in some way the counterpart is also involved. Abel Lluch (2009: 144) states: 'With the party's expert opinion, the party submits the report and addresses its points, without the intervention of the other party or the judge. In the case of a court-appointed expert, notwithstanding the legal silence, in addition to the points made by the party requesting the expert's opinion, the other parties must be notified in person if they wish to extend the expert's opinion on certain points.'

opinion, it should be provided for in the legislation itself and not simply assumed (even implicitly) as an evaluation criterion. Judicial control does not depend in any way on the parties, because they cannot demand judicial checks on the expert evidence they offer with the experts they select. The law itself does not allow this!

Undoubtedly, communication between the parties, the expert and the judge could be critical to clearly defining the work to be done by the expert, including the ends of the expert opinion as well as the information on the case provided for that purpose. These controls could be established irrespective of who selects the expert. They can be established for the court-appointed expert, as is the case in France, where an ongoing relationship between experts and judges obliges experts to keep judges informed throughout the course of their work (Article 161 of the French Code of Criminal Procedure). They can also be established for expert witness chosen by the parties, as is the case in England, where experts are entitled to ask the court for instructions to do their job (paragraphs 28 and 29 of the Guidance for the Instruction of Experts in Civil Claims) and have access to all the relevant information provided by the parties, including that being considered by the expert of the adversary (paragraph 30). In my opinion, these regulations show that the court's interest in the work and the quality of experts cannot be limited solely *to the person that selected them* or the selection method. In both legislative and judicial contexts, the definition of the ends of the expert opinion and the information provided for it must be taken into account.

One last point to highlight regarding the information given to experts to conduct their activities and write their reports is cognitive bias, which also clouds the selection of an impartial expert even from a list of good experts. In a recent article, Dror (2018) stressed how in criminal justice, the 'irrelevant contextual information' to which several experts, especially institutional experts, are exposed can cause biases in their thought processes: knowing the defendant's criminal record, identifying witnesses and even taking confessions. Cognitive bias occurs not only because the parties can influence the thought process of an expert in very different ways, but because of a very varied set of circumstances that have nothing to do with the parties.[53] For this very reason, it is somewhat dangerous to anchor the concept of the reliability of expert evidence to the relationship between the court and the expert (Appazov,

---

[53] A very interesting empirical analysis of these cognitive biases at the international in *forensic science examiners* can be found in Kukucka, Kassin, Zapf and Dror, 2017. Something on the subject of expert partiality/impartiality in general can also be seen in Vázquez, 2018.

2016: 162). Cognitive bias can occur in expert witnesses chosen by parties and in those appointed by courts.

Another aspect traditionally regarded as a source of partiality among expert witnesses is the financial remuneration they receive for their services. As has been seen, in Spain, at least some court-appointed expert witnesses are paid by the requesting parties, and the expert will ultimately negotiate the cost of their work with them. Once again, if this is the source of concern, then the compensation to be received and the reporting of that amount itself could be controlled (to the extent possible) so as not to become excessive. For example, after working on the Law Reform Commission of Tanzania, sub-section 10.6, Allen (2015: 384) suggested this in 'A Proposed Evidence Law': 'An expert witness shall disclose any and all compensation received directly or indirectly from the parties'. Obviously, informal payments made to experts outside judicial settings may not be possible to control, but such futility applies to both expert witnesses chosen by the parties and those appointed by courts.[54]

Following analysis of the Spanish case, one of the most important conclusions about the reliability of expert opinions is that big labels, such as 'the impartiality of court-appointed experts', are useless. Not only because they hide practices that contribute nothing to the quality of the expert evidence, but because, regardless of who selects the expert, the important issue seems to be how experts are selected and, perhaps more pointedly, the information provided to them and even their compensation. Despite all the efforts that could be made to improve these aspects, an expert's assertions in a specific case must still be evaluated.

A genuine and rational evaluation of experts' assertions about a case requires that judges understand them in the context for or in which they are made. In other words, it requires that they go into detail about what experts do and say, not merely select one of them or simply use big labels that release them from the substantial cognitive work involved in availing themselves of expert information to reach a court finding. And for this purpose, thought should be given to the procedural tools that are available to motivate such understanding, irrespective of how lawyers protect their experts. As we saw at the beginning of this chapter, this is another of the issues considered

---

[54] Cf. Nieva, 2017: 94 ff., who asserts that 'although these cases have seldom been committed to paper, there exist real stories about court-appointed experts who, following their appointment, receive telephone calls virtually immediately from the parties' lawyers to offer them more money if they find in their favour. Many of these opinions have been produced in the following way: the expert drafts an opinion, forwards it to the lawyer, who rewords it to suit their interests, and the opinion is eventually submitted to the court as if it were the work of the expert alone.'

fundamental to the preconception that an expert witness chosen by a party is worse than a court-appointed one.

Thinking about procedural mechanisms is difficult without thinking about the kind of specific problems that, in theory, they should help us resolve. Expert appraisals or evidence do not always involve the same kinds of problems, and perhaps consideration should be given to regulating different situations of varying complexity. For example, in cases in which the expert evidence is exceptionally complex, an advisor could assist the judge in very basic questions pertaining to the type of expertise involved, or even conceptual questions, with neither knowledge of the specific case nor access to the evidence provided.[55] Another possibility is a kind of meta-expert in cases in which the disagreement between the experts who provided the expert evidence is highly complex. The purpose would not be to provide new expert evidence or to hear the disagreement, but rather to help the judge understand the actual disagreement. There would always be time to apply the burden of proof as a rule of decision if the judge, after making all the necessary efforts to draw legal consequences from the disagreement, considers that what has been said by any of the experts cannot be used to reach a decision, assuming that the case is to be decided on the basis of the expert evidence alone.

Focusing so heavily on a big label such as the 'impartial selection of an expert' has had certain consequences. It has promoted a culture or understanding of expert evidence that is far removed from the epistemic requirements that can reasonably be placed upon it. This focus not only assumes that the impartial selection of an expert will guarantee the reliability of the evidence, it also avoids at all costs disagreements or confrontations between experts, and overlooks the fact that, at least in some cases, the best solution would be *to understand the reason for the disagreement* rather than simply avoid it.[56] Thus, not all legal systems provide for the possibility of discussion between experts; it is not included in the Spanish legal system, for example. However, virtually none of the legal systems that do provide for this possibility regulate the dynamics of such meetings and/or establish their objectives. One excellent exception is the English system. Before any debate, the experts in

---

[55] Like the 'technical advisors' in the United States, provided for in FRE 104 and in certain precedents, who are requested in very exceptional cases, who do not carry out any expert operations but simply help the judge to understand the information already available. They do not give an opinion about the case and cannot be cross-examined.

[56] That is to say, before summoning a third expert using the lists again and entering further information that has not been analysed. Converting court proceedings into a kind of sports tournament where the party that runs up the highest score wins: two experts versus one. Identified in the Spanish setting as the 'the principle of coincident plurality', cf. Abel Lluch, 2009: 148.

disagreement are asked to provide the judge with a report in which they both agree on the specific points and basis of their dissent.[57] This would allow the judge to better oversee the confrontation and draw conclusions from it. The points would have been clearly established in advance, preventing the meeting from degenerating into a purely theoretical debate.

Nevertheless, the aforementioned procedural tools do not have to be activated always or in all cases. In most legal procedures, it will probably suffice for judges to be able to clarify doubts about the expert witness's assertions in the course of the proceedings in order to understand what an expert, either chosen by a party or court-appointed, is saying about the case in hand. Many scholars who follow this line of thinking maintain that judges cannot remain passive before experts and their expertise, whereas others say that judges should remain passive, and act as mere onlookers. In my opinion, the latter stance fails to consider that, in the best of cases, judges who have queries about the expertise provided will consult external sources, bringing in information that has not been discussed by the parties. And in the worst cases, judges will eventually defer to one of the experts because they are incapable of reasonably appraising all the information.

Mechanisms such as the ones referred to above should not be difficult to introduce into systems in which the court-appointed expert has enjoyed greater influence due to the emphasis that has always been placed on how they should assist the judge. However, it should be clearly understood that it is not a matter of the origin of the expert opinion making a difference, but of experts and judges both meeting the specific obligations entrusted to them and of providing them with the necessary tools to do the work that corresponds to each one. And evidently, this must be designed to protect the procedural guarantees of the parties at all times, which means that they will have a say in approving the participation of any expert in the court procedure.

12.5 A BRIEF CONCLUSION

The term 'court-appointed expert' seems to be based on a set of assumptions about how this type of expert evidence should work. However, when we analyse how it actually works in today's systems, we may find big problems that have a very important impact on its quality and are ignored by those who simply assume that court-appointed experts deserve greater

[57] See the Civil Procedure Rule 35.12; Practice Direction 35 ('Experts and Assessors') issued by the Ministry of Justice, paragraphs 9.1 to 9.8; and the Guidance for the Instruction of Experts in Civil Claims issued by the Civil Justice Council (2014), paragraphs 70 to 83.

probative value because the parties do not participate in their appointment. Therefore,

(1) If a genuine epistemic difference is to be made between an expert chosen by a party and one appointed by the court, attention should be paid to how courts appoint experts. Who is responsible for selecting them? What information and/or mechanisms do they have to do it?

(2) Systems that guarantee the quality of a sufficient pool of experts willing to provide expert opinion can be expensive and, of course, not without problems.

(3) The information given to expert witnesses to conduct their inquiries and produce reports, the compensation they deserve for their work and the court's interpretation of their assertions without regard for either party's interests do not necessarily depend on the origin of the expert opinion. They are all situations that can be anticipated, legislatively and judicially, even in the case of experts selected by one of the parties.

A good system of expert evidence would take us on a path other than the one predicted by Wigmore (1904: 970): 'legislative progress in the adoption of [authorization of court appointed experts in any context] has been slow. But it is inevitably the way of the future'. It seems that educational models of expert opinion[58] should be examined now and with an eye toward the future. Extensive information about the expertise of the expert witnesses would be welcome, as would procedural tools to fully understand the expert information available in specific cases, irrespective of who is presenting it. Needless to say, the wise use of expert opinion is economically and cognitively costly, but ignorance will always be costlier.

REFERENCES

Abel Lluch, X. (2009). La prueba pericial. In Abel Lluch and Picó i Junoy, eds., *La prueba pericial*, Barcelona: J. M. Bosch, pp. 15–248.

Allen, R. (2015). A Proposed Evidence Law. *Boston University International Law Journal*, vol. 33(2), 359–94.

Allen, R. and Miller, J. S. (1993). The Common Law Theory of Experts. Deference or education?. *Northwestern University Law Review*, 87(4), 1131–47.

---

[58] As Allen has been asserting for some time now, in different works. The source was Allen and Miller, 1993.

246 *Carmen Vázquez*

Appazov, A. (2016). *Expert Evidence and International Criminal Justice*, Copenhagen: Springer.

Bachmaier, L. (2009). Dos modelos de prueba pericial penal en el derecho comparado: Estados Unidos de Norteamérica y Alemania. *Jueces para la democracia*, 66, 118–37.

Dror, I. E. (2018). Biases in forensic experts. *Science*, 2360(6386), 243 ff.

EGLE- European Guide for Legal Expertise. (2015). *Guía de buenas prácticas de la pericia judicial civil en la Unión Europea*. https://experts-institute.eu/en/pr ojects/the-guide-to-good-practices-in-civil-judicial-expertise-in-the-european-union/

Gross, S. R. (1991). Expert Evidence. *Wisconsin Law Review*, 1991, 1113–232.

Hooper, L., Cecil, J. and Willging, T. (2001). *Neutral Science Panels: Two Examples of Panels of Court-Appointed Experts in the Breast Implants Product Liability Litigation*, Washington, DC: Federal Judicial Center.

Kukucka, J., Kassin, S. M., Zapf, P. and Dror, I. E. (2017). Cognitive Bias and Blindness: A Global Survey of Forensic Science Examiners. *Journal of Applied Research in Memory and Cognition*, 6, 452–9.

Laguna, M. del P. and Palomo, J. (2008). *La prueba pericial económica en el ámbito procesal español*, Madrid: Universidad Rey Juan Carlos.

Muñoz Sabaté, L. (2001) *Fundamentos de prueba judicial civil, L.E.C 1/2000*, Barcelona: J. Ma. Bosch.

Nieva Fenoll, J. (2017). Repensando Daubert: Elementos de convicción que debe tener un buen dictamen pericial. In J. Picó i Junoy, ed., *Peritaje y prueba pericial*, Barcelona: J. M. Bosch.

Orellana de Castro, R. (2017). Un estudio crítico sobre los diferentes sistemas de designación de peritos y sobre las listas de peritos en la LEC. In J. Pico i Junoy, ed., *Peritaje y prueba pericial*, Barcelona: J. M. Bosch.

Pardo, M. S. (2010). Evidence Theory and the NAS Report on Forensic Science. *Utah Law Review*, 2, 367–83.

Picó i Junoy, J. (2001). *La prueba pericial en el proceso civil español, Ley 1/2000 de Enjuiciamiento Civil*, Barcelona: Bosch Editor.

Saltzburg, S. A., Martin, M. M. and Capra, D. (2006). *Federal Rules of Evidence Manual*, 9th ed., vol. 3, San Francisco: Lexis Nexis.

Serra Domínguez, M. (2000). La prueba pericial. In J. Alonso-Cuevillas, ed., *Instituciones del nuevo proceso civil. Comentarios sistemáticos a la Ley 1/ 2000 sobre Enjuiciamiento Civil*, Barcelona: Difusión Jurídica.

Taruffo, M. (1996). La prova scientifiche nella recente esperienza statunitense. *Rivista Trimestrale Di Diritto e Procedura Civile*, 50(1), 219–49.

Vázquez, C. (2015). *De la prueba científica a la prueba pericial*, Barcelona-Madrid: Marcial Pons.

Vázquez, C. (2016). La prueba pericial en la experiencia estadounidense. *Jueces para la democracia*, 86, 92–112.

Vázquez, C. (2018). La im/parcialidad pericial y otros conceptos afines. Confiabilidad, desacuerdos y sesgos de los expertos. *Isonomía*, 48, 69–107.

Wigmore, J. H. (1904). A *Treatise on the System of Evidence in Trials at Common Law*, 2nd ed. (1923), Boston: Little, Brown.

13

Latent Justice

Fingerprint Evidence and the Limits of Adversarialism in England, Australia and New Zealand

Gary Edmond

13.1 INTRODUCTION: TESTING ADVERSARIALISM

This chapter offers a critical review of reported fingerprint cases in three common law jurisdictions covering the period from the beginning of the twentieth century until the time of publication. It considers how the tools of adversarialism were applied to the admissibility and use of fingerprint evidence in criminal proceedings. It provides a detailed survey of the manner in which defence and appellate counsel contested fingerprint evidence, how courts responded to these challenges in trials and appeals and, implicitly, how examiners testified and prosecutors presented this evidence. In order to facilitate analysis, the chapter draws upon mainstream scientific research and recommendations. This scientific knowledge operates as a standard that can be used to evaluate legal representations and uses of fingerprint evidence as well as the effectiveness of legal rules, procedures and personnel. The chapter concludes that legal institutions in each of these jurisdictions were basically inattentive to the epistemological dimensions of latent fingerprint evidence. Adversarial trial safeguards, including appeals, did not bring the lack of testing and systematic over-claiming to the attention of courts.

Following a brief exposition of the method of data collection and my approach to categorisation, the chapter provides seriatim reviews of reported accounts of latent fingerprint evidence in England and Wales, Australia and New Zealand. Each section reviews the earliest appeals and the manner in which the evidence is routinely expressed, provides an indication of the dominant types of challenges over the course of more than a century and then, in a little more detail, examines the most sustained challenges. Each jurisdiction displays idiosyncratic contours although the overall patters are similar. It is remarkable how challenges were overwhelmingly focused on *legal* rather than *epistemological* issues.

In the following discussion the cases are divided into two rough categories. First, the heading of '*legal* engagement' captures the range of challenges to fingerprint evidence that are not substantially concerned with the accuracy of the identification. These are focused on the admissibility of the fingerprint evidence because of the way reference prints were collected, fingerprint examiners testifying about something beyond identity (such as the age of a print), fingerprint evidence being presented in a manner that draws attention to prior criminality and risked unfair prejudice to the defendant, whether a guilty plea was made prior to the suspect being presented with fingerprint evidence to secure the full sentencing discount, and so on. Relying heavily on legal rules and values and contests over the significance of fingerprint evidence, they make up the vast majority of the reported cases that refer to fingerprint evidence other than in passing.[1] The second group is more *epistemologically* oriented. It is composed of the tiny number of reported cases that more directly engage with the identification, particularly around point standards and the sufficiency of prints for comparison. These cases sometimes touch upon epistemological issues, but as we shall see, almost never engage with scientific literature and research.

Legal reports of fingerprints start as early as 1905 but there were no appeals concerned with admissibility per se. The evidence was already in use before appellate courts were called upon to consider specific legal issues. The early decisions capture examiners categorically identifying a specific person (i.e. individualising) on the basis of fingerprint comparison and courts not merely receiving the evidence but actively lending their imprimatur. This informal collaboration continued for more than a century, even as attentive scientists began to describe categorical identification and claims about a zero error rate as 'not scientifically plausible' and 'indefensible' (National Research Council, 2009: 142–3; AAAS Report, 2017: 71).

This chapter summarises more expansive studies of each of the jurisdictions.[2] The data was collected using a combination of public legal repositories (e.g. BAILII, AustLii and NZLii) and commercial publishers such as LexisNexis and Westlaw. These databases were searched for

---

[1] It is not my intention to suggest that legal challenges are inappropriate. In some cases, they represent the best way of advancing a defendant's interests and rights. However, inattention to validity and reliability is revealing.

[2] Edmond, 2019: 301–65; Edmond, 2020: 1–29; Edmond et al., 2020: 1287–327.

references to 'fingermark' and 'fingerprint' and their variations located alongside the roots of words such as 'admissibility', 'reliability' and 'challenge'. Searches returned hundreds of cases for each jurisdiction and these were read and analysed. A qualitative synthesis of these cases is reproduced in the pages that follow.

The focus on reported cases (and readily accessible judgments) overlooks many encounters in trials, including the very first appearances of latent fingerprint evidence in each of these jurisdictions. Nevertheless, it confers a range of benefits. It concentrates focus on those cases that were conceived as important and provided accessible resources for generations of lawyers and judges. Reported decisions capture both legal authority and legal understanding of latent fingerprint evidence. Some of the decisions, notably *R v. Smith* (2011) in England and Wales, *Bennett v. Police* (2005) in Australia and *The Queen v. Carter* (2005) in New Zealand, represent the current law in relation to fingerprint evidence. As we shall see, authoritative legal perspectives are difficult to reconcile with contemporary scientific knowledge and the recommendations of mainstream scientists.

Because this chapter is concerned with adversarial practice and raises serious and unanswered questions about the effectiveness of legal assumptions, procedures and protections, it is important to draw attention to precepts that seem fundamental to reliance on forensic science evidence in common law criminal proceedings. Self-evidently, these are informed and even condition by the commitment to factual rectitude (i.e. getting the outcome right) and fairness to all participants.[3] First, it is the responsibility of the parties, respectively, the state (through the prosecutor) and the defendant (usually through lawyers) to have the resources and inclination to assemble evidence, make relevant legal submissions and prosecute their case. This applies to locating, adducing and challenging forensic science evidence (see, e.g. Devlin, 1979; Duff et al. 2004). Secondly, non-trivial limitations with forensic science evidence should be disclosed and, where appropriate, tested by defence counsel and explained by trial judges. All of the participants involved – though especially fingerprint examiners, prosecutors and judges – have formal obligations to present the evidence accurately and to facilitate comprehension. Thirdly, rules and procedures regulating the admission, presentation and evaluation of expert evidence – such as admissibility standards, rules for expert reports, provision for cross-examination, access to expert assistance, judicial directions and instructions – are assumed to

3 In England and New Zealand these are to some extent aligned with formal rights instruments (e.g. ECHR and New Zealand Bill of Rights Act 1990) and section 6 of the New Zealand Evidence Act 2006, s. 6.

be effective.[4] Fourthly, adversarial systems assume that decision-makers (including jurors) will be placed in a position to understand and evaluate the evidence presented during the trial, including forensic science evidence. There are other legal commitments, around the burden and standard or proof, avoiding wrongful convictions, the importance of finality, efficient use of resources, to name just a few, but the four aforementioned precepts seem to be fundamental to meaningful routine reliance on forensic science evidence.

13.2 ENGLAND AND WALES

This section and the two that follow provide succinct overviews of reported responses to fingerprint evidence in England and Wales, Australia and New Zealand. Each has its own trajectory but they share common law commitments and are strikingly similar in the way that there is no meaningful exploration of the value of this ubiquitous evidence. What these reviews expose is how legally trained personnel accepted identifications and focused instead on legal and procedural issues, without considering the validity of underlying procedures, the proficiency of individual examiners, the impact of cognitive bias and the frequency of errors.

13.2.1 *Early Appeals and the Form of Expression:* Castleton *and Beyond*

The very first prominently reported appeal was *R* v. *Castleton.*[5] By 1909 admissibility was taken for granted, in *Castleton* the issue was whether fingerprint evidence could support proof beyond reasonable doubt, and perhaps whether the latent fingerprints were sufficiently similar to Castleton's. Speaking for the Court of Criminal Appeal, the Lord Chief Justice dismissed the appeal. His reasoning is reproduced in full below:

> We are clearly of opinion that this application must be dismissed. The suggestion has been made that these finger-prints may have been put there by someone else, but that suggestion was disposed by the jury, who decided upon the evidence before them. Our attention has been drawn to the photographs of the impressions of the finger-prints. Looking at the middle finger particularly, as well as to the index finger of the right hand, we agree with the evidence of the expert at the trial.[6]

---

[4] Or, capable of being effectively operationalised. Ineffectiveness is routinely attributed to deliberate (i.e. tactical) decisions, and on rare occasions legal incompetence.
[5] *R* v. *Castleton* [1909] 3 Cr. App. R. 74.
[6] Ibid.

Castleton was convicted of burglary when fingerprints on a candle recovered from the crime scene were identified to him. The judges were personally satisfied by, indeed agreed with, the fingerprint examiner. The fact that Castleton consorted with thieves and the candle, as a readily movable object, might have been used and abandoned by another person, were dismissed. One of the appeal judges, Justice Darling, is reported to have asked: 'Can the prisoner find anybody whose fingerprints are exactly like his?'[7] There was already an expectation that a defendant would need to locate a person with the same print (or an error) if they sought to challenge the identification. Failure is used to imply guilt.

Fingerprint evidence was also relied upon to resolve identity and in the process address the vexed issue of recidivism.[8] In the absence of more reliable forms of identification, repeat offenders often sought to avoid more severe sentences by inventing pseudonyms and claiming that a conviction was their first offence.[9] Identification by fingerprints, in conjunction with rapidly expanding police records, was used to unveil such deception in *R v. Bacon* (1915):

> At the trial eight previous convictions were proved against him, but it turns out that some of them were in names other than that of Bacon – namely Cox, Barnes, Llewellyn, and Barrell. It is said, however, that they and Bacon were all names of the same man. The appellant denied these previous convictions, except in one case: but on the production of fingerprints, which we have examined, and on which we have heard the evidence of Detective-Inspector Alden, we have no doubt that they are all the same, and that they tally with the finger-prints of the appellant.[10]

Over time, the criminal histories of suspects, defendants and appellants were resolved through fingerprint records.[11]

From the earliest cases and continuing to the modern-day latent fingerprint evidence has been continuously presented in England as categorical evidence of identity. For example:

> ... his fingerprint was found on the door.[12]

---

7   Ibid. In *R v. Parker* [1912] VR 152 at 155, the Chief Justice of Victoria insinuates that this question 'cannot have been seriously meant'.

8   Cole, 2001; Beavan, 2001; Sengoopta, 2003. More generally, see Groebner, 2007; Torpey and Caplan, 2001.

9   Prior to the collection of fingerprints police officers inspected the ranks of prisoners hoping to identify repeat offenders.

10 *R v. Bacon* (1915) 11 Cr. App. R. 90 at 90–91.

11 Ibid. Other early cases include: *R v. Pearson* (1910) 5 Cr. App. R. 188 at 188–9; *R v. Headley* (1979) 1 Cr. App. R. (S.) 158; *James Harris, alias Robert Desmond* (1913) 8 Cr. App. R. 30.

12 *R v. Foster* [2018] EWCA Crim. 93 at 2.

And,

> ... the appellant maintained that he had been mistakenly identified, and he maintained his denials even after his fingerprints were found on Mrs White's pension book.[13]

13.2.2 A Century of Legal Engagement

Castleton should be understood as a *legal* challenge, the single ground of appeal was whether the evidence satisfied the standard of proof burdening the Crown. Now we move to consider the most prominent types of legal challenge in its aftermath.

Quite a few of the reported challenges sought to have fingerprint evidence excluded on the basis of some kind of non-compliance with common law rules, enabling legislation, or because of unfairness in the way the evidence was collected. Consider *Callis v. Gunn*. When in custody at the police station a detective said: 'I want to take your fingerprints. All right?' Callis replied: 'Yes'.[14] The fingerprint evidence was excluded because Callis had not been cautioned. The Crown appealed. The Court of Appeal held the fingerprint evidence admissible. Distinguishing confessions, regulated by the Judge's Rules, it 'was quite unnecessary to give any caution' when taking fingerprints.[15] Fingerprint evidence was admissible subject to discretion and the evidence being 'obtained oppressively, by false representations, by a trick, by threats, by bribes, anything of that sort'.[16]

The case of *R v. Tottenham Justices, Ex parte ML* was directly concerned with the specific provisions of enabling legislation. Police sought the print of the leading edge of ML's hand in relation to the death of a police officer. ML, was a minor who was in custody and had already been fingerprinted. He was resisting the application. Collecting the prints of a minor was governed by section 49 of the Magistrates' Court Act 1980. The issue for the Court was whether 'finger-prints' in the statutory regime – which expressly included 'palm-prints' – extended to the edge of a hand. The Court of Appeal was satisfied that 'when Parliament authorized the taking of palm-prints it left it to the good sense of magistrates to decide whether in the particular circumstances of any individual case what was sought to be taken was in reality a palm-print'.[17]

---

[13] *R v. Buck* [2000] 1 Cr. App. R. (S.) 42, 43.
[14] *Callis v. Gunn* (1964) 48 Cr. App. R. 36, 37.
[15] Ibid., 40.
[16] Ibid.
[17] *R v. Tottenham Justices, Ex parte ML* (1986) 82 Cr. App. R 277, 280.

Some of the challenges revolved around the adoption of new technologies, though there was remarkably little interest in their validity and reliability. We can observe limited engagement in *R* v. *Rhodes*.[18] Through the use of 'modern computerized science techniques' Rhodes was identified as an armed robber three decades after a robbery.[19] Precisely what the 'modern' techniques involve is not considered in the judgment. Instead, the trial and appeal focus on the disadvantage to the defendant from the delay in prosecution. In warning the jury about potential unfairness the trial judge observed that 'the fingerprints are not suffering from memory problems'.[20] The Court of Appeal was satisfied that 'as a whole' the summing-up was 'fair and balanced'.[21]

Several of the challenges alleged police misconduct and even the fabrication of evidence. Investigators misled Mason and his solicitor when they 'set out deliberately to make the defendant believe [they] had a fingerprint on some of the glass fragments from the bottle' used to start a fire. Police reasoned that if Mason was innocent 'there was no way he would produce a confession'.[22] Mason made admissions and was convicted. The appeal focused on the admissibility of the confession in light of the deception:[23]

> It is obvious from the undisputed evidence that the police practiced a deceit not only upon the appellant, which is bad enough, but also upon the solicitor whose duty it was to advise him. In effect, they hoodwinked both solicitor and client. This was a most reprehensible thing to do.[24]

The Court of Appeal explained that the confession should have been excluded and expressed the hope 'never again to hear of deceit such as this being practiced on an accused person'.[25]

R v. *Martin and others* followed a reference from the Criminal Cases Review Commission (CCRC). The original evidence had been assembled by the discredited 'Flying Squad'. The case against Martin included video of the robbery and a 'good palm print' lifted from the crime scene.[26] Martin

18 *R* v. *Rhodes* [2014] EWCA Crim. 1434. See also *Public Prosecution Service of Northern Ireland* v. *Elliott* [2013] UKSC 32, at 5–6; *The Queen* v. *Clarke* [2012] NICA 2, at 4.
19 *R* v. *Rhodes* [2014] EWCA Crim. 1434 at 2. See also *The Queen* v. *Rodgers* [2013] NICA 71 at 8; *The Queen* v. *Clarke* [2012] NICA 2 at 4.
20 *R* v. *Rhodes* [2014] EWCA Crim. 1434 at 20.
21 Ibid. at 24.
22 *R* v. *Mason* (1988) 86 Cr. App. R. 349, 352. On false confessions, see Gudjonsson, 2003; Leo and Drizin, 2004: 891.
23 Under PACE ss. 76 and 78.
24 *R* v. *Mason* (1988) 86 Cr. App. R. 349, 353. See also *Callis* v. *Gunn* (1964) 48 Cr. App. R. 36.
25 *R* v. *Mason* (1988) 86 Cr. App. R. 349, 353. Such deceit is permissible in many US jurisdictions.
26 *R* v. *Martin and others* [2000] 7 WLUK 298 at 21.

denied having been to the shop and 'said that his palm print *must* have been covertly taken from another source (e.g. his parked car)'.[27] An initial appeal was unsuccessful but 'everything changed ... when a Police Complaints enquiry investigating the [Flying] Squad revealed massive corruption within it'.[28] Several of the investigators were convicted of serious criminal offences – including perverting the course of justice. These revelations and the real possibility of fabrication led to the case being reconsidered. The Court allowed the appeal even though it was 'not easy to divine the precise nature of the police misconduct in respect of the palm print'.[29]

Many of the challenges contested what the finding of a person's fingerprints at a specific location or on specific item signified in terms of the Crown's case. The case of *Atkinson* is representative.[30] Atkinson initially denied having been to an apartment where a woman was assaulted. When a palm print located on the inside of the door was matched to him, his version of events changed. Rather than dispute the identification, Atkinson offered an explanation that was inconsistent with participation in the assault. He said that while looking for premises to burgle he noticed an apartment with a door ajar. Upon entering Atkinson realised that an assault was in progress. He left so as to avoid being implicated. There was other evidence against Atkinson and the Court of Appeal had no doubt about the safety of his conviction.

While the significance or meaning of prints was often in issue, the failure to locate prints and/or find other, frequently unidentified, prints was often raised, particularly by defendants, as consistent with non-guilt. Prosecutors and courts were inclined to emphasise, sometimes proactively, that the failure to find latent fingerprints might not be very significant because prints were not always deposited and could be avoided through premeditation (e.g. wearing gloves), cleaning or destroying a scene. In R v. *Howell and Howell*, the trial judge explained that:

It must be remembered that it is commonplace in criminal trials for a defendant to rely on 'holes' in the prosecution case, for example, a failure to take fingerprints or a failure to submit evidential material to forensic examination. ... Often the absence of a video film or fingerprints or DNA material is likely to hamper the prosecution as much as the defence.[31]

[27] Ibid. at 6.
[28] Ibid. at 8.
[29] Ibid. at 21. Alleged in R v. *Moore and Boyfield* [2005] EWCA Crim. 3650 at 13. See also R v. *Slade* 2000 WL 33116508 at 5, 10, where alleged police misconduct involved the planting of a glove with the appellant's fingerprint and R v. *Zomparelli* 2000 WL 35801961 at 8, where police misconduct and planting of evidence were successfully raised.
[30] *Atkinson* (1988) 86 Cr. App. R. 359. See also DPP v. *Douglas* [2016] NICA 14.
[31] R v. *Howell and Howell* [2001] EWCA Crim. 3009 at 27.

In *R* v. *Humphries* the jury inquired about the absence of fingerprints on a baseball bat allegedly used in an assault.[32] They asked about the possibility that the bat was cleaned and how surfaces effected the deposition and recovery of prints. The trial judge responded: '[T]here is no evidence on this topic. You must not speculate, but you are entitled to use your experience of the world and your common sense when you approach your job as jurors.'[33] The appeal was successful on the basis that they should have been 'precluded ... from drawing any adverse inference' against the defendants.[34] There was no expert evidence on these subjects and 'any suggestion of cleaning or rubbing ... should have been put to the appellants'.[35]

Judicial directions were also criticised in *R* v. *Skinner* following jury questions about the absence of prints on an item. The trial judge's explanation of the evidentiary (in)significance was criticised in the Court of Appeal:

> The findings of the forensic science laboratory should not have been expressed as saying 'does not show that the defendant's fingerprints were not upon the canister'. What should have been said is that 'the appellant's fingerprints were not found to be on the canister'; in other words a positive statement in his favour, rather than in the double negative way in which it had been expressed by the learned judge.[36]

The Court was, nevertheless, 'not of the view that the way in which the learned judge expressed the matter was so fundamentally wrong as to affect the justice of the conviction in the case'.[37]

In *R* v. *Fratson* the Home Secretary referred a conviction to the Court of Appeal when it was determined that a bloody fingerprint 'found on the premises of the murdered man ... was not caused by any part of the appellant's hands'.[38] According to the Lord Chief Justice: '[T]he effect of the [fingerprint on the] piece of cardboard on the appellant's case appears to be nothing at all. The matter is purely negative, and could not be important except on the unproved assumption that nobody other than the appellant was concerned in the commission of the crime.'[39] The prosecutor 'leant to the view that the

[32] *R* v. *Humphries* [2006] EWCA Crim. 558. See also *Regina* v. *Skye Case* [2015] EWCA Crim. 2080 at 8.
[33] *R* v. *Humphries* [2006] EWCA Crim. 558, at 10.
[34] Ibid. at 12.
[35] Ibid. at 12.
[36] *R* v. *Skinner* (1994) 99 Cr. App. R. at 212, 214–215.
[37] Ibid. at 212, 215.
[38] *R* v. *Fratson* (1931) 22 Cr. App. R. at 29, 30.
[39] Ibid. at 29, 30. Interestingly, this decision was handed down just years before *Woolmington* v. *DPP* (1935) AC 462.

impression was made by the hand of a police-sergeant ... investigating the case'.[40] The record does not disclose whether the evidence suggested that more than one person was involved, or whether the fingerprints of investigators were compared.[41]

Trial fairness also looms large among the challenges (as in *Mason*). There is the perennial difficulty of presenting fingerprint evidence without implying a defendant was already known to police. Usually studiously avoided, in *R v. Howes* the issue surfaced when the prosecutor explained that a false name provided by Howes was discovered when his fingerprints were compared with police records. The Court of Appeal explained that:

> it really depends on the effect that the offending words may have on the jury, and it is to be observed that the Deputy-Chairman in this case took very good care in his summing-up not to refer to the matter of fingerprints at all. ... notwithstanding the unfortunate course this case took in regard to the appellant not being represented for the Court of Appeal 'there has been no miscarriage of justice'.[42]

In general, fingerprint examiners, prosecutors and judges endeavour not to draw attention to the source of reference prints. But the issue is frequently lurking.

Another fairness issue concerns the willingness of the state to fund defence challenges to latent fingerprint evidence, conspicuously defence experts. Defence counsel was routinely resourced to challenge legal (particularly procedural) aspects of the evidence. It seems that there was typically less support for cases where defendants sought to argue mistaken identification.[43] The case of *R v. O'Brien* is revealing. The Court of Appeal quashed a conviction in part because legal aid declined to fund the defence.[44] Legal Aid had declined because 'it was a fingerprint case' and, using circular reasoning, characterised the defendant's alibi as 'phoney'.

Among the largest set of legal challenges in England and Wales were appeals from sentence.[45] In these cases, the main issue was whether the

---

[40] *R v. Fratson* (1931) 22 Cr. App. R. at 29, 30.

[41] Fratson was later reprieved from his capital sentence when another man, Walter Prince, confessed.

[42] *Howes* (1964) 48 Cr. App. R. at 172, 178–9. See also the Privy Council decision in *Culpepper v. Trinidad and Tobago* [2000] 12 WLUK 563.

[43] See e.g. *R v. O'Brien* [1967] 1 WLUK 496.

[44] Ibid.

[45] See e.g. *R v. Winter* [2013] EWCA Crim. 2488 at 10; *Attorney General's Reference (No.9 of 2013) (Robert Rees)* [2013] EWCA Crim. 597 at 13; *R v. RH* [1998] 1 Cr. App. R. 220; *R v. Brewster* (1980) 71 Cr. App. R. at 375, 376.

suspect made a timely guilty plea. To obtain the maximum sentence discount, guilty pleas should be offered at the earliest opportunity, but before a suspect's culpability is *confirmed* by latent fingerprint evidence. An untimely plea may result in the loss of a discount because latent fingerprint evidence is conceived as practically infallible evidence of identity (and often as synonymous with guilt).[46]

R v. *Magee* is typical.[47] The 'late' plea was considered in relation to the failure to acknowledge the theft when interviewed by police: '[T]he mitigating features, which the learned Recorder noted, were his guilty plea, albeit not at the first reasonable opportunity (which would have been when he was initially questioned by the police). He had, in fact, only accepted his guilt when confronted with the fingerprint evidence.'[48] In R v. *Lang*, the sentencing judge also questioned the value of the plea: 'I give such credit as I can for your plea of guilty and the admissions you made to the police. However, the fingerprint evidence, of course, meant that such a plea was virtually unavoidable.'[49] In sentencing, processes of collection and identification are treated as unproblematic.

There were also challenges to the retention of fingerprints collected before and after the ECHR came into effect.[50]

None of these *legal* challenges engages with the accuracy of the identification.

13.2.3 *The Major 'Challenges': McNamee, Buckley and* Smith

There have only been three reported English decisions substantially engaged with the standards used by fingerprint examiners (in R v. *Buckley*) or the possibility of a mistake that drew upon questions of interpretation and practice (in R v. *McNamee* and R v. *Smith*).

R v. *McNamee* is the first reported decision that engages with the accuracy of a latent fingerprint match in English history.[51] McNamee was convicted in

---

[46] R v. *Blaydes* [2014] EWCA Crim. 798; R v. *Dooley* (1994) 15 Cr. App. R. (S.) 703.

[47] R v. *Magee* [2011] EWCA Crim. 1574.

[48] Ibid. at 10.

[49] R v. *Lang* [2001] EWCA Crim. 2690 at 4, 9 (sentence reduced for other reasons).

[50] Challenges to biometrics include: *Gaughran* v. *Chief Constable of Northern Ireland* [2015] UKSC 29; R. *(on the application of RMC)* v. *Commissioner of Police of the Metropolis* [2012] EWHC 1681 (Admin); R. *(GC)* v. *Commissioner of Police of the Metropolis (Liberty and Another intervening)* [2011] UKSC 21; *Mark Richardson* v. *The Chief Constable of West Midlands* [2011] EWHC 773 (QB); S v. *United Kingdom* (2009) 48 E.H.R.R. 50 (*On the Application of S*) v. *Chief Constable of South Yorkshire Police*; R. *(On the Application of Marper)* v. *Chief Constable of South Yorkshire Police* [2004] UKHL 39.

[51] R v. *McNamee* [1998] 12 WLUK 408; [1998] EWCA Crim. 3524.

1987 of conspiracy to cause explosions in relation to the IRA bombing campaign.[52] Three partial prints linked McNamee to an explosive device recovered from an IRA weapons cache. The question at trial was whether McNamee was involved in the manufacture of bombs or might have innocently touched a battery and insulating tape, used in their manufacture, during the course of his regular employment. On appeal, the Court refused to hear from fingerprint examiners engaged by the appellant and the conviction was upheld.

In a second appeal prompted by a reference from the CCRC (set up in the wake of the Runciman Royal Commission) there was a challenge to one of the prints relied upon to identify McNamee. The Court of Appeal received testimony from fourteen fingerprint examiners 'in relation to this single thumb print over no less than 7 full court days'.[53] The Court's assessment is revealing: '*Remarkably, and worryingly,* save for those who said that the print was unreadable, there was no unanimity between them, and very substantial areas of disagreement. All the experts, save Mr. Swann who is retired, are currently employed in various police forces.'[54] The examiners could not agree on whether the latent print was sufficient for analysis and comparison, let alone whether it matched McNamee's thumb. Four of the examiners – respective heads of bureaux (from Cambridgeshire, Norfolk, Thames Valley and Devon and Cornwall) – testified 'that there was insufficient ridge detail on the thumb mark for it to be safe to make any comparison with the control set of prints'.[55] There was marked variation in the number of points observed by examiners – ranging between five and sixteen. There was also controversy as to the number of touches. The original examiner referred to two touches, for the first time, a week before the second appeal and acceded to three in testimony before the Court.

In summary, the Court concluded:

> There was much disagreement between the experts *in relation to this print* and it is impossible to know what evidence a jury would be likely to accept and what evidence they would be likely to reject. A case on 11 coincident markings [or points] is a case different from a case based on 16 coincident markings. ... Evidence of fewer than 16 characteristics is not inadmissible as evidence of identification. As we were told by the experts,

[52] The Runciman Royal Commission on Criminal Justice was established because of the crisis of confidence arising from the miscarriages of justice following IRA bombings. See Runciman, 1993; Roberts, Wilmore and Davis, 1993; Walker and Starmer, 1999.
[53] *R v. McNamee* [1998] 12 WLUK 408; [1998] EWCA Crim. 3524.
[54] Ibid. (italics added).
[55] Ibid.

much depends on the quality of the print itself and the quality of the matching characteristics ...

Having heard all the expert evidence called before us, it is impossible to say with confidence which conclusion a jury would have reached.[56]

The Court quashed the conviction.

The case of *R* v. *Buckley* was not a formal challenge but is nonetheless enlightening. The substantive appeal was abandoned but the Court of Appeal elected to provide an overview of latent fingerprint evidence because of its perceived 'wider importance'.[57] The judgment relies on a history, prepared by the prosecutor, concerned with the introduction, acceptance and scientifically influenced abandonment of point standards. It documents arbitrariness in the number of points required (by police) to report an identification. In 1924 New Scotland Yard introduced a sixteenth point standard based on research by Alphonse Bertillon.[58] Though, this standard was based on forged fingerprints and, for the Court, 'adopted on a false basis'. The sixteenth point requirement was accepted as a national standard in 1953, but later modified so that where a scene produced one latent with sixteen points, 'any other mark at the same scene could be matched if ten ridge characteristics were identified'.[59]

Over time, we are told, fingerprint examiners came to a consensus that the sixteenth point standard was unnecessarily high:

considerably fewer than 16 ridge characteristics would establish a match beyond any doubt. Some experts suggested that eight would provide a complete safeguard. Others maintained that there should be no numerical standard at all. We are told, and accept, that other countries admit identification of 12, 10 or eight similar ridge characteristics and, in some countries, the numerical system has been abandoned.[60]

In 1983 the examiners agreed that 'there would be rare occasions where an identification fell below *the* standard, but the print was of such crucial importance in the case that the evidence about it should be placed before the Court'.[61] In 'such extremely rare cases' the evidence should be given 'only by an expert of long experience and high standing'.[62]

---

[56] Ibid. (italics added).
[57] R v. *Buckley* (1999) 163 JP 561.
[58] Ibid. at 5.
[59] Ibid. at 5–6.
[60] Ibid. at 6.
[61] Ibid. at 6 (italics added).
[62] Ibid. at 6.

In 1988 the Home Office and Association of Chief Police Officers commissioned scientists – Evett and Williams (1996) – to review the prevailing standard(s). The review concluded that 'there was no scientific, logical or statistical basis for the retention of any numerical standard'.[63] In response, the Court explains that the examiner community was working towards 'clear procedures and protocols' and to developing nationwide training, management and audit systems. The *Buckley* Court characterised all this as 'excellent work by the police and fingerprint experts' but said nothing about the implications for past identifications and continuing practice.

As for admissibility, the Court held that fingerprint evidence 'is admissible . . . if it tends to prove the guilt of the accused'. Moreover, it 'may so tend, even if there are only a few similar ridge characteristics but it may, in such a case, have little weight'.[64] The trial judge must 'in every case' warn the jury that fingerprint evidence is an opinion, and is not conclusive. Such warnings are the only express safeguard set out in a decision heavily dependent on experience and consensus.

In *R v. Smith* the Court of Appeal quashed a murder conviction. At trial, the jury heard that a fingerprint examiner discerned a fingerprint in what appeared to be blood found at the crime scene. This print was identified to the defendant by an examiner, and verified by two others. The jury heard that the examiner had originally considered the mark unsuitable for analysis, but used new technology to obtain better images after Smith was charged. These images were then used for the comparison and identification (of a known person).[65] The examiner kept no working notes of his process, nor did he record the points on which he relied in making the identification.[66] His report stated: '[I]n forming my opinion I have considered the amount of detail, its relative position and sequence and general quality. I have no doubt that the area of friction ridge detail indicated in the photograph was made by [the appellant].'[67]

The defence briefed two fingerprint experts to review the police examiners' work, but called only the UK-trained examiner after the Crown indicated it would challenge the qualifications of its primary witness.

---

[63] *R v. Buckley* (1999) 163 JP 561 at 7.

[64] Ibid. at 8.

[65] That is, the examiner knew the identity of the suspect when undertaking this difficult comparison.

[66] The examiner was expected to use a process known as ACE-V – discussed in Section 13.5. Toward the end of the twentieth century ACE-V emerged as the dominant 'method' used by latent fingerprint examiners in the UK and beyond. The case of *R v. Smith* [2011] EWCA Crim. 1296, [20] is the only reported reference, albeit tangential, to ACE-V in England and Wales.

[67] *R v. Smith* [2011] EWCA Crim. 1296 at 19. Contrast the New Zealand case of *The Queen v. Carter* [2005] NZCA 422.

The case against Smith was not limited to the fingerprint evidence, though he sought and obtained fresh evidence for the appeal. This included two additional statements by UK-trained fingerprint examiners. There was considerable disagreement between the respondent's witnesses – the original examiner and those who had 'verified' his identification – and the testimony of the appellant's two new witnesses.' The Court of Appeal characterised this as 'a clear conflict between the experts'.[68]

The Court of Appeal was critical of the police monopoly on fingerprint training and certification that made it difficult for the defence to access expert assistance: '[I]t is essential for the proper administration of justice that there are independent persons expert in fingerprint examination; almost all who do this are retired from police Fingerprint Bureaux. The position is in marked contrast to other forensic science disciplines.'[69] The Court also criticised the dearth of documentation; 'it was not possible' in consequence to determine if the fingerprint examiner's reasoning was stable.[70]

Despite the circumstantial case against him, Smith's conviction was quashed on the basis that the fresh fingerprint evidence 'might reasonably have affected' the jury's decision. According to the Court there 'is plainly a need for the points that have arisen in this case to be the subject of wider examination'.[71] The judgment alluded to the ongoing Fingerprint Inquiry in Scotland and the need for: 'the ACPO [Association of Chief Police Officers], the Forensic Science Regulator and the recently established Fingerprint Quality Standards Specialist Group to examine as expeditiously as possible the issues we have identified, to assess the position and to ensure that there are common quality standards enforced through a robust and accountable system'.[72]

Smith's appeal does not address the underlying method of fingerprint comparison. Instead, like *McNamee*, it focuses on interpretive disagreements between experienced examiners, alongside poor documentation, in relation to a specific match decision. Notwithstanding some critical commentary on the practice and institutional arrangements and reference to the work of Evett and Williams (1996) in Buckley, none of the cases cite or discuss relevant scientific research.[73] None of these cases is subsequently referred to in an appeal concerned with fingerprints after *Smith*.

[68] *R* v. *Smith* [2011] EWCA Crim. 1296 at 56.
[69] Ibid. at 61.
[70] Ibid. at 61.
[71] Ibid. at 62.
[72] Ibid. at 62.
[73] Cole and Roberts, 2012.

13.3 AUSTRALIA

13.3.1 *Early Appeals and the Form of Expression: Blacker and* Parker

The first challenges in Australia were reported in the years immediately after *Castleton. Rex* v. *Blacker* was heard in the New South Wales Court of Appeal in 1910 and *R* v. *Parker* was decided in 1912 in the Victorian Court of Appeal. Both cases, respectively, an assault and a robbery, were resolved through fingerprint evidence. The appeals were not concerned with admissibility but rather the imagery in *Blacker* and in *Parker* whether a single print could support guilt to the criminal standard. *Parker* is the only case, across the three jurisdictions, where a judge questioned the scientific pretensions of fingerprint comparison.

The appeal in *Blacker* was primarily directed towards the admissibility of partial enlargements of the images of the fingerprints on the ground that they reproduced only that part of the print relied upon by the examiner. Dismissing the appeal, the Chief Justice of New South Wales (NSW) had no doubts about fingerprint evidence and its foundations.[74]

> This new *science of identification* by fingerprints is *based on experiments* which show that the portion of the body most likely to be identified without probability of mistake is the bulbous portion of the thumb, and if similarity is found to exist *the test is a very reliable one*. In the present case the evidence of the expert showed that the similarity was sufficiently strong to justify the admission of evidence upon the point.[75]

Chief Justice Cullen explained that the fingerprint evidence 'was carefully given and thoroughly tested'. The jury was 'very carefully directed by the learned Judge as to the risk of error to which evidence of this class is open' and 'every precaution was taken to guard against any wrongful impression being conveyed to the jury'.[76] Following its examination of the images, the Court of Appeal was satisfied that the fingerprints were made by the same person.

Parker was convicted solely on the basis of a fingerprint on a ginger beer bottle recovered from premises that had been burgled. A Victorian detective had observed nine points of similarity and identified Parker:

> he was of opinion that the prisoner's finger must have made the print on the bottle. He had examined tens of thousands of finger-prints, and never found two alike. The markings on a person's fingers remain the same through life.

[74] *R v. Blacker* [1910] SR (NSW) 357 360.
[75] Ibid. (italics added).
[76] Ibid.

Inspector Child [from *Blacker*], of the New South Wales police, gave evidence to the same effect. No two individuals had the same finger-prints.[77]

On the question of whether the fingerprint evidence could support identification and conviction, the Court of Appeal was divided. Justice Hodges characterised fingerprint evidence as 'the strongest, the most satisfactory, and the most conclusive proof of identity that could be produced'. The encomium continued:

> In my opinion, it may be the safest of all evidence, as it does not depend upon the impressions caused by a momentary glance, but the impression is put on record, and the jury can see and judge for themselves as to the identity of the finger-marks and the expert be merely a help to enable the jury to use the evidence of their own eyes.[78]

Justice Cussen concurred: '[i]t now seems that this much is established – that there is a very high degree of probability that a finger-print corresponding with that of the prisoner was made by his finger'.[79] It seemed to follow that 'finger-print evidence of identity may be undoubtedly sufficient to justify the conviction of the accused'.[80]

The Chief Justice of Victoria, in contrast, adverted to the 'extreme danger' of allowing fingerprint evidence to satisfy criminal proof.

> The extreme danger of arriving at such a conclusion warrants me in not deferring to their opinions. We are asked to accept the theory that the correspondence between two sets of finger-prints is conclusive evidence of the identity of the person who made those prints as an established scientific fact, standing on the same basis as the proposition of Euclid or other matters vouched for by science and universally accepted as proved. If this finger-print theory were generally recognised by scientific men as standing on this basis, there would be no more to be said. ... My difficulty arises from the fact that the subject of finger-prints has not been sufficiently studied to enable these propositions to be laid down as scientific facts. Finger-prints have been studied by Monsieur Bertillon in France from an anthropometrical point of view, and by Sir Francis Galton and a few others, doubtless highly intelligent persons, from the standpoint of mere observers. But the matter has not been investigated by scientists generally so that we can say that the propositions relied on by the Crown are accepted scientific facts.[81]

[77] *R v. Parker* [1912] VR 152, 153.
[78] Ibid., 153.
[79] Ibid., 161.
[80] Ibid., 158.
[81] Ibid., 154.

For Chief Justice Madden decision-makers were dependent on the 'ipse dixit' of the examiner.[82] How could his evidence be 'tested' when 'the detectives swear that no two men's finger-prints could possibly be alike, I think that that is apt to be accepted by the jury, who have no personal knowledge to test it by'.[83]The Chief Justice was not satisfied that 'there is any marked similarity' between the images of the latent fingerprint and Parker's fingerprint.[84] He characterised the decision in R v. *Castleton* as 'most unsatisfactory' and noted the possibility that the prisoner had innocently touched the bottle had not been excluded (by the prosecutor). He was of the opinion that the case should have been withdrawn.

There are two additional features of *Parker* worthy of note. First, there was uncertainty as to whether the police examiners were presenting expert evidence or merely introducing the images of prints for the jury to consider. Justice Cussens considered the examiners 'are not, in one sense, speaking as experts . . . but merely pointing out to the jury matters which the jury could determine for themselves'.[85] Justice Hodges required the jury to be 'satisfied with the witness under examination and cross-examination to arrive at the conclusion'. If satisfied with the expertise and credibility, 'that was sufficient to justify a conviction'.[86] Questions around the allocation of responsibilities would re-emerge.

Secondly, notwithstanding the dissent, all of the judges agreed that 'the statement made by the expert witnesses that there could not be two fingerprints alike should not have been admitted, because . . . their knowledge or the knowledge of anyone else on the subject does not profess to be based on any universal law, but is merely empirical'.[87] Indeed, this was reported in the headnote in the *Argus Law Reports* as: '*Semble, per Curiam*, – Evidence by experts that no two finger-prints can be identical is not admissible as being the statement of a scientific fact based upon a universal law'.[88] The full Court of Appeal seems to have proscribed claims that fingerprints are unique. Notwithstanding this early prohibition – which is not easily reconciled with the categorical identification and statements by the majority judges – fingerprint examiners continued to identify specific persons.

Bennett v. *Police* captures both modern Australian authority and continuity in the way fingerprint evidence is represented and understood. At trial the

[82] Ibid., 154. This term reappears in *Kumho Tire Co., Ltd.* v. *Carmichael* 526 U.S. 127 (1999).
[83] R v. *Parker* [1912] VR 152, 155.
[84] Ibid., 155.
[85] Ibid., 160.
[86] Ibid., 159.
[87] Ibid., 155 (Madden CJ), 159 (Cossens J), 158 (Hodges J).
[88] R v. *Parker* in The Argus Law Reports, vol. xviii (14 May 1912).

examiner testified that 'the impressions were made by the one person excluding all others'.[89] Bennett was convicted. On appeal, before the South
Australian Supreme Court, there was no dispute about the examiner being
'qualified to express the opinion that he gave'.[90] The Court insisted that there
was 'no suggestion that the process of comparison that he followed is not
a recognised and appropriate process'.[91]

13.3.2 A Century of Legal Engagement

None of the reported Australian challenges, apart from the dissent of Madden
CJ in *Parker*, engage with the validity or reliability of identification by latent
fingerprint. Every reported challenge was focused on legal and procedural
issues.

From the very beginnings in *Blacker*, Australian appellate courts heard
submissions about the mis-use and eventually non-disclosure of images of
prints. This issue was dismissed in *Blacker*, where copies of prints were
characterised as 'necessary' and the partial enlargements were deemed to
have been adequate. More recently, in *Bennett*, the failure to 'describe in
detail what the witness observed, or to produce an image or representation of
what the witness observed' was not 'an obstacle to the admissibility of the
opinion'.[92] The examiner was entitled to report what he had observed and
oversights and omissions were for weight. The opportunity to cross-examine
the examiner was said to have made proceedings fair.[93]

Tardiness in relation to the production of images seems in part a response to
the emergence of an orthodox position around who was entitled to interpret
and compare the fingerprints. Through a series of not always clear decisions,
the Victorian Court of Appeal explained that responsibility for interpretation
and comparison rested with the examiners: '[I]t is a matter for expertise not
possessed by the ordinary run of mankind to identify characteristics of fingerprints and their patterns in each of two prints and make a comparison and form
a conclusion as to whether they are identical or not and the jury could not be
invited or allowed to act as experts.'[94] It was the responsibility of the jury (and
where appropriate, judges) to assess the expert, her opinion and reasoning.
The Court of Appeal in *Bennett* agreed. The jury 'may find the evidence

[89] *Bennett* v. *Police* [2005] SASC 415, [16].
[90] Ibid., [5].
[91] Ibid., [5].
[92] Ibid. at 35–7, 44.
[93] Ibid. at 47.
[94] *R* v. *Lawless* [1974] VR 398; *R* v. *O'Callaghan* [1976] VR 676.

unconvincing; they may have doubts as to the independence or qualifications of the expert; *they may not be satisfied that there are sufficient points of similarity*; there may be a conflict of expert evidence; they may suspect police tampering with the evidence'.[95] Though, these seem to be theoretical possibilities.

As in our other jurisdictions, a significant group of Australian challenges focused on enabling legislation and collection. Though largely unsuccessful, these challenges offered the possibility of keeping potentially incriminating identification evidence out of proceedings. *Sernack v. McTavish* (1971) affords a useful illustration. Sernack was charged and convicted of being without lawful excuse on the US embassy premises during an anti-Vietnam war protest. At the police station Sernack identified herself but refused to have her fingerprints taken. She was subsequently convicted of hindering a police officer in the execution of his duty. The question on appeal was whether 'Standing Instructions', issued by the Commissioner of Police, requiring that fingerprints be collected, was consistent with section 353A of the Crimes Act 1900 (NSW). Justice Fox explained that the 'power under S. 353A (3) is only to be exercised when the officer in charge forms the view that the finger-prints are necessary for the "identification" of the person in custody. . . . It is to be remembered too that the word is "necessary"; it is not sufficient that finger-printing is thought desirable'.[96] The Commissioner's standing instructions were found to be 'unlawful' and the conviction was set aside.[97]

As in England, there were also many challenges around the significance or meaning of fingerprints.[98] In *Dhanoa v. R*, a case reviewing convictions for kidnap and assault, both the NSW Court of Criminal Appeal and the High Court accepted that 'once the appellant was confronted with the fingerprint evidence he was bound to, and did concede that he had at some relevant time been in [the] flat'.[99] The main issues were whether Dhanoa was in the flat when the assault occurred, what was the significance of an initial denial (before he was confronted with the fingerprint evidence), as well as the need to warn the jury about the complainant's identification evidence.

---

[95] *Bennett v. Police* [2005] SASC 415 at 4–5 (italics added).
[96] *Sernack v. McTavish* [1971] ALR 441; 384.
[97] See also *Carr v. The Queen* (1973) 127 CLR 662, 663.
[98] See, e.g. *R v. Clapham* [2017] QCA 99 at 17–18; *Jubraeel v. R* [2015] NSWCCA 131 at 51; *Lam v. R* [2015] NSWCCA 87 at 19; *Young and Ors v. The Queen* [2015] VSCA 265 at 54–5; *Oncev v. The State of Western Australia* [2012] WASCA 178, at 42–3; *R v. Delgado-Guerra* [2001] QCA 266 at 18–19.
[99] *Dhanhoa v. R* [2003] HCA 40 at 63, 95.

Where fingerprint examiners offered testimony that trespassed onto issues beyond an identification (of the *source*), such as the age of a print or the *activity* leading to deposition, courts were usually resistant to receiving this evidence, especially if it was central to the prosecution case. An opinion about the likely age of a latent fingerprint on a library book found at the complainant's house was said to have been inadmissible but its expression did not threaten the conviction.[100] In *Hillstead v. The Queen*, however, an opinion about the timing of the deposition of a fingerprint and palmprint (apparently) in blood was successfully appealed where the examiner did not know how much blood was spilled, the depth of the blood, prevailing conditions or the rate at which blood dries.[101] Given that timing was important, the unqualified opinion, that the fingerprints were contemporaneous with the castoff blood, was said to have been beyond the examiner's expertise.

There were also challenges to the propriety of investigations. Allegations of a planted matchbox, featuring a fingerprint identified to the appellant, recovered from the murder scene, were dismissed by several courts and an inquiry following the conviction of Lawless.[102] In the saga surrounding a notorious gold robbery from the Perth Mint, the Mickelberg brothers were eventually acquitted when serious police impropriety surfaced, that may have extended to fabricating fingerprint evidence against the brothers.

Several appeals asserted that the fingerprint evidence introduced unfairness because it implied prior criminality. These appeals were almost universally unsuccessful, notwithstanding quite strong historical concerns about unfair prejudice posed by bad character and propensity (or tendency) reasoning.[103] Fairness was also raised in a number of appeals in response to summings-up, judicial directions and warnings. Though courts of appeal were not particularly sympathetic to submissions alleging that trials had been unfair because trial judges had, in effect, suggested that an identification required 'some explanation as to how the fingerprints got there' (as in *Dhanoa*).[104]

13.3.3 *Unreported (and Unknown) Challenges: JP and* Nguyen

There have been no reported epistemological challenges in Australia. Though there have been two scientifically inspired challenges during

---

[100] *R v SMR* [2002] NSWCCA 258.
[101] *Hillstead v The Queen* [2005] WASCA 116.
[102] *R v. Lawless* [1974] VR 398; *Lawless v. The Queen* (1979) 142 CLR 659.
[103] *R v. Fennell* [2017] QCA 154 at 91ff.; *R v. Ahola (No 6)* [2013] NSWSC 703; *Kuehne v. R* [2011] NSWCCA 101 at 20–8.
[104] *Maniaci v. The Queen* [2000] WASCA 195 at 8, 24; *O'Grady v. The Queen* [2012] NSWCCA 62; *O'Grady v. The Queen* [2012] NSWCCA 62.

trials.[105] The specifics of the epistemologically sensitive challenges have not been reported because of the way the case was run and appealed in *JP* v. *DPP* and because the defendant accepted a guilty plea in *Nguyen* v. *R*.

Drawing heavily on a recently published article – 'How to Cross-Examine a Forensic Scientist' – the junior barrister representing JP in a fingerprint-only prosecution in the Children's Court in regional NSW, may have been the first person in Australian history to ask a fingerprint examiner about the validity and reliability of the procedure supporting his opinion (Edmond et al., 2014). Defence counsel objected to the admissibility of the examiner's report because it was non-compliant with the requirements of the Code of Conduct for Expert Witnesses (Edmond et al., 2017).

In order to obtain some sense of the challenge consider the following exchanges from the cross-examination:

Q. Do you agree that because the ACE-V[106] technique depends on your capability as a human being to make observations and make subjective decisions that it is actually vulnerable to a number of sources of error?
A. Again if ACE-V is done correctly and by a person in the right mind and with the correct tools and apparatus I don't believe that there would be an error.

. . .

Q. But you say because of the method that you use that you're always right when you make an identification is that what you say?
A. Me personally yes.
Q. So you would say that the ACE-V method is infallible is that what you say?
A. In the correct – used in the correct method and way and by myself yes.[107]

And,

Q. Is it possible that you have made a mistake or mistakes in your examination of fingerprint impressions in this case?
A. No I haven't.

[105] These are cases that might have been missed by my research methods, though it is unlikely that such challenges preceded the NRC report.
[106] The acronym describes the modern process of fingerprint comparison. It stands for the stages Analysis, Comparison, Evaluation and Verification (by a second examiner), and is considered in Section 13.5.
[107] Transcript of Proceedings, *R* v. *JP* (Childrens' Court, 27 January 2015) 12–13.

. . .

Q. In every case in which you've identified a latent print to a known print have you been a hundred per cent certain?
A. Yes I have.
Q. You've never had any doubt?
A. Never.[108]

And,

Q. Do you claim to be immune to any form of bias in your work as a fingerprint examiner?
A. In my own mind yes.
Q. Are you familiar with the term cognitive bias?
A. I've heard of the term but I'm not quite familiar with it exactly what it means no.[109]

. . .

Q. Are you aware of the scientific literature in relation to fingerprint examination and identification being vulnerable to a number of forms of bias?
A. I am aware that there is bias involved or can be involved.
Q. Including when ACE-V is used?
A. If ACE-V is used correctly bias shouldn't be taken into account at all.[110]

This seems to have been the first time an examiner was questioned about mainstream scientific reports – discussed in Section 13.5 – in an Australian court. When asked if he was aware of the seminal National Research Council (NRC) report published in 2009, the examiner replied: 'No, I'm not.' He was then asked about the following recommendation from the NIST report:

Q. One of the recommendations by the United States National Institute of Standards and Technology [from the NIST report] was this, 'Because empirical evidence and statistical reasoning do not support a source attribution to the exclusion of all other individuals in the world latent print examiners should not report or testify directly or by implication to a source attribution to the exclusion of all others in the world.' What do you say about that recommendation?

[108] Ibid., 11.
[109] Ibid., 4.
[110] Ibid., 9–11.

A. Well it's someone's opinion in America.[111]

The examiner's ignorance, and a curious reluctance to acknowledge the authority of the NRC and NIST and their reports – given the requirement to be impartial – prevented these documents, including the findings and recommendations, from becoming evidence and having a bearing on the case. *JP* reveals the limits of cross-examination, particularly when the individual recognised by the court as an expert expresses opinions that are inconsistent with mainstream scientific research and advice (Edmond et al., 2019).

Remarkably, the examiner's responses were not considered by decision-makers to have weakened the evidence. Rather, the magistrate concluded: 'his evidence was unshaken ... As an expert his expertise was not shaken, his opinion was not shaken'.[112] The only scepticism was directed toward the NRC and NIST reports – pejoratively dismissed as 'arguments' and 'articles'. On appeal, the expert report was found to be non-compliant with the Code of Conduct, yet somehow was said to have been repaired by the answers provided in cross-examination. The magistrate was said to have had the benefit of observing the examiner directly. How direct observation compensated for fundamental scientific oversights was not explained: 'it was open to his Honour to conclude that there was no material to indicate that, to the extent the criticisms were sustained, they materially affected the weight to be attached to Sergeant W's opinion that the fingerprints were identical'.[113]

In the subsequent case of *The Queen* v. *Nguyen*, a more tutored examiner provided answers that confounded a not entirely sophisticated cross-examination by a barrister relying heavily on notes from *JP*. The testimony was a mixture of fingerprint dogma and engagement with supportive scientific studies, albeit presented in a way overly favourable to the Crown; with many limitations and contingencies elided. *Nguyen* was not an ideal case for a challenge because there were multiple fingermarks identified to the defendant. This important point, and the very small possibility of mis-identification in consequence, did not assume appropriate significance in the examiner's testimony on the *voir dire*.

There are no direct references to any of the scientific materials raised in these cases in written judgments. 'Lessons' or insights from *JP* and the unreported *Nguyen* case are largely lost to Australian legal consciousness.

---

[111] Ibid., 17, see also 16; NIST, 2012. This testimony (and the expression) is inconsistent with the Australian standards for reporting forensic science testimony: Standards Australia, 'Forensics Analysis: Part 4: Reporting' (Standard No AS 5883.4, 2 May 2013).

[112] Transcript of Proceedings, *R* v. *JP* (Childrens' Court, 27 January 2015) 29–30.

[113] *JP* v. *DPP* (NSW) [2015] NSWSC 1669 at 90.

13.4 NEW ZEALAND

13.4.1 Early Appeals, Summings-Up and the Form of Expression: Clancy, Krausch and Gunn

The first reported case from New Zealand is *Rex* v. *Clancy* (1905). It was published in a Circular. The report states:

> **Rex v Clancy**
>
> At the Supreme Court, Wellington, on the 4th May, 1905, before His Honour the Chief Justice, Sir Robert Stout, John Clancy was indicted with breaking and entering the house of Mrs. M. A. Williams on the 23rd February, 1905, and with theft therefrom. Mr. Wilford appeared for the accused. Mr. Myers prosecuted. Evidence showed that entrance was effected by breaking a window and forcing back the catch. The detective investigating the complaint, on visiting Mrs. Williams's house on the morning following the robbery, from careful examination, discovered on the glass of the window through which entrance was effected a finger-print. The portion of the pane with the print thereon was carefully removed and taken to the Finger-print Branch. On the same date, the Finger-print Branch reported that the impression on the glass was identical with the third right finger of John Clancy, whose finger-prints had been received in the Branch from Auckland Gaol some months previously. On this information alone Clancy was arrested, and on evidence as to the identity of the print on the glass with that of Clancy's being given he was committed for trial. At the Supreme Court the Finger-print Branch experts proved positively that the print on the glass was identical with that of Clancy's third right finger, and must have been made by him. Lengthy cross-examination failed to shake that evidence in the slightest degree. On this evidence alone prisoner was found guilty and sentenced to three years' imprisonment with hard labour.[114]

Already, as this short report makes clear, there is a Finger-print Branch, reference fingerprints of prisoners were being collected (apparently before enabling legislation was enacted) and the fingerprint evidence is treated as admissible. The appeal seems to have been a review of conviction, where in a fingerprint-only prosecution (before *Castleton* and *Parker*) the defendant was convicted on testimony that the fingerprints were 'identical' and 'must have been made by [Clancy]'. Significantly, the conviction is safe and the proceedings are implicitly fair because 'cross-examination failed to shake that evidence in the slightest degree'.

---

[114] Reproduced in *The King* v. *Gunn* (1920) 2 New Zealand Police Law Reports (Supplement) i.

The next two reported cases – *Rex* v. *Krausch* (1913) and *The King* v. *Gunn* (1920) – are not appeals but rather reproductions of a trial judge's 'charge to the jury'. Presented by the same judge within a decade, they share many features. Justice Chapman repeatedly insists that latent fingerprint evidence is compelling evidence of identity.

> So many of these cases have now been tried in this Court, and reference has so often been made to *expert testimony and books of authority* on this subject, that *the leading facts of it may well be taken to be established scientific facts.* . . . The *leading facts* respecting finger-markings such as have been proved in this case may be regarded as *established biological facts*.[115]

The accuracy of identification by fingerprint is grounded in the permanence and uniqueness of fingerprints. These are said to be 'established scientific facts',[116] though there are no references to any books or articles supporting the propositions.

Notwithstanding the categorical identification by examiners in both *Krausch* and *Gunn*, when summarising the evidence the trial judge explained that the jury was entitled 'to treat the matter as one of probability'.[117] Having described the rarity of individual points on a fingerprint, and how quickly the improbability of sharing multiple points accumulated, Chapman J showed the jury his keys and by analogy asked about the chances of another person in New Zealand having exactly the same set.

Summarising the respective cases, the trial judge endorsed the Crown's position, lending the imprimatur of the Court, and dismissed points raised by the defence. In *Gunn*, he reminded the jury of the Crown's contention that in terms of reliability of the fingerprint evidence, the defence 'might as well try to produce a conflict about the multiplication table'.[118] Defence recourse to the dissent in *Parker* was contrasted with the unanimous acceptance of the New Zealand judiciary.

> In my very long experience on this Bench no one has hitherto produced a conflict of evidence on the subject. So far as the witnesses are able to inform you of the history of the last seventeen years, and so far as the views of other Judges are concerned, no conflict of evidence has ever been heard of.[119]

115 *Rex* v. *Krausch* (1913) 32 NZLR 1229, 1230.
116 Ibid., 1230.
117 Ibid., 1231.
118 *The King* v. *Gunn* (1920) 2 New Zealand Police Law Reports (Supplement) i, vi.
119 Ibid., i, v–vi. See also *Rex* v. *Krausch and others* (5 September 1913) XV *Gazette Law Reports* 664, 665.

The response was to reiterate 'the immense value' of the fingerprint evidence.[120]

Attempts to suggest that police fingerprint examiners might be biased, like some experts in civil proceedings, led the trial judge to remind the jury that the examiners had no personal or professional interests in the case and to reinforce the value of the evidence.

> If you do not see evidence of bias, or any straining on the professional side, you will have to weigh that evidence most carefully to see whether it does or does not support the suggestion of the Crown that when a man places his hand on a smooth surface he leaves upon it something as certain as his signature, or, in the words of Chief Justice Sir Samuel Griffith, of Australia, 'his unforgeable signature'.[121]

The trial judge also drew attention to Gunn's unwillingness to step down from the witness box and provide a palm print to see if it matched a print recovered from the crime scene.[122]

References to evidence being unshaken and there being no expert evidence available to the defendant, in combination with the collective experience of the Court, are used as evidence (really proxies) for the accuracy of the identification. After these cases, there are no reports of judges offering probabilistic analogies or explaining the evidence, through appeals to scientific foundations.[123] As identification by fingerprint established itself in the popular imagination, latent fingerprint examiners made categorical claims that passed without challenge and without the need for judges to support or even explain the evidence, though the endorsement of the courts is a persistent feature of this evidence.

The reported cases occasionally provide a glimpse of the pre-trial investigatory processes where latent fingerprints are also represented and understood as incontestable evidence of identity. Consider the following account of a police interview from later in the century:

> I said, your prints have been found on some of the cannabis inside the case. He said, what do you want me to say. I said, how did they get there. He said I don't know. I said, I believe they're palm prints. He said, I'm in the shit aren't I. I said *prints don't lie*. He said I don't know how they got there.[124]

[120] *The King* v. *Gunn* (1920) 2 New Zealand Police Law Reports (Supplement) i, v–vi.
[121] Ibid., i, viii–ix, quoting *Parker*.
[122] Ibid., i, vii.
[123] *R* v. *Buisson* [1990] 2 NZLR 542 and *The Queen* v. *Carter* [2005] NZCA 422, discussed below, might be considered partial exceptions.
[124] *R* v. *Samuels* [1985] 1 NZLR 350, 353 (uncorrected, italics added)

Fingerprints were routinely presented as unerring evidence of identity. Recent cases perpetuate that legacy: 'A latent fingerprint in the diary was later *identified as being that of* Mr Wallace.'[125] This use from *Wallace v. R* is revealing because the 'strength of the' DNA and the fingerprint evidence were grounds of appeal. The DNA evidence (nuclear, LCN and Y-STR) was presented in probabilistic terms and supported by references to validation, domestic databases and defence expert witnesses. The challenge to fingerprint evidence as categorical identification was perfunctorily dismissed.

13.4.2 A Century of Legal Engagement

Unremarkably, there are significant overlaps with the legal challenges launched in England and Australia, although New Zealand appears to have been especially concerned with the collection of reference fingerprints. As in our other jurisdictions, there are hardly any cases that directly challenge the identification or address underlying epistemological issues.

Police and others were empowered to collect the fingerprints of prisoners and persons in custody under a variety of acts, beginning with the Prisons Amendment Act 1912, though in *Clancy* (1905) the police were already collecting and circulating the fingerprints of prisoners. The power to collect and store prints expanded over the years, notably under the Police Force Act 1947 section 47, the Police Act 1958 section 57 and its various incarnations, prior to the Policing Act 2008. Compliance with these powers was challenged through a succession of appeals, substantially commencing with *Duffield v. Police (No. 2)*, where the Court of Appeal's strict reading limited the collection of fingerprints to circumstances where they were 'necessary for the identification'.[126] *Duffield* led to the revision of the Police Act 1958 and in *Keenan v. Attorney-General* the Court of Appeal accepted that fingerprints 'may be taken and used for any legitimate police purpose',[127] though the courts were unwilling to read the power to collect fingerprints into proceedings under the Extradition Act 1999, where identity was not in issue.[128] Similarly, legitimate purposes did not extend to arresting and fingerprinting a former police officer for a minor offence that was alleged to have occurred eighteen months earlier.[129]

---

[125] *Wallace v. The Queen* [2010] NZCA 46 at 12 (italics added).
[126] *Duffield v. Police (No. 2)* [1971] NZLR 710.
[127] *Keenan v. Attorney-General* [1986] 1 NZLR 241, 245, 247–78.
[128] *Kim v. Attorney-General (NZ)* [2014] NZHC 1383 at 97–102.
[129] *Neilsen v. Attorney-General* [2001] 3 NZLR 433, 441 at 30. See also *Everitt v. Attorney-General* [2002] 1 NZLR 82 at 14.

Questioning the significance of fingerprints was a prominent means of defence inoculation. New Zealand features several cases where the possibility of innocence touching required the Crown to produce evidence suggesting that the age of prints was inconsistent with an innocent version of events.[130] In *Cockburn v. New Zealand Police*, an ex-employee was prosecuted for stealing oil and converting a company truck in the process. A fingerprint on the door of the vehicle was identified to Cockburn. Detailed records of vehicle cleaning along with the orientation of the latent print were presented as incompatible with innocent touching. In *Fenton v. The Queen* a cabinet maker was prosecuted for a series of burglaries when he was identified to a fingerprint on a kitchen cabinet manufactured by his company several years earlier.[131] The cleaning of cabinets at the factory, the inspection and cleaning of the area by a police officer (prior to the second robbery, after which the latent fingerprint was found), the likely touching of the area when the cabinets were installed and the improbability of the persistence of the fingerprint, given touching and cleaning over a course of years, were said to eliminate the potentially innocent explanation.

There were quite a few cases where the meaning of fingerprints in relation to the alleged manufacture of drugs was in issue. Appellants fared inconsistently. In *The Queen v. Wheatley*, fingerprints on a beer mug and a chemical catalogue were deemed to raise 'a considerable degree of suspicion, but that is insufficient'.[132] Whereas in *David v. The Queen*, fingerprints on chemicals and equipment as well as drug smoking paraphernalia at the site of a clandestine laboratory 'obviously required an explanation', though the possibility that David was merely a user who visited the house to obtain and smoke methamphetamine was not accepted.[133]

New Zealand also has its share of implausible explanations.[134]

Perhaps the most notorious challenge to fingerprint evidence emerged out of the prosecution, conviction and eventual acquittal of David Bain. Though part of a much larger evidentiary array, fingerprints were central to the prosecution and domestic appeals that upheld his conviction. There was no dispute that Bain's fingerprints were on the rifle used to murder four members of his family. A fingerprint examiner testified that the fingerprints were bloody

[130] See *Simon v. R* [2017] NZHC 1235 at 5–7.
[131] *Fenton v. The Queen* [2011] NZCA 110 at 1–6. See also *R v. Harbour* [1995] 1 NZLR 440.
[132] *The Queen v. Wheatley* (NZHC, CRI 2006-019-8509, 6 September 2007), at 23.
[133] *David v. The Queen* [2013] NZCA 507.
[134] *T v. New Zealand Police* (NZHC, CRI 2009-470-27, 30 September 2009) at 11; *Nairn v. The Queen* [2008] NZCA 553 at 36, 55; *The Queen v. Voice* (NZCA, 13 October 1978) at 2, 8.

and very likely to have been contemporaneous with the shooting deaths. He accepted that: 'it was not possible to age fingerprints with scientific accuracy' but thought it was 'highly unlikely the prints were 4–6 months old, given their condition'.[135] This was a deliberate response to Bain's account of the last time he had been hunting. The Court of Appeal accepted that it was unlikely the gun would have been stored without having been cleaned.[136]

In the appeals following conviction, Bain raised the possibility that the fingerprints might have been in animal blood, possibly from hunting varmits. The actual bloody fingerprints had not been tested, though adjacent blood on the rifle was confirmed as human. When traces of the fingerprints were eventually tested for blood the results were inconclusive.

The trial judge had characterised the 'bloody' fingerprint evidence as a key point against Bain and the Court of Appeal described this evidence as one of three points 'of such cogency' that, notwithstanding the new evidence, proved the case against Bain beyond reasonable doubt.[137] The Court of Appeal summarised the evidence: '[T]he bloodstained condition of the rifle was such that the uncontaminated area associated with the fingerprints on the forearm leads to the almost inescapable conclusion that the hand that made the prints was in a position contemporaneously with the murders. That hand was David's.'[138]

Bain is interesting because the Privy Council did not agree with the Court of Appeal's assessment. For it,

The trial proceeded on the assumption that David's fingerprints on the forearm of the rifle were in human blood. It is now known that although blood from other parts of the rifle had been tested before trial and found to be human blood, the fingerprint material had not been tested. When it was tested after the trial it gave no positive reading for human DNA. Thus the blood analysis evidence was consistent with the blood being mammalian in origin, the possible result of possum or rabbit shooting some months before. ... There are a number of highly contentious issues arising from this evidence ... But these were not issues which the trial jury had any opportunity to consider, and they are not, with respect, issues which an appellate court can fairly resolve without hearing cross-examination of witnesses giving credible but contradictory evidence.[139]

[135]   *R v. Bain* [2004] 1 NZLR 638 at 66.
[136]   Ibid. at 68, although the family otherwise lived in squalid conditions.
[137]   Ibid. at 165.
[138]   Ibid. at 165, 135, see also 62.
[139]   *Bain v. R* [2007] NZPC 1; [2007] UKPC 33, [112].

On the basis of numerous evidentiary issues, extending well beyond problems with the significance of Bain's fingerprints, the Privy Council quashed the conviction and ordered a re-trial. Bain was subsequently acquitted.

Another case reinforces just how contingent fingerprint evidence is on explanations (see Lynch et al., 2008: 237–41). Moore was found not guilty of murder when a fellow gang member testified that he and Moore had been to the crime scene on a previous occasion, so the presence of Moore's fingerprints had a potentially innocent explanation. Following acquittal the gang member abjured and Moore was prosecuted for perjury.[140]

In terms of age and activity, fingerprint examiners typically accepted that fingerprints could not be aged, but that did not prevent them offering (and being allowed to offer) opinions on the likely age of prints based on common sense and crude experiments.[141] Following a burglary in R v. Tuporo, a senior crime scene officer testified about the age of a palmprint on a farm gate:

> there is no scientific way of giving an exact time frame . . . However, given these prints were located on a gate that is exposed to the weather what (sic) wouldn't be a long time at all . . . It was June so that was winter so probably until the next time there was a lot of moisture in the air and they would have been washed away. Very misty in that area as well especially in the morning.[142]

The defence sought, unsuccessfully as it turned out, a mis-trial because they were obliged to rely on the Crown's fingerprint examiner – who identified the palmprint 'as having come from the appellant's right palm' – to 'undo her damaging testimony'.[143] The Court of Appeal described the crime scene officer's testimony as 'reasoned comment' that was 'cured by' the fingerprint examiner reiterating the difficulty of aging prints.[144]

There were not many allegations of fraud or fabrication, but there were cases where police and prosecutors compromised the evidence – such as where the suspect was handed drug packaging during the investigation and where the Crown lost the fingerprint exhibit during proceedings.[145]

Each of these cases involved a challenge that did not question latent fingerprint comparison or the accuracy of the specific identification.

140   R v. Moore [1999] 3 NZLR 385.
141   See e.g. R v. Harbour [1995] 1 NZLR 440, 445–6.
142   R v. Tuporo (NZCA, BC200662930, 5 December 2006) at 18–19.
143   Ibid. at 7, 18–22.
144   Ibid. at 24.
145   R v. Reed [1980] 1 NZLR 758; The Queen v. Moore and Moore (NZCA, CA159/00 and CA160/00, 27 July 2000). See also R v. W [2006] (BC200662563, Court of Appeal, 18, 31 October).

13.4.3 *The Major 'Challenges': Buisson and Carter (and Wells)*

From time to time in all three jurisdictions there are references to the number of points of similarity observed between two prints. There were twenty-one in *Clancy* and fifteen in *Krausch*. The police in New Zealand appear to have settled upon twelve points (cf. *Buckley* in England) before they would report a match as an identification. This seems to have been based on the belief that twelve points would provide a guarantee of accuracy and perhaps the misunderstanding that courts required twelve points before an identification would be admissible.[146] The issue occasionally surfaced, as in *R* v. *Samuels*, where a 'junior technician' inadvertently suggested that a print with less than twelve points had been matched to Samuels, but not reported. Then, in *R* v. *Redmile*, an examiner purported to have relied upon fifteen points for an identification, but accepted that four 'could not be clearly demonstrated to the jury'.[147] The Court of Appeal indicated that the number of points 'went, not to admissibility, but to weight'.[148] The issue was argued more expansively in *R* v. *Buisson*.[149]

Indeed, *Buisson* was the main challenge of the twentieth century. The senior examiner called by the Crown offered his understanding of the prevailing point standard:

> it was necessary to establish at the beginning of fingerprint science a system which was beyond doubt in the minds of Courts and members of the public. This is the so-called, in my opinion, safety factor because 12 points throughout the world are acknowledged as an extremely safe number about which any two competent experts wouldn't disagree.[150]

The defence sought to have the evidence excluded in a pre-trial ruling contending there were not twelve points of similarity.[151]

Buisson was unusual because: the actual identification was in issue; it focused attention on that part of the prevailing 'method' concerned with the number of points required (by courts); the defence had access to experts, albeit retired fingerprint examiners (operating within the prevailing metaphysics); and the defence submitted that relying on less than twelve points created a 'prejudicial effect that exceeds the probative value' of the evidence.[152] The Crown and defence each called two examiners. The Crown examiners

[146] *R* v. *Buisson* [1990] 2 NZLR 542, 456: 'competent experts wouldn't disagree'.
[147] *R* v. *Redmile* (NZCA, CA272/86, BC8660134, 17 December 1986) at 4.
[148] Ibid.
[149] *R* v. *Buisson* [1990] 2 NZLR 542.
[150] Ibid., 546.
[151] Crimes Act 1961 s. 344A.
[152] *R* v. *Buisson* [1989] 2 NZLR 370, 371.

testified that they had identified twelve to fifteen points. The defence witnesses, in contrast, found less than twelve.[153] One testified that he could only see 'eight discernible points' that would be apparent to a jury. He accepted that there was no 'magic' in the requirement of twelve points but insisted that an identification should not be made with less than six. The other defence witness 'found seven points' and was 'adamant that anything less than 12 points of identity would not have been acceptable for evidence in Court in his experience, although he conceded that he had made many identifications on eight or nine points to other police officers'.[154]

Drawing attention to the fact that neither of the defence witnesses 'went so far as to say the print could not belong to Buisson', the Court inadvertently endorsed the position in *Redmile*:[155]

> Certainly, in the experience of most – if not all – judges, it is the practice for police experts to put forward at least 12 points in common, and if a witness endeavoured to support identity on less he or she might well be asked for an explanation. However, there is no rule that an opinion based on a lesser number is inadmissible. No doubt a judge would reject such evidence if the similarities on which it were based were so few or unremarkable that they could have no probative value in determining identity.[156]

The identification was admissible. It was for the defence to expose weaknesses.

The only other case to engage with the underlying methodology, though really only requiring production of some of the fingerprint community's documents, is *The Queen v. Carter*. The main issue on appeal was the examiner's failure to offer reasons, an expectation burdening experts following *R v. Calder*.[157] At trial the examiner identified a single fingerprint from a recipe for methamphetamine recovered from a clandestine laboratory to Carter. The examiner made no contemporaneous notes and provided limited explanation. When questioned he explained (accurately as it turns out) that the 'identification is occurring in the head' and 'it happens in the mind'. He also placed considerable reliance on peer review (or verification) and did not accept that he could be wrong. The trial transcript records:

> ... – In my opinion I have made an identification, that identification has been verified.

[153] *R v. Buisson* [1990] 2 NZLR 542, 545.
[154] Ibid., 546.
[155] Ibid.
[156] *R v. Buisson* [1990] 2 NZLR 542 (CA) 546.
[157] *R v. Calder* HC Christchurch T154/94, 12 April 1995.

By whom? – We have a form of peer review. It is part of the methodology.
ACE. The correct application of the science will lead to the correct result.
...

I put the question again, do you accept you could be wrong? – No.
Never wrong? – No, in other things but not in the identification process
itself.
Why should the jurors simply accept your opinion? – I have been trained,
I have 5 years of training and experience and 8 years of built up experience,
training courses and so on and I have been proficiency tested.[158]

Carter's counsel submitted that the failure to provide reasons 'rendered his
evidence of no value'.[159] The Court of Appeal agreed that the examiner had '[i]n
effect ... asked the jury to accept his conclusory observations based solely on his
own experience and the fact of peer review, the latter not being proved independently of his evidence. No other reasons were given."[160] In response, the Crown
drew attention to the fact that fingerprint procedures had recently changed;
having moved from the point standard to a holistic approach associated with
ACE-V.[161] In an effort to support the revised procedures the Crown produced
a range of documents including '[G]uidelines issued by the Scientific Working
Group on Friction Ridge Analysis, Study and Technology [or SWGFAST]' and
an article from an English law journal.[162]
Without clearly explaining the relationship between the previous points-
based approach and the new holistic ACE-V process, or reviewing the new
procedures in any detail, the Court found that the supplementary materials
supported them. The fingerprint examiner's description of his method was
characterised as 'consistent with recent developments' and he was said to have
alluded to the Guidelines – 'in his evidence'.[163] Vague judicial instructions,
where the emphasis was on the issue being for the jury rather than experts, and
reference to the fingerprint evidence as 'damning', were said to be clear and
appropriate. The appeal was dismissed.[164]

---

[158] *R v. Carter* [2005] NZCA 422 at 58 (punctuation not corrected).
[159] Ibid. at 42.
[160] Ibid. at 61.
[161] This is the first reported reference to ACE-V in New Zealand, even though it had been in use for years.
[162] The Scientific Working Group on Friction Ridge Analysis, Study and Technology (SWGFAST) has been transformed into the Organization of Scientific Area Committees (OSAC) Friction Ridge Subcommittee (FRS) under the oversight of, initially the Forensic Science Commission and, more recently, NIST.
[163] *R v. Carter* [2005] NZCA 422 at 65, 66, 71.
[164] The Court of Appeal suggested that the appropriate course of action was for defence counsel to challenge the value of the evidence, particularly reliance on verification, given that the Crown did not call any verifier. Reliability issues were effectively transformed into tactical

In 2014, in *Wells* v. *R*, appellate counsel sought to challenge fingerprint evidence on the basis of incompetent legal representation because trial counsel had not cross-examined about: the Bradley Mayfield misidentification and inquiry; confirmation bias; known errors; and the subjective nature of identification by fingerprint. Defence counsel also sought to call an FBI fingerprint examiner who appeared in the Mayfield inquiry. The Court of Appeal noted that the FBI examiner was not contending that there is 'no correlation at all' between the prints (re-call *Buisson*) and concluded that this evidence was not sufficiently cogent to support admission on appeal.[165] *Carter* was affirmed as authoritive even though these issues and emerging scientific interventions were not considered.

13.5 A LITTLE SCIENCE

Now, having reviewed legal responses to latent fingerprint evidence, including the major epistemological challenges in our three jurisdictions, it is time to introduce mainstream scientific perspectives. This section provides a very brief summary of recent reviews focused on the forensic sciences. The studies were produced by the National Research Council of the National Academy of Sciences (NRC report),[166] Sir Anthony Campbell, following an inquiry into mistaken identifications in the McKie case in Scotland (The Fingerprint Inquiry),[167] the National Institute of Standards and Technology and the Department of Justice (the NIST report), the President's Council of Advisers on Science and Technology (PCAST Report), the American Association for the Advancement of Science (AAAS Report), as well as guidance documents prepared by the UK's Forensic Science Regulator.[168] To place the legal reception and use of latent fingerprint evidence as well as the way examiners report their evidence into a scientific context, this section directs attention to important findings and recommendations beginning with validity and reliability.[169]

Fingerprint examiners have not used the same procedures, equipment and technologies across the twentieth century. This is not a trivial observation, but

decisions (and issues of hearsay) for the defence. See also *R* v. *Mokaraka* [2002] 1 NZLR 793 at 38–41.

[165] *Wells* v. *The Queen* [2014] NZCA 479.
[166] For an overview, see Edmond, 2015: 33.
[167] Campbell, 2011. See also United States Department of Justice, 2006.
[168] See e.g. Forensic Science Regulator, Guidance: Validation: Friction Ridge Detail (Fingerprint) Search Algorithm (FSR-G-230, 2019).
[169] See also Saks and Faigman, 2008: 149; Saks and Koehler, 2005: 892.

here we focus upon the most recent iteration of their subjective 'method', namely ACE-V. The NRC report made several important remarks about fingerprint comparison. The first was indirect but surprisingly critical: '[W] ith the exception of nuclear DNA analysis, however, no forensic method has been rigorously shown to have the capacity to consistently, and with a high degree of certainty, demonstrate a connection between evidence and a specific individual or source.'[170] This came as a devastating blow. For, it is questioned precisely what latent fingerprint examiners had been purporting to do – with certitude – for more than a century.

The NRC made direct reference to ACE-V. Claims about a zero error rate were dismissed out of hand as 'not scientifically plausible' and in the AAAS report as 'indefensible'.[171] The NRC and NIST both concluded that:

> ACE-V provides a broadly stated framework for conducting friction ridge analyses. However, this framework is not specific enough to qualify as a validated method for this type of analysis. ACE-V does not guard against bias; is too broad to ensure repeatability and transparency; and does not guarantee that two analysts following it will obtain the same results. For these reasons, merely following the steps of ACE-V does not imply that one is proceeding in a scientific manner or producing reliable results.[172]

The Committee searched in vain for research supporting the abilities and claims of fingerprint examiners. It turned out that latent fingerprint comparison had never been formally evaluated. The NRC called for epistemological humility in response.[173] The NIST report concluded that because 'empirical evidence and statistical reasoning do not support a source attribution to the exclusion of all other individuals in the world, latent print examiners should not report or testify, directly or by implication, to a source attribution to the exclusion of all others in the world'.[174] And, The Fingerprint Inquiry recommended that: '[E]xaminers should discontinue reporting conclusions on identification or exclusion with a claim to 100% certainty or on any other basis suggesting that fingerprint evidence is infallible.'[175] The PCAST report went further insisting that federal prosecutors and judges should not adduce or admit forensic science evidence that is not demonstrably reliable – that is, validated.[176]

[170] NRC report, 7–8.
[171] NRC report, 142–3, AAAS report, 71.
[172] NRC report 142; NIST report, 9.
[173] NRC report, 142, 184.
[174] NIST report, 197: Recommendation 3.7. See also NRC report, 106.
[175] SFI, Recommendation 3.
[176] PCAST report, 18: Recommendation 6.

These criticisms and recommendations led to the first scientifically rigorous validation studies, conducted with the support of the FBI (Tangen et al., 2011: 995–7; Ulery et al., 2011: 7733). Published from 2009, these studies were significant for a number of reasons. First, they confirmed that trained latent fingerprint examiners are markedly more accurate than novices. Formal validation studies demonstrated genuine expertise. Secondly, when tested under controlled conditions where the correct answer was known, trained latent fingerprint examiners (using ACE) made small numbers of false positive and false negative errors.[177] Studies confirmed that the method is not infallible and examiners occasionally make mistakes when undertaking their subjective assessment of whether two prints match or do not match. Additional testing confirmed that examiners regularly disagree about whether latent prints are suitable for comparison (Ulery et al., 2012; Ulery et al., 2014).

These studies led PCAST to, somewhat controversially (based on just two sets of studies), accept that latent fingerprint comparison is *foundationally* valid, though the President's Council was not persuaded that fingerprint comparison was consistently valid in the way it was *applied* in practice. This reflected concerns about the lack of standards, not performing ACE-V in sequence, and examiners (and verifiers) being unnecessarily exposed to domain-irrelevant information and suggestive processes. The upshot, for PCAST, the AAAS, and more recently, the UK's Forensic Science Regulator, is that it is incumbent on latent fingerprint examiners and courts (through prosecutors and trial judges) to correct widespread misconceptions – especially around categorical identification and practical infallibility. PCAST explained:

> PCAST finds that latent fingerprint analysis [has] *a false positive rate that is substantial* and is likely to be higher than expected by many jurors based on longstanding claims about the infallibility of fingerprint analysis. The false-positive rate could be as high as 1 error in 306 cases based on the FBI study and 1 error in 18 cases based on a study by another crime laboratory. In reporting results of latent-fingerprint examination, it is important to state the false-positive rates based on properly designed validation studies.[178]

For PCAST, the provision of this information would 'appropriately inform jurors that errors occur at detectable frequencies, allowing them to weigh the probative value of the evidence'.[179] This stands in stark contrast to the

---

[177] Review has not been adequately studied, and there is limited evidence about the effects of non-blind review.

[178] PCAST report, 9–10, 26, 74; AAAS report, 9, 73.

[179] PCAST report, 74, 26.

presentation of opinions as categorical identification that, if questioned, are defended as certain or infallible.[180]

The various reports, though most conspicuously the NRC report, the NIST report and the AAAS report, also directed attention towards previously unrecognised risks posed by human factors, especially a range of unconscious biases. These risks became notorious after an entrepreneurial cognitive scientist managed to persuade four of five experienced fingerprint examiners to change their opinion about whether two prints matched by exposing them to context information – notably suggestion (Dror et al., 2006).

> Observers' expectations have been shown to influence judgment in a broad range of tasks. Especially when confronted with ambiguous stimuli, people tend to see what they hope or expect to see. . . . some information about the origin of a latent print can facilitate accurate results, but other contextual information can produce confirmation bias. Extraneous information can influence people acting in good faith and attempting to be fair interpreters of the evidence.[181]

Historically, like almost all forensic scientists, fingerprint examiners were routinely exposed to case information and suggestive processes, such as only verifying matches. Examiners were inclined to consider themselves immune from human factors on the basis of training and experience. Attentive scientists dismissed such claims as naïve, at best. It is no coincidence that highly trained biomedical researchers employ double-blind clinical trials.

This leads to two important supplementary issues. First, legal institutions have historically placed a great deal of reliance on the experience of forensic scientists. Attentive scientists dismissed these (more sociological) commitments and insisted on the need to attend to validation studies and error. Consider the firm advice from PCAST:

> We note, finally, that neither experience, nor judgment, nor good professional practices (such as certification programs and accreditation programs, standardized protocols, proficiency testing, and codes of ethics) can substitute for actual evidence of foundational validity and reliability. . . . Similarly, an expert's expression of *confidence* based on personal professional experience or expressions of *consensus* among practitioners about the accuracy of their field is no substitute for error rates estimated from relevant studies. For forensic feature-comparison methods, establishing foundational validity based on empirical evidence is thus a *sine qua non*. Nothing can substitute for it. (White et al., 2014)

[180] PCAST report, 87.
[181] NIST report, 10.

Finally, and of significance leading into a discussion of these findings, the NRC, PCAST and AAAS reports were all highly critical of the performance and abilities of lawyers and courts. In our attempt to understand legal responses to fingerprint evidence and the profound failure to recognise these limitations across more than a century of routine use, we should not overlook the complicity of lawyers and judges.[182]

> Public perceptions of latent print examination have undoubtedly been shaped by *decades of overstatement*. One of the problems that examiners now face when attempting to convey a more realistic and appropriate sense of the value of latent print evidence is that people generally think a reported association between a latent print and reference print constitutes a virtually infallible identification. In our view latent print examiners should take affirmative steps, when reporting their findings, to address these common misconceptions.[183]

Latent fingerprint evidence was admitted and endorsed by prosecutors and judges (and, implicitly, defence counsel). Our legal institutions and personnel are complicit in more than a century of systematic overstatement.

13.6 NON-PRINCIPLED DIS-ENGAGEMENT, UNFAIRNESS AND IGNORANCE

This section endeavours to make some sense of the discordant state of affairs in terms of the precepts governing adversarial reliance on forensic science evidence.

Though, before proceeding, one further indication of epistemological insensitivity is the remarkable lack of engagement with the tremendous changes occurring in the organisation and practice of fingerprint comparison and the forensic sciences more generally over the course of the twentieth century. Just to provide a taste of the kinds of developments and changes that might have inspired questions, if not necessarily challenges, consider: the move from dusting and tape lifts to photography and digital capture; the abandonment of point systems and the move to holistic analysis; the introduction of electronic databases and algorithms for searching; the adoption and validity of ACE-V; changes to training and personnel, including the introduction of civilian and some scientifically trained examiners; the development of new chemical processes to visualise prints; public inquiries and royal commissions (e.g. Runciman, 1993; Morling, 1987) which exposed systematic problems with the forensic sciences; the introduction of scientifically predicated DNA profiling and population databases to facilitate

[182] NRC report, 53: 'courts have been utterly ineffective'.
[183] AAAS 2018, 71, italics added.

probabilistic reporting; the appearance of scholarly critiques of latent finger-print comparison (e.g. Cole, 2004); sustained admissibility challenges in the United States from the late 1990s (e.g. *US* v. *Mitchell; Llera Plaza*); high profile mis-identifications in Mayfield and McKie; 'laboratory' accreditation under international standards such as ISO 17025 (requiring validation); the formation of professional societies with ethical obligations; the public release of the scientific reports discussed in Section 13.5; as well as expanded disclosure and reporting obligations and changing admissibility conditions in each of our jurisdictions.[184]

Hardly any of these issues or developments led to a challenge, let alone a challenge informed by scientific knowledge.

13.6.1 *Lax Admissibility: Then and Now*

Fingerprint evidence first appeared at a time when the standards governing expert evidence were quite lax.[185] They were focused on persons having skills or experience that were considered capable of assisting fact-finding. The early reported decisions, with the notable exception of Chief Justice Madden in *Parker*, take the admissibility of fingerprint evidence for granted.

While admission at the beginning of the twentieth century might be comprehensible, even reasonable given persistent problems with proof and identification, the terms of admission were never revisited as procedures and technologies changed, as databases expanded, as algorithms were introduced, and as the rules governing expert reports and expert opinion evidence were criticised or revised in each of our jurisdictions.[186]

While there is no doubt that, as a foundationally valid procedure, finger-print evidence should be prima facie admissible, questions of whether comparison is valid as applied, what fingerprint examiners are entitled to say, and how opinions should be qualified warrant sustained legal attention.

13.6.2 *Systematic Over-Claiming: Then and Now*

From its first appearances in courts in all of these jurisdictions, fingerprint evidence was equated with categorical identification of a specific person.

---

[184] *US* v. *Mitchell*, 365 F.3d 215 (3d Cir. 2004); *US* v. *Llera Plaza*, 188 F. Supp. 2d 549 (E.D. Pa. 2002).

[185] See e.g. *Folkes* v. *Chadd* (1782) 3 Dougl 157; 99 ER 589 and *R* v. *Silverlock* [1894] 2 QB 766.

[186] See e.g. Law Commission, 2011 and subsequent revisions to Criminal Practice Directions and Criminal Procedure Rules; the introduction of the Uniform Evidence Law (e.g. NSW Evidence Act 1995) in most Australian jurisdictions from 1995, and the New Zealand Evidence Act 2006.

Castleton was categorically identified. Clancy was categorically identified. Blacker and Parker were categorically identified. Notwithstanding his probabilistic analogies, police examiners categorically identified Krausch and Gunn, and Chapman J characterised the process as based on 'established scientific facts' and 'biological facts'. Attempts to have the first appeals reviewed in the High Court of Australia were unsuccessful. In refusing leave to appeal, the Chief Justice of Australia described the fingerprint evidence as an 'unforgeable signature'.[187] Probabilistic analogies and 'scientific' explanations were quickly dropped as latent fingerprint evidence took on a life and reputation of its own.

This state of affairs continues (Cole, 2009; Cole, 2014). Fingerprint examiners report and, when occasionally called, categorically identify specific persons without qualification. If asked, they are likely to describe their confidence as absolute and insist that their procedures are practically infallible. Such representations are not just misleading, they are systematically biased in favour of the state. Historical review confirms that misleading impressions are rarely, perhaps never, corrected. Legal practices are inconsistent with mainstream scientific advice and reveal a good deal about the effectiveness of our trial safeguards.

13.6.3 *Law's (Almost) Invisible Hand: Trial Safeguards*

Trial safeguards have not worked effectively in the hands of (technically illiterate) lawyers and judges. It is not my contention that trial safeguards are necessarily ineffective, although we cannot ignore the fact that they did not expose limitations or bring scientific knowledge to the attention of the courts. For over a century, some of the finest legal counsel in these three jurisdictions, along with the most senior judicial officers (with the exception of a single judge), have failed to expose or address fundamental limitations with latent fingerprint evidence.

Not only did examiners swear oaths and have formal obligations, but prosecutors were obliged to act as 'ministers of justice' in the presentation of fingerprint evidence. Presenting the fingerprint evidence as complete proof of identity was inconsistent with these responsibilities. Experienced defence barristers had opportunities to question fingerprint examiners in exquisite detail about their procedures, the scientific research supporting them and scientific criticisms, but apart from a couple of recent cases in Australia (*JP* and *Nguyen*), do not appear to have taken the opportunity to

---

[187] *Parker v The King* (1912) 14 CLR 681, 682.

do so. Cross-examination has not been a great engine for the discovery of truth.

Where trial safeguards and appeals did uncover issues (as in *McNamee*, *Smith* and *Carter*), the myopia of the common law restricted appellate focus to the instant case. Though, there are few reasons to believe that the messiness, disagreement and lack of access to advice exposed in these appeals were unrepresentative.

One powerful example of the ability of courts to deceive themselves, to declare and believe their processes fair, can be gleaned from *Blacker*. Reviewing the proceedings, the Chief Justice of NSW assured the appellant (and the wider audience) that:

> The jury also were very carefully directed by the learned Judge as to the risk of error to which evidence of this class is open, and as far as the conduct of the trial is concerned every precaution was taken to guard against any wrongful impression being conveyed to the jury.[188]

But this was mistaken. This was not a 'new science of identification' and it was not 'based on experiments' that were oriented toward understanding accuracy or improving comprehension. Latent fingerprint comparison and the range of 'methods' and assumptions underpinning it had not been tested and would not be tested for another century. The Chief Justice's assessment is based largely on impressions and ignorance. It assumes conventional trial safeguards are effective. Like many similar judicial assertions it is misguided and misleading.

On the rare occasion when an identification was questioned, courts, beginning with Darling J in *Castleton*, have expected defendants to identify someone with the same fingerprint or to expose an error. Such expectations are fanciful. They impose an impossible burden on defendants in circumstances where if an error has been made it is exceedingly difficult to demonstrate. Fingerprint comparison remains a subjective process that takes place, as the examiner in *Carter* conceded, 'in the head'. How do you identify mistakes in examiners' heads and how do you cross-examine examiners about unconscious bias or interpretative processes that they are not necessarily conscious of?

13.6.4 Decision-Makers Not Positioned for Rational Evaluation

It is a fundamental expectation that legal decision-makers, whether jurors, lawyers or judges, will be placed in a position to rationally evaluate forensic science evidence. This study reveals that latent fingerprint evidence was rarely,

---

[188] *R v. Blacker* [1910] SR (NSW) 357, 360.

if ever, presented in a way that facilitated evaluation. Rather than present the evidence in an empirically based probabilistic form, with an indicative error rate, its value was overstated by examiners, prosecutors and judges.

The impact of overstatement on rectitude depends on the case and the evidence assembled against particular defendants. In cases where there were multiple fingerprints identified to a person, or fingerprint evidence was combined with independent evidence, the risk of error will generally have been quite low (see Edmond et al., 2014: 1). In cases such as *Parker*, where the only admissible evidence was a single latent fingerprint on a movable object, the risk of error was non-trivial. In no case is there a credible reason for overstating – in favour of the state – the value of fingerprint evidence. Such over-claiming, along with the courts' imprimatur, increased the risk that innocent persons would be convicted. In all these proceedings, the mis-representation produced unfairness to defendants and appellants. Over-claiming is unfair. It threatens rational evaluation and denies defendants the benefit of doubts that may be neither remote nor fanciful. We might reflect on what it means for a system of justice to repeatedly fail to present expert evidence in a manner that captures its value and facilitates rational evaluation. We should be especially concerned when legal practices are not modified in response to mainstream scientific 'interventions'.

13.6.5 *Principled Derogation from Scientific Knowledge and Advice?*

This chapter starkly illustrates the disjuncture between mainstream scientific knowledge and conventional legal practice. Scientists who have formally studied or reviewed the procedures used by latent fingerprint examiners (and many other forensic scientists) and the research supporting them have been remarkably critical. In proceeding, it is important to acknowledge that courts are not purporting to do science, so there may be good reasons why they persist with traditional approaches and (effectively) ignore mainstream scientific advice, although it is difficult to imagine what they might be.

The primary reason we allow experts into courts is epistemological. We admit expert evidence to enhance the accuracy of decision-making. Centuries ago, Saunders J explained that '[i]f matters arise in our law which concern other sciences or faculties, we commonly apply for the aid of that science or faculty which it concerns'.[189] Incorporating exogenous forms of knowledge is conceived to improve legal decision-making and to reduce the risk of wrongful conviction, thereby enhancing legal institutional legitimacy. Reliance on

---

[189]   *Buckley* v. *Rice* (1554) 175 Eng. Rep. 182, 192.

expert evidence is directly contingent on the evidence having value and the decision-maker being able to assess its value in the context of the case.[190]

Given that legal engagement with scientific and technical evidence is primarily, and perhaps exclusively, for epistemological purposes, if legal institutions wish to derogate from mainstream scientific recommendations and advice then there must be compelling institutional reasons and these reasons must be identified.[191] As things stand, our courts have clearly derogated but have offered no explanation, compelling or otherwise.

13.6.6 *The Costs of Non-engagement: Perpetuation of Legal Myths*

Apart from mis-managing the most ubiquitous forensic science evidence, the other serious cost of non-engagement with mainstream scientific research and advice is the failure to recognise that legal rules, procedures and safeguards do not always work well, or at all. For more than a century, lawyers and courts in each of these jurisdictions celebrated the adversarial criminal trial. They relied heavily upon a range of rules, around disclosure, the obligations of lawyers, rules of evidence and procedure, directions and instructions, as well as appeals to sustain claims about rectitude and fairness. And yet, none of these brought the lack of testing and the indefensible claims into prominence.

This survey suggests that those working in, but particularly the judges presiding over, adversarial systems should be less credulous. They should not assume that forensic sciences have been formally evaluated (and have trivial rates of error). They should not assume that real limitations, uncertainties and even levels of accuracy and error will be known and disclosed, let alone raised and considered. They should not assume that the defence is in a position to address them, or that failure to raise issues was deliberate (i.e. tactical). They should also be concerned about new legal procedures, such as streamlined forensic reporting (in England and Wales), restricted disclosure and the limited resources provided to defendants, in relation to their ability to understand and where appropriate explore epistemological dimensions of forensic science evidence (Edmond et al., 2019: 764).

---

[190] Historically, there was a tendency to assume that juries could deal with any reliability issues in context of the trial. Now, it seems that the trial cannot deal with expert evidence, and there are continuing issues with the jury. Recent cases have tended to recognise the importance of reliability, see e.g. *Tuite v. The Queen* [2015] VSCA 148 and *Lundy v. The Queen* [2018] NZCA 410 at 239.

[191] On the application of the US reports to other jurisdictions employing the same (or similar) procedures, consider the following comment by PCAST's co-chair, Lander, 2017.

Lawyers and judges must be more sophisticated consumers of science and technology (see, e.g. Jasanoff, 2005). They need to play regulatory roles and should not leave issues of validity and reliability to laypersons to resolve in the context of fact-finding in contested cases. Courts should not be early (or late) adopters of technology.[192] Reliance on forensic science evidence should be firmly grounded in independent research that confirms the procedure does what is claimed, that the particular witness is demonstrably proficient in the particular task, and opinions are expressed in scientifically defensible terms.

We have a very long way to go.

REFERENCES

Beavan, C. (2001). *Fingerprints: The Origins of Crime Detection and the Murder Case that Launched Forensic Science* (London: Hyperion).
Campbell, A. (2011). *The Fingerprint Inquiry Report* (Edinburgh: APS Group).
Cole, S. (2001). *Suspect Identities: A History of Fingerprinting and Criminal Identification* (Cambridge, MA: Harvard University Press).
Cole, S. (2004). Grandfathering Evidence: Fingerprint Admissibility Rulings from *Jennings* to *Llera Plaza* and Back Again. *American Criminal Law Review*, 41 (3), 1189–276.
Cole, S. (2009). Forensics Without Uniqueness, Conclusions Without Individualization: The New Epistemology of Forensic Identification. *Law, Probability, and Risk*, 8(3), 233–55.
Cole, S. (2014). Individualization Is Dead, Long Live Individualization! Reforms of Reporting Practices for Fingerprint Analysis in the United States. *Law, Probability and Risk*, 13(2), 117–50.
Cole, S. and Roberts, A. (2012). Certainty, Individualisation and the Subjective Nature of Expert Fingerprint Evidence. *Criminal Law Review*, 12, 824–49.
Devlin, P. (1979). *The Judge*, Oxford: Oxford University Press.
Dror, I. et al. (2006). Contextual Information Renders Experts Vulnerable to Making Erroneous Identifications. *Forensic Science International*, 156, 74–78.
Duff, A., Farmer, L., Marshall, S. and Tadros, V., eds. (2004). *The Trial on Trial: Towards a Normative Theory of the Criminal Trial*, Oxford: Hart Publishing.

---

[192] Compare Lord Steyn in *R v. Clarke* [1995] 2 Cr. App. R. 425, 429–30: 'It would be entirely wrong to deny to the law of evidence the advantages to be gained from new techniques and new advances in science.'

Edmond, G. (2015). Forensic Science Evidence and the Conditions for Rational (Jury) Evaluation. *Melbourne University Law Review*, 39(1), 77–127.

Edmond G. (2019). Latent Science: A History of Australian Fingerprint Evidence in Australia. *University of Queensland Law Journal*, 38(2), 301–65.

Edmond, G. (2020). Fingerprint Evidence in New Zealand Courts: The Oversight of Overstatement. *New Zealand Universities Law Review*, 29, 1–29.

Edmond, G. and Cunliffe, E. (2016). Cinderella Story? The Social Production of a Forensic 'Science'. *Journal of Criminal Law and Criminology*, 106(2), 219–73

Edmond, G. and San Roque, M. (2012). The Cool Crucible: Forensic Science and the Frailty of the Criminal Trial. *Current Issues in Criminal Justice*, 24 (1), 51–68.

Edmond, G. et al. (2014). Evidence-Based Forensic Initiative. How to Cross-Examine Forensic Scientists: A Guide for Lawyer. *Australian Bar Review*, 39, 174–97.

Edmond, G., Hamer, D. and Cunliffe, E. (2016). A Little Ignorance Is a Dangerous Thing: Engaging with Exogenous Knowledge Not Adduced by the Parties. *Griffith Law Review*, 25(3), 383–413.

Edmond, G., Martire, K. and San Roque, M. (2017). Expert Reports in the Forensic Sciences. *UNSW Law Journal*, 40(2), 590–637.

Edmond, G., Tangen, J., Searston, R. and Dror, I. (2014). Contextual Bias and Cross-Contamination in the Forensic Sciences: The Implications for Investigations, Plea Bargains, Trials and Appeals. *Law, Probability & Risk*, 14, 1–25.

Edmond, G., Carr, S. and Piasecki, E. (2018). Science Friction: Streamlined Forensic Reporting. *Oxford Journal of Legal Studies*, 38(4), 764–792.

Edmond, G., Cunliffe, E. and Hamer, D. (2020). Fingerprint Comparison and Adversarialism: The Scientific and Historical Evidence. *Modern Law Review*, 83(6), 1287–327.

Edmond, G., Cunliffe, E., Martire, K. and San Roque, M. (2019). Forensic Science Evidence and the Limits of Cross-Examination. *Melbourne University Law Review*, 42(3), 858–920.

Evett, I. and Williams, R. (1996). Review of the Sixteen Points Fingerprint Standard in England and Wales. *Journal of Forensic Identification*, 46, 49.

Groebner, V. (2007). *Who Are You? Identification, Deception and Surveillance in Early Modern Europe* (New York: Zone).

Gudjonsson, G. (2003). *The Psychology of Interrogations and Confessions: A Handbook* (Oxford: Wiley).

Jasanoff, S. (2005). Law's Knowledge: Science for Justice in Legal Settings. *American Journal of Public Health*, 95(S1), 49–58.

Lander, E. (2017). Response to the ANZFSS council statement on the
    President's Council of Advisors on Science and Technology Report.
    Australian Journal of Forensic Science, 49, 1.
Law Commission of England and Wales. (2011). *Expert Evidence in Criminal
    Proceedings in England and Wales*, 34 Law Commission Report No 325
    (HMSO, London).
Leo, R. and Drizin, S. (2004). The Problem of False Confessions in the Post-
    DNA World. *North Carolina Law Review*, 82, 891.
Lynch, M., Cole, S., McNally, R. and Jordan, K. (2008). *Truth Machine: The
    Contentious History of DNA Evidence* (Chicago: University of Chicago
    Press) 237–41.
Morling, T. (1987). *Report of the Commissioner the Hon Mr Justice TR
    Morling: Royal Commission of Inquiry into the Chamberlain Convictions*
    (Canberra: Government Printer).
National Institute of Standards and Technology. (2012). *Latent Print
    Examination and Human Factors: Improving the Practice Through
    a Systems Approach* (US Department of Commerce).
National Research Council. (2009). Strengthening Forensic Science in the
    United States: A Path Forward (National Academies Press), 142–3 (NRC
    Report).
President's Council of Advisors on Science and Technology, Forensic Science
    in Criminal Courts: Ensuring Scientific Validity of Feature-Comparison
    Methods (Report, 20 September 2016).
Roberts, R., Wilmore, C. and Davis, G. (1993). *The Role of Forensic Science
    Evidence in Criminal Proceedings*. Royal Commission on Criminal Justice
    Research Study No 11 (London: HMSO).
Runciman, V. (1993). *Royal Commission on Criminal Justice* (London:
    HMSO).
Saks, M. and Faigman, D. (2008). Failed Forensics: How Forensic Science
    Lost Its Way and How It Might Yet Find It. *Annual Review of Law & Social
    Science*, 4, 149–71.
Saks, M. and Koehler, J. (2005). The Coming Paradigm Shift in Forensic
    Identification Science. *Science*, 309, 892–5.
Sengoopta, C. (2003). *Imprint of the Raj: How Fingerprinting Was Born in
    Colonial India* (London: PanMacMillan).
Tangen, J., Thompson, M. and McCarthy, D. (2011). Identifying Fingerprint
    Expertise. *Psychological Science*, 22, 995–7.
Thompson, W. (2005). Analyzing the Relevance and Admissibility of
    Bullet-Lead Evidence: Did the NRC Report Miss the Target? *Jurimetrics
    Journal*, 46(1), 65–89.
Thompson, W. et al. (2017). Forensic Science Assessments: A Quality and Gap
    Analysis – Latent Fingerprint Examination (AAAS) (AAAS Report).

Torpey, J. and Caplan, J. (eds). (2001). *Documenting Individual Identity: The Development of State Practices in the Modern World* (Princeton, NJ: Princeton University Press).

Ulery, B. et al. (2011). Accuracy and Reliability of Forensic Latent Fingerprint Decisions. *Proceedings of the National Academy of Sciences*, 108, 773–8.

Ulery, B. et al. (2012). Repeatability and Reproducibility of Decisions by Latent Fingerprint Examiners. *PloS One*, 7, e32800.

Ulery, B. et al. (2014). Measuring What Latent Fingerprint Examiners Consider Sufficient Information for Individualization Determinations. *Plos One*, 9, e110179.

United States Department of Justice. (2006). *A Review of the FBI's Handling of the Brandon Mayfield Case* (US Department of Justice, Office of the Inspector General, Oversight and Review Division).

Walker, C. and Starmer, K. (eds.). (1999). *Miscarriages of Justice: A Review of Justice in Error* (London: Blackstone).

White, D. et al. (2014). Passport Officers' Errors in Face Matching. *PLoS ONE*, 9(8), 1–6.

14

Prevention and Education

The Path towards Better Forensic Science Evidence

Marina Gascón Abellán

14.1 FORENSIC SCIENCE: 'BOOM', MYTH AND ERRORS

Forensic scientists are influential players in the justice system. Experts in forensic odontology, fingerprinting, forensic serology, DNA, bloodstain patterns, handwriting, ballistics, toxicology and drug analysis, microscopic hair analysis, fibres and fire debris analysis, voice comparison, firearms, bite marks, explosives residue, gunshot residue, questioned documents, glass, paint, metals, soil and other trace evidence, shoeprints, tire tracks, tool marks and other emerging forensic science disciplines (such as digital and multimedia analysis) give daily assistance to the courts in answering complex evidentiary issues in the service of the criminal justice system and civil litigation. Actually, forensic evidence has been critical to resolve crimes that might not otherwise been resolved, and demand for it has risen significantly.

The enthusiasm for forensic science evidence at trials is most likely due to its alleged contrast with other types of evidence. Traditional types of evidence are seen as problematic, uncertain and fallible. For instance, assessing an eyewitness's credibility is not an easy task, and in fact most judges concede the inherent subjectivity and fragility of such a judgement. On the contrary, forensic evidence is considered as 'scientific' and consequently objective and conclusive. People in general and legal actors in particular place the highest confidence in it, and as forensic science disciplines become more high-tech so too does their sheen of invincibility.[1]

At least two reasons may account for the great confidence placed in forensics. On the one hand, most people (and judges) have a rather poor science education that leads them to put exaggerated expectations on the analysis coming from

---

[1] The idealised vision of forensic science (as a symbol of certainty) is widely spread. In Spain it has been noticed some years ago by Igartua, 2007.

forensic science labs. There is an unrealistic vision of what most forensic science disciplines can do in actual terms. It is vaguely assumed that forensic science evidence is always based on rigorous, scientific methodology which brings objective and conclusive results. And it is often ignored that in most cases the conclusions of the forensic tests express a probability judgement in a particular case that, relying on the analyst's personal opinion, has a strong subjective component, hence it is difficult to speak of 'objectivity' let alone 'infallibility' regarding them.[2] In short, the idea has taken root that the knowledge obtained in courtrooms is fragile whereas that obtained in forensic labs is something quite different.

On the other hand, DNA profiling has contributed decisively to the prestige of forensic science. After years of intensive research, nuclear DNA analysis has been shown to have the capacity to consistently, and with a high degree of certainty, demonstrate a connection between an evidentiary sample and a specific individual or source. There are, of course, many concerns relating to this technique.[3] However, there must be no surprise that the huge success achieved by forensic DNA (the 'gold standard' of human identification) has projected, as a sort of 'radiation effect', on many other forensic disciplines whose methodology is not as developed and their accuracy not as high as those of the former.

The so called CSI effect captures this situation. The effect refers to the tremendous impact that some television booms, such as the American series *CSI (Crime Scene Investigation)* and other high-tech forensic shows, have on the population. Purportedly the watchers of these series hold exaggerated expectations regarding forensic science evidence. With an effect in judicial practice, demand for forensic evidence at trial is increasing significantly and there is even a reluctance to convict when such evidence is lacking. It is true that some studies have questioned the existence of a 'CSI effect', and some of them have even claimed that watchers of these TV shows used to be more critical of forensic science.[4] In any case, regardless of whether or not there is a 'CSI effect', there is no doubt about the great deal of confidence placed in the 'white-coat experts'.

---

[2]   'Any probability judgement in a particular case, even when the judgement is frequency based, has a component based on personal knowledge.' That is the same as saying that any probability judgement is essentially personal and hence subjective. Understanding statistical data as objective data, in the sense that they are incontrovertible and universally achievable, shows an unreal conception of the possibilities of science. It is possible to speak of objectivity as an intersubjective agreement. In this sense it is easier for scientists to accept a result if it is based upon relevant statistical data than if it is based upon subjective assessments of probabilities, but this does not amount to saying that scientists believe that result to be incontrovertible Taroni et al., 2006: 21.

[3]   On the problems and controversial questions concerning forensic DNA, see Murphy, 2015. Thompson, 2006: 10–16; or Balding and Bucleton, 2009: 1–10.

[4]   Cf. Schweitzer and Saks, 2007; Cole and Dioso-Vila, 2009; Chin and Workewych, 2016.

Unfortunately, there is no reason for such a strong confidence, and experience shows that forensic science errors are also possible.

14.1.1 *The Mayfield Error*

In the year 2004 we knew one of the most serious mistakes and likely the most damaging to the prestige of forensic science. I am referring, of course, to the erroneous identification of Brandon Mayfield following the 2004 Madrid train bombing. The mistake affected one of the most broadly used and prestigious forensic techniques: latent fingerprint analysis. In addition, The Federal Bureau of Investigation (FBI) – arguably the best of the best in the forensics world – made it.

The story is very well known. An unknown print was found on a plastic bag containing the detonation materials in Madrid. As part of international assistance requested with identifying potential suspects, the FBI laboratory investigated the print using its IAFIS system (Integrated Automated Fingerprints Identification System). IAFIS permits computer searches of FBI databases containing the fingerprints of over forty-seven million individuals. A list of twenty candidates was obtained and one investigation was launched on them. Number fourth on the list was Brandon Mayfield, an attorney from Portland, Oregon. Acting upon this suggestion, three separate fingerprint examiners at the FBI compared successively the unknown print with Mayfield's print (one made the first examination, and the other two verified the identification) and all three concluded that there was a definite match. With no other evidentiary basis, Brandon Mayfield was arrested as a material witness in relation to the bombing attacks.

Mayfield claimed that the identification had to be a mistake, since he had never been in Spain, had remained entirely in the United States during the relevant period and, in addition, lacked a passport. Indeed, following the FBI report, the Spanish National Police re-examined the prints and concluded they did not match. However, all the three FBI examiners were reluctant to change their report and insisted that it was a '100 per cent match', an 'absolute-incontrovertible match' and there was 'no doubt about it'. An independent court-appointed examiner also confirmed the match. Several weeks later Spanish Authorities located another suspect in a different database, an Algerian national who – they claimed – was the actual source of the print. Eventually, the FBI concurred and Mayfield was released. The FBI was deeply embarrassed.[5]

---

[5] See a detailed description of the case in the report issued by the Office of the Inspector General. US Department of Justice: *Report on Mayfield: A Review of the FBI's Handling of the Brandon Mayfield Case* (2006).

What happened? How could an error like this occur? The Report issued by the US Department of Justice on the case identifies several possible causes of the error.[6] It is worth mentioning some of them.

Firstly, the intrinsic weakness of the method used to analyse latent fingerprints. The AFIS system suggested the possible match between Mayfield's print and the latent print found in Madrid. But upon that 'suggestion' it is the examiner who has to compare the two prints to determine if they actually match. The FBI examiners concluded that Mayfield's print matched the latent print because there was a strong degree of similarity between them: an 'unusual similarity'. But the problem is that there is no information about the likelihood that two prints selected at random would have that similarity (so we have no basis for interpreting the meaning of the similarities), and there is not an agreement on how much similarity should exist for determining a match, and we do not know either the error rates associated with the method. At root, the conclusion reached in a latent fingerprints' comparison is a matter of subjective judgement by the trained and experienced examiner. So to speak, the expert is the method. It is therefore surprising that lacking sound data supporting the reliability and accuracy of the method, examiners referred to the match in absolute terms: '100 per cent certainty'; 'no doubt about it', 'o per cent error rate'. The concern though is that they expressed the match in those terms because they used to do so.

But also, *cognitive biases* most certainly played a role. In reviewing the case, J. Mnookin describes it as follows: 'It seems that once the first FBI examiner declared the prints to match, the verifying examiners *expected* to find a match. It is not great surprise, then, that they found precisely what they expected to find, likely the result of a mixture of peer pressure and expectation bias's' (Mnookin, 2010: 1230). On the other hand, contextual information also seems to have produced a bias. When the Spanish Police objected to the match the three FBI examiners knew that Mayfield had converted to Islam some time earlier, and that he had also represented a known terrorist in a child custody dispute. He was the perfect suspect. And that could explain their reluctance to reopen the issue or contemplate the possibility that they had made a mistake. In fact, Mayfield later claimed he was a victim of religious persecution.

The Mayfield error is highly interesting because it indicates that if in a relatively well-established and broadly used forensic discipline such big errors can occur, there are reasons to suspect that same errors can occur – a fortiori – in other forensic techniques worse founded than fingerprint analysis.

---

[6] See again *Report on Mayfield* (2006). There is abundant literature on the Mayfield error. An excellent study of the case is the one by Mnookin, 2010, which I refer to for complete analysis.

Marina Gascón Abellán

14.2 MORE TRANSPARENCY AND LESS EXAGGERATION: CRITICISM
OF FORENSIC SCIENCE

In fact, four years after the Mayfield error this suspicion was confirmed. In 2009, The National Academy of Sciences (NAS) of the United States released its report on forensic science, which reads:

> For decades, the forensic science disciplines have produced valuable evidence that has contributed to the successful prosecution and conviction of criminals as well as to the exoneration of innocent people ... Those advances, however, also have revealed that, in some cases, substantive information and testimony based on faulty forensic science analyses may have contributed to wrongful convictions of innocent people. This fact has demonstrated the potential danger of giving undue weight to evidence and testimony derived from imperfect testing and analysis.[7]

The Report found serious deficiencies in most forensic disciplines in a variety of issues.

14.2.1 *Poor (or No) Scientific Basis*

To begin with, although some of the forensic science disciplines (such as DNA analysis, serology, forensic pathology, toxicology, chemical analysis and digital and multimedia forensics) are built on solid bases of theory and research, many other kinds of forensic science fields (particularly those based on expert interpretation of observed patterns, such as fingerprints, writing samples, tool marks, bite marks, and specimens such as fibres, hair and fire debris) are essentially built on practitioners' experience but lack proper validation using the usual methods and approaches of science (NAS Report 2009: 128). So, we do not know how reliable and accurate they are. Their empirical assertions are not based on rigorous collection of data; there has been little formal validation of their methods; the error rates remain unknown; and there has also been too little study of how often and for what reasons experts might make mistakes. Consequently, experts in these forensic fields, 'have regularly testified in court to matters that are both less proven and less certain than they are claimed to be. They have overstated their degree of knowledge, underreported the chances of error, and suggested greater certainty than is warranted' (Mnookin, 2010: 1210). Under such circumstances,

---

[7] National Research Council Report, 2009, *Strengthening Scientific Evidence in the United States: A Path Forward* (hereinafter NAS Report, 2009): 4.

reliance upon evidence produced by those non-scientific forensic disciplines is rather a 'matter of faith'.

14.2.2 *Cognitive Biases*

Insufficient attention has also been given to the risk that some information might bias expert's interpretation of findings. Biases come largely from contextual information. Frequently, experts are exposed (for example through the police or the prosecutors) to some information related to the case which – if true – would have a strong probative value. For instance, that the suspect has an alibi, or has confessed, or has been previously convicted, or his/her analysis is the only relevant evidence in the case, etc. Such information is irrelevant for the analysis that expert has to perform but can potentially cause bias in the conclusions reached, as it is clear and quite well established that we have a cognitive tendency to see what we expect to see. Ignoring the risk of biases that can influence experts' interpretations of data does not permit to assure the quality of expert' conclusions.

Concerns for cognitive biases are not mere speculation. From the Cognitive Psychology, some experiments have been made that, although not conclusive, suggest that biases may affect significantly expert's conclusions.[8] Evidently, experts may need to know some information to perform their tests. For example, for analysing a latent fingerprint it may be necessary to know on which surface (a knife, a crystal, a plastic bag) the print was found, and such information may be potentially biasing. But apart from that necessary information, the expert should remain blind to any other data surrounding the case.

Additionally, a sort of bias may also derive from the institutional role experts are believed to play. In this respect, Sandra Guerra Thompson suggests that with the vast majority of forensic labs being located within a state's police department, many forensic analysts view themselves as 'cops in lab coats', working for the purposes and goals of police and prosecution, rather than

---

[8] For example, the experiment carried out by Itiel E. Dror and his collaborators to demonstrate that experts are relatively 'unreliable and biasable'. The experiment is now very well known. They took two sets of fingerprints that have previously been examined and assessed by a number of latent print experts as a clear and definite match. Then they presented these same fingerprints again, to the same experts, but gave a context that suggested that they were a no-match (they labelled the first set of prints as belonging to the Madrid bomber and the second set as those of Mayfield). hey then asked the analysts to determine if the prints matched, and most of them determined they did not match, thus contradicting their own previous identification decision. The experts reached different conclusions because the labels – and not the actual print evidence – indicated that 'no match' was the correct finding (Dror, 2006).

strictly making the scientific analysis in an impartial, independent way. With the result that forensic findings are presented in court as neutral, yet they are definitively discovered and discerned on only one side of the case.[9]

14.2.3 *Deficiencies in Labs*

Quality of practices in forensic laboratories is also far from satisfactory. The report stresses the lack of *autonomy* of most crime laboratories (part of the statewide network of institutes linked to the government and possibly biased for the purposes of police and prosecution) (NAS Report, 2009: 183–4), their failure to adhere to robust *performance standards*, the absence of uniform, mandatory accreditation programmes, and the lack of *effective oversight* (NAS Report, 2009: 193 ff.). It also underlines the gross shortage of adequate training and continuing education of practitioners, and the absence of rigorous *proficiency testing*.[10] In addition, *transparency* is very much absent. Transparency implies that legal actors (judges, defence attorneys and prosecutors) must have access to all the data that may influence the quality of the analysis results, as well as the failures and mistakes found. However, all this precious information is not publicly disclosed beyond the walls of the laboratory. Indeed, many laboratories lack quality control protocols to identify mistakes, fraud and bias, and to improve laboratory performance (NAS Report, 2009: 201 ff.).

14.2.4 *Misleading Testimony: The Rhetoric of Individualisation*

The presentation of forensic evidence to the courts is of the most importance. However, experts in the forensic fields having as their goal the identification of the source of a specific evidence item from a particular crime scene (e.g., shoe and tire impressions, dermal ridge prints, tool marks, firearms and handwriting) often exaggerate, overstate or overrepresent the significance of their findings.

The critical problem here is the use of imprecise terms and expressions that can be misunderstood to imply *individualisation*. Namely, they suggest that

---

[9]   See Guerra Thompson, 2015: 183, 187 ff. The same is pointed to by Itiel Dror, who writes that forensic experts are too often exposed to irrelevant contextual information that might bias their analysis of the evidence, 'largely because they work with the police and prosecution' (Dror, 2018: 243).

[10] While testifying in court, a fingerprint examiner with twenty-five years prior service at New Scotland Yard, referred to the FBI's proficiency tests as 'too easy'. Adequate for trainees but not for real experts. 'If I gave my experts these tests – he said – they'd fall about laughing' (*Llera Plaza (II)*, 188 F. Supp. 2d 549).

the expert, by analysing an evidence item, has 'individualised' the specific source (an individual or a particular object) where that item comes from.[11] For example, when fingerprint examiners declare a 'match', they use to assert that the latent fingerprint examined 'coincides with' or is 'consistent with' or 'is identical to' or presents 'an unusual similarity to' a specific known fingerprint, implying that they come from a common source. In addition, quite often forensic examiners claim their conclusions are supported 'to a reasonable degree of scientific certainty'; and in some other cases they even claim their conclusions are '100 per cent certain', or their technique has a '0 error rate'. All this wording suggests the capacity of a forensic method to demonstrate (to a high degree of certainty) a connection between a trace material and a specific individual or source to the exclusion of all other possible sources in the world, and thus gives fuel to the misconception that the method is infallible.

Yet there is no reason for such strong claims. Individualisation is settled on the assumption that *uniqueness* exists. Uniqueness – put in simple words – means that 'nature never repeats' (a subject can be identical only to itself; all subjects are different from each other). However, uniqueness has not been established in any of the traditional, low-tech forensic disciplines, such as fingerprints, firearms, shoe and tire impressions and handwriting (Saks and Koehler, 2010: 1189). And, moreover, even if it were held to exist, such disciplines have epistemological constrictions that prevent them from interpreting a *match* (between a questioned and a known sample) in individualisation terms.[12] That is why the NAS Report reads: 'with the exception of nuclear DNA analysis, no forensic method has been rigorously shown to have the capacity to consistently, and with a high degree of certainty, demonstrate a connection between evidence and a specific individual or source' (NAS Report, 2009: 7). It means that individualisation statements rest more on rhetorical grounds than on scientific grounds, and experts should therefore abandon them and exhibit a greater degree of epistemological humility. Forensic disciplines, in a nutshell, are needed of more transparency and less exaggeration.[13]

[11] 'The concept of individualization is that an object found at a crime scene can be uniquely associated with one particular source' (NAS Report, 2009: 184).
[12] 'The question is less a matter of whether each person's fingerprints are permanent and unique – uniqueness is commonly assumed – and more a matter of whether one can determine with adequate reliability that the finger that left an imperfect impression at a crime scene is the same finger that left an impression (with different imperfections) in a file of fingerprints' (NAS Report 2009: 43).
[13] In addition, 'when experts exaggerate the state of their science and their exaggerations find acceptance in the courtroom, researchers have less incentive for conducting the basic and applied research needed to put these assertions to the test' (Saks and Joehler, 2010: 1207).

The diagnostic made by the NAS Report has been devastating. The investigation has shown that, with the exception of nuclear DNA analysis, forensic identification techniques are 'no more than a house of cards built on unvalidated hypotheses and unsubstantiated or non-existent data' (Fabricant and Carrington, 2016: 1), and consequently their claims are clearly overvalued and oversold. With a concerning corollary: not only miscarriages of justice when using forensic evidence are possible but, according to that diagnostic, the number of them could be also worrying.

This concern has been confirmed in the past years.

Although it is not easy to measure the prevalence of miscarriages of justice in the system (cf. Cunliffe and Edmond, 2017; Cole, 2012), several studies have revealed that faulty forensic science (including insufficient validation of a method, mistakes in the laboratories, errors when interpreting the data – such as the prosecutor's fallacy – or exaggerated or misleading testimonies) is one of the most significant contributing factors to judicial errors.[14] In 2009, a first study reviewing 137 cases of innocent people wrongfully convicted found that in the bulk of cases (60 per cent) forensic analysts provided invalid testimony at trial (mainly involving serological analysis and microscopic hair comparison, but also bite marks, shoe prints, fingerprints comparisons, and other forensic techniques).[15] And according to the *Innocence Project*, 'misapplication of forensic science' (including unreliable or invalid forensic discipline, insufficient validation of a method, misleading testimony, mistakes and misconduct) was found in nearly half (45 per cent) of the more than 350 DNA exoneration cases.[16] Even the FBI has admitted flaws in hair analyses over decades and has agreed to review thousands of closed criminal cases for errant and faulty forensic testimony.[17]

---

[14] For analytical discussion of the role of forensic science in wrongful convictions, see Garret, 2014; Cooley and Turvey, 2014. A documentation of cases in which faulty forensic evidence seems to have played a critical role can be seen in Champod and Vuille, 2011, a comparative study on scientific evidence drawn up for the Council of Europe. For the phenomenon in China, see Jiang, 2016.

[15] The study was made by Garret and Neufeld, 2009: 9.

[16] The Innocence Project was started in 1992 by Barry Scheck and Peter Neufeld at the Cardozo School of Law and is committed to exonerating wrongly convicted people through the use of DNA testing. Data and statistics are available on the www.innocenceproject.org. Aside misapplication of forensic science, other factors contributing to wrongful convictions are eyewitness misidentification, false confessions, inadequate defence, government misconduct and incentivised informants.

[17] See, for example, Spencer S. Hsu, 'FBI Admits Flaws in Hair Analysis Over Decades', *The Washington Post* (18 April 2015). www.washingtonpost.com/local/crime/fbi-overstated-forensic -hair-matches-in-nearly-all-criminal-trials-for-decades/2015/04/18/39c8d8c6-e515-11e4-b510-962 fcfabc310_story.html?utm_term=.4a7cacoa8d25 (accessed on 21 September 2018).

These statistics and other scholar studies raise a very serious concern: the risk of judicial errors based on faulty forensics is real. *Bad* forensic science, *misleading or misapplied* forensic science and *soft* forensic science may well lead to curtail and compromise the liberty and lives of real people. But judicial errors –and much more wrongful convictions – are the epitome of an 'unfair justice'. Therefore, it is not surprising that wrongful convictions are now viewed as a social problem globally, and an *innocence movement* has been developed (cf. Zalman, 2018). There is a political and moral obligation to avoid judicial errors. So, there is an obligation to take action in that direction.

14.3 PROGRESS AND CHALLENGES

The need to act to avoid judicial errors concerns both fields involved in a forensic analysis: forensic disciplines that perform the analysis and courts that receive and assess the results. Forensic science and law.

'What it should be done' to improve the contribution of forensic science to the judicial system could be expressed in two simple words: prevention and education. *Prevention* for avoiding that faulty forensic evidence reaches the courts. *Education* for equipping judges with the adequate cognitive toolkit to assess the reliability and accuracy of expert testimony and thus decide intelligently. Prevention is the path forward for forensic science. Education is the challenge for the law.

14.3.1 *The (Ethical) Path Forward for Forensic Science: Prevention*

Forensic science has a definite moral dimension: forensic findings reported to the courts have a practical effect on people's lives. So *epistemic* issues involved in forensic evidence are also *ethically relevant*, and thus a forensic science politically and morally committed must do as much as possible to increase the quality of forensic evidence that reaches the courts. Indeed, the 'path forward' for forensic sciences that the NAS Report-2009 identified is a paradigm shift that represents a unique ethical challenge.[18] Improving the 'quality of forensic evidence' is, in a way, improving 'the justice of the justice system'.

The forensic community must do more rigorous systematic research on the several forensic techniques (mainly on those scientifically weaker) to establish their *reliability*, measure their *error rates* and reinforce their *accuracy*. It is necessary that all forensic laboratories follow robust *protocols* to perform the

---

[18]   See Fabricant and Carrington, 2016: 2. Also Mnookin states that 'the danger of erroneous conviction provides both a moral and practical perspective on why reliable and valid forensic science is so important' (Mnookin, 2010: 1212).

analysis, and practitioners pass good *proficiency testing* and receive training to guarantee that the alleged expert is not a pseudo-expert. This is a very important issue for lawyers since proficiency tests reveal clearly what experts can do and how often they make mistakes.[19] Further research is needed to identify the factors that may cause cognitive and contextual biases in experts' judgements and implement pertinent countermeasures to keep forensic examiners from potentially biasing information. Finally, and very importantly, substantial progress needs to be made in the way forensic experts report their findings to the courts.[20] Much of the misunderstandings and misrepresentations between forensic experts and courts are due to the lack of a consistent, appropriate *terminology* in the several fields of forensics. The wording used by experts to convey their findings and conclusions have a significant impact in the courtroom. So, words matter.[21] Particularly numbers have a powerful effect. Numbers and statistics may seem impressive or insufficient.[22] What expert witnesses say may well differ from what fact finders hear. In addition, the practice not only varies among countries and across disciplines but also among (and even within) laboratories. Therefore, it is necessary to standardise the terminology and develop guidelines for reports and testimony, at least, within particular disciplines and, at the best, across them.[23] If forensic experts do not consistently use a common language to report their findings to the courts, the risk to misinterpret the forensic reports and testimonies will not diminish.

Over the past ten years significant progress has been made, and important developments are underway to raise the quality of forensic science in many aspects.

---

[19]   See Mnookin, 2010: 1268, who also suggests that 'these proficiency tests ought to be appropriately difficult and should mirror the range of difficulty found in actual casework'.

[20]   The need for experts to interpret and report their findings to the courts in a right way had already been strongly emphasised by Aitken and Taroni, 2004.

[21]   'Studies with mock jurors indicate that conviction rates systematically vary as a function of minor variations in the wording used to describe forensic science evidence' (Koehler, 2014: 8). See also Garret and Mitchell, 2013.

[22]   An experiment conducted by Mcquiston-Surrett and Saks, 2009 revealed that judges and jurors alike were most impressed with the *qualitative* forms of *testimonial presentation* than they were with quantitative testimony, inferring a higher probability that the defendant was the source of the crime scene mark. This might explain why *conclusion testimony* (experts explicit, ultimate opinion that the defendant was the source), when offered, had a higher effect when findings were presented *quantitatively*: when findings are presented in qualitative forms conclusion testimony has little to add.

[23]   The NAS Report also stresses this point: most forensic science disciplines 'critically need to standardize and clarify the terminology used in reporting and testifying about the results' (NAS Report, 2009: 189). On the need to standardise the terminology used in the forensic science reports (and also – and even more importantly – for a consensus on the evaluation of forensic science results), see Biedermann et al., 2015.

The scientific basis of some forensic disciplines is increasingly improving. For example, studies are already under way to determine the reliability and error rates of fingerprinting analysis (one of the most important and widely used evidence in law enforcement and forensic agencies worldwide) (see Ulery et al., 2011; Cao and Jain, 2017). Conversely, some other disciplines are progressively falling into discredit because their methods lack sufficient validity to continue to be offered as evidence. Actually, several methods have been laid to rest in the recent past and some others are likely next candidates.[24] Important steps have been also taken in the standardisation of forensic laboratories and in the accreditation of practitioners. Crime labs are adopting now more rigorous protocols and also more stringent proficiency tests. Several studies have already been made on contextual and cognitive biases. Procedures have been developed to identify the potential biasing factors and measure experts bias ability and reliability,[25] and efforts are also being made to develop tools for reducing bias ability keeping experts from unnecessary, potentially biasing information; for example, establishing what is the right balance of information necessary for forensic testing and how can unnecessary information be sequentially unmasked to prevent subconscious bias.[26] Finally, significant progress is also being made in a critical issue: forensic report and testimony. Forensic examiners (particularly in the field of pattern-matching techniques, such as fingerprinting, footwear impressions, tool marks, handwriting analysis, and the like) are reaching conclusions in new ways and changing the language they use in reports and testimony (see Thompson et al., 2018). Among other achievements, at the European level it is to be noted the adoption of a common framework for evaluating and reporting forensic findings.[27]

Yet there is still a long way to go. Despite positive progress, more substantial efforts to improve the quality of forensics in the justice system are still to be

[24] This is the case of bitemarks comparison. Other forensic arenas scientifically deficient, such as comparative bullet lead analysis and arson, have been progressively laid to rest. See Saks et al., 2016.

[25] As the method developed by Itiel E. Dror and his collaborators by examining if, when experts judge the same case in two different moments, they reach the same conclusions, e.g., identify the same suspect (see Dror and Rosenthal, 2008). For further development of the method used for quantifying experts reliability and bias ability, see Dror, 2016: 121–7.

[26] The work of Dror and his collaborators is also important in this point. See Dror et al., 2015.

[27] I am referring to the ENFSI Guideline for Evaluative Reporting in Forensic Science. Strengthening the Evaluation of Forensic Results across Europe (STEOFRAE), of 2015, created by ENFSI (European Network of Forensic Science Institutes), a key organisation in Europe bringing together more than sixty laboratories with a vision to share common quality standards and exchange knowledge and expertise. Available at http://enfsi.eu/wp-content/upl oads/2016/09/m1_guideline.pdf.

done. Actually, same concerns expressed by the NAS Report (2009) have been reiterated by the PCAST Report (2016) on *Forensic Science in Criminal Courts: Ensuring Scientific Validity of Feature Comparison Methods.*[28] The Report stresses once again important gaps in some specific feature-comparison methods (such as fingerprinting, firearms, complex DNA mixtures or bite marks analysis) and makes recommendations to strengthen these disciplines. According to the Report, further studies are necessary to test and improve the reliability of those forensic methods and to inform the courts of their error rates. Such research is critical, since 'the claim that two objects have been compared and found to have the same property (length, weight, or fingerprint pattern) is meaningless without quantitative information about the reliability of the comparison process' (PCAST Report, 2016: 62). There is also a need to develop more rigorous proficiency testing (ideally blind proficiency testing, that is, with samples inserted into the flow of casework such that examiners do not know that they are being tested) (PCAST Report, 2016: 158), and similarly it should be assured that all the laboratories and examiners meet the necessary standards to perform the analyses. Ultimately, greater transparency in the labs is crucial. Labs should reveal their mistakes and publicly report quality issues that arise in forensic casework, in a manner similar to the 'quality issue notification system' used by the Netherlands Forensic Institute (NFI) (see Kloosterman et al., 2014: 77–85; Kloostroom, 2014).

In any case, despite the remaining gaps and challenges, there is no doubt that forensic science community is striving to strengthen and reform their disciplines from within, and it could be said that 'a paradigm shift' is underway.[29]

14.3.2 *The Challenge for the Law: Education*

However, this is not enough. Despite the advancement in forensic disciplines and research, a significant obstruction remains to restoring reliability in our criminal justice systems: the courts. The reforms under way in the forensic field will not assure the quality of judicial decisions if there is no actual change in legal culture. Also judges, not just forensic experts, should be key players in ensuring that judicial decisions are based on reliable, accurate forensic science evidence. Actually, that is the real meaning of the *Daubert* ruling in the

---

[28] Report released to the President Barack Obama by the President's Council of Advisors on Science and Technology (PCAST) on September 2016. For the risks remaining in forensic science despite progressive reform, see also Carr et al., 2016.

[29] That is affirmed in the significant title ('The Shifted Paradigm') of a recent study by Fabricant and Carrington, 2016. The new paradigm was anticipated by Zaks and Koeler, 2005.

United States: a call for judges to carefully examine how reliable and accurate expert testimony is.[30] The role of the judiciary in preventing miscarriages of justice based on faulty forensics is critical.

The challenge faced by courts to address the problems raised by forensic evidence at trial may be examined in light of the conceptual opposition *deference* versus *education* as put by Ronald Allen.[31] I consider this approach to be particularly interesting in a threefold sense. Firstly, because *deference* and *education* are respectively consistent with the *uncritical* and *critical* vision of forensic disciplines marked by the hard criticism made within forensic science, so what might be termed the *pre-criticism* and *post-criticism* paradigm in forensic science. Secondly, because it applies to all expert testimonies, not just the forensic science testimonies, thus making it possible to account for a wider variety of proofs. Finally, and most importantly, because it makes it very clear that only *education* (and its parallel in forensic science: the *post-criticism stage*) conforms to the epistemic orientation of adjudication in the rule of law.

14.3.2.1 Deference

Courts tend to be highly deferential to forensic science testimony. They largely (if not blindly) rely on what expert witnesses declare *without critical scrutiny*. To be sure, the only scrutiny they do is mostly superficial or formal, consisting of verifying that experts have the pertinent qualifications (e.g., as a chemist or doctor or engineer) or sufficient training or experience in a legally recognisable field (cf. Martire and Edmond, 2017: 969). Sometimes additional

---

[30] *Daubert v. Merrell Dow Pharmaceuticals, Inc.*, 509 U.S. 579 (1993). In *Daubert* the Supreme Court required an independent judicial assessment of the reliability of expert testimony and pointed to several factors that might be considered by a trial judge: (1) whether the theory or technique on which the proffered expert testimony is premised 'can be (and has been) tested'; (2) whether the theory or technique has been 'subjected to peer review and publication'; (3) 'the known or potential rate of error ... and the existence and maintenance of standards controlling the technique's operation'; and (4) the scientific technique's 'degree of acceptance" within a relevant scientific community. But other than setting the factors, the importance of Daubert lies in the fact that it involves an exhortation to judges to examine more critically scientific expert testimony. For a clear presentation of Daubert's factors, as well as criticism on confusion and misunderstandings concerning them, cf. Haack, 2015: 50 ss. Eloquently Champod and Vuille express this idea: 'The Daubert, Joiner and Kumho trilogy of decisions implicitly emphasises the scepticism which the judge must maintain vis-à-vis the expert, who is thus no longer considered a member of an authoritative elite but a social agent comparable to any other, possibly subject to pressure of a political and economic kind that may impair his discernment' (Champod and Vuille, 2011: 39).

[31] This approach was first exposed by Allen and Miller, 1993. Further development in Allen, 2013.

factors may be considered, such as how long the technique has been in use or whether the technique or the expert had previously been admitted.[32] Indeed, very often judges deal with challenges to expert testimony by looking at what other judges have said.

In a way, strong deference to forensic expert testimony is understandable. Deference is the general attitude towards all kinds of expert testimonies (and not just the forensic science ones), since, lacking sufficient knowledge and experience in a particular area, judges have no capacity to call into question and challenge expert claims, and then, as a matter of logic, they are prompted to rely on them. If, additionally, such expertise is considered to be 'scientific' (as is the case of expertise concerning forensic science techniques and methods), and given the great faith in 'science', then it may be no surprise that courts place heavy (if not blind) reliance on forensic science testimony.[33] In short, confidence in science makes deference to forensic science witnesses quite much stronger.

But an additional reason is likely to account for (and reinforce) deference, namely the fact that experts frequently report their findings to the courts making individualisation claims.[34] Judges and attorneys want clear and definite answers from forensic experts. They expect experts (with their knowledge) to tell them what they need to know to make their decision. For example, they want to know whether 'a latent fingerprint comes (or does not come) from the suspect', and naturally they want the greatest possible certainty. So, when expert witness declares that he or she has found a match between the latent fingerprint and a known exemplar 'with a great degree of certainty', courts are prone to accept that expert has succeeded in identifying the source of the latent print, without asking how reliable and accurate the technique is. In the end, for one reason or another, considerable forensic science evidence makes its way into the courtroom without any scrutiny.

However, there are no reasons for such a strong confidence. Rather, the harsh criticism undergone by forensic science pushes judges to examine the many things that could have gone wrong when forensic science evidence has been obtained and reported to them. Therefore, the legal community has to do what the forensic community has already done: wake up and take notice of their responsibilities in the use of forensics in the courtroom. Courts bear the responsibility to decide by themselves, which means that, before making their

[32] 'Judges are more comfortable repeating past practice (what has been admitted in the past continues to be admitted)' (Koehler, Schweitzer, Saks and Macquiston, 2016: 402).
[33] I have elaborated further on this point in Gascón, 2016: 347 ff.
[34] See the above said about the frequent use of individualisation statements in the identification forensic disciplines: Section 14.2.4.

decision, they must scrutinise (rather than blindly rely on) expert opinions. They have to adopt a non-deferential attitude.

Particularly, when deciding the admissibility of expert testimony, courts should take account of how reliable the technique used is and how accurate are their results. So, they should know if it is based on a reproducible and consistent procedure and what are its error rates (*foundational validity*). If they do not know the performance relative to expert claims, expert assertions about the significance of similarities may be meaningless. Therefore, given the present lack of an adequate research basis supporting validity in most pattern identification arenas, 'exclusion should have a central place in the judicial toolkit' (Mnookin, 2010: 1265). Courts should also ensure that the technique has been reliably applied to the facts of the case (*validity as applied*).[35] So, they should make sure that laboratories met the accepted standards, experts have the adequate competence and performance to rely on their work[36] and no decisive practical aspect in the analysis went wrong.[37] Additionally, courts cannot continue ignoring the risk of bias that can impact experts' judgement. Since biases arise largely from exposure to contextual information, they should do any effort for keeping the expert from all the irrelevant, potentially biasing information on the case. And finally, but very importantly, courts should pay also attention to the risk of overestimating or misinterpreting the findings of the analysis, and so they should check that experts do not make claims or implications beyond the empirical evidence. In essence, similarly to the paradigm shift occurring in the forensic science community, courts need to adopt a new and more rigorous approach to expert evidence. A non-deferential approach.

---

[35] The recommendation for judges to examine the *foundational validity* and the *validity as applied* is explicitly made by the PCAST Report, 2016: 145 ff.

[36] George Reis, a certified analyst in photogrammetry (the technique of determining the form, measurements and position in the space of an object based on visual evidence) says his fellow analysts agree that their science is valid and reliable when it's done well, but *judges tend to be too permissive in terms of who they let testify*. 'The problem is that judges don't want to exclude experts', he says. See 'Forensic video analysis goes under the microscope in Texas', *The Texas Tribune* (15 December 2016), www.texastribune.org/2016/12/15/video-analysis-goes-under-microscope/ (accessed on 24 September 2018).

[37] When a forensic analysis is run, many factors can affect the quality of the results. For example, relating to DNA analysis, evidence must be found in a usable state and properly preserved. When collecting DNA at a crime scene, it is sometimes difficult to obtain samples that are not contaminated with another person's DNA, making results unreliable. The DNA can be degraded or of poor quality; the laboratory analysts who run the tests sometimes make mistakes; the final determination about whether a DNA profile matches that of a suspect is subject to interpretation, etc. On the several problems that may affect the results of a DNA tests, see Murphy, 2015.

Unfortunately, although forensic science has never experienced greater scientific scrutiny than it does today (Saks et al., 2016: 540), things have not changed much in courts. The wave of reforms attendant to the forensic science disciplines seems to have eluded lawyers. Legal culture relating forensic science remains very much intact, and courts continue to pay strong deference to expert testimony. Even once a field of forensics or a particular expert has been discredited, courts continue to trust them, which shows how poorly they scrutinise expert testimony.[38] In addition, that recalcitrant attitude has a sort of accumulative effect, because if reliability of a forensic technique is challenged at trial the answer is a judicial precedent: other courts have expressed the same confidence on it.

Yet deference must be abandoned. On the one hand, for institutional reasons. Deference is not consistent with a system that attributes to the judges (independent and impartial) the institutional role of making decisions on the facts of the case. According to that role, it is the judges (not the experts) to assess all the evidence, including forensic evidence. However, when courts pay considerable deference to expert testimony, namely when they accept their claims without previously examining how reliable and accurate they are, it could be said that it is the expert himself (not the court) who makes the decision on the facts in issue. The role of fact-finder shifts to the expert, and therefore a new system of proof grounded on experts' authority is being adopted. In a nutshell: deference implies that experts usurp the role of fact-finders.

But there is a more decisive reason to abandon deference: deference is at odds with the epistemic orientation of adjudication in the rule of law.[39] Immanent in the concept of rule of law – as developed by contemporary western legal systems – there is the idea that only decisions based on accurate statements on the facts in issue are legitimate. However, when courts act

---

[38]   The history of bite mark jurisprudence shows this recalcitrant deferential attitude. As it reads in an editorial of *The Washington Post*, 'In the 1990s, DNA testing began to show that bite mark analysis wasn't as reliable as its practitioners claimed. We now know that such analysis has led to more than two dozen wrongful arrests and convictions. And a growing number of studies have found no scientific evidence to support its two core assumptions – that teeth are as unique as fingerprints and that human skin can record this uniqueness with enough detail to identify someone. Yet to date, every time a defendant has challenged the scientific validity of bite mark analysis, the court has upheld it. Judges point out that lots of other courts across the country have ruled that bite mark evidence is legitimate.' See Balko and Carrington, 'Bad science puts innocent people in jail and keeps them there', *The Washington Post* (21 March 2018). Available at www.washingtonpost.com /outlook/bad-science-puts-innocent-people-in-jail–and-keeps-them-there/2018/03/20/fifffd08-263e-11e8-b79d-f3d931db7f68_story.html?noredirect=on&utm_term=.c7946e5bc438 (consulted on 22 September 2018).

[39]   This is the central point raised by Ronald J. Allen to abandon deference (Allen, 2013).

deferentially factual accuracy is not granted, and thus the chances of mistakes increase. Deference, indeed, implies that judges decide without further scrutiny on expert testimony, and thus unintelligently, without understanding the reasons for their decision. That amounts to saying that deferential decisions are not based on knowledge, and thus they may well lead to accept flawed or invalid science (*junk science*, to quote the famous expression made popular by Peter Huber, 1991), data based on poor or spurious science or faulty analysis which can contribute to judicial errors. Actually, as said above, legal community is starting to concede (with varying degrees of urgency, depending on the countries) that our systems produce erroneous convictions based on discredit or poor-quality forensics (cf. Metzger, 2006: 475, 491). So, for epistemic but also political and moral reasons deference should be overcome.

Again, no matter the advancement in the forensic science field, as long as judges fail to decide by themselves, understanding why they decide what they do, the quality of judicial decisions based on forensic evidence will not be entirely guaranteed. If courts keep on relying on expert testimonies without further scrutiny, if they do not push for rigour in the courtroom, if they keep on refusing to examine the expert's competence and performance or permitting them to testify beyond the scope of their ambiguous findings, the accuracy of their decisions will not be assured.

14.3.2.2 Education

However, there is a difficulty for overcoming deference. In general, judges are scientifically illiterate. They usually lack the necessary knowledge and skills to evaluate the forensic expert testimony.[40] They are not adequately equipped to determine how reliable the forensic method used in the analysis is or how much weight – if any – to give to the evidence obtained, which impedes them from questioning or scrutinising expert testimony and lead them to rely on external cues, such as the expert's credentials.[41] They are trained to do legal

---

[40] It has also been highlighted by NAS Report 2009, at 12: 'The judicial system is encumbered by, among other things, judges and lawyers who generally lack the scientific expertise necessary to comprehend and evaluate forensic evidence in an informed manner.'

[41] It is the disinformation about the soundness of the methodology used to obtain the evidence which lead the judges to rely on expert testimony under the assumption that the expert's credentials in a particular field of knowledge guarantee his/her competence (Igartua, 2007: 1). And it is also the disinformation which may account for the fact that 'expressing limitations of forensic science' (e.g. telling the jurors that a forensic science method has not been thoroughly and scientifically tested) seems to have little influence on the way jurors weight the evidence provided, as revealed by the experiments conducted by Mcquiston-Surrett and Saks, 2009; and Koehler et al., 2016: 401–13.

analyses, not scientific ones, and thus they have a difficulty in evaluating and responding to unreliable and unscientific evidence.

Remarkably, lack of some statistical understanding may raise serious problems, as it may lead judges astray when interpreting the meaning of the evidence. Statistics plays a critical role in the interpretation of the forensic findings. Forensic science disciplines are based on mainly probabilistic laws, and data expressed in expert reports and testimonies are often statistical data which interpretation may be complex and counterintuitive. Additionally, it is well demonstrated that statistical data has a major effect on people in general and judges in particular. Therefore, lacking some statistical knowledge misinterpretations of statistical data (such as the *source probability error* and the *prosecutor's fallacy*)[42] are very common and can result in a wrongful conviction.[43] Even someone as seasoned and quantitative-skilled as Richard Posner, one of America's most renowned, influential judges and legal writers, makes this kind of flawed probability arguments.[44]

Therefore, if we want judges to decide rationally, so if we want them to overcome deference and decide intelligently, then it is self-evident that they must be better educated. There is no other solution to the problems posed by expert testimony: either judges must be provided somehow with the necessary

[42]   There is abundant literature on these two very similar probability fallacies. See, for example, Koehler, 2014. The author says, concerning the *source probability error*, that many people use to think that the probabilities associated to a DNA match (such as one in one billion) identifies the probability that the matched is or is not the source of a recovered DNA sample. However, 'this latter probability cannot be identified absent a factfinder's estimate of the "prior probability" (i.e., prior to the DNA analysis) that the matched is the source of the evidence. The prior probability depends on non-forensic factors including, but not limited to, the strength of the non-forensic evidence presented in the case (e.g., eyewitness testimony, motive). In other words, counter-intuitive though it may seem, the results of a DNA analysis cannot be translated directly into a probability that someone is or is not the source of DNA evidence ... Since the earliest days of DNA evidence, judges, attorneys, jurors and experts alike have been committing the source probability error' (Koehler, 2014: 6). On the source probability error, see also Aitken and Taroni, 2004: 81–2; Jamieson and Boder, 2016: 300. On the prosecutor fallacy, see Thompson and Schumann, 1987: 167 ff; Thomson, 2009; Leung, 2002: 44–50; Jamieson and Boder, 2016: 300; Carracedo, 1999.

[43]   According to some studies, the majority of wrongful DNA matches and errors originated in the *post-analytical stage* (i.e., statistical evaluation of the analysis results or reporting the conclusions). See Kloostroom, 2014. Some of the most high-profile judicial mistakes associated to the use of forensic evidence are due to the misuse or misinterpretation of statistical data. In Europe, the case of Lucia de Berk, in the Netherlands, is very well known. For a description of the case, see Meester et al., 2006.

[44]   See Koehler, 2014. Posner's ruling examined by Koehler is *U.S. v. Herrera*, 704 F.3d 480 (2013). Of course, it is not just Posner to commit that kind of mistakes. Another example of the source probability error that was considered by the US Supreme Court, in *McDaniel v. Brown*, 558 US 120 (2010).

background to decide by themselves, or they must defer to the judgement of others (Beety, 2016: 20; Allen, 2013: 50). Judicial decision will only be rational if based on knowledge and understanding, and for that some education is needed.[45]

Education to properly understand what forensic analyses can provide and be aware of its limits. So, education to evaluate the reliability of the evidence (whether the method or procedure used are controversial, or error rates are known, or the results have been overstated or overvalued in transmission, or expert judgement can be biased, or expert is competent, etc.) and assess its probative weight, without undervaluing or overvaluing it. Just with *awareness* of what forensic science can provide in actual terms and *knowledge* for understanding what expert testimony is saying courts will be able to transform themselves and keep their decisions from unreliable forensic evidence. And just an informed judiciary can contribute to a better-quality justice. Conversely, without some educational basis for understanding expert testimony the evidence becomes literally uninterpretable and this should argue in favour of deference.

The fact that an opposing expert may contradict expert testimony is of the most importance, but it does not change things much. It may appear that confrontation of testimonies and vigorous cross-examination does assure a more rational, impartial decision. But the fact is that judges have to choose between them,[46] and lacking the scientific background to make such judgement their decision *will not be based on knowledge* but otherwise. Usually, on the ability of one of the parties to 'persuade' them, for example by presenting a large number of expert witnesses that the other party is not capable to counteract because of its cost. In addition, this situation embodies an unequal position of the parties depending on the costs that each one can (or is willing to) assume, and thus the principle of equality of arms will also be broken.[47] So, summing up, if judges lack the adequate education to understand the expert testimony they have to assess, their decisions will not be epistemically grounded. They will not be rational.

---

[45] Carmen Vázquez seems to be of different opinion. She advocates for education only for systems where expert witnesses are presented by the parties but defends a deferential model for expert witnesses designated by the court (Vázquez, 2015).

[46] The problem courts have to face when there is a disagreement between experts about a relevant evidentiary issue is thoroughly examined by Roberts (2013: 169 ff.) taking as a case-study *Henderson*, which resolved conjointly the appeals of three different convictions for the death of babies supposedly shaken.

[47] For analytical discussion on the violation of equality of arms in both inquisitorial and accusatorial systems due to the lack of scientific knowledge and resources of the part of the defence, see Champod and Vuille, 2011: 30–1.

Educating judges aims to *increase and strengthen their cognitive basis to permit them an informed, rational decision.* Therefore, education may be achieved in different ways.

Expert reports may and must be a precious source of information. So, in a way, they may and (according to the most thoughtful and critical approach in forensic science) must have an educational dimension. Reports *complete* (describing methods and materials, procedures, results, and conclusions) and *thorough* (identifying the sources of uncertainty in the procedures and conclusions along with estimates of their scale to indicate the level of confidence in the results) will provide sufficient content 'to allow the nonscientist reader to understand what has been done and permit informed, unbiased scrutiny of the conclusion'.[48] Therefore, judges should require the experts, when necessary, to provide them with this kind of educational reports.

But complete and rigorous expert report, being critical, may not be sufficient, and parallel sources of education can be tried. For example, it could be beneficial to have some *scientific independent entity* which may assist courts in hard or complicate cases, such as the one suggested by The Law Commission for the United Kingdom[49] or that suggested by Christophe Champod and Joëlle Vuille for Europe, consisting in establishing a European body 'to act as the main adviser to political and judicial authorities on the reliability of the scientific techniques that are used'.[50] And, of course, it would also be of most benefit to establish public *education programmes* to train the members of the judiciary on the challenges raised by forensics[51] and to push *law schools* to incorporate courses in forensic science in their curricula:[52] education on the

---

[48] NAS Report, 2009: 186 underlines this requirement for expert reports.

[49] In the Report: *The Admissibility of Expert Evidence in Criminal Proceedings in England and Wales. A new Approach to the Determination of Evidentiary Reliability* (2009), The Law Commission suggested the possibility that, in hard or complicate cases, the courts may call upon the assistance of an independent assessor to help them to determine whether the expert evidence is sufficiently reliable (paragraph 6.67).

[50] 'Such a body would not have binding powers, but could nevertheless issue recommendations to domestic courts that would assist judges when they had to rule on the admissibility of a new forensic technique or the reliability of a new form of evidence, or when it seemed appropriate to abandon a form of evidence that had become obsolete' (Champod and Vuille, 2011: 54).

[51] Significantly, among the recommendations made by PCAST Report (2016) was the need for better resources to support judicial training in the evaluation of forensic evidence (at 144–5). In Spain, for example, the General Council of the Judiciary could include that training in its frequent ongoing judicial training programmes.

[52] Explicitly, the NAS Report 2009 (at 236) pointed to law schools as 'the best way to get lawyers and judges up to speed' in forensic science. Also William Twining, under the suggestion of 'taking facts seriously' (Twining, 2009), and taking account of the interdisciplinary nature of many important aspects of 'evidence in law' (Twining, 2013), push for incorporating the study of forensic science to the law education programmes.

nature and methods of science; on the several forensic techniques, or at least the most commonly used; on the technical terms used; and on the meaning of statistical data. On the other hand, given the fact that scientific knowledge is not state-constricted, perhaps the call for education should be expanded to include an international or cosmopolitan dimension.[53]

With regard to the latter (educating the judiciary), it is sometimes objected that it would be 'quite impracticable to provide the judges with sufficient expertise of its own to avoid deference'.[54] To put it simply: science education for judges is not considered a realistic purpose. However, this is a somewhat hasty objection. Education does not aim to transform judges into mathematicians or experts in the several fields of expertise they may handle. The purpose of education is not (because it cannot be) to turn judges into amateur scientists. Education aims only to equip judges with sufficient information to understand what the expert witness is saying, and thus decide intelligently. Namely, to understand what has be done, permit informed scrutiny of the conclusions, and understand what can go wrong: techniques that are in discredit or lack sufficient validation, poor quality of practice in the labs, relevant evidence that has been neglected or distorted in transmission, biases that can have influenced expert judgement, supposed experts who are plausible but untrustworthy pseudo-experts, or blatant reasoning errors or fallacies when interpreting and reporting statistical data.[55] This is a modest goal, and there is no reason to underestimate the ability of judges to achieve this understanding and spot flaws to forensic science work.[56]

Naturally, educating judges is not a panacea for ensuring the quality of the decisions based on expert evidence, since it can be assumed that education will always be imperfect, and in any case it would be difficult to keep judges permanently educated in all kinds of expertise they may face. And naturally

[53] In the book edited by Roberts and Redmayne, 2007, Callen (at 159), and Jackson (at 291) stress the cosmopolitan dimension of law of evidence. Much more – it could be said – when it comes to the scientific evidence.

[54] That reads in the report *The Admissibility of Expert Evidence in Criminal Proceedings in England and Wales*, 2009 (paragraph 2.5, at 8). Susan Haack also writes: 'there's simply no way to bring (let alone keep) judges up to speed on every kind of expert testimony with which they may be faced. There are just too many potentially legally relevant fields of expertise. It's impossible to solve the problem . . . by making judges experts on everything' (Haack, 2015: 66).

[55] For example, though statistical education may seem a complicated issue to many, some of the mistakes related to statistics could be certainly avoided with just a limited understanding of the probability theory. In any case, there is also the possibility (and even the necessity) for experts to assist the courts in the tricky cases. See Lucena et al., 2015.

[56] See Allen, 2013: 51: 'The deficits of juridical fact finders do not appear to be cognitive; they are informational. Judges and jurors lack knowledge about many things, like science and technology, but there is no reason that they could not adequately master the relevant fields'.

education is not the only way to face the problems raised by potentially faulty forensic evidence. For example, Susan Haack suggests as a better strategy to shift our focus to earlier in the process to reduce the incidence of bad stuff reaching the courts (malpractices in the research and the promotion of a technique, frauds in the laboratories, incompetent experts, avoidable biases, etc.) and to increase the likelihood that it will get exposed quickly if it does (Haack, 2015: 69). In short, she claims that *prevention is better than cure.* I cannot agree more with her. In fact, I have argued before that prevention is the (ethical) 'path forward' that forensic community has to go, which among others implies strengthening the foundation of the forensic techniques, ensuring the quality of the practice in laboratories, and reporting the findings in a complete and rigorous way (including all the relevant information and avoiding confusing or misleading expressions). *But still, education is necessary.* Without suitable education there will always be the risk of accepting as sound evidence what in actual fact lacks any serious foundation, which ultimately undermines the fairness of the decision.[57] Without education the cognitive basis of judicial decisions weakens and risk of error increases.

REFERENCES

Allen, R. J. (2013). The Conceptual Challenge of Expert Evidence, *Discusiones filosóficas*, 14(23), 41–65.

Aitken, C. and Taroni, F. (2004). *Statistics and the Evaluation of Evidence for Forensic Scientists*, 2nd ed., Chichester: John Wiley and Sons Ltd.

Allen, R. J. and Miller, J. S. (1993). The Common Law Theory of Experts: Deference or Education? *Northwestern University Law Review*, 87, 1131–47.

Balding, D. J. and Bucleton, J. (2009). Interpreting Low Template DNA Profiles, *Forensic Science International: Genetics*, 4(1), 1–10.

Beety, V. E. (2016). Cops in Lab Coats and Forensic in the Courtrooms, *Ohio State Journal of Criminal Law*, 13(2), 543–65.

Biedermann, A., Vuille, J., Taroni, F. and Champod C. (2015). The Need for Reporting Standards in Forensic Science, *Law, Probability and Risk*, 14 (2), 169–73.

Cao, K. and Jain, A. K. (2017). Automated Latent Fingerprints Recognition, *IEEE Transactions on Pattern Analysis and Machine Intelligence*, 41(4), 788–800.

Carr, S., Piasecki, E., Tully, G. and Wilson, T. J. (2016). Opening the Scientific Expert's Black Box, *Journal of Criminal Law*, 80(5), 364–86.

---

[57]   See for example, Grace et al., 2011, who advocate for educating judges and juries so that they are correctly informed of the uncertainty margins regarding the results of the forensics tests.

Carracedo, A. (1999). Valoración de la prueba del ADN, in *La prueba del ADN en la medicina forense. La genética al servicio de la ley*, B. Martínez Jarreta ed., Barcelona: Masson.

Champod, C. and Vuille, J. (2011). Scientific Evidence in Europe. Admissibility, Appraisal and Equality of Arms, *International Commentary on Evidence*, 9 (1), 1–68.

Chin, J. and Workewych, L. (2016). The CSI Effect, *Oxford Handbooks Online*, DOI 10.1093/oxfordhb/9780199935352.013.28.

Cole, S. (2009). Forensics without Uniqueness, Conclusions without Individualization: The New Epistemology of Forensic Identification, *Law, Probability and Risk* 8(3), 233–55.

Cole, S. (2012). Forensic Science and Wrongful Convictions: From Exposer, to Contributor to Corrector, *New England Law Review*, 46, 711–36.

Cole, S. and Dioso-Villa, R. (2009). Investigating the CSI Effect: Media and Litigation Crisis in Criminal Law, *Stanford Law Review* 61(6), 1335–74.

Cooley, C. and Turvey, B. (2014). *Miscarriages of Justice. Actual Evidence, Forensic Evidence and the Law*, Oxford: Academic Press.

Cunliffe, E. and Edmond, G. (2017). Reviewing Wrongful Convictions in Canada, *Criminal Law Quarterly*, 64 (3–4), 473–86.

Dror, I. (2016). A Hierarchy of Expert Performance, *Journal of Applied Research in Memory and Cognition*, 5(2), 121–7.

Dror, I. (2018). Biases in Forensic Experts, *Science*, 360 (6386), 243.

Dror, I. E., Charlton, D., and Péron, A. E. (2006). Contextual Information Renders Experts Vulnerable to Making Erroneous Identifications, *Forensic Science International*, 156(1), 74–8.

Dror, I. and Rosenthal, R. (2008). Meta-Analytically Quantifying the Reliability and Biasability of Forensic Experts, *Journal of Forensic Sciences*, 53(4), 900–3.

Dror, I., Thompson, W., Meissner, Kornfield, I. , Krane, D., Saks, M. and Risinger, M. (2015). Context Management Toolbox: A Linear Sequential Unmasking (LSU) Approach for Minimizing Cognitive Bias in Forensic Decision Making, *Journal of Forensic Siences*, 60(4), 1111–12.

Fabricant, C. and Carrington, W. T. (2016). The Shifted Paradigm: Forensic Sciences's Overdue Evolution from Magic to Law, *Virginia Journal of Criminal Law*, 4(1), 1–115.

Garret, B. L. (2014). Wrongful Convictions and the Role of Forensic Science, in Jamieson, A. and Moenssens, A. eds., *Wiley Online Encyclopaedia of Forensic Science*, Chichester: John Wiley and Sons.

Garret, B. and Neufeld P. (2009). Invalid Forensic Science Testimony and Wrongful Convictions, *Virginia Law Review*, 95 (1), 1–97.

Garret, B. and Mitchell, G. (2013). How Jurors Evaluate Fingerprint Evidence: The Relative Importance of Match Language, Method

Information, and Error Acknowledgment, *Journal of Empirical Legal Studies*, 10, 484–511.

Gascón, M. (2016). Conocimientos expertos y deferencia del juez. Apuntes para la superación de un problema, DOXA. *Cuadernos de Filosofía del Derecho*, 39, 347–65.

Grace, V., Midgley, G., Veth, J. and Ahuriri-Driscoll, A. (2011). *Forensic DNA Evidence on Trial: Science and Uncertainty in the Courtroom*. Litchfield Park, AZ: Emergent Publications.

Guerra Thompson, A. (2015). *Cops in Lab Coats. Curbing Wrongful Convictions through Independent Forensic Laboratories*, Durham, NC: Carolina Academic Press.

Haack, S. (2015). The Expert Witness: Lessons from the U.S. Experience, *Humana Mente*, 28(2015), 39–70.

Huber, P. (1991). *Galileo's Revenge: Junk Science in the Courtroom*, New York: New York Basic Books.

Igartua, J. (2007). Prueba científica y decisión judicial: unas anotaciones propedéuticas, *Diario La Ley*, 6812 (2/11).

Jamieson, A. and Boder, S., eds. (2016). *A Guide to Forensic DNA Profiling*, Chichester: John Wiley and Sons.

Jiang, N. (2016). *Wrongful Convictions in China. Comparative and Empirical Perspectives*, Berlin: Springer.

Kaye, D. H. (2010). Probability, Individualization and Uniqueness in Forensic Science: Listening to the Academies, *Brooklyn Law Review*, 75(4), 1163–86.

Koehler, J. (2014). Forensic Fallacies and a Famous Judge, *Jurimetrics*, 54(3), 211–19.

Koehler, J., Schweitzer, N. J., Saks, M. J. and Macquiston, D. E. (2016). Science, Technology, or the Expert Witness: What Influences Jurors' Judgments About Forensic Science Testimony? *Psychology, Public Policy and Law*, 22(4), 401–13.

Kloosterman, A., Sjerps, M. and Quak, A. (2014). Error Rates in Forensic DNA Analysis: Definition, Numbers, Impact and Communication, *Forensic Science International: Genetics*, 12, 77–85.

Kloostroom, A. (2014). *Framework for Registration, Classification and Evaluation of errors in the Forensic DNA Typing Process*, Nederlands Forensich Instituut. Available: www.nist.gov/forensics/upload/Kloosterma n-DNA.pdf.

Leung, W. C. (2002). The Prosecutor's Fallacy – A Pitfall in Interpreting Probabilities in Forensic Evidence, *Medicine Science and the Law*, 42(1), 44–50.

Lucena, J. J., Gascón, M. and Pardo, V. (2015). Technical Support for a Judge when Assessing A Priori Odds, *Law, Probability and Risk*, 14(2), 147–68.

Martire, K. A. and Edmond, G. (2017). 'Rethinking Expert Opinion Evidence', *Melbourne University Law Review*, 40 (3), 967–98.

Mcquiston-Surrett, D. and Saks, M. J. (2009). The Testimony of Forensic Identification Science: What Expert Witnesses Say and What Facfinders Hear', *Law and Human Behaviour*, 33(5), 436–53.

Meester, R., Collins, M., Gill, R., and Van Lambalgen, M. (2006). On the (ab) Use of Statistics in the Legal Case against the nurse Lucia de B. Law, Probability and Risk, 5(3–4), 233–50.

Metzger, P. (2006). Cheating the Constitution, *Vanderbilt Law Review*, 59 (2),475–538.

Mnookin, J. (2010). The Courts, the NAS, and the Future of Forensic Science, *Brooklyn Law Review*, 75 (4), 1208–75.

Murphy, E. (2015). *Inside the Cell: The Dark Side of Forensic DNA*, New York: Nation Books.

National Research Council of the National Academy of Sciences (NAS) (2009). Report, *Strengthening Scientific Evidence in the United States: A Path Forward*, Washington DC: The National Academies Press.

Office of the Inspector General. US Department of Justice, 2006: Report on Mayfield: A Review of the FBI's handling of the Brandon Mayfield Case. www.justice.gov/oig/special/s0601/final.pdf.

President's Council of Advisors on Science and Technology (PCAST), (2016) Report, *Forensic Science in Criminal Courts: Ensuring Scientific Validity of Feature-Comparison Methods.* https://obamawhitehouse.archives.gov/sites/d efault/files/microsites/ostp/PCAST/pcast_forensic_science_report_final.pdf.

Roberts, P. (2013). ¿Fue el bebé sacudido? Prueba, pericia y epistemología jurídica en el proceso penal inglés, in *Estándares de prueba y prueba científica*, C. Vázquez, ed., Madrid: Marcial Pons, 135–80.

Roberts, P. and Redmayne M., eds. (2007). *Innovations in Evidence and Proof: Integrating Theory, Research and Teaching*, Oxford: Bloomsbury Publishing.

Saks, M. J. and Koehler, J. (2005). The Coming Paradigm Shift in Forensic Science, *Science* 309(5736), 892–5.

Saks, M. J. and Koehler, J. (2008). The Individualization Fallacy in Forensic Science Evidence, *Vanderbilt Law Review*, 61(1), 199–219.

Saks, M. J. and Koehler, J. (2010). Individualization Claims in Forensic Science: Still Unwarranted, *Brooklyn Law Review*, 75(4), 1187–208.

Saks, M. J., Albright, T., Bohan, T. L., Bierer, B. E., Bowers, C. M., Bush, M. A. et al. (2016). Forensic Bitemark Identification: Weak Foundations, Exaggerated Claims. *Journal of Law and the Biosciences*, 3(3), 538–75.

Schweitzer, N. J. and Saks, M. J. (2007). The CSI Effect: Popular Fiction About Forensic Science Affects Public Expectations About Real Forensic Science, *Jurimetrics* 47, 357–64.

Taroni, F., Aitken, C., Garbolino, P. and Biedermann, A. (2006) *Bayesian Networks and Probabilistic Inference in Forensic Science*, Chichester: John Wiley and Sons Ltd.

The Law Comission (2009) Report *The Admissibility of Expert Evidence in Criminal Proceedings in England and Wales. A New Approach to the Determination of Evidentiary Reliability*, www.lawcom.gov.uk/expert_evidence.htm.

Thompson, W. C. (2006). Tarnish on the 'Gold Standard': Understanding Recent Problems in Forensic DNA Testing. *The Champion*, 30(1), 10–16.

Thompson, W. C. (2009). Letter to the Editor – The Prosecutor's Fallacy in George Clarke's. Justice and Science: Trials and Triumphs of DNA Evidence, *Journal of Forensic Sciences*, 54(2), 504–5.

Thompson, W. C. and Chumann, E. (1987). Interpretation of Statistical Evidence in Criminal Trials. The Prosecutor's Fallacy and the Defense Attorney Fallacy, *Law and Human Behaviour* 11(3), 167–87.

Thompson, W. C., Vuille, J., Taroni, F., Biedermann, A., (2018). After Uniqueness: The Evolution of Forensic Science Opinions, *Judicature*, 102 (1), 18–27.

Twining, W. (2009). De nuevo, los hechos en serio, *DOXA*, 32, 317–39.

Twining, W. (2013). Moving Beyond Law: Interdisciplinarity and the Study of Evidence', in *Evidence, Inference and Inquiry*, Dawid, P., Twinning, W. Vasilaki, M. , eds., British Academy Scholarship Online.

Ulery, B. T. et al. (2011). Accuracy and Reliability of Forensic Latent Fingerprint Decisions, *Proceedings of the National Academy of Sciences*, 108 (19). DOI: 10.1073/pnas.1018707108.

Vázquez, C. (2015). *De la prueba científica a la prueba pericial*, Madrid-Barcelona: Marcial Pons.

Zalman, M. (2018). Wrongful Convictions: Comparative Perspectives. *Cambridge Handbook of Social Problems*, Cambridge: Cambridge University Press, 448–80.

15

Evidentiary Practices and Risks of Wrongful Conviction

An Empirical Perspective

Mauricio Duce J.

15.1 INTRODUCTION

There is no criminal justice system in the world that can prevent mistakes from being made in some cases.[1] Not only would it be an illusion to claim that the system is infallible, it would also reveal a lack of understanding of how it actually works and indeed of what happens in any human enterprise. In effect, criminal justice forms part of a very complex system, in which a large number of actors with very different objectives intervene, in which serious and very dissimilar events are investigated, and in which the number of interacting factors can generate defects that increase the chances of wrong decisions being made. This is without taking into consideration that judicial systems usually have structural limitations when it comes to reconstructing past events and clarifying the truth.[2]

In this scenario, the problem does not lie in a theoretical possibility that criminal justice systems may make mistakes. At the end of the day, the risk of erring is a variable that must be lived with. The problem, rather, is that the empirical evidence in recent years indicates that errors are more frequent than

---

[1] Among these mistakes, those that are probably more serious and paradigmatic occur at opposite extremes. On the one hand, there are cases in which an innocent person is convicted (also called false positives) and, at the other extreme, in which a guilty party is acquitted ('false negatives'). In between, there are many other types of error. As I will note below, the focus of this work is on the wrongful conviction of innocent people and other similar mistakes.

[2] The reasons are multiple, and it is impossible to make an exhaustive list of them. By way of example only, one can mention the difficulty involved in reconstructing past events that have often occurred long ago; others without clear evidence at the beginning of the investigation, and not infrequently with scarce investigative resources. To this must be added that processes of reconstructing the truth are regulated, with many rules that impose limitations on reaching the truth in order to safeguard other relevant values (e.g., the exclusion of evidence obtained by infringing fundamental rights).

is intuitively believed, cause enormous damage to those who suffer them, and arise for perfectly avoidable reasons. We know today, then, that mistakes are more common than we usually believe, and go beyond the mere possibility that criminal justice systems have in the abstract to be wrong. Moreover, errors occur as a result of system practices that could be corrected if we had identified them in advance.

At present, both in the Anglo-Saxon world and in continental Europe the study of one type of error – the conviction of innocent people – has gained enormous importance, attracting growing academic research[3] and indeed giving birth to an activism aimed at obtaining the exoneration of innocent victims of unjust court convictions.[4] This has generated a level of information that we lacked until a couple of decades ago. One of the issues that has produced the greatest number of studies has been identifying factors that increase the probability that convictions of innocent people will occur.[5] Among its results is a consensus that a group of 'evidentiary practices'[6] exists that may explain the errors. In other words, when such practices are present,

[3] The literature that reviews academic research in the field is very extensive. By way of example, I refer to two recent books that contain chapters with research and comparative analysis of the problem, including countries like Germany, Canada, Spain, the United States, Holland, England, Italy, Israel, Poland, and Switzerland (Huff and Killias, 2010; Huff and Killias, 2013). This concern has reached distant latitudes as in the case of China (Jiahong, 2016). As can be seen, these works show that it is a concern that goes far beyond the systems of the Anglo-Saxon tradition.

[4] The best-known work is that carried out by the Innocence Project. Created in the United States in 1992 by Barry Scheck and Peter Neufeld, this institution is dedicated to exonerating people wrongly convicted by demonstrating their innocence, mainly through the use of DNA evidence. More information is available at: www.innocenceproject.org (last accessed on 21 May 2018). Less known, but with more international work, is the Innocence Network, which is a network of institutions dedicated to providing free legal and investigative services to exonerate people wrongly convicted. In addition to affiliates in the United States, it includes institutions from Australia, Canada, France, Holland, Italy, Ireland, New Zealand, the United Kingdom and South Africa. www.innocencenetwork.org/members (last accessed on 21 May 2018). Others estimated that by 2016 there were fifty-five 'innocence projects' or related organisations in the United States and another fourteen outside the country (Gould and Leo, 2016: 7).

[5] The literature with empirical research on the subject is also very extensive. One of the texts that I most recommend for those starting their study has a detailed analysis of cases, including a study of the background of, and transcripts from, the first 250 cases exonerated by the Innocence Project of the United States (Garret, 2011).

[6] For the purposes of this chapter, I will understand by 'evidentiary practices' the group of behaviours of the criminal justice system that are associated with the production, incorporation, litigation and evaluation of different means of proof or sources of information of the system. My intention in using this expression is not to establish a conceptually rigorous or sophisticated category but to have a sufficiently broad umbrella under which I can group different system behaviours.

the likelihood of an error or the outright conviction of an innocent increases significantly.[7]

In this context, the present chapter aims to describe, from the evidence available, the most problematic evidentiary practices in relation to the use of expert evidence. According to the empirical data available this is one of the most relevant factors in the system's production of wrong decisions. Based on a more refined diagnosis of which practices are most problematic in the use of this evidence I hope to make it possible, first of all, to gauge the system's weaknesses. This will allow me to develop proposals and strategies for risk prevention and minimisation (reduction of unnecessary damage). Diminishing and anticipating errors (not eliminating them) not only seems a realistic goal or a reasonable aspiration, but also an imperative for the system.

To achieve the objective described, the chapter is divided into three sections. In the first, I very briefly review, in general, the main findings of the available research on the incidence of errors in the criminal justice system and the factors that increase the likelihood of their occurrence. The second section reviews knowledge accumulated by research in the field of expert evidence. With this purpose is mind, I use both the evidence available at a comparative level, particularly but not solely in the United States, as well as the results of my own empirical research conducted in Chile. Finally, the third section concludes with some brief thoughts on the type of proposals that we need to aim at in efforts to solve the problems identified.

15.2 ERRORS OF THE CRIMINAL JUSTICE SYSTEM AND FACTORS INCREASING THEIR LIKELIHOOD

It is very difficult to determine precisely the number of cases in which there is a conviction of innocent people, and even more difficult in those cases in

---

[7] Until now I have spoken indistinctly of system errors and wrongful conviction, even though these concepts are different. When I speak of system errors, I refer to a much broader category of problems in the functioning of criminal justice in which, as I suggested previously, cases can be included in which an innocent person is wrongly convicted. However, but others also belong to it in which there is no such sentence. Thus, for example, system errors would include situations such as the acquittal of the guilty; failure to prosecute crimes that have actually been committed; and the arrest and detention in custody during trial of innocent people without their subsequent conviction, among others. I share the opinion of Forst, who maintains that while many cases of systemic error do not answer to the same problem as the conviction of innocents, if they concern people who have suffered deprivation of liberty without sentence, the factors causing them are similar and their effects equally devastating. For this reason, I include this last category in my analysis, to which I will refer as cases of 'wrongful accusation' to distinguish them from convictions (Forst, 2013: 17).

which errors are committed with serious consequences for the accused, but without there necessarily having been a conviction – cases that I group in the category of 'wrongful accusations.' A first calculation method (statistical evidence) has been through studies that attempt to identify a statistical error rate based on certain categories of crimes where information is available about wrongful convictions. The second method (anecdotal evidence) has been by listing individual cases in which it was established, through the use of some mechanism of exoneration, that an innocent person was convicted. Unfortunately, neither of these two estimates can give us a very accurate picture of reality since the real number of wrongful convictions and other types of error is estimated to be far greater than those formally recorded.

In the United States, efforts have been made to generate what I call statistical evidence, even though this is a relatively underdeveloped line of research that has been questioned on several grounds. For example, in 2007 Risinger was able to work out a rate at which wrongful convictions could occur, based on cases with death sentences for crimes of rape-homicide during the 1980s. His analysis led him to conclude that the error rate in the United States for this type of case varied between 3.3 per cent of the cases (the most conservative figure) and 5 per cent (the highest reasonable figure) (Risinger, 2007). In 2008, Gross, for his part, estimated that in cases punishable by the death sentence between 1973 and 1989, the error rate would be between 2.3 per cent and 5 per cent of convictions, and in rape crimes it would rise to a percentage between 3.2 and 5 per cent (Gross, 2008: 7). Again, in 2014, Gross together with other researchers established a rate of 4.1 per cent of wrongful convictions in death penalty cases in the United States between 1973 and 2004, considering this a conservative figure (Gross et al., 2014).

As can be seen, all these figures show percentages that are by no means negligible but are restricted to some categories of crimes, and in any event have important methodological limitations if extended to other categories of case. Thus, for example, there is growing information in the same country indicating that, in the case of charges for less serious crimes, the risk of conviction of innocent people is even greater.[8] This is suggested by the growing research on a specific topic – the possible impact on this phenomenon of negotiated procedures in crimes of lesser gravity – which claims that a frequent occurrence in them is that innocent people declare themselves

---

[8]   Risinger himself, who appears very cautious about extending the results of his investigation to other crimes, states nevertheless that there were no good reasons to think that the rate was substantially different in less serious crimes – given for example that the system does not invest the same efforts and resources in their clarification (Risinger, 2007: 782–8).

guilty. Analysing the total number of people who confess responsibility, Blume and Helm affirm that the largest category corresponds precisely to that of innocent people accused of relatively minor offences (Blume and Helm, 2014: 173). One problem, to be sure, is that there are no exact figures about the scale of this phenomenon. Although, as I have said, in all types of cases it is difficult to identify wrongful convictions, the problems seem all the greater in the area of minor offences due to the much more informal treatment they receive from criminal justice systems, and the poorer record-keeping and follow-up with respect to them, among other reasons. This is explicable because in these crimes the possibility of controlling the error after conviction is very limited compared to more serious accusations, for example, by inter-posing post-conviction habeas corpus or other functional equivalents (Natapoff, 2012: 118; King, 2013: 22).[9] The effect would be a far higher number of unrecorded wrongful convictions in these cases than in normal procedures.[10] Apart from these difficulties, it is clear that the problem is huge due to the sheer number of minor criminal cases that are processed in the United States.[11] Similar evidence is reported also in some countries of continental Europe (Killias, 2013: 66), such as Switzerland (Gilliéron, 2013).

A second way of measuring the problem of wrongful convictions can be explored through what I have referred to as anecdotal evidence, that is, the systematic recording of specific cases in which an exoneration has occurred. This could provide at least an image of the reality. Again, the most renowned databases worldwide are those in the United States. The best known of these is the one maintained by the *Innocent Project*, which as of May 2018 listed 356 cases of innocent people convicted, corresponding to the cases that themselves have litigated.[12] Less known, but more extensive, is the database of the

---

[9] In this same direction, the empirical investigation available in Chile shows that, on average, the cases of post-conviction review granted by the Supreme Court are for more serious crimes (with higher penalties) than those that in average are convicted as a whole in the system (Duce, 2017a: 16–17).

[10] Gross points out that in this type of crime, wrong convictions are almost undetectable, although they are likely to be much more frequent than in common crimes (Gross, 2008: 180). Citing a report prepared by defenders on lesser crimes, Roberts points out that there is no study to quantify the number of innocent people convicted in these cases, but they could be in hundreds of thousands (Roberts, 2011: 286).

[11] Data for 2016 produced by the National Center for States Courts show that in the three highest income states that appear in their database, the percentages of misdemeanours over the total number of cases are around or over 80 per cent. This occurs in Texas (86 per cent), North Carolina (82 per cent) and California (80 per cent). The figures of these and other states can be reviewed in: www.ncsc.org/Sitecore/Content/Microsites/PopUp/Home/CSP/CSP_Intro (last visited 21 May 2018).

[12] See www.innocenceproject.org/ (last visited 21 May 2018).

National Registry of Exonerations (NRE)[13] that records cases of innocent
people convicted and then exonerated by every method (not exclusively
DNA), starting in 1989. As of May 2018, it listed 2,218 cases.

There are also registries of cases in other latitudes. For example, in the
United Kingdom, the Criminal Cases Review Commission records that
between April 1997 (its creation) and March 2018, it received 23,516 requests,
of which it ordered that 650 cases be referred to the Courts of Appeal due to
a suspicion of judicial errors. Of these, appeals were admitted on 422
occasions.[14] My own investigation in Chile based on data of judicial post-
conviction reviews resolved by the Supreme Court between 2007 and 2016
allowed me to identify 48 cases out of a total of 601 applications in this 10-year
period (approximately 8 per cent) that were accepted, declaring that people
convicted in a final judgment under the new accusatory system were
innocent.[15]

While the number of cases registered through these mechanisms in all the
countries that I have mentioned as examples are by no means negligible,
neither are they a good measure of the real situation. Anecdotal evidence
covers only a small portion of the cases in which one may think that the system
is making big mistakes with serious consequences for the person under
investigation. For one thing, the focus in these cases leaves out all those
situations in which errors occur without a conviction ('wrongful accusations,'
as I have called them). Also excluded are those in which a person may have
been wrongfully convicted without being able to exercise an action that could
lead to their exoneration. We should also add cases in which there is evidence
that the conviction was dubious, the convicted person was not in a position to
prove their innocence beyond reasonable doubt, which is normally
a requirement of this type of mechanism. An important agreement in the
comparative literature points in the same direction – that cases of formal
exoneration are only the tip of the iceberg of a much larger problem. This is
because there are many others that never reach these formal instances for
various reasons or because of access barriers (Findley, 2011–12: 918).

---

[13]   This is a joint project originally carried out by the law faculties of the universities of Michigan
       and Northwestern. More information at: www.law.umich.edu/special/exoneration/Pages/abo
       ut.aspx (last visited 21 May 2018).
[14]   These data can be viewed at: https://ccrc.gov.uk/case-statistics/ (last visited on 21 May 2018).
       This commission was created in March 1997 as an autonomous public organisation whose
       objective is to review cases where there were possible judicial errors in the United Kingdom.
       Background at: https://ccrc.gov.uk/ (last visited on 21 May 2018).
[15]   It should be noted that other applications were also admitted during the same period, but they
       dealt with cases adjudicated under the previous inquisitorial system and therefore were not
       analysed in my work (Duce, 2017a).

The available evidence about the factors that influence wrongful convictions changes the scenario. As indicated in the introduction, this has been one of the topics that has generated more research than any other in the comparative field. In the more traditional literature, there seems to be a consensus that the main factors affecting the production of wrongful convictions are six: (1) problems with the visual identification of defendants by victims and witnesses; (2) use of expert evidence of low reliability and quality; (3) use of false confessions; (4) use of mendacious or unreliable witnesses; (5) poor work of criminal prosecution agencies; (6) inadequate legal representation of those convicted.

It should be kept in mind that this literature agrees decisively that no single factor is responsible, but several factors commonly converge in these accredited erroneous conviction cases. Thus, the conviction of innocent people and the most paradigmatic cases are explicable as a consequence of several problems that arise simultaneously (Simon, 2012: 7).[16]

The most recent literature in the United States has led to an interesting methodological debate about the limitations of the studies published on the subject as faithful reflections of reality. In particular, bias resulting from establishing a causal link from samples based on exoneration cases (Gould et al., 2014) is posed as a potential problem. For this reason, interesting empirical research has been done in which researchers work in parallel with cases of wrongful convictions and so-called near misses. The particularity of the latter is that the system was able to discern the innocence of the accused before a conviction (in this sense they assimilate to the cases I have called 'wrongful accusations'). The idea of these investigations is to verify what happens in cases where the criminal justice systems had the possibility of discovering the errors before a conviction and compare these cases with those in which that did not happen. The results of this new line of research confirm that the six factors mentioned above increase the probability of system error, but they have added new elements to consider. These, such as the punitive culture of the state in which the innocent is convicted; the existence of convicts' prior criminal records, among others, also have relevance and weight in explaining criminal justice system errors.[17]

---

[16] Simon adds that although in some cases the set of factors can occur by chance, in the vast majority he suspects that they arise rather as a product of the dynamics of the police investigation process. He states that from an investigative error a cascade of other problems can follow that end in the conviction of someone innocent.

[17] The main research in this new line of work is a study financed by funds from the National Institute of Justice of the United States, whose results were published in March 2013. The study involved the analysis of 460 cases (260 of the conviction of innocent persons and 200 near misses) that took place between 1980 and 2012 (Gould et al., 2013).

Beyond the nuances, all the investigations mentioned highlight the enormous influence of the different evidence on the conviction of innocent people or on the production of errors in the system. Among them is expert testimony. To this I turn in the next section.

15.3 THE USE OF EXPERT TESTIMONY AND SYSTEM ERRORS

A broad consensus that the use of expert evidence in judicial systems is increasingly frequent is evident from a panoramic review of the specialised literature. Authors belonging to different legal traditions and writing from various analytical perspectives emphasise that judicial systems increasingly resort to the use of this type of evidence to decide the cases they adjudicate. Thus, for example, both the relevant doctrine in the Anglo-Saxon[18] and the continental European traditions[19] make basically the same point, there being no significant differences whether it is expressed from a criminal[20] or civil procedure perspective[21] or from perspectives with a different emphasis, for

---

[18] Within this tradition, the number of authors who refer to the subject is extraordinary. I will limit myself to examples from four countries. In the United States, Mauet has stated that 'We see more and more experts in every type of trial. It is a daily event. Almost all trials now have experts' (Mauet, 2007: 20). In Canada, Gold states that 'Knowledge and expertise have grown exponentially in our society, and our courts' increased consumption of expert evidence reflects that reality of our modern world' (Gold, 2003: 4). In the context of Great Britain, Dennis emphasises that 'there are a great many other matters on which expert evidence can be given, and the list is growing' (Dennis, 2010: 887). In Australia, Freckelton describes this same phenomenon with an emphasis on the increase in supply, stating that. 'The pages of *Expert Evidence* (subscription service) show that the extent to which the "forensic sciences" have proliferated and evolved and have become specialised and professionalised' (Freckelton, 2009: 1120).

[19] In Italy, Federico Stella describes this phenomenon, pointing out that 'the wave of judicial procedures that relate to science and technology in recent decades has led to a spectacular increase in the number and type of experts called to participate in trials'.

[20] For example, on this point Roxin, perhaps one of the main referents in the criminal area of the continental tradition, points out, 'In modern criminal procedure, in which the scientific clarification of issues that are not juridical plays an increasingly important role, the expert has frequently reached a dominant position in practice' (Roxin, 2003: 240).

[21] Taruffo has pointed out, specifically referring to civil proceedings, that 'more and more often civil litigation matters involve facts that go beyond the borders of a common or average culture, which is the kind of non-juridical culture of a judge or a jury' (Taruffo, 2008: 90). Referring to scientific evidence, he adds that 'in reality, the frequency with which science is used to provide proof of the facts of a case is growing in all the procedural systems' (Taruffo, 2008: 97). In the Anglo-Saxon tradition Beecher-Monas notes that 'Scientific evidence is an inescapable facet of modern litigation. It is fundamental to criminal justice system and civil litigation' (Beecher-Monas, 2007: 4).

example those that accentuate the legal,[22] epistemological[23] or scientific problems generated by the use of this type of evidence.[24] In my opinion, this consensus is due to the social, technological and economic development experienced globally by our societies, and it is foreseeable that the phenomenon will even increase in the future for the same reason.

On this point, a relevant finding of my research in the case of Chile[25] was that the system devotes considerable resources to the production of expert evidence, at least in terms of its preparation.[26] Yet this appearance can be deceptive. A more detailed analysis of these figures shows that a significant portion of these reports do not correspond to expert testimony as such, but rather to different technical research activities such as analysis of incident sites, social worker reports, crime reports, among others. The largest part of what could indeed be considered expert evidence consist of standardised tests

---

[22] Many of the authors that I have previously cited placed this emphasis on their analysis of the expert evidence, so I will not repeat the quotes.

[23] As Marina Gascón, who writes from this perspective points out, 'the constant scientific and technical advances in recent years have had a profound impact in the field of evidence and play an increasingly important role in every trial' (Gascón, 2013: 181).

[24] In this sense, the most relevant text is the report prepared by the National Academy of Sciences of the United States in 2009 (National Research Council, 2009). Referring to the reality of the United States in a specific area such as forensic psychology, Cutler and Zapf point out that 'Psychological knowledge is now regularly used in trial, appellate, and supreme court cases at state and federal levels and is used to craft laws on relevant topics. Psychologists routinely provide testimony about criminal defendants, litigants, and psychological issues in trial courts' (Cutler and Zapf, 2014: xix).

[25] This was a qualitative empirical investigation and is based on the opinions of a significant number of expert informants on the criminal procedure system. These were opinions obtained through semi-structured interviews with a total of fifty-two actors in the criminal justice system of the Metropolitan Region, including private attorneys (six), public criminal justice defenders (eight), prosecutors from the Public Prosecutor's Office (thirteen), guarantee judges (nine), criminal trial court judges (nine) and experts (seven). The interviews were conducted between the months of May 2015 and November 2016. They were complemented by a compilation of other sources. The first consisted of statistics and data from the institutions of the system, some published in various texts or general access websites, and others obtained thanks to specific information requests made as the investigation progressed through transparency applications. The second comes from the findings from two exploratory empirical studies based on the review and analysis of judgments handed down by Oral Criminal Courts (hereinafter OCC) of the city of Santiago. Both were prepared by the authors of master's theses; the development of whose work had the support of this project. The publication of the detailed findings can be found in Duce, 2018.

[26] In fact, according to the statistics of the laboratories of the Investigations Police and of Carabineros of Chile, the Legal Medical Service, and the Institute of Public Health, in 2015 about 330,000 requests for expert evidence were issued. To these must be added those produced by other public and private institutions working for the system and others provided by defenders (for example, in 2015 the Public Defender's Office alone ordered the preparation of 11,319 expert opinions). See Duce, 2018: 51–9.

performed by laboratories.[27] This explains, in part, that only a portion of this total is duly translated into expert evidence in criminal trials. Thus, in a recent empirical evaluation of the functioning of the Chilean criminal justice system it was possible to determine that prosecutors presented expert evidence in 28 per cent of the cases that they bring to trial in the most serious cases (Arellano, 2017: 65). This would account for the fact that despite the investment of considerable resources in this area, Chile's capacity to produce expert evidence for trials in which the most serious and complex cases are heard continues to be limited.

15.3.1 *The Size of the Problem: Evidence in Some Paradigmatic Countries*

Comparative studies on the conviction of innocent people tend to emphasise that the improper use of expert evidence is one of the main factors that explain system errors. Given the aims of this work, to cover rigorously all the countries where there is information on the topic is an impossible task. So, I will limit myself to presenting information on two paradigmatic cases in which this issue has been discussed in greatest depth: one of them because of the very significant empirical information available, and the other due to the debate generated in various official fora about the problem.

The country where this topic has been most researched empirically is the United States. Thus, the data from the Innocence Project show consistently over time that the improper use of expert evidence is the second most relevant factor in the cases of wrongful convictions they have represented. This aspect is present in about 45 per cent of the cases in which convicted persons were exonerated and their innocence later proven, exceeded only by incorrect visual recognition, the most frequently occurring cause.[28] A second database showing the size of the problem in the United States is that of the NRE, which coincides with the Innocence Project in finding misuse of expert evidence to be one of the main factors contributing to the production of wrongful convictions. It ranks fourth in order of statistical frequency, being found in 24 per cent of the cases.[29] The results of empirical studies dealing with

---

[27] On this last point, the Legal Medical Service is the agency that produces the greatest number of expert reports, and in 2015 70 per cent of those within the institutions analysed were produced by them. Within this universe, 81.5 per cent corresponded to laboratories and 70 per cent of those were alcohol tests (that is, almost 52 per cent of the total of expert reports produced during the year, considering the five institutions analysed in my research). See Duce, 2018: 54–5.

[28] See www.innocenceproject.org/causes/misapplication-forensic-science/ (last visited 21 May 2018).

[29] See www.law.umich.edu/special/exoneration/Pages/ExonerationsContribFactorsByCrime .aspx (last visited 21 May 2018). Analysed by type of crime, this factor would increase to

so-called near misses confirm that the use of expert evidence is an important factor increasing the probability of system error (Gould et al., 2013: 410). In short, different databases and research conducted in the United States concur in identifying the use of expert evidence as a relevant factor in explaining errors in the criminal justice system.

The United Kingdom is another example in which the impact of expert evidence in the production of wrongful convictions has been a subject of concern and study. It is true that there have been no initiatives in the UK to systematise cases comparable to the one implemented in the United States that would allow us to measure the probable scale or statistical magnitude of the problem (Naughton, 2013: 105). However, the UK is an interesting case to review since public awareness of this problem has generated action by various official bodies to implement different types of policy – including legal reforms and jurisprudential changes – aiming to minimise the risks of system errors entailed by the use of this evidence. In this context, a series of high-profile wrongful convictions over the last twenty years generated enormous debate and a series of initiatives aimed at reviewing the treatment of expert evidence in the United Kingdom. The first development was the preparation of a report in 2005 by the House of Commons Science and Technology Committee. This set out a series of proposals for improving the use of forensics to avoid errors in the criminal justice system, assuming that misuse of this evidence was a cause of wrongful convictions.[30]

In response to this – but also a product of the concern caused at the time by cases of the conviction of innocent people due to mistaken use of expert evidence – the Law Commission of England and Wales[31] produced a report whose focus was to generate debate and obtain feedback for drawing up a legal reform proposal aimed at establishing more stringent rules for the admissibility

---

31 per cent in cases of sexual assault, which helps explain the differences from the results of the Innocence Project. In fact, rape crimes are much more frequent in the Innocent Project database than that of the NRE since they usually include forensic evidence obtained from the victims themselves (Garret, 2011: 89 and 313). On the other hand, the Innocent Project estimates that between 90 to 95 per cent of the cases known to the criminal justice system cannot lead to a DNA-based exoneration due to the impossibility of finding biological evidence on which to carry out the respective test. See: www.innocenceproject.org/causes/u nvalidated-or-improper-forensic-science/ (last visited 21 May 2018).

[30] Among other things, measures were recommended to improve the training of judges and lawyers and the development of institutional bodies to promote better communication between expert communities and members of the criminal justice system (House of Commons Science and Technology Committee, 2005).

[31] This is an autonomous body created by law in 1965 with the purpose of supervising that the legislation of both countries is fair, modern, simple, and cost-effective. More information can be found on its website www.lawcom.gov.uk/ (last visited 21 May 2018).

of expert evidence in criminal proceedings. In the proposal's preamble, special emphasis is placed on the need to raise admissibility standards for this type of evidence, given the *laissez-faire* practice very widespread in the criminal courts.[32] After responses received from various institutions and experts, this first proposal was transformed into a definitive draft legal reform bill and presented to the government in a new report published in 2011 (The Law Commission, 2011: 211).[33] In this draft, the authors insist again that the new legislation does not respond to a merely theoretical problem but to a real one, evident in a series of wrongful convictions in England and Wales that demonstrate the risks in the use of this type of evidence (The Law Commission, 2011: 3–4). The expectation on which the reform bill rests is that stricter standards of admissibility could prevent expert evidence of low reliability – such as those that led to mistaken convictions in the cases analysed – from being accepted into trial and lead to a determination of the accused's guilt.

In 2013, the government rejected the legislative proposal made in the 2011 Law Commission report, even though it recognised the risks posed by improper use of untrustworthy forensic evidence and acknowledged that the proposals contained in the report could reduce this risk.[34] Despite this, its response recommends reviewing the Criminal Procedure Rules in order to provide more information in the early stages of the trial about the forensic reports to be introduced as evidence, in order to enhance litigants' and judges' capacity to contest them and thereby reduce the risks of judicial error. This reform was finally introduced on 14 October 2014 through a change to rule 33.4 (h), which states that the expert's report must include information necessary to allow the court to decide whether 'the expert's opinion is sufficiently reliable to admit it as evidence' (Freckelton et al., 2016: 41–2).[35]

---

[32]   In this report, several of these cases of the conviction of innocent people generated by improper use of expert evidence are analysed in an exemplary manner (The Law Commission, 2009: 10–17).

[33]   The proposal raises the need to pass specific legislation on expert evidence in criminal matters (Criminal Evidence (experts) Bill), that would harness the jurisprudential and normative developments already experienced in England and Wales into a single legal body, as well as perfect these in a proposal that would address the central problems based on the Commission's diagnosis.

[34]   In the document, the government expresses doubt about the benefits of introducing the proposed legal reforms given the dearth of robust data demonstrating the real scale of the problem and, especially, considering that the proposals would generate more operating costs for the system, for example for the holding of new and longer hearings (Ministry of Justice, 2013).

[35]   This has been complemented by changes in the Criminal Practice Directions 33.A.4, 33.A.5 and 33.A.6 of England, which – although without standing as law – reflect the concern to advance in the normative regulation of the use of expert evidence.

In parallel with this debate over reform of the rules, the Law Commission's proposals have been incorporated increasingly and by different channels into judicial practice, since judges in England and Wales largely share concerns about the size of the problem of wrongful convictions generated by misuse of expert evidence in the country.[36]

I add a brief analysis of the situation in Chile to these two cases. Even with the limited information available on the subject, the use of expert evidence has been identified in Chile also as a relevant factor in known cases of error in recent years. I start with those identified by the Innocents Project, an initiative created by the Public Defender's Office in 2013.[37] The project selects paradigmatic cases of people who have suffered the consequences of a criminal prosecution in which there have been errors of various kinds, which would have avoided drawn out trials and harmful results for the individuals concerned had they been promptly detected. In other words, it covers mainly cases that I have previously called 'wrongful accusations'. Of the fifty-nine cases registered by April 2018, the project identified 'expert error or limited science' as the main cause in four of them. These were cases of people who spent between 60 and 220 days in custody due to improper use of expert evidence against them.[38]

Added to these is the case of Rodrigo Saavedra, which is not included as it was tried under the inquisitorial system. Saavedra was sentenced in 2007 to serve fifteen years in prison after being found guilty of the rape of his daughter, who was nine years old at the time of the events.[39] Saavedra had spent four years in jail

---

[36] As the Lord Chief Justice of England and Wales pointed out to the press in November 2014. *The Guardian*: 'Are Juries Being Blinded by Science', October 15, 2014, in: www.theguardian.com/la w/2014/oct/15/juries-blinded-science-lord-chief-justice-primers (last visited 21 May 2018). A brief summary of the recent development of jurisprudence in England that shows how reliability has effectively been accepted as an admissibility criterion can be seen in (Freckelton et al., 2016: 228–30).

[37] According to its website, the project aims to raise awareness in society about the possibility of error by the criminal justice system by identifying and documenting cases in which this has occurred. Available at: www.proyectoinocentes.cl/ (last visited 21 May 2016).

[38] I cannot dwell on the specifics of each case, but they include those of Fernando Vasquez Mamani, whose case was dismissed in 2003 after he had been held in custody for 60 days on drug trafficking charges. www.proyectoinocentes.cl/casos/detalle/10/fernando_vasquez-mamani (last visited 21 May 2018); Alonso Etcheverría Martínez, who was absolved in 2007 by an Oral Criminal Court after having spent 123 days in preventive detention on charges of the sexual abuse of a child. www.proyectoinocentes.cl/casos/detalle/8/alonso-etcheverria_martinez (last visited 21 May 2018); C.P.P.F who was acquitted in oral trial in 2013, after having spending 220 days in preventive detention accused of raping his partner's 8-year-old daughter. www .proyectoinocentes.cl/casos/detalle/26/c-p_p-f (last visited 21 May 2018); and Elías Cartes Parra who was acquitted by an oral criminal court in 2014, after 160 days in preventive custody and 90 days under house arrest, charged with murder. www.proyectoinocentes.cl/casos/detalle/42/elias-cartes_parra (last visited on 21 May 2018).

[39] Supreme Court sentence of 28 July 2011 in case no. 2827–2011.

before obtaining his release after the Supreme Court granted his post-conviction appeal. Key evidence in his conviction was a forensic report stating that the child had 'old ruptures of the hymen, now healed, that is, she was deflowered at a not recent date'.[40] Added to this was a prior medical examination by four doctors at the Calvo Mackenna hospital who maintained that the girl also had a sexually transmitted disease (gonorrhoea). In the review appeal, the Supreme Court gave special consideration – in addition to psychological evidence and the victim's statement that she was already a legal adult at the time – to the opinion expressed in a new gynaecological forensic report that indicated no elements of sexual activity and that the alleged sexually transmitted disease that had originally been diagnosed could be transmitted even in pregnancy and childbirth. The court finally considered, on the basis of various pieces of evidence attached to the review appeal, that what had been detected was a vaginal infection that the alleged victim had had since she was three years old, as documented in the trial, and that the infection was still present at the time the original exams were conducted, due to poor treatment.

As can be seen in this brief account of the examples analysed, the problems that the use of expert evidence causes in producing mistaken convictions are relevant in the comparative field and accumulating empirical information increasingly demonstrates this. Moreover, some emerging reactions from various criminal justice system authorities testify to the enormous concern that this issue is generating. Far from being isolated cases, I believe them to be a constant, with manifestations in several countries. It suffices to mention three more examples from different regions and legal traditions that point in the same direction: Canada,[41] Germany[42] and China.[43] Of course in this work

---

[40]   Apart from the review sentence, detailed information on the case is available in an extensive report by *The Clinic* in October 2013. *The Clinic*: 'The 1,302 days of Rodrigo Saavedra in the former Penitentiary', 14 October 2013. Available at: www.theclinic.cl/2013/10/14/los-1-302-dias-de-rodrigo-saavedra-en-la-ex-penitenciaria/ (last visited 21 May 2018).

[41]   The impact of expert evidence on wrongful convictions in Canada has been so great that, from the perspective of criminal prosecutors themselves, two reports by prosecutor working groups (in 2004 and 2011) aimed at preventing them have addressed it as one of the most relevant problems (FPT Heads Of Prosecutions Committee Working Group, 2004: 115–32 and FPT Heads Of Prosecutions Committee, 2011, 133–59).

[42]   Concern about this issue has been present in the doctrine in this country for over fifty years. For example, Hirschberg analyses several cases of wrongful convictions handed down in Germany which he places in the category of 'uncritical assessment of forensic opinions', pointing out that numerous erroneous judgments arise mainly out of 'that blind faith of the courts in the expert, especially in the official investigator, and in the deficient instruction of the majority of judges and defenders' (Hirshberg, 1969: 69–92, original publication in German in 1960).

[43]   Jiahong has recently drawn attention to how incorrect use and interpretation of scientific evidence in that country has been the cause of wrongful convictions in a series of cases analysed in his text (Jiahong, 2016: 31–51).

I cannot analyse each case exhaustively. I am more interested in taking further a description of the reasons that research shows to cause the phenomenon described. To that I turn in the next section.

15.3.2 *Specific Problems Identified in the Comparative Literature*

From the comparative literature we can identify a series of problems in the use of expert evidence that explain the risks of producing the conviction of innocent people. I pause very briefly to consider the four main ones.

15.3.2.1 The Use of Unreliable Expert Evidence

The first problem detected is the tendency of criminal justice systems to use a set of very low reliability forensic tests. This generally occurs as a result of the use of expert opinions based on disciplines of little methodological or scientific rigour. The Anglo-Saxon literature groups these cases under the notion of 'Junk Science'.[44] The central point to emphasise is that on many occasions expert evidence is used at trial that has an aura of scientific or methodological rigour that it does not really possess, leading judges to make mistakes in the final decision.

Garret, in an analysis based on the Innocent Project database, points out that many of those exonerated by this project have been convicted as a result of unreliable forensic methods (Garret, 2011: 90). Similarly, the Law Commission of England and Wales devised a proposal for legal reform based on its view that a frequent problem in those countries and that explains the conviction of innocent people has been the use of unreliable evidence on the part of criminal prosecutors (The Law Commission, 2011: 1). Evidence from Canada (ROACH, 2010: 339) and Australia (Freckelton et al., 2016: 31–3) on the incidence of this factor points in the same direction.

A central contribution from the scientific community on this issue has come from work by the National Academy of Sciences (NAS) of the United States. In 2009 the institution's National Research Council published a report intended to contribute to improving the quality of forensic sciences in that country. The report identified serious deficiencies in forensic work in areas of common use in criminal courts. They included bite marks analysis, the microscopic analysis of hairs, the marks of shoe prints, voice comparisons,

---

[44] Thomas explains how this term became popular in the United States through a work published by Peter Huber in 1991. In this he described junk science as 'the mirror image of real science, with much of the same form but none of the same substance' (Thomas, 2015: 1039).

and the use of fingerprints. The report establishes that these disciplines present problems of reliability due to the scientific research evidence on which they are based, which is too scanty to permit validation of the basic premises and techniques on which they are built (National Research Council, 2009: 1–33). In short, such evidence has a weak and debatable scientific basis. Evidently, it is not surprising that if regularly used expert evidence has no real scientific support, such evidence could be an engine of wrong conviction decisions. The reader can imagine the impact that a report of this nature, produced by an institution with great credibility in the scientific world, has had in that country and worldwide.[45]

My own empirical research on evidentiary practices in Chile also shows that this is an issue that exposes us to various risks. Thus, my research demonstrated several elements that create doubts about the reliability and quality of the expert evidence submitted in trial.

On the question of reliability, we found that some frequently presented expert skills are from disciplines that have been subject to much debate and questioning in the comparative scientific field. For example, it was possible to establish that more than half the expert evidence presented at trial in the case of sexual crimes (55 per cent) rested on what are called psychological story credibility tests (based on the SVA method), whose reliability is widely debated in science, or that a not inconsiderable percentage (10.7 per cent) of the forensic reports produced by Carabineros (Chile's uniformed police force) in 2015[46] were on fingerprints (Duce, 2018: 61–2).[47]

---

[45] For example, the FBI in the United States has recently admitted mistakes made in hundreds of cases in which the technique of hair analysis was applied. Thus, a 2015 report by the institution's Office of Inspector General found there to have been irregular behaviours in the hair analysis unit. See: BBC News: FBI Admits Forensic Evidence Errors in Hundreds of Cases, 20 April 2015. Available at: www.bbc.com/news/world-us-canada-32380051 (last visited 21 May 2018). See also: *The Washington Post*: 'Convicted Defendants Left Uninformed of Forensic Flaws Found by Justice Dept.', 16 April 2012. Available at: www.washingtonpost.com/local/crime/convicted-defendants-left-uninformed-of-forensic-flaws-found-by-justice-dept/2012/04/16/gIQAWTcgMT_st ory.html (last visited 21 May 2018).

[46] By 2017, this figure had risen to 12.5 per cent of the total number of expert reports carried out by the Carabineros laboratories and 18.9 per cent of those performed by the laboratories of Chile's Investigative Police (PDI).

[47] These findings coincide with the results of a subsequent empirical study conducted by Dirección de Estudios de la Corte Suprema de Chile (hereinafter the Studies Department of the Supreme Court of Chile), which carried out a massive survey of judges, experts and attorneys on expert evidence. One of the findings was that the attorneys surveyed (more than 4,000) rated the reliability and validity of the methodology used in criminal investigations at 3.6 out of a maximum of 7.0 (the grade means failure in the Chilean educational system). The criminal judges surveyed (60 guarantee judges and 87 oral criminal court judges) rated them a little more generously at 4.8 (Direction of Studies of The Supreme Court, 2017: 29).

Added to this were severe quality defects in forensic work that could also affect the reliability of the results. Thus, I detected many criticisms by the actors of the system about the scanty or sometimes non-existent information provided by the experts and their reports on the methods they used to arrive at their conclusions – that is, serious deficiencies in the justification of their opinions or conclusions and also severe problems of completeness of the same (Duce, 2018: 65–8).[48]

I add to these deficiencies some important problems we detected concerning the experts' specialisation in certain matters, as for example in the area of forensic psychology and forensic medicine. This is relevant because if the expert does not have the minimum competences required, it is highly probable that the results obtained will not be valid within his discipline. The evidence collected showed that those who practice these forensic investigations do not, as a rule, have the training or experience to ensure their quality and reliability (Duce, 2018: 69–73).[49] A dramatic example illustrates the above. I obtained the composition of the forensic sexology unit of the Medical Legal Service (SML) in the Metropolitan Region, having chosen this example since it is a very important and frequent forensic procedure in the case of sexual crimes (20.3 per cent of the total number of forensic reports submitted according to the investigation). As of April 2016, the unit was composed of eleven members, seven of whom had no specialty, while two had forensic medicine and two gynecology as their specialty. To have an idea of the scale of this unit's work, during 2015 they reported that they were responsible for more than 50 per cent of the total number of forensic assessments carried out by the SML at the national level in cases of sexual crime.

On the other hand, one of the areas in which the interviewees identified greater strengths in terms of the quality and reliability of expert reports was in the work of the laboratories. In this context, I investigated some indicators that

---

[48] Likewise, these findings coincide with the results of the empirical study of the Studies Department of the Supreme Court of Chile. Thus, the attorneys surveyed rated the quality of the explanation and justification of methodology in the expert reports at 3.6 out of a maximum of 7. It should be noted that in the Chilean educational system the minimum pass grade is 4.0. The criminal judges surveyed, on the other hand, rated those same attributes at 4.8. The attorneys also evaluated the correspondence between the premises and the conclusions of expert opinions, again rating them with a failure grade (3.9) while the judges rated them a little higher (4.8) (Direction of Studies of The Supreme Court, 2017: 29–30).

[49] The investigation was able to detect serious problems in the development of some forensic specialities in the country such as forensic medicine, and important problems that we might call the political economy of the system (incentives for the training and retention of specialised personnel in the state institutions that produce expert evidence, among others). This finding is also reiterated in the empirical study that I have already quoted from the Justice Studies Center of the Americas, that is, an evaluation of the operation of the Legal Medical Service (Arellano, 2017: 171).

340   *Mauricio Duce J.*

could justify this perception and suggest it was not simply due to a favourable bias based on the supposed scientific rigour of what appear to be 'technical' data. At an international level, the main developments in this area have been linked to the establishment of accreditation systems for forensic laboratories that allow verification of whether their working procedures comply with quality standards, which ensures the reliability of their results.[50] For this purpose, requests for access to public information were presented, requesting details of the laboratories' accreditations. The answers received show that the accreditation process of Chilean forensic laboratories in the criminal area is still in its infancy and, therefore, the positive perception of the actors in this regard should be read with extreme caution (Duce, 2018: 64–5).

15.3.2.2 Invalid forensic testimony

A second problem identified in the comparative literature is what Garret and Naufeld describe as invalid forensic testimony (Garret and Naufeld, 2009: 7–8). By this they refer to experts, even those belonging to disciplines that do not have significant reliability problems, who tend in trial to make statements and reach conclusions that have no empirical support in their respective discipline. That is to say, the problem is due to the way in which the experts report and interpret the results obtained in their operations when delivering their testimonies in the trial hearings (Garret and Naufeld, 2009: 6–8).[51] The study of both authors analyses 137 cases of people exonerated by the Innocent Project (from a total universe of 232 exonerees at the date of the study) in which forensic evidence was produced in court. Based on this sample, they found that in 60 per cent of them (eighty-two cases) the analysts submitted invalid testimony. This testimony basically includes two hypotheses for the errors: improper use of empirical data about the general population, and conclusions about the probative value of the respective evidence that had no support in the empirical evidence available in the discipline itself (Garret and Naufeld, 2009: 9). The scale of the problem allows these authors to

---

[50] The current standard-setting document has been developed by the International Laboratory Accreditation Cooperation for institutions that operate according to the ISO/IEC 17011 norms, also known as ILAC: http://ilac.org/about-ilac/ (last visited 21 May 2018). In August 2014 this institution published the ILAC G19-2014 standard, a guide for forensic units with responsibility for the examination and testing of forensic samples (basically laboratories) to ensure the application of ISO/IEC 17025 and ISO/IEC 17020 standards, available at: http://ilac.org/lates t_ilac_news/ilac-g19082014-published/ (last visited 21 May 2018).
[51] For example, the study found that in 27 per cent of the cases in which analysts of DNA – a technology widely validated in science – appeared, statements in the hearing by the expert witnesses were invalid (p. 15).

identify this as not only a common behaviour of forensic experts in trials, but a prevalent practice (Garret and Naufeld, 2009: 14).

Equally, the problem described by Garret and Naufeld seems to be a common pattern in comparative experience, as can be seen in reviews of cases in countries as diverse as England (Naughton, 2013: 103–5), Canada (Roach, 2009: 72–3) or China (Jiahong, 2016: 31–42). The enormous risk these behaviours of the experts generate for the correctness of judges' decisions seems obvious.

Due to the nature of my empirical research in Chile, it was a practice on which I was unable to obtain much information. Nonetheless, as a common practice associated with this problem, I was able to identify a phenomenon that I identify as 'experts who speak more than they write'. These are situations in which the experts include in their testimony in the trial hearing aspects of relevance to the case that had not been previously mentioned in their written report. My research was able to establish that this was a frequent problem. When the differences exceed those changes of detail or those additional elements that an oral statement in court will naturally include and could hardly be included in the previous written report, this generates significant risks to the system similar to those that occur with the practice of giving invalid testimony. This is because it makes it extremely difficult to submit these new contents to a robust test of plausibility and seriousness, by not giving the counter party a real chance of challenging them. For this reason, it is an indirect way of weakening the quality control of information (Duce, 2018: 80–1).

15.3.2.3 Bad Conduct by Experts

A third problem relates to bad conduct by experts working for criminal justice systems. By bad conduct I refer not to the specific deficiencies of an expert in a particular case, but rather to behaviours aimed explicitly at causing an error. This would include conduct like not disclosing to the accused evidence favourable to their case; fabricating forensic evidence against them; and, presenting the forensic opinion in order to improperly assist the work of the police or prosecutors (Naugthon, 2013: 65).[52] While there are cases of extremely serious misbehaviour documented in countries such as the United States[53] and

---

[52] The last of these three improper conducts of the experts – undue assistance to the police or prosecutors – intersects with the second of the problems described, that is, the rendering of invalid testimony at trial.

[53] One of the most infamous cases is that of Fred Zain. Zain worked for thirteen years in the West Virginia police laboratory in the United States, where he even became supervisor of the serology unit. During these years he provided key testimony for the conviction of various defendants in his state and in Texas. After a series of exonerations obtained by DNA tests of the people he had found guilty, the Supreme Court of West Virginia began an investigation against him. This led to the discovery of more wrongful convictions as a result of his testimony and a long sequence of

England,[54] where some experts have had decisive influence on dozens or hundreds of cases over several years of work, there is some debate about the real scale of the problem. Thus, the Garret and Naufeld study published in 2009 detected that about 10 per cent of the cases analysed included failures in the discovery of exculpatory evidence or the plain fabrication of evidence (Garret and Naufeldt, 2009: 76). That figure would rise to about 14 per cent in Garret's studies of the year 2011 (Garret, 2011: 108).

Despite the relatively limited number, Garret considers the problem not to be one of some 'bad apples' but something rather more systematic and therefore more widespread. In this context, he cites studies purporting to show that forensic analysts could be exposed inadvertently to significant biases due to their work for the police or prosecutors (Garret, 2011: 92–3),[55] the product of phenomena that translate into 'cognitive biases' of one kind or another.[56] On the other hand, as Edmond points out, experts' biases are not only produced consciously but also on many occasions as a result of their exposure to irrelevant or prejudicial information that is not required for them to form their opinion. This can generate unconscious cognitive biases that are equally harmful to others (Edmond, 2013: 256–7). To conclude this point, the comparative evidence shows that we are faced by a problem of some importance, and one that also offers a clue to why criminal justice systems wrongly condemn innocent people in hypotheses of this type.

To this problem another issue could be added that is typical of the operating environment of adversarial criminal systems: the role played by the parties themselves, whose incentives are to optimise their possibilities in the trial rather than reach the truth. This would lead them to favour using experts more motivated to be faithful to the interests of those who hire them rather than to the science, art or trade they profess. On this point, after describing the differences and showing

---

irregularities in his work that revealed what was not a casual but a systematic problem in his performance. Greater detail in Naugthon, 2013: 65–6 and Garret, 2011: 252–5.

[54] Naughton mentions as an example the case of Dr Frank Skuse, a British Home Office forensic expert who testified in the famous case of the conviction of innocent people known as the Birmingham Six (Naughton, 2013: 66–8).

[55] On the same point, there are also authors who make a general analysis about the influences and biases that forensic professionals who work in laboratories acquire (Sacks and Spellman, 2016: 209–10).

[56] Garret explains that psychological research shows that cognitive biases occur because our beliefs, desires and hopes influence the things we perceive, and how we reason and behave. This would result, among other things, when we identify our behaviour with noble ends. For example, when the police believe that when they catch someone guilty, they are doing justice regardless of the way they have done it (Garret, 2011: 266–7).

the tensions between the professional cultures of scientists and attorneys at the forefront of adversarial models, Susan Haack points out:

> the legal system often gets less from science than science could give: attorneys are motivated by the demands of their profession to seek out experts willing to shade or select the evidence as their case demands, and may encourage maverick, marginal or less-than-honest scientists into the lucrative business of the professional expert witness . . . (Haack, 2003: 208).

The problem of bad conduct by experts is not foreign to Chile. One of the best-known cases fits under the logic of the 'manufacture' of expert evidence. The 'Larraín case', which made headline news in 2013, involved a senator's son who was accused of a homicide while driving under the influence of alcohol. In this case, after a second forensic examination was performed on the victim's body, it was discovered that the original autopsy report carried out by a Legal Medical Service specialist incorporated false information about procedures that were never performed on the victim's body, since neither body cavities nor the skull were opened, as was visible to the naked eye.[57] The expert in question ended with a conviction for forging a public instrument in January 2016, in an abbreviated procedure.[58]

There have also been cases that point to problems of a systemic nature. In the final months of 2017, the case known as 'Operation Hurricane' came to public attention, after the discovery that an intelligence unit, with expert support, had fabricated and implanted false evidence on a massive scale, supposedly by intercepting electronic communications (in messaging systems such as Telegram and WhatsApp) to a group of Mapuche community members who were accused of committing a terrorist crime. Beyond the fabrication problem, what is publicly known about the investigation shows that the Carabineros laboratory experts who analysed the telephones that were seized after the interceptions presented the preliminary results of their findings to their superiors in the same institution and eventually also to the prosecutors themselves before they prepared their final reports. In the latter, they followed the comments and suggestions received in their consultations and validated

---

[57] When the case was revealed to public opinion, the expert acknowledged to different media that he had made mistakes in the preparation of his evidence, but that even so he had complied 'as always' and drafted his report 'in the usual way' after having more than twenty years' experience in the field. See: *Forensik*: 'Larraín Case: Questioned Expert Admits Errors in Autopsy', 29 October 2013, at www.forensik.cl/novedades-de-forensik/noticias/836-caso-larrain.html (last visited 21 May 2018).

[58] *La Tercera*: 'Doctor Who Forged Victim Autopsy of Martín Larraín Convicted', 14 January 2016. Available at: www.latercera.com/noticia/nacional/2016/01/680-664173-9-condenan-a-medico-que-falsifico-autopsia-de-victima-de-martin-larrain.shtml (last visited 21 May 2018).

the result of intercepts that were later shown to be false. This case clearly shows the risk that forensic analysts may be exposed to influences from the institutional structures on which they depend, especially in institutions with a hierarchical structure such as Carabineros de Chile.[59] This has initiated a debate in Chile on the need to discuss the institutional dependence of the bodies responsible for forensic evidence.

15.3.2.4 Difficulties in Assessing and Challenging Forensic Evidence Produced in Court

The problems just described may be aggravated by two relevant phenomena identified by the comparative literature that have to do with the production and evaluation of forensic evidence in oral trials: the difficulties judges experience in properly assessing forensic evidence, and the difficulties litigants have in contesting the quality of information emanating from experts during the trial. I briefly explain each.

DIFFICULTIES IN ASSESSMENT Notwithstanding the fact that most countries have systems providing freedom to evaluate evidence, there is a major concern in the comparative doctrine and jurisprudence – also with empirical support – about the risk that judges and juries may overvalue forensic evidence.[60] This concern is reflected very clearly in the reflection noted by the Supreme Court of the United States in the *Daubert* case, stating: '[e]xpert evidence can be both powerful and quite misleading because of the difficulty in evaluating it' (Garret and Naufeldt, 2009: 9). The doctrine expresses similar concerns in the continental procedural tradition.[61]

The concern, then, is that in practice judges give more decisive weight to expert evidence than to the remainder of the evidence. This occurs, among

---

[59] Detailed information on the case can be found in a series of newspaper reports. An interesting collection has been made by CIPER Chile and can be seen at the following link: http://ciperchile.cl/especiales/operacion-huracan/ (last visited 21 May 2018).

[60] The risk of overestimating the value of the expert evidence is one of the basic explanations, according to some, of the special treatment in admissibility this test has in countries such as the United States (Schauer and Spellman, 2013: 3–4).

[61] Thus, for example, according to Taruffo, 'as is said traditionally, the judge is *peritus peritorum* and, therefore, must be able to assess and control the grounds and opinion of the expert. However, this is only in theory; in practice, the judge or jury often does not have the necessary technical or scientific training to control the work of the expert effectively. Therefore, the free assessment of forensic evidence by the court may be nothing more than a fiction, since the court may be conditioned by an "epistemic deference" towards the expert and, therefore, it may be that the expert actually determines the content of the judicial verdict' (Taruffo, 2008: 96–7).

other factors, because of the special aura attached to opinions from experts, or difficulties that can arise in correctly understanding the scope of this evidence in certain matters.[62] The risk, then, is that such evidence may unduly influence findings of guilt beyond the real value that should be given to it. In this context, Edmond has stressed that the rational evaluation of evidence based on the use of forensic disciplines and legal medicine means having a minimum of information, without which there is a risk that the reasoning of judges, whether juries or professional judges, is based on speculative arguments or built on mere impressions (Edmond, 2015). Specifically, he states that this minimum consists of information about: (1) the value of the technique (usually based on it being independently validated); (2) the limitations and margin of error of the technique used in the specific case; and (3) the expert's competence in the use of the respective technique (Edmond, 2015: 83–6). Optimally, to this must be added information about what he calls complementary criteria, such as the existence of standards and protocols in the discipline; information that can identify experts' contextual biases; and appropriate language and forms of expression in communicating results, among others (Edmond, 2015: 86–90). The basic problem of criminal justice systems is that normally such information does not appear in trials, greatly increasing the possibility of a mistaken evaluation of this type of evidence (Edmond, 2015: 93).

On the same point, a recent empirical study on jury behaviour shows that, in evaluating the credibility of a forensic report, consideration is given to both the type of expertise and the characteristics of the expert. In addition, in weighing both aspects there is wide scope for considering elements that are neither reliable or relevant, significantly increasing the risk of reaching wrong decisions based on an incorrect assessment of this evidence (Freckelton et al., 2016: 202–3). Edmond himself identifies the use of unreliable criteria such as the use of speculative arguments about the reliability and validity of the technique, the expert's appearance of impartiality, impressions based on the expert's trial performance, among others (Edmond, 2015: 95–103).

Some literature has questioned the empirical basis for this fear that judges in practice overvalue expert evidence, claiming that the available evidence is ambiguous at the very least (Schauer and Spellman, 2013: 13–18). However, subsequent evidence – in some cases coming from studies that were unavailable at the time of the work cited – has shown that this risk must be taken seriously (Freckelton et al., 2016: 27–8, 191–2). Moreover, the authors who

---

[62] On this point, it is interesting to recall evidence that shows that professional judges are not significantly different in how they understand proof compared to juries and, therefore, that the former perform as well or as badly as the latter (Sacks and Spellman, 2016: 217).

question the risk of overvaluation have clarified their opinion by arguing that the risk is much reduced when there has been a real possibility of questioning this evidence in the trial, either through cross-examination by litigants or the production of other forensic evidence (Schauer and Spellman, 2013: 16). In this way, the risk can be minimised in contexts where the system allows strict scrutiny of forensic evidence. But if such control does not exist or is weak, they recognise that the risk is a real one. As I observe in the next point, the risk seems to be a norm in criminal justice systems.

My empirical research in Chile has uncovered evidence pointing in the same direction as the above. In the first place, I was able to establish that expert evidence is very important for judges and in practice is given significant weight.[63] Then, on analysing how their evaluate it, I found that the actors interviewed were critical of the work done by the judges, both in their ability to understand the contents of forensic reports correctly, the way in which they justify their reasoning in making judgments, and even for some potential biases in the assessment of forensic evidence (for example, a certain preference for 'official' expert evidence). These concerns are partly shared by the judges themselves, who recognise the importance of this evidence, the weight that is normally given to it, and their lack of relevant training to do a better job of evaluating it.[64] Nevertheless, they add that the poor contribution of litigants with their work in the hearings does little to help improve the outlook (Duce, 2018: 81–3).

These perceptions coincide with the findings of studies of verdicts made as an adjunct to my research. These studies note that there are almost no arguments in the judgments to accredit the experts' suitability or to address the methodology used to arrive at their conclusions. For example, in a study on crimes against life and health it was found that in only 4 per cent of the cases did the court address the methodology when evaluating this evidence in its verdict. This percentage rises to 13 per cent in another study of verdicts in sexual crimes.[65] The key question is whether with such sparse information on the methodological support of expert evidence presented at trial it is possible for the judges to assess it correctly.

[63] This coincides with a later finding of the empirical research carried out by the Studies Department of the Supreme Court of Chile that I have already mentioned: 92 per cent of the attorneys and 83.1 per cent of the criminal judges interviewed argued that the expert evidence was relevant or very relevant (Studies Department of The Supreme Court, 2017: 34).

[64] In the Supreme Court investigation, 73 per cent of the criminal judges interviewed considered it imperative to have greater training in evaluating expert evidence (Studies Department of the Supreme Court, 2017: 37).

[65] I refer to the research of Catalán and Santibáñez, respectively, which is widely cited in my research (Duce, 2018: 82–3).

There is also evidence indicating that in many cases the judges do not really evaluate expert evidence as they rely on what the experts declare in court, as if they were effectively delegating their jurisdictional function (Dirección de Estudios de la Corte Suprema, 2017: 37).

DIFFICULTIES IN CHALLENGING EXPERT EVIDENCE The evidence available in the comparative field shows that litigating attorneys have limited capacity to question the quality of forensic work and experts' statements through cross-examination.[66] For example, Garret and Naulfeld's 2009 study concludes that defence attorneys rarely question invalid testimony presented by expert witnesses in court and very rarely cross-examine the latter successfully. They also find that defence attorneys display weaknesses at the moment of addressing the evidence in their opening arguments, and furthermore that only a small percentage (in 19 out of 137 cases) themselves produce experts able to question those of the prosecution. In practice, therefore, the presentation of forensic evidence is one-sided (Garret and Naufeldt, 2009: 89–90). In the Garret study of 2011, there are similar findings. For example, in 50 per cent of the cases in which an invalid testimony was given by an expert witness, the defence attorneys did not even raise a question in the area where there was mistaken testimony (Garret, 2011: 113). This leads Garret to conclude that one cannot depend exclusively on the adversarial process as a way to prevent errors generated by the use of expert evidence (Garret, 2011: 114).[67] Moreover, there is also much information that shows the limitations of presenting expert counter-testimony as a mechanism for challenging the expert evidence used for incrimination.[68]

Once again, my empirical research showed that these practices described in the comparative literature as risk factors in wrong decisions are reproduced in Chile. The evidence shows that only in a small percentage of cases are experts

---

[66] Citing various studies on the true ability to question expert evidence through cross-examinations, Edmond concludes: 'Rather than a vehicle or engine capable of exposing weakness and uncovering truth, the effects of cross-examination are inconsistent and often mundane' (Edmond, 2011: 184).

[67] In a similar vein, the report of the National Academy of Sciences of the United States has concluded that due to the serious shortcomings of judges and lawyers in dealing with the presentation and evaluation of forensic evidence, the controls of the legal system are insufficient to correct all problems (National Research Council, 2009: 53).

[68] These limits are to do with the difficulties that the defence normally faces in obtaining quality experts in certain areas who are willing to give testimonies that contradict other experts; with judges' biases when evaluating these experts; and finally, with the difficulties involved in challenging expert evidence of dubious quality effectively, when it is part of the coherent and more complex narrative that prosecutors usually present in trial (Edmond, 2011: 184–6).

cross-examined. Although there are differences by type of expertise (for example, there seem to be more challenges to psychological assessments in sexual crimes than in other matters), the final average is poor.[69] In addition, my research also established that in cases in which cross examinations are carried out, attorneys have limited ability to question expert evidence effectively. There are various reasons for these phenomena. Actors of the system interviewed acknowledge the lack of specialised training and specific skills, but also mention insufficient time for proper preparation.[70]

This deficit in challenging prosecution forensic evidence is not compensated by the presentation of expert counter-evidence since this only occurs in a small percentage of cases.[71] Consequently, expert evidence submitted to trial is not subject to strict scrutiny by the litigants in the regular operation of the system.

In conclusion, the sum of all these practices described generates the risk of faulty verdicts. While there is some debate over this, the available evidence seems to suggest that it is an environment that is produced by the actual functioning of criminal justice systems, one that is replicated in realities like that of Chile.

15.4 SOME FINAL THOUGHTS

Despite geographical distance and differences in criminal procedure design, the research available in the comparative literature and what I have been able to carry out in Chile into evidentiary practices associated with expert evidence show very similar results. The indication is that that we are in an area of operation of criminal justice systems in which serious risks increase the probability of making wrong decisions. It seems to me that this is due to certain dynamics shared by criminal justice systems as a result of how they work, regardless of their specific design differences at a legal or theoretical level.

Solving the problems identified in this investigation involves the development of public policies at very different levels and not all of them are

---

[69] In the empirical studies of sentences, it was found that there was cross-examination of only 23 per cent of the experts on sexual offenses and 11 per cent of those in crimes against life and health (Duce, 2018: 78).

[70] The Supreme Court study coincides with these findings. For example, 86 per cent of criminal judges interviewed and 89 per cent of attorneys consider that the latter lack sufficient training to deal with experts (Dirección de Estudios de la Corte Suprema, 2017: 36).

[71] In sexual crimes, the empirical study shows that this occurred in 22.7 per cent of the cases, and in 11.1 per cent of crimes against life and health (Duce, 2018: 79–80).

necessarily articulated through reforms to the criminal procedure law. Thus, for example, my research in Chile reveals enormous deficiencies and training needs of judges, prosecutors and defence attorneys in playing a more active role and making better quality decisions when faced with expert evidence. It is not just that there is no training, but also problems of focus and priorities in the training they currently have. There are also needs to strengthen the work done by professionals and experts in the forensic world, who could play a more dedicated role in setting work parameters and quality control for this evidence. Finally, it is also necessary to think about capacity building policies for the public apparatus that generates expert knowledge, including, among other things, developing policies for the generation of advanced human capital specialised in forensic matters as well as in academic research. As is evident from these examples, it is a complex tangle of issues that surpasses the scope of intervention that those of us who work in criminal justice from the legal point of view are accustomed to.

Despite this, I think there is a sensitive area in the working of criminal justice systems that could be subject to improvements at the level of legal reforms. A relevant finding in my research was that, despite there being very debatable and problematic evidentiary practices in the production of expert evidence – which result in evident deficiencies in a sizeable proportion of evidence of this type introduced at trial – in the daily functioning of the system there is nothing to filter those sources to prevent information of low quality and reliability from entering trial. In effect, I was able to confirm that the Oral Trial Preparation Hearing (hereinafter the OTPH), which is designed in the Chilean model to discuss the admissibility of evidence to trial, has not provided a real opportunity to debate the admissibility of expert evidence. The reason is that it is uncommon for litigants to insist on a discussion, nor do judges play a role as filters, except in exceptional situations (Duce, 2018: 73–6).[72] My experience working in other countries of the region is that their intermediate hearings, functional equivalents to Chile's OTPH, are not fulfilling a role like this either, even though I suspect that their evidentiary practices in these matters are, at least, similar to those of my country. In short, we are exposing ourselves rather recklessly to evident risks that can later translate into erroneous decisions, with enormous consequences for those who suffer them.

I think there are several reasons that explain this behaviour in the Chilean case and my impression is that they are also applicable regionally. All of them, it seems to me, are generally associated with basic problems that reflect the

---

[72] I obtained identical findings in similar research into the use of visual recognition of victims or witnesses (Duce, 2017 b: 347–8).

shallowness with which evidentiary issues have traditionally been studied and understood in my country (this contrasts with the first and principal explanation usually given by system actors: the lack of resources/time to do their job well). Let us look at some of these reasons more specifically.

I think there are several reasons that explain this behaviour in the Chilean case and my impression is that they are also applicable regionally. All of them, it seems to me, are generally associated with basic problems that reflect the shallowness with which evidentiary issues have traditionally been studied and understood in my country (this contrasts with the first and principal explanation usually given by system actors: the lack of resources/time to do their job welSl). Let us look at some of these reasons more specifically.

The first, as I was able to verify in my research (Duce, 2017b: 345–8), is that a dominant conception seems to exist according to which the potential problems of this evidence are a matter of its 'evaluation' as trial evidence, and not of its admissibility. It is an idea very typical of the evidentiary culture that feeds our legal tradition, one that has traditionally placed a great faith in the ability of professional judges to solve these problems without affecting their decision-making capacity in cases. The problem with this vision is that today we know that professional judges are equally exposed to making mistakes and also have big problems evaluating this type of evidence. This is without taking into account the various cognitive biases that derive from our common humanity, including those who develop specific professions.

A second reason has to do with the installation of a rather superficial conception of the principle of free proof that has resulted in very little rigour in the development of evidentiary practices. How did this come about? The introduction of an accusatory prosecutorial model in Chile, as in almost all the countries of the region, meant the abandonment of a system of legal or weighted proof that prevailed under the inquisitorial system, where the law established categorically the means of proof that could be used. In its replacement, the accusatory process established a system of probative freedom, according to which the introduction of any means sufficient to produce conviction is allowed, without the need for it to be specifically regulated by law in advance.[73]

---

[73] Thus, Article 295 of the Code of Chile's Criminal Procedure of Chile (hereinafter the CPP) states: 'Freedom of evidence. All relevant facts and circumstances for the proper resolution of the case submitted for prosecution may be proved by any means produced and incorporated in accordance with the law.' The installation of systems of probative freedom has been a notable trend in the context of criminal justice reform processes in Latin America. Thus, standards very similar to Article 295 of the CPP can be identified in almost all the region's codes. For example, in articles 170 of the Criminal Procedure Code of the Dominican Republic; 157.1 of the Peruvian Criminal Procedure Code; 373 of the Colombian Criminal Procedure Code; 182 of the Criminal Procedure Code of Guatemala; 182 of the Criminal Procedure Code of Costa

This is a very profound change in how evidentiary logic is understood and it has often been grasped only superficially, giving rise to various problems of interpretation. One of these problems has been the reasoning that free proof makes the introduction of evidence so flexible that the entry of any type of information source, in any way, is permissible, which would prevent guarantee judges from rejecting evidence except for those cases specifically contemplated in the criminal procedure legislation.[74] The logic of this reasoning is simple: if there is free proof, any means suitable to convince that does not fall within the grounds of exclusion provided for in our criminal procedure system should be accepted as evidence in trial.[75] Without rehearsing the counter-arguments as I have done in other works (Duce, 2016), it seems to me that the doctrine coincides in identifying a natural limit to free proof when relevant values of procedural systems are affected. For this reason, if there is an attempt to present a source of information in the trial that compromises these values (for example, prejudices the quality of the decision or the rights of one of the parties), the system should not admit it. In other words, free proof does not confer on trial participants an unlimited right to present anything as proof in trial that they consider best serves their interests. Lack of clarity and understanding on this point, therefore, has meant that there are practically no controls on the admissibility of the evidence intended for introduction prior to trial.

A third factor has to do with ambiguities in the criminal procedural legislation as to whether criteria exist that allow judges to justify decisions to filter expert evidence or declare it inadmissible. Thus, for example, although I myself have proposed in other works an interpretation of the current rules according to which it can be argued that the CPP of Chile[76] and of other

---

Rica; Article 376 of the Procedural Code of Panama; and, 209 of the Criminal Procedure Code of the Province of Buenos Aires.

[74] In the Chilean case, these are regulated in Article 276 of the CPP and include evidence that is manifestly irrelevant; that which falls on public and well-known facts; over-abundant evidence with dilatory effects and evidence obtained as a result of the infringement of fundamental rights.

[75] This kind of interpretation, as Jordi Ferrer points out, is part of a certain abolitionist doctrinal tradition in probative law (Ferrer, 2010: 5).

[76] I have argued that the CPP contemplates at least three specific requirements of special admissibility: the need for expert evidence, the suitability of the expert, and the reliability of the evidence (Duce, 2010). Some decisions of appellate courts in the country have referred to these criteria. Thus, there are decisions that have validated exclusion due to the lack of accreditation of the suitability of experts – for example, Court of Appeals of San Miguel, case No. 1392-2007, of 12 October 2007, and Court of Appeals of Valparaíso, case No. 644-2018, of 29 April 2016. There have been others in which the problem is that the forensic evidence was of low reliability and the lack of any need for the evidence – for example, Court of Appeals of Rancagua, case No. 199-2013, of 23 May 2013.

countries of the region (Duce, 2013) contemplate special rules for the admissibility of expert evidence – similar to those included in the comparative legislation – the rules have not been read as a way of producing a strong control of admissibility.

To this factor I would add an additional element. To introduce a robust practice for the discussion of admissibility would require, apart from special rules dealing with quality and reliability issues, providing the hearing with the conditions needed to facilitate an in-depth discussion. This means, among other things, regulating precisely early access to quality information on this evidence so that litigants can prepare questions about its admission in advance, and not simply improvise them in the course of the hearings. It also means ensuring that the hearing is a place where these debates can effectively be carried out. The problematic phenomenon observed, as things stand, is that the hearing has increasingly lost its role of making itself into a serious instance of quality control of the information introduced at trial.[77]

Finally, a factor that I think may explain the deficient filter of admissibility carried out, and especially defence attorneys' un-proactive behaviour on the issue, is a defeatist attitude that is a product of the poor results regularly obtained in the OTPH due to all the above explanations. At the end of the day, if the probability of success is low, a natural tendency is to avoid any effort that will not bring positive results.[78] This gives rise to a vicious circle that prevents improvements in the quality of evidentiary practices.

Working from the perspective of devising legal reforms that touch key 'nerves' of the system and promote the development of practices different from the current ones may, I think, be a way to help overcome these problems, at least in part. One of the central ones would be to introduce new rules that establish explicit admissibility criteria for this type of evidence, with rules to the effect that the consequence of non-compliance would be its exclusion from the trial. It also seems to me that much more precise and demanding standards for the discovery of relevant information must be established, to

---

[77] Data from Chile's judicial branch show how over time the OTPH has turned into an increasingly formal instance of debate. This is reflected in a substantial reduction in its average duration time. In effect, while in 2006 this was 37.4 minutes, in 2014 it dropped to much less than half of that: 16.4 minutes. It is necessary to consider that in this time interval a summary of public prosecutor's accusation is also made, its formal defects are remedied, the evidence to be introduced into the trial is presented, among other aspects that necessarily have to be resolved for preparation of the trial. Evidently, these data point to the existence of a serious problem (Arellano, 2017: 64).

[78] This is one of the explanations given in the United States regarding defenders' poor performance in the exclusion of visual recognitions, and I think this can be extended to the forensic issue (Wells et al., 2012: 179).

ensure that there is a real possibility of a fruitful debate on the subject.[79] Finally, the filtering role of judges in this matter should be reinforced.

It would be ingenuous to believe that a legal reform by itself will have the capacity to change reality and practices if it is not accompanied by other elements of a more structural nature. I also know the enormous difficulties that special admissibility rules have had in their practical application in countries like the United States, the important critique of their scope, and the debate that exists about their real impact. Nevertheless, given the present state of affairs as described in this chapter, a legislative reform could send a strong political signal for the different institutions of the criminal justice system to deal more intently with the problems they face in terms of expert evidence and visual recognitions. I pause on this point since it is a crucial one. It seems to me that the greatest value of a legal regulation on this matter will not be found in the courts' capacity to exclude necessarily a large amount of the evidence presented to them. I believe, rather, that its potential lies in the strong signal the legislature would be sending to the parties and judges to take more seriously the problem of the quality and reliability of the evidence they present at trial and of the evidentiary practices associated with its production. In the medium and long term, this should translate into incentives for the development of behaviours that would prevent the most problematic cases – as seen in the Chilean courts in my research – from occurring.[80]

Along with this 'political' effect, a good legal design should, in addition, allow spaces for litigation that have not been developed at present due to the lack of regulation and that could serve as a control of the quality and reliability of expert evidence. That would give more space for the development of jurisprudence that is rather more sophisticated than the current one and that addresses the most problematic practices. In short, all this could translate

---

[79] The poor overall quality of the discovery that is currently made in the OTPH is reflected in a fact revealed in the CEJA study, which found that only in 40 per cent of the cases observed did the Public Prosecutor's Office specifically indicate the facts or points of evidence for which it offered each piece of evidence (Arellano, 2017: 65).

[80] It seems to me that the Supreme Court of Canada points to this logic in a relatively recent case in which it established for the first time that the impartiality of the experts could also be required as a criterion for the admissibility of such evidence to trial. In April 2015, the court noted that experts' impartiality, understood as their ability to fulfil their duty to report objectively regardless of the party that produces them in trial, is not only a problem of assessment of the evidence at trial but also of its admissibility. Then it established a standard that they themselves consider should not be an obstacle or impediment for the admission of most experts, recognising that their decision rather tries to send a signal to litigants and judges to improve their practices. See *White Burgess Langille* v. *Abbott and Haliburton*, 2015 SCC 23, at https://scc-csc.lexum.com/scc-csc/scc-csc/en/item/15328/index.do (last visited 21 May 2018).

into a refinement and improvement of practices and overcome the 'defeatism' over these matters that I have identified. Finally, a legal regulation could also serve to set the floor or basic parameters for the development of protocols for the action of institutions like the police and forensic laboratories so that it is more consistent with the available scientific evidence, thus improving quality and reliability in the production of expert evidence. In addition, it would give these protocols greater normative weight and enforceability, as they would be backed by a legal norm and not simply by institutional volition, as is the case with the current protocols.

It is clear to me that the roadmap for solving the problems identified in my research is long and complex. A first step is to be aware, at least, of the problems we face and to have a more precise diagnosis of them. I hope that this work will help in part to meet these initial, but no less important, objectives.

REFERENCES

Arellano, J. (2017). *Desafíos de la reforma procesal penal en Chile: análisis retrospectivo a más de una década*, Santiago: Centro de Estudios de Justicia de las Américas.

Beecher-Monas, E. (2007). *Evaluating Scientific Evidence: An Interdisciplinary Framework for Intellectual Due Process*, New York: Cambridge University Press.

Blume, J. and Helm, R. (2014). The Unexonerated: Factually Innocent Defendants Who Plead Guilty. *Cornell Law Review*, 113, 157–91.

Castillo, I. (2013). Enjuiciando al Proceso Penal Chileno desde el Inocentrismo (algunos apuntes sobre la necesidad de tomarse en serio a los inocentes). *Revista Política Criminal*, 8(15), 249–313.

Cutler, B. and Zapf, P. (2014). Introduction: The Definition, Breadth, and Importance of Forensic Psychology, in Cutler, B., Zapf, P. (editors in chief), *APA Handbook of Forensic Psychology (Vol. 1)*, Washington: American Psychological Association, xvii–xxii.

Dennis, I. (2010). *The Law of Evidence*, England: Sweet and Maxwell.

Dirección de Estudios de la Corte Suprema (2017). *Peritajes en Chile*, Santiago: Corte Suprema.

Duce, M. (2010). Admisibilidad de la prueba pericial en juicios orales: un modelo para armar en la jurisprudencia nacional, in D. Accatino, ed., *Formación y valoración de la prueba en el proceso penal*, Santiago: Abeledo Perrot, 45–86.

Duce, M. (2013). *La prueba pericial*, Buenos Aires: Ediciones Didot.

Duce, M. (2015). Algunas lecciones a partir de cuatro casos de condenas de inocentes en Chile. *Revista de Derecho Universidad Católica del Norte*, 22 (1), 149–208.

Duce, M. (2016). Los informes en derecho nacional y su inadmisibilidad como prueba a juicio en el proceso penal chileno, *Revista de Derecho Universidad Austral*, XXIX(1), 297–327.

Duce, M. (2017a). Los recursos de revisión y la condena de inocentes en Chile: Una aproximación empírica en el período 2007–2016. *Doctrina y Jurisprudencia Penal*, 30, 3–40.

Duce, M. (2017b). Los reconocimientos oculares: una aproximación empírica a su funcionamiento y algunas recomendaciones para su mejora. *Política Criminal*, 12(23), 291–379.

Duce, M. (2018). Una aproximación empírica al uso y prácticas de la prueba pericial en el proceso penal chileno a la luz de su impacto en los errores del sistema. *Política Criminal*, 13(25), 42–103.

Edmond, G. (2011). Actual Innocents? Legal Limitations and Their Implications for Forensic Science and Medicine. *Australian Journal of Forensic Sciences*, 43(2–3), 177–212.

Edmond, G. (2013). Introduction: Expert Evidence in Report and Courts. *Australian Journal of Forensic Sciences*, 45(3), 248–62.

Edmond, G. (2015). Forensic Science Evidence and the Conditions for Rational (Jury) Evaluation. *Melbourne University Law Review*, 39(1), 77–127.

Ferrer, J. (2010). La prueba es libertad, pero no tanto. Una teoría de la prueba cuasi-benthamiana, in D. Accatino, ed., *Formación y valoración de la prueba en el proceso penal*, Santiago: Abeledo Perrot, 3–19.

Findley, K. (2011-2012). Adversarial Inquisitions: Rethinking the Search for the Truth, *New York Law School Law Review*, 56, 912–41.

Forst, B. (2013). Wrongful Convictions in a World of Miscarriages of Justice, R. Huff and M. Killias, eds., *Wrongful Conviction and Miscarriages of Justice: Causes and Remedies in North American and European Criminal Justice Systems*, New York: Routledge, 15–43.

Freckelton, I. (2009). Scientific Evidence, in I. Freckelton, and H. Selby, eds., *Expert Evidence*, 4th ed., Victoria: Thomson Reuters, 1120–36.

Freckelton, I., Goodman-Delahunty, J., Horan, J. and McKimmie, B. (2016). *Expert Evidence and Criminal Jury Trials*, Oxford: Oxford University Press.

FPT Heads of Prosecutions Committee Working Group (2004). *Report on the Prevention of Miscarriages of Justice*, Canada: Department of Justice.

FPT Heads of Prosecutions Committee (2011). *The Path to Justice: Preventing Wrongful Convictions*, Canada: FPT Heads of Prosecutions Committee.

Garret, B. (2011). *Convicting the Innocent*, Cambridge MA: Harvard University Press.

Garret, B. and Naufeld, P. (2009). Invalid Forensic Testimony and Wrongful Convictions. *Virginia Law Review*, 95(1), 1–97.

Gascón, M. (2013). Prueba Científica. Un Mapa de Retos, in C. Vázquez ed., *Estándares de Prueba y Prueba Científica*, Madrid: Marcial Pons, 181–202.

Gilliéron, G. (2013). Wrongful Convictions in Switzerland: A Problem of Summary Proceedings. *University of Cincinnati Law Review*, 80(4), 1145–65.

Gold, A. (2003). *Expert Evidence in Criminal Law: The Scientific Approach*, Canada: Irving Law.

Gould, J., Carrano, J., Leo, R. and Hail Jares, K. (2014). Predicting Erroneous Convictions. *Iowa Law Review*, 99, 471–522.

Gould, J., Carrano, J, Leo, R. and Hail Jares, K. (2014). Innocent Defendants: Divergent Cases Outcomes and What They Teach Us, in M. Zalman and J. Carrano, eds., *Wrongful Conviction and Criminal Justice Reform*, New York: Routledge, 73–89.

Gould, J., Carrano, J, Leo, R. and Young, J. (2013) *Predicting Erroneous Convictions: A Social Science Approach to Miscarriages of Justice*, USA, National Institute of Justice. Available at: www.ncjrs.gov/pdffiles1/nij/grant s/241389.pdf.

Gould, J. and Leo, R. (2016). The Path to Exoneration, University of San Francisco Law Research Paper, 2016-3.

Gross, S. (2008). Convicting the Innocent. *Annual Review of Law and Social Science*, 4, 173–92.

Gross, S. (2008). Convicting the Innocent, Working Paper no. 103, University of Michigan Law School.

Gross, S., O'Brien, B., Hu, C. and Kennedy, E. H. (2014). Rate of False Convictions of Criminal Defendants Who Are Sentenced to Death. *Proceedings of the National Academy of Sciences of the United States of America*, 11(20), 7230–5.

Haack, S. (2003). Inquiry and Advocacy, Fallibilism and Finality: Culture and Inference in Science and the Law. *Law, Probability and Risk*, 2, 205–14.

Harris, D. (2012). *Failed Evidence*, New York: New York University Press.

Hirshberg, M., (1969). *La Sentencia Errónea en el Proceso Penal*, Banzhaf T. trans., Buenos Aires: Ediciones Jurídicas Europa-América.

House of Commons Science and Technology Committee (2005). *Forensic Science on Trial*, London: The Stationery Office Limited.

Huff, R. and Killias, M., eds. (2010). *Wrongful Conviction: International Perspectives on Miscarriages of Justice*, Philadelphia: Temple University Press.

Huff, R. and Killias, M., eds. (2013). *Wrongful Convictions and Miscarriages of Justice: Causes and Remedies in North American and European Criminal Justice Systems*, New York: Routledge.

Jiahong, H. (2016) *Back from the Dead: Criminal Justice and Wrongful Convictions in China*, Honolulu: University of Hawaii Press.

King, J. (2013). Beyond Life and Liberty: The Evolving Right to Counsel. *Harvard Civil Rights-Civil Liberties Law Review*, 48, 1–48.

Mauet, T. (2007). *Estudios de técnicas de litigación*, K. Ventura and L. M., trans., Perú: Jurista Editores.

Ministry of Justice (2013). *The Government's Response to the Law Commission Report: Expert Evidence in Criminal Proceedings in England and Wales*, England: Ministry of Justice.

Natapoff, A. (2012). Misdemeanors. *Southern California Law Review*, 85, 101–63.

National Research Council (2009). *Strengthening Forensic Science in the United States: A Path Forward*, Washington, DC: The National Academy of Sciences.

Naughton, M. (2013). *The Innocent and the Criminal Justice System. A Sociological Analysis of Miscarriages of Justice*, United Kingdom: Palgrave Macmillan.

Risinger, M. (2007). Innocent Convicted: An Empirically Justified Wrongful Conviction Rate. *The Journal of Criminal Law and Criminology*, 97(3), 761–806.

Roach, K. (2009). Forensic Science and Miscarriages of Justice: Some Lessons from a Comparative Perspective. *Jurimetrics*, 50, 67–92.

Roach, K. (2010). Wrongful Convictions: Adversarial and Inquisitorial Themes, *North Carolina Journal of International Law and Commercial Regulation*, 35 (2), 387–446.

Roberts, J. (2011). Why Misdemeanors Matter: Defining Effective Advocacy in Lower Criminal Courts. *University of California Davis Law Review*, 45, 277–372.

Roxin, C. (2003). *Derecho Procesal Penal*, 25th ed., G. Córdoba and D. Pastor, trans., Buenos Aires: Editores del Puerto.

Sacks, M. and Spellman, B. (2016). *The Psychological Foundations of Evidence Law*, New York: New York University Press.

Schauer F. and Spellman B. (2013). Is Expert Evidence Really Different? *Notre Dame Law Review*, 89, 1–26.

Simon, D. (2012). *In Doubt: The Psychology of the Criminal Justice Process*, Cambridge MA: Harvard University Press.

Taruffo, M. (2008). *La Prueba*, L. Manríquez and J. Ferrer Beltrán (translators), Madrid: Marcial Pons.

The Law Commission (2009). *The Admissibility of Expert Evidence in Criminal Proceedings in England and Wales*, Consultation Paper no. 190, London: The Law Commission.

The Law Commission (2011). *Expert Evidence in Criminal Proceedings in England and Wales*, Law Com. No. 325, London: Stationary Office.

Thomas, S. (2015). Addressing Wrongful Convictions: An Examination of Texas's New Junk Science Writ and Other Measures for Protecting the Innocent, *Houston Law Review*, 52, 1037–68.

Wells, G., Greathouse, S. and Smalarz, L. (2012). Why Do Motions to Suppress Suggestive Eyewitness Identifications Fail? in B. Cutlered ed., *Conviction of the Innocent*, Washington, DC: American Psychological Association, 167–84.

PART V

STANDARDS OF EVIDENCE AS DECISION-MAKING RULES

16

Burdens of Proof and Choice of Law

Dale A. Nance

16.1 THE PROBLEM

Consider the following hypothetical case: the court in one state or country, what I will call the "forum state," is called upon to decide a civil case the events and parties of which have contacts with another state or country, the "non-forum state." Assume that, because of these contacts with the non-forum state, the forum state court decides that the proper choice of law is to apply the non-forum state's substantive law governing the cause of action. My question, then, is: Which state's rules regarding the burden of proof should control?[1] Alternatively, one can isolate the issue even further by supposing the law of the forum state and non-forum state are the same except for the burden of proof, yet the contacts with the non-forum state are such that the forum court would apply non-forum substantive law, were it different. The question in this case is whether the difference in the burden of proof is the kind of difference that warrants applying the non-forum proof rule.

16.2 THE TRADITIONAL APPROACH

The traditional answer to these questions invoked the familiar substance/procedure distinction, the forum court selecting the procedural rules of the forum. Procedure was taken to include burdens of proof, so burdens of proof would be supplied by forum law. This is the position taken, at least nominally, by the first Restatement of Conflict of Laws, published by the American Law

---

[1] I have assumed a civil claim because of the long-established principle that one state will not apply the criminal law of another, so the question of choosing proof rules does not arise. See, e.g., Restatement (First) of Conflict of Laws § 427 (1934).

Institute in 1934,[2] an approach still followed in a minority of American states and many other countries.[3]

To illustrate, one of the leading American cases in the early twentieth century was a decision by the highest court of Massachusetts in a negligence case brought there based on an automobile accident that had occurred in the neighboring state of Rhode Island.[4] At the time, both states had a cause of action for negligently causing injury, and both states recognized the plaintiff's contributory negligence to be a bar to recovery. If the suit had been brought in Rhode Island, the plaintiff would have been required to bear the burden of proving both the defendant's negligence and his own freedom from fault, whereas under Massachusetts law, the plaintiff was required to prove the defendant's negligence, but the burden was on the defendant to prove the plaintiff's contributory negligence as an affirmative defense. The highest Massachusetts court, in a one-page opinion, held that, while "the law of the place where the injury was received determines whether a right of action exists," the burden of proof rule was procedural, governed by forum law, so the burden was properly placed on the defendant to prove the plaintiff's contributory negligence in accord with Massachusetts law.[5]

This principle for burdens of proof was problematic in those situations where the non-forum cause of action did not have a direct analogue in forum law. In that case, there would not be any forum rule for the burden of proof: without a cause of action, there would have been no occasion for the courts (or the legislature) of the forum state to specify a burden of proof. Courts faced with such unusual non-forum causes of action would often say that the non-forum proof rule was inextricably intertwined with the non-forum substantive claim.[6] The traditional choice-of-law preference for the forum rule was thus subject to an exception. This exception is not to be found in the Restatement's formal statements of principle, however, but only in the accompanying "comments" by the drafters.[7]

Moreover, this exception never adequately accounted for the full range of American case law. Some cases selected the non-forum proof rule even when the forum state had the same cause of action except for a difference in the

---

[2] See Restatement (First) of Conflict of Laws § 595 (1934).
[3] See, e.g., *Shaps v. Provident Life and Accident Ins. Co.*, 826 So.2d 250, 254 (Fla. 2002).
[4] See *Levy v. Steiger*, 124 N.E. 477 (Mass. 1919).
[5] The opinion also states that "the law of the place where the action is brought regulates the remedy and its incidents, such as pleading, evidence, and practice." Ibid. This reflects an early, now largely obsolete, conflation of the substance/procedure distinction with the right/remedy distinction. This confusion results in giving a very wide scope to the application of forum law. For the best discussion of this history, see Risinger, 1982: 190–203.
[6] See, e.g., *Fitzpatrick v. International Ry. Co.*, 169 N.E. 112 (N.Y. 1929).
[7] See Restatement (First) Conflict of Laws § 595(1) comment a (1934).

burden of proof.[8] Sometimes these courts would try to avoid rejecting the conventional syllogism – that is, a burden of proof rule is procedural, so it must be governed by forum law – by characterizing the burden of proof rule in the non-forum state as a "condition" on the cause of action itself, thus making the proof rule look more substantive.[9] But rarely was there any explanation of why this made sense in one context but not in another. The cases applying the general rule and those applying the exception were simply irreconcilable.

16.3 TWENTIETH-CENTURY NORTH AMERICAN DEVELOPMENTS

Around the time of the publication of the first Restatement, a sea change of ideas was beginning in the United States. Part of it was a rejection of the kind of formalism that these early cases represented. Scholars pressed courts to give up the substance/procedure distinction as a tool for deciding choice-of-law questions, replacing it with direct consideration of the policies that determine whether a particular rule should be governed by forum law (see, e.g., Cook, 1933: 333). This meant that a rule that was conventionally considered procedural might very well be considered important enough to the substantive right being litigated that the two would be taken together for choice-of-law purposes. For example, the rule clearly solidified that the measure of damages is ordinarily governed by the law of the state governing the cause of action (Felix and Whitten, 2011: 231–3).

Another part of this sea change was doctrinal: in 1938, the United States Supreme Court decided *Erie R. Co. v. Tompkins*,[10] which radically changed the law of federal courts exercising jurisdiction not based on the application of federal statutory or constitutional claims, based instead merely on the fact that the parties are from different states or countries, which is known as "diversity of citizenship" jurisdiction. *Erie* was understood as requiring that federal courts in diversity jurisdiction apply state substantive law but federal procedural law. This became a central premise of what is called "vertical choice of law" in our federal system. Although the grounds of the decision in *Erie* are still debated, one of the undeniable goals of the new doctrine was to prevent out-of-state plaintiffs from obtaining a more favorable governing rule merely by filing in federal courts than they would encounter had they filed in state courts, and also to prevent in-state defendants from doing the same sort of thing by "removing" a claim initially filed in state court to federal court based on diversity of citizenship, a removal authorized by statute.[11]

---

[8] See, e.g., *Precourt v. Driscoll*, 157 A. 525 (N.H. 1931).
[9] See, e.g., *Redick v. M.B. Thomas Auto Sales*, 273 S.W.2d 228, 232–5 (Mo. 1954).
[10] 304 US 487 (1938).
[11] So important is this consideration that the Supreme Court quickly held that among those state rules that the federal court was obligated to apply are the state's rules regarding conflict of laws.

Yet differences in *procedural* rules between state and federal courts also created serious incentives to engage in such "forum shopping." This forced the federal courts in diversity cases gradually to expand what was considered "substantive" to embrace a variety of state rules that would normally have been considered procedural.[12] In particular, early in this process, most rules regarding the burden of proof were recognized as substantive for such vertical choice-of-law purposes,[13] even though still nominally considered procedural for ordinary "horizontal" choice-of-law purposes.[14]

This vertical choice-of-law jurisprudence has placed considerable pressure on the substance/procedure distinction in horizontal choice of law, always in the direction of expanding what is considered substantive. The basic principle expressed by academics has been that, once the forum court chooses to apply non-forum substantive law, the forum court should employ as much of the law of the non-forum state pertaining to the issue as is possible, whether that law is ordinarily thought to be substantive or procedural. The only limits usually acknowledged are that it is unnecessary to adopt non-forum procedural rules that have minimal impact on the result or would be excessively costly or inconvenient to replicate in the forum.[15]

16.4 THE SECOND RESTATEMENT

While an expansive recognition of non-forum "procedural" rules as appropriate candidates for choice of law is probably the dominant academic preference among American conflicts scholars, the case law is only partially cooperating.

See *Klaxon Co. v. Stentor Mfg. Co.*, 313 U.S. 487 (1941). This has meant that horizontal choice of law in the United States is essentially state law; federal horizontal choice-of-law doctrine is mostly limited to cases that are based on federal subject matter jurisdiction. See, e.g., *Lauritzen v. Larsen*, 345 U.S. 571 (1953) (admiralty claims).

[12] See, e.g., *Guaranty Trust Co. v. York*, 326 U.S. 99 (1945) (statute of limitations). The principal exceptions – rules as to which the federal courts will *not* defer to state law – are those governed by an explicit federal statute, such as the Federal Rules of Civil Procedure or the Federal Rules of Evidence – see, e.g., *Hanna v. Plumer*, 380 U.S. 460 (1965) (federal rule of civil procedure) – or by policies supported by an explicit provision of the federal Constitution – see, e.g., *Byrd v. Blue Ridge Rural Elec. Coop., Inc.*, 356 U.S. 525 (1958) (right to jury trial).

[13] See, e.g., *Cities Services Oil Co. v. Dunlap*, 308 U.S. 208 (1939) (allocation of burden of persuasion); *Dick v. New York Life Ins. Co.*, 359 U.S. 437 (1959) (presumption shifting the burden of persuasion).

[14] See, e.g., *Sampson v. Channell*, 110 F.2d 754 (1st Cir.), *cert. denied*, 310 U.S. 650 (1940) (holding, in a diversity case, that the burden of persuasion on contributory negligence is substantive in the vertical choice context, and thus governed by state law, but procedural in the horizontal context, and thus governed by Massachusetts law even though the governing substantive law was that of Maine).

[15] See, e.g., Morgan, 1944; Sedler, 1962. See also, Mosteller et al., 2020, § 349.

Consider the main principle on the subject in the second Restatement of Conflict of Laws, published in 1971, trying to capture the evolving case law:

§ 122 (*Issues Relating to Judicial Administration*): A court usually applies its own local law rules prescribing how litigation shall be conducted even when it applies the local law rules of another state to resolve other issues in the case.

Notice that § 122 drops the conceptual category of "procedure," replacing it with the somewhat more descriptive phrase, "rules prescribing how litigation shall be conducted." This section says that the forum court *usually* applies its own rules of this type, and the accompanying "comments" justify this by noting the inconvenience of doing otherwise. Here the drafters explicitly refer to rules of pleading, service of process, discovery, mode of trial (for example, jury or non-jury), and of execution of judgments.[16] This corresponds reasonably well to the prevailing academic opinions about sound choice-of-law policy.[17]

But the Restatement drafters explicitly note that burden of proof rules are special, constituting a close case that must be resolved differently in different situations. Reflecting the diversity of judicial opinions, the second Restatement provides, in §§ 133–5, the same default principle, one still favoring forum law, regarding the various issues relating to the burden of proof:

§§ 133–135: (*Burden of Proof; Burden of Production; Sufficiency of Evidence*): The forum will apply its own local law [concerning the burden of proof, the burden of production, or sufficiency of evidence] unless the primary purpose of the relevant rule of the state of the applicable law is to affect decision of the issue rather than to regulate the conduct of the trial. In that event, the rule of the state of the otherwise applicable law will be applied.[18]

As compared to the first Restatement, here the acknowledgment of exceptional treatment – a court's potential escape vehicle – is articulated in the conflicts principles themselves, not merely in the comments. Instead of the substance/procedure distinction, many American courts now invoke a distinction between "rules designed to affect the decision of the issue" and "rules designed to regulate the trial," only the former being governed by the non-forum state law.

Commentators have not found the second Restatement's articulation to be particularly helpful, given that all rules that affect the decision do so by

---

[16] See Restatement (Second) of Conflict of Laws § 122 comment a (1971).
[17] There is little doubt that the availability of a jury trial may affect a party's choice of forum, yet this is not considered a matter governed by the *lex causae*. That demonstrates that the concern about forum shopping is not necessarily controlling.
[18] See Restatement (Second) of Conflict of Laws §§ 133–5 (1971) (emphasis supplied). I have consolidated these rules into one because they all state the same principle for choice of law.

regulating the trial, and all rules that regulate the trial have at least the contemplated potential to affect the decision. In particular, it seems hard to imagine a burden of proof rule that is *not* designed to affect the decision.[19] What else could it mean to say that one party, rather than the other, bears such a burden?

16.5 THE ANALYTICAL ISSUES

In thinking this way, commentators seem to presuppose that what it means for a rule merely to "regulate the trial" is for that rule to have *no significant effect* on the decision in the case about which party prevails, such as a rule that simply reduces the public cost of litigation, or a rule that coordinates the parties' conduct so as to reduce both private and public costs.

I think this is a mistake. In order to see why, one must distinguish between two variants of what it means to "affect the decision of the issue":

(1) Some rules are designed to systematically favor one side of the dispute or one class of litigants over another in the final decision; while

(2) Some rules are designed to affect the final decision, but without regard to whether that effect will benefit some class of plaintiffs or defendants.

The important observation here is that, for choice-of-law purposes, type 2 rules should be grouped together with rules that are designed merely to "regulate the trial." Such type 2 rules are designed to affect the decision of the issue, to be sure, but not to favor one side or the other. What the opinions no doubt mean, when they refer to proof rules or other rules that are designed to "affect the decision" is rules that are designed to affect the decision *in a certain way*, in the manner of type 1 rules, by intentionally favoring one class of litigants over another, rules specifying or altering the law's preference for one such class.[20] Most American commentators in this field neglect the importance of type 2 burden of proof rules.[21]

---

[19]   See, e.g., Mosteller et al., 2020, § 349.
[20]   This surfaces clearly in only one of the many illustrations provided by the drafters of the Restatement. In Illustration 5, the drafters considered the application of a statute interpreted by the courts of state X, in which it was enacted, as placing the burden of persuasion on an employer to prove that an injury to an employee occurring during the scope of employment was not caused by the employer's negligence. The drafters state: "This statute, as so interpreted, will be applied in an action brought by [an employee] in a court in state Y to recover for his injuries [in state X] if the Y court finds, as it probably will, that the X statute was primarily designed to affect decision of the issue of the employer's negligence *in favor of the injured employee.*" Restatement (Second) of Conflict of Laws § 133 illustration 5 (1971) (emphasis supplied).
[21]   Part of the explanation of this failure of perception may be a belief that procedural neutrality is largely a myth. From the perspective of the litigant – i.e., considering only whether a given rule might have an effect that would enter a litigant's calculation about where to file suit – that may

But are there any type 2 burden of proof rules? The most important examples of type 2 rules are rules that are designed to improve the accuracy of the resulting judgment. The existence of such rules is readily acknowledged outside the burden of proof context. Most admissibility rules, other than privileges, are of this type, applying indiscriminately to both plaintiff and defendant. Whether any such rule is wise or unwise is usually debatable, but what is rarely seriously challenged is the idea that such rules are intended to improve the accuracy of the resulting verdict, without regard to which side of the dispute is favored thereby. And it is generally conceded that this means that most forum court admissibility rules apply even when a non-forum doctrine of tort or contract law is selected to govern the dispute.[22]

But what about burdens of proof? Is there some aspect of proof burdens that is analogous to admissibility rules in this respect? If not, if all burden of proof rules are type 1 rules, then the choice-of-law principle, at least the default principle, ought to be the *opposite* of what the second Restatement provides. And that is the conclusion of most American conflicts scholars.

Now, the second Restatement does at least recognize a distinction that Anglo-American evidence scholars routinely emphasize, the distinction between the burden of persuasion (or the risk of non-persuasion) and the burden of production (see generally, Park et al., 2022: §§ 2.02–2.06). But the Restatement provides the same default principle, and the same escape principle, for both kinds of burdens. Here are the pertinent sections:

§ 133 (*Burden of Proof*): The forum will apply its own local law in determining which party has the burden of persuading the trier of fact on a particular issue unless the primary purpose of the relevant rule of the state of the applicable law is to affect decision of the issue rather than to regulate the conduct of the

---

be true. See, e.g., Tidmarsh, 2011: 877, 891–2 (2011). But the litigant's perspective is not the correct one here; the proper perspective is that of the policy maker. See Illmer, 2009. Dr Illmer's quest for neutrality is sound, though I think his criterion of neutrality is not quite right. He draws a distinction between rules "affecting the decision on the merits" and those "concerned with the decision on the merits," with only the latter being referred to the *lex causae*. Ibid. at 246. In so doing, Illmer seems essentially to have replicated the distinction, such as it is, to be found in the Restatement. This may be because he considers the critical difference to be one of focus: "Neutrality is determined by the abstract nature of the matter in question, not by reference to the concrete case." Ibid. This is also a mistake. Abstraction is not the key; rather, the key is whether the rule is designed to favor one side or the other. All the rules at issue, even those of type 1, are articulated in abstract terms, so as to apply to a range of cases. Conversely, type 2 rules are certainly "concerned with the decision on the merits," in that they are *designed* to affect the decision; they do not merely affect the decision incidentally. It is not surprising, therefore, that some scholars have found Illmer's suggested criterion unhelpful. See, e.g., Garnett, 2012: 39 n. 155.

[22] See Restatement (Second) of Conflict of Laws § 138 (1971).

trial. In that event, the rule of the state of the otherwise applicable law will be applied.

§ 134 *(Burden of Going Forward with the Evidence; Presumptions):* The forum will apply its own local law in determining which party has the burden of going forward with the evidence on a particular issue unless the primary purpose of the relevant rule of the state of the applicable law is to affect decision of the issue rather than to regulate the conduct of the trial. In that event, the rule of the state of the otherwise applicable law will be applied.[23]

One wonders why the need to have two choice rules when the same choice principles apply to both categories of proof rules. Perhaps the articulation of distinct (albeit identical) rules for the burden of persuasion and the burden of production reflects a latent recognition that different choice-of-law results might be appropriate, perhaps that the escape principle works out differently in the two contexts. We should look more closely at these two kinds of burden.

Each of them has two parts: an allocation, and a specification of severity. The burden of persuasion, or risk of non-persuasion, is allocated to one side or the other and rarely moves during the entire proof process. It is applied by the fact-finder during deliberation. Its severity is specified by what is usually called the "standard of proof," such as proof by a preponderance of the evidence, or proof by clear and convincing evidence, or even proof beyond reasonable doubt, which is on rare occasions encountered in civil cases. All this is determined by statute or judicial decision for each cause of action. And by allocating the burden with regard to certain ultimate material facts, the law determines whether each such fact is part of the plaintiff's prima facie case or, instead, part of an affirmative defense.[24]

This burden is surely a type 1 rule: it specifies the degree to which the law favors the plaintiff or defendant. By making the standard of proof relatively high, say by invoking the standard of proof by clear and convincing evidence (as is common when the plaintiff alleges fraud or malice, for example), the law favors defendants with regard to those claims. Similarly, by placing the burden of persuasion on the defendant rather than the plaintiff, thus making the fact in question a matter of affirmative defense (such as the expiration of the statute of limitations), the law favors the plaintiff with regard to that factual finding. And so on. Making these decisions is not unlike choosing whether or not to

---

[23] Restatement (Second) of Conflict of Laws §§ 133, 134 (1971).
[24] See Park et al., 2022: § 2.03. A careful reader will have noticed that neither § 133 nor § 134 of the Restatement expressly addresses what I have called the "severity" issue; both are written to address only the allocation issue. The comments do not suggest otherwise. To be sure, § 135 addresses "sufficiency" issues, but these are issues related to the severity of the burden of *production*, not the severity of the burden of persuasion. A distinct lacuna results.

add an additional element to what the plaintiff must prove: adding an element favors the defendant, and intentionally so. Removing an element favors the plaintiff. To this extent, the mainstream American conflicts scholars are correct: the default principle of the second Restatement is backwards. It should specify that non-forum law governs the burden of persuasion on an issue that is otherwise controlled by non-forum substantive law. In fact, the modern decisions generally so hold.[25]

Now consider the burden of production. This burden, of course, takes on very different forms in Anglo-American adversarial trials than in trials conducted on the civil-law model. In Anglo-American trials, this burden compels a party to produce evidence at trial. The allocation of this burden can shift back and forth during the trial, and when the case is ultimately submitted by the court to the fact-finder for decision, there is no longer any production burden at all. The burden of production is a collection of rules used to assess whether each party has done what it must do in terms of the presentation of evidence in order to be entitled to have a fact-finder rule on the merits. These "sufficiency" rules, which allocate, reallocate, and determine the severity of the production burden, serve numerous purposes: sometimes they allow trial courts to place pressure on a party to present evidence that the party would not otherwise choose to present; sometimes, they allow the trial courts to save time and expense by terminating easy cases without the necessity of jury deliberation; sometimes, they allow the trial courts to remind the jury not to be overly legalistic in its assessment of evidence, not to check their common sense at the door; sometimes they allow trial courts to preclude irrational decisions by juries; and sometimes they allow appellate courts or legislatures to control the trial courts' conduct in doing the foregoing things (see Park et al., 2022: § 2.06).

In contrast, it is often said that there is no burden of production in the civil-law model of adjudication, because the parties do not select and present evidence like they do in Anglo-American trials (see, e.g., Taruffo, 2003: 659, 672). Instead, based on (but certainly not limited to) witness lists and documents provided by the parties, a judicial magistrate undertakes to obtain the evidence needed to resolve the case. To be sure, the failure of a court of first instance to pursue an appropriate line of investigation may be the basis for an appeal. Appellate courts in civil-law jurisdictions, at least those at the first level

---

[25] See, e.g., *Kabo v. Summa Corp.*, 523 F. Supp. 1326, 1331 (E.D. Pa. 1981); *DeSantis v. Wachenhut*, 732 S.W. 2d 29, 34–6 (Tex. App. 1986), rev'd on other grounds, 793 S.W. 2d 670 (Tex. 1990); *In re IBP, Inc. Shareholders' Litigation*, 789 A.2d 13 (Del. Ch. 2001); *DaimlerChrysler Corporation Healthcare Benefits Plan v. Durden*, 448 F.3d 918 (6th Cir. 2006); *Otal Inv. Ltd. v. M/V Clary*, 494 F.3d 40, 50 (2d Cir. 2007); *Arkoma Basin Exploration Company, Inc. v. FMF Associates 1990-A, Ltd.*, 249 S.W.3d 380 (Tex. 2008).

of appeal, sometimes return such cases to the original trial court for consideration of additional evidence, but more often they simply take the additional evidence and render a new judgment.[26] So, rather than concluding that there is no burden of production in civil-law jurisdictions, it would be more accurate to conclude that no such burden rests *on the parties*, but a similar burden rests on the judiciary itself, and its satisfaction is tested by appeal, rather than by a motion imposing a sanction on an opponent at trial. In any event, such a burden works quite differently than the analogous notion in Anglo-American trials.

Anglo-American courts and commentators addressing the conflict of laws question express divergent views about the role of burden of production rules. Some emphasize that, in the absence of any evidence on an issue, the burden of production cannot be met, so it is "outcome-determinative"; these commentators infer that the burden of production is type 1, designed to favor defendants (see, e.g., Mosteller et al., 2020: § 349 at 785). This *Erie*-inspired argument is unconvincing. It is little different from observing that, under the right conditions, an admissibility rule will be outcome-determinative and favor the defendant. True enough, but under the right conditions, either an admissibility rule or the burden of production can also result in a judgment *for the plaintiff*. That is just the necessary consequence of using rules that must be enforced.[27] It does not mean that the rule is there to favor one side over the other in regard to the decision on the merits.[28]

On the other hand, some of these courts and commentators emphasize that one of the parties must go first in presenting evidence in an adversarial trial, and it really does not matter much which one does. It is like choosing whether to drive on the right side or the left side of the street: one must pick a convention so that everyone knows how to do things, a simple coordination problem. By this logic, the burden of production is merely a matter of the order of presenting evidence. That is, it is neither a type 1 nor a type 2 rule, but rather a rule regulating the conduct of the trial. That may have been the thinking of the drafters of the second Restatement. But it ignores the many functions I have noted, functions that relate instead to improving accuracy and

---

[26]   See e.g., Murray and Stürner, 2004: 373–86; Herzog and Weser, 1967: 397–408.

[27]   See Garnett, 2012: 21. ("[P]otentially any procedural rule in a given context may affect the rights and duties of the parties and so alter the result.")

[28]   The objection might be made that, statistically speaking, directed verdicts are more commonly given against the party bearing the burden of persuasion, i.e., usually the plaintiff. But even if this contingent fact is true, this merely reflects the fact that the allocation of the burden of persuasion *is* designed to favour one side over the other. So long as the burden of persuasion is appropriately selected, any statistical bias in the non-forum state derives from the alignment of the initial burden of production with the burden of persuasion.

monitoring the respective roles of judge and jury, as well as merely reducing costs and achieving coordination. These effects are real. And the accuracy effects, in particular, can result in changing which party wins. Still, they are not type 1 rules; they are type 2 rules.[29] The following discussion places this observation in a broader perspective.

16.6 THE BURDEN OF PRODUCTION AND THE WEIGHT OF EVIDENCE

In a monograph I published in 2016, I placed the burden of production within the context of a wide variety of rules the collective purpose of which is to manage what I called the *Keynesian weight* of the evidence (Nance, 2016: 201–12). (The name comes from some fascinating suggestions by John Maynard Keynes in his early book on probability.) Keynesian weight is different from the weight of evidence that lawyers are accustomed to talking about. We usually think of weight of evidence as the degree to which the evidence favors one side over the other. Keynesian weight, on the other hand, is a measure of the degree of completeness of the evidence, the extent to which the tribunal has been provided the evidence that is available to be obtained and considered. Augmenting Keynesian weight may or may not affect weight in the first sense; that is, it may or may not affect the degree to which the evidence favors one side or the other. Except in unusual circumstances, however, it necessarily increases expected accuracy.[30]

In adversarial adjudication, rules managing Keynesian weight include, but are certainly not limited to, rules of mandatory disclosure and discovery, most rules of admissibility, some rules requiring corroboration, rules permitting a court to invite adverse inferences from a party's withholding or destruction of evidence, and many rules about the sufficiency of the evidence. The main and intended effect of such rules is to augment the flow of relevant information to the fact-finder. Without attempting to summarize the lengthy arguments presented in that book, I just observe that the burden of production is one component part of an integrated and evolved system for practically optimizing the evidence considered by the fact-finder. By "practically optimizing,"

---

[29] The drafters of the Restatement at least seem to have been aware of this in the context of rebuttable presumptions that shift (only) the burden of producing evidence. Here, they write in terms of augmenting the accuracy of decisions. *See* Restatement (Second) of Conflict of Laws § 134 Rationale (1971).

[30] The unusual circumstances are those in which the relevant evidence that is thereby added is misleading or prejudicial. See, e.g., Fed. R. Evid. 403 (permitting trial judges to exclude evidence that is clearly misleading or prejudicial).

I simply mean attempting to attain the best tradeoff possible between improved accuracy and the costs (of various kinds) of obtaining additional evidence. Again, whatever the extent and nature of these tradeoffs, augmenting the available relevant evidence generally improves expected accuracy of decision. That sometimes affects which side wins, but that fact does not mean its point is to favor one side over the other. Rather, the point is to improve the expected gains, or reduce the expected losses, of decision-making, regardless of which side wins as a result (Nance, 2016: 111–17, 264–70).

Now each legal system, however adversarial it may be, makes its own judgment – explicitly or implicitly – about how to accommodate the interest in maximizing accuracy and other competing procedural goals, whether they be respecting the autonomy of litigants, incorporating the practical judgment of lay jurors, creating a highly structured decision process that minimizes the discretion of decision-makers, keeping litigation costs down, or something else. Some commentators have observed, I think correctly, that the differences between legal systems in terms of their procedures can be greater than the differences in the substantive norms that they recognize (see, e.g., Lowenfeld, 1997: 649). Without passing judgment on these tradeoffs, each system's accommodation of these procedural goals is entitled to be respected by its own courts, even when one of them chooses to apply the law of a non-forum state.[31] While some disturbance of the system is almost inevitable when applying non-forum substantive law, each legal system will and should try to keep this disruption to a minimum.

So what is called the burden of production is a set of rules that does more than merely regulated the order for the presentation of evidence. Yet it is also not a set of rules designed to specify the degree to which the law will favor one side over the other. It is a type 2 rule that ordinarily should be governed by the law of the forum (cf. Seibl, 2017: 237–9). On this point, the common view among American conflicts scholars is wrong, and the second Restatement's default principle is essentially correct, even though it was not adequately explained. In any event, a long line of cases reflects the application of forum rules regarding the burden of production and the sufficiency of the evidence to support a verdict.[32]

---

[31] This is not a counsel against domestic improvements, nor against the recognition of the importance of comparative insights in informing such change. But the adjudication of a particular dispute that happens to involve interstate or international components is ordinarily not the appropriate occasion to undertake such reform.

[32] See, e.g., *Richardson* v. *Pacific Power and Light Co.*, 118 P.2d 985, 996–7 (Wash. 1941); *Sylvania Electric Products* v. *Barker*, 228 F.2d 842, 848050 (1st Cir. 1956); *Maryland Casualty Co.* v. *Williams*, 377 F.2d 389 (5th Cir. 1967); *Hysto Products, Inc.* v. *MNP Corp.*, 18 F.3d 1384, 1387–8 (7th Cir. 1994); *Healthtronics, Inc.* v. *Lisa Laser USA*, Inc., 382 S.W.3d 567 (Tex. App. 2012).

16.7 CONCLUSION

Thus, my recommendation, supported more by the results in the case law than by the opinions of American conflicts scholars, is that the choice-of-law rule, or at least the default preference, should be that the burden of persuasion follows the relevant non-forum law, while the burden of production follows the law of the forum.[33] If United States law continues to move in this direction, moreover, it will be converging on the private international law norms in Europe. Under both Rome I (for contractual disputes) and Rome II (for non-contractual disputes), what Americans evidence scholars usually call the burden of persuasion, as well as presumptions that would shift that burden, are now governed by *lex causae* rather than *lex fori*.[34]

The extension of this idea to litigation with both European and non-European components makes sense. Given the universal recognition of the problem of decision making under uncertainty, the idea of a risk of non-persuasion, and the necessity of articulating some rule to address it, are unavoidable concerns. The varying answers to the question thus raised help define parties' relative rights and duties and are appropriately subject to choice of non-forum law. But whether an American court is resolving a dispute governed by European contract or tort law or a European court is resolving a dispute governed by American contract or tort law, the forum court should not attempt to deal with the intricacies of the burden of production. It plays out differently in each system of adjudication in accord with its place in a broader regulation of the weight of evidence that reflects how important accuracy is in comparison to other process values.[35]

---

[33] There are a number of important counterarguments that must be considered. The most important is how to deal with legal rules that govern the burden of persuasion but are not intended to favour one class of litigants (even though they may) and, conversely, legal rules that govern the burden of production but are intended to favour one class of litigants (even though they may not). My thesis is developed more extensively, and counterarguments are considered, in a separate paper. See Nance, 2021.

[34] See Regulation (EC) 593/2008 (Rome I) art. 18 [2008] OJ L177/6; Regulation (EC) 864/2007 (Rome II) art. 22 [2007] L199/40.

[35] Although there would be less dissonance when an American forum state adjudicates rights using the tort or contract law of a sister state, whose procedural system is much less different than a European one, even here the distinct role of the burden of production and its interactions with other procedural norms should not be ignored. A uniform rule in American states is preferable to having one rule for international conflicts and another for interstate conflicts.

REFERENCES

Cook, W. W. (1933). "Substance" and "Procedure" in the Conflict of Laws, *Yale Law Journal*, 42(3), 333–58.

Felix, R. L. and Whitten, R. U. (2011). *American Conflicts Law*, 6th ed., Durham, NC: Carolina Academic Press.

Garnett, R. (2012). *Substance and Procedure in Private International Law*. Oxford: Oxford University Press.

Herzog, P. and Weser, M. (1967). *Civil Procedure in France*. Dordrecht: Springer Science.

Illmer, M. (2009). Neutrality Matters—Some Thoughts About the Rome Regulations and the So-Called Dichotomy of Substance and Procedure in European Private International Law, *Civil Justice Quarterly*, 28, 237–60.

Lowenfeld, A. F. (1997). Introduction: The Elements of Procedure: Are They Separately Portable? *The American Journal of Comparative Law*, 45(4), 649–55.

Morgan, E. M. (1944). Choice of Law Governing Proof, *Harvard Law Review*, 58(2), 153–95.

Mosteller, R. P. et al., eds. (2020). *McCormick on Evidence*, vol. 2, 8th ed., St. Paul, MN: West Academic Publishing.

Murray, P. L. and Stürner, R. (2004). *German Civil Justice*. Durham, NC: Carolina Academic Press.

Nance, D. A. (2016). *The Burdens of Proof: Discriminatory Power, Weight of Evidence, and Tenacity of Belief*. Cambridge: Cambridge University Press.

Nance, D. A. (2021). Choice of Law for Burdens of Proof, *North Carolina Journal of International Law*, 46, 235–313.

Park, R. C., Orenstein, A. A., and Nance, D. A. (2022). *Evidence Law a Student's Guide to the Law of Evidence as Applied in American Trials*, 5th ed., St. Paul, MN: West Academic Publishing.

Risinger, D. M. (1982). "Substance" and "Procedure" Revisited: With Some Afterthoughts on the Constitutional Problems of Irrebutable Presumptions, *UCLA Law Review*, 30, 1621–50.

Sedler, R. A. (1962). The Erie Outcome Test as a Guide to Substance and Procedure in the Conflict of Laws, *New York University Law Review*, 37, 813–80.

Seibl, M. (2017). Burden of Proof, in *Encyclopaedia of Private International Law*, vol. 1, Cheltenham: Edward Elgar Publishing.

Taruffo, M. (2003). Rethinking the Standards of Proof, *The American Journal of Comparative Law*, 51(3), 659–77.

Tidmarsh, J. (2011). Procedure, Substance, and Erie, *Vanderbilt Law Review*, 64(3), 877–924.

17

Is It Possible to Formulate a Precise and Objective Standard of Proof?

Some Questions Based on an Argumentative Approach to Evidence

Daniel González Lagier

17.1 INTRODUCTION

In the Latin American context, evidence theory has progressed in a few years from being a subject hardly dealt with by jurists and philosophers to become a highly active, flourishing, thriving field of study, with important advances and intriguing proposals (this development occurred long beforehand in the English-speaking world). However, I believe that, as in any expanding discipline, in order to have a solid base it is necessary to have precise terminology that does not result in serious errors, and to share a series of concepts allowing us to clearly formulate problems and avoid confusion due, not to the difficulty of the problems dealt with but to the lack of univocality in the language used. It is in relation to this aspect that I think it is possible and necessary to make further progress, particularly in relation to what might be considered one of the central planks of this discipline: the evaluation of evidence and the decision on which hypothesis must be accepted as proven. Our legal systems normally use quite similar terminology to refer to the laws of logic, the lessons of experience, scientific knowledge and the rules of reasoned judgment as evaluation criteria, but without specifying these rather vague concepts. To these criteria would be added the standard of proof, the subject of so many discussions in our recent literature. However, in my opinion, despite these discussions, the relationships and differences between the standard of proof and the evaluation criteria remain unclear. This lack of precision can make it difficult to discuss which evaluation criteria and which particular standards are appropriate, or even to discuss the possibility of formulating a precise, objective standard of proof. In this study, I will try to offer a set of conceptual suggestions that could be used to make progress in the search for a shared terminological and conceptual basis on this point. To do this, I will adopt an argumentative perspective on evidence, focusing on three points: (1) The structure of evidentiary inference; (2) which reasons count as good ones for establishing the degree of corroboration of a hypothesis and (3) the possibility of formulating a precise, objective standard of proof.

17.2 THREE WAYS OF ARGUING ABOUT FACTS

One of the many senses in which the word 'evidence' is used is 'evidence as argument' (González Lagier, 2014: 109 ff.). From this point of view, 'proving' something consists of constructing an argument to justify a certain hypothesis as the factual premise for a legal decision. As I see it, this kind of argument always consists of correlating two types of facts (or statements about facts): the facts we want to prove and the facts we use to prove them (the elements of judgment). This argument therefore consists of a set of premises (the elements of judgment); a conclusion (the hypothesis on the facts we want to prove); and a connection or relationship between the premises and the hypothesis. This link or connection between the elements of judgment and the hypothesis may be empirical, normative or conceptual.

In the first case, the link is an empirical generalisation correlating facts like those described in the premises with facts like those described in the conclusion, based on the observation of a past association between the two types of facts. These generalisations can include scientific knowledge, and we can call them 'maxims of experience', although sometimes this term refers only to the empirical generalisations attempted based on common sense and general acceptance. In these cases, we can speak of empirical evidential inference (in some contexts it would be appropriate to restrict the word 'evidence' to these circumstances). For example:

(1) The defendant was arrested near the house where the burglary was committed shortly after the time that it happened, carrying the objects removed from the house together with a metal lever (elements of judgment).

(2) If someone is surprised at the scene of the crime or nearby immediately after the event carrying items or the proceeds of the crime and/or items necessary for committing it, they are probably responsible for the crime (lesson of experience).

(3) The defendant is responsible for the crime (proven fact).

In the second case, the link is a rule (normally from legislation or jurisprudence) establishing that, if there are facts like those described in the premises (the basic fact), a certain hypothesis must be considered proven (the consequential fact). We can call these rules the 'rules of presumption' or the rules of the weighted evaluation of evidence and these inferences are known as normative evidential inferences.

For example:

(1) Subjects x and y (father and son) died in the same car accident and there is no evidence of who died first (elements of judgment).
(2) 'If there is any doubt as to which of two or more people who succeed one another died first . . ., and if there is no proof, they are presumed to have died at the same time' (legal presumption established in Article 33 of the Spanish Civil Code).
(3) x and y died at the same time (proven fact).

In the third case, the connection is established by a conceptual definition or rule establishing that the facts of the kind described in the hypothesis 'count as' (in other words, 'can be subsumed in') a certain category of facts (an action, an intention, a causal relationship, etc.). In these cases, what is at stake is not so much whether a particular fact has occurred but rather its interpretation; in other words, its classification in a particular general category of facts.

For example:

(1) Everyone who contracted the toxic syndrome had eaten rape-seed oil, but not everyone who ate rape-seed oil contracted the toxic syndrome. In other words, rape seed oil was a necessary but not sufficient condition of the toxic syndrome (elements of judgment).
(2) When one fact is a necessary condition of another (even if it is not necessary and sufficient) the former is a cause of the latter (definition).
(3) The rape-seed oil caused the toxic syndrome (proven fact).

In all cases, as might be expected, empirical evidential inferences are prioritary. It is impossible to make one of the other types of inference without proving that the basic fact of the presumption or the definition has occurred (which will have to be done by using an empirical generalisation). In the following discussion, I will leave aside evidential inferences based on definitions, which raise different difficulties to the ones I want to deal with here.

17.3 CONCERNING THE EVALUATION OF EVIDENCE
AND THE CONFIRMATION OF A HYPOTHESIS

17.3.1 *Evaluating Evidence*

It is clear that the type of argument we call 'evaluation of evidence' occurs only as a result of empirical evidential inference. In the case of normative evidential inference – in other words in cases of weighted evidence – the evaluation is already predetermined in the rule[1]. Inferences based on empirical generalisations correspond to free evidence evaluation systems, while normative evidential inferences belong to weighted evidence systems. A 'perfect' free evidence evaluation system would have no rules for establishing presumptions. By contrast, a 'perfect' weighted evidence system is clearly impossible unless it is completely circular, because at some point the basic fact of a rule of presumption must be empirically proven. In fact, although our systems are considered to be free evidence evaluation systems, within them there are cases of 'free evidence' (or freer evidence) and cases of 'weighted evidence' (or less free evidence). The use of free evaluation or weighted evidence is a question of degree.

It is, then, in cases where the judge is free to examine whether the elements of judgment make it possible to support the hypothesis and to what degree this can be done that we can properly speak of the evaluation of evidence. However, empirical evidential inference does not allow an absolutely certain conclusion to be drawn. On the contrary, it allows us to know the truth only in a limited and rather approximate way. This is the case even if we formulate the inference as a deduction, because it is not possible for us to be more certain of the conclusion than we are of the premises – we must not confuse the logical validity of the argument with the material certainty of its conclusion. From the point of view of argument, the evaluation of evidence can be identified with the degree to which the empirical evidential inference is correct or solid; in other words, the degree to which the evidence confirms or corroborates the hypothesis. We might also say that the evaluation of evidence consists of determining the level of inductive probability with which the hypothesis/conclusion follows from the premises (in other words, from the elements of judgment and the lesson of experience). We therefore need rational criteria to determine the degree to which

---

[1]   When we use a rule of presumption, we will have to prove the basic fact of the presumption and also (if accepted) any possible evidence in rebuttal, but this will be done by empirical evidential inference.

the conclusion is solid. These criteria are not formal, or are not only formal. Formal criteria would be the logical rules also alluded to by our systems as evaluation criteria. Seen from the point of view of argument, the rules of reasoned judgment can be interpreted as informal criteria for the solidity of empirical evidential inference.

17.3.2 *The 'Rules of Reasoned Judgment'*

In previous studies I have suggested the following criteria or rules for rational evidence evaluation (González Lagier, 2005):

(1) The more elements of judgment we have in favour of a hypothesis, the better the confirmation of the hypothesis.

(2) The more varied the elements of judgment (in other words, if they add information making it possible to eliminate alternative hypotheses), the better the confirmation of the hypothesis.

(3) The more relevant the elements of judgment (the better related they are to the hypotheses through reliable empirical generalisations), the better the confirmation of the hypothesis.

(4) The more reliable the elements of judgment (the better founded they are in other elements of judgment and previous inferences or direct observations or firm knowledge), the better the confirmation of the hypothesis.

(5) The better founded the lessons of experience in inductive generalisations, the firmer the hypothesis.

(6) The greater the probability expressed in the lesson of experience, the firmer the hypothesis. (Lessons of experience have the following structure: 'If p, then probably q'; the degree of probability with which the two types of fact are correlated is important for the confirmation of the hypothesis.)

(7) The hypothesis must not have been refuted either directly (no fact incompatible with the hypothesis must have been proved) or indirectly (hypotheses that are true must not be refuted if the truth of the main hypothesis is accepted).

(8) If the hypotheses derived from the main hypothesis (in other words, hypotheses that would be true if the main hypothesis was true) can be confirmed, the better the confirmation of the main hypothesis (by means of abductive argument).

(9) The more coherent the hypothesis from a narrative point of view, the better the confirmation of the hypothesis.

(10) The more elements of judgment explained by the hypothesis, the better the confirmation of the hypothesis.

(11) The fewer unproven facts required for the hypothesis to be true, the better the confirmation of the hypothesis.

(12) The fewer existing alternative hypotheses incompatible with the main hypothesis, the better the confirmation of the main hypothesis.

I believe it is enlightening to identify the 'rules of reasoned judgment' to which our systems allude with criteria of epistemological rationality like these. There is room for discussion on many of my proposed points: there may be a rule missing; they may not be well formulated; some of the rules are redundant (2 and 12, for example, are the same rule seen from the point of view of elements of judgment and from the point of view of the hypothesis, while 3 and 5 also point towards the same idea, from the point of view of elements of judgment and the point of view of the lesson of experience); some of them may be superfluous, incorrect, or defective in other ways. They can probably be presented more clearly, economically and precisely. However, what I want to suggest is that what in our culture we call rules of reasoned judgment must be rules of this kind if the aim is for the evaluation of evidence to be epistemologically rational (and, therefore, tend to ensure conclusions that are probably true, or that minimise error). They certainly cannot differ very much from them.

Does it make sense for legislators or jurisprudence to regulate or positivise this kind of rule? I believe it is important to realise that, whether or not they are positivised, these methodological rules are necessary in terms of trying to infer rationally correct hypotheses based on the available elements of judgment. Moreover, the fact that this is necessary does not depend directly on judicial authority. It does indirectly, however, in that the design and purpose of the process of proof depends on the judicial authorities. In other words, what the Law establishes as *compulsory* is the requirement of rationality in the evaluation of evidence; the evaluation rules are *necessary* means to this end. Just as the logical principle of non-contradiction must be respected, whether the legislator spells this out or not, the intrinsic nature of the laws of logic does not change. Nor do the rules of epistemological rationality need to be positivised to make them binding or necessary. They would only be included in normative texts, therefore, in the form of guidelines, examples and indications. The question of what the rules of epistemological rationality are is, in itself, a methodological and philosophical issue open to discussion and dependent on the epistemological theory assumed. It is therefore not advisable to positivise it, except perhaps for the more flexible jurisprudential route.

One clarification: I believe it is important to point out that, while the evaluation of evidence is identified with estimating the degree of solidity of evidential inference, the subject of evaluation is not merely the *evidence* (the elements of judgment) but rather the *proof* – the evidential argument as a whole. In other words, as we have seen, it concerns the criteria covering the elements of judgment, the hypothesis and the connection between these.

17.3.3 *Rules of Reasoned Judgment and Lessons of Experience*

The rules of reasoned judgment are different from the lessons of experience. The former are normative (although not judicial – as we have just said they are requirements for rationality determining which forms of argument are correct and which are not, and they can be seen as a set of rules determining the framework of theoretical rationality). Their basis is also not empirical (unless some type of naturalised epistemology is maintained, like that proposed by Quine, for whom epistemology must be reduced to cognitive psychology) (Quine, 2002). A rule establishing that 'the more elements of judgment there are in favour of a hypothesis, the firmer it is' is not something we could ultimately justify with experience (although it is possible that we might have learned from observing the criteria used by others). Trying to justify this kind of rule of inductive rationality from experience would raise various problems. If we try to show that these rules are successful in finding the truth there would be a problem of circularity, because to show that they are normally successful we would have to use the principles or rules that we are trying to justify; if we simply try to justify them by showing that they are in fact the criteria used by the majority to justify beliefs, they would also lose their normative dimension (as they would be no use in determining whether or not an argument is correct, they would simply indicate whether or not an argument conforms to a habit). Meanwhile, the lessons of experience are empirically based descriptive statements (and therefore either true or false). We arrive at them through general argument (using the rules of epistemological rationality) based on examining particular cases. These are necessary to correlate evidentiary facts and the facts that require proof, but it is not a logical or inductive need: they are required as premises of evidentiary inference, not as methodological rationality criteria.

17.3.4 *The Gradual Nature of the Confirmation of Hypotheses*

The rules for evaluating evidence are gradual in at least two senses: firstly concerning the criteria, which are themselves gradual (varying number of elements of judgment, varying degree of reliability, varying degree of coherence of hypotheses, varying degree of foundation of the maxims of experience and so on). Secondly, one hypothesis could be justified by several rules, and it would be too demanding to require that it should meet all of them to a relevant degree.

There are two consequences of this gradual nature. The first, which establishes the degree of confirmation of a hypothesis, requires an overall judgment in the light of all these criteria, which means it is necessarily the result of a holistic evaluation.

None of these criteria alone is a necessary or a sufficient condition of a certain degree of confirmation. They are not a necessary condition because if one of them is absent it can always be made up for by other criteria. For example, it cannot be said that, as the number of elements of judgment in favour of a hypothesis is very small, the hypothesis necessarily has a very low degree of confirmation, because this could be compensated for by the fact that the lessons of experience connecting these elements of judgment with the hypothesis are very solid and that it has been possible to eliminate a good number of alternative hypotheses. Nor is it a sufficient condition for a certain degree of confirmation, because the criteria it has in its favour can always be counteracted by a deficit in others. For example, it cannot be said that the fact that the lessons of experience are very well-founded guarantees that the hypothesis is properly confirmed, because this could be undermined by the fact that the elements of judgment themselves are not very reliable. As we will see, this is important in the discussion about the plausibility of a standard of proof used as a sufficiency threshold.

The second consequence is that these criteria make it possible to determine the relative probability (in logical or inductive terms) of one hypothesis compared with another, but not how much more probable it is.[2] In other words, they allow the comparison and ordering of the degree of justification of different particular hypotheses but not a numerical quantification of their probability. So now, once the evidence has been evaluated, the problem of making the decision arises: is the degree of confirmation obtained sufficient to consider the hypothesis proven? Answering this question requires a new criterion: the standard of proof. This criterion must operate as a threshold (although a certain degree of vagueness is acceptable) allowing us to discriminate between what we consider to be (sufficiently) proven and what we do not consider to be (sufficiently) proven.

Therefore, the evaluation criteria and the standard of proof have different objectives and purposes: what we evaluated using the evidence evaluation

---

[2] For an influential analysis of the notion of inductive probability, see Cohen, 1977.

rules is the evidentiary argument or inference to try to establish their degree of confirmation or justification. Meanwhile, the standard of proof does not attempt to evaluate the evidence against. Instead, we use it to evaluate the degree of justification obtained (in other words, the result of previous argument) to answer the question of whether it is sufficient for the decision to be made. Of course, we do not need just one standard of proof, it may also be different – more or less strict – depending on the type of decision involved. However, the evaluation criteria are the same for all cases (although some may be more relevant or more often used for some types of facts).

17.4 STANDARDS OF PROOF

17.4.1 *Practical Standards and Decisions*

Standards of proof (or decision) are not exclusively a judicial problem. As we know, our decisions and actions can be seen as the result of the combination of a desire and a belief about how to satisfy it. That means our knowledge of the world (our beliefs) has practical and not just theoretical relevance. We need beliefs to know how to act. However, the consequences of our decisions and actions may be relevant to different degrees. The more far-reaching the decision I have to make, the more serious its consequences, and the more certain I need to be of the beliefs guiding that decision. If my life depends on arriving in Madrid on time, my belief that the plane leaves at nine in the morning based only on what I have read in the paper seems not to be sufficiently justified. The reasonable thing to do would be to try to reach a higher level of certainty, so I should look for more evidence. The level to which we demand that a belief should be justified depends on the context and the practical relevance of the belief. So the same belief with the same inductive support may or may not be sufficiently justified depending on the context. For example (Grimaltos, 2009: 35–50):

- Context 1: On Friday, Michael and his wife go to the bank to pay money in. As there is a long queue, Michael says: 'I'll come back on my own tomorrow.' His wife says: 'Perhaps the bank isn't open tomorrow. A lot of banks are closed on Saturdays.' Michael answers: 'No. I know it will be open: I came on Saturday two weeks ago and they're open until lunchtime.'
  - Context 2: This time they need to pay the money in before Monday as some cheques they have signed will be drawn on that day. If the funds are not paid in by Monday, they are going to have real problems. As in context 1, there is a long queue and Michael says he will come back the next day. His wife reminds him that, if they do not pay the money in before Monday, they are

going to have difficulties and tells him: 'Banks change their opening times. Are you sure the bank is open tomorrow?' Michael, who is just as convinced as before that the bank is open on Saturday, replies: 'Well, no. We'd better stay and pay the money in today.'

In context 1, Michael says he knows the bank is open on Saturdays; in context 2 he says he does not. The evidence in favour of his belief is the same in both cases. This evidence is sufficient to consider his belief justified in 1 but not to consider it justified in 2. From this, the philosophical view known as contextualism draws the conclusion that the attribution of knowledge (justified true beliefs) is sensible in the context. However, another way of looking at this relativity of the degree to which beliefs are justified with respect to the context, which avoids certain problems of contextualism, can be to introduce the distinction between *belief* and *acceptance* as two different types of propositional attitudes. Using this distinction, it should be said that it is not the case that in context 1 the belief is justified and in 2 it is not. In both cases the belief is equally justified, but this degree of justification in context 1 is sufficient for it to be accepted (to act in accordance with it), while in context 2 it is not.

17.4.2 Belief and Acceptance

I cannot *believe* something I know to be false; by contrast I can *accept* something even though I have doubts, or even if I believe it to be false, and act as if it were true. Acceptance is therefore a propositional attitude which is also related to truth, but in a different way to belief. A person who believes something considers that their belief is true, but this consideration is not necessarily present in acceptance. A person who accepts something can only consider that there are reasons to act as if the statement were true, even if it is not. According to L. J. Cohen, 'Accepting *p* means having or adopting a policy of judging, suggesting or postulating *p* – that is, including this proposition or rule among a one's own premises for deciding what to do or think in a particular context, whether or not *p* is actually true' (Cohen, 1992: 4). We can sketch out the differences between belief and acceptance in the following way:

(1) Belief is gradual (we can be convinced of something to different degrees): acceptance is all or nothing.

(2) Belief is determined by epistemic reasons – reasons for believing – but not by practical reasons (that it is wise to believe p is not a suitable reason to make one believe p). Acceptance is determined by epistemic and/or practical reasons.

(3) Belief is not an action; in other words, it is not entirely within our control. (Beliefs can be consequences of our actions but they are not actions in themselves. For example, we cannot cease to believe *p*, for which we have overwhelming evidence, although if we do not yet believe *p* we can avoid looking for this evidence. And we cannot force ourselves to believe *p* if we do not have epistemic reasons for it, although we can look for evidence). Acceptance, on the other hand, is the result of a deliberate decision.

It follows from the above, then, that belief is a reason for acceptance, but it is not the only one. Acceptance can occur for epistemological or other reasons (prudence, for example). However, when we accept something for epistemological reasons, a certain degree of justification is necessary, and that degree of justification is a practical criterion related to the context and the purposes of the agent.

17.4.3 *Standard of Proof and Acceptance*

The concept of acceptance can be useful to take account of some of the propositional attitudes present in the evidence. For example, when we argue through normative evidentiary inference (in other words, when we do not evaluate the evidence but simply subsume the elements of judgment in the factual situation of a rule establishing a presumption or determining an evidentiary result), it makes no sense pretending that rules can force us to have a particular belief, as beliefs are not entirely under our control. However, if acceptance is a deliberate action, rules can force us to accept a particular hypothesis as the factual premise for a judicial decision (Mendonca, 1998). Some of these rules require acceptance of a particular evidential result for epistemic reasons (they force us to accept something because there are reasons to believe it). Others require acceptance for practical reasons (protection of a legal asset). In weighted evidence systems, then, the judge is required to accept the proven facts without wondering whether there are reasons to believe them.

The idea of acceptance can also shed some light on standards of proof. We must remember that the evaluation of evidence makes sense only in the case of empirical evidentiary inferences. Similarly, the problem of standard of proof arises only in this type of inference. A rule that establishes the obligation to consider a fact proven if a certain combination of elements of judgment are present (which we have called a presumption rule) establishes, as we have seen, that it must be accepted that this fact has occurred. That, in itself, is an acceptance criterion, so no new criterion – or standard – is required in order to know whether the fact has to be accepted. In legal or weighted evidence systems, the problem of determining the standard of proof does not arise (or, we might say, the legislator has already established a rigid standard of proof for each case). But in cases of free evidence evaluation we need criteria to tell us the degree to which the hypothesis must be justified so that it has to be accepted (or used as a guide for the judicial decision). In these free evaluation systems, there are two types of reasons for accepting the guilty hypothesis: firstly there are reasons for believing it in order to reduce error, which are those indicated by the evidence evaluation criteria. Secondly, there are what we might call secondary reasons for considering the degree of certainty or justification achieved – in other words reasons for acceptance. These secondary reasons are practical ones, related to how we want to distribute the cost of mistakes. In criminal law, for example, it is assumed that it is more serious to find an innocent person guilty than to acquit a guilty one, so the degree of sufficiency demanded must be higher. In other words, the hypothesis accepted must be epistemologically founded, but with a degree of justification that must exceed a certain threshold or meet certain requirements. For this reason, it is possible that, in cases of free evaluation, the judge believes the hypothesis is correct but does not accept it (it does not reach the standard of proof). But the judge cannot accept it without reasons to believe it (even though the judge may not, in fact, believe it).

Finally, the distinction between 'belief' and 'acceptance' can also shed light on an ambiguity in the expression '*p* being proven'. This could refer to there being reasons for believing 'p' (in which case it has a descriptive meaning) or to there being reasons for accepting 'p' (in which case it is once again ambiguous: it can be a description stating the existence of these reasons or it can express the performative that establishes 'p' as proven).[3]

17.4.4 *Is a Precise, Objective Standard of Proof Possible?*

The great problem raised by the standard of proof concerns finding an objective formulation for it. According to Larry Laudan's well-known critique (Laudan, 2005), the formulas offered by our judicial systems, at least in the criminal sphere ('beyond all reasonable doubt', 'sufficient incriminating evidence', 'deep conviction') are vague ad imprecise. In the end they depend on

---

[3]   This is relevant for the discussion of the illocutionary force of evidentiary statements. See Dei Vecchi, 2014.

the subjective considerations of the judge or jury, without guidance from rational criteria.[4]

To consider this kind of criticism in detail it seems important to distinguish two types of problems with standards of proof concerning the ambiguity of the terms 'objective' and 'subjective'. Sometimes by 'subjective' we mean the subjective attitudes or discretionary mental states of the person judging, as is the case with the standard of 'deep conviction'. It is enough for the judge to be convinced, without such a conviction needing to be rational in order to justify a statement that the facts are proven. This makes the criterion an arbitrary one. Other times, we use 'subjective' in the sense of 'vague' or 'imprecise' (because, if it is imprecise, the judge ends up deciding by using his own discretion, in accordance with his own subjective criteria). Now, a concept can be affected by two types of imprecision or vagueness. We might call these intensional vagueness (the necessary and sufficient conditions for the application of the concept are not properly determined: for example, the defining notes of 'book' and 'vehicle', are not determined) and gradual vagueness (one of the defining notes of the concept is gradual – in other words it can be possessed to different degrees – as with 'baldness', 'tallness', 'heat' or 'degree of confirmation'). For example, when we speak of 'reasonable doubt', although this term is given objective meaning, what is meant by 'reasonable' remains to be specified, and using another gradual property must be avoided. A satisfactory standard of proof should, then, determine whether the 'degree of confirmation' of a hypothesis is sufficient to be accepted. Some conditions are necessary to achieve this: (1) it must be done appealing to objective criteria rather than mental states, (2) it must be intensionally precise and (3) it must deal with the problem that 'degree of confirmation' is a gradual (and unquantifiable) concept. If this issue is not resolved, this consideration cannot be used as a 'threshold' or sufficiency criterion. Is all this possible? I believe it is possible to interpret the standards so that they do not depend on subjective mental states, but I am much more sceptical about the possibility that the two forms of vagueness can be satisfactorily reduced so that the judge's discretion is rendered unnecessary.[5] I will try to demonstrate the reasons for my scepticism.

---

[4] To summarise it in the words of Juan Carlos Bayón, the standard must not be subjective, or express this even covertly. See Bayón, 2008.

[5] Laudan has offered various examples of a standard of proof which would be preferable to traditional ones; they include the following:

(a) 'If prosecution evidence or testimony that would be difficult to explain if the defendant was innocent is credible, and exculpatory evidence or testimony that would be very difficult to explain if the accused was guilty is not credible, then find him guilty. Otherwise acquit him.'

17.4.4.1 The 'Mathematical Probabilism' Route

An initial route consists of trying to quantify the level of credibility of the hypotheses. That means finding a method for mathematically expressing the confidence we have in them. Susan Haack has called the attempt to do this in the sphere of judicial proof 'legal probabilism'. If it were objectively possible to mathematically quantify the support that the elements of judgment provide for the hypothesis to be proved (if we could say, for example, that, given certain evidence, the hypothesis is 70 per cent or 90 per cent confirmed, for example) then an objective standard of proof could be established, although the actual figure would have to be specified. The problem with this attempt to offer an objective standard is that it lacks satisfactory instruments for making the calculation. Attempts to apply Bayes' Theorem to the calculation of the degree of credibility of a hypothesis (which are the most serious attempts at 'legal probabilism') seem to arouse tremendous difficulties. Bayes' theorem tries to measure the impact that a particular piece of evidence (or a set of them) has on the probability initially attributed to a hypothesis, without taking into account the evidence in question. To use it as a standard of proof, the *a priori* probability assigned to the hypothesis of guilt would first have to be established. The application of the formula would then indicate, given the impact of the new evidence, the *a posteriori* probability of this hypothesis. If we established the standard of proof at 95 per cent, for example, we would pass the test if the *a posteriori* probability was the same or higher. So how do we assign the *a priori* probability? In some cases, statistical data can be obtained to help with this initial assignment of probability but in the vast majority of cases, the assignment of the *a priori* probability which finally determines the *a posteriori* probability is utterly subjective. Therefore, the standard of proof constructed in this way does not overcome the problem of subjectivity, it just transfers it to another point. The

(b) 'If the prosecution's story concerning the crime is plausible and you cannot imagine a plausible story showing the accused to be innocent, then find her guilty. Otherwise acquit her.'

(c) 'Decide whether the facts established by the prosecution refute any even marginally reasonable hypothesis you can think of concerning the defendant's innocence. If they do, you must find him guilty. Otherwise, you must acquit' (Laudan: 2005, 108).

I believe it is clear that these proposals do not manage to overcome the use of subjective factors (such as the capacity to imagine stories or think of plausible hypotheses in favour of innocence). Nor do they make much progress in reducing intensional vagueness (they refer to vague notions such as 'if it is credible', 'plausible', 'difficult to explain' without indicating when it must be credible, plausible, and so on). Finally, they do not solve the problem of gradual vagueness, as the concepts referred to – credibility, plausibility and so on – are clearly gradual concepts.

criticisms of authors like J. Cohen, Susan Haack, Michele Taruffo, Larry Laudan or Jordi Ferrer show the implausibility of this method of constructing an objective standard of proof (see, for all these, Taruffo, 2002 and Cohen, 1977).

17.4.4.2 The Problem of Intensional Vagueness: Formulating a Standard Based on a Selection of Evidence Evaluation Criteria

Let us suppose we have reached a consensus with respect to a closed list of evaluation rules (for example, the twelve already proposed). We could then require that the evidentiary argument should meet a minimum number of criteria depending on how strict we want the standard to be. However, for this to work we would need to be convinced that the conclusion of an inference complying with a greater number of these rules would always be more justified than one complying with fewer of them. And this is not the case. We have already seen that each of these rules can be complied with to different degrees, so it would be possible for hypothesis H1 to meet nine criteria, but to a lesser degree, and another hypothesis, H2, to meet just five, but to such a high degree that this would make up for the lower number of rules complied with. That could make H2 more justified than H1. Solving this requires having criteria to determine the degree necessary for *accepting* that a rule has been complied with. However, then we run up against the need for a 'standard of compliance' with each rule, which would reproduce our problems (and begin a regression to the infinite).

Another possibility would be to select some of these evaluation rules as particularly relevant (or strict) and make acceptance of the hypothesis depend on compliance with these. The criterion would then no longer be quantitative (complying with a particular number of rules), it would be qualitative: rules 7, 10 and 12 must be complied with, for example. This strategy raises similar difficulties. Firstly, it is difficult to determine which criteria or rules are more important or why, because this involves deciding that compliance with the other rules cannot make up for failing to comply with those chosen. Secondly, once again a standard would have to be established to determine whether the rules have been complied with sufficiently (we must remember that different degrees of compliance are possible). Thirdly, if acceptance requires only three rules of epistemological rationality, does this mean that the others, however intuitive they appear, are irrelevant?

I think Jordi Ferrer's proposed standards of proof run into these same problems. One of his formulations, for example, would be the following conditions have to be met for the hypothesis of guilt to be considered proven:

1) The hypotheses must be proved to a high standard, explain the available data and be capable of predicting new data which has, in turn, been corroborated.
2) All other plausible hypothesis explaining the same data and compatible with innocence must be refuted.

(Ferrer, 2007)

It is easy to see that Ferrer's strategy consists of formulating the standard of proof based on certain evidence evaluation criteria. In the example mentioned, these are that hypothesis makes it possible to predict new data (coinciding with our evaluation rule 8), that it has explanatory capacity (rule 10) and that it eliminates alternative hypotheses (rule 12). My argument, again, is that, *given the fact that the determination of the degree of confirmation of a hypothesis requires holistic evaluation, no subset of the evidence evaluation criteria is, on its own, a sufficient or necessary condition for achieving a certain degree of confirmation. Therefore, it is impossible to be sure that this standard requires a higher (or lower) degree of confirmation than would be required by a standard based on other evaluation criteria.* The confirmation threshold that a standard of this kind attempts to set can also be reached by a hypothesis that does not meet that standard. It therefore gives us no assurance that we are minimising the risk of error in finding guilt to a higher degree than another standard based on a subset of the evaluation criteria. In the words of Susan Haack: 'As the quality of evidence has various different dimensions ... and there is no way of ordering relative success or failure through these different factors, there is not even any assurance of a linear order of degrees of guarantee' (Haack, 2013: 80). Any standard of this kind would involve setting arbitrary conditions with no guarantee that we are making proof more (or less) difficult. On the contrary, if we try to formulate the standard including all evaluation criteria it either leads to vague formulations (choosing the hypothesis that is the best or most credible explanation, for example) or prevents a distinction between the evaluation of evidence and the standard of proof.

17.4.4.3 The Problem of Gradual Vagueness: Refuting Alternative Hypotheses, an All-or-Nothing Principle?

It might be thought that the degree of strictness involved in refuting or eliminating the hypotheses in favour of innocence included in the third of Laudan's and Ferrer's proposals is a more precise standard and could operate as a 'threshold'. The idea of refuting all alternative hypotheses is intriguing because, firstly, it looks like a strict criterion and, at the same time, it might be thought that refuting a hypothesis was an 'all-or-nothing' matter. However, it is not that simple. Refuting a hypothesis consists of showing that there is a fact incompatible with the hypothesis (direct refutation) or with a hypothesis deriving from it (indirect refutation). The pattern of these arguments is as follows:

Direct refutation of hypothesis A:

(1) We assume Hypothesis A.

(2) Hypothesis B is incompatible with Hypothesis A (they cannot simultaneously be true).

(3) Hypothesis B is accepted as proven (it is sufficiently confirmed).

Hypothesis A is therefore false.

Indirect refutation of hypothesis A:

(1) If Hypothesis A is true, Hypothesis B will be too (Hypothesis A implies Hypothesis B).

(2) Hypothesis B is incompatible with Hypothesis C (they cannot simultaneously be true).

(3) Hypothesis C is accepted as proven (it is sufficiently confirmed).

(4) Hypothesis B is false.

Therefore (by modus tollens) Hypothesis A is false.

As can be seen in both cases, to refute or eliminate a hypothesis a supposedly incompatible fact must be *proved*, but because of the nature of evidentiary argument we will not have absolute certainty about it. When we say that hypothesis H1 has been refuted, what we are really saying is that it is not the most probable hypothesis, because we concerned here with probabilities rather than certainties. Instead, we are saying that hypothesis H2, which assures the existence of a fact directly or indirectly incompatible with H1, seems to us more probable. So, refutation is also a comparison between various hypothesis, it is also gradual, and it once again requires a standard of proof. Moreover, if refuting the hypotheses compatible with innocence means showing that another hypothesis (that of guilt) is more plausible, it might then be thought that refuting the acquittal hypotheses is no more than the other side of the coin to confirming the conviction hypothesis, rather than being a different judgment.

17.4.4.4 The Problem of Measuring the Effectiveness of the Standards for Distributing the Risk of Error

There is another problem raised by the above strategies (including the one using mathematical probability): once the standard has been chosen, how can we know the consequences of the intended result for the distribution of error? If the purpose of the standard is to try to fix a certain ratio between the number of false convictions and the number of false acquittals, we need a criterion (which must be different from the one provided by the standard) to check that the standard is producing the desired effect. But in the case of trials, we do not have these criteria. Once the evidence has been evaluated and it has been established that hypothesis H is the best confirmed and that its degree of confirmation is sufficient, we no longer (except in the few cases where new more solid evidence appears and case is reopened) have another way of establishing whether or not H is true. As Bayón says, once the standard has been formulated 'there would be no guarantee that the distribution of risk considered to be correct would be the exact result of its application'. This is an important difference between acceptance criteria or standards from other spheres (medicine, science or even everyday life) and law. During my life, I have learned through experience (sometimes hard experience) that if I rely on the cinema opening time information given in newspapers to find out what time the film I want to see starts, or on what the weather forecast says to find out what the weather is going to be like in a couple of days' time, I might end up missing the film or organising a disastrous picnic in the country. But I learn from reality. In Law we rarely have this chance of confirmation.

It seems to me that the above considerations point to the fact that, although it is possible to eliminate directly subjective references from the standards intended to indicate the degree of proof required, it is not possible to formulate them precisely so that the associated intensional vagueness and gradual vagueness can be overcome. The route towards a precise standard of proof appears to be blocked.

However, not all the standards we have are entirely useless or counterproductive and some are at least minimally informative. Everyone understands that the confirmation criterion 'beyond all reasonable doubt' is more demanding than that of 'overwhelming evidence' or 'clear and convincing evidence'.[6] Or that when incriminating evidence is required in gender violence crimes the fact that the victim 'does not lack credibility' and the 'corroboration with other information' of a statement establish stricter requirements than if a simple statement were enough.[7] Standards should at least provide information on whether the judicial authorities want them to be strict or not, even though they do not specify how strict, so that the idea of sufficient proof still depends on the good judgment and consideration of judges.

17.5 FINAL REFLECTION

As we have seen, the problem of formulating the standard of proof arises basically in cases of free evaluation of evidence. Moreover, it is a problem caused by abandoning weighted evidence systems. The excessive rigidity of these systems leads to judges being delegated (1) the responsibility of evaluating the evidence and (2) the responsibility for determining whether the hypothesis is sufficient to be considered proven. The current search by evidence theorists for a more precise standard of sufficiency is, perhaps paradoxically, an attempt to maintain (1) but reduce (2). Now, if it is not possible to satisfy (2) by means of a precise standard of proof, one way of reducing discretion concerning the estimation of sufficiency consists of reducing discretion in evaluation. If rules are introduced to authoritatively determine the evidentiary result, they will simultaneously do (1) and (2). I am not suggesting here that weighted evidence and the standard of proof are the same thing, but I am alluding to the fact that one solution to reducing discretion in determining the sufficiency of the degree of confirmation consists of going back to legally or jurisprudentially weighted evidence or similar procedures. But then we once again run up against the reasons for avoiding legally weighted evidence, such as excessive rigidity. Perhaps freedom in the evaluation of evidence is simply not compatible with the precise regulation of decision-making standards and we must find other ways of distributing the costs of error.

---

[6] The standard of reasonable doubt is not as useless as it might seem. Daniela Accatino has shown that the best interpretation of this standard is not the subjectivist one – there must be a conviction if the judge, in fact, has no reasonable doubt. He advocates an objective interpretation – the doubt must be justified – which could be identified with the elimination of the acquittal hypotheses.' See Accatino, 2011.

[7] Along these lines, Mercedes Fernández López has proposed abandoning the attempt to specify a general standard of proof. Instead, she calls for the specification of requirements that must be met by the means of proof in each type of case so they can be considered incriminating evidence. See Fernández López, 2006.

REFERENCES

Accatino, D. (2011). Certezas, dudas y propuestas en torno al estándar de la prueba penal, *Revista de Derecho de la Pontificia Universidad Católica de Valparaíso*, 37, 483–511.

Bayón, J. C. (2008). Epistemología, moral y prueba de los hechos. hacia un enfoque no benthamiano, *Analisi e Diritto*, 2008, 15–34.

Cohen, L. J. (1977). *The Probable and the Provable*, Oxford: Clarendon Press.

Cohen, L. J. (1992). *Belief and Acceptance*, Oxford: Clarendon Press.

Dei Vecchi, D. (2014). Acerca de la fuerza de los enunciados probatorios. El salto constitutivo, *Doxa*, 37, 237–61.

Fernández López, M. (2006). La valoración de las pruebas personales y el estándar de la duda razonable, *Cuadernos Electrónicos de Filosofía del Derecho*, 15.

Ferrer, J. (2006). Los estándares de prueba en el proceso penal español, *Cuadernos Electrónicos de Filosofía del Derecho*, 15.

González Lagier, D. (2005). *Quaestio facti. Ensayos sobre prueba, causalidad y acción*. Lima: Editorial Palestra-Temis.

González Lagier, D. (2006). Hechos y conceptos, *Cuadernos Electrónicos de Filosofía del Derecho*, 15.

González Lagier, D. (2014). Presunción de inocencia, verdad y objetividad, in J. A. García Amado and P. Bonorino, eds., *Prueba y razonamiento probatorio en Derecho*, Granada: Comares.

Grimaltos, T. (2009). Creencia, aceptación y conocimiento, *Episteme*, 29(1), 35–50.

Haack, S. (2013). El probabilismo jurídico. Una disensión epistemológica, in C. Vázquez ed., *Estándares de prueba y prueba científica. Ensayos de epistemología jurídica*, Barcelona: Marcial Pons.

Laudan, L. (2005). Por qué un estándar de prueba subjetivo y ambiguo no es un estándar, *Doxa*, 28, 95–113.

Mendonca, D. (1998). Presunciones, *Doxa*, 21(1), 83–98.

Quine, W. O. (2002). *Naturalización de la epistemología, in La relatividad ontológica y otros ensayos*, Madrid: Tecnos.

Taruffo, M. (2002). *La prueba de los hechos*, Madrid: Trotta.

18

Prolegomena to a Theory of Standards of Proof

The Test Case for State Liability for Undue Pre-trial Detention

Jordi Ferrer Beltrán[*]

18.1 INTRODUCTION

The traditional tendency in the Spanish-speaking legal culture to abandon evidential legal reasoning and the general theory of evidence which has characterised procedure law and philosophy of law studies has clearly changed over the last few decades. However, the general theory of evidence continues to present a major gap, which it shares with the theories of the criminal fair trial. Both theories, different in scope but evidently interrelated, are seriously incomplete if they fail to address the problem of how to establish the standard of proof for each procedural phase and for every type of proceedings. And this lack of theorising is mirrored in the legislation, where the absence of standards of proof becomes the Achilles' heel of a procedural design which seeks to limit arbitrariness and promote control over decisions on evidence. A system without standards of proof is a system that lacks the rules to justify factual findings, rendering numerous procedural rights (such as the presumption of innocence) useless, and even the duty to state the grounds on which the judgment is based. I will therefore present an initial theoretical outline of the way in which standards of proof should be established and will analyse the legal regulation and case law regarding the right to compensation for undue pre-trial detention as a test case for the need for standards of proof establishing different evidential thresholds.

[*] This chapter was supported by the *Seguridad jurídica y razonamiento judicial* (DER2017-82661-P) research project of the Spanish Ministry of the Economy and Competitiveness. I would like to thank all my colleagues in the Philosophy of Law research group of the University of Girona for their highly insightful comments on a previous version of this chapter, and more particularly Edgar Aguilera, Jorge Baquerizo, Diego Dei Vecchi, Carolina Fernández Blanco, Daniel González Lagier, Laura Manrique, Esteban Pereira, Pablo Rapetti and Carmen Vázquez.

I will use the following assumptions, which are current axioms of the rationalist theory or tradition of proof, as my initial premises:[1]

(1) Evidence and truth have a teleological relationship, whereby truth is the institutional objective to be achieved through the use of evidence in legal proceedings.[2]

(2) The concept of truth at issue, which is useful in explaining this teleological relationship, is that of the correspondence theory of truth, meaning that a statement of fact (raised to be prove in court) is true if, and only if, it corresponds to what actually occurred in the world (outside the proceedings).[3]

(3) A body of evidence, however rich and reliable, will never make it possible to reach rational – not psychological or subjective – certainties about the occurrence of an event. Hence, statements of fact are inevitably true or false, but our epistemic limitations always oblige us to make decisions in situations of uncertainty.

(4) Evidential legal reasoning is, therefore, by necessity probabilistic. Saying that a statement of fact is proven is asserting that it is probably true (on a level to be established) in view of the available evidence.

While these premises are broadly shared in the literature on evidence and proof, the relevant consequences are not always extracted from them. More specifically, and as I stated previously, the Spanish-speaking and continental legal cultures have generally overlooked the need for rules that establish

---

[1] A description of this tradition can be found in Ferrer Beltrán, 2007: 64–6. For an excellent presentation of the rationalist tradition in the English-speaking culture, see Twining, 1990: 32 ff.

[2] In the terms of Anderson, Schum and Twining (2005: 79): 'The central tenet of the Rationalist Tradition is that the primary objective of adjective (or procedural) law is the achievement of "rectitude of decision" in adjudication, that is to say the correct application of law to facts proved to be true. . . . With respect to disputed questions of fact, the tenet assumes that realization of that objective involves the pursuit of "truth" through rational means.' The foundations of the objective of ascertaining the truth as a guarantee of the proper enforcement of substantive law may be found in Bentham, 1827: 17–19. For a more in-depth analysis and rationale of this premise, see Ferrer Beltrán, 2002: 55 ff.

[3] In this regard, see Taruffo, 1992: 145; and Gascón, 1999: 59 et seq. It should be added that throughout his work, Taruffo has maintained that in trials, and perhaps in other areas of knowledge, we can only achieve relative or contextual truths. He thereby rules out the existence of absolute truths (see Taruffo, 1992: 146 ff.). As we shall see later, I believe there may be good context-specific reasons to use different levels of evidentiary threshold to accept a factual assumption as true (and therefore proven), but that does not mean that the actual truth is relative. If we adopt, as I do, the notion of truth as correspondence, then truth is always absolute: Peter either did or did not cross the street when the light was red; or Maria either killed or did not kill Philip. There are no relative truths; what is relative is the degree of corroboration and the evidence that these facts have taken place. Relativity is therefore epistemological and not ontological.

a sufficient degree of probability to accept a statement of fact (or a hypothesis) as proven in legal proceedings.

If evidential legal reasoning is probabilistic, and rational certainty about a factual hypothesis is unattainable, then we need rules, called 'standards of proof', to determine the degree of probability required to be able to deem the assumption as proven. In other words, that establish what degree of support is sufficient to accept the hypothesis in question as true (and be able to use it as such in our reasoning).

The type of probability capable of shaping evidential legal reasoning is inductive and cannot be calculated mathematically.[4] Therefore, standards of proof will not be able to put a number on the degree of probabilistic sufficiency required to prove a hypothesis.

Only if we have standards of proof that indicate evidential thresholds (i.e., the degree of probability needed to prove a hypothesis) will we be able to use other decision-making rules, such as burdens of proof or presumptions. Indeed, the purpose of burden of proof rules is to determine who loses the case if there is insufficient evidence of any of the hypotheses at issue. However, to apply these rules we need to know when the evidence is sufficient. The same is true of rebuttable (*iuris tantum*) presumptions, which require that a hypothesis be admitted in court (and used in the reasoning) in the absence of (sufficient) proof to the contrary. Therefore, for example, the presumption of innocence as a procedural rule means that defendants must be found innocent unless there is sufficient proof of their guilt.[5] But when is the proof of a defendant's guilt sufficient? Once again, implementing the presumption of innocence (like any other rebuttable presumption) presupposes the existence of a rule that establishes the evidentiary threshold.

18.2 HOW CAN A STANDARD OF PROOF BE ESTABLISHED?

The formulations of the level of evidentiary threshold in procedural rules and in case law tend to present two serious problems. On the one hand, they usually refer to psychological or mental aspects of the decision-maker (including the strength of belief, the *'intime conviction'*, 'subjective certainty' and 'conscientious assessment'), which preclude intersubjective control and are therefore not suitable for reviewing the correctness of a previous decision or for guaranteeing, for example, the presumption of innocence in criminal proceedings (see

---

[4] Many authors have argued this impossibility. See, for all of them, Cohen, 1977: 58–67; and a general presentation in Ferrer Beltrán, 2007: 98–120.

[5] Or what Mendonca terms the strategy of destruction ('estrategia de destrucción') of presumption (which must be distinguished from the blocking or rebuttal strategy ('estrategia de bloqueo'). In this regard, see Mendonca, 2000: 229; and also Ullmann-Margalit, 1983: 149.

Laudan, 2005: 99 ff.). I shall return to this point later. On the other hand, the
formulations of standards of proof currently in use in most systems present
a degree of vagueness inconsistent with their purpose of establishing (even
approximately) the evidentiary threshold. Two examples of this would be: (1)
Article 641 of the Spanish Criminal Procedure Act (*Ley de Enjuiciamiento
Criminal*, LECr), which regulates temporary stays of proceedings in various
situations, the second situation (Article 641.2) being 'when a crime has been
committed and there are *insufficient grounds* to accuse an individual person or
persons as perpetrators, accomplices or aiders and abettors'. (2) Article 503 of the
same Act, which governs the circumstances in which the defendant should be
held in pre-trial detention, the second condition (Article 503.2) being expressed
in the following terms: 'when there are *sufficient grounds to believe* that the
person to be held in detention is guilty of the offence'. The language of these
examples utterly fails to establish when and under what conditions *sufficient* (or
insufficient) grounds exist to make an accusation, or when and under what
conditions *sufficient* grounds exist to believe that someone is responsible for
a crime. This presupposes what the actual rules should eventually decide.

However, affording substance and effectiveness to procedural rights is impossible if the rules that govern the factual decision are unknown or are extremely
vague. The presumption of innocence, for example, can never be effective as
a rule about the factual decision if it is undetermined when the evidence provides
sufficient corroboration of the accusatory hypothesis to rebut it.[6] It is therefore
essential to understand the requirements in order to properly establish a standard
of proof and to radically improve our legislation and case law in this regard.

Establishing standards of proof must fulfil two different kinds of requirements: firstly, those related to a proper formulation from the epistemological
or methodological standpoint and, secondly those pertaining to the grounds
for establishing a specific evidentiary threshold in the standard. Let us consider them separately.

18.2.1 *Methodological Requirements for Standards of Proof*

Three requirements must be met for a rule to be properly called a 'standard of
proof':

(1) It must address criteria about the probative force of evidence, that is, the
    evidence's capacity to justify the evidentiary conclusions. This obviously

---

[6] One paradigmatic example of the failure to safeguard the presumption of innocence resulting from
     an undefined standard of proof is to be found in the judgment of the Spanish Supreme Court 124/
     1983 (F.J. [legal ground] 1). This is analysed in greater depth in Ferrer Beltrán, 2013: 179–83.

excludes the use of subjective criteria specific to the decision-makers, hence any formulation of a standard of proof that refers to their mental or psychological state does not meet this requirement. A judge's or jury's psychological conviction with regard to 'p' does not imply anything about the truth of 'p' or about the degree of corroboration provided by the evidence for 'p'. Therefore, and from the justificatory standpoint of the verdict, whether or not the decision-maker is convinced is irrelevant. However, examples of procedural legislation that undermines this basic requirement abound, using criteria such as '*intime*' or deep conviction or other psychological aspects linked, in one way or another, to the decision maker's beliefs. On other occasions, case law doctrine relates formulations of standards of proof refer to mental states that do not refer directly to them. That is the case of the interpretation made by North American case law of the 'beyond all reasonable doubt' standard[7] By rejecting the possibility of establishing intersubjective criteria for the reasonableness of the doubt, it affirms that the latter is self-evident and that only the conviction of each member of the jury can establish the existence of a reasonable doubt.[8] In other words, with this interpretation, 'beyond all reasonable doubt' and '*intime conviction*' are two ways of saying the same thing.[9]

Irrespective of who has the authority to issue the ruling and of the possibility of appeal, the ruling must be guided by intersubjectively controllable criteria, which would make errors in the application of the criteria conceptually possible. The finality of the decision and its infallibility are, as Hart insisted, different matters (see Hart, 1961: 141–7). For instance, if the criterion used to purchase a car is the buyer's taste, then under no circumstances can we say that they made a wrong decision. However, if the criterion for deciding between one model and the other is greater engine power, even although the decision falls entirely to the buyer and there is no possibility of returning the car, conceptually the buyer may be said to have been wrong if the car chosen is not the most powerful one on the market.

---

[7] See, in this regard, the analysis by Laudan, 2003; and in Laudan, 2006: 59–102. For English interpretation of de standard, see also Roberts and Zuckerman, 2004: 361 et seq.

[8] Lowey (2009: 68) identifies, in US case law, two schools: one, as was said in the text, holds that reasonability of doubt does not need to be and should not be defined; the other one posits the usefulness of giving the jury a definition of the reasonability of the doubt (albeit, unfortunately, I would add) in terms of the degree of the degree of confidence they should have in the factual hypothesis.

[9] The same conclusion is reached by Solan, 1999: 106.

(2) Standard of proof criteria must establish a threshold that is as precise as possible, on the basis of which a factual assumption may be regarded as sufficiently corroborated for making the decision in question. Obviously, this criterion is not met by rules of sound Judgment (which in the best of cases would be a form of assessment but not an evidentiary threshold), by the generic reference to induction (for the same reasons) or respect for the laws of science or logic. It is therefore obvious that evidential legal reasoning must always be inductive, it must respect the laws of logic or science and it should be applied in each procedural stage. On the other hand, in these different stages (e.g., deciding when the case may go to trial, taking interim measures or regarding the facts as proven in the final sentence), the required evidentiary burden is and must be different. It does not suffice to say that these decisions must be inductively justified, etc.; rather, the threshold as of which they will be deemed justified must be defined.

(3) Since the structure of evidential legal reasoning is based on logical and inductive, and not mathematical, probability,[10] numbers or mathematical formulas cannot be used to establish evidentiary thresholds and qualitative criteria must be used instead.

18.2.2 *Justification of the Required Evidentiary Thresholds in the Standards of Proof*

The point of departure for understanding the type of constraints involved in establishing a standard of proof is to realise that its purpose is to distribute the risk of error between the parties.[11] For example, if we raise the evidentiary

---

[10] For a detailed discussion of this thesis, see Ferrer Beltrán, 2007: 98–120.

[11] The general theory of proof must target two strategies, for which purpose there are different instruments. The first one is the reduction of errors. Basically, procedural mechanisms must be designed to facilitate the inclusion of as much relevant evidence as possible into the body of evidence, as well as information about its reliability. The second strategy is the distribution of the risk of error between the parties, underpinned by moral or political preferences as to who should bear the risk and to what extent. For this purpose, the most important procedural mechanisms are burdens of proof, presumptions and especially standards of proof. For more on the role of standards as proof as mechanisms of error distribution, see Stein, 2005: 133–4, and Laudan, 2006: 66 et seq. Laudan's strategy is based on the need to determine a suitable distribution of errors (of false acquittals and false convictions) to subsequently establish the standard of proof that is capable of producing such a distribution. However, in my opinion, this strategy assumes the impossible. Indeed, to ascertain what standard of proof is capable of producing a distribution of errors that we consider appropriate, we need a mechanism to identify false acquittals and false convictions that does not depend on the actual object of

burden in criminal proceedings, all things being equal, fewer innocent people will be convicted (since it will be more difficult to amass sufficient incriminating evidence against them), although more guilty people will be acquitted[12] (since it will also be more difficult to reach the required evidentiary threshold established by this standard of proof to convict the person(s) who actually committed the crimes).[13] Conversely, if the evidentiary burden of the standard of proof is lowered, all things being equal, we can expect to have fewer guilty people acquitted (as it will be easier to gather evidence of guilt that allows us to reach this level of certainty), but more innocent persons convicted (because it will be easier to exceed the required level of corroboration). This is why standards of proof and other rules, such as those that establish burdens of proof or presumptions, distribute the risk of error between the parties.

The theory that a demanding standard of proof reduces the number of factual errors has its fair share of advocates. This, however, is a somewhat hasty conclusion. It is based on the observation of a single type of errors, that is, wrongful convictions, and does not take into consideration, whether unknowingly or unaware, that false acquittals are also wrong in terms of evidence. In other words, if we accept that the institutional purpose of evidence in judicial proceedings is to ascertain the truth, then any discrepancy between what happened and what was proven is a material error (although, as we shall see

---

analysis: the evidence produced at the trial and the evidential legal reasoning applied to it. For example, if we wish to ascertain the ratio of false positive and false negative results for a home pregnancy test it will suffice to have a broad enough sample of women use it and then observe how many of them are actually pregnant and finally compare this number to the test results. Pregnancy can be accurately detected independently of the test, thus making it possible to ascertain the error rate of false positives and false negatives of the test. But what mechanism can we use to establish the ratio of false positives and false negatives resulting from the application of a standard of proof in judicial proceedings? In my opinion, it is impossible to design a mechanism that is independent of the actual evidential information, of the evidential legal reasoning and of the type of standard of proof applied (attention has been drawn to this problem by Bayón, 2008: 26 et seq.).

However, this problem does not prevent us from asserting that standards of proof have a direct effect on the distribution of the *risk* of error. For this purpose, it will suffice to demonstrate that, with regard to the same body of evidence, applying a demanding standard of proof might result in acquittal, whereas a less demanding standard would lead to conviction. In the first case, the accusation would bear the risk of error, whereas in the second one the defence would.

[12] Let it be understood that I am using the expressions 'guilty' and 'innocent' in the material sense, to refer to defendants who, respectively, did and did not commit the offence of which they are accused (irrespective of the evidence against them).

[13] In many cases it may actually transpire that proceedings are not initiated because the prosecution, or the judge who decides when to go to trial, consider that the available evidence would never meet the established standard of proof to convict the person who committed the offence.

presently, it may not be an inferential error). Having, in certain circumstances, a preference for one of these types of errors (to a certain extent a false acquittal could be preferable to a false conviction) has no ultimate bearing on all of them being regarded as such.

Of course, legal epistemology should not be solely or primarily concerned with distributing errors, but above all with reducing them. However, the appropriate procedural instruments to maximise the probability of correct decisions on evidence are not rules of decision, like standards of proof: specifically, they are those intended to build a body of evidence that is as quantitatively and qualitatively rich as possible. Some of the aspects that affect the weight of the body of evidence include who can make a request for admission of evidence in court (as well as when and how), what evidence is admissible and how its reliability can be controlled (taking and handling it properly or admitting other evidence about it). The greater the amount and reliability of the information, the stronger the probability of reaching correct findings.

If this is so, determining the evidentiary threshold by means of a standard of proof does not affect the reduction of errors but rather the distribution of the risk of error between the parties. Therefore, the main reason for determining the evidentiary threshold at which we will establish the standard of proof is related to the distribution of the risk of error (false convictions and false acquittals) that we consider acceptable,[14] which is clearly a political and moral decision.[15]

---

[14]   As I mentioned in note 12, the question is not (*à la* Laudan), after we have determined the ratio of errors of one kind or another that we deem desirable, that we can go on to establish a standard of proof capable of achieving this ratio. It is more a question of determining, for each type of case, at what level of evidentiary burden we are willing to allow the risk of error (i.e., a false conviction) to fall upon the defence (or, from the opposite standpoint, at what level of evidentiary burden we are willing to allow the risk of error, i.e., false acquittal, to be shouldered by the prosecution). Evidently, a more demanding evidentiary threshold will also increase the risk of error of false acquittal, and vice versa.

[15]   In this regard, see Stein, 2005: 121–2. As opposed to the psychologistic or subjectivistic conception of proof, in which evidential reasoning is based on deep conviction or on the judge's subjective beliefs, the rationalist tradition of proof assumes the axiom whereby conviction and acquittal cannot both be justified at the same time by the same body of evidence, depending on the judge involved. This is suggested by the evidentialist theory in epistemology (see Feldman and Conee, 1985). This theory holds that the epistemic justification of beliefs depends solely on the evidence on which they are based. Thus, two judges who have the same evidence should always reach the same justified evidentiary findings. However, the epistemological theory of evidence is incapable of accommodating the notion that the required evidentiary threshold (i.e., the standard of proof) may be different depending on what is at stake, and therefore, when confronted with the same evidence, a civil judge and a criminal judge, for example, could justifiably reach different conclusions about evidence.

One way of providing a theoretical basis for the contextual relativity of the degree of evidentiary burden to justify an assumption of fact is contextualism. According to this theory, the justification of a belief on which we base a practical decision is contextual and depends on

However, what arguments can be used to decide about the evidentiary burden? Clearly, the list is an open-ended one, and under no circumstances will the items on it be objective (since they reflect political preferences). Nevertheless, the following five arguments should be emphasised.

(1) The seriousness of the error in the event of a wrongful conviction, which is essentially related to the relative importance of the particular legal right affected by the legal consequences and the extent to which it is affected. We may agree that a financial penalty is not as serious as imprisonment and that house arrest on weekends is not the same as a twenty-year prison sentence. When the legal rights at stake are more important and are affected to a greater extent, a more demanding standard of proof is usually recommended, since a wrongful conviction would have more serious consequences.[16]

the importance of what is at stake in the decision. An example given by Fantl and McGrath (2002: 67–8) may be of use here. Imagine that we are in the Boston train station and are about to take a train to Providence to visit some friends. We would rather take a direct train, if possible, although this is not crucial. We ask another passenger waiting for the same train if it is direct and she says no. Now, imagine that we are in the same situation and place but, for reasons that our professional careers depend upon, we need to go urgently to Foxboro, a small station en route to Providence. We ask the same passenger waiting for the train and she tells us that the next train stops at all stations. The dilemma is as follows: in the first situation, is the information provided by the passenger sufficient enough for us to decide to board the train? What about the second situation? Since both the information and the source are the same, evidentialism or the epistemic justification of beliefs should answer yes or no in both cases. Contextualism, on the other hand, is sensitive to the practical aspect of the decision when determining the amount of information that is regarded as sufficient to justify the belief that supports the decision. According to this theory, even with the same available information, in the first situation we would be justified in believing that the train stops in Foxboro but not in the second one. In view of the importance of what is at stake in the second situation, justification of the belief would call for further and more reliable information (see Fantl and McGrath, 2002: 78–9).

One important point remains: Who evaluates the importance of what is at stake in each decision? If it is the decision-maker, in our case the judge, then we run the risk of lapsing once again into the subjective nature of decision-making. Two judges, faced with the same evidence and with the same legal rights at stake, may evaluate the importance of those rights differently and therefore apply different levels of evidentiary burden. To avoid this, the only solution is that this evaluation, due to its political and moral nature, and in order to avoid judicial subjectivism, should be made by lawmakers and include the standards of proof that determine the evidentiary burden for each type of case in procedure law. For a more exhaustive discussion of contextualism, see, among others, Cohen, S. (1999), Folley (2000), Rysiew (2001), Stanley (2005) – particularly chap. 5 – and Hawthorne and Stanley (2008).

[16] Moreover, we must also remember that a wrongful conviction includes both the assumption in which someone was convicted of a crime that did not actually occur and the one in which the crime did occur, but the perpetrator was not the person who was convicted. This second example contains two errors that should be taken into account: an innocent person is convicted, and the actual perpetrator of the crime goes free.

For this reason, for example, the Anglo-Saxon legal systems have traditionally distinguished between the standard of proof for criminal trials and the
standard (or standards) for civil proceedings. In view of this first argument,
however, I believe that the distinction should be much more subtle. Indeed,
in the last few decades, criminal law has undergone a major transformation
by abandoning the minimal intervention model and including a wide range
of crimes in the penal codes. At the same time, the range of legal consequences or penalties has also grown exponentially to include fines, professional disqualification or ineligibility for public office, community service
and restraining orders, as well as traditional prison sentences, which are not
only highly varied in length, but also include house arrest as an alternative to
prison time. Of course, some of these consequences are no different to those
that may arise from civil, administrative-contentious or labour proceedings.
The legal consequences of an inaccurate determination of the facts are not
always as serious as they are in criminal cases. This makes it advisable, taking
the first argument into account, to have different standards of proof available
for these types of cases depending on the severity of the established legal
consequences. Similarly, an error in a criminal case does not always have to
be more serious than in a civil case. In other words, a wrongfully imposed
financial penalty in a criminal case is not clearly more serious than the
undue loss of child custody rights in a civil action. Therefore, and according
to this first argument, it would not be appropriate to establish a harmonised
standard of proof for all criminal proceedings, although these standards need
not be more demanding than the ones applied in civil, administrative-
contentious and other cases.

Consequently, and irrespective of the serious ambiguity of the 'beyond all
reasonable doubt' standard, it should cease to be applied indiscriminately in
all criminal proceedings. Moreover, if the argument we use to make the
criminal standard of proof more demanding is the severity of the penalty,
and consequently of a wrongful conviction, this does not apply to establishing
the standard of proof for a presumption of innocence, which makes it possible
to regard the innocence of the defendant as proven (no longer presumed). If
this is so, it would seem reasonable to have different standards of proof in
criminal cases for the hypotheses of innocence and guilt.[17]

---

[17] Evidently, on many occasions, the defence will simply need to ensure that the body of
evidence for prosecution does not reach the demands of the standard of proof for the
hypothesis of guilt, in which case the presumption of innocence would prevail. However,
there are other occasions in which it is highly relevant (not only personally or socially, but also
traditionally) that innocence not only be presumed, but also proven, as we shall see later
regarding compensation for undue pre-trial detention or offences such as false accusation.

(2) The cost of false acquittals. It is clear that if our only interest lies in avoiding wrongful convictions, the best (and only) way of guaranteeing this is to not convict anyone. In doing so, we would fully satisfy one of the demands we make upon the State: that it not use its power to impose penalties to harm innocent persons However, we would also be totally ignoring another demand that we as a society make upon the State: that it protect our rights (to life, physical well-being, freedom, property, sexual freedom, etc.) and prevent other people from doing us harm.[18] We must therefore be aware that as the evidentiary burden for the standard of proof is raised, so too will the number of false acquittals, or, to put it another way, the number of guilty people that go free. To the extent that such people may be repeat offenders or that the lack of convictions may diminish or eliminate the deterrent effect of the law, the standard of proof would have a considerable impact on the State fulfilling its function of protecting our rights.

(3) The third argument to be considered when setting standards of proof is related to evidentiary difficulties in the types of cases to which the standards are to be applied, as characterised by the lawmaker.[19] One example to illustrate this is the evolution of the definition of sexual offences in many countries. Physical resistance is no longer required to ascertain lack of consent; a simple refusal to have sexual intercourse now suffices. However, undeniable progress in one regard introduces serious evidence-related problems in another: a scenario in which there is evidence of physical resistance is much more straightforward than one in which an absence of consent,

---

[18] Some time ago, Laplace (1814: 133) highlighted this twofold intention with regard to the State addressing the evidentiary burden (likelihood) that the prosecution's hypothesis should have in order to justify the conviction: 'does the proof of the defendant's crime have the high degree of probability required for citizens to fear court errors less if an innocent person were found guilty than they would if the actual culprit were acquitted and committed further offences and unfortunate people were made to feel exasperated at the culprit's impunity?'. This approach was also pursued by Laudan, 2016: 27 et seq. Among many others in the area of criminal law, Roxin also insisted upon the twofold objective of protecting citizens' rights through criminal law and against criminal law (see Roxin, 1994: 137). See also Roberts and Zuckerman, 2004: 9 et seq., 351.

[19] Contextualism, as a theory of the justification of beliefs on whose foundations our decision is based, also assumes that evidentiary difficulties may be one of the factors to be taken into account to determine the degree of evidentiary burden (see Fantl and McGrath, 2002: 81). The classification of the types of cases that pose evidentiary difficulties can be found in Hunter, 2015: 213 et seq. It should be noted that Hunter distinguishes between evidentiary difficulties that pertain to the type of facts and those that pertain to the availability of evidence or ease of proof of one party in the trial but does not consider lowering the standard of proof regardless of the type of difficulty. Ormazábal, on the other hand, does consider that possibility, 2004: 14–5. I limit my consideration to evidentiary difficulties pertaining to the type of facts that may give reason to establish the degree of sufficiency of the standard of proof.

which may be only verbal or even non-verbal, has to be proven. What is more, sexual offences are not usually committed in public, making them even more difficult to prove.

Another clear example of this type of problem can be found in crimes of corruption. Linking financial transactions to political bribes, for example, can be very difficult because of the considerable obstacles involved in following the movement of money (very often with intermediaries, between accounts in different countries, particularly in tax havens).

In these types of cases,[20] evidentiary difficulties provide a reason to lower the standard. As a result, impunity is avoided but the legal definition of the crime is pointless because the class of offence becomes unenforceable. In other words, the particular evidentiary difficulties in these types of cases tend to result in a large number of false acquittals, with the corresponding lack of protection of the rights that the class of offence sought to protect. If we wish to avoid this outcome, we can either modify the definition of the class of offence so that it does not create these serious evidentiary problems or lower the standard of proof.[21]

Evidently, it is not at all strange for arguments to be put forth for raising the evidentiary threshold (or for keeping it high) and for reducing it at the same time. This occurs, for example, when cases that present major evidentiary difficulties have particularly serious legal consequences (e.g., a long-term prison sentence). In the absence of an objective method to ponder these opposing arguments, the decision can only be political. However, any eventual legislation that defines factual assumptions in such a way as to create serious evidentiary difficulties and attaches grave legal consequences to them runs a serious risk of becoming ineffectual and/or ineffective.

(4) As mentioned previously, standards of proof are not the only rules that affect the distribution of evidentiary risk in our legal systems. Among others, the rules that establish burdens of proof and presumptions also have an impact (see Allen and Callen, 2003: 5). The burden of proof determines which party loses the case if neither one manages to corroborate their respective factual hypotheses in accordance with the level of the applicable standard or standards of proof. Consequently, this party will run the risk of a wrongful decision

---

[20] It is important to stress that I am talking about types of cases, not individual cases which, for whatever reason have to contend with evidentiary difficulties. For the simple reason of the consistency of the laws by which we are judged, standards of proof must be designed as general and abstract rules.

[21] This will reduce the number of false acquittals, although it will also increase the number of wrongful convictions. On the other hand, it is also clear that this third reason is actually instrumental to the second.

due to lack of evidence. By observing the overall impact of the different rules of distribution of evidentiary risk, we can ascertain, for example, how the so-called preponderance of evidence standard does not necessarily distribute the risk of error equally, unlike what is often claimed. This depends not only on the standard, but also on the distribution of the burden of proof. Thus, although the standard is the same for both parties' factual hypotheses and only requires preponderance of evidence, one of the parties will be jeopardised by the burden of proof, that is, they will lose if there is insufficient evidence, and it is therefore this party alone that runs the risk of having insufficient evidence.

Presumptions, on the other hand, can be of two types:[22] *stricto sensu* and the so-called apparent presumptions. The first are conditional, and given a certain underlying assumption, take a presumed fact as true unless proven otherwise. For example, many civil codes provide for the so-called presumption of simultaneous death (the Commorientes Rule) in the event that two or more persons who would be successors die in the same accident.[23] These civil codes establish that if an underlying assumption is proven (multiple deaths in the same accident), another fact will be presumed (that the different persons died at the same time) unless proven otherwise. This is a very useful legislative technique for resolving situations of evidentiary difficulty. Indeed, proving the exact moment when two people died may be very complicated if it happens within a short time and there are no witnesses (a very common situation in natural disasters or accidents). In this case, it will suffice to prove another much simpler fact, namely death in the same accident. Unless it can be proven otherwise, all the victims will be presumed to have died at the same time. In terms of evidence, the effect is twofold. First, the *thema probandum* (the fact to be proved) changes, which, once proven, changes the burden of proof of the non-occurrence of the presumed fact. An example of how this technique can be used in situations involving evidentiary difficulty can also be found in some penal codes that include illicit enrichment. In these laws, the existence of an underlying assumption (increased wealth during the exercise of public office that cannot be accounted for by the office holder's known lawful income), unless proven otherwise, leads to the presumption of another fact (illicit enrichment).[24]

---

[22] I voluntarily omit the so-called irrebuttable (*iuris et de iure*) presumptions, which have no bearing on evidential legal reasoning, since they operate by excluding it.

[23] See, for example, Article 95 of the Civil and Commercial Code of Argentina or, less clearly so in terms of identifying the underlying assumption, Article 33 of the Spanish Civil Code.

[24] At this point I will not get into the otherwise interesting debate as to whether this technique is consistent with the presumption of innocence in criminal proceedings.

Like *stricto sensu* presumptions, apparent presumptions admit evidence to the contrary and place the burden of proof on the party that does not benefit from the presumption. However, they differ from *stricto sensu* presumptions in that underlying assumptions do not need to be proven to make the presumption. The presumption of innocence and that of good faith in civil matters are clear examples of this type of rule. Their practical effect is not at all different to that of the rules that establish burdens of proof.

It is easy to see that if we wish to distribute evidentiary risk using standards of proof, we also need to take other rules that affect distribution into account. For example, if, in an effort to favour the weaker party in consumer relations, we establish that the burden of proof in cases of liability for defective products falls to the manufacturer and at the same time we greatly reduce the standard of proof, the result may be exactly opposite to the one sought. In other words, when taking into account the reasons related to the seriousness of the conse-quences of a wrong decision on evidence or the evidentiary difficulties of a certain case we must also consider where the burden of proof lies and the effects of any possible assumptions about the case.[25]

(5) Finally, the preceding arguments would appear to point to the need for standards of proof for factual findings when the ruling in the case is issued. However, this is not the only point in the proceedings when evidentiary concerns should be postponed to evaluate factual findings.[26] Let us take a look at some examples taken from the *Ley de Enjuiciamiento Criminal española* [Criminal Procedure Act] [LECr]:

> *Pre-trial detention* (Art. 503.1 LECr): 'The following circumstances will be necessary to order pre-trial detention:
>
> . . .
>
> 2. That there are *sufficient grounds for believing* that the person against whom the detention order is to be issued is criminally responsible for the offence'

---

[25]   Laudan (2006: 118 ff.) has defended the position whereby once a preference for a given distribution of errors (of false acquittals and false convictions) has been incorporated into the standard of proof, no other evidentiary rule should modify this distribution. Laudan's critique is aimed explicitly at exclusionary rules concerning relevant evidence that only benefit the defence in a criminal procedure, and it makes a great deal of sense within that context. More broadly, however, I find the idea that the distribution of the risk of proof should fall exclusively to standards of proof is disproportionate. As I have already pointed out, the rules that establish burdens of proof and presumptions should also distribute the risk of error. And since we cannot disregard burdens of proof and presumptions, they should be taken into consideration to ensure the most suitable distribution.

[26]   See Anderson, Schum, and Twining, 2005: 230 ff.

Dismissal of the case (Art. 637 LECr): 'The case will be dismissed:
1. When there is *no rational prima facie evidence that the act* that gave rise to the proceedings *has been committed.*
. . .

Temporary stay of proceedings (Art. 641 LECr): 'A temporary stay of proceedings will be issued:
. . .

2. When it emerges from the proceedings that an offence has been committed and *there are not sufficient grounds* to accuse any individual or individuals as perpetrators, accomplices, or accessories, aiders and abettors'.

As can be seen, lawmakers have realised that judges must use evidentiary sufficiency at different points in trials to make decisions: to continue with the proceedings (and not dismiss the case), to go to the trial, to order preventive measures such as pre-trial detention. However, the criteria applied by Spanish lawmakers do not meet the methodological requirements described in Section 18.2.1 of this chapter; more specifically, they are not inter-subjectively controllable and are not suitable for establishing a threshold for evidence.

In addition to all the aforementioned methodological and political requirements, another methodological prerequisite must be taken into consideration if interim provisional standards of proof for proceedings are to be properly established. The evidentiary threshold required by the different standards of proof for the different phases of the proceedings must be ordered from lowest to highest, whereby the evidentiary threshold required to order a stay (or not) of proceedings must be lower than that which is required to go to the trial, which in turn must be lower than that which is required to prove the claims under consideration in the final decision. Otherwise, the interim or provisional rulings would do little more than anticipate the final decision, rendering all subsequent proceedings useless. The same applies to rulings on preventive measures, such as pre-trial detention, as well as measures related to assets and restrictions on movements. As the importance of the legal right involved varies, so does the degree of affectation, also altering the seriousness of a judicial error. Moreover, under no circumstances should preventive measures require the same degree of corroboration of evidence as final decisions. As we shall see later, this has an important impact on deciding what counts as an error in each case.

18.2.3 *Some Examples of Standards of Proof*

We have just seen how deficient some of the so-called standards of proof in Spanish criminal procedure law are. Besides the ones already mentioned, we might add that which has been established for final decisions by Article 741 of the LECr.: 'The court, *assessing according to its conscience the evidence* examined in the trial, the arguments of the prosecution and the defence and the testimony of the defendant, will issue its decision within the term provided for by this Law' (italics added). Finally, in terms of case law, both the Supreme Court and the Constitutional Court have established that a conviction can only be handed down if the evidence substantiates the guilt of the defendant beyond a reasonable doubt. Here, one example will suffice:

> The right to the presumption of innocence involves the right not to be convicted without valid evidence, which means that any conviction must state the evidence on which the declaration of criminal liability is based; moreover, such evidence must have been obtained in accordance with constitutional guarantees, taken properly in the trial and assessed and justified by the Courts in accordance with the rules of logic and experience, so that it may be asserted that the declaration of guilt *has been established beyond any reasonable doubt*' Constitutional Court Judgment 43/2003, F.J. [legal basis] 4. (italics added).[27]

However, as has already been mentioned, it hardly seems a good idea to assume that the same standard of proof will govern the final decision about the prosecution's case in all criminal proceedings. This, compounded by the problems resulting from a lack of criteria regarding the reasonableness of the doubt, renders it imperative to enact different rules to establish thresholds for sufficient evidence for each type of decision regarding the facts of a trial.

In the preceding sections, I identified the methodological and political requirements to be considered when standards of proof are defined. In this section, I will merely offer a series of proposals that would fulfil all the aforementioned requirements, and will establish the degree of corroboration from highest to lowest. I do not mean to suggest that these proposed standards should be used, not least because this would require a decision on the distribution of evidentiary risk deemed politically expedient at any given time. I merely intend to show how it would be possible to establish standards of proof that avoid the problems of current formulations.

Standard of proof (1)

Both of the following conditions must be met to prove a factual hypothesis:

(a) The hypothesis must be capable of explaining and integrating the available data in a consistent way, and any predictions of new data based on the hypothesis must have been confirmed.

---

[27] A similar opinion is clearly expressed by the Constitutional Court Judgment 66/2009, F.J. [legal ground] 6. To cite but two Supreme Court Judgments, see the Judgments 258/2003, of 25 February, F.J. [legal ground] 3 and 1991/2002, of 25 November, F.J. [legal ground] 13.

(b) All other plausible hypothesis that explain the same data and are consistent with the defendant's innocence, excluding mere *ad hoc* hypothesis, must have been refuted.[28]

Standard of proof (2)
Both of the following conditions must be met to prove a factual hypothesis:

(a) The hypothesis must be capable of explaining and integrating the available data in a consistent way, and any predictions of new data based on the hypothesis must have been confirmed.
(b) The alternative hypothesis formulated by the defence, if plausible, that explains the same data and is consistent with the defendant's innocence, excluding mere *ad hoc* hypothesis, must have been refuted.

Standard of proof (3)
Both of the following conditions must be met to prove a factual hypothesis:

(a) The hypothesis is the best explanation available for the facts to be proven, in the light of the evidence existing in the court proceedings.
(b) The evidential weight of the body of relevant evidence supplied to the proceedings is complete (the redundant evidence having been excluded).[29]

---

[28] A presentation of this standard of proof and an explanation thereof is to be found in Ferrer Beltrán, 2007: 147 ff. In any event, here it should be pointed out, to avoid subjective misinterpretations, that the plausibility referred to in the second clause of the standard is essentially understood as compatibility with the knowledge that we have of the world.

[29] A presentation of this standard of proof and an explanation thereof can be found in Ferrer Beltrán, 2014: 227 ff. I would like to highlight the mention of the evidential or probative weight, a notion that must be carefully distinguished from that of probative value. The concept of evidential weight I am referring to originates from Keynes (1921: chap. IV, 71 ff.) and was adapted to the context of inductive probability by Cohen (1986). Evidential or probative value is the degree of confirmation that a set of evidence provides to a hypothesis. On the other hand, evidential weight measures the comprehensiveness (i.e., the wealth) of the set of evidence with which the decision is taken. In Keynesian terms, the evidential weight is the sum of relevant, favourable and unfavourable evidence that make it possible to confer an evidential value on each one of the hypotheses at issue. Thus, whereas the evidential value of a hypothesis accounts for the probability that this hypothesis is true compared to its rival hypotheses, the evidential weight accounts for the probability of the decision being right, depending on the wealth of the evidence taken into consideration in the decision. In this regard, it may be said that the greater the amount of information available, the greater the probability of the right decision being taken. Hence, with regard to any hypothesis about facts, we may ask what evidence is necessary to substantiate each one of the elements. The question about weight is whether or not this evidence is contained in the proceedings (irrespective of its evidential value, i.e., as to whether or not the evidence is reliable enough to prove what we are trying to prove).

Standard of proof (4)

Both of the following conditions must be met to prove a factual hypothesis:

(a) The hypothesis offers a better explanation of the facts to be proven than the adversary's hypothesis in the light of the evidence existing in the proceedings.

(b) The evidential weight of the body of relevant evidence supplied to the proceedings is complete (the redundant evidence having been excluded).

Standard of proof (5)

A hypothesis about the facts of a trial will be considered proven when:

The hypothesis is the best explanation available for the facts that have to be proven in the light of the evidence existing in the proceedings.

Standard of proof (6)

A hypothesis about the facts of a trial will be considered proven when:

The hypothesis offers a better explanation of the facts to be proven than the adversary's hypothesis in the light of the evidence existing in the proceedings.

With these or other proposed standards, lawmakers would have a range of choices, depending on the evidentiary thresholds they want to stipulate for each decision on the facts of the case. And these proposals have another advantage: making the other rules of distribution of evidentiary risk (burden of proof and presumptions) applicable. In effect, and this is very important, in my opinion none of them have any bearing whatsoever on the evidentiary threshold, although they presuppose that we have a rule that establishes this. It is not possible to apply the burden of proof in the event of lack of

---

The two proposed clauses of the standard seek to capture dimensions that are similar to the distinction made by Haack (1993; 82 et seq.) between the degree of support offered by the evidence to a hypothesis and the degree of comprehensiveness of the evidence, which answers the question as to the amount of relevant proof that we have. In the same line as Keynes, Stein (1997: 581 ff.) makes the distinction between the probability of a hypothesis and evidential weight and considers that decisions about proven facts must be based on both dimensions.

The proposed standard would make it possible to avoid the problem pointed out by Laudan (2007: 302 et seq.) regarding the use of inference for the best explanation as a standard of proof; in short, that the best explanation available could be a bad one, since, even if, in comparison to another hypothesis, it is more corroborated, it may be supported by a very poor set of evidence. Thus, requiring comprehensive evidential weight would no longer mean having to declare a hypothesis that has a very scant evidential support as proven simply because it is relatively better than the adversary's.

evidence if we have not yet determined when to consider that evidence is lacking. And similarly, there is no way to apply a rebuttable presumption, such as the presumption of innocence in legal proceedings, if we have not established under which conditions the presumption is regarded as disproven, that is, when there is sufficient evidence to the contrary.

18.3 STANDARDS OF PROOF AND TYPES OF JUDICIAL ERRORS INVOLVING EVIDENCE

Up until this point, I have consistently used the notion of error to refer to the discrepancy between what is declared proven or not proven in court and events in the world. In this regard, errors take place when innocent persons (who did not commit the deeds with which they are charged) are convicted but also when guilty persons (who did commit the deeds) are acquitted. And in the case of acquittals, whether the defendants are acquitted for lack of evidence of guilt or for proof of innocence does not matter.

However, this type of error, which I will call material, is not the only possible one. There is another type, the inferential error, which does not result from a direct conflict between the evidentiary findings of the proceedings and the world external to them but rather from the analysis of the actual evidential reasoning of the proceedings. Inferential errors occur when, on the basis of provided evidence and taking the applicable standard of proof into account, the court's evidentiary findings cannot be justified.

If we take 'p' as any statement of fact, there are three possible evidentiary findings: proven 'p', not proven 'p' and proven 'non-p'. If 'p' designates the commission of a criminal act, proof thereof will involve a conviction, whereas lack of evidence or evidence of non-commission will mean acquittal. It is important to emphasise that inferential errors depend on purely procedural aspects: the evidence provided to the proceedings and the applicable standard of proof. If either aspect varies, evidently the justified finding may also change. Therefore, the same body of evidence may lead to the justified finding that 'p' is proven if the standard is of an intermediate level of sufficiency or that 'p' is not proven if we apply a higher standard to the same evidence. In this way, it may be inferentially justified to convict a person who is materially innocent (if the existing evidence corroborates of the indictment at the level of the standard required) or to acquit someone who is materially guilty (if the evidence does not make it possible to reach the same standard).

The following combinations of the two types of errors are possible:[30]

(1) Inferentially justified (accurate inference) conviction of an innocent person (material error)
(2) Inferentially unjustified (error of inference) conviction of an innocent person (material error)
(3) Inferentially justified (accurate inference) acquittal of a guilty person (material error)
(4) Inferentially unjustified (error of inference) acquittal of a guilty person (material error)
(5) Inferentially unjustified (error of inference) conviction of a guilty person (materially correct)
(6) Inferentially unjustified (error of inference) acquittal of an innocent person (materially correct)

18.4 PRESUMPTION OF INNOCENCE AND PRE-TRIAL DETENTION: THE STATE'S RESPONSIBILITY FOR 'UNDUE' PRE-TRIAL DETENTION

Having provided a very superficial outline of the general theory of standards of proof, it would be useful to analyse a specific problem that involves the need to distinguish between very different degrees of evidentiary threshold: the determination of the State's civil responsibility for 'undue' or 'wrongful' pre-trial detention. In regard to this question, we stand at a crossroads of different stages in the criminal process with their specific rules (that which governs pre-trial detention and that which governs the final decision in the case), the determination of civil liability, the holding of proceedings in different jurisdictions, etc. In other words, this is a good test case for a theory of standards of proof.

In previous works, I have analysed the compatibility between presumption of innocence as a rule on how the defendant is to be regarded and subsequently treated in the criminal proceedings and preventive measures, focusing particularly on pre-trial detention (see Ferrer Beltrán, 2013 and 2017). Here,

---

[30] Evidently, there are actually eight logical combinations of materially correct and material error or accurate inference (because material error can in turn be subdivided into two kinds: conviction of an innocent person and acquittal of a guilty person). The two combinations missing from the following list are: (7) inferentially justified (accurate inference) conviction of a guilty person (materially correct) and (8) inferentially justified (accurate inference) acquittal of an innocent person (materially correct). I do not address these two cases here as I wish to analyse only the cases in which there is an error in either of the two kinds. The possibilities may be further complicated if, as we shall see is useful for the purpose of compensation for undue pre-trial detention, we distinguish between insufficient evidence of guilt (not proven 'p') and proof of innocence (proven 'non-p').

I would like to emphasise the relationship between the presumption of innocence as a rule which instructs the fact-finder decision and its implications for
the ruling following acquittal with regard to a possible claim for undue pre-
trial detention. For this purpose, it is essential to understand the theoretical
guidelines on standards of proof and types of judicial error presented so far.
Before drawing any conclusions from the analysis, however, it would be
advisable to present the original doctrine of the Spanish Supreme Court, on
the basis of the provisions of the Ley Orgánica del Poder Judicial [LOPJ,
Organic Statute of the Judiciary] regarding the legal regulation of compensation for 'undue' pre-trial detention and the crucial amendment to it based on
the case law of the European Court of Human Rights (ECHR).

18.4.1 *The Supreme Court's Original Doctrine*

Article 121 of the Spanish Constitution establishes that 'damages caused by
judicial errors, as well as those arising from irregularities in the administration
of justice, shall be subject to compensation by the State in accordance with the
law'. This constitutional clause was developed by the LOPJ, establishing
a general rule (Article 293) and a specific regulation for certain cases of
'undue' pre-trial detention (Article 294), which in any event does not rule
out appeals to the general rule for other cases. Thus, the specific rule of Article
294 of the LOPJ established that:[31]

> 1. Any persons who, following pre-trial detention are acquitted due to non-
> occurrence of the alleged act or if the charges have been dismissed, will be
> entitled to compensation provided that damages have been caused.

On the other hand, according to the general rule, any allegations of
judicial error require a specific ruling by the Supreme Court, which has
always ruled that the error must be 'objective, patent and unquestionable',[32]
or in other words, that it be blatant. Regardless of the conditions under which
such an error might occur, it is both procedurally and substantively evident
that the general rule is more restrictive than its specific counterpart with
regard to pre-trial detention.[33] The latter only requires an acquittal or
dismissal issued in the same criminal proceedings in which the pre-trial

---

[31] We will see below that the wording has been amended by a recent ruling of the Spanish
Constitutional Court, but for the moment it is important to take into account the original
wording of the Article.

[32] See the Spanish Supreme Court Judgments of 12 September 1991 (Second Chamber), and of
7 June 2011 (Fourth Chamber), among the many in this regard.

[33] A critique of this restrictive interpretation may be found in Tolivar Alas, 2009: 203 et seq.

detention was ordered. Surprisingly enough, however, the exact wording of Article 294 of the LOPJ limited this eventuality to cases in which acquittal is due to the non-occurrence of the supposed crime, whereby it would not include the eventuality in which the act did occur but was not committed by the person who was held in pre-trial detention (which accounts for the vast majority of cases of pre-trial detention with subsequent acquittal).

This strange restriction, hardly compatible with the right to equality,[34] was quickly lifted by subsequent case law interpretations. Thus, the Supreme Court, after receiving the opinion of the Council of State,[35] found that the non-occurrence of the crime should be understood in both its 'objective' (or literal) sense as well as in its 'subjective' sense, namely that the criminal act committed by the defendant did not occur (thus including 'acting subject' in the definition of the actual deed).[36] In essence, the Supreme Court understood that compensation should be provided for undue pre-trial detention when the defendant is acquitted or the case is dismissed because there is proof of the non-occurrence of the crime or the non-involvement of the subject held in pre-trial detention for the crime.[37] When dealing with subjects of rights, there are three options:

(1) The crime and the defendant's involvement are proven (proven that 'p') and, consequently, the defendant is convicted.

(2) It is proven that the crime did not occur or that the subject did not participate (proven that 'non-p') and consequently the subject's innocence has been proven, the subject is acquitted and compensation for undue pre-trial detention is warranted.

---

[34] See, in the same regard, the Constitutional Court Judgment 98/1992, of 22 June, F.J. [legal ground] 2, and using the same argument as a criticism of the jurisprudence of the ECHR which will be analysed subsequently, see Díaz Fraile, 2017: 68. This argument is also crucial in the declaration of unconstitutionality of the two limitations of Article 294.1 of the LOPJ by the Constitutional Court Judgment 85/2019, of 19 June (F.J. [legal ground] 7), which I will refer to later, and in two previous decisions under appeal, Constitutional Court Judgments 8/2017 and 10/2017.

[35] See the decision of the Council of State of 9 October 1986, no. 49283.

[36] See, for example, the Spanish Supreme Court Judgment of 27 January 1989 (Third Chamber), a case law that, as we shall see, remained constant until the *Tendam v. Spain* decision issued by the ECHR.

[37] As in most legal problems, there is very little empirical information available on this subject in Spain. One exception, which may be indicative, is the study by Guerra Pérez (2010: 371), which analyses 250 cases from the province of Malaga, during 2003 and 2004, in which the defendant was held in pre-trial detention. In the study, 16 per cent of them were ultimately not convicted: 12 per cent were acquitted and 4 per cent were not convicted when the case was dismissed.

(3) There is insufficient evidence as to either the guilt or innocence of the subject, who is acquitted but not entitled to compensation for undue pre-trial detention.

In the light of the points addressed in Sections 18.2 and 18.3 of this chapter, this system of compensation is deserving of further analysis. First of all, it must be related to the different types of judicial error identified previously, taking into consideration that claiming an inferential error in some or any of the decisions will depend on the standard of proof applicable to the specific decision and on the evidence available at that time. Given that the standard of proof for pre-trial detention of a subject accused of participating in a crime[38] must necessarily be lower than the standard of proof required for the final decision on the indictment and that the evidence available at the time of the decision does not have to be the same as that which is available when the final decision is taken, it is perfectly possible that the court's decision to order pre-trial detention is inferentially correct, even although the final decision to acquit the subject (even through proof of innocence) may also be correct. That is to say, both decisions may be inferentially correct, even if they reach different conclusions, since they are based on bodies of evidence that are also different and apply different standards of proof. In that case, even when acquittals consider that the innocence of subjects was proven, we could conclude that material errors were committed in the decisions to order pre-trial detention, albeit not inferential errors that could be ascribed to the judge. Deciding that compensation should be provided in that case places such redress within the sphere of the State's objective liability. If, on the other hand, inferential errors in decisions to order pre-trial detention were also substantiated (i.e., the decisions were not justified in the light of the evidence available at that time and the applicable standard of proof), the State would be responsible for the judge's negligence (or malicious intent in the event of malfeasance).

However, the most interesting eventuality is that of final acquittal due to lack of evidence because neither the standard of proof established for the hypothesis of guilt nor the standard established for the hypothesis of innocence (neither 'p' nor 'non-p' are proven) are met. In that case, it is commonly accepted that the presumption of innocence as a rule of Judgment requires

---

[38] It is important to point out that ordering pre-trial detention must be substantiated by two very different facts: a certain threshold of sufficient evidence regarding the commission of the crime in question must be reached, and the existence of any of the procedural dangers provided for in the legislation (flight, destruction of evidence, criminal recidivism) must be substantiated. This chapter will only address the first aspect mentioned.

that the defendant be acquitted, although if pre-trial detention was ordered during the procedure, we can neither assert that a material error has taken place (because innocence is not proven) nor that an inferential error has taken place (because the fact that the degree of substantiation of the hypothesis of guilt does not exceed the standard established for conviction does not allow us to infer that the standard established for pre-trial detention, which is by necessity lower, was not exceeded at the time). Therefore, acquittal due to the presumption of innocence would be applicable without the pre-trial detention being regarded as wrongful in either material or inferential terms. And this is why the solution provided by the case law of the Supreme Court is appropriate: in such cases, acquittal should be ordered (because guilt is not proven) but no compensation for pre-trial detention should be provided for (because judicial error, in the material or inferential sense, is not proven). In other terms, in these cases, there would be no compensatory damages.

18.4.2 *The Case Law of the European Court of Human Rights*

The European Court of Human Rights (ECHR) responded to this case law of the Spanish Supreme Court, mainly through the *Tendam* v. *Spain* ruling,[39] which already had a somewhat less clear precedent in the *Puig Panella* v. *Spain* ruling.[40] The doctrine established by the ECHR in this and other decisions in this regard may be summarised as follows:[41]

(1) Neither Article 6.2 of the European Convention on Human Rights, which acknowledges the right to the presumption of innocence, nor any other provision of this Convention requires States to provide compensation for time spent in legal pre-trial detention even when the person involved is ultimately acquitted.

(2) However, if a State decides to acknowledge the right to be compensated for undue pre-trial detention, it must do so in a way that reflects the full

---

[39]   ECHR Judgment of 13 July 2010, which was upheld by the ECHR Judgment of 16 February 2016 on the joined cases *Vlieeland Boddy and Marcelo Lanni* v. *Spain*.

[40]   ECHR Judgment of 25 April 2006; previously, although the Spanish State was not party to the proceedings, the ECHR had issued a similar ruling with regard to an Austrian regulation that is very similar to the case law of the Spanish Supreme Court, in the ruling in the *Asan Rushiti* v. *Austria* case of 21 March 2000.

[41]   There is an excellent presentation of the Puig Panella ruling in Martín Rebollo (2009) and of the latter and the Tendam ruling in Cobreros Mendazona (2012). The same doctrine was reproduced with regard to Article 48.1 of the Charter of Fundamental Rights of the European Union by the Court of Justice of the EU: in this regard, there is a good presentation in Lupária, 2017: 203 et seq.

scope of the presumption of innocence and of the other rights recognised in the Convention.

(3) The right to the presumption of innocence as a rule on how the defendant is to be regarded and subsequently treated in the criminal proceedings is not only applicable up until the moment the final ruling on the case is issued, but, moreover, if subjects are acquitted, it requires that they be treated as innocent of the crimes they had been accused of in any subsequent interaction with the State.

(4) For this reason, the State cannot take any decision after the criminal proceedings, either in court or administratively, that questions the innocence of an acquitted person.

(5) This being so, for the purpose of establishing compensation for pre-trial detention, making a distinction between cases in which acquittal was based on proof of innocence and cases in which the grounds are based on the lack of evidence of the hypothesis of guilt is contrary to the presumption of innocence. For these purposes, the ECHR considers that 'there should be no qualitative difference between an acquittal based on lack of evidence and an acquittal resulting from the demonstration of a person's innocence beyond any reasonable doubt'.[42]

Given the arguments underpinning rulings for violations of the presumption of innocence of persons acquitted in criminal trials in Spain, there would be two ways out: acknowledgement of the right to compensation of all subjects held in pre-trial detention and subsequently acquitted (irrespective of the

---

[42] ECHR Judgment *Tendam* v. *Spain*, of 13 July 2010, § 37, which already had precedents pointing in the same direction since the ECHR Judgments *Englert* v. *Germany* and *Nölkenbockhoff* v. *Germany*, both of 25 August 1987, *Sekanina* v. *Austria*, of 25 August 1993 and *Rushiti* v. *Austria*, of 21 March 2000. Various rulings of the ECHR on this matter against Norway are also very illustrative. This country had a legal system in place (Articles 444 and 446 of the Norwegian criminal code) to provide compensation for pre-trial detention followed by an acquittal, according to which defendants who were acquitted would have had to apply for compensation and prove their innocence before the same court that tried them, with a preponderance of the evidence standard. That is, if the hypothesis of guilt was more probable than that of innocence but did not reach a sufficient degree of corroboration in light of the standard of criminal evidence, defendants were to be acquitted, but were not entitled to compensation if they were held in pre-trial detention. If, on the other hand, the hypothesis of innocence was more likely than that of guilt, innocence was understood to be proven, giving rise to entitlement to compensation for the pre-trial detention suffered. The ECHR also considers this regulation contrary to the presumption of innocence: see, for example, *O.* v. *Norway*, of 11 February 2003 (§ 33–41).

grounds justifying the acquittal) or denial of the right to compensation of all subjects acquitted (due to subjective non-occurrence of the offence).

The Supreme Court quickly opted[43] for the second option, applying a literal interpretation of Article 294 of the LOPJ and acknowledging only the right to compensation in cases in which the objective non-occurrence of the criminal act is proven.[44]

The doctrine has highlighted the perverse and paradoxical effect of how an interpretation that purportedly provides greater guarantee of the presumption of innocence has led to a serious restriction on compensation for undue pre-trial detention.[45] It should be added, however, that this was corrected by ruling 85/2019 of the Spanish Constitutional Court, which declared the clauses of Article 294.1 of the LOPJ, which limit compensation to cases of acquittal or dismissal of the criminal case due to the non-occurrence of the alleged act, to be unconstitutional. Thus, the Constitutional Court accepted the doctrine of the ECHR regarding the presumption of innocence and, in addition, considered that distinguishing between assumptions of non-occurrence of the act and non-participation in it by the defendant is contrary to the right to equality. Finally, as a result of this ruling, legal regulations in Spain have been configured in such a way that compensation is due in all cases in which a person has been held in pre-trial detention and the case is finally dismissed or the defendant acquitted.

However, in this final part of my chapter, I would like to stress the profound lack of understanding of how standards of proof work in the approach that lies at the core of the doctrine of the ECHR (and of ruling 85/2019 -F.J. 10°-, of the Constitutional Court of Spain, which fully endorses it). Allow me to elaborate.

The first of the political or moral reasons, and perhaps the most important one, for establishing the evidentiary threshold of a standard of proof, is the seriousness of the judicial error (false positives and false negatives) in the kind of case in question, which largely depends on the seriousness or the importance of the established legal consequences and of the effects on the law's capacity to motivate behaviour. It would therefore be reasonable to have different standards of proof for different kind of cases (even criminal cases) based on the possible penalty: for example, a fine, a ban on exercising a professional activity or imprisonment. This being so, raising the evidentiary threshold in certain kind of criminal cases due to the severity of the possible

---

43   See the Supreme Court Judgment of 23 November 2010 and, in this regard, De Mateo Menéndez, 2011: 80 ff.
44   Although in theory it remains possible to appeal to the general system of judicial error of Article 293 of the LOPJ, which, we should recall, is very narrowly interpreted.
45   See, for all, Cobreros Mendazona, 2012 and Díaz Fraile, 2017: 190 ff.

penalty and of any potential judicial error regarding the facts has nothing to do with any subsequent administrative or judicial proceedings in which the envisaged legal consequences are far less serious.

This would seem to be a good reason to apply different standards of proof to criminal liability for a certain deed and civil liability that may be derived from such a deed. There is no reason that can justify it being easier, in terms of evidence, for a victim to obtain compensation for damage that does not constitute a crime than to obtain compensation for damage that does. However, this is what would happen if the civil liability for a deed which, if proven, would constitute a crime were judged necessarily and solely in criminal proceedings according to the standard of proof specific to a criminal ruling. The varying severity of the misattribution of legal consequences (civil redress and a prison term, for example) is one good reason for judging them with different standards, although this allows someone who is acquitted of a crime to be convicted in a civil court for the same act.[46] That, however, would be contrary to the presumption of innocence according to ECHR doctrine. Nevertheless, it must be said that ECHR case law has been excluded this consequence in a large number of cases and in a manner hardly consistent with the doctrine discussed here. For example, in the ECHR ruling *Ringvold* v. *Norway*, of 11 February 2003 (§ 38), criminal acquittal is considered compatible with the subsequent attribution of civil liability for the same acts, *given the different standards of proof applicable* to the two proceedings and provided that the civil sentence does not use language that might lead to doubts about the subject being innocent of the crime.[47]

The same occurs in cases of compensation sought for undue pre-trial detention. As the Spanish Supreme Court noted in its original doctrine, acquittal may be due to the specific threshold of the criminal standard of proof that is applied, although nothing seems to suggest that the reasons for raising the standard of proof in such criminal proceedings should require that

---

[46] See, in this regard, among others, the Supreme Court Judgments (Civil chamber) of 28 November 1992 and 21 March 2005. Also, the excellent presentation and analysis by Doménech Pascual, 2015: 24 ff.

[47] The same criterion is found in many ECHR rulings, including ECHR rulings in the cases Y. v. *Norway*, of 11 February 2003 (§ 41–2), *Diacenco* v. *Romania*, of 7 February 2012 (§ 58), *Allen* v. *United Kingdom*, of 12 July 2013 (§ 123) and *Vlieeland Boddy and Marcelo Lanni* v. *Spain*, of 16 February 2016 (§ 44). However, given that irrespective of which standard governs civil liability, it appears that at the very least the hypothesis that the defendant has committed the acts must be more likely than the hypothesis of innocence, it is difficult to see how the conditions required by the ECHR can be met and even more difficult to find the differences that make civil conviction after criminal acquittal acceptable and not the denial of compensation for pre-trial detention, even subject to the same standard of proof.

the same standard be used in subsequent contentious-administrative or civil proceedings.

This same lack of understanding of the role of standards of proof by the ECHR is demonstrated in other examples. I will mention but one of many.[48]

The ECHR ruling on *Stavropoulos v. Greece*, of 27 September 2017, resolves a case involving both contentious administrative and criminal aspects. The main aspects of the case are as follows: Mr Stavropoulos applied for social housing, with the requirement that he could not be the owner of a house in the region, which he certified. A house was granted to him, but it was later discovered that Mr Stavropoulos did own another house, whereupon his right to social housing was revoked in an administrative action and criminal charges were brought against him for fraud. In the criminal trial, Mr Stavropoulos was ultimately acquitted because the intention to commit fraud was not duly substantiated. On the basis of the criminal acquittal, Mr Stavropoulos applied to have his right to social housing restored by the administration, but it was rejected because the criminal sentence had no effect on the administrative appeal and because it had not been proven in the criminal proceedings that Mr Stavropoulos did not intend to commit fraud (or, in other words, his innocence had not been proven).

The ECHR ruling considers that the presumption of innocence was violated, because the Greek State, following the acquittal, was obligated to treat Mr Stavropoulos as innocent (i.e., not the perpetrator of the deeds) in all areas of relevance to the same facts that had been tried in the criminal procedure. Of course, this also overlooks what is at stake in criminal and administrative proceedings, as well as the varying severity of the potential errors, meaning that the applicable standards of proof do not need to be the same. In other terms, if criminal charges had not been brought against Mr Stavropoulos, would the administrative decision to withdraw the social housing have been correct? If the answer is yes, as I believe it should be, then what reasons are there for the evidentiary threshold in the administrative setting to change and assume an unfamiliar and more demanding standard of proof simply because the act committed may have additional criminal penalties?[49]

---

[48]   A list of ECHR cases in the same vein can be seen in Doménech Pascual, 2015: 28.

[49]   One variant of this problem is: on the one hand, the presumption of innocence is assumed to be linked to a particularly high standard of proof, and on the other it is assumed that the application of the presumption of innocence can and must be extended to other areas, such as punitive administrative law and disciplinary and grievance procedures in employment law. Given both assumptions, it also follows that these other areas require a particularly demanding standard of proof, similar to that of a criminal procedure. As I have strived to show in this chapter, such a conclusion is totally inappropriate, but in order to reject it we must also abandon some of the initial premises or assumptions. Therefore, my proposal is to reject the link between the presumption of innocence and a given standard of proof. The hypothesis of

In summary, the ECHR's doctrine extends the applicability of the right to the presumption of innocence as a rule on how the defendant is to be regarded and treated within the criminal proceedings to all state actions following a criminal acquittal and related to the same facts. Of course, in this event, it is clear that we are no longer dealing with a rebuttable presumption, but rather an irrebuttable (*iuris et de iure*) presumption, or even with fiction. Moreover, the extension of this unquestionable presumption to any other subsequent procedure, such as the determination of the applicability of compensation for 'undue' pre-trial detention, involves, in practice, considering the standard of proof in these other proceedings to be the same as the criminal standard of proof, and consequently that the question of proof has already been decided in this jurisdiction. All of this, which I trust I have demonstrated, is based on a serious confusion about the role of standards of proof in judicial proceedings and their relationship to the presumption of innocence.[50]

REFERENCES

Allen, R. J. and Callen, C. R. (2003). The Juridical Management of Factual Uncertainty. *The International Journal of Evidence and Proof*, 7, 1–30.
Anderson, T., Schum, D. and Twining, W. (2005). *Analysis of Evidence*, 2nd ed., Cambridge: Cambridge University Press.
Bayón, J. C. (2008). Epistemología, moral y prueba de los hechos: hacia un enfoque no benthamiano. *Analisi e diritto*, 2008, 15–34.

guilt must be proven in order to override the presumption of innocence. However, the evidentiary threshold for the hypothesis to be considered proven depends on the political reasons presented in Section 18.2.2 of this chapter and not on the actual presumption of innocence.

[50] The ECHR's doctrine has a further consequence, which appears to have gone unnoticed in the doctrine of the Spanish Supreme Court and by the Court itself. Indeed, the Spanish criminal justice system (like systems in many countries around us) has made false accusation, false reporting and simulation of crime illegal (Article 456). Both the literal wording of the provision and its case law interpretation require that the accusation be false, and that the accuser knew that it was. This being so, the judicial proceedings resulting from the accusation must have proven that the latter. In other words, the innocence of the defendant must be proven, not just that they were acquitted for lack of evidence. Therefore, in accordance with the ECHR doctrine expounded, once the defendant has been acquitted, distinguishing between acquittals for lack of evidence and acquittals based on proven innocence is not consistent with the presumption of innocence, thus leaving only two options for the offence of false accusations: (1) consider that all accusations that conclude in acquittal for lack of evidence are false, which is evidently absurd; or (2) abolishing the offence of false accusations, which would lead, yet again, to no protection from malicious accusations of having committed crimes.

Bentham, J. (1827). *Rationale of Judicial Evidence*, 7 vols., J. Stuart Mill ed. and cited from the edition included in Bentham, J. : *The Works of Jeremy Bentham*, 11 vols., edited by J. Bowring, Bristol: Thoemmes Press, 1995.

Cohen, L. J. (1977). *The Probable and the Provable*, Oxford: Clarendon Press. Cited from the reprint of Gregg Revivals, Aldershot, 1991.

Cohen, L. J. (1986). Twelve Questions About Keynes's Concept of Weight, *The British Journal for the Philosophy of Science*, 37(3), 263–78.

Cohen, S. (1999).Contextualism, Skepticism, and the Structure of Reasons, in Tomberlin, J. ed., *Philosophical Perspectives*, Cambridge: Blackwell.

Cobreros Mendazona, E. (2012). Los paradójicos efectos de la protección de la presunción de inocencia sobre el sistema indemnizatorio por prisión provisional indebida. (Las sentencias Puig Panella y Tendam del Tribunal Europeo de Derechos Humanos), in E. García de Enterría and R. Alonso García, eds., *Administración y Justicia (Un análisis jurisprudencial). Liber Amicorum Tomás-Ramón Fernández*, vol. II, Madrid: Civitas.

De Mateo Menéndez, F. (2011). Responsabilidad patrimonial por prisión preventiva indebida: nueva jurisprudencia. *Jueces para la Democracia*, 70, 80–91.

Díaz Fraile, F. (2017). *La presunción de inocencia y la indemnización por prisión preventiva*, Valencia: Tirant lo Blanch.

Doménech Pascual, G. (2015). ¿Es mejor indemnizar a diez culpables que dejar a un inocente sin compensación? Responsabilidad patrimonial del Estado por los daños causados por la prisión preventiva seguida de absolución o sobreseimiento. *InDret, Revista para el análisis del Derecho*, 4/2015.

Fantl, J. and McGrath, M. (2002). Evidence, Pragmatics, and Justification, *The Philosophical Review*, 111(1), 67–94.

Feldman, R. and Conee, E. (1985). Evidentialism, *Philosophical Studies*, 48 (1), 15–34.

Ferrer Beltrán, J. (2002). *Prueba y verdad en el derecho*, Madrid: Marcial Pons, 2nd ed. 2005.

Ferrer Beltrán, J. (2007). *La valoración racional de la prueba*, Madrid: Marcial Pons.

Ferrer Beltrán, J. (2013). Una concepción minimalista y garantista de la presunción de inocencia, in J. L. Martí and J. J. Moreso, eds., *Contribuciones a la filosofía del derecho. Imperia en Barcelona 2010*, Madrid: Marcial Pons.

Ferrer Beltrán, J. (2014). La prueba de la causalidad en la responsabilidad civil, in D. M. Papayannis, ed., *Causalidad y atribución de responsabilidad*, Madrid: Marcial Pons.

Ferrer Beltrán, J. (2017). Presunción de inocencia y prisión preventiva, in J. M. Asencio Mellado and J. L. Castillo Alva, eds., *Colaboración eficaz, prisión preventiva y prueba*, Lima: Ideas-Universitat d'Alacant.

Foley, R. (2000). Epistemically Rational Belief and Responsible Belief, in R. Cobb-Stevens, ed., *Proceedings of the Twentieth World Congress of Philosophy*, Bowling Green, Ohio: Philosophy Documentation Center, 5, 181–8.

Gascón Abellán, M. (1999). *Los hechos en el derecho. Bases argumentales de la prueba*, Madrid: Marcial Pons, 3rd ed. 2010.

Guerra Pérez, C. (2010). *La decisión judicial de prisión preventiva (Análisis jurídico y criminológico)*, Valencia: Tirant lo Blanch.

Haack, S. (1993). *Evidence and Inquiry: Towards Reconstruction in Epistemology*, Oxford: Blackwell Publishers, revised ed. 2001.

Hart, H. L. A. (1961). *The Concept of Law*, Oxford: Clarendon Press, 2nd ed. 1994.

Hawthorne, J. and Stanley, J. (2008). Knowledge and Action. *Journal of Philosophy*, 105(10), 571–90.

Hunter, I. (2015). Las dificultades probatorias en el proceso civil. Tratamiento doctrinal y jurisprudencial. Críticas y una propuesta. *Revista de Derecho – Universidad Católica del Norte*, 22(1), 209–57.

Keynes, J.M. (1921). *A Treatise on Probability*, London: Macmillan and Co. Cited from the edition of Watchmaker Publishing, 2007.

Laplace, P. S. Marquis de (1814): *Essai philosophique sur les probabilités*, Paris. Cited from the English translation of Truscott, F. W. and Emory, F. L.: *A Philosophical Essay on Probabilities*, London: John Wiley and Sons, 1902.

Laudan, L. (2003). Is Reasonable Doubt Reasonable? *Legal Theory*, 9(4), 295–331.

Laudan, L. (2005). Por qué un estándar de prueba subjetivo y ambiguo no es un estándar. *Doxa*, 28, 95–113.

Laudan, L. (2006). *Truth, Error, and Criminal Law: An Essay in Legal Epistemology*, Cambridge: Cambridge University Press.

Laudan, L. (2007). Strange Bedfellows: Inference to the Best Explanation and the Criminal Standard of Proof. *The International Journal of Evidence and Proof*, 11(4), 292–306.

Laudan, L. (2016). *The Law's Flaws: Rethinking Trial and Errors?*, Milton Keynes: College Publications.

Lowey, A. H. (2009). Taking Reasonable Doubt Seriously. *Chicago-Kent Law Review*, 85(1), 63–75.

Lupária, L. (2017). La presunción de nocencia en la Carta de los Derechos Fundamentales de la Unión Europea. *Revista Vasca de Derecho Procesal y Arbitraje*, 29(2), 199–214.

Martin Rebollo, L. (2009). Presunción de inocencia y responsabilidad del Estado: una relación ambigua (a propósito de la sentencia TEDH de 25 de abril de 2006), in AA.VV., *Derechos fundamentales y otros estudios, en homenaje al prof. Dr Lorenzo Martín-Retortillo*, vol. II, Zaragoza: El Justicia de Aragón.

Mendonca, D. (2000). Las claves del derecho, Barcelona: Gedisa.

Nance, D. A. (2016). The Burdens of Proof. Discriminatory Power, Weight of Evidence, and Tenacity of Belief, Cambridge: Cambridge University Press.

Ormazábal, G. (2004). La carga de la prueba y sociedad del riesgo, Madrid: Marcial Pons.

Roberts, P. and Zuckerman, A. (2004). Criminal Evidence, Oxford: Oxford University Press.

Roxin, C. (1994). Strafrecht. Allgemeiner Teil, Band I: Grundlagen. Der Aufbau der Verbrechenslehre. 2. München: Auflage Beck. D. M. Luzón Peña, M. D. García Conlledo and J. de Vicente Remesal (trans.), Derecho Penal. Parte General, Civitas, 2003.

Rysiew, P. (2001). The Context-Sensitivity of Knowledge Attributions, Noûs, 35(4), 477–514.

Solan, L. M. (1999). Refocusing the Burden of Proof in Criminal Cases: Some Doubt About Reasonable Doubt. Texas Law Review, 78, 105–47.

Stanley, J. (2005). Knowledge and Practical Interest, Oxford: Clarendon Press.

Stein, A. (1997). Against Free Proof, Israel Law Review, 31, 573–89.

Stein, A. (2005). Foundations of Evidence Law, Oxford: Oxford University Press.

Taruffo, M. (1992). La prova dei fatti giuridici, Milano: Giuffrè.

Tolivar Alas, L. (2009). La adjetivación reductora del error judicial: ¿un fraude de Constitución? Revista Española de Derecho Administrativo, 142, 203–24.

Twining, W. (1990). Rethinking Evidence. Exploratory Essays, cited from the 2nd ed., Evanston IL: Northwestern University Press, 1994.

Ullmann-Margalit, E. (1983). On Presumption. Journal of Philosophy, 80(3), 143–63.

Index

specialities of expert witnesses, 226, 232
specific causation
  in cases concerning toxic torts, 168–9
specification of crimes, 198–211
standard of proof
  distinction from other standards of
    decision, 21
  for non-specified wrongs, 198–211
  for toxic torts, 168–9
  formulation, 375–93, 395–423
  in Singapore, 175–7
  in Spain, 408–10
  necessity, 396–7
  probability, 60–2
  relation
    to burden of persuasion, 368
    to inferential errors, 413–14
    to miscarriages of justice, 405
    to presumption of innocence, 211, 395–423
    See also probability; statistical evidence.
State liability
  for undue pre-trial detention, 395–423
statements
  logic of connections, 162
  role in decision making, 150, 159
  See also propositions.
statistical evidence,
  for non-specified wrongs, 198–211
  for toxic torts, 166–8
  for wrongful convictions, 326–7
  objectivity, 297
  ostensive aspect, 145
  understanding, 211, 314, 317
  See also probability; standard of proof.
status crimes, 207–8
statutory intrusion, 40
Stavropoulos *v.* Greece (2017), 422
Stein, Alex
  principle of maximal individualization,
    150
  view on evidential weight, 412
Stella, Federico
  view on expert evidence, 330
Steyn, Lord Justice
  view on forensic evidence, 292
story model, 46, 338
StPO (Strafprozeßordnung)
  on expert reports read in absence of
    expert, 221
strength of evidence. *See* weight
stricto sensu presumptions, 407–8

structural remedies
  facilitation of virtuous deliberation, 134, 135
structure of trials, 41
subject development, 35
subjectivity
  in an adversarial process, 78, 79
  influence of background assumptions,
    76
  interaction between subject and object,
    56, 57–8
  meaning, 387
  of statistical data, 297
  overcoming, 77, 403
substance blind approach, 16
substance/procedure distinction, 361–73
sufficiency of evidence, 367, 369–72
summings up. *See* directions
SWGFAST (Scientific Working Group on
  Friction Ridge Analysis, Study and
  Technology), 281
Swiss National Science Foundation (SNSF)
  Trial Observation Project, 86
Switzerland
  prohibition on use of evidence, 86–7, 93,
    94, 96
syllogisms, 162
synergy of group
  contribution of deliberative virtues, 126–8
system errors, 325, 330–48

Tarski, Alfred
  view on truth, 57
Taruffo, Michele
  on expert evidence, 330, 344
  on inferences, 5–6, 159–69
  on relative truth, 396
technical advisors, 243
Tendam *v.* Spain (2010), 416, 418–19
terminology
  in field of evidence, 2, 14, 375–6
  in field of forensic science, 306
terrorism
  fair trial rights, 116–17, 120
testimony
  comparison with first-hand knowledge,
    149–50
  ostensive aspects, 144–6
  See also expert evidence.
testing of factual inferences, 71, 72, 78
Thayer, James Bradley
  triumph, 19

view
  on admissibility, 25
  on law and logic, 23, 99–100
theorising about evidence, 14
  gap in relation to standard of proof, 395
  in law, 26
theory of guilt, 175–7
Thomas, Sabra
  view on junk science, 337
Thompson. *See* Guerra Thompson
thought control, 205
three-attribute theory of evidence, 66
Three Strikes laws, 208
torts. *See* toxic torts
torture
  prohibition on use of evidence, 85
    approach of ECtHR, 104
    in Singapore, 173
total process model
  application
    to materiality, 22
    to relevance, 23
  in Anglo-American tradition, 28
Toulmin, Stephen
  inferential model, 162–3
  view on field of evidence, 13
toxic torts, 168–9
training
  in forensic science, 302, 306, 307, 308, 313–18
  in virtuous group deliberation, 135, 302
  See also qualifications.
traits of character. *See* group-deliberative
    virtues
transparency
  of forensic laboratories, 302, 308
Trial Observation Project, 86
trials
  as complex adaptive system, 46–7
  enforcement of codes, 42
  from perspective of complexity theory, 44
  functions, 42
  mistakes. *See* bias; errors; miscarriages of
    justice
  organization, 41
  outcomes, 41, 42, 43, 44
  See also adjudication model; disputes; jury
    trials; litigation.
truth
  correspondence theory, 57, 159, 396
  of propositions, 56, 159, 161
  relation to evidence, 396

Twining, William
  on definition of evidence, 148, 150–1
  on development of new subjects, 35
  on field of evidence, 3, 13–30, 35
  on generalizations, 59, 152–3
  on purpose of fact finding, 151
  on rationalist tradition, 396
  on rules of evidence, 47
  on scientific evidence, 316
two-attribute theory of evidence, 66

UCL (University College London)
  evidence project, 18
ultimate *probandum*
  in relation to materiality, 20
  in relation to relevance, 23
uncertainty. *See* 'beyond all reasonable doubt'
    standard; forensic science; probability;
    standard of proof; statistical evidence
unconscious prejudices. *See* non-volitional
    prejudices
undue pre-trial detention, 395–423
unexamined statements. *See* hearsay evidence;
    right: to examine witnesses
UNHRC (United Nations Human Rights
    Council)
  Universal Periodic Review (UPR), 185
uniqueness, 303
United Kingdom
  wrongful convictions, 333–5
United Nations Human Rights Committee
  regulation of law of evidence, 102
United Nations Human Rights Council
    (UNHRC)
  Universal Periodic Review (UPR), 185
United States
  adverse inferences from silence, 179
  burden of proof, 361–73
  error rate of trials, 61, 326–7, 332–3, 338
  evidence of prior similar acts, 199
  expert reports read in absence of expert, 221
  level of peacefulness, 48
  selection of court-appointed experts, 223,
    229
  technical advisors, 48, 243
  See also Anglo-American tradition; Federal
    Rules of Evidence; New York.
United States v. Woods (1973), 206
Universal Periodic Review (UPR), 185
universe
  as complex adaptive system, 37

Printed by Printforce, United Kingdom